PUBLIC POLICY

PUBLIC POLICY

Perspectives and Choices

THIRD EDITION

Charles L. Cochran
Eloise F. Malone

LYNNE
RIENNER
PUBLISHERS

BOULDER
LONDON

Published in the United States of America in 2005 by
Lynne Rienner Publishers, Inc.
1800 30th Street, Boulder, Colorado 80301
www.rienner.com

and in the United Kingdom by
Lynne Rienner Publishers, Inc.
3 Henrietta Street, Covent Garden, London WC2E 8LU

Library of Congress Cataloging-in-Publication Data
Cochran, Charles L.
  Public policy : perspectives and choices / by Charles L. Cochran and
Eloise F. Malone.—3rd ed.
      p. cm.
    Includes bibliographical references and index.
    ISBN 1-58826-375-4 (pbk. : alk. paper)
  1. Policy sciences.   I. Malone, Eloise F.   II. Title.
  H97.C6   2005
  320.6—dc22

                                                2005010767

British Cataloguing in Publication Data
A Cataloguing in Publication record for this book
is available from the British Library.

Printed and bound in the United States of America

         The paper used in this publication meets the requirements
  ∞   of the American National Standard for Permanence of
         Paper for Printed Library Materials Z39.48-1992.

    5   4   3   2   1

Contents

Illustrations

Figures

Preface

Understanding the implications of public policy choices is essential for every citizen. For over two centuries, the United States has been an example to the rest of the world representing what an informed and involved citizenry could achieve. The potential for democratic government to be regarded as a positive instrument in promoting the general welfare appeared victorious after the Great Depression. Since then, interest groups that flourish in our democratic state have attracted broad support for issues like environmental protection, energy conservation, protection of civil liberties, national health care, or homeland security. Other interest groups promote narrower objectives—for example, support or opposition for gun control, the death penalty, freedom of choice, or immigration reform. Today, political entrepreneurs find it necessary to constantly take the political pulse through polling to determine how to react to specific policy issues on the agenda. Other activists with an ideological bent try to build winning partisan coalitions through the use of focus groups to shape the debate in a way that attracts citizens to their "perspective" while making the opposing party appear less attractive.

We often hear that the people rule in our "democracy" and we would like to think it were true. In the first decade of the new century many Americans have become increasingly detached from public life. The general interests of ordinary citizens are frequently drowned out by the clamor of special interest groups. A growing cynicism often results, leading to an ironic alliance between the average citizen, who comes to believe that the democratic process is largely a mockery, and the financial elites, who believe that it is best to entrust as little to government policymaking as possible. Attacks on the institutions of U.S. government as *the problem* make it more difficult to craft the compromises needed to produce effective policies. Unfortunately, well-financed groups often resort to this tactic in an effort to block policies that may pose a threat to their interests. Growing economic inequality in the United States and the evolving political paradigm that supports it is one of the most important trends in the modern United States. Often, the policies associated with support for the most well-off result in policies that negatively affect those less well-off. Nevertheless, public policy as a discipline is optimistic. It is based on the profoundly significant belief that the citizens in a democratic society can take responsible actions to improve the national well-being.

Why This Book?

Like the preceding editions, the primary purpose of this text is to tell the story of public policy in a clear, scholarly, balanced, and interesting manner. We believe that it is a narrative of great importance—one that sharpens our focus and clarifies our understanding of the society we live in and the rules that govern it.

Public policy continues to grow as a subfield of political science. At the same time, the study of public policy transcends the boundaries of academic disciplines, and, in recent decades, interdisciplinary techniques have contributed important, but often controversial or competing, new perspectives. In the best of circumstances, arriving at a collective public policy decision—whether as an academic exercise or on Capitol Hill—is very difficult to achieve.

Public policy texts often ignore basic concepts used by political scientists and policy analysts. Some texts begin by encouraging students to "debate" controversial policy issues without any development of theory. Others study public policy primarily as a process, or they encourage the use of basic models used to examine policy. These approaches have a long and useful history.

We, however, have chosen to base our text on contributions from all the disciplines that are of concern to policy studies. We believe it is important for students to be thoroughly grounded in basic economic arguments such as market failures, free riders, externalities, economic rents, and moral hazards. We emphasize that practically everything is for sale in economic markets—but in a political society, many things should be beyond price. Relying too heavily on markets frequently produces results that offend our sense of justice and fairness. Other contributions such as democratic theory, rational public choice, international relations theory, and psychology are also necessary to understand the complexity of public policy problem solving.

The Plan of the Third Edition

The first five chapters provide a tour of the fundamental elements of a political scientist's way of thinking about policy issues and the policymaking process. Although leading professional journals in public policy now routinely deal with topics such as scarcity, rational self-interest, the tragedy of the commons, the free rider problem, and market and government failures, they are frequently ignored in public policy texts. We believe that these topics should be presented as the essential core of public policy, something that students will remember long after the course is over. We also develop the difference between the often idealist goals of the policymaker and the reality of the circumstances in which public policy is hammered out; policy analysts, after all, are rarely constrained by the need to raise money and win votes, unlike the politicians who actually make public policy.

Making sense of these principles is important because, though fundamentally logical, they are often misunderstood. We have done our utmost to explain public policy ideas clearly and in understandable language. At the same time we try to avoid oversimplification and to elevate the policy problems by highlighting the political, philosophical, and economic issues that permeate even the most seemingly straightforward problems. We find that interweaving theoretical perspectives and real-life practical choices into our discussion offers the reader a well-rounded understanding of the policy issues at hand.

In addition to rewriting the text to take into account changes in the policy environment over the past several years, we have updated boxed areas to include contemporary case studies. The boxed areas also illustrate policy application and implementation, and offer additional explanations of concepts and problems addressed in the text. In some instances, the boxed material serves as a medium for introducing or developing important ideas and issues that may be tangential to the main flow of the chapter, and are therefore best treated separately.

Frequently we compare U.S. approaches to policymaking with those of other advanced countries, especially the nations of the Organization for European Cooperation and Development. Today what goes on in the rest of the world has a growing impact on policy issues in the United States; in the aftermath of September 11, 2001, we are discovering how extensive an impact it is. Now more than ever, we must be aware that other countries have faced the same policy dilemmas as the United States and frequently they have made alternative choices that can inform our policy decisions.

Finally, we have tried to emphasize that the appeal to the individual for democratic decisionmaking is based on the ability of the collective to achieve goals that individuals cannot achieve acting separately. In this sense, government is a necessary good in promoting the general welfare. Capitalism, in contrast, appeals to the individual's self-interest and tends to see government as a necessary evil. The capitalist perspective is to emphasize market decisions as being more efficient than the collective decisions of democracy. All capitalist societies recognize that market failures contribute to outcomes that are incompatible with society's values. Policy studies must inevitably raise issues about the ethical relationship between the individual and the collective. The study of public policy thus involves the thoughtful use of interdisciplinary insights and empirical evidence in pursuit of social justice. To achieve a humane society as well as an efficient economy, wise government involvement is inevitable.

Acknowledgments

We are indebted to so many people for their help in writing this book that it is difficult to know where to begin thanking them. Our parents imparted a strong sense of social justice and fairness to us. We were also encouraged by them to be informed about political issues and to be open to new ways of seeing things. This debt cannot be repaid, only acknowledged.

Second, our spouses, Mimi and Dave, have continued to encourage us in undertaking the third edition. Others have helped in numerous ways. We owe special thanks to Glenn Gottschalk, Linda Hull, Michael Malone, Barbara Breeden, and Florence Todd. Many of our colleagues helped by providing information, sources, and articles, and (frequently unknowingly) through conversations that stimulated new ideas or resulted in the modification of our own.

Throughout the entire process there were many reviewers, too numerous to mention, who read earlier drafts and made many useful comments. Particular acknowledgment must be made to the staff at Lynne Rienner Publishers, who have been very helpful. In particular, Leanne Anderson and Lesli B. Athanasoulis took a special interest in the project and saved us from public humiliation. For any other errors that remain, the authors blame each other.

—Charles Cochran
Eloise F. Malone

CHAPTER 1

Basic Concepts in Public Policy

We begin this book by introducing you to the vocabulary of public policy. The following pages define concepts students need to know to understand the policy process. The driving force pushing public policies comprises **scarcity*** and **rational self-interest**. In a diverse society that embraces different values and points of view, interests collide and compromises are unavoidable. The policy analyst must deal with practical questions of who will gain and who will lose by any given policy. Will government intervention improve on a market solution? How are policy choices made without compromising values important to society in general?

What Is Public Policy?

Public policy emerged as a prominent subfield within the discipline of political science in the mid-1960s. In a broad sense, the analysis of public policy dates back to the beginning of civilization. Public policy is the study of government decisions and actions designed to deal with a matter of public concern. Policy analysis describes the investigations that produce accurate and useful information for decisionmakers.

Policy Analysis as a Subfield of Political Science

The social sciences emerged from the humanities and the natural sciences during the latter part of the nineteenth century. The commitment to the methods of the natural sciences, with their concern for methodological and analytical rigor in the study of human behavior, has been critical to the development of social science.

---

*Key concepts are indicated in **boldface** on first definition in the book.

Social scientists share the conviction that rational scientific methods can be used to improve the human condition. The scientific method began to be applied to a wide range of social activity, ranging from the efforts of Frederick A. Taylor's studies on scientific management to the politics of the Progressives. Legislation in the Progressive era was delegated to "experts" in such new and presumably independent regulatory agencies as the Federal Trade Commission and the Federal Reserve Commission.

Positive policy analysis and value neutrality.   Although the social sciences emerged in an environment of social reform, by the early twentieth century there was a general retreat from any sort of policy advocacy. The social sciences in general adopted a value-neutral position under the guise of scientific objectivity. Scientific thought is probably one of the most prestigious activities in modern life. And those engaged in policy studies from a variety of social science disciplines were attracted to the idea that their studies would be more scientific if they eliminated values and merely focused on social behavior. As a result, many policy studies were confined to empirical descriptions. Such studies may prove useful in a variety of ways.

Positive policy analysis.   Emphasis on value-free policy analysis is referred to as **positive policy analysis**, which is concerned with understanding how the policy process works. It strives to understand public policy as it is. It also endeavors to explain how various social and political forces would change policy. Positive policy analysis tries to pursue truth through the process of testing hypotheses by measuring them against the standard of real-world experiences. Positive policy analysis usually deals with assertions of cause and effect. A disagreement over such analysis can usually be resolved by examining the facts. For instance, the following is a positive statement: "If the U.S. government raises interest rates, then consumers will borrow less." We can check the validity of this statement by measuring it against real-world observations. Other positive policy statements, such as "If long-term welfare recipients were required to finish their high school education as a condition of continuing to receive their welfare checks, a high percentage would develop employable skills and become self-sufficient," may be tested by setting up an experiment within a state. The results may confirm or refute the statement.

The attempt to become more scientific by excluding values has several major effects. First, by narrowing the focus to largely empirical studies, it reduced the relevance of policy analysis for policymakers, who must be concerned with preferred end-states such as "reduced ethnic antagonisms." Second, it reduced the importance of values in policy debates by shifting the discussion to cost-benefit analysis or the appropriate way to test a hypothesis. Finally, by glossing over the normative issues, the field of values was abandoned to business interests and social conservatives. Applying models based on market efficiency while ignoring issues of "justice and fairness" played into the hands of business interests and social conservatives, who never stopped touting the values of right to property, and the virtues of self-reliance, independence, thrift, and hard work.

Normative analysis. The Great Depression and Franklin Roosevelt contributed to a major change in policy approaches. The Roosevelt revolution swept aside any suggestion that promoting the general welfare could be divorced from normative goals. Nevertheless, there were many of the New Deal who preferred to think of themselves as a rather elite group of experts engaged in administering programs remaining above petty partisan bickering. Until the depression, during which 25 percent of the labor force was unemployed, many thought that unemployment was a personal problem, not a matter for government action. The Roosevelt administration changed that perception by fighting excessive unemployment through a variety of government policies. Government planning during the New Deal gave great impetus to operations research, systems analysis, and cost-benefit analysis as techniques for efficient management. After World War II, debates within the social sciences forced a search for more inclusive policy models. During the Kennedy administration new techniques such as the Planning, Programming, and Budgeting System (PPBS) were used by the "whiz kids" brought into government service by Secretary of Defense Robert McNamara in the Pentagon.

The applied orientation of these techniques in the Department of Defense earned public recognition and acceptance of policy analysis while it encouraged debate among social scientists that they should become more active contributors to policy analysis and policymaking.[1] The techniques noted above, along with survey research, had wide applicability not only in public policy, but also in private industry. The result was increased debate between those in the social sciences who wished to maintain a more theoretical approach of positive analysis and those who wished to see the policy sciences applied to society's problems. In 1966, Hans J. Morgenthau, a well-known political scientist, summed up the views of those in favor of applying quantitative techniques to achieve practical outcomes, in a statement that could just as well apply to all the policy sciences:

> A political science that is neither hated nor respected, but treated with indifference as an innocuous pastime, is likely to have retreated into a sphere that lies beyond the positive or negative interests of society. The retreat into the trivial, the formal, the methodological, the purely theoretical, the remotely historical—in short, the politically irrelevant—is the unmistakable sign of a "noncontroversial" political science which has neither friends nor enemies because it has no relevance for the great political issues in which society has a stake.[2]

David Easton, in his presidential address to the American Political Science Association in 1969, signaled this momentum when he called for a "postbehavioral" approach that used techniques, methods, and insights of all relevant disciplines in dealing with social issues.[3]

Policy analysis, with a view toward resolving public issues, is *prescriptive* rather than *descriptive* when it recommends action to be taken rather than merely describing policy processes. It is referred to as **normative policy analysis**. Normative policy analysis is directed toward studying what public policy ought to be to improve the general welfare.

Normative analysis deals with statements involving value judgments about what *should* be. For example, the assertion that "the cost of health care in the United States is too high" is a normative statement. This statement cannot be confirmed by referring to data. Whether the cost is too high or is appropriate is based on a given criterion. Its validity depends on one's values and ethical views. Individuals may agree on the facts of health care costs but disagree over their ethical judgments regarding the implications of "the cost of health care."

It is important to be aware of the distinction between positive and normative policy analysis, and not to substitute the goals or methods of one for those of the other. This is because the value of policy analysis is determined by the accurate observation of the critical variables in the external environment. Only an accurate rendering of factual relationships can indicate how best to achieve normative goals. For example, a normative view that we should improve the educational system in the United States does not indicate how to achieve that goal most effectively or most efficiently. If we have limited resources to add to the education budget, how should we spend the funds? Would higher salaries attract more capable teachers? Should we extend the school year? Should we improve the teacher-to-pupil ratio by hiring more teachers? Should we add alternative educational programs? Only a rigorous study of the costs and benefits of various alternatives can indicate a preferred solution. In a republican form of government such as our own, such questions are settled by voting and through decisions made by those elected to run the institutions of government.

Frequently, however, normative statements can be used to develop positive hypotheses. Generally, most people do not feel strongly about the value of a capital gains tax cut. Their support or opposition to such a change in the tax law depends on a prescriptive belief about a valued end-state. Many politicians press to reduce the federal tax on capital gains. They argue that a reduction in the capital gains tax would increase incentives to invest in the economy and thus fuel economic growth. However, computer estimates have shown that this change in the tax structure would reduce government revenues after several years and raise the federal deficit. Estimates also have shown that upper-income groups would receive a significantly larger per capita benefit than would other income groups. The result of these estimates, when publicized, was an increased popular perception that the tax cut would be "unfair." Republicans have had difficulty in pressing the proposal for this reason.

In the decision to study public policy, there is an implicit ethical view that people and their welfare are important. We must try to learn about all the forces that affect the well-being of individuals and of society in the aggregate. The desire to improve the current system is the basis for public policy. To achieve that goal, students of public policy must first understand how the current system works.

In democratic societies, the decisionmaking authority is characterized by varying degrees of decentralization. When decisionmaking authority is distributed between different power centers, such as the different branches of government—executive, legislative, and judicial as well as local, state, or national levels and including various interest groups and the general public—no single group's will is totally dominant. Policy analysts therefore study how the actors in the policy process make decisions: how do issues get on the agenda, what goals are developed by the various groups, how are they pursued. Political elites must share power. They often differ concerning not only which problems must be addressed, but also how they should be addressed. The policy that results is often the result of different powerful groups pulling in different directions. The outcome often differs from what anyone intended. Policy analysts therefore study how individuals and groups in the policy process interact with each other.

Policy analysts also attempt to apply rational analysis to the effort to produce better policy decisions. Thus, through empirical and rational analysis, a body of research findings opens up the possibility of policy analysts providing valuable input to promote the general welfare.

Decisions and Policymaking

Public opinion polls confirm that people worry about their economic well-being more than any other concern. People worry about educating their children and meeting mortgage payments. They worry about the high cost of health care, the needs of an elderly parent, the threat of unemployment. These concerns cut across age groups. Students worry about finding a job when they graduate, paying their rent, making insurance payments. Many people express concern for economic problems like federal budget deficits, taxes, and inflation. Many are increasingly aware that personal well-being is somehow related to broader social trends. This relationship is the domain of public policy, though few really understand how the public policy process works or how it affects them personally.

Public policy comprises political decisions for implementing programs to achieve societal goals. These decisions hopefully represent a consensus of values. When analyzed, public policy comprises a plan of action or program and a statement of objectives, in other words, a map and a destination. The objectives tells us what we want to achieve with policy and who will be affected by policy. Public policy plans or programs outline the process or the necessary steps to achieve the policy objectives. They tell us how to do it. For example, a newly proposed public policy for national health care would include an objective statement explaining why a health care policy matters, along with a detailed health care program or procedure. The program might be "managed competition," or perhaps a "Canadian single-payer" program. Usually the program stage provides the "moment of truth" and people are forced to face up to the values and principles they espouse.

Ultimately public policy is about people, their values and needs, their options and choices. The basic challenge confronting public policy is the fact of scarcity. We cannot have everything we want. Unfortunately, available resources are limited, while for practical purposes human wants are limitless. Scarcity is an ever-present attribute of the human condition. The combination of limited resources and unlimited wants requires that we choose among the goods and services to be produced and in what quantities. Because of scarcity, government may intervene to ration the distribution of certain goods and services thought to be in the public interest. Thus, because of scarcity, there is a need for governmental organizations (such as the Departments of Education, Energy, Defense, Health and Human Services, and Treasury) to allocate resources among competing potential users. Conversely, if there were no scarcity, we would not have to make choices between which goods or services to produce.

Poverty and *scarcity* are not synonymous. Scarcity exists because there are insufficient resources to satisfy all human wants. If poverty were eliminated, scarcity would remain, because even though everyone might have a minimally acceptable standard of living, society still would not have adequate resources to produce everything people desired.

Opportunity Costs

Public policy focuses on the choices individuals and governments make. Because of scarcity, people and societies are forced to make choices. Whenever we make a choice, costs are incurred. When the unlimited wants of individuals or society press against our limited resources, some wants must go unsatisfied. To achieve one goal, we usually have to forgo another. Policy choices determine which wants we will satisfy and which will go unsatisfied. The most highly valued opportunity forfeited by a choice is known as the **opportunity cost**. This cost equals the value of the most desired goods or services forgone. In other words, to choose one alternative means that we sacrifice the opportunity to choose a different alternative. For example, when you decide to enroll in college rather than get a job, the opportunity cost of college includes not only the cost of tuition and other expenses, but also the forgone salary.

People grouped in societies face different kinds of choices. The opportunity cost of any government program is determined by the most valuable alternative use. One tradeoff society faces is between national defense (guns) and social goods (butter). A fixed amount of money, say $100 billion, can be used to buy military goods, or an equivalent amount of social goods (education or health care), but it cannot be used to purchase both goods simultaneously. A decision to have more of one good is also a decision to have less of other goods. Another policy tradeoff society faces is between a cleaner environment and more income. Laws requiring reduced pollution result in higher production costs, which simultaneously squeezes profits, puts a downward pressure on wages, and puts an upward pressure on prices. Laws to reduce pollution may give us a cleaner, healthier environment, but at the cost of reducing corporate profits, and workers' wages, while raising costs for consumers.

The saying that there is no such thing as a free lunch indicates that, because of scarcity, choices must be made that preclude other alternatives.[4] This may seem an obvious point, but many often assume that there is a free lunch. For instance, many people speak of "free public schools" or the need for "free medical care" or "free highways." The problem is that "free" suggests no opportunities forfeited and no sacrifice. This is not the case, however, as the resources that provide education, health care, or highways could have been used to produce other goods. Recognizing that we face choices with tradeoffs, as individuals and collectively in society, does not tell us what decisions we will or should make. But it is important to recognize the tradeoffs in our choices because we can make astute decisions only if we clearly understand the options. The opportunity cost principle can be illustrated. Figure 1.1 summarizes the hypothetical choices in what political econo- mists call a **production possibilities curve** (PPC). This production possibilities curve, or **production possibilities frontier** (PPF), provides a menu of output choices between any two alternatives. Think of it as a curve representing tradeoffs. It illustrates the hard choices we must make when resources are scarce, or the opportunity costs associated with the output of any desired quantity of a good. It also illustrates the indirect effect of **factors of production**, defined as land, labor, and capital. Our ability to alter the mix of output depends on the ease with which the factors of production can be shifted from one area to another. For example, with the collapse of communism the government shifted some production from the defense industry to the civilian sector.

Figure 1.1 Production Possibilities Curve

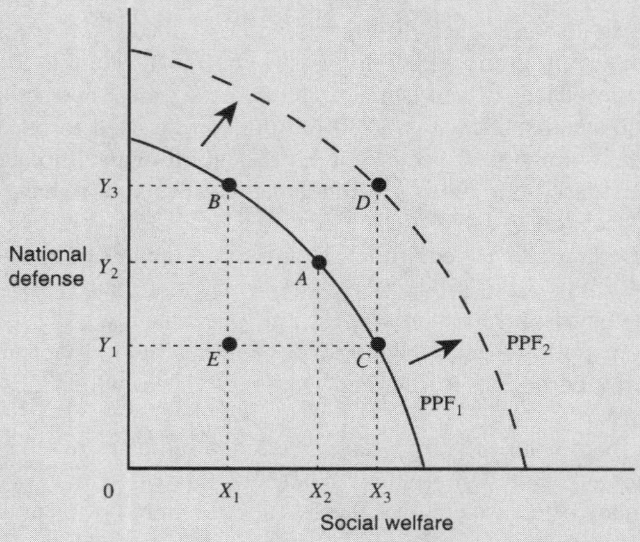

In Figure 1.1 the economy is at point A but conservatives want to pull it to point B while liberals prefer point C, resulting in a political struggle. Both could get the quantity they want through economic growth (point D). Even at point D, both soon find that their wants are greater than the scarce resources available. And the tug-of-war would soon begin on the new PPF. Keep in mind that points on (not inside) the production possibilities frontier indicate efficient levels of production. When the economy is producing at point A, for example, there is no way to produce more of one good without producing less of the other. When a policy decision moves the production from point A to point B, for instance, society produces more national defense but at the expense of producing less social welfare.

The economy cannot operate outside its production frontier with current resources and technology. It is not desirable to operate inside the frontier. Note that point E is a feasible output combination but not a desirable one. Why? Because by moving to point B, for instance, the economy could produce as much social welfare as at point E, but it could also produce considerably more national defense. Or by moving to point C, more social welfare could be produced without sacrificing the production of defense. Production at point E means that the economy's resources are not being used efficiently.

As we move more factors of production from the production of national defense toward social welfare, we must give up ever-increasing quantities of defense in order to get more social welfare, and vice versa. This is so universal a phenomenon that it is referred to as the **principle of increasing costs**. It states that the opportunity costs of producing additional units of one good increase as more resources are used to produce that good. Or, stated differently, in order to get more of one good in a given period, the production of other goods must fall by ever-increasing amounts.

Production potential is not fixed for all time. As more resources or better technology becomes available, production possibilities increase. As population increases, the number of potential workers increases production possibilities. An improvement in the quality of the labor force, such as through improved education or investment in new plants and equipment, can also increase production possibilities. The outward shift of the PPF is at the heart of an expanding economy. This also means a reduction of opportunity costs and a potential increase in an overall standard of living.

The points along the production possibility curve or frontier indicate that many bundles of goods can be produced with the same resources. Consequently, movement along the PPF demonstrates that most changes in public policy are modest or **incremental** shifts. Policy changes are usually, but not always, relatively small, and are typically made with current conditions in mind. Hence the best predictor of what the federal budget will be next year is the current budget. The decision to change the budget is made **at the margin**. Essentially, decisions at the margin mean that we focus on the effects of small changes in particular activities. Policymakers usually consider marginal not total benefits and costs, and as a result we are not faced with all-or-nothing choices. An important principle for anyone studying public policy is the significance of **marginal analysis**. Marginal analysis is a decisionmaking process that is concerned with the additional benefits that a plan of action will provide and the additional costs that will be incurred. A policy analyst would recommend that a proposed action be taken if and only if the marginal benefit of the action exceeds the marginal cost.

Studying the PPF helps us see that choosing what mix of goods and services to produce is the essence of public policy considerations. A nation may face a guns-versus-butter choice in a period of high threats to national security, and environmental protection versus health care might come to the fore in peacetime. Shifts outward in the PPF represent growth; however, the production possibilities curve says nothing about the desirability of any particular combination of goods and services. To understand this, we have to know more than what choices have been made. We must also know why and how individuals and groups make choices and who benefits.

Social Choice

Resource scarcity sets up the conditions for social choice. It is important to emphasize that choices are ultimately made by individuals. The press may report that "the Congress passed a bill" or that "a divided Supreme Court decided," but these are summary expressions of a group decisionmaking process. Actually a majority of the individual members of Congress voted for a bill, or a majority of the individual members of the Court decided a case before it. The mechanism for aggregating individual choices to arrive at collective decisions is democratic majority rule. The democratic process translates the private interests of individual human beings into group decisions. Interested individuals freely express their preferences and decide, in the aggregate, what the public policy decision will be. However, as we shall examine later, public opinion and the voting process may provide very weak guidance to political elites.

While individual choice is the basic unit of public policy analysis, there are often situations in which we treat an organization, such as a government agency, a lobbying group, or even a family, as a "black box"—a gadget whose output is known even though its internal workings are not completely known. Mechanisms such as television sets or computers are, for most, black boxes. In the public policy realm, in some instances, we will open the black box to examine exactly how and why certain individual and group decisions are made. It is of crucial importance that, as students of public policy, we understand what goes on within the black box of the "political system." We need to know how policy is produced within the institutional processes of the political environment and how voters, interest groups, and political parties behave.

More important, public policy originates in our understanding of the public interest. Appealing to that public interest is difficult because it mirrors the disagreement among competing concepts of social morality and justice. In many situations there may be no conflict between acting in one's self-interest *and* the interest of others, or the common good, simultaneously. More frequently, however, if people act in their narrow self-interest, it becomes impossible to achieve the common good. A healthy public spirit, the social form of altruism, sometimes referred to as "social responsibility," is essential for a healthy democracy. A willingness to accept the general interest as one's own is what President John Kennedy referred to when he said, "Ask not what your country can do for you, but what you can do for your country."

Social Justice

Normative policy analysis is concerned with how the individual justifies the use of state authority to pursue one purpose rather than another. Because self-interest inevitably conflicts with the interest of others, it is impossible to achieve an absolute moral consensus about appropriate government policy. A fundamental problem is that the U.S. polity lacks a practical agreement on the meaning of justice. The result is that conflict and not consensus is at the center of modern politics and public policy.

To illustrate the problem, consider a controversy between two individuals. One individual, Joan, is concerned with what she believes is the arbitrary nature of the distribution of wealth and income. She is particularly distressed over the accompanying inequality of power between those with considerable wealth and those without. She concludes that the poor are virtually powerless to improve their condition, while the wealthy are able to increase their wealth and power with ease. The great inequalities in wealth and power are considered unjust by Joan. She concludes that government efforts to redistribute wealth in the direction of the poor through taxes are demanded by simple justice. This help by government activity will lead to greater individual freedom and justice. Joan therefore decides to vote for political candidates who support such taxes and her notion of justice.

The second individual, Robert, has worked hard to achieve certain goals in life. These include financial independence that permits him to purchase a house, to travel, to send his children to college, and sufficient investments to permit a comfortable retirement. He now finds his goals jeopardized by proposals to raise taxes to reduce the deficit and to provide housing for the indigent. He regards these policies that threaten his goals as unjust because they deprive him of his financial resources against his will. He believes that justice demands the full entitlement of each person to the fruits of his or her own labor, and that each individual should have the complete rights to use and control them.

If the economy is growing rapidly enough, Joan's projects may be implemented without threatening Robert's goals. In that case they may both vote for the same political candidates. But if the economy is stagnant, and either Joan's or Robert's policies must be sacrificed to the other, it becomes clear that each has a view of justice that is logically incompatible with the other. In such cases each will use their competing concepts of justice to promote incompatible social goals.

John Rawls received considerable attention for his treatise *A Theory of Justice,* in which he addressed the question of what constitutes a just distribution of goods in society.[5] He held that principles of just distribution may limit legitimate acquisition. If applying principles of just distribution requires a redistributive tax or the taking of property through eminent domain, that acceptance of the taking of property is the price that must be paid to achieve a broader justice in the community.

Robert Nozick argued in his book *Anarchy, State, and Utopia,* in response to Rawls, that each individual has a right in justice to the product of his or her labor unless or until that individual chooses to give some part of it to another person (or to a central authority for redistribution).[6] If the result of individual acquisition is a gross inequality between individuals, justice requires that the disparity be accepted.

The price to be paid for justice in each definition must be paid by another group. Neither of these contending principles of justice is socially neutral.[7] U.S. culture has no accepted rational criterion for deciding between rights based on lawful entitlement versus claims based on need. However, Rawls and Nozick both suggest rational principles to appeal to the contending parties. Some, like Rawls, define justice in relation to an equitable distribution in society. For them, justice is based on a consideration of the present-day distribution. Justice should have priority over economic efficiency. This leads them to an appeal against absolute entitlement. Others, like Nozick, argue that legal acquisition of wealth and income in the past is alone relevant; present-day distribution is irrelevant.[8] They appeal against distributive rules to a justice based on entitlement.

Neither Rawls nor Nozick refer to what is deserved based on justice. But concepts of what is deserved or merited are implied. Nozick argues that individuals are entitled in justice to their wealth and property, and not that they deserve this wealth and property. However, groups supporting this position invariably argue that they are entitled to what they have acquired through their efforts, or the efforts of others who have legally passed title to them. Rawls protests on behalf of the poor that their poverty is undeserved and therefore unwarranted. The child born to the migrant worker is no less deserving than the child born to a family of wealth and privilege. Rawls called this the "natural lottery."

The debate over taxes further illustrates this difference in values between Rawls's distributive justice and Nozick's entitlement theory. The modern opposition to any tax increases or government expenditure policies originates in the strongly negative attitude toward taxation among those who must pay them. Taxes, they argue, are paid primarily by the haves, while benefits accrue primarily to the have-nots. Many of the more fortunate members of society oppose all taxation, but their opposition to the redistribution of wealth through tax policy is not put so crudely.

A concern for liberty, the requirements of justice, efficiency, or the virtues of **laissez-faire** (noninterference) are the most frequently cited justifications. Indeed it is perhaps naive to expect the privileged to respond sympathetically to policies that transfer resources from themselves to others, particularly since there is no community consensus on virtue. The affluent attack government as an arbitrary, profligate liability that is held in check only by relentless attention to its defects. Those with the temerity to promise increased services for the needy are promptly labeled "big spenders." The Rawls-Nozick philosophical debate is an extension of the economic and political rift between different groups in society. Not only is there no value consensus in public policy, but modern political competition is a less violent form of civil war.

Politics and Economics

How societies decide to utilize their scarce resources is determined by a variety of factors. Along with values, they include the history, culture, socioeconomic development, forms of government, and economic organization of those societies. The classic definition of **political science** is a study of "who gets what, when, and how in and through government."[9]

Consequently, politics involves the struggle over the allocation of resources based on the values of the society. Public policy is the outcome of the struggle in government over who gets what.[10] **Economics** has been defined as "the science of how individuals and societies deal with the fact that wants are greater than the limited resources available to satisfy those wants."[11]

These definitions of the two disciplines of political science and economics have a great deal in common. Both are concerned with studying human behavior in competition for scarce resources. **Public policy** exists at the confluence of these disciplines (see Chapter 2). As such, any definition of public policy will reflect these origins. Most definitions of public policy are rather imprecise and we will offer only a working definition. For our purposes, public policy includes actions of government to convert competing private objectives into public commitments, and includes decisions not to take action. Public policies are purposeful decisions made by authoritative actors in a political system who have the formal responsibility for making binding choices among societal goals.[12] Public policy is a form of government control usually expressed in a law, a regulation, or an order. Since it reflects an intent of government, it is backed by an authorized reward or incentive or a penalty.

The assumption voiced in the Declaration of Independence that individuals create government to secure their rights poses a paradox in contemporary U.S. public policy. Men and women can advance their individual freedom only by giving up the anarchistic freedom of no government. Government policy must be coercive and constrain the individual in order to promote the general welfare and secure order and predictability. People organize out of a fear of uncertainty.

Public Policy Typology

One practical means of categorizing policies is based on the method of control used by policymakers. Control can be exerted through patronage, regulatory, and redistributive policies.[13]

Patronage policies (also known as promotional policies) include those government actions that provide incentives for individuals or corporations to undertake activities they would only reluctantly undertake without the promise of a reward. As distinct from policies that threaten punishment for noncompliance, this kind of policy motivates people to act by using "carrots." Not surprisingly, it is the recipients of the rewards who often convince the government to subsidize individuals or corporations to act. These promotional techniques can be classified into three types: subsidies, contracts, and licenses.

The use of **subsidies** has played a central role in the history of the United States. Alexander Hamilton wrote in his *Report on Manufactures,* one of the first policy planning documents in the administration of George Washington, that subsidies for U.S. business should be provided by "pecuniary bounties" supplied by the government. Subsidies to business quickly became commonplace in the United States, ranging from land grants given to railroad companies, to cash subsidies for the merchant marine fleet, for shipbuilders, and for the airline industry.

Other subsidies to businesses have included loans to specific companies like the Chrysler Corporation or the more recent savings and loan "bailout." Subsidies have also been provided to individuals through such policies as land grants to farmers in the nineteenth century, or through the current tax deductions allowed for interest on home mortgage payments.

Subsidies are typically made possible through the largesse of the U.S. taxpayer. Since the cost is spread out among all the population, each person bears only a minuscule portion of the whole cost. There is little opposition to these kinds of subsidies, yet the threat of their removal can arouse intense reactions from their recipients, for whom their loss could entail significant financial hardship. Because subsidies are often attacked as "pork-barrel" programs, every effort is made to tie such projects to some "high national purpose" (such as military defense).

Contracts are also an important means of promoting particular policies. Contracts can be used to encourage corporations to adopt certain behaviors, such as equal employment opportunity, which they might otherwise find burdensome.

Through **licenses**, governments can grant the privilege of carrying on a particular activity. Licensing allows corporations or individuals to conduct a business or engage in a profession (e.g., a licensed pilot) that without the license is illegal. Licensing allows the government to regulate various sectors of the population and, indirectly, the economy.

Regulatory policies allow the government to exert control over the conduct of certain activities. If patronage policies involve positive motivation (the use of "carrots"), then regulatory policies involve negative forms of control (the use of "sticks"). The most obvious examples of regulation techniques include civil and criminal penalties for certain behaviors. The immediate example that comes to mind is regulating criminal behavior. Other forms of conduct are regulated, not to eliminate the conduct, but to deal with the negative side effects. For example, a public utility may provide a community with the "desired good" of electricity, but it can also seek monopoly profits. The conduct of the utility is "regulated" rather than "policed" in a criminal sense, in that the company is given an exclusive license to provide electrical energy to a given geographical area, but in return the government holds the right to regulate the quality of service and the rates charged.

Other forms of regulatory policies that generate more controversy include environmental pollution, consumer protection, or employee health and safety concerns. Tax policy often may have as its primary purpose not raising revenue but regulating a certain type of behavior by making that behavior too expensive for most individuals or companies to engage in. By taxing a substance like gasoline, tobacco, or alcohol, the government encourages a reduction in the consumption of these products. Likewise, "effluent taxes" may raise the price of goods and services that pollute, which encourages companies to reduce their pollution to reduce or avoid the tax.[14]

Some environmentalists are critical of the use of market mechanisms to control pollution, even though they may reduce pollution efficiently. They feel that pollution is morally wrong and a stigma should be attached to the deed. If market mechanisms alone are used to reduce pollution, it is increasingly perceived as morally indifferent, a good to be bought or sold in the market like any other good. Environmental policy is thereby transformed from an expression of the current generation's trusteeship responsibility over the environment for future generations, to an area where economic self-interest is the guiding standard. Regulatory decisions frequently reallocate costs for those affected. Unlike promotional policies that provide only benefits, regulatory policies are usually thought of in terms of winners and losers. The losses they cause are as obvious as their benefits.

Redistributive policies control people by managing the economy as a whole. The techniques of control involve fiscal (tax) and monetary (supply of money) policies. They tend to benefit one group at the expense of other groups through the reallocation of wealth. Changing the income tax laws from 2001 to 2003, for example, significantly reduced the taxes of upper-income groups compared to other income groups in society, although some of those at the very bottom were taken off the tax roles altogether. The result was a decline in the middle class.[15] Since those who have power and wealth are usually reluctant to share those privileges, redistribution policies tend to be the most contentious. Many past policies aimed at redistributing wealth more equitably, even when initially successful, faced severe obstacles in their long-term viability. The most obvious examples are those of the Great Society and War on Poverty programs of the 1960s. Programs with widely distributed benefits, such as Social Security, have enjoyed more success, because of the larger number of people with a stake in their continuation.

Fiscal techniques use tax rates and government spending to affect total or aggregate demand. Each particular approach to taxing or spending can have a different impact on the overall economy, so political entrepreneurs often propose or initiate policies with the goal of achieving specific impacts. For example, in the late 1980s, President George H.W. Bush, faced with a sluggish economy in an election year, proposed a policy of stimulating the economy by cutting taxes to increase demand (and thereby employment). He also proposed cutting taxes on capital gains, a policy that would have benefited primarily higher-income people, with the claim that it would encourage real investment.[16]

Monetary techniques, used by the Federal Reserve Board (the "Fed"), also try to regulate the economy by changing the rate of growth of the money supply or manipulating interest rates (for more on this see Chapter 6).[17]

Basic Economic Systems

If political science is the study of who gets what, when, and how, then public policy may begin by examining the current state of affairs of who already has what, and how it was obtained. There are three basic types of economic organization. The oldest form of economic organization, with only a few examples still remaining throughout the world, is the traditional economy. **Traditional economies** are those in which economic decisions are based on customs and beliefs handed down from previous generations. In these societies the three basic questions of *what, how,* and *for whom* to produce are answered according to how things have been done in the past. Today, in countries like Bolivia, the peasant economy outside of a city like La Paz is predominantly traditional.

Command economies (also known as planned economies) are characterized by government ownership of nonhuman factors of production. Since the government allocates most resources, it also makes most of the decisions regarding economic activities. In socialist economies, for example, the government may own most resources other than labor. Governments then decide what, how, and for whom goods are to be produced. Such governments generally follow policies resulting in wages being more evenly distributed than in capitalist economies.

Pure market economies (also known as capitalistic economies) are characterized by private ownership of the nonhuman factors of production. Decisionmaking is decentralized and most economic activities take place in the private sector. In a market economy, *what* to produce is left up to entrepreneurs responding to consumer demand. *How* to produce is determined by available technology and entrepreneurs seeking the most efficient means of production in order to maximize their profit. And *for whom* the goods are produced is determined by consumer demand, or "dollar votes": if you have the money you can buy it. Prices are the signals in a market economy for what and how to produce goods.

In command economies the government determines to whom the goods will be distributed. In theory this occurs according to "one's needs." In practice it has often been charged that what is produced is distributed according to political or party loyalty. In a market economy, on the other hand, to whom the goods are to be distributed is again ignored by the government and public policy. The goods are distributed to those having what can be labeled as "rationing coupons" (dollar bills). If you have sufficient dollar bills, you can purchase whatever you demand in the marketplace: food, cars, health care, education, or homes. If you do not have these rationing coupons, the system will not recognize your needs, since entrepreneurs respond only to those having the means to demand (i.e., those willing and able to pay for the good in question). Thus, members of a pure market system with no government intervention would have to be willing to watch people starve to death in the streets, unless those starving could prevail on some private charity to provide minimum support.

Of course, the real world is much more complex than these simple definitions indicate; there are no examples of pure capitalism or pure command economic systems. While there are some examples that are closer to the definitions than others, it is not possible to draw a line between pure capitalism and pure command (or socialist) economies and place countries squarely on either side.

Mixed capitalism combines some features of both types of economic organization. It is a system in which most economic decisions are made by the private sector, but the government also plays a substantial economic and regulatory role.

Clearly, economic systems that rely on command are significantly less efficient than those that rely primarily on the market. Most noteworthy in this regard is the former Soviet Union, which became notorious for shoddy goods, shortages and surpluses in the market, absenteeism among the labor force, and an overall lack of innovation in products and production techniques. Former Soviet president Mikhail Gorbachev finally proclaimed that he supported the dismantling of the command economy in favor of mixed capitalism. Today, most countries that undertook planned economies have abandoned this system in favor of mixed capitalism.

While command systems are very inefficient, pure market systems do not allocate resources in a way that most people are willing to tolerate. Hence mixed capitalism in the United States, and increasingly in the rest of the world, is the basis for an increasing number of politico-economic organizations. John Maynard Keynes (see Chapter 6) was the theoretician of a partnership between government and private enterprise. In Keynesian economics, government is responsible for initiating policies that lead to full employment, while ownership of the means of production, as well as profits, remain in private hands.

The perceived legitimate public policy role for government is much greater in those countries that are emerging from command economies, or other varieties of socialism, than in countries living under a mixed capitalism that evolved from more libertarian origins, such as the United States. The U.S. political and economic system begins with a bias in favor of a laissez-faire attitude, which has come to mean a minimal role for government in private lives and distributional policies.

This is significant because, as we shall see, the existence of certain public policies that are taken for granted in many nations (such as a system of national health care) may be challenged by many in the United States as not being the legitimate domain of government.

Why Governments Intervene

While markets are usually the most efficient way to organize economic activity to provide goods and services, there are some exceptions to the rule. Sometimes market forces do not work as the theory would suggest. Policy analysts use the term **market failure** to refer to those situations where the market does not allocate resources efficiently.

The market mechanism works well as long as an exchange between a buyer and a seller does not affect a bystander, or third party. But all too often a third party is affected. Examples are everywhere: people who drive cars do not pay the full cost of pollution created by their vehicles. A farmer who sprays his crop with pesticides does not pay for the degradation of streams caused by the runoff. Factory owners may not pay the full cost of smokestack emissions that destroy the ozone layer. Such social costs are referred to as **externalities**, because they are borne by individuals external to the transaction that caused them. In these cases, the government may improve the outcome through regulation.

Markets also fail in the face of excessive power through oligopolies or monopoly power. In such instances the invisible hand of the market does not allocate resources efficiently because there is little or no price competition. For example, if everyone in a town needs water, but only one homeowner has a well with potable water, the owner of the well has a monopoly and is not subject to competition from any other source of drinking water. Government regulation in such cases may actually increase efficiency.

The market mechanism does not distribute income or wealth fairly. The market system certainly does not guarantee equality. To the contrary, the market ensures inequality, since one source of its efficiency is to be found in the way that it distributes rewards and penalties. Many believe that the market is overly generous to those who are successful and too ruthless in penalizing those who fail in market competition. Thus capitalist markets provide for great opulence to exist next to abject poverty and may reduce overall economic efficiency. The goal of many public policies is to provide a system that is closer to our ideas of social justice than capitalism provides (see Chapter 7).

A final area in which the market fails to perform adequately is in the provision of what policy analysts call **public goods**. Consumers in the marketplace express their collective answer to the question of *what* to produce by offering to pay higher or lower prices for certain goods, thus signaling their demand for those goods. The market mechanism works efficiently because the benefits of consuming a specific good or service are available only to those who purchase the product. A **private good** is a good or service whose benefits are confined to a single consumer and whose consumption excludes consumption by others. If it is shared, more for one must mean less for another. For example, the purchase of a hamburger by one individual effectively excludes others from consuming it. If the purchaser shares the hamburger with someone else, the portion shared cannot be consumed by the purchaser.

Certain other products in our society do not have the characteristic of private goods because they never enter the market system, so the market does not distribute them. These public goods are indivisible and nonexclusive—that is, their consumption by one individual does not interfere with their consumption by another. The air from a pollution-free environment can be inhaled by many people simultaneously, unlike a hamburger, which cannot be consumed simultaneously by many individuals. No one can be excluded from the use of a public good. You can be denied the use of your neighbor's swimming pool, but you cannot be denied the protection provided by the nation's national defense network. If the national defense system works, it defends everyone under its umbrella whether they have contributed to its purchase or not.

Another characteristic of public goods is that policy regarding them can be provided only by collective decisions. The purchase of private goods depends on an individual decision as to whether to spend one's income on hamburgers or swimming pools. But it is not possible for one person to decide to purchase national defense, dams, or weather services. The decision or agreement to buy a public good, and the quantity to buy, is made collectively. There are few examples of pure public goods, but clean air and national defense come as close to meeting the definition as any. Other examples of public goods, though they do not meet the criteria as clearly, include police protection and education. Police protection generally provides a safer environment for everyone living in an area, even if one does not contribute to the purchase of that protection. Education is a similar good. The primary beneficiary of an education is the person educated. However, there are secondary benefits to society that result from a better-educated work force. Moreover, the amount of education allotted to one person does not affect the amount left over for others. The same could be said for highway space or the administration of justice.

The communal nature of public goods leads to a major problem in public policy known as the **free rider**—someone who enjoys the benefits of someone else's purchase of a public good while bearing none of the costs of providing it. If two people both will benefit from national defense, good public education, or clean air, the question arises as to who should pay for it. Each individual has an incentive to avoid payment, hoping to take a free ride on other people's "purchase." As a result, all parties will profess little interest in purchasing the good, hoping others will step forward, demand the good, and pay for it. This is a rational response for individuals with limited resources. Everyone will benefit from the good by more than their proportionate cost, but they would benefit even more if others paid the entire cost. Thus the good will not be purchased unless the government makes the purchase and requires everyone to pay his or her fair share through mandatory taxes.

How do we determine how many and what mix of public goods the government should purchase? By relying on a specific means of public decisionmaking: voting. Because voting is a very imprecise mechanism that limits us to a "yes" or a "no" for candidates, it does not make any distinctions regarding the myriad of issues that must be acted on collectively. Nor does it register the intensity of preferences by various individuals or groups. Therefore, we sometimes find ourselves with an oversupply and sometimes with an undersupply of public goods.

Some conservatives tend to believe that certain public goods could be treated as private goods and brought into the market system, reducing the role of government. For example, tolls could be charged on all roads and bridges for their maintenance. This would limit the building and repair of highways to the amount of demand expressed by those paying the tolls. An admission fee to public parks might be charged to cover the services they provide—a fee that could simultaneously reduce congestion while funding maintenance and even development.[18] Public libraries could charge fees for their services to provide the budgets needed for salaries and the purchase of books and materials. Public transportation systems might charge fees necessary for them to operate profitably, or reduce their service and provide only the amount demanded by those paying the fares. According to conservatives, other areas of government operations could also be reduced through privatization. For example, the operation and maintenance of prisons could be contracted out to private companies rather than being managed by public employees.

The privatization of public goods and services in this manner would certainly result in their being produced, more or less, as if they were private goods. However, there are many difficulties associated with this approach. First, there are the technical difficulties of making some public goods private. How do we make national defense a private good? Also, this approach offends our sense of justice and equity. Do we really think that national or state parks should exist to be enjoyed only by those with sufficient income to pay for their upkeep?

Imperfect Information

The market system is built on the assumption that individuals are rational and do not act capriciously, and that they have roughly accurate information about the market. Without adequate, correct information, people cannot make decisions in their rational self-interest. In fact, most people do not have adequate information to make rational decisions. Developing or finding the information has a significant opportunity cost associated with it. Very few people have the resources or time to do a complete research job.

Information, then, can be considered a public good, or a good with **positive externality**. Once the information is provided, it can be shared by any number of people. Once in the public domain, it is impossible to exclude anyone from using it.

Manufacturers of consumer products, such as cigarettes, do not have an interest in advertising the health hazards associated with the use of their products. But ignorance about those hazards can be reduced by informing consumers, through mandatory labels on cigarette packages, that smoking is dangerous. The manufacturers may still advertise their cigarettes. But the mandatory labels attempt to mend omissions in the market system by introducing information so that individuals can make better choices.

Many people believe the government has a role in researching and disseminating various kinds of information relevant to consumer choices. For instance, the government might investigate and publicize information about the safety of different consumer products such as cars, drugs, food additives, microwave ovens, and other potentially dangerous products.

There is a debate regarding how this remedy for market failure should be applied. If one accepts the proposition that the individual is the best judge of his or her own welfare, then one may argue that governmental actions should be limited to the provision of information. The government, having produced the information, should not regulate the behavior of individuals, according to this view. Once people have been supplied with all the relevant information, they should be permitted to make their own choices—to consume dangerous substances (e.g., to purchase tobacco products) or to purchase potentially dangerous products. Only if the risks extend beyond the user—meaning that **negative externalities** exist involving third parties—may there be an argument for expanding the role of government beyond providing information. For example, those in favor of the right to a smoke-free work environment argue that the spillover effect of inhaling secondary smoke is hazardous to nonsmokers' health.

This view of the informational role of government is not followed consistently in practice. For example, the Pure Food and Drug Act prohibits the sale of certain harmful products but does not provide the option of informing consumers of a product's harmful effects.

Equity and Security

Public goods, externalities, and ignorance all cause resource misallocation. They result in the market mechanism failing to produce the optimal mix of output. Beyond a failure of *what* to produce, we may also find that *for whom* the output is produced violates our sense of fairness.

These are situations, however, when markets fail to achieve the ideal economic efficiency. In a very literal sense, in fact, markets always "fail" because economic efficiency is a fabricated definition based on a normative model of how the world *should* be. Market failure indicates that supply and demand forces have resulted in a mix of output that is different from the one society is willing to accept. It signifies that we are at a less than satisfactory point on the production possibilities curve. Some cases of market failure are so extreme, and the potential for corrective public policy action is sufficiently available, that most people would support some form of governmental intervention to achieve a better output mix. Because of these limitations, no country relies exclusively on the free market to make all of its socioeconomic policy decisions.

Not everyone agrees that turning the decisionmaking over to the public policy mechanism of government constitutes a good solution. Many people believe that governmental processes to alter production choices or to redistribute goods and services do not promote efficiency. Therefore, in their view, whatever the deficiencies of market mechanisms, the market is still to be preferred over government intervention in matters of distribution.

In general, the market mechanism answers the question of for whom to produce by distributing a larger share of output to those with the most rationing coupons (dollars). While this method is efficient, it may not accord with our view of what is socially acceptable. Individuals who are unemployed, disabled, aged, or very young may be unable to earn income and need to be protected from such risks inherent in life in a market economy. Government intervention may be sought for income redistribution through taxes and programs like unemployment compensation, Social Security, Medicare, and Temporary Assistance for Needy Families that shift those risks to taxpayers as a whole.

Redistribution of income to reduce inequities also falls under the theory of public goods because it adds to public security. Without some redistribution, we could expect more muggings and thefts to occur as people sought to escape the consequences of poverty. Moreover, leaving inequalities of wealth solely to market mechanisms would produce the phenomenon of the free rider again. Some individuals would no doubt contribute to charities aimed at reducing poverty, and everyone would benefit from somewhat safer streets. But those who did not so contribute would be taking a free ride on those who did.

Society is therefore forced to confront tradeoffs between the inefficiencies of the market system and views of justice and equity. For example, policies implemented in the 1960s to provide welfare benefits for unemployed women with dependent children were criticized for breeding dependency on government "handouts," so they were changed during the Clinton administration. Bill Clinton's welfare reform increased incentives for finding gainful employment and penalized those who failed to try. Critics of the reform claim that in solving one problem, it created others, like the need for affordable day care and access to transportation. Proponents of the reform argue that it reduced the incentive to save money for retirement, which, although more risky and less predictable than a policy of "forcing" people to save money for retirement, provided capital formation for greater economic growth.

Every society has to deal with the question of what constitutes an equitable distribution of income. It is clear that no government policy is neutral on the question. Income distribution tends to reflect the biases of governments, ranging from traditional laissez-faire to planned economies. The political process by which any society governs itself must ultimately decide what constitutes an acceptable inequality of wealth and income.

Although government *can* improve on market outcomes, it is by no means certain that it always *will*. Public policy is the result of a very imperfect political process. Unfortunately, policies are sometimes designed as a quid pro quo for campaign contributions. At other times they merely reward society's elites or otherwise politically powerful individuals. Frequently they are made by well-intentioned political leaders forced into so many compromises that the resulting policy bears little resemblance to the original proposal.

A major goal of the study of public policy is to help you judge when government action is justifiable to promote specific ends such as efficiency or equity, and which policies can reasonably be expected to achieve those goals and which ones cannot.

Conclusion

The crux of all our public policy problems is to be found in the hard reality of limited (scarce) resources. The free market has proven a superb device for efficiently producing goods and services, based on individual rational self-interest. Problems of scarcity, which are universal, require intervention. This suggests that solutions, whether left to market forces or government intervention, reflect values. There are a variety of possible solutions reflecting the biases and choices of the individuals proposing them.

People face tradeoffs when they make choices. The cost of any action, whether individual or collective, is measured in terms of what must be given up. People as well as societies tend to make decisions by comparing their marginal costs against their marginal benefits. People and societies will adjust their behavior whenever incentives change.

It is important to keep in mind that although markets are a good way to organize many of society's activities, there are several areas where markets fail or produce outcomes unacceptable to society's collective values. In those cases, government can improve on market outcomes. Government efforts to relieve market imperfections (failures) by public policy may also be flawed, however. The question is whether government, which was created to "promote the general welfare," will provide solutions that will be less imperfect than market mechanisms.

Government may be the only actor that can improve market efficiency or alter economic and social costs, risks, and income distribution in a positive way. Some argue that these problems can be solved, but that most solutions mean someone must accept significant economic losses. No one willingly accepts a loss. So people struggle to veto any solution that would impact negatively on them, or at minimum have the cost transferred to someone else or another group. The effect is to produce "veto groups" waiting to aggressively fight any proposed public policy that would result in a loss to their position. Often, the political struggle that results causes a larger cost than gain for those attempting to effect the change. The result is often political and economic paralysis.

However, not all public policy solutions must be **zero-sum solutions**, where one group's net gains must be offset by another group's losses. There are non-zero-sum solutions, which usually involve increasing economic growth so there is more for everyone. But even this solution requires the intervention of government in the form of industrial policies, and many people see this as just another effort to have government provide a remedy no more promising than any the market itself can provide. The major economic competitors of the United States, including both Japan and Germany, have incorporated industrial policy as a key component of their public policies, but it is a controversial issue in the United States.

Questions for Discussion

1. If society desires health care and a clean environment for everyone, why does the free market not provide it?
2. Explain how scarcity, choice, and opportunity cost are related and make public policy inevitable.
3. Give several examples of significant tradeoffs that you face in your life. What are the major considerations in your decisionmaking?
4. Should you consciously think about your values and goals when analyzing important tradeoffs and choices that you face? Why?
5. Explain the difference between self-interest and selfishness. How is it possible for some self-interested behavior to be selfish while other self-interested behavior may be altruistic?
6. Explain why policymakers should consider the importance of incentives.
7. Is reliance on the market to resolve policy issues inherently conservative, or is it inherently progressive?
8. Explain the different types of economic organization and how they answer the questions of what, how, and for whom to produce.

Suggested Readings

Aaron, Henry J., Thomas E. Mann, and Timothy Taylor, eds. *Values and Public Policy.* Washington, D.C.: Brookings Institution, 1994.

Anderson, James E. *Public Policymaking.* 3rd ed. New York: Houghton Mifflin, 1997.

Ben-Ner, Avner, and Louis Putterman, eds. *Economics, Values, and Organization.* Cambridge: Cambridge University Press, 1998.

Berman, David R. *American Government, Politics, and Policy Making.* 3rd ed. Englewood Cliffs, N.J.: Prentice-Hall, 1988.

Demmert, Henry. *Economics: Understanding the Market Process.* New York: Harcourt Brace Jovanovich, 1991.

Dionne, E. J., Jr. *Why Americans Hate Politics.* New York: Simon and Schuster Touchstone, 1991.

Heilbroner, Robert. "The Embarrassment of Economics." *Challenge: The Magazine of Economic Affairs,* November–December 1996.

Heineman, Robert A., William T. Bluhm, Steven A. Peterson, and Edward N. Kearny. *The World of the Policy Analyst: Rationality, Values, and Politics.* Chatham, N.J.: Chatham House, 1990.

Herson, Lawrence J.R. *The Politics of Ideas: Political Theory and American Public Policy.* Prospect Heights, Ill.: Waveland Press, 1984.

Nagle, Stuart. *Public Policy: Goals, Means, and Methods.* New York: St. Martin's Press, 1984.

Reich, Robert B. *The Resurgent Liberal and Other Unfashionable Prophecies.* New York: Vintage Books, 1989.

Rhoads, Steven E. *The Economist's View of the World: Government, Markets, and Public Policy.* New York: Cambridge University Press, 1990.

Rushefsky, Mark E. *Public Policy in the United States: Toward the Twenty-First Century.* Belmont, Calif.: Wadsworth, 1996.

Shonfield, Andrew. *In Defense of the Mixed Economy.* New York: Oxford University Press, 1984.

Stone, Deborah. *Policy Paradox: The Art of Political Decision Making.* Rev. ed. New York: W. W. Norton, 2001.

Thurow, Lester C. *The Zero-Sum Society: Distribution and the Possibilities for Economic Change.* New York: Basic Books, 1980.

Tomlinson, Jim. *Public Policy and the Economy Since 1900.* New York: Oxford University Press, 1990.

Notes

1. Robert A. Heineman et al., *The World of the Policy Analyst: Rationality, Values, and Politics* (Chatham, N.J.: Chatham House, 1990), p. 17.

2. Hans J. Morgenthau, "The Purpose of Political Science," in James C. Charlesworth, ed., *A Design for Political Science: Scope, Objectives, and Methods,* Monograph no. 6 (Philadelphia: American Academy of Political and Social Science, 1966), pp. 67–68.

3. David Easton, "The New Revolution in Political Science," *American Political Science Review* 63 (December 1969): 1051–1061.

4. The statement is accurate when referring to the market in the long run. However, it is not necessarily true in the polity in the short run. There are many public policies in which taxes paid by some people are redistributed to provide benefits for others. For example, middle-income taxpayers may provide funds for food stamps for the poor. Those providing the largesse for others usually want spending reductions, while the recipients of the benefits favor more resources.

5. John Rawls, *A Theory of Justice* (Cambridge: Harvard University Press, 1971).

6. Robert Nozick, *Anarchy, State, and Utopia* (New York: Basic Books, 1974). This work is primarily a response to John Rawls. The extension of Nozick's thought leads to a view that the only form of economic life compatible with individualism is laissez-faire capitalism. Nozick's position is in the tradition of writers in the anarcho-capitalist tradition. His response to Rawls has attracted more comment than the writings of others with similar views.

7. See Alasdair MacIntyre, *After Virtue: A Study in Moral Theory,* 2nd ed. (Notre Dame, Ind.: University of Notre Dame Press, 1984), esp. chap. 17, "Justice as a Virtue: Changing Conceptions," for an excellent comparison of the theory of John Rawls and Nozick's countering view.

8. Nozick's critics point out that his thesis assumes that legitimate entitlements can be traced back to rightful acts of earliest acquisition. Based on that criterion, however, there are few legitimate entitlements, as most property has been inherited from those who originally used force or theft to steal the common lands of the first inhabitants.

9. Harold Lasswell, *Politics: Who Gets What, When, How* (Cleveland: Meridian Books, 1958).

10. Thomas R. Dye, Harmon Zeigler, and S. Robert Lichter, *American Politics in the Media Age,* 4th ed. (Pacific Grove, Calif.: Brooks/Cole, 1992), p. 2.

11. Roger A. Arnold, *Macroeconomics* (St. Paul, Minn.: West, 1996), p. 6.

12. See Larry N. Gerston, *Making Public Policy: From Conflict to Resolution* (Glenville, Ill.: Scott, Foresman, 1979), pp. 4–6. See also Jay M. Shafritz, *Dictionary of American Government and Politics* (Chicago: Dorsey Press, 1988), p. 456.

13. See Theodore Lowi, "American Business, Public Policy, Case Studies, and Political Theory," *World Politics* (July 1964): 677–715. See also Theodore Lowi, *The End of Liberalism: The Second Republic of the United States* (New York: W. W. Norton, 1979).

14. Taxation for the purpose of discouraging certain conduct or eliminating certain activities is often opposed on the grounds that the affluent can buy the right to behave in a manner that is prohibitive to the less wealthy. The charge is correct in that the affluent may be less deterred by the higher price of gasoline, alcohol, tobacco, or other products that cause pollution, than will the poor, who may be eliminated from the market by the repressive features of the tax. However, exercising the right to buy the products will make the wealthy poorer. It should also be pointed out that, by discouraging the purchase of certain products, public health should improve and the environment should become cleaner. The repressive nature of the tax may also be beside the point if the extra amount that the affluent pay exceeds the value we place on the harm caused by alcohol or tobacco consumption, or if a cleaner environment caused by less consumption of gas or other products that cause pollution results in the transference of real income to the population as a whole.

15. See Richard Morin, "America's Middle-Class Meltdown," *Washington Post,* December 1, 1991, p. C1. Reporting on several studies, Morin stated that "the boom years of the 1980s were a bust for fully half of all Americans. At the same time, the safety net of social programs for the nation's poor was replaced by a safety net for the rich, speeding the decline of the middle class."

16. A **capital gain** is the realized increase in the value of an asset. **Real investment** refers to the accumulation of real capital, such as machinery or buildings, rather than financial investment (which refers to the acquisition of such paper instruments as bonds).

17. The Federal Reserve System's control over the money supply is the key aspect of U.S. monetary policy. The Fed has three primary levers of power. The first concerns the reserve requirement. The Fed requires private banks to keep some fraction of their deposits in reserve. The reserves are held in the form of cash or as credits at its regional Federal Reserve Bank. By changing the reserve requirement, the Fed can directly affect the ability of the banking system to lend money. The second lever concerns the Fed's discount rate; the Fed changes the cost of money for banks and the incentive and ability to borrow. The third and most important lever involves the Fed's open market operations, which directly alter the reserves of the banking system. When the Fed buys bonds, it increases the deposits (reserves) available in the banking system. If the Fed sells bonds, it reduces the reserves and restricts the amount of money available for lending.

18. See, for example, Dan Bechter, "Congested Parks: A Pricing Dilemma," *Monthly Review* (Federal Reserve Bank of Kansas City), June 1971. Overcrowding at public parks may reflect a distortion in the recreation market by charging too little for their use. It is suggested that such low pricing amounts to a misallocation of resources. Raising the price would help "clear" the market and relieve congestion. If the price of visiting national parks were increased, more people would substitute other leisure activities.

CHAPTER 2

Methods and Models for Policy Analysis

Although public policy has been recognized as a subfield of political science for only a few decades, the study of ways to "promote the general welfare" goes back centuries. Policy is made in the present, based on the past, with the purpose of improving the well-being of society's future. It utilizes both normative and scientific methodologies to achieve this. Public policy is action-oriented. The purpose of studying public problems is to provide insight into a range of policy options in order to take some control over the future.

Policy Analysis as a Subfield of Political Science

Every academic discipline has its own language and its own specialized way of thinking based on its specific subject matter and goals. Physicists analyze matter and energy and their interactions. Economists talk about inflation, unemployment, comparative advantage, and income distribution. Chemists examine the composition and chemical properties and processes of substances. Psychologists talk about personality development, cognitive dissonance, and perception. Sociologists focus on the collective behavior and interaction of organized groups of human beings in social institutions and social relationships.

Political science is no different. Political scientists focus on people with conflicting interests competing for governmental power. As noted in Chapter 1, political science is about who gets, what, when, and how. In other words, it focuses on what decisions are made by those in authority and why those decisions were made. Political scientists are concerned with the exercise of **political power**. Many observers of humankind's condition see human nature as one-dimensional. Aristotle put forward a biological explanation for political power when he said: "It is evident that the state is a creation of nature, and that man is by nature a political animal."[1] To Aristotelian thinkers, the state and political power are as natural and innate as the instinctual behaviors among herd animals. Still, refusal to accept prevailing authority, or even any governmental authority, has always been prevalent.

A number of political scientists have developed sociological explanations for the transmission of cultural values that hold a political society together, through child rearing, religious education, and socioeconomic class. These scholars see people in plastic terms. People are pliable and are molded by their social environment. Political power and even legitimacy are threatened when those in authority lose touch with the cultural values the masses have been taught to accept. Politicians frequently calculate strategies where one group competes for power by claiming that its political opponents could destroy the cultural values on which society is built. For example, former president Bill Clinton maintains that Republicans had been working to embed negative stereotypes of Democrats in the nation's consciousness since the administration of Richard Nixon in 1968. In the 1994 elections, House Speaker Newt Gingrich tried to confirm the negative stereotypes of Democrats. Clinton wrote in his autobiography: "The core of his [Gingrich's] argument was not just that his ideas were better than ours; he said that his *values* were better than ours, because Democrats were weak on family, work, welfare, crime, and defense, and because being crippled by the self-indulgent sixties, we couldn't draw distinctions between right and wrong."[2]

Karl Marx and other political economists argued that economic foundations of society determine the culture and what the law recognizes as legitimate. Some countries with very similar cultures have developed very different political systems, undermining the Marxist claims about cultural development. Subsequently, Sigmund Freud suggested that culture is transmitted by the interactions between parents and children. B. F. Skinner held that through "operant conditioning"—providing positive rewards for individuals engaging in behavior deemed "good," and negative rewards for behavior deemed undesirable—we could improve society. Finally, some Darwinian biologists see all human behavior as being driven by genes.

Political philosophers such as John Locke have argued that human beings are rational. Individuals use their mental faculties to try to rise above mere conditioned behaviors or emotional attachment to past practices. Locke certainly agreed that the human mind is shaped as an individual grows and matures. Experiences develop the human capacity for reasoning. Ideas stem from experiences, which act on our senses. Subsequent behavior flows from the rational ideas thus developed. Locke was aware that most rulers, if not checked, would favor their own selfish interests over those needed to promote the general welfare. Since everyone is equal and self-interested, and most are rational, a social contract may be agreed on to limit power and ensure the general welfare. A government is formed to protect individuals and their property. Power resides with the citizenry, who can dissolve the contract if the government abuses its authority.

It was only a small step from the political theory of the rational human being acting to promote the general welfare, to the theory of the modern economic human being, who, while still rational, acts to promote his or her self-interest. This economic theory is now frequently applied to political, sociological, and psychological models of human nature as well.

Policy analysts recognize the complexity of human nature and avoid any attempt to analyze it using just one or two of these theories. For example, to reduce human beings, as some economists do, to actors who pursue material self-interest, or as some sociologists might, to actors completely defined by culture, is a mistake. A single theory of the individual, whether based in biology, sociology, economics, or psychology, results in a misleading oversimplification of human nature, although each theory may have an element of truth.

The purpose of this book is to introduce you to the political scientist's way of thinking. In particular, this book is about the political scientist as a **policy analyst**, someone who describes investigations that produce accurate and useful information for decisionmakers. Learning to approach political problems as an analyst is a developmental process and does not occur quickly. This book will provide a combination of social science theory, case studies, and examples of notable public policy issues to help you to develop these skills. To begin, it is important to understand why the field of public policy is interdisciplinary, and why policy analysts must be eclectic in their methodology.

In the Middle Ages all study was under the rubric of *philosophy,* which means "to seek wisdom." As shown in Figure 2.1, philosophy was divided into two parts: moral and natural. **Moral philosophy** focused on human existence and has evolved into the field that we today call the **humanities**. The subject matter of the humanities is our social world, or in other words, the human condition and human values. Because the social world is a projection of human nature, individuals can no more completely understand or control it than they can completely understand and control themselves. Indeed, it is the very intimacy of human involvement with the social world that inhibits both comprehension of and authority over it.[3]

Natural philosophy has evolved into the field that we today call the **natural sciences**. Since it is focused on aspects of the outside world that can be observed, weighed, and measured, it is viewed as being **value-free**. It is a paradox that the natural world, which humans did not create, is much more susceptible to human understanding than is the social world, which is created by humans themselves. Through the discovery of the laws by which the universe is ordered, people can

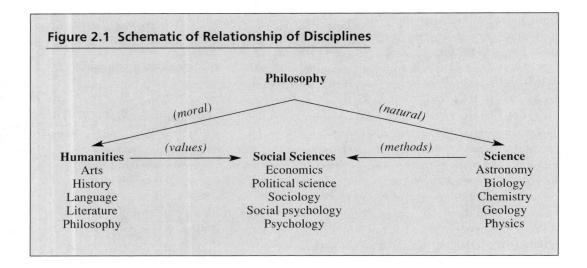

Figure 2.1 Schematic of Relationship of Disciplines

Philosophy

(moral)   *(natural)*

Humanities   —— *(values)* ——▶   Social Sciences   ◀—— *(methods)* ——   Science

Humanities	Social Sciences	Science
Arts	Economics	Astronomy
History	Political science	Biology
Language	Sociology	Chemistry
Literature	Social psychology	Geology
Philosophy	Psychology	Physics

look back into the past and project into the future. Through this understanding, they can control and even harness the forces of nature as they wish.

More recently, a new set of disciplines existing between the humanities and the natural sciences, the **social sciences**, have matured and made significant contributions to our understanding of society through the systematic study of various aspects of the human condition. The social sciences have a split personality. They not only exist between the humanities and the natural sciences, but also borrow freely from both. The social sciences developed from the historical cultural values and conditions of the social community, while at the same time adopting the methods of the natural sciences. Many believe that political science, of which the study of public policy is a subfield, exists at the confluence of the social sciences. It is not an independent discipline within the social sciences. In this view, a political scientist focuses on the political ramifications of the other social sciences.

As a consequence, political scientists use methods of investigation that span the range of intellectual and scientific disciplines. The criterion for using a particular method is whether the tools of inquiry from the other disciplines match the particular problems the political scientist is addressing. Political science is not the only social science that uses a borrowed toolbox, and this practice of utilizing a toolbox of methodologies borrowed primarily from the physical sciences has caused considerable concern.[4] Since the social sciences, especially political science, economics, sociology, and to a lesser extent psychology, are generally moving toward greater involvement in policymaking, it may be appropriate to think of them more generally as "policy sciences." This is most frequently said about economics. In the view of policymakers, John Maynard Keynes's theories in the 1930s moved economics well ahead of the other social sciences as a source of relevant ideas for public policy.

Statistical inference is widely used in public policy, as is historical inquiry. Likewise, the use of historical investigation is somewhat different when undertaken by those interested in public policy than when carried out by historians. Students of public policy must study the present with an understanding of the past, for the purpose of guiding the future. In this regard, no part of humanity or civilization is beyond their concern.

Policy analysis owes its birth to the development of the social sciences, but the physical sciences are an increasingly important part of the policy agenda. There are increasing concerns in all levels of government for science policy. Issues regarding such questions as the environment, including the ozone layer, pollution, global warming, nuclear energy, and population issues, to name just a few, require the policy analyst to not only be cognizant of, but also take part in, scientific studies. Policy analysts today must have more than an appreciation of prevailing interpretations of scientific theory relevant to policy issues. This means that a political scientist in the role of policy analyst must be increasingly prepared to work with specialists in the natural as well as the social sciences.

The political scientist's perspective, scholarly interests, and manner of thought are heavily influenced by the society of which he or she is a member. Every society has biases that encourage an acceptance of and conformity to its political culture. However, the political scientist's obligation to seek the truth about the world of politics will necessarily result in he or she being the messenger of things that society will not want to hear.

A civilization's prevailing socioeconomic culture and the political institutions that grow out of that culture contain an elaborate articulation of the culture's ideals, which are pursued through the political system. An existing political system is usually defended with the concession that it has problems, but that these problems can best be dealt with in terms of the existing system. Consequently, a society that styles itself as Marxist, like the People's Republic of China, cannot allow an investigation into the assumptions on which communist theory is based. Conversely, societies whose economies are basically capitalist in nature are biased against inquiries regarding the goal of equal distribution of property. A society based on a caste system, or some other type of ethnic or racial discrimination, cannot accept such issues as proper subjects for scientific inquiry. Likewise, in republican forms of government, it is taken for granted that the voting mechanism of the nation reflects fairly the "will of the people."

Since every society fosters support for the premises on which the community is based, a commitment to truth in studying a society leads to questions and controversy regarding the values and institutions of that society. Thus the influence of political scientists and economists on policymakers goes beyond their role as policy analysts. As John Maynard Keynes wrote:

> The ideas of *economists* and *political philosophers,* both when they are right and when they are wrong, are more powerful than is commonly understood. Indeed the world is ruled by little else. Practical men, who believe themselves to be quite exempt from intellectual influences, are usually slaves of some defunct economist. Madmen in authority who hear voices in the air, are distilling their frenzy from some academic scribbler of a few years back.[5]

The Political Scientist as Scientist

The **scientific method** was developed in the natural sciences as a way to help understand phenomena by developing theories or models to explain and predict them. The same is true in the social sciences, of which political science and policy studies are a part. To those outside the social sciences it may seem unnatural and even a bit pretentious to claim that political science is a science. After all, political scientists do not utilize the equipment and other trappings of science. The essential element of science, however, is found in the method of investigation. It requires the impartial construction and testing of hypotheses regarding the social world. The method of developing theories and testing them with regard to the effect of gravity on embryo development is just as applicable to studying the impact of a proposed tax subsidy to create additional housing.

Why Theory Development Requires Simplification

While policy scientists use theories and observation like natural scientists do, they face a complication that makes their effort especially difficult: experiments are sometimes impossible in the policy sciences. Biochemists testing a theory about the effect of pollutants on fish embryos can obtain many fish eggs to generate the data they need. In contrast to natural scientists, policy analysts usually do not have the luxury of being able to freely conduct experiments. At best, many social science experiments are difficult to carry out. People do not willingly let themselves become the laboratory subjects for someone else's experiment. For example, if policy scientists wanted to study the relation of imports to total employment, they would not be allowed to control imports to generate data. The risks and cost to society would be deemed too great. In this sense, policy scientists are not unlike astronomers in that although the latter can observe distant galaxies to generate data for analysis, their ability to conduct controlled experiments is very limited.

The difficulty in conducting controlled experiments in political science and public policy means that these social scientists will pay very close attention to the events of history as a type of informal, spontaneous experiment. For example, turbulence in several Asian economies once vaunted as models of economic development to be emulated, causes concern in financial markets throughout the world. In affected Asian countries it depresses living standards. For policy analysts it poses difficult problems of how to respond to contain the problem and reverse the economic decline. But it also provides policy scientists with an opportunity to study the relationships between banking, barriers and subsidies to international trade, currency speculation, and domestic savings and consumption. The lessons learned from such as episode continued long after the particular crisis has passed. Such events provide important case studies because they improve our theoretical understanding of these critical variables and suggest ways to monitor and evaluate current economic policies.

Public Policy and Theory

The first step in the scientific method is to recognize, or identify, the problem to be addressed. Isaac Newton, a seventeenth-century mathematician, observed an apple fall from a tree. Newton's thinking over the problem of explaining "why" the apple fell led him to develop a theory of gravity that applies not only to apples but also to other objects in the universe. Policy analysts must likewise identify the problem to be addressed, such as how to improve the labor skills of the average worker.

Scientists must make **assumptions** to cut away any unnecessary detail. Assumptions are made to help us get to the heart of the problem by reducing its complexity. Assumptions help make a problem easier to understand. In Chapter 1, for example, we looked at a production possibilities frontier that assumed there were only two types of goods in an economy when in fact there might be dozens or even thousands. By assuming that there are only two types of goods, military and social, for example, we can concentrate on the relationship between them. Once the relationship is understood, we are in a better position to understand the greater complexity of a world with other goods.

A critical skill for anyone engaged in scientific inquiry is the ability to decide which assumptions to make. For example, suppose that we want to study what happens to the quality of health care provided to the indigent if Medicaid funding were increased. A key factor in the analysis would be how prices respond to increased funding. Since many Medicaid fee schedules are set by the government, we might assume that prices would not change in the short run. But in the longer run, we would expect physicians and other health care providers to demand higher prices or payments for their services covered under Medicaid. Thus in the longer run we would have to assume price increases. A physicist may assume away the effect of friction when dropping a feather and a baseball in a vacuum, but different assumptions would be necessary in calculating the effect of friction in the atmosphere when dropping a feather and a baseball over the side of a building; so too policy scientists must modify their assumptions when conditions change. Models and theories are similar to assumptions in that they also simplify reality by omitting many details, so that by refining our concentration we can better understand reality.

If we wished to provide policymakers with a complete description of "income distribution," we could go out and collect all the data we could find, present it to decisionmakers, and "let the facts speak for themselves." But a complete description, gathering data from millions of households, thousands of separate federal, state, and local governments, and thousands of firms, is unworkable and would be ineffective as a guide to public policy.

Theories help make sense of the millions of facts. Theories help explain how the political and economic aspects of society work by identifying how basic underlying causal relationships fit together. A **theory** in a scientific sense is a set of logically related, empirically testable hypotheses. Theories are a deliberate simplification of related generalizations used to describe and explain how certain facts are related. Their usefulness derives from this ability to simplify otherwise complex phenomena. Thus a theory is not a mirror image of reality.[6] A theory will usually contain at least one **hypothesis** about how a specific set of facts is related. The theory should explain the phenomena in an abstract manner. The inclination to abstract from nonessential details of the world around us is necessary because of the awesome complexity of reality. **Abstraction** is the process of disregarding needless details in order to focus on a limited number of factors to explain a phenomenon. As an abstraction, a theory is useful not because it is true or false, but because it helps analysts understand the interactions between variables and predict how change in one or more variables will affect other dependent variables.

Theories attempt to do the same thing—bring order and meaning to data that without the theory would remain unrelated and unintelligible. For example, a policy analyst might wish to explain why some people have very high incomes while others barely survive economically. To do so, the analyst must try to separate or abstract the meaningful data from the insignificant data. Thus, variables such as gender, age, education, and occupation may be considered meaningful. Other variables, such as educational level or parents' income, may be considered interesting but less significant. Still others, such as eye color, height, or weight, may be considered unimportant and not be included among the explanatory variables. The theory developed by the analyst is built on all these assumptions and makes up a simplified, logical account of income inequality and its causes.

A theory must be consistent with the facts that it draws together. And the facts, in turn, must lend themselves to the interpretation that the theory puts upon them. Finally, the conclusions derived from the theory must flow logically from the theory's premises or assumptions.

The policy analyst, therefore, must determine which variables to include and which to ignore when conducting social analysis. Although events and forces in a socioeconomic setting reflect all the intrinsic ambiguity of human nature in motion, policy analysts assume that, under comparable circumstances, events and forces will appear in a similar manner. As Michel de Montaigne said:

> As no event and no shape is entirely like another, so also is there none entirely different from another. . . . *If there were no similarity in our faces, we could not distinguish man from beast; if there were no dissimilarity, we could not distinguish one man from another.* All things hold together by some similarity; every example is halting, and the comparison that is derived from experience is always defective and imperfect.[7]

From theories—interpretations of variables—we are able to formulate hypotheses: tentative assumptions or generalizations that have not yet been tested. Because hypotheses, like theories, are abstractions, it is necessary to test them. The hypothesis must be stated as an affirmative proposition (i.e., not as a question) that is capable of being tested against empirical evidence. Accordingly, a hypothesis is most useful when it relates two or more variables in terms of a comparison. For example, we might develop a hypothesis such as: "Cost-control incentives in health care proposed by the private sector are more effective than those imposed by government agencies." The analyst will include only those variables in the hypothesis that are critical in explaining the particular event.

Hypotheses contain variables that can take on different values. A **value** is a measurable characteristic of a variable (such as "strong," "neutral," or "weak"). We might hypothesize: "Strong (value) support for a president will vary positively with low (value) inflation and low (value) unemployment." In this hypothesis, "support for a president" is the dependent variable. "Inflation" and "unemployment" are independent variables. The variables or values selected depend on the questions being asked or the problems to be resolved. Variables are the most basic elements in theories. A **variable** is a term in a hypothesis that can assume different values. In the hypothesis above we could have substituted the variables "support for a member of the Senate" or "support for a member of Congress" for "support for a president." All this is part of the scientific method as applied to the social sciences, as shown in Figure 2.2.

Figure 2.2 Deductive Theory and Measurement: Thinking Scientifically

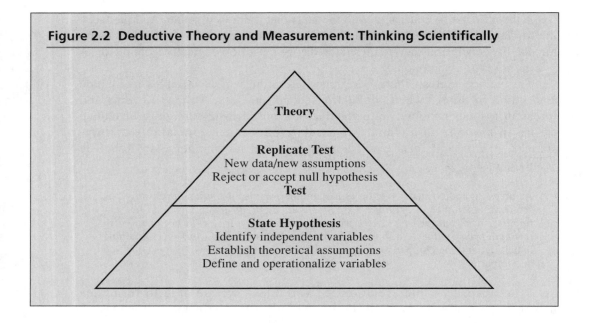

The Scientific Method in the Social Sciences

The scientific method as applied to the social sciences progresses along the pathway of theory and observation suggested in Figure 2.2. The variables are defined, assumptions noted, and hypotheses framed. Various implications and predictions are deduced and stated from the hypotheses. These three steps make up the building of a theory. In the fourth step, the theory is tested. The data either fail to reject the theory or do reject it. If the data fail to reject the theory, this still does not prove it true. It merely fails to disprove it. This can increase one's confidence in the theory, but a theory must continue to be evaluated by seeking additional tests. If, on the other hand, the evidence rejects the theory, there are two possibilities. Either the theory can be amended based on the evidence obtained from the test, or it can be abandoned altogether, in which case those who formulated the theory must return to the first step and start developing a new one. Usually political scientists prefer simple theories to complicated ones. The preference for the simplest of competing theories over more complicated theories when both are consistent with the data is known as **Ockham's razor**, named after fourteenth-century philosopher William of Ockham, who urged its use to "shave away" superfluous theoretical complexities.

When a theory cannot better predict the consequences of the actions than can alternative explanations, it must be modified or replaced. The scientific method requires setting up a theory to explain some phenomenon and then ascertaining if that theory can be disproven by evidence. The danger in this approach is that the world is so complicated that *some confirming evidence* can be found for almost any theory—which is why conspiracy theories abound in U.S. politics.

The Role of Theory in Policy Science

One of the most humbling aspects of the study of public policy is how complex it actually is. Dividing the policymaking process into stages of agenda setting, selection of an alternative, adoption, implementation, and evaluation simplifies it into workable segments for inquiry. Most researchers feel forced to concentrate their efforts on just one stage of the process, to reduce their studies to manageable size. In the past two decades, process studies have contributed to understanding what goes on in policymaking, but by themselves do not show the causal relationships between the policymaking stages. There has been a considerable effort by those in the rational public choice school to develop a theory of policymaking within that tradition.[8]

It is important to bear in mind that theories are abstractions, based on assumptions. This means the resulting predictions are *theoretical* predictions, and will hold true only as long as the basic assumptions of the theory are valid. Policymakers are not so much interested in theoretical predictions as they are in broader factual forecasts. That is, they are more likely to be interested in cosmopolitan views rather than narrower political or economic theories in a given situation. For example, a theory can correctly claim that a competitive labor market erodes wage discrimination based on gender. But this is clearly not an accurate description of events in markets where gender discrimination is institutionalized, making it difficult for the erosion of wage discrimination predicted by competitive labor theory to make itself felt. Policy research shows that gender discrimination acts as an intervening variable. For the maker of public policy, then, economic forces that are offset by social forces are only of theoretical and not of actual value in making predictions.[9] The policymaker must understand social reality as well as economic theory to develop appropriate policy. In the case of wage discrimination based on gender, the policymaker must have a broad knowledge of the institutional arrangements and cultural aspects involved in order to find a viable solution.

Policy theory has developed a disreputable public image—partly because of its inability to predict future outcomes with the same precision as do the natural sciences, partly because of some theorizing that is irrelevant or trivial, and partly because many politicians have found it expedient to ridicule theory in policy analysis. We must distinguish between policy theory and actual public policy. **Policy theory** can develop rules and principles of policy that can serve as a guide for action in a given set of circumstances. **Public policy** refers to the actual action taken. In an ideal world, public policy would always be consistent with the policy theory put forward. Policy problems and issues, by definition, have political ramifications. The result is that policy theory is modified by political realities. For instance, theory might indicate that we should raise taxes to reduce inflation, but during an election year the theory may yield to political realities resulting in reduced taxes to win votes.

But it is exactly the importance of public policy that makes policy theory so critical. If there were no possibility of changing the general social welfare through public policy, political science and economics might both be disciplines asking merely historical questions such as, "How did the U.S. government react to the stagnant economy during the Great Depression of the 1930s?" or "How have health or education policies changed since the mid-1970s?"

Human Behavior and Predictability

The policy sciences deal with the behavior of people, which is not so neatly categorized as other phenomena. How does one find order given so many variables that cannot be isolated? A variation of this view holds that human beings are the least-controllable or least-predictable of subjects for scientific inquiry.[10] However, even if one accepts the argument of the great complexity of the social sciences, one cannot conclude that the discovery of relationships is impossible, only that there are more variables, making it more difficult to discover the critical ones.

Another argument runs that, while the natural sciences deal with inanimate matter subject to natural laws, the social sciences focus on humans with free will and passions not subject to such laws. Consequently, generalizations formulated in the social sciences lack predictive power. It is true that free will and passions like love, hate, pride, envy, ambition, and altruism are more unpredictable in their effects on human behavior than natural causes are on the behavior of atoms. All of these influences, which are extremely difficult to understand, interact within individual humans and affect their behavior. Nevertheless, having free will and passions does not mean that individuals do not act rationally on the basis of their values, disposition, character, and external restraints, and that these actions cannot be understood.[11]

For the natural sciences, if hydrogen and oxygen are mixed under specific conditions, then water will always result. However, for the social sciences, if the government decides for budgetary reasons to reduce welfare payments (and incidentally support the self-help work ethic), then some individuals will adopt the desired behavior pattern but others will not. Some people, faced with reduced benefits, will work very hard to find a job and become self-sufficient. Others, seeing few options, may adopt a life of crime as their avenue of escape. And the same individuals may react differently at different points in time.

The social sciences have developed ways to predict group behavior even though they cannot predict individual behavior. For example, social scientists cannot predict which particular individuals will be killed by handguns or automobile accidents on a given weekend, but they can predict with surprising accuracy the total number who will be killed. Pollsters are likewise able, through sampling techniques, to learn the major concerns of voters. Political candidates can use this knowledge to place themselves in a favorable position to gain the support of potential voters. This predictive ability is of course crucial for policymakers who wish to know how people will react to a change in, for example, the capital gains tax. One's reaction to a capital gains tax cut will depend on several factors, such as income level, expectations regarding how one's own position will be helped or hurt by the proposed tax change, and awareness of the law and its effect. Some individuals will react in surprising ways, but the overall response will be predictable within a small margin of error.

Public policy analysis bases its predictive efforts on the assumption that individuals act so consistently in their rational self-interest that they can be said to obey "laws" of behavior. Several such generalizations provide a logical matrix for understanding human behavior similar to the laws used to account for events in the material world. But social scientific generalizations have their limitations. Human beings bent on maximizing their self-interest may behave in a number of different ways, depending on their understanding of their situation.

Nevertheless, the unpredicted or random movements—the errors—of individuals tend to offset each other. Knowledge of this fact makes possible the **statistical law of large numbers**, which states that the average error (irregularity) of all individuals combined will approach zero. Since the irregularities of individual behavior will tend to cancel each other out, the regularities will tend to show up in replicated observations.

The Policy Analyst as Policymaker

Policy experts are often asked to explain the causes of certain events. Why, for example, has violent crime declined in almost every U.S. city in the past few years? At other times, policy analysts are asked to recommend policies to reduce crime. When social scientists are explaining why violent crime has declined, they are acting in their role as scientists. When they are proposing policies to reduce criminal activity, they are acting in their role as policymakers.

As noted in Chapter 1, it is important to understand the difference between positive and normative analysis. Positive analysis tries to explain the world as it exists. While policymakers may value scientific analysis, they have an additional goal. Someone involved in normative analysis is trying to bring about a different and presumably better end-state. For example, two individuals might be involved in a discussion of drug usage in the United States. The following exchange might be heard:

> Jim: Current drug laws contribute to urban decay.
> Colleen: Most drug laws should be rescinded.

The important distinction between the two statements is that the first is *descriptive* of a social condition, at least as perceived by Jim. The second is *prescriptive* in that it describes the legal order as it *should be,* that is, the law ought to be changed. We can gather evidence to support or counter Jim's positive statement. Colleen's normative statement about what the policy ought to be cannot be confirmed or refuted by merely gathering evidence. Deciding on the appropriate policy will involve our philosophical views and personal values. This is not to deny that our evaluation of the evidence about drug laws and urban decay will influence our value judgments about what the policy ought to be. Specialists in public policy spend a great deal of time trying to determine what the critical relationships are and exactly how society works. But the whole purpose of government, and public policy, is to improve society by promoting the general welfare.

Why Policy Analysts Disagree

The fact that policy is dependent on values results in the community of policy scholars being no more unified in outlook than is the political community. Policy scholars generally agree on various analytical aspects of policy, yet they hold different views about what is best for society. Since public policy analysts come from across the political spectrum, they hold different opinions about the "best" or "right" solution to problems.

For example, in the mid-1990s, some policymakers were determined to reduce the federal deficit. Some analysts disagreed about the accuracy of the different theories regarding the impact of the deficit and the importance of balancing the budget. Analysts also disagreed on what the policy goals should be. Some believed that a full employment deficit would help create jobs, which they thought ought to be a major goal of public policy. Other analysts believed that the deficit would result in rising inflation, which they thought ought to be avoided as the primary responsibility of government. Some policymakers in Congress and in the executive branch found political advantage on either side of the question and staked out their position largely along the lines of appealing to their traditional constituents. As the deficit fell faster than most had anticipated, the disagreement shifted to the issue of whether there should be a tax cut and a further reduction in the role of government, or a reduction in the national debt. Once again many analysts honestly disagreed on which policy should be adopted based on the theories and data available. Their disagreements were undoubtedly influenced by their individual values and which theories they believed would best address the problem.

Another perennial issue is tax policy. Are Americans taxed too much? In the long run, would individual saving and spending be a better stimulus for the economy than government spending? Public policy analysts are no better at answering this question than are physicians in determining whether the right to abortion is justifiable. Such judgments in the United States are determined by the people through the democratic process of voting into office those with specific policy goals.

Increasingly there are cases in which policy experts agree, but the role of special interest groups obscures the consensus. For example, even though independent scholars were unanimous in their findings about the health risks of smoking, for years the tobacco companies funded research that downplayed their significance. Similarly studies were funded as the result of the Civil Rights Act of 1964 to assess the extent to which individuals were being denied educational opportunities because of race or other attributes. The research was not politically neutral. It was limited to questions that provided information helpful to one side of the issue. Studies are vulnerable to manipulation by the choice of alternatives considered, or the interpretation of the findings.

The result is that policy analysis research is often used in the U.S. political process to advocate opposition. Political entrepreneurs and special interest groups examine the research not for overall utility in improving policy so much as for selective findings that may undercut an adversary's position or strengthen one's own. Politicians and lobbyists often look for support for preformed political and ideological positions rather than information to help shape and guide policy. Administrations are distressed to find that the results of analyses hinder the pursuit of policies on which they have already embarked. The more ideologically motivated the administration or bureaucracy, the more policy is made on the basis of ideological inputs rather than analysis. In recent years, for example, conservatives have backed and buttressed their aims by funding policy analysis groups such as the Heritage Foundation or the American Enterprise Institute as an alternative to institutes perceived as having a more liberal orientation.[12]

The Policymaking Process

Public policy did not appear as a subfield of political science until the mid-1960s. The effort to provide an abstract framework for the entire policy process was presented by David Easton.[13] Since that time, effort has concentrated on the analysis of specific substantive areas of public policy. Research has focused on topics such as health care, education, the environment, welfare, and national security. Much of this research has provided very detailed historical case studies of the development and evolution of policy. More recently, there have been greater efforts to apply theoretical models to these case studies, focusing on the factors that affect policy formulation and implementation. This evaluation research judges the formulation of the policy proposal, the process of policy adoption, and the operation of the policy program.

Public policy analysis has not progressed in developing scientifically lawlike propositions. Similarly, the current understanding of the policy process is really a heuristic model, not a theory that allows explanation and prediction. This model separates the policymaking process into five stages: problem identification, policy formulation, adoption, program operations, and evaluation. The model contains no clear and consistent postulates about what drives the process from one stage to the next. Its primary value has been that it divides the policymaking process into manageable units of analysis. Thus the model has resulted in research projects that focus almost exclusively on a single stage without tying results into other projects. Little theoretical coherence exists from one stage to the next.[14]

Problem Identification

The first stage, shown in Figure 2.3, simply indicates that public policy begins when a problem is perceived and gets on the **policy agenda**. There are many problems in society that are not part of the policy agenda because they have not come to the attention of the authoritative actors in the government and therefore do not cause any policy response.[15] The desire for policies to provide for individual needs is insatiable, while room on the agenda is scarce. This raises the question as to why some issues get on the agenda while others do not. The dynamics of a changing political environment, new political players, policy entrepreneurs, and new windows of opportunity are major elements in new issues gaining a place on the agenda. For instance, the Great Depression provided the opportunity for legislation that ushered in various policies such as Social Security and minimum-wage laws. The conservative reaction that swept Ronald Reagan to the presidency provided a window of opportunity for the reduction of social welfare legislation and the introduction of supply-side economics on the policy agenda.[16]

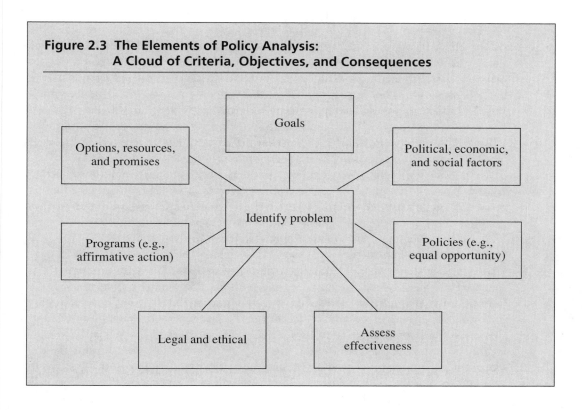

**Figure 2.3 The Elements of Policy Analysis:
A Cloud of Criteria, Objectives, and Consequences**

But in truth, success in getting on the policy agenda does not ensure that an issue will receive a policy response. Some issues manage to get on the agenda yet drift along for years without getting beyond the first stage. For example, health care reform has been accepted as a policy item because of the strength of voter attitudes on the issue. However, both political parties are in disarray as to how to proceed in implementing any reforms. The two major alternatives proposed are a universal plan administered by the government, and a plan that would require coverage but use existing structures of private insurance. Neither political party has coalesced around any firm proposals. Intense lobbying by special interest groups, ideological biases, and questions regarding costs have made it difficult to get beyond the initial agreement that something should be done. The lack of consensus on how to proceed has resulted mostly in considerable debate and posturing by political entrepreneurs (see Chapter 10).

Other items may get on the policy agenda only to disappear into a black hole by the crush of other issues, then resurface later in slightly modified forms. Thus the question as to whether the United States should develop an **industrial policy** to promote a resurgence of U.S. business growth was placed on the agenda in the early 1980s. The idea was brushed aside by the Reagan White House, which viewed industrial policy as inappropriate interference with an unfettered free market, one of the goals of that administration. More recently, the administration of Bill Clinton quietly instituted an industrial policy designed to strengthen business and U.S. exports as part of his overall economic program.

The first step in the policymaking process is a prerequisite for all the steps that follow. So even though getting on the policy agenda provides no assurance that an issue will go any further, failure to get on the agenda guarantees it will not go anywhere at all. For that reason, getting on the policy agenda is the most critical step, and also the most nebulous and amorphous, in the entire process.

Some researchers suggest that the policy agenda should be thought of as consisting of a systemic agenda and an institutional agenda. The **systemic agenda** is made up of those issues perceived by the political community as meriting public attention and resolution.[17] However, the systemic agendas of national and state governments are largely symbolic in nature. The issues they contain are often controversial, and some items may be on one systemic agenda but not another. For example, some believe that the "right to bear arms" is guaranteed by the Constitution, and that it should be beyond the authority of Congress or the states to regulate in any way. Therefore, the issue of gun control has until very recently remained on the systemic agendas of the federal government and most state governments, with many gun control opponents urging its removal altogether. Another subset of items on the systemic agenda are those subject to nothing more than discussion; these are termed "pseudo-agenda items."

The **institutional agenda** consists of those items that receive the powerful and earnest attention of decisionmakers, though they are not always easily identified or agreed upon. They include those issues that are actively pursued through the various institutions of government.

Items may shift from the systemic to the institutional agenda as a result of a variety of events. For example, Congress may prefer to keep an item such as an abortion bill on the systemic agenda because it may be perceived as a no-win situation for members to take a stand on by voting. However, a decision by the Supreme Court, such as *Roe v. Wade,* may force the issue back to the national legislature and require some action. Policy issues typically move from private decisionmaking to the public agenda when they progress from the systemic to the institutional agenda.

Scope of the conflict. If policy is not made through public decisions by the government, it will be made through private decisions, primarily by businesses or financial elites. Traditionally, the principle of laissez-faire meant that government should not interfere with business. As a practical matter, it meant that government supported business decisionmaking through legislation and court decisions that legitimized and reinforced corporate interests. Thus corporations made policy that provided pervasive control over the lives of individuals unhindered by government interference. Businesses were given a free hand to set the terms of employment, wages, hours, and working conditions for employees, and those terms were supported by government stipulations regarding the rights to private property and freedom of contract.

Under laissez-faire doctrine, business provided for individual economic needs through free enterprise, and was loosely supervised by lower levels of government. But with the rise of giant corporations in the late nineteenth century, the power of business organizations over the lives of individuals grew correspondingly. The result was an overwhelming popular demand for government action to correct the perceived abuses of power by corporate interests.

This demand for reform expanded the scope of the conflict from the private arena of management versus labor to the public arena of government versus business. For example, the national government took the lead in legislating worker compensation and child labor laws. With the Great Depression came even more pressure for the government to take an active role in managing the economy and business.

Despite this expansion of governmental regulation, businesses still have a privileged position in U.S. politics even today. They can often make major decisions with only a minimum of government control. In arguing for corporate autonomy from government regulation, executives point out that business must submit first of all to the discipline of the marketplace if it is to be successful. When an issue affecting business does get on the public policy agenda, business organizations are well represented in the public and governmental debates. Corporate leaders are effective proponents for their companies and for the interests of capitalism in general. They also provide many people for government positions, which encourages a probusiness bias in government policymaking.

As long as decisions are made in the private sector, they are outside the realm of politics, even though those decisions may affect many people and the allocation of vast resources. Indeed, private conflicts are taken into the public arena precisely because someone or some group wants to make certain that the power ratio among the private interests shall not prevail in the final decisionmaking (see Chapter 4).[18] In fact, politics may be defined as the socialization of conflict:

> The political process is a sequence: conflicts are initiated by highly motivated, high-tension groups so directly and immediately involved that it is difficult for them to see the justice of competing claims. As long as the conflicts remain *private* . . . no political process is initiated. Conflicts become political only when an attempt is made to involve the wider public. Pressure politics might be described as a stage in the socialization of conflict.[19]

Enlarging the scope.   As noted earlier, democracies provide the political means for private controversies to spill over into the public arena. An issue or condition must attract sufficient attention and interest to expand the scope of the conflict into the public arena if there is to be any hope of changing its current disposition or status.

Some of those involved in the issue will prefer the status quo, and attempt to limit the scope of the conflict to keep the issue off the public policy agenda. And those with interests already on the public policy agenda will not welcome new items that threaten to displace their own. Since only a finite number of items can be considered at any given time, there is always tension when new issues erupt into public consciousness. Those items already on the agenda have a public legitimacy by virtue of having been accepted onto it. New items have not yet established their public legitimacy. For all of these reasons, the political system has a bias in favor of the status quo and will resist the addition of new issues to the policy agenda.

Who sets the public policy agenda?   Determining which issues move from the systemic to the institutional agenda is an extremely important part of the entire policymaking process. The policy agenda is overburdened with a wide assortment of foreign policy issues, national security affairs, economic questions, and domestic concerns. For a problem to become a salient agenda item, it is important that it have an influential advocate, especially the president. Another route for an issue to move onto the institutional agenda is for it to be regarded as a crisis. The perception of a problem as being serious may even be more important than its actual seriousness. A triggering event, for example, the single act of a terrorist, may focus attention on an issue.

Increasingly, policy agendas are determined by tightly knit groups that dominate policymaking in particular subject areas. **Iron triangles** are the reciprocal bonds that evolve between congressional committees and their staffs, special interest groups, and bureaucratic agencies in the executive branch.[20] Members of Congress have incentives to serve on committees that deal with special interest constituencies from their districts. Senators and representatives will bargain for such appointments. And over time, committees in Congress tend to be dominated by members who are highly motivated to provide generous support for the agencies they oversee. These congressional committees make up one side of an iron triangle; they tend to be insulated from many party pressures and develop committee-member alliances that cross party lines.

The special interest groups form a second side of the triangle. These lobbyists and political action committees provide experts in the special interest area. They provide committees with resources for public relations and media coverage, and supply campaign financing to committee members. Finally, the bureaucracies of federal agencies in the executive branch are the third side of the triangle, with their own entrenched interests in particular issues or programs. Congressional hearings provide excellent opportunities for government representatives and lobbyists to build imposing cases for their positions.[21] Iron triangles exemplify disturbing problems in public policy. Policy alternatives that challenge the established interests of the triangle may never receive serious attention.

Responses to the situation created by iron triangles have been based mainly on two different approaches to understanding the nature and functioning of government: elite theory and pluralism or group theory. Those who espouse **elite theory** are critical of iron triangles, pointing to their power as proof of the victory of greedy special interest groups over the general welfare. Those who espouse **pluralism**, on the other hand, are more likely to conclude that such triangles simply reflect strategies developed to promote policies in a diverse nation whose subgroups have different interests.

Getting from the systemic to the institutional agenda. According to elite theory, elites who are powerful in their own right have relatively little trouble getting their issues before the public. Those who own the media can publish stories or air television shows.[22] A member of Congress or the president, together with their respective bureaucracies, can propose a policy. Special interest groups also frequently approach the government with their perceptions of problems and proposed solutions.

Ordinarily an individual must enlarge the scope of the conflict by mobilizing public opinion. This might be done by enlisting the aid of experts who are knowledgeable about the issue and how to publicize it. Frequently, the simplest solution is to seek out an interest group that already deals with a related topic. For example, if one is concerned that local public school students appear to be falling below national standards in testing, one might approach the local parent teacher association regarding remedial steps that might be taken. Getting the local newspaper to write an article might elicit support for new school policies designed to improve the quality of education in the local schools.

The number of people affected by an issue, the intensity of the effect an issue has on the community, and the degree to which everyone's self-interest can be

Case Study: The Issue-Attention Cycle

Anthony Downs contends that many issues appear on the policy agenda in a standardized process that comprises an **issue-attention cycle**. In his view, key domestic problems leap into prominence and remain the center of public attention for a short time, then fade from concern even though they remain largely unresolved. It is in part the length that public attention stays focused on any given issue that determines whether enough political pressure will be brought to bear to effect a change. This cycle is rooted in the nature of many domestic problems and the way the communications media interact with the public. The cycle has five stages, each of variable duration, which usually occur in the following sequence:

1. *The preproblem stage.* Some major problem arises, and although policy experts and special interest groups may be alarmed by the situation, the general public is generally not aware of the problem or its magnitude. The general press has given it prominent coverage. It is not unusual for some problems, such as racism or malnutrition, to be worse during the preproblem stage than they are by the time the public's interest is aroused.

2. *Alarmed discovery and euphoric enthusiasm.* Often as a result of some dramatic event (like a riot or demonstration), the public becomes aware of the problem. Authoritative decisionmakers then make speeches, which are enthusiastically received by the public, regarding the politicians' determination to resolve the problem. This optimism is embedded in U.S. culture, which tends to view any problem as *outside* the structure of society, and naively believes that every problem can be resolved *without any basic reordering of society itself.* U.S. optimism in the past has clung to the view that we as a nation could accomplish anything. Since the late 1960s a more realistic awareness that some problems may be beyond a complete "solution" has begun to develop.

3. *Realization of the cost of significant progress.* A realization that the cost of solving the problem is extremely high sets in. The solution would not only take a great deal of money, but also require that some groups give up some economic security (through taxes or some other redistribution of resources in favor of others). The public begins to realize the structural nature of the problem, and a human inconsistency regarding public policy makes itself felt: we favor collective coercion to raise our personal standard of living, and oppose it when it is used to limit our own actions and raise someone else's income.

Many social problems involve the exploitation, whether deliberately or unconsciously, of one group by another, or people being prevented from benefiting from something that others want to keep for themselves. For example, most upper-middle-income people (usually white) have a high regard for geographic separation from poor people (frequently nonwhite). Consequently, equality of access to the advantages of suburban living for the poor cannot be achieved without some sacrifice by the upper-middle class of the "benefits" of that separation. The recognition of the relationship between the problem and its "solution" is a key part of the third stage.

4. *Gradual decline of intense public interest.* As more people realize how difficult and costly to themselves a solution would be, their enthusiasm for finding a "solution" diminishes rapidly. Some come to feel that solving the problem threatens them; others merely get bored or discouraged with the per-

F

continues

Case Study   continued

ceived futility of grappling with the issue. Also by this time, another issue has usually been discovered by the media and is entering the second stage, and it claims the public's attention.

5. *The postproblem stage.* Having been replaced by successive issues at the center of public interest, the issue moves into a stage of reduced attention, although there may be a recurrence of interest from time to time. This stage differs from the preproblem stage in that some programs and policies have been put in place to deal with the issue. A govern-

ment bureaucracy may have been given the task of administering a program and monitoring the situation. Special interest groups may have developed a symbiotic relationship with the bureaucracy and have had a successful impact even though the "action" has shifted to other issues.

Source: Anthony Downs, "The 'Issue-Attention Cycle,'" *Public Interest,* no. 28 (1972): 38–50; Anthony Downs, "Up and Down with Ecology: The Issue-Attention Cycle," *Public Interest,* no. 32 (1973): 39–53.

---

aroused to confront the problem are all factors to be considered when trying to get an issue on the institutional agenda. An analysis of what will happen if nothing is done about a problem, in terms of who will be affected and in what ways, can be a powerful inducement to action.

Using symbols to get an issue on the agenda. Ultimately the need to attract broad support to get an issue on the political agenda, and to try to move it to the institutional agenda, encourages the use of symbols. A **symbol** legitimizes issues and attracts support for the proposed policy goals. Symbols help people to order and interpret their reality, and even create the reality to which they give their attention. A major attribute of successful symbols is ambiguity. A symbol may be a slogan, an event, a person, or anything to which people attach meaning or value. Symbols can mean different things to different people. They permit the translation of private and personal intentions into wider collective goals by appealing to people with diverse motivations and values.[23] Ambiguity permits maneuvering room to reduce opposition to a policy. For instance, in the 1980s, "welfare" came under increasing attack in a period of tight budgets and declining support for egalitarian policies. Calling the programs "workfare" rather than "welfare" reduced some of the opposition to them, since the new term implied welfare recipients would not be getting a free ride.

Civil rights efforts in the 1960s were initially known primarily for their use of slogans and symbolic marches rather than for any solid achievements. When marchers appealing to "equal rights," the "Constitution," and "justice and equality" were shown on television being attacked by police using dogs and fire hoses, the news reports had a powerful impact on the nation. After a relatively brief period, several effective pieces of legislation passed Congress. It is doubtful that the legislation could have passed without the powerful symbols that preceded it.

Policy Formulation

Success in getting a problem accepted onto the policy agenda may depend in part on the ability to convince others that it is amenable to some governmental solution. Once the problem is on the agenda, however, specific plans for attacking it must be addressed. The problem has been clearly identified, and the need to do something about it accepted; policy formulation is then concerned with the "what" questions associated with generating alternatives. What is the plan for dealing with the problem? What are the goals and priorities? What options are available to achieve those goals? What are the costs and benefits of each of the options? What externalities, positive or negative, are associated with each alternative?

The first option after looking at the proposed solutions may well be to do nothing. Most, but not all, public policy proposals cost money. Currently there are severe economic constraints on new policy initiatives at the state level and particularly at the national level. The economic costs of new programs at the national level have made it extremely difficult to add any new programs.

The result of huge federal deficits during the mid-1980s, budgetary problems dwarfed all other issues as the president and Congress wrestled with the gap between revenues and demand. The result was that few new policies were added to the public agenda, and old programs were reauthorized at the same or reduced spending levels.

Increasingly, programs are expected to be financed by their recipients. For example, the Medicare Catastrophic Coverage Act, which was passed with bipartisan support prior to the 1988 election, provided insurance against catastrophic illnesses for those on Medicare by imposing a ceiling on medical bills and paying 100 percent of the costs through Medicare. The goal was to relieve worry among the elderly that they would be impoverished by the high costs of medical care, especially hospitalization. This insurance was to be paid through a surtax on the income taxes of the elderly. The wealthiest elderly would pay the most, the poorest the least. The theory was that the elderly, as the program's beneficiaries, should bear the cost.[24]

Another major concern for entrepreneurs are the political costs associated with taking action. Since many policies will alter the distribution of income, it can be expected that those whose incomes will be adversely affected will generally oppose them, while those who will be helped will generally favor them. Political entrepreneurs sometimes find themselves caught between doing what they think is right and choosing the alternative that is the least costly from a political perspective.

Case Study: The Dilemma of Tax Cuts, Deficits, and Social Welfare

The huge budget deficits that started in the 1980s were a continuous problem for policymakers. When President Ronald Reagan took office in 1981 he was committed to a reduction in tax rates, especially for the affluent. He found reducing government expenditures more difficult politically than cutting taxes. The result was a period of massive budget deficits that continued through his and George H. W. Bush's administrations and well into Bill Clinton's.

The government ran budget deficits through most of the years from the 1950s through the 1970s. The deficits were modest, however, and the overall economy grew faster than the deficits. The fact that the national debt was actually declining when measured against gross domestic product (GDP) during this period translated into no cause for alarm, as the government was living within its means. When the Reagan tax cuts were not accompanied by cuts in government spending, the growth in government debt relative to GDP began rising. The government had to finance the growing deficit by borrowing the money (selling bonds). This had the effect of pulling money away from investment in new capital equipment, which slowed economic growth and depressed the living standards of Americans. Policymakers of whatever political persuasion accepted this basic theory and saw persistent deficits growing relative to GDP as a significant policy problem. They disagreed on the question of how to reduce the deficit.

There are three ways to reduce a deficit: raise taxes, cut spending, or promote a more rapid growth in GDP than in government spending. When Bill Clinton took office in 1993, deficit reduction was his major goal. In fact, Clinton later boasted that the deficit had declined in each year he was in office. His first action was to raise taxes among upper-income groups while reducing the rate of growth of the budget. When the Republicans took control of Congress in 1995, they opposed any further tax increases, and pressed for more tax cuts to encourage private sector savings (which might be translated into capital investment). The result was a reduction in spending for many welfare programs as Clinton proposed to "end welfare as we know it." Modest cuts in military spending and a long, steady growth in the economy reduced the size of the deficit, and the debt relative to GDP.

Clinton later proposed using the surge in tax receipts, taken in as the deficit gap decreased, for a modest tax cut and an increase in spending for education and other social welfare programs. Republicans in Congress proposed greater tax cuts and were committed to a smaller government. The budget issue continues to test policymakers' metal. After President George W. Bush was elected, he acted quickly to provide "tax relief" particularly to those at the higher end of the income bracket. Those supporting the tax breaks could not have anticipated the extraordinary costs of the terrorist strikes and subsequent invasion of Iraq. The unfortunate consequence is a renewal of the deficit that policymakers had worked to reduce.

Like many policy issues, the debate over budget deficits has several facets. Policymakers agree on the general theory, but disagree on the best solution. The outcome is incremental changes at the margins resulting from compromise. It should also be noted that it took several years before the issue got on the agenda for serious debate and action. Budgets and economic policy will be discussed more fully in later chapters.

Selecting alternatives. The formulation of a policy proposal ordinarily includes not only a statement of the goals of the policy, but various alternatives (or programs) for achieving the goals. How the problem is formulated will often suggest how the alternatives are proposed.

Some policy theorists promote **rational analysis** as a plan for achieving government efficiency through a comprehensive review of all the policy options and an examination of their consequences. Rational analysis selects the option that maximizes utility.

Much of the animosity surrounding the budgetary process is claimed to result from its *lack* of rationality. Everyone from the person-in-the-street, to bureaucrats, to special interest groups, to Congress, to the president believes that he or she can produce a better, more rational budget. However, rational analysis of the budgetary process implies that each option be considered, and no analyst can do this nor can any analysis of the budget be completely comprehensive.[25] Some things are inevitably left out of every analysis. There is not even a basis for constructing a satisfactory list of criteria to determine which goals or alternatives are the most reasonable and which could be left out.

A model of all social problems that included their ranking by importance would be very expensive and difficult to keep up-to-date. People's and society's concerns change constantly. For instance, until about 1980, most Americans outside the medical profession were unaware of Alzheimer's disease. It is now generally known to be a relatively common form of dementia that afflicts a significant percentage of the elderly population. It causes memory loss, personality disorders, and a decrease in other mental capabilities. After research helped to define Alzheimer's as a particular pathology, an organization was formed by people who had family members diagnosed with the disease. The Alzheimer's Association has since opened an office in Washington, D.C., to lobby Congress to double the amount of federal funds currently dedicated to Alzheimer's research. However, a complete analysis of the appropriate amount of federal money to spend for Alzheimer's research would have to include an analysis of all other possible ways to spend the money. That is, every other item in the budget, such as aid to education, the space program, cancer research, environmental protection, even deficit reduction and lowering taxes, would have to be considered.[26]

Only the political process can do this. Budgetary decisionmaking is a political process regarding choices about values. The suggestion that this process could be replaced with an apolitical rationality is disingenuous. Several presidents have argued in favor of Congress giving the executive the power of a **line-item veto**, as though this would take politics out of the process. But nothing can take politics out of the budgetary process.[27] In 1996 Congress handed the president additional power to cut the budget by providing a limited line-item veto. The first time it was used, by President Clinton in the fall of 1997, court challenges were instituted arguing that this was an unconstitutional delegation of power to the executive.

Other policy theorists therefore contend that an incremental approach is actually much more rational. Incrementalism is an approach to decisionmaking in which policymakers change policy at the margins. That is, they begin with the current set of circumstances and consider changing things in only a small way. Particularly in budgeting, this is the typical approach. Just note that the best predictor of what next year's federal budget allocations will be is this year's allocations. Incrementalism assumes that public policy decisions will usually involve only modest changes to the status quo and not require a thorough inspection of all the available options.

Incrementalism assumes the rational self-interest approach of individuals and groups. Since individual and group interests usually conflict, compromise will be required in which everyone will have to settle for less than they hoped for. This results in relatively small changes in existing policy. The budgetary process is thus simplified into a task that assumes each existing program will continue to be funded at its existing level because this level is perceived as fair. If the budget is growing, each program gets approximately the same percentage increase, with those programs having unusually strong support getting a slightly larger increase and those whose support or visibility are waning receiving slightly less. These new funding levels become the bases for the next year's budget.

The late Aaron Wildavsky maintained that **incrementalism** is the best technique for reaching budgetary decisions, because it reduces the decisionmaking process to manageable size. It focuses only on the changes to existing programs rather than requiring a complete justification of the entire program annually. The result is also an allocation of money according to each program's political strength. Since the selection of programs is a normative decision, according to Wildavsky, it is about as good a measure as we have regarding which programs are most deserving.[28]

The result of incrementalism is **satisficing**, or adopting a policy acceptable from all viewpoints rather than seeking the best solution possible. The "best" solution might prove unacceptable to so many decisionmakers that it would be voted down if proposed. For example, many public policy experts recommended a significant tax increase on gasoline at the pump as the "best" way to reduce gas consumption and U.S. reliance on imported oil. Fear of consumer reaction and Republican opposition forced President Clinton to reduce a proposed gasoline tax increase from 20¢ to 5¢ a gallon. When the tax kicked in during the fall of 1993, few even noticed. In the fall of 1994, after inflation, gasoline prices were actually lower than before the tax increase. Since politics is the art of the possible, a negotiated compromise that wins some, if not all, support is preferred to defeat.

Incrementalism works, then, because it is in some ways the most rational approach to policymaking. Time and resources are too limited to permit an examination of all the alternatives. There is a legitimacy in previous policies and programs, while the feasibility of new ones is less predictable. Incrementalism also permits quicker political settlements, particularly when disputes are at the margins regarding the modification of programs.

Adoption

Getting a proposed policy from the institutional agenda through the adoption process is crucial to effecting a change. In the late 1960s many public policy scholars focused on the question of how a bill becomes a law and the many veto points in the process. The process of proposing a bill and getting it passed is very straightforward in that it must follow a standardized procedure. However, the pitfalls that can befall a bill in the process are well known.

The definition of an issue and its impact on different portions of the population usually change in the debate during the policy process. Political entrepreneurs try to redraw the dimensions of the dispute so they can reconfigure political coalitions and gain a winning edge. Party leaders and senior members of the congressional committee considering the issue often bide their time, waiting for other members of the committee or of Congress to become familiar with the issue. They generally then move when they sense the time is ripe for action, based on their experience in dealing with such matters.

The separation of powers in government allows each branch to judge the legitimacy, and if necessary to take action to check the moves, of the other branches. The actors involved here are clearly political elites and must be persuaded not of the wisdom of the proposed policy, but of its chances of success politically. For this reason the major concern at this point is whether the proposed policy is politically viable. The broadest support for the policy must be in evidence here to convince political entrepreneurs that it is in their own interests to promote it through their votes.

Program Operations

In the policy process, once a problem has been identified, alternatives have been examined, and a solution has been selected and legitimized through the adoption of legislation, one part of the policymaking process has been completed. But this is also the beginning of another part of the process—implementing the policy. **Implementation** means carrying out the policy or program operations. Or as Robert Lineberry asserts, implementation is "a continuation of policy making by other means."[29] Implementation has attracted a significant amount of research, because policies often do not accomplish what they were designed to achieve.[30] There are a series of decisions and actions that are necessary to put a policy into effect, and as in chess, miscalculation in the original design strategy or in implementation may bring the entire effort to naught.

Policy advocates have come to realize that the time to plan for the implementation phase is during the formulation and policy selection stage. All the earlier phases, if done well, will reach this state where the proposal is to be translated into action. Several factors in the design phase will facilitate the implementation stage. Perhaps most critical is the question of **policy design**. That is, has the problem been accurately defined? Only if the problem is accurately understood do the causal relationships become evident and allow the analyst to correctly perceive the connections between a particular policy's operation and its intent. For example, the Americans with Disabilities Act of 1990 prohibited discrimination against people with disabilities. The Equal Employment Opportunity Commission and other federal agencies held lengthy hearings to create the regulations spelling out the standards of compliance.[31]

Congress can reduce the discretion of administrators by providing very detailed legislation. For example, Social Security legislation provides very precise terms for eligibility and levels of benefits and formulas for additional earnings. Even so, eligibility for benefits under Social Security Disability Insurance (SSDI) cannot be set forth with such precision. The general definition of *disability* states that an individual is unable to engage in significant gainful employment by reason of a medically diagnosable mental or physical impairment expected to last at least twelve months or result in death. This definition of necessity leaves much room for subjective judgments and interpretation.[32] Implementation of SSDI benefits has resulted in significant controversy and thousands of cases of litigation.

It is usually much easier to implement a policy if it is clearly stated and consistent with other policy objectives. Vague and ambiguous language will be received by the state officials handling the implementation quite differently than will crisp, lucid legislation. Vaguely worded laws may be subject to varying interpretations by bureaucrats or state officials tasked with implementing a program. Vagueness may even permit opponents to effectively sabotage the policy. On the other hand, there are times when vagueness may be preferred to clarity, if the alternative would be no program at all. An excellent example of this is the Constitution, which as the basic framework of the U.S. government is also a policy statement. When the Founding Fathers were unable to agree on clear statements on several issues, they compromised on vague, broad statements and agreed to let later practice determine the outcome. The "necessary and proper" clause is an obvious instance.

Another factor that facilitates the implementation of a policy is its perceived legitimacy. For instance, a program that passes both houses of Congress with large majorities or a decision by the Supreme Court that is unanimous or nearly so will generally also have the support of those tasked with its implementation. Even those who have misgivings will be more inclined to go along with the perceived mandate.

Implementation is the most important part of the policymaking process for students of public administration. Much of the important work of implementing policy is done by the "street-level" bureaucrats, including judges, public health workers, school teachers, social workers, and other federal, state, and local government employees.

Evaluation

The last stage of the policymaking process is evaluation. Every stage involves a purposeful effort to bring about some change in the political environment. But in particular the process of formulating a proposal and choosing among alternatives to achieve the policy's objectives suggests the need for some criteria or standard to determine if the implemented policy has achieved it objectives.

Evaluation is the assessment of how a program achieves its intended goals. All the earlier stages of the policy process look toward a future goal to be achieved; evaluation looks backward. It is a tool whose primary purpose is to appraise the operation of a program and provide feedback to those involved in the earlier stages. This feedback permits modifications in the policy to improve its efficiency and effectiveness. Evaluation also pinpoints unintended effects of a policy and allows adjustment in the implementation process to avoid those that are undesirable. In addition, it can be used to monitor the expenditure of funds to see that they were spent according to the terms of the law or grant. Thus, such assessments focus on the implementation of a program and how it has met the goals and objectives spelled out in the selection and adoption phases of the policy process.

Evaluation of public policy programs came into its own during the 1960s. Under Great Society legislation, there was a surge in government programs to deal with a variety of social ills. At the same time, critics charged that these programs resulted in many government failures, and at a significant cost to taxpayers. The media reported cases of waste and inefficiency, as well as programs that were not achieving their intended goals. Congress began requiring more vigorous evaluations of programs by agencies like the General Accounting Office.

It is useful to make a distinction between policymaking and policy analysis. This book is primarily concerned with the policymaking process. Policy analysts, however, emphasize the evaluation process and use a variety of different methods to assess policy, including laboratory studies, simulations, case studies, sample surveys, and cost-benefit analyses, to name just a few. The process often also involves the use of analytical techniques, such as applied statistical analysis, to measure program effectiveness in meeting goals.

Conclusion

Public policy has developed as a subfield within the discipline of political science since the mid-1960s. As a social science, it draws on the humanities, and history in particular, for its data. It also utilizes the scientific method in an effort to explain and predict underlying causal relationships in policymaking and uses empirical methodology to test the validity of causal relationships. Existing at the confluence of the social sciences, public policy draws on theoretical developments in the various social sciences.

Policy analysts utilize the scientific method in order to understand the social world in which they work. Like other scientists, they must make assumptions and construct models to simplify a very complex world to provide greater understanding. Policy analysts study all the issues that are of interest to policymakers, which is to say that policy analysis is wide ranging and interdisciplinary.

When policy analysts are engaged in positive analysis, they are concerned with understanding the world as it *is*. When policy analysts are concerned with normative issues (how the world *ought* to be), they are acting more in the role of policymaker. An objective understanding of how the world *is* will influence one's values.

Specialists in public policy issues may not always agree, because they have different scientific judgments regarding theories developed from studies. They also disagree because they have different value systems about what *ought to be* to improve society. Sometimes there may be wide agreement among policy scientists but a public perception of a lack of consensus, because special interest groups often provide studies and spokespersons claiming expertise to support almost any position imaginable.

The complexity of the problems in policy analysis has made the development of public policy theory difficult. Predictions that may be valid solely in terms of the underlying assumptions of a discipline such as economics or political science are often not based on data broad enough in scope to ensure their accuracy in the larger policy scheme. Such predictions fail to take into account all the significant phenomena that influence the politico-economic variables related to a problem. This means that any effective theory development must begin at the micro level and take into account individual rational actors and their decisionmaking preferences, then move toward the macro level and take into account aspects of institutional constraints and the societal effects of policy.

Scholarship over the past two decades has resulted in a significant accumulation of knowledge regarding the policymaking process. Dividing the process into stages—getting an issue on the public agenda, formulating the policy proposal, achieving its adoption, implementing the policy as a program, and evaluating the program's effectiveness in achieving the original policy goals—has been the standard analytical approach. This has resulted in uncovering phenomena, such as "critical actors," that were previously overlooked.

The political system transfers private disagreements into public disagreements. Getting an issue on the public policy agenda is a critical procedural process. Elites in the society have far more influence than the average citizen.

Questions for Discussion

1. Discuss the role of theory in understanding phenomena from the natural sciences. Does it differ from the role of theory in the social sciences? Why?
2. Why is the development of theory in the social sciences more difficult than in the natural sciences?
3. What are the special problems in developing theory in the policy sciences?
4. Should theories and models be a completely accurate reflection of reality?
5. Why are the contributions of policy analysts often not held in high regard by policymakers?
6. What if anything can be done to strengthen the role of policy analysts?
7. Why is it so difficult to get a proposed policy adopted and implemented? How would you suggest streamlining the process?

Suggested Readings

Adams, Bruce. "The Limitations of Muddling Through: Does Anyone in Washington Really Think Anymore?" *Public Administration Review* 39 (November–December 1979).

Bailey, John J., and Robert J. O'Connor. "Operationizing Incrementalism: Measuring the Muddles." *Public Administration Review* 35 (January–February 1975).

Connally, William E., ed. *The Bias of Pluralism*. New York: Atherton, 1971.

Dahl, Robert. *Who Governs?* New Haven: Yale University Press, 1961. This is the classic pluralist work.

Dye, Thomas R. *Who's Running America? The Bush Era*. 5th ed. Englewood Cliffs, N.J.: Prentice-Hall, 1990.

Furnival, John S. *Colonial Policy and Practice*. New York: New York University Press, 1956.

Kingdon, John W. *Agendas, Alternatives, and Public Policies*. Boston: Little, Brown, 1984.

Lindblom, Charles E. "The Science of 'Muddling Through.'" *Public Administration Review* 19 (Spring 1959).

Mills, C. Wright. *The Power Elite*. New York: Oxford University Press, 1956.

Truman, David B. *The Governmental Process*. New York: Knopf, 1971.

Notes

1. From Aristotle, *Politics,* in William Ebenstein and Alan Ebenstein, *Great Political Thinkers,* 5th ed. (New York: Harcourt Brace, 1991), p. 93.

2. Bill Clinton, *My Life* (New York: Alfred A. Knopf, 2004), p. 635.

3. Hans J. Morgenthau, "The Purpose of Political Science," in James C. Charlesworth, ed., *A Design for Political Science: Scope, Objectives, and Methods,* Monograph no. 6 (Philadelphia: American Academy of Political and Social Science, 1966), pp. 67–68.

4. The concern is that humans are the makers of the tools that shape their environment, guide their vision, and help make their destiny. When people use these tools on themselves and other people, it is important to ask how these tools affect their vision of humanity. Charles Hampden-Turner, in *Radical Man: The Process of Psycho-Social Development* (New York: Anchor Books, 1971), argues that the scientific method has a very conservative bias when applied to the human environment.

5. John Maynard Keynes, *The General Theory of Employment, Interest, and Money* (New York: Harcourt Brace Jovanovich, 1966; originally published in 1936), p. 383.

6. A model is a simplified representation of how the real world works. Its usefulness is judged by how well it represents reality. Models may be depicted by mathematical equations, charts, and graphs, or may be descriptively stated.

7. Michel de Montaigne, *The Essays of Michel de Montaigne,* edited and translated by Jacob Zeitlin (New York: Alfred A. Knopf, 1936), vol. 3, p. 270 (emphasis in original).

8. See, for example, Larry Kiser and Elinor Ostrom, "The Three Worlds of Action," in Elinor Ostrom, ed., *Strategies of Political Inquiry* (Beverly Hills: Sage, 1982), pp. 179–222.

9. Theories require modification when **masked variables** are detected. A typical example of price discrimination that has been frequently used is doctors' pricing of health care services. A patient with fewer alternative providers, the theory postulates, can be charged a higher price for medical care. However, masked variables have caused trouble for this theory. Take the issue of race. Suppose that black patients have lower average incomes than whites. Some physicians might be less willing to accept black patients because of racism or because of a fear that black patients will be less able to pay for medical services. If that were true, according to the theory, then those physicians willing to treat black patients could charger higher prices and be less likely to lose black patients to other physicians. Some studies in the 1970s found support for that hypothesis. More recent studies using more extensive data have found no evidence of physician price discrimination on the basis of race. Earlier studies had not included region of the country, which masked cost of living and fee differentials and misattributed those effects to the racial composition of a physician's patients. The point is that this example illustrates the importance of not ending analysis at the theoretical level. The question must be pursued in the real world to determine if the theoretical argument is an accurate explanation of what is really happening. Accordingly, basing our understanding of the world and public policy on empirically empty theory is dangerous. See Alvin E. Headen Jr., "Price Discrimination in Physician Services Markets Based on Race: New Test of an Old Implicit Hypothesis," *Review of Black Political Economy* 15, no. 4 (Spring 1987): 5–20.

10. Russell Kirk, a critic of the scientific study of politics, has argued that "human beings are the least controllable, verifiable, law-obeying and predictable of subjects."

Russell Kirk, "Is Social Science Scientific?" in Nelson W. Polsby, Robert Dentler, and Paul Smith, eds., *Politics and Social Life* (Boston: Houghton Mifflin, 1963), p. 63.

11. For example, democratic society is based on the assumption that rational people acting "freely" may decide to violate the law. The cost of such action is determined by the probability of being punished. The sanction of the law makes sense in part because it presumes that most people will freely decide to obey the law. In fact it is only because we can act freely that we can be held responsible. For example, deranged individuals are less accountable precisely because they do not freely choose their actions. These, then, are research problems, not unbeatable methodological barriers.

12. In addition to institutes funded to conduct policy research, such as the American Enterprise Institute and the Brookings Institution, Congress employs thousands of staff members who also do such research. There are several thousand more analysts who work for other government support agencies, such as the General Accounting Office, the Office of Technology Assessment, the Congressional Research Service, and the Congressional Budget Office. These agencies generally respond to requests by congressional representatives and their staffs for specific studies. They also may engage in studies on their own initiative. As such, they are a significant source of policy agenda items.

13. David Easton, *A Systems Analysis of Political Life* (New York: John Wiley and Sons, 1965).

14. Paul A. Sabatier, "Political Science and Public Policy," *PS: Political Science and Politics* 24 (June 1991): 145.

15. For a sophisticated and sound theoretical treatment of agenda setting, see John Kingdon, *Agendas, Alternatives, and Public Policies* (Boston: Little, Brown, 1984). See also Barbara Nelson, *Making an Issue of Child Abuse* (Chicago: University of Chicago Press, 1984).

16. See Kingdon, *Agendas,* pp. 183–184.

17. See Roger W. Cobb and Charles D. Elder, *Participation in American Politics: The Dynamics of Agenda Building,* 2nd ed. (Baltimore: Johns Hopkins University Press, 1983), p. 85.

18. E. E. Schattschneider, *The Semi-Sovereign People: A Realist's View of Democracy in America* (New York: Holt, Rinehart, and Winston, 1960), p. 38.

19. Ibid., p. 39 (emphasis in original).

20. See Jeffrey M. Berry, "Subgovernments, Issue Networks, and Political Conflict," in Richard Harris and Signey Milkis, eds., *Remaking American Politics* (Boulder: Westview, 1990), pp. 239–269.

21. The lobbying on behalf of the B-1 bomber is an excellent example of an iron triangle at work. Although various studies over thirty years recommended against its production, the U.S. Air Force formed an alliance with various defense contractors to build the B-1. They were able to rouse political support for the program, valued in excess of $28 billion, in part because of the anticipated jobs the program would create across the country in forty-eight states. The U.S. Air Force and defense contractors lobbied many members of Congress who were not on any of the armed services committees, emphasizing the jobs and the money that would flow into each congressperson's state. See Nick Kotz, *Wild Blue Yonder: Money, Politics, and the B-1 Bomber* (Princeton: Princeton University Press, 1988).

22. A number of works make the point that the media, popular opinion to the contrary, tend to be conservative and supportive of the conservative bias of elites. See, for example, W. Lance Bennett, *News: The Politics of Illusion,* 2nd ed. (New York: Longman, 1988).

23. Charles D. Elder and Roger W. Cobb, *The Political Uses of Symbols* (New York: Longman, 1983), pp. 28–29.

24. It may be surprising to some that an administration committed to tax reduction would propose such a program. It was put forth in part to secure the support of the elderly, whose backing of the Republicans had been weak. The pay-as-you-go plan flopped, however. Retirees who had procured insurance benefits in the private sector led an effort to repeal the bill. The wealthier elderly did not want to trade some of their economic independence to help less-well-off retirees reach an equal plane regarding health care. They resented subsidizing the less wealthy. Those leading the opposition, however, appealed to the less wealthy retirees by arguing that the medical costs of the elderly should be the responsibility of younger Americans as well. They argued successfully that to make the elderly alone pay more, regardless of economic circumstances, was unfair, and the beginning of a reduction in benefits for all retirees was to be firmly resisted.

25. See Charles E. Lindblom, "The Science of 'Muddling Through,'" *Public Administration Review* 19, no. 2 (Spring 1959): 79–88.

26. Other supporters of the rational model agree that it is impossible to find the best of all possible courses of action. They would instead reduce the number of courses of action to a reasonable set of contenders. Then, statistical decisionmaking models might be used to decide on a final rational allocation of budgetary resources. However, critics point out that the initial selection of contenders is a political decision and arbitrary.

27. The budgeting process in the federal government is known as **line-item budgeting**. Congress presents to the president a budget, which is then broken down by organizational units, such as the Department of Energy, and then by subunits, such as renewable energy, solar energy, and so forth. Within all the subcategories, spending is broken down by accounts to include salaries, research, grants, and the like. A president using a line-item veto would merely be substituting one individual's judgment for the collective will of Congress—and a judgment presumably based just as much on ideology, special interest group pressure, partisan concerns, and personal views about the nature of the general welfare as that of any senator or congressional representative. To suggest taking politics out of the budgetary process is rather like saying one should take doctors out of medicine or pilots out of flying. That is, the budget is inherently a political document.

28. Aaron Wildavsky, *The Politics of the Budgetary Process* (Boston: Little, Brown, 1964; rev. 4th ed., 1984).

29. Robert Lineberry, *American Public Policy* (New York: Harper and Row, 1977), p. 71.

30. See Paul Sabatier, "Top-Down and Bottom-Up Models of Policy Implementation: A Critical Analysis and Suggested Synthesis," *Journal of Public Policy* 6 (January 1986): 21–48. See also Laurence O'Toole, "Policy Recommendations for Multi-Actor Implementation: An Assessment of the Field," *Journal of Public Policy* 6 (April 1986): 181–210.

31. See Peter C. Bishop and Augustus J. Jones, "Implementing the Americans with Disabilities Act of 1990: Assessing the Variables of Success," *Public Administration Review* 53 (March–April 1993): 121–128.

32. See Martha Derthick, *Agency Under Stress: The Social Security Administration in American Government* (Washington, D.C.: Brookings Institution, 1990).

CHAPTER 3

Rational Public Choice

This chapter is concerned with the theory of **rational choice**, which was originally developed by economists but was quickly adapted to other policy science disciplines. Indeed, there is nothing especially economic about rational behavior. There are several differences between the economic marketplace and political markets. In most economic markets, firms compete to sell products to the consumer, who makes the final choice. Theoretically at least, the consumer is sovereign. Production matches itself to the demand of consumers based on their willingness and ability to pay. Political markets are typically decided by a one-time choice at the ballot box in which a majority wins. Interested parties may continue to pressure an elected official for the duration of the term of office following the election, but all consumers get the same political goods whether it is health care, public schools, or national defense.

This chapter is concerned with how individuals and elected policymakers make decisions. Can we develop a set of assumptions regarding individual preferences, and from these derive principles of political behavior for individuals as well as those seeking election? Do elected officials' decisions reflect the will of the voters? Is the competition in the political marketplace as responsive to consumers' wishes as it is in the economic marketplace?

Rational Choice

Rational choice theory, sometimes called public choice, is the study of the collective decisions made by groups of individuals through the political process to maximize their own self-interest. Public choice assumes that individuals are just as rational and self-interested in the political sector as they are in the economic marketplace.[1] According to public choice theory, when people behave differently in the political sector than in the marketplace, it is because the institutional arrangements are different and not because of a lack of self-interest.

Many political scientists defend public choice as being wholly value-free and scientific.[2] Rational public choice attempts to provide an analysis and an explanation of the society as it is and not necessarily as it should be. That is, it explains actual social behavior. It explains why individuals with high incomes are more likely to vote than those with low incomes, and why they are more likely to be active members of special interest groups. The theory also suggests why there are built-in social and political supports for the status quo, because despite the claim of many of its practitioners that the theory is value-free, positive science, the conclusions of public choice have a definite modern-day conservative cast.

Personal Decisionmaking

In Chapter 2 we pointed out that human beings are multifaceted creatures. Human nature is too complex to be explained in one or two dimensions. But we do assume that people are *motivated* to engage in goal-directed actions to satisfy their needs. Each individual has a unique set of needs that are influenced by his or her own history, including gender, age, ethnic background, intellectual abilities, family situation, and financial status, to name just a few. Motivation theories tell us that we all are motivated to fulfill a variety of needs. Abraham Maslow proposed that there is a hierarchy of needs that is common to mentally healthy adults. Any of the five needs are capable of motivating behavior (see Figure 3.1).[3] He believed that these needs arranged themselves in a distinct order. According to his theory, as long as a lower-level need is unsatisfied, an individual will be highly motivated to choose actions calculated to satisfy that need.

According to this theory, once lower needs, like the physiological needs, are satisfied, a person will direct their attention toward satisfying their safety needs and so on. Research on Maslow's model has resulted in several criticisms, although none of the criticisms have been fatal. First, a person's needs may change over time. The needs of a young adult embarking on a new career and starting a family will differ from those of a veteran employee preparing for retirement. And changes in society may result in changes in the significance of different needs. For example, an economy falling into recession with rising unemployment may cause one to shift his or her attention from esteem needs to safety and physiological needs. A second criticism suggested by research is that people often work to satisfy several needs at the same time. For example, a person's employment may satisfy the physiological need to acquire money to provide for the survival needs, while simultaneously providing for safety needs through insurance and pension programs. One's peers at work may also satisfy esteem and self-actualization needs through friend-

Figure 3.1 Maslow's Need Hierarchy

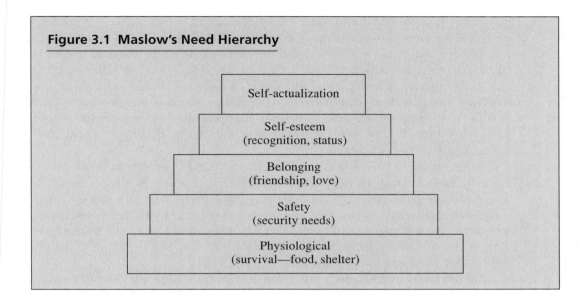

ship and the mutual participation in creative work endeavors. Despite these criticisms, Maslow's theory retains a certain popularity because of its intuitive appeal and because understanding how individual needs appear is critical in understanding what motivates individual behavior.

The conventional view of policymaking in the United States is that people act on the basis of self-interest in public and private affairs. The "public interest" may be understood as the entirety of these individual preferences expressed as choices. Society is improved when some people's preferences can be satisfied without making other people worse off. Usually we assume the economic market will serve best to improve society. Public policies are needed when a policy makes improvements more efficiently than does the market.[4] This is not a statement of how public policies are actually made, but how they are justified.[5]

Public policy is interested in purposeful rational choice. In this sense, rational behavior simply means making choices the consumer believes will maximize personal satisfaction or utility. Adam Smith described this as "the desire of bettering our condition," which begins at birth and never ends until we go to our graves.

Since the concept of rational self-interest is often a source of misunderstanding, it is important to clarify its meaning.[6] Rational self-interest means that individuals have preferences. People *intend* to act in such a way to achieve those preferences when the expected benefits exceed the costs of available choices. Since people try to make decisions by comparing costs and benefits, their behavior may change if the costs or benefits they face change. Rational choice follows the basic rule of logic that holds that behavior is rational as long as its marginal benefit is equal to its marginal cost. A rational actor is expected to choose the action that will *maximize* expected benefits. This simple rule of logic is central to rational choice thinking. The **marginal benefit** from taking certain action is the increase in total benefit from doing it once more, while the **marginal cost** is the increase in total costs from doing it once more. Behavior is maximized by making decisions until the net benefit equals the net cost.

Some rational choices may seem irrational. For example, a rational choice made by an individual with limited information may not appear rational to someone with more information. A consumer may pay a high price for a product when the identical item may be for sale at a much lower price at another store nearby. But the consumer may not be aware that the other store carries the product, let alone at a lower price. Decisions are often made with less than perfect information. Information has a cost in time, and sometimes in money.

Rational self-interest does not mean that people make the best decisions. Mistakes will still be made. Decisions are usually made under conditions of limited information. The costs associated with acquiring all the relevant information may be too high, or the information required for utility-maximizing behavior may not be available. For example, the government spends close to $30 billion a year to acquire the best information available regarding other countries' capabilities and intentions. Much of the information is gathered despite the attempts of other countries to maintain their secrecy. The government may formulate foreign policy based on the best available intelligence findings. Failures of foreign policy occur when there is an incorrect assessment of the intelligence information, or an inability to uncover all critical information.

Even if the full range of information needed to make a truly rational, self-interested choice is unavailable or too great for a person to adequately assimilate, the *process of choice* rather than the outcome of the process can still be considered rational. Behavior may be procedurally rational when it is the outcome of appropriate consideration based on incomplete information. Rational behavior does not mean that individuals never make a bad decision. Still, only a self-destructive individual will knowingly choose an inferior alternative to a more preferred one.

People may make irrational decisions, for example, by ignoring opportunity costs. An individual who squanders his money gambling and is then unable to pay his rent or mortgage has acted irresponsibly, and to a public choice theorist, irrationally. There is evidence that people learn from their experience and, when faced with a repeated situation, learn to consider opportunity costs. The concept of rational self-interest only holds that an individual would never knowingly choose a higher-cost means of achieving a given end when a lower-cost alternative is available. The notion that people will respond to incentives in predictable ways is central to rational choice and to public policy. If the cost of health care rises in real terms (adjusted for changes in inflation), less will be demanded. Drivers will buckle their seat belts if the perceived benefit (reduced risk of injury) outweighs the cost (the time spent buckling and the discomfort of the restraint). But if the cost of their use is viewed as exceeding the benefit, seat belts will remain unbuckled. People will try to reduce costs and increase benefits to themselves.

Rational self-interest arouses ambivalence in many people. It evokes images of reason and informed decisionmaking on the one hand, but on the other hand suggests a sophisticated self-centered behavior. Rational self-interest is not the same as selfishness or greed. An individual who is injured in an accident and seeks medical attention is acting in his or her self-interest, but we would not accuse the individual of being selfish because of that action. By the same token, obeying the law may be in one's self-interest, but it is not selfish conduct. Selfish conduct is behavior that disregards the interest of others in situations in which their interests should not be ignored. For example, to take an ample supply of food and water on a camping trip is not selfish, but to refuse to share some of one's excess food to a hiker who has been lost and without food would be.

Rational self-interest does not deny altruism. Individuals may act out of altruism in working in soup kitchens or in homeless shelters. However, rational self-interest does suggest that the altruistic behavior of individuals will be affected by changing perceptions of costs and benefits. For example, if tax deductions for charitable contributions are reduced or eliminated, such contributions will decline. Conversely, increasing the tax benefit for charitable contributions will result in an increase in such constributions.[7] The corollary to the point that rational self-interest does not coincide with selfishness is the observation that rational self-interest does not mean individuals are motivated solely by the pursuit of material goods. Individuals may be motivated by love, justice, power, and other abstract influences. It is still true, however, that economic welfare may often be the basis for achieving even many nonmaterial goals.

None of the foregoing is meant to suggest that individuals consciously calculate benefits and costs before selecting an alternative. Rational self-interest describes *behavior,* not thought processes.[8] A physicist would describe the forces involved in achieving balance in riding a bicycle quite differently than the average adolescent riding one. However, the child riding a bike will act as if he or she has a physicist's understanding when, in fact, he or she does not.

Rational self-interest is an assumption about the way people do behave, and is not a judgment about how they should behave. The term *rational* does not indicate approval or disapproval of the goal itself.

Calvin and Hobbes © 1990 Watterson. Reprinted with permission of Universal Press Syndicate. All rights reserved.

The Tragedy of the Commons

Any discussion of rational self-interested behavior should point out that individual rationality and group rationality are not identical and may even be opposed. To understand this dilemma, we consider a metaphorical story written by biologist Garrett Hardin. Hardin asks us to assume that several farmers use a common pasture to graze their sheep. As the common meadow is owned by everyone, it is the responsibility of no one. The total number of sheep grazing this pasture is at the maximum sustainable amount of grass the pasture can yield to maintain the sheep. It is in the farmers' collective interest not to allow any additional sheep to graze in this pasture and to try to secure an agreement among themselves to that effect.

But since the sheep are the sole means of livelihood for each farmer, the number of sheep each farmer has directly relates to the income his family has. For each farmer, therefore, the rational strategy is to sneak additional sheep into his flock to graze in the common meadow. The point is that it is always in the individual's self-interest to exploit the commons to the maximum (whether it is public grazing land, the environment, or fisheries), because the individual will receive all the benefits of his action, while the cost will be shared by all members of the community. The triumph of rational egoism through market capitalism has the effect of aggravating the **tragedy of the commons**. It may also serve to reduce trust and the feeling of community between the members of society.

Each farmer has an incentive to act according to a short time horizon to improve his personal well-being. But at some point in the future this behavior, though individually rational, will result in the disintegration of the entire commons from overgrazing. The individual farmer is seeking immediate large gains over what appear to be smaller losses in the remote future. The tragedy of the commons is found in the conflict between individual interests and the well-being of the collective. If the meadow were privately owned, the farmer with title to the property would have an incentive not to overgraze his meadow. The moral of the metaphor is that individual rational self-interested behavior to maximize private gain may be suboptimal in the long run.

The story concerns what policy analysts call "the public interest" and what economists call "collective goods." The ideas revealed in the tragedy of the commons undermine Adam Smith's laissez-faire assumption that self-interested behavior will maximize social benefit. Many of those who identified themselves as libertarian in the 1990s were drawn from conservative circles and the "New Left" of the 1960s and 1970s, both of which applied the same laissez-faire logic to politics that others applied to economics.

From Individual to Group Choice

We have looked at the behavior of individuals when they act to maximize their utility. Now we turn our attention to consider how the model might be applied to explain or predict the behavior of government. Rational choice theory when applied to government or public policy decisionmaking is often referred to as **public choice theory**. For our purposes, we can use "rational choice" and "public choice" interchangeably.

A basic premise of rational public choice is that "political man/woman" (political entrepreneurs, voters, and members of special interest groups) and "economic man/woman" (producers and consumers) are one and the same person. The person who votes or runs for political office is also the consumer of economic goods and concerned with opportunity costs. In both roles people decide on their preferences based on their rational self-interest, and act purposefully to bring about outcomes that are desirable to them. Again this is not to deny that people may also have social consciences or value altruism. But it suggests why it may be difficult to develop a broad commitment in society to transfer benefits from contributors to noncontributors—that is, from the privileged to the poor. It also suggests why the haves acquire more power with which to further their self-interest than do the have-nots.

It is based on the premise that competition takes place in the political arena. Although the coercive power of government is imposing, it is still limited by several factors. It is constrained, first, by the resources that it can command. The government relies on its taxing and spending powers in many instances to conduct public policy. The function of taxes is to transfer control over capital from the private sector to the public sector. By using this purchasing power to buy goods and

---

Case Study: The Tragedy of the Commons and Common Resources

As the tragedy of the commons illustrates, when people own resources in common, they have little incentive to use them efficiently. Private decisionmakers have an incentive to overuse the common resource. Government's policy response is to impose a cost for the use of the resource to reduce its overuse.

Fisheries are the classic example of overuse of a common resource. Fish and whales have commercial value, which every fisher has an economic incentive to exploit. But no one has an economic incentive to manage or protect these fisheries. Fish and mammals in the ocean are often considered a common resource. Cod, tuna, mackerel, and many other species are being seriously depleted by overfishing. The natural tendency is for every fishing vessel to take as many fish as possible from the oceans.

The United Nations has found it extremely difficult to develop a global system to manage the common fishery and repropagate depleted species. The difficulty in reaching an agreement on how a treaty regulating fishing rights would be policed and enforced, especially among newly independent states that are very sensitive to issues of national sovereignty, makes it difficult to reach a negotiated settlement. Within a country's internal waters, governments may pass laws with relative ease, placing limits on the size or total catch of fish, charging a fee for a license to catch fish, and limiting fishing seasons. Some entrepreneurs have tried to control their exclusive access to privatized stocks by developing "fish farms."

Note that many animals with commercial value have been threatened with extinction when viewed as a common resource (buffalo and elephants, for example). Many other animals with commercial value (cattle, chickens, and cows) are not threatened with extinction. In fact, their commercial value provides a sufficient incentive for private ownership. And it provides the owners with an incentive to conserve these resources for future generations.

Pollution of the environment is another example of market failure in dealing with a common resource. An environment with clean water and clean air is a common resource for all to enjoy. Excessive pollution that degrades the environment beyond its ability to naturally replenish itself demonstrates the tendency to overuse a common resource to the detriment of all.

---

services for the public, the government is altering the mix of goods and services that would be demanded if everything were left to the private sector. This inevitably means a move to a different point on the production possibilities curve (see Chapter 1).

The government is also constrained by the political landscape. For example, there are only two major political parties in the United States, which constrains the selection of alternatives by the voters. In the private sector, if there were only two firms producing a good, we would define the market as a shared monopoly with no competition to give consumers a choice.

The public choice theory of government stresses that government actions result from the effort of politicians and government workers attempting to maximize their own interests rather than the public interest. To understand how and why the government operates as it does, it is necessary to understand the complex network of individuals each attempting to maximize their own objectives.

We often think of government officials as motivated by the desire to follow policies that promote the general welfare. The government is made up of a collection of individuals, most of whom are sincerely dedicated to promoting the perceived general welfare. They may have different views about what constitutes the general welfare, and their views on the subject may change. Dedicated officials may have conflicting goals. For example, an elected official's views may clash with the majority that elected him or her, which may create a dilemma around the desire to be reelected. Similar conflicts may arise when a candidate for office has an opportunity to receive a campaign contribution from an organization that favors certain policies different from his or her own. The problem is made more difficult if a much needed contribution will go to an opponent if the candidate will not support the contributing organization's policies. The final decision will be based on cost and benefit calculations.

Since every elected official will be subjected to his or her own conflicting pressures, it is not accurate to think of the government as a single entity having a well-defined set of objectives. The U.S. government acts through a distinctive assortment of institutional arrangements to develop public policy. Our representative democracy is based on majority voting, frequently focused through special interest groups, and its policies and programs are implemented by a government bureaucracy. Rational public choice theory makes it clear that government policy-making, like market allocation, may not result in the best attainable outcome. A society may be faced with the dilemma of choosing between a market solution that is imperfect and a government policy that is also not perfect. Simplistic notions demanding that we should return to basics and "let the market do it" or that we should abandon the market and "let government do it" must themselves be abandoned. Instead, the costs and benefits of market solutions to social problems, government solutions, or a combination of the two must be examined in order to select policies that will be the most effective in meeting society's needs.

Whenever market performance is judged to be defective, we speak of market failure. Market failure does not mean that nothing good has happened, but only that the best attainable outcome has not been produced. There are two senses of "the best attainable outcome has not been produced." One relates to the inability of the market to achieve efficiency in the distribution of the community's resources. The other sense concerns the failure of the market to further social goals, such as achieving the desired distribution of income or providing adequate health care for everyone. Consequently, a private market that functions without government intervention may lead to consequences a society is unwilling to accept.

Cost-Benefit Analysis

Public policy is the political decision by a state to take action. The increasing use of cost-benefit analysis to gauge the appropriateness of a policy decision typifies the application of market-based criteria to gauge the appropriateness of state action. **Cost-benefit analysis** is one of the most widely used tools of policy analysts. Cost-benefit analysis finds and compares the total costs and benefits to society of providing a public good. When several options are being considered for adoption, the one with the greatest benefit after considering the costs should be selected.

The need for public goods compels government intervention to provide a variety of goods and services that the market will not produce on its own in an optimal quantity for the society. The government must then decide not only what kinds of goods to provide but also what quantity to provide. However, the government cannot easily obtain the required information to decide which public goods to provide or the correct quantities. Since consumers of public goods or services have incentives not to disclose their true preferences and to downplay their willingness to pay in the hopes that others will be taxed, how is the government to decide how much to provide? Moreover, when government moves to use resources to alter the mix of goods and services produced, there will inevitably be conflicting goals and constituencies between which political choices must be made. Government finds itself in the middle of the adversarial relationship between those private sector forces that stand to lose as a result of government action and those that stand to gain.

In theory, determining the optimal mix of output is uncomplicated. More government sector endeavors are advisable only if the gains from those activities exceed their opportunity costs. So cost-benefit analysis as applied to government activities is used to calculate and compare the difference between the costs and the benefits of a program or project. Basically, the benefits of a proposed public project are compared to the value of the private goods given up (through taxes) to produce it. But while the notion that the benefits or utility of a project should exceed its costs is uncomplicated enough in principle, determining this ratio in practice is exceedingly complex.

In theory, all the costs and benefits of a program should be identified and converted into monetary units covering the life of the proposed project. Ideally, an attempt is made to consider the negative externalities resulting from the program, such as the roadside businesses that will be lost due to the construction of a new limited-access highway. In theory also, with benefits and costs measured in the same units, the benefits and costs of alternative policies can be determined not just within a policy sector, but also across diverse sectors. For example, cost-benefit analysis could be used to determine policy alternatives in health care such as whether funds would be more efficiently spent on prenatal care for pregnant women who are indigent, on AIDS research, or on a screening and preventive medicine program to reduce mortality from cardiovascular disease. Such analysis then could also be used to determine if the funds to be allocated to the health care program with the highest benefit-to-cost ratio would be more efficiently spent if allocated to the construction of a dam.

Political Entrepreneurs

Politicians play a role similar to business entrepreneurs when they seek votes for political office and when they make collective political decisions. In markets, consumers register their opinions about the value of a product by the simple decision of whether to buy it or not. Consumers register their votes with dollar bills. In political markets, politicians demand votes supplied by citizens. Technically, votes cannot be bought and sold in electoral markets. Instead, politicians must accumulate or purchase (bribe?) votes by carefully positioning themselves on a variety of policy issues in order to appeal to more voters than can opposing candidates. All politicians appeal to voters with an argument that suggests a bribe: "You should vote for me because I will do more for your welfare than will my opponent."

Positioning includes conveying impressions of greater talent, higher moral

---

Case Study: The Difficulty in Applying Cost-Benefit Analysis

The most efficient use of public resources would be to rank proposed programs from highest to lowest in terms of their benefit-cost ratios, and proceed to implement those programs in priority order, beginning with those having the highest ratios. This would meet one goal of cost-benefit analysis: determining the most efficient way of using public funds. But cost-benefit analysis has a second goal: determining the merit of specific government policies, such as discouraging the use of disposable containers, encouraging higher average mile-per-gallon standards for use of gasoline by automobiles, promoting transportation safety, and establishing honesty in product labeling. "Merit" is different from "efficiency," but it also has economic consequences.

In dealing with private market goods, the demand for a particular good determines the benefits of its production. But in regard to some public goods, the benefits generated by their "output" are less clear. For example, government control over air quality usually involves political tradeoffs between a healthy and aesthetic environment and the loss of production of other economic goods. Reducing air pollution from automobiles increases the price of cars, which results in the decreased production of automobiles and

continues

Case Study   continued

therefore fewer jobs. In this case, the losers from this government policy are those whose jobs are lost or who cannot afford to buy a higher-priced car. The winners are those who advocate environmental protection, and those who will suffer fewer illnesses (or perhaps will not die) because of a cleaner atmosphere. The objective of public policy is to promote the welfare of society. The welfare of society must depend on the welfare of individuals. It is people that count.

Cost-benefit analysis emphasizes measurement and tangible factors. Its insistence on quantifying measures almost invariably stresses costs over benefits. The main reason for this is that in areas such as education, environment, and health, policies produce benefits that cannot be quantified, while the costs are much more easily calculated. How does one put a value on human life, for example? To the individual or a spouse or one's child, human life is priceless in that no amount of money would be accepted for those lives. However, lives are not priceless or we would provide everyone with unlimited health care, require cars to be much safer, and require much lower speed limits. Some courts have determined the value of a life by estimating what the individual might have earned if they had had a normal life expectancy. But this leads to the absurd conclusion that a disabled or retired person's life has no value. Another method is to examine the risks people voluntarily take in their jobs and how much they must be paid to agree to take them. Or how does one put a value of the survival of the spotted owl, which has little or no economic value, against the value of harvesting the trees in the state of Washington, the value of which can be easily assessed?

Citizens may be aware of the costs of programs in terms of their taxes paid, but may not be aware of noticeable benefits for a recession or flood averted, or a healthier environment. In some cases then, leaders may be punished for their planning and judgment.

Another defect of cost-benefit analysis is that it does not consider the distributional question of who should pay the cost and who should receive the benefits. It may be that a new highway will displace residents in a low-income housing project, while it will benefit affluent business investors who own commercially zoned land along the proposed highway route.

The most serious defect of cost-benefit analysis, however, is that it seeks to maximize only the value of efficiency when other values such as equity, justice, or even the environment might deserve inclusion in the consideration of public policy decisions. Since it is not possible to reduce moral or ethical concerns to the requirements of cost-benefit analysis, this means the analysts who use this approach must go beyond it in making their policy recommendations; not to do so will have the effect of positively excluding normative concerns. In a period of tight federal budgets, government officials often defend their reliance on cost-benefit analysis by claiming that they should not be involved in controversial "ideological" debates, but rather only with the most efficient policy. They may even assert a moral obligation to apply cost-benefit analysis in order to save taxpayers money. Such analysis is useful for clarifying approaches to problems, but it is not without methodological difficulties and it is certainly not "value-free."

character, and a preferred vision of the nation's future. Politicians with strong policy views on some issues may try to put them in a new context and suggest new arguments that voters may find appealing. Persuasion may be more successful with new issues about which many voters have not formed strong opinions.

An elected official also is expected to reflect the views of his or her constituents, not merely his or her own personal views. But unlike business, wherein consumers clearly "vote" on products by buying or not buying them, in politics the voting mechanism is not well suited to determining how constituents want to be represented on any given issue. Take education as an example. In theory, one votes for more education by electing the candidate committed to initiating new educational programs or putting more resources into the sector. Nonetheless, in practice it is much more complicated than this, since every candidate campaigns on a whole series of issues, of which education is only one, and the winning candidate may have been elected on the basis of issues other than his or her position on education or even despite it. This makes constituent views on any issue difficult to discern, nor is there any reliable way to assign weights to the different views of voters.

Furthermore, fewer than half of those eligible to vote usually participate in any given election. Presidential elections draw the highest voter turnout, while for off-year congressional and state elections the turnout rarely exceeds 40 percent of those registered to vote.[9] Presidential voter turnout peaked at 63 percent of persons over twenty-one years of age in 1960, but has declined since. In 1992, voting turnout increased to 55 percent due in part to the high level of interest sparked by a strong third-party candidate, but declined in 1996 to 49 percent of eligible voters. In 1996, Bill Clinton was elected with 49.2 percent of the votes cast for president. Of 196.5 million eligible voters, 151.7 million (about 77 percent) were actually registered to vote. Of those registered, 95.8 million actually turned out on election day to cast their ballots. The participation rate was just 63 percent of registered voters and less than half (48.8 percent) of eligible voters. Thus Clinton was elected by about 23 percent of eligible voters. The 2004 election witnessed another high tide of voter turnout, with 61 percent of eligible voters casting a ballot. President George W. Bush won 50.8 percent of the 122 million votes cast, compared to Senator John Kerry's 48.3 percent. Without question, the 2004 election turnout was affected by the extraordinary battle for the White House in 2000. The prolonged contest that resulted in a victory for Bush in 2000 was beset with voting irregularities throughout the country, though mainly in the state of Florida. Ultimately, Bush defeated opponent Al Gore by just 537 votes, according to the University of Chicago's National Opinion Research Center. This confused chapter in U.S. voting history saw many people going to the polls planning to vote for one candidate and realizing that they had cast an invalid ballot. Such anomalies cast such a shadow on the Bush White House that voting turnout in the 2004 election grew significantly as considerable numbers of otherwise disinterested Americans acted on their civic duty and voted. Therefore, since the first task of political entrepreneurs is to get elected and the second is to get reelected,[10] and since they are expected to reflect the views of their constituents, this means they are likely to reflect the views of constituents who actually vote or who make their views known to their political representatives in other ways (writing letters, lobbying, etc.).

The voting records of congressional representatives, senators, and even presidents reflect a heightened awareness of constituent interests as elections draw nearer. Conversely, their voting records show more independence immediately after they are safely in office. Senators show the most independence after an election, since they are safely in office for six years. Members of the House of Representatives, who run for reelection every two years, are the most closely attuned to the views of the constituents who voted for them. Their high return rate to Congress may reflect this to some extent. Presidents also respond to the political market pressures exerted by the not-so-invisible hands of voters at the ballot box. The late H. R. Haldeman, Richard Nixon's chief of staff, noted how political self-interest dominated that administration's policymaking when he wrote the following in his diary on December 15, 1970:

> K [Henry Kissinger] came in and the discussion covered some of the general thinking about Vietnam and the P's [President Nixon's] big peace plan for next year, which K later told me he does not favor. He thinks that any pullout next year would be a serious mistake because the adverse reaction to it could set in well before the '72 elections. He favors, instead, a continued winding down and then a pullout right at the fall of '72 so that if any bad results follow they will be too late to affect the election.[11]

President Nixon understood that the United States could not "win" in Vietnam and that after a U.S. pullout, the South Vietnamese army would disintegrate. In the end, he agreed with Kissinger and delayed that outcome for political reasons. After the election in 1972, an agreement was signed in January 1973 on terms that quickly led to the inevitable North Vietnamese victory. In the private marketplace, communications between consumers and producers are much more direct and time-sensitive.

Ballots and Decisionmaking

Political discussions often make references to the "will of the people." But ascertaining what that will is, when people make conflicting demands, is not an easy task. Different voting rules have been suggested, including unanimity voting, simple majority voting, and two-thirds majority voting.

Case Study: Voting and Choice

Do people vote based on rational choice? There are three major factors, which often overlap, that go into the voting choice. **Party identification** is the sense of an affiliation with a perspective on politics and an evaluation of policy issues. Party identification is often acquired during childhood from the family. It is reinforced or subverted by the socialization process in college and subsequently within one's career and peer groups. **Candidate appeal** has grown in importance alongside the growth of media coverage and the ability to package and market a candidate. The ability to focus on a candidate's strengths (or an opponent's weakness) through the press is extraordinary. Television sound-bites can be used to emphasize the positive elements of one candidate's character and the negative elements in an opponent's background. Personal qualities may be more easily assessed than the candidates' positions on complicated issues. This is especially so since candidates frequently and deliberately obscure their positions on issues so they cannot be easily attacked. The impact of **issues** as assessed by voters is also significant. Voters typically do not vote based on one specific policy issue such as national health care or education. During the Cold War, Republicans were able to capitalize on such issues as foreign policy and fear of the Soviet Union. By 1992, with the collapse of the Soviet Union, George H. W. Bush was vulnerable for his handling of the economy, which most described in negative terms. Bill Clinton emphasized the state of the economy and the deficit in his campaign. To maintain the campaign's focus, a sign at Clinton's campaign headquarters reminded the staff that, "It's the economy, stupid!" Many voters cast *retrospective votes*— that is, judging the incumbent on how he *has* performed—rather than voting *prospectively* on what he promises to do if elected.

As Table 3.1 suggests, the higher a person's socioeconomic status as measured by income, education, employment, and other demographic characteristics, the more likely the person will be to register and vote. These same characteristics also influence *how* they vote. Age is a significant factor affecting voter turnout. Older voters may be more settled in their lives and have experienced voting as an expected activity, and so are more likely to vote than the young. Ethnic background is also important in determining the level of voter turnout. Whites are most likely to vote, followed by blacks and then Hispanics. Women have recently been more likely to vote than men. Generally speaking, the more education one has the more likely one is to vote. Differences in income levels also lead to differences in voter turnout. Wealthier voters are overrepresented among those who actually vote. Low-income and less-educated people are less likely to vote. Of course, these demographic characteristics may reinforce each other. White voters are more likely to have a higher income and (closely related) more education. The issues that bound the 2004 election differed from those in previous years. While the 2000 election was fractured by voting anomalies, the 2004 election swung on issues of terrorism and moral values.

Nonvoting is also a choice. The most frequently cited reasons for nonvoting are that people think their vote does not count, and that they do not know enough about the candidates or the issues. About a fourth of nonvoters indicate that they are disgusted with the government or the choice of candidates. Can the decision not to vote be a result of cost-benefit calculations? Can a decision to remain ignorant of the candidates and the issues really be considered **rational ignorance**?

Table 3.1 A Demographic Portrait of Voters, 2004

Characteristic	All Voters (%)	Bush (%)	Kerry (%)	Nader (%)
Gender		51	48	1
Men	46	55	44	0
Women	54	48	51	0
Race				
White	77	58	41	0
Black	11	11	88	0
Hispanic	8	44	53	2
Age				
18–29 years old	17	45	54	0
30–44 years old	29	53	46	1
45–59 years old	30	51	48	0
60 and older	24	54	46	0
Education				
No high school diploma	4	49	50	0
High school graduate	22	52	47	0
Some college	32	54	46	0
College graduate	26	52	46	1
Postgraduate education	16	44	55	1
Religion				
White Protestant	54	59	40	0
Catholic	27	52	47	0
Jewish	3	25	74	< 1
Party				
Republican	37	93	6	0
Independent	26	48	49	1
Democrat	37	11	89	0
Family income				
Under $15,000	8	36	63	0
$15,000–$29,999	15	42	57	0
$30,000–$49,999	22	49	50	0
$50,000–$74,999	23	56	43	0
$75,000–$99,999	14	55	45	0
Over $100,000	18	60	38	1
Other issues				
Born again[a]		78	21	< 1
Gay, lesbian, bisexual		23	77	< 1
Economy, jobs		18	80	< 1
Terrorism		86	14	< 1
Moral values		80	18	< 1

Source: http://www.cnn.com/Election/2004.
Note: a. Fundamentalist Christians who claim to have been born again in religious truth.

Unanimity

In an ideal world, there would be no conflict. Public choice would result from the unanimity of views from the population. The great advantage of the **unanimity rule** ensures that no one is misused, since every voter must approve each proposition. The difficulty with a unanimity rule is that each voter has a veto power. Anyone likely to be made worse off by the proposal would veto it. Thus a government's public policies would have to meet the condition of a **Pareto improvement**, which occurs when a reallocation of resources causes at least one person to be better off without making anyone else worse off.[12] Unanimity is at the base of any policy agreement between two individuals in that, when two people agree on a policy, they do so because it makes both of them better off. That is, they are unanimous in agreeing to the exchange or they would not have agreed on it. But in the world of public policy matters, unanimity is not likely to lead to useful outcomes.

Suppose, for example, that a remote community is considering the construction of a satellite dish to receive otherwise inaccessible television programming. Suppose also that the dish is to be financed by dividing the cost equally among the members of the community. Sensing how much the project means to everyone else, one villager who greatly desires access to satellite television may nevertheless profess a preference for keeping the intrusions of the outside world out of the community's peaceful valley. He or she may then demand a large bribe not to veto the project. A unanimity rule is an invitation to bribery because it offers individuals an incentive to hide their true preferences regarding public goods in order to reduce personal costs or to gain something at the expense of others. The costs of reaching a decision under such conditions are prohibitive, and government paralysis results, with no practical decisions able to be made. Therefore it is necessary to accept some principle for public decisionmaking short of unanimity.

Majority Voting

The excessively high cost of decisionmaking associated with unanimity voting leads to a search for lower-cost alternatives. The **majority voting rule** provides that in the choice between alternatives, an action or decision is approved if it receives a majority of the votes. Majority rule is a basic principle of decisionmaking in democratic societies.

Unfortunately, majority rule also has serious problems. For example, under it, a bare majority may get some benefit no matter how slight, while a ponderous sacrifice is exacted from the minority. Thus majority rule may result in a situation in which a society is worse off in that the benefit to the majority may fall far short of the total costs imposed on the minority.

For example, suppose there are 100 villagers in the aforementioned remote community considering the investment in the satellite dish. Each would require a line from the dish to their cottage to receive the benefit of the cost to the community. Suppose under majority rule that 51 villagers vote to invest in the satellite dish and connect their cottages by cable to it, and also to assess every villager an equal amount to pay for the dish and the hookups. The minority 49 villagers who voted against the measure must pay the tax but will get no benefit and thus will suffer significantly, while the majority 51 villagers may well receive a benefit that barely exceeds their assessment. Consequently, there is an overall loss to this community because of majority rule.

Majority rule can be inefficient also because a policy that may benefit a minority a great deal may be defeated if it makes the majority slightly worse off. For instance, most people will not contract AIDS. But for the minority who do, the cost of treatment is extremely high. The majority may resist paying a relatively small tax to cover the cost of health care for those so afflicted, however.

This example depicts the major weakness of majority rule, and one long recognized: *it places minority rights at risk.* Thus, most democratic forms of government that employ majority rule try to protect the rights of minorities against "overbearing" majorities by constitutional means.[13]

The Voting Paradox

Majority rule does not generate such manifestly unfair results if voters act rationally in their decisions. But for rational behavior to occur, **transitivity** is necessary.[14] However, majority rule may not necessarily generate a transitive group decision, even though each individual chooses rationally.

Table 3.2 shows an example of what happens when transitivity is violated. In this example, the situation is perfectly symmetrical in that all three voters rank their preferences for three different issues. Every policy is one person's first choice, another person's second choice, and yet another's third choice. But if two policy issues are voted on at a time, it will result in an intransitive ranking. Each person presumably ranks the issues in order of importance to themselves.

As shown in Tables 3.2 and 3.3, if education is paired against health care, education wins, as it is Colleen's first choice and Cassie prefers it to health care. If health care is opposed to housing, health care wins, as it is Mike's first choice and Colleen's second choice. If housing is paired against education, housing wins, as Mike prefers it to education and joins Cassie in a winning coalition. Here majority rule has resulted in incompatible results. It is this inconsistency that is the **voting paradox**: majority rule can produce inconsistent social choices even if all voters make consistent choices. If the second and third choices of one of the voters were reversed in Table 3.2, the paradox would disappear. Nonetheless, majority rule may

Table 3.2   The Voting Paradox

Program	Colleen	Mike	Cassie
Education	1st choice	3rd choice	2nd choice
Health care	2nd choice	1st choice	3rd choice
Housing	3rd choice	2nd choice	1st choice

result in no clear winner. When majority rule does not result in transitive preferences, any policy choice is somewhat arbitrary. The final choice will be determined by the political process. Table 3.3 illustrates the outcome based on the pairings of the voters.

The majority party in the legislature usually can determine the agenda and the order of voting, and thereby control the outcome. Regardless of the option selected, a political entrepreneur can argue that he or she followed the popular mandate. This inconsistency leads to incongruous policies in which, for example, the government provides agricultural subsidies that raise the prices of food items and then provides food stamps to assist poor people in purchasing the higher-priced foodstuffs.

In the example shown in Tables 3.2 and 3.3, if limited funds mean only one or two programs can be funded, which program is funded will depend entirely on the arbitrary order in which they are taken up. The result highlights the importance of how the voting agenda is set.[15] The outcome of voting between several alternatives will often depend on the order in which the choices are considered.

Table 3.3   Opposing Choices and Outcomes

Opposing Choices	Outcome
Education versus health care	Education
Health care versus housing	Health care
Housing versus education	Housing

Logrolling: Rolling Along or Getting Rolled

Majority voting rules allow voters to vote either "yes" or "no" on an issue. The vote disregards the intensity of the views held by the voters. The votes of those who are fervently in support of a bill count the same as the votes of those only mildly in favor. And while ordinary voters seldom trade their votes, it is not unusual for legislators to trade votes. This form of vote trading is often used to organize compromises that include several policy issues in one informal understanding. **Logrolling** is vote trading by representatives who care more intensely about one issue, with representatives who care more intensely about another issue. Legislator A may agree to vote for a bill that Legislator B feels strongly about in return for B's promise to vote for a bill that is very important to A. This logrolling provides a way for a minority group on one issue to win the vote and become a majority in return for changing a vote on another issue that the minority finds less important.

With single issues, the intensity of preference in voting is not important. However, in the political process, the issues being considered are always multiple, and each involves varying degrees of support by minorities. Some people are very concerned about some issues, while other people are indifferent regarding those particular policies. By trading votes, representatives can register just how strongly they feel about various issues. Suppose Katherine and Chip tend to be slightly negatively inclined toward more defense spending (see Table 3.4). Christy, however, strongly feels the need for more defense spending. In a system that permits logrolling, Christy may be able to convince Katherine to vote for more defense spending if Christy promises to vote for a health care bill sponsored by Katherine.

Logrolling can increase or decrease government program efficiency depending on the circumstances. But the practice has its defenders. They contend that logrolling can potentially lead to public policies of benefit to society that otherwise would not be produced. Such vote trading also has the advantage of revealing the intensity of preferences. And finally, compromises, such as those implicit in logrolling, are necessary for a democratic system to function.

Table 3.4 illustrates the advantages of logrolling. If both policies—health care and defense—were put to a simple majority vote, both would lose. But passing them is a Pareto improvement in that everyone is better off relative to not passing them. In this case, logrolling can overcome the problem of an "oppressive majority."

Logrolling can just as easily lead to negative outcomes for society. Table 3.5 illustrates the same programs as those shown in Table 3.4. However, Chip opposes both more intensely. The sum of the preferences indicates that Chip's intense opposition will count for more than the combined support by Christy and Katherine. Thus logrolling among the three will hurt the chances of both programs being

Table 3.4   Logrolling—Positive Outcome

	Christy	Katherine	Chip	Net Benefit to Society's Welfare
Health care	+20	−5	−3	+12
Defense	−5	+20	−3	+12

Note: Logrolling can produce an efficient outcome when the benefits (+) exceed the costs (−) to each individual or society. Each project would lose with simple majority voting. Yet with logrolling, each project can pass, improving the general welfare.

passed. If neither program passes, there will be a net loss to society's welfare, even if Christy and Katherine logroll as before because the net benefit to them individually is greater.

Tying two bills together can be very convenient for legislators, who can then claim they do not support policies opposed by their constituents even though they voted for them. They defend themselves by arguing that they did not want the health care bill, for example, but had to vote for it to get the defense bill they and their constituents did want.

In general, logrolling has a negative reputation. Called "pork-barrel" legislation, it may lead to policies that are not only inefficient, but also opposed by the majority of voters. For example, the United States maintains many military bases that do not contribute significantly to national security. Unneeded military bases

Table 3.5   Logrolling—Inefficient Result

	Christy	Katherine	Chip	Net Loss to Society's Welfare
Health care	+20	−5	−17	−2
Defense	−5	+20	−17	−2

Note: If the costs (−) exceed the benefits (+), logrolling can lead to an inefficient outcome.

are notoriously difficult to close down, however, because congressional representatives in effect become lobbyists for special interest legislation to keep the bases in
their districts open. Many military bases continue to exist because votes are traded
to keep them in congressional districts to maintain certain levels of economic
activity and numbers of jobs in those districts. On the other hand, the Pentagon has
lobbied occasionally for the closing of bases so that the savings could be used for
higher military salaries and more weapons systems.[16] It is apparent, then, that
logrolling may lead to an improvement in the results of simple majority voting, but
it may as frequently lead to inefficient outcomes.

The Median Voter: In the Eye of the Storm

We have noted that political entrepreneurs have a particular incentive to be responsive to voters rather than to nonvoters. One way to accomplish this is by identifying and paying attention to the **median voter**. The median voter is the voter whose
preferences lie in the middle of an issue, with half the voters preferring more and
half preferring less. The theory predicts that under majority rule the median voter
will determine the decision.[17]

To illustrate the principle of the median voter, suppose that five people must
vote on a tax increase to provide more police protection for their community, as
shown in Table 3.6. Since each voter's preference has a single peak, the closer
another voter's position is to one's own, the more the second voter prefers it.
Christy does not perceive a need to increase expenditures for police protection at
all and would prefer no tax increase for that purpose. A movement from zero
expenditures to $25.00 would be approved by Collie, Cassie, Chip, and Jim, how-
ever. And an increase to $75.00 would be approved by Cassie, Chip, and Jim. A
movement to $125.00 would be thwarted by a coalition consisting of Christy,
Collie, and Cassie. A preference for either extreme will be outvoted by four votes,
and a preference for the second or fourth position will be blocked by three votes.
But a majority will vote for an assessment of $75.00, which is the median voter's
preference. Notice that the median voter in this example does not prefer the average amount of the proposed expenditures, but is merely the voter in the middle.

Since each voter will vote for the candidate who is closest to his or her own
position, the candidate who is closest to the median position will win the election.
This is not lost on candidates for public office. Politicians need to get elected, so
they are inclined to take positions that will increase their vote. If both political parties want to maximize their vote, they will try to take positions close to the median
voter. The theory of the median voter also helps to explain why many voters feel
that elections do not provide them with a real choice: both political parties try to
capture the middle to avoid defeat.

Table 3.6   The Median Voter

Voter	Most-Preferred Annual Tax Increase for Added Police ($)
Christy	0.00
Collie	25.00
Cassie	75.00
Chip	125.00
Jim	300.00

To illustrate this theory, the threat of H. Ross Perot in the 1992 presidential election encouraged George H.W. Bush to move from the centrist position. To strengthen his support on the right, he stressed opposition to abortion and gay rights, and support for "traditional family" values. This permitted Bill Clinton to grab the strategic center, which is often difficult for a challenger to do. When Perot dropped out of the race, it became impossible for Bush to regain the center by credibly portraying Clinton as being out of the mainstream.

Median positions maximize the vote-getting potential. The disruptive potential of major third-party candidates to challenge the centrist political party's control of government provides the major parties with an incentive to make it difficult for third parties to get on the ballot, either by erecting election-rule barriers or by incorporating variations of the third parties' positions into a more moderate setting.

Now consider a situation in which there are just two candidates a Republican and a Democrat. The Republican is concerned with keeping taxes low and wants to increase per capita expenditures by $25.00 a year. The Democrat wants to increase per capita spending by $125.00 per year. With an eye on public opinion polls and sensing the potential to gain the necessary majority, the Democrat proposes a $120.00 per capita increase. The Republican, not to be outdone, proposes a $35.00 increase. In short, both candidates will try to move toward the middle in order to attract the median voter. In truth, they will try to move to the center sooner rather than later to preempt their opponents from seizing the middle ground. Figure 3.3 (p. 90) illustrates how candidates move toward the middle as campaigns progress toward election day.

What does the model of the median voter predict? There are several conclusions that follow:

Case Study: A Single-Peaked Ideological Spectrum

Let us assume that political competition mobilizes public opinion along a political spectrum from the far left to the far right, as shown in Figure 3.2. In a normal distribution of opinions, there is a split down the middle, at *M*, indicating those at the "middle of the road." The voter at *M* is the median voter. Each candidate will try to get to the middle of the spectrum to increase his or her chances of winning. If either party's candidate moves away from the median and adopts an extreme such as the liberal *(L)* position, that office seeker will get less than half the vote. As voters will vote for political candidates closest to their own positions, less than half the voters will be closer to a candidate positioned at *L* than to a candidate positioned at *M*. If one candidate is at *L* and one is at *M*, the candidate at *L* will receive all votes to the left of *L*, while the candidate at *M* will receive all votes to the right of the median and the larger percentage of the votes under the curve between *M* and *L*. Clearly, each candidate will move toward the center.

If a third candidate enters the race, the possibilities change dramatically. If the new candidate adopts a position just to the right of *M* and the other candidates are at *M*, he or she will get all the votes to the right of *M* and defeat the two centrist candidates. However, the entry of the third candidate will probably encourage the more liberal of the two centrist candidates to move toward *L*. The candidate still at *M* will be boxed in with a small portion of the vote between *L* and *C*. That candidate then has an incentive to move just outside the *L-C* portion, thereby trapping one of the other candidates. In a three-party contest in which all three start at the center, there will be an incentive for one to move away. There are limits, however. As long as the voter distribution is **single-peaked**, with its center at *M*, an office seeker can increase his or her portion of the vote by moving toward *M*. And with three candidates, at *L, M,* and *C*, additional political contestants can increase their votes by shifting toward the center.

1. *Public choices selected may not reflect individual desires.* The system will result in many frustrated voters who feel that their views are not being considered. Many, perhaps the entire minority, will not have their views accepted.

The principle of the median voter will permit, and perhaps even require, that the views of those on the extreme left or right be neglected at least to the extent that no political entrepreneurs can overtly court those views beyond listening sympathetically and pointing out that they themselves are closer to those on the far right (or left) than are their opponents, who are "dangerously out of touch"—that is, at the other end of the spectrum.

Since the median voter determines the outcome, the intensity of the views of the other voters is irrelevant. Only the intensity of the median voter's view is significant. Thus the most dissatisfied voters will likely be those on the far right or left. This is in distinct contrast to the market in private goods, where demand counted in terms of "dollar votes" clearly records the intensity of preferences.

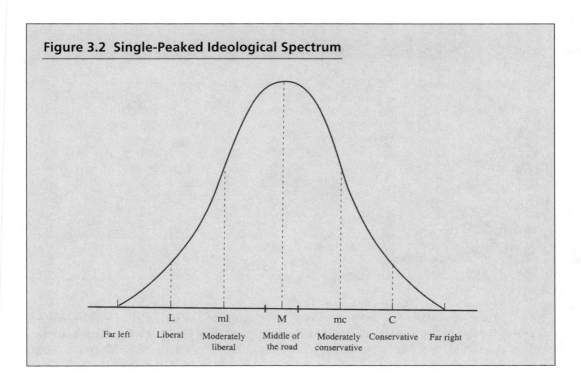

Figure 3.2 Single-Peaked Ideological Spectrum

L	ml	M	mc	C
Far left	Liberal	Moderately liberal	Middle of the road	Moderately conservative	Conservative	Far right

2. Candidates will try to seize the middle ground first, and claim to be moderate, while labeling their opponents as "out of the mainstream" on the right or left. In their effort to command the vital middle, candidates will portray themselves as moderates. Some conservative Republicans, believing the spectrum had shifted in 1996, boldly proclaimed themselves in favor of a "conservative agenda." This sent the wrong message to many voters who identified as being more moderate. A seizing of the middle also offers an explanation as to why the nonincumbent party is often put in the position of running a "me-too" campaign: "We can do the *same* job as the incumbents, only better."

This is not to suggest that all candidates are actually alike. Candidates, as political activists, usually do have political philosophies and positions that can be labeled as more or less conservative, or more or less liberal. But as political entrepreneurs, they are forced to mask them during campaigns to seize the middle. Once elected, they may try to support their philosophical inclinations so long as they can still position themselves to maintain their majority support in the next election.

President Clinton's extraordinarily high favorable rating after six years in

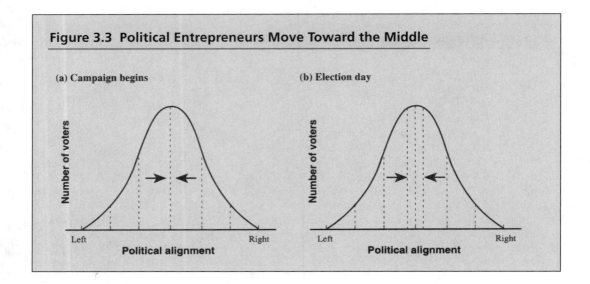

Figure 3.3 Political Entrepreneurs Move Toward the Middle

office was attributed to his having taken control of the political center by, among other policies, reforming federal welfare programs (made easier by a booming economy), supporting the death penalty, and providing additional funds for police protection. While many liberals in the Democratic Party felt he had betrayed basic party commitments going back to the New Deal, they had no alternative. Republicans felt many of their issues had been taken away from them, but could not criticize him too harshly without sounding "too far right."

3. *Candidates will constantly monitor public opinion through polling. They will make slight modifications in the direction of their opponents' positions on those issues for which the opposing candidates are preferred in the polls.* When polls tell a candidate that they would lose the race if the election were held today, they cannot afford to do nothing. They must change their position to attract more voters. In order to successfully sell themselves in the political market, political entrepreneurs try to make position adjustments as subtly as possible to avoid the charge of "political opportunism." Political opponents are always quick to seize on shifts of position to question the integrity of each other. That is, they question whether those they are running against are just "waffling" or, in a more sinister fashion, not being honest regarding their actual positions. Position adjustments also tend to blur the distinction between candidates, which presumably no one wants.

The positions of parties will not be identical. In part this is because political entrepreneurs are not able to identify the median positions perfectly, since public opinion, and the median voter, are moving targets. Also, since there are many non-voters, candidates may stake out positions that they believe will appeal to the median of the population that is expected to vote. In some instances, a candidate may stake out a position to appeal to the median of a group that includes a set of nonvoters precisely because he or she hopes to increase voter turnout by appealing to that group.

4. *Political candidates will prefer to speak in general rather than specific terms.* Voters (and candidates for public office) are inclined to agree on the ends much more than on the means to achieve those ends, or in some cases the feasibility of reaching the ends. For instance, voters across the political spectrum agree that an expanding economy is preferable to a contracting economy. They agree that low unemployment rates are preferable to high unemployment rates. There is also a consensus that lower taxes are preferable to higher taxes, and that a good educational system is preferable to a bad educational system. However, there are great differences between how those we might label "conservative" and those we might label "liberal" think these goals might be accomplished. Conservatives tend to prefer pursuing them through less governmental intervention and private means, while liberals are more likely to perceive a positive role for government in seeking what they perceive as public goods. Candidates will therefore be more likely to talk about the ends, on which there is more of a consensus, than the means, on which there is wide disagreement.

Voting and the Political Marketplace

If politicians are the entrepreneurs of the political marketplace, voters are the consumers, looking out for their best interests by voting for the candidates promising them the most benefits. As noted above, many people who are eligible to vote do not. The key question is: What motivates a person to vote? There is a cost to voting, and the probability of a single voter determining the outcome of an election is extremely small. Therefore, the marginal costs of learning about the issues and the candidates' positions, registering to vote, and going to the polls may exceed the marginal benefit of voting. If, however, the candidates have staked out contrasting positions on certain issues and there are indications the election will be close, the marginal benefit of voting increases and voter turnout also rises.[18] In essence, it appears that individuals do make a cost-benefit analysis of their interests in resolving to vote. And in addition to the benefits hoped for from a candidate's promises, voters also receive the psychological "benefit" of knowing they have performed their civic duty.

A concern in the formation of public policy is whether people make informed choices when they vote. We can expect voters to gather information about candidates that will influence their decisions about whom to vote for as long as the benefits of gathering additional information exceed the costs. Often, though, voters decide that it is not cost-effective to gather information. Anthony Downs labels the shortage of information gathered on the part of the public that does vote "rational ignorance," which is the decision not to actively seek additional information because people find the marginal cost of its acquisition exceeds the marginal benefit of possessing it. This feeling of excessive marginal cost, in turn, can arise because information gathering is more complicated for public choices than for private choices. There are several reasons for this.

In the political market, voters must evaluate and select a package deal. This is unlike the commercial marketplace, where in buying apples or shirts you can decide to buy one item more or one item less; that is, you can engage in making decisions at the margin. When you place an additional item in your shopping basket, you register a clear plebiscite for its production. However, when you vote in a political election your vote is registered not for a single item supported by the political entrepreneur, but for the entire package of issues the candidate or party supports. Like many voters, you may vote for a candidate because of his or her support for a particular issue that is of intense interest to you, such as defense spending. You are likely to find several other items in the candidate's bundle that you really do not want.

Voting occurs infrequently and irregularly, in contrast to buying in the commercial marketplace, where consumer choices are registered frequently and repetitively. In the commercial market, consumers communicate very effectively when they cast millions of votes every day to producers by deciding to buy or not to buy the products offered. But the electorate does not have the opportunity, or perhaps the inclination, to vote frequently enough to send a clear signal to political entrepreneurs regarding its political desires. Voters typically get to vote for candidates only every two, four, or six years. This makes it difficult to find candidates who will support public wants reliably for their entire term and over the range of issues that often emerge after the election. It is impossible to know in advance whether a candidate will support a particular position on issues that were not foreseen at the time of the election. It is also impossible to know the final shape of future bills to be voted on by representatives.

This means political entrepreneurs are relatively free of control by the electorate. The main control voters have is in elections in which an incumbent is running for reelection, where they can retrospectively sanction or reject the candidate's record in the voting booth. Voters can use indicators that provide clues about how someone might vote on unanticipated issues, such as claims by a candidate that he or she is "conservative" or "moderate" or "Republican." But picking someone based on a label is a very inexact system.

The infrequency of elections also requires that many different choices be made at the same time. The many candidates and the many different issues at the local, state, and national levels inevitably lead to great complexity for voters trying to make informed choices.

There is also little incentive for voters to be informed. The political realities noted above make it difficult for the best-intentioned voter to evaluate candidates and issues with confidence. The cost of acquiring useful information is very high. For example, suppose the government suggests it is necessary both to spend billions of dollars on a savings and loan bailout to protect confidence in the U.S. banking system, and to provide aid to a foreign government to provide assistance for a president's continued leadership there, and that those expenditures will require a cutback in unemployment compensation for U.S. workers laid off from their jobs. How can the average voter obtain information to make a rational choice in such a situation?

Some voters will decide to remain rationally uninformed because they decide that the costs exceed the benefits of being fully informed on these issues. Others may choose to become free riders, not only by refusing to gather any information but also by not even voting. If the choices of those who vote are beneficial to the nonvoters, the nonvoting free riders will benefit without incurring any costs. More likely, the political entrepreneurs will soon discover who the nonvoters are and ignore those items in the package that would most benefit them.

Many voters reduce the cost of gathering information for themselves by relying on the "brand names" in the political marketplace: Republican and Democrat. Brand names are at least as important in the political market as in private markets. They provide information regarding general public philosophies. The packaging of a candidate as well as factors like incumbency also provide brand-name information regarding quality. An incumbent has a track record that can be evaluated and has a brand-name identification usually not found among challengers. Voters tend to support incumbent reelection bids just as consumers tend to develop brand-name loyalty to products they buy in stores.

In conclusion, there are important differences between the political and the private marketplaces. Communicating demands in the political marketplace through the process of infrequent voting is more problematic than communicating them on a daily basis through the process of buying and selling. In this area the political marketplace is less efficient than the private marketplace, due in part to the way the political marketplace is designed.

Since any one person's vote is unlikely to affect the outcome of an election, there is less of an incentive for the average person to stay informed than if his or her vote would likely affect the outcome. This increases the power of special interest groups, because unorganized voters have more diffuse interests and are less likely to become informed.

Interest Groups: Added Muscle in the Policy Market

An **interest group** is a collection of individuals with intensely held preferences who attempt to influence government policies to benefit its own members. Because their interests are strongly affected by public policies in a particular area, their members keep themselves well informed regarding legislation in that area. This contrasts with the general voter, who is often uninformed on many issues because the cost of acquiring information is deemed too high relative to its benefit. And if a proposed policy will confer benefits on one group while imposing costs on another, both affected groups will probably organize, one to support and the other to oppose the policy. For example, teachers will be well informed about tax laws and programs that support public education or hurt it. Members of the teaching profession usually know much more about the laws affecting education than does the general public, so as individuals they make informed voting decisions and through teacher organizations they lobby for or against specific laws.

The existence and importance of special interest groups lie in the principle of rational ignorance. Individuals, and members of groups, are more likely to have incentives to seek information concerning candidates' stands on issues that affect them personally. They are more likely to try to influence other people to adopt their positions, to take an active part in campaigning for candidates supporting their interests, and to vote. Political entrepreneurs seeking election thus try to court special interest groups at the expense of the general welfare. And thus special interest groups are likely to have significant effects on policy decisions in areas where they think they have the most to gain or lose by the outcomes.

The high costs of running modern campaigns, necessitated by television advertising and so forth, makes political candidates more eager for offers of campaign contributions from special interest groups. The more the general public is uninformed, the more likely cost to a politician for supporting special interest group policies, related to the benefit of the campaign contribution, diminishes.

There are limits on the influence of special interests, though. Politicians seeking election or reelection typically take money from interest groups in return for supporting positions favorable to those groups. Although they need contributions to mount successful campaigns, they may be wary of accepting money from groups whose positions may be unacceptable to **unorganized voters**. Interest groups themselves are aware that it may be best not to press legislators in causes to which the unorganized voters are hostile. Thus legislators often vote as the unorganized, but interested, voters want, and congressional decisionmaking often takes into account the wishes of voters who are not members of interest groups. This can even diminish the possible number of special interest groups, since by not antagonizing unorganized voters it encourages them to remain unorganized.[19]

Special interest groups propose and support legislation they perceive as important to their interests; in general, voters who are not members of such groups are not likely to oppose such legislation or to lobby politicians against it if they do not think it will affect them adversely or at all. As an example, assume that a state proposes to reduce the budget for its state-supported university system because of a shortfall of tax receipts. The state may propose a reduction in the faculty and staff, to be accompanied by an increase in tuition for the students. Since the faculty, staff, and students will bear the brunt of this decision, they may form an interest group to propose an increase in taxes within the state to be used not just to avoid layoffs, but also to maintain low tuition and even increase faculty and staff salaries. In other words, this interest group is petitioning the state to raise the wealth of its members at the expense of general taxpayers. They are demanders of a transfer of wealth from the state.

The suppliers of this wealth transfer are the taxpayers, who probably will not find it worthwhile to organize to oppose having their wealth taken away by the state university system. General taxpayers probably will be less well informed about this legislation than members of the special interest group. But even if they are well informed, they will have to calculate the costs and benefits of opposing the legislation. Say that if the tax increase passed, the average taxpayer would have to pay out approximately $2. But he or she might have to spend $10 to defeat the proposal. Thus, even those knowing of the legislation and aware that its passage would cost them money would probably conclude it was not worth the cost of opposing it.

The role of special interest groups in the making of public policy cannot be overemphasized. In a large and complex economy such as that of the United States, a high number of interest groups is to be expected. Many of the interest groups overlap. There are, for example, woman's rights groups, minority rights groups, religious groups, physician groups, lawyer groups, farmer groups, and so forth. And special interest groups are responsible for much of the misallocation of public resources. However, legislation drafted for the benefit of special interest groups is not necessarily bad. Much of it may even benefit the general public. In the example above, education is a public good and the citizens of the state may be well served by having a good state university system for the general population. The point to be stressed is that the costs and benefits of being informed on certain issues and the marginal costs and marginal benefits for lobbying for or against those issues are different for members of a special interest group than they are for the general public. It is this difference in the allocation of the costs and benefits of being informed and taking an active political stance that usually influences the type of legislation proposed and implemented.

James Madison denounced interest groups ("factions," he called them) as being the cause of instability, injustice, and confusion in democratic politics. He defined factions as "a number of citizens . . . who are united and actuated by some common impulse of passion, or of interest, adverse to the rights of other citizens, or to the permanent and aggregate interests of the community."[20] Since that time, every interest group has claimed to represent *the national interest* rather than a parochial interest. And each group has looked suspiciously at every other interest group as aggregations of conniving, self-seeking individuals.

Mancur Olson accepts the Madisonian standard model of human nature, which says that individuals know their self-interests and act rationally to further them.[21] He concludes that **collective goals** are seldom rationally pursued. If, as noted above, broadly dispersed interests find it difficult to organize for political action, then in all likelihood small, narrow interest groups will engineer a redistribution of benefits toward themselves and away from the dispersed interests. However, since individuals discover the benefits of group organization for themselves, a stable society gradually accumulates an increasing number of special interest groups. Each will have a disproportionate political influence on the areas of its needs. The implications for society are ominous, in that special interest groups redistribute national wealth to themselves, which reduces society's overall efficiency. In other words, special interest groups seek to preserve their benefits at the cost of general economic stagnation.[22]

For example, neither Herbert Hoover nor George H.W. Bush wanted a depressed economy, but there were many in their constituencies who were financially secure and not threatened with unemployment. Many in this more affluent element preferred those conditions to taxing and spending policies to reduce unemployment and stimulate economic activity, which they feared might reduce their status.

The Bureaucratization of the Polity

The legislative branch of government passes laws and approves specific levels of public policy spending. The actual implementation of the laws and the actual distribution of funds are delegated to various agencies and bureaus of the executive branch. Bureaucrats, like politicians and the average voter, have a variety of interests.

In reality, bureaucrats are often attacked for being unresponsive to the public they serve. Still other critics complain that politicians make their bureaucracies too responsive to special interest groups instead of allowing them to impartially administer the programs for which they were created.

Bureaucrats are the unelected U.S. government officials tasked with carrying out the program approved by Congress and the president. Many laws are passed that are more symbolic than substantive insofar as they indicate the "intent" to ensure automotive safety, guarantee safe working conditions, or protect the environment, for example, without specifying exactly how to accomplish these goals. Bureaucrats must use their administrative authority to give meaning to vague platitudinous legislation and determine how the law will actually be applied.

Those working in bureaus tend to be supportive of the legislature's goals. They also prefer a growing budget, which usually correlates with opportunities for promotion and higher salaries for themselves. In public bureaucracies there are no incentives to minimize budgets. Instead, bureaucrats try to maximize the sizes of their agencies through high salaries and the perquisites of office, power, and patronage. Within these organizations, in fact, a person's prestige and authority are measured by the number of personnel under his or her authority. (Even if bureaucrats did operate very efficiently, the general voter would be unaware of this due to the principle of rational ignorance.) Therefore, bureaucrats compete with other bureaucrats for a larger share of the available funds. Bureaus typically do not end each fiscal year with budget surpluses, but rather spend all their revenues before the end for fear of appearing not to need as much money in the future. Bureaucrats try to increase the size of their agency by influencing politicians who provide their budget. This leads them to typically exaggerate their claim of a mismatch between their responsibilities and their limited resources.

They may indeed be providing efficient services to the special interest groups that were responsible for the legislation creating the bureaus, and they may even be serving the public that is their clientele efficiently. But they must also answer to the legislature that funds and oversees them. It should be noted that in doing this, bureaucracies have significant information advantages over the typical legislator, who must be concerned with literally hundreds of different programs. And bureaucracies themselves provide the information the legislators need to oversee the bureaus.

Those who criticize bureaucracies for being less efficient than private firms miss a fundamental point of the purpose of a bureaucracy. Typically its existence is the result of some market failure—a situation in which market competition could not resolve some issue or issues. Consequently, it cannot be measured by normal market criteria. Many government bureaucracies provide services for which there is no competition. For example, there is only one place to get a driver's license or a zoning permit.

Public bureaucracies associated with high national purposes of the state, such as the military, the Central Intelligence Agency, or the Federal Bureau of Investigation, are generally held in high regard as patriotic public servants. Ironically, the members of the largest governmental bureaucracy, the military, often do not even consider themselves bureaucrats. Bureaucracies associated with domestic regulatory or redistributional programs that adversely affect the more privileged members of society are generally condemned as being wasteful and inefficient, while the individual bureaucrats tasked with enforcing those policies are usually held in contempt as incompetent bumblers.

A Critique of Rational Choice

Rational choice theory began as an explanation of how a rationally self-interested person behaves in the marketplace. To the extent that individuals choose what they most prefer among potential choices in the market, they are engaging in rational behavior. It claims a scientific objectivity in alleging that it is descriptive of how people actually behave in markets without making any value judgment about that behavior. As a model of decisionmaking, the logic of rational choice has widespread application throughout the social sciences and has found increasing applicability in the policy sciences. Its strength is to be found in its illustration of how to make efficient choices and in the model's ability to explain individual as well as group behavior. Rational egoism, as a general rule, may be perfectly acceptable in the market. There is no reason for the individual contemplating a choice between purchases to be committed to any particular political philosophy. Democratic forms of government require that rational man/woman be concerned not just with his or her own personal well-being, but to concern him- or herself with the general welfare of the community of citizens. The invasion of narrowly self-interested economic rationality into the political thought and behavior of individuals overwhelms and ravages democratic politics.

Universal rational egoism assumes that individuals will act just as rationally, and just as self-interestedly, in political arenas as in economic markets. In economic thinking there is a strong bias in favor of free markets, with a great concern that any government intervention will reduce efficiency. This same bias against government is evident in the thought of many policy scientists who have adopted rational choice thinking. Supporters of the rational choice model claim the analysis describes government and political behaviors *as they are,* free from any wishful notions about how they *should be.*[23] Nevertheless, the conclusions of public choice have a clear bias in favor of free market principles and limited government. Critics point out that rational choice disregards the role that culture plays in modifying and restricting decisionmaking. Rationality can mean different things in different cultures.[24]

Social choice theory shows that if individuals actually behave the way the theory describes, all collective voting mechanisms are subject to manipulation in which the popular will may be thwarted. In other words, whoever controls the voting order can determine the results. Even bureaucracy is interpreted as being

rationally concerned primarily with increasing its budget and power. The conclusion is that most government agencies are not in the public interest. The obvious implication for anyone suspicious of government is that all bureaucratic organizations and budgets are too large, so budgets may be cut without fear that the affected agencies cannot still carry out their responsibilities. The main problem for "responsible" government, then, is little more than to rein in out-of-control agencies.

The average citizen has a modest interest in policy issues, but the costs are too high relative to the benefits for him or her to become well versed on either the specific issues or the policy positions of elected officials. Politicians have a positive incentive not to inform the voters on specific policy proposals, but only to speak in general of the goals of "peace and prosperity." Rather than speaking to the public about policy issues, they can be expected to espouse ethical principles and humbly acknowledge their own moral rectitude while castigating that of their opponent.

Citizens are usually rationally ignorant and not well positioned to monitor public policies in a manner assumed by democratic theory. Political elites formulate policies in a way that maximizes their benefits in the theory.

In the rational choice model, which is descriptive of what *is,* without passing judgment, politics is little more than a game in which all participants seek to maximize their benefits while treating the cost as a negative externality to be transferred to the commons (all taxpayers). The world of politics as viewed through the lens of rational choice is almost unrecognizable to the student of liberal democratic thought. There is no doubt that the economic calculus of public choice (rational egoism) explains one facet of the human psyche. This explanation has grown, and is accepted, to the point that it threatens to crowd out other approaches.

Rational choice theory has a difficult time explaining altruistic behavior. Why do individuals who perceive no benefit to themselves for helping others nevertheless do so? Rational choice theory would not predict that individuals would engage in "good Samaritan behavior." Nor do rational choice theorists have an easy explanation for collective action for the general welfare. For example, even though the cost of collecting information and going to the polls to vote outweighs the likelihood that the vote will have any influence on the outcome of the election, millions of people do go to the polls.

Finally, many cognitive psychologists argue that individuals usually do not have complete information and therefore cannot ascertain the "best" choice from a rational perspective. As a result, individuals are more likely to seek a minimum level of satisfaction (rather than the maximum) from their decisions. This is referred to as "satisficing."

On the positive side, a contribution of the theory has been to suggest to policymakers one avenue to develop public policies. We agree that a competitive market can allocate resources efficiently and without any guidance from government. At the same time, we recognize that the market has several weaknesses. The market is unable by itself to cope with business cycles and unemployment, income inequality, or the consequences of a concentration of market power and money. A market does not protect the commons. The market is incapable of providing public goods. Many of society's most urgent public policy issues—urban decay, pollution, the social unrest that is attributable to poverty—are to some degree the result of some market shortcoming.

Many market imperfections can be treated by policies that make use of the market's mechanisms. Policymakers increasingly attempt to take the incentives of the free market into account when designing public policy. Privatizing government operations is one such effort to use the profit motive to increase efficiency. Deregulation of some industries, such as airline and trucking, is an example. The effort to use market mechanisms to control pollution is another example. As noted earlier, many critics of this approach feel that to permit businesses to pay a fee to pollute removes the moral stigma from the act. The right to pollute is reduced to any other market good that can be bought or sold. In the case of the tragedy of the commons, each individual acts rationally in their self-interest, with the result being collective irrationality. The basic consequence of public choice is that of "rational man, irrational society."[25]

Adam Smith, writing in an earlier age, thought of economics as a part of moral philosophy. It never occurred to him that economics might be thought of as value-free (see Chapter 5). On the contrary, his theory was based on the desire to improve the situation of the masses. As he wrote in *Wealth of Nations:* "Consumption is the sole end and purpose of all production; and the interest of the producer ought to be attended to, only so far as it may be necessary for promoting that of the consumer."[26]

Robert Heilbroner has pointed out that economists today claim to engage in value-free scientific thinking because the prestige associated with pursuing a science resembles the grandeur of religious pursuits in an earlier age. He holds that all "economic analysis is shot through with ideological considerations whose function is to mask the fullest possible grasp of some of the properties of a capitalist social order."[27] The social sciences cannot achieve the rigor (or objectivity) of the natural sciences as long as the worth of the individual is valued. Normative values regarding the worth of life, health, and human dignity permeate public issues. In fact, as members of a social order, it is impossible for us to describe this order without using the feelings of attachment and identification that make us a part of the fabric of society. A nonideological being could not exist as a sentient member of society.

This is as it should be, especially in public policy, since its purpose is to promote the general welfare. The next two chapters explore the relationship between the individual and society.

Conclusion

Markets fail to produce ideal outcomes in the best-attainable allocation of goods and services. Democratic governments are asked to intervene to correct the deficiencies of market outcomes, but must do so through the institutions of representative democracy, with voting procedures, political entrepreneurs, and interest groups serving as intermediaries.

The process is one in which individuals in politics act, as people are assumed to do in the marketplace, on the basis of their preferences based on their views of their rational self-interest. Rational public choice theory offers an explanation regarding how individuals act in the political marketplace. It should be seen as a view about how the system actually works and not how the system *should* work.

In some ways the government is even less efficient than the private market-place. This is particularly true in limiting voters to infrequent elections and in requiring the political "package deals" achieved through logrolling.

The principle of the median voter results in the "middle ground" of the electorate being critical in any election. Since both candidates in a two-way race must compete for the median voter's position and portray their opponent as being an extremist and "out of touch with the mainstream," campaigns usually fail to produce any bold initiatives for change. Rather they eschew substance in favor of efforts by candidates to tar their opponents with negative symbols.

The voting paradox also allows political entrepreneurs to take almost any position on an issue and claim that this was supported by a majority. Consequently, whoever controls the voting agenda on several related items will have a powerful influence on the voting outcome.

Special interest groups are organized voters who see their self-interest bound up with a specific issue, are informed about it, and are therefore inclined to vote based on that issue. The general population of potential voters, following the principle of rational ignorance, is likely to be uninformed about and indifferent to most political issues. Special interest groups, then, have a political influence out of proportion to their numbers, although politicians are reluctant to antagonize the general voting population needlessly because they too have the potential to mobilize and retaliate through their own interest groups.

The accumulation over time of legislation for the benefit of special interest groups redirects public resources toward those groups at the expense of the unorganized and less-likely-to-vote general public, particularly the poor. This may result in further movements away from the ideal of government correction for market failures.

Rational choice thinking is a valuable tool for policy scientists. An overemphasis on the model can legitimize an approach to public policy that treats all issues and positions as of equal value. In such a scenario the role of policy scientists is reduced to tabulating wins and losses for different groups.

Questions for Discussion

1. What is public choice theory? How does it help in analyzing public behavior and policy?
2. How can democratic voting behavior lead to undemocratic results? How can this be squared with the idea of justice? Is there a solution to this problem?

3. Why do political candidates move to the center in a single-peaked two-party system? Why are parties more likely to have more fixed ideological points in multiparty systems?

4. Why do candidates prefer to campaign on general terms rather than specific issues? Conversely, why do candidates reduce an opponent's general stands into specific positions?

5. What is the idea of rational ignorance? How can this be squared with the democratic ideal of an informed citizenry?

6. The democratic ideal also contains the concept of each citizen having an equal voice in government. How then can special interest legislation be justified?

7. Are there ways to make government bureaucracies more concerned about the efficiency of their programs?

8. Why must policymakers be concerned with the use of common resources? How can policymakers best regulate the usage?

Suggested Readings

Arrow, Kenneth. *Social Choice and Individual Values.* New York: John Wiley, 1951.

Austen-Smith, David, and Jeffrey Banks. "Elections, Coalitions, and Legislative Outcomes." *American Political Science Review* 82 (June 1988).

Downs, Anthony. *An Economic Theory of Democracy.* New York: Harper, 1957.

Dryzek, John S. *Democracy in Capitalist Times: Ideals, Limits, and Struggles.* New York: Oxford University Press, 1996.

Lasswell, Harold D. *A Pre-View of Policy Sciences.* New York: American Elsevier, 1971.

Lovrich, Nicholas P., and Max Neiman. *Public Choice Theory in Public Administration: An Annotated Bibliography.* New York: Garland, 1982.

Mueller, Dennis C. *Public Choice.* New York: Cambridge University Press, 1979.

Shepsle, Kenneth A., and Mark S. Bonchek. *Analyzing Politics: Rationality, Behavior, and Institutions.* New York: W. W. Norton, 1997.

Shepsle, Kenneth, and Barry R. Weingast. "Political Preferences for the Porkbarrel: A Generalization." *American Journal of Political Science* 25 (February 1981).

Strom, Kaare. *Minority Government and Majority Rule.* Cambridge: Cambridge University Press, 1990.

Tribe, Laurence H. "Policy Science: Analysis or Ideology?" *Philosophy and Public Affairs* 2 (Fall 1972).

Tullock, Gordon. *Private Wants, Public Means: An Economic Analysis of the Desirable Scope of Government.* New York: Basic Books, 1970.

Weschler, Louis F. "Public Choice: Methodological Individualism in Politics." *Public Administration Review* 42 (May–June 1982).

Vanberg, Viktor, and James M. Buchanan. "Rational Choice and Moral Order." In James H. Nichols Jr. and Colin Wright, eds., *From Political Economy to Economics and Back?* San Francisco: Institute for Contemporary Studies, 1990.

Notes

1. The adaptation of this theory from economics to political science began with William Riker at the University of Rochester in the 1950s. But it has developed most broadly in the Virginia state university system, especially at George Mason University, Virginia Tech, and the University of Virginia, and is sometimes referred to as the Virginia school. James M. Buchanan Jr., an economist from George Mason University, won a Nobel Prize for his work in this area (1986).

2. See William H. Riker, *Liberalism Against Populism: A Confrontation Between the Theory of Democracy and the Theory of Social Choice* (San Francisco: Freeman, 1982). See also William C. Mitchell, *Government As It Is* (London: Institute of Economic Affairs, 1988).

3. Abraham Maslow, "A Theory of Human Motivation," *Psychological Review* 50 (1943): 370–396.

4. As an economic term, *efficiency* is defined as maximizing output with given resources (costs). It implies the impossibility of gains in one area without losses in another.

5. Robert B. Reich, *The Resurgent Liberal and Other Unfashionable Prophecies* (New York: Vintage Books, 1989), p. 259.

6. For an excellent summary of rational self-interest, see Henry Demmert, *Economics: Understanding the Market Process* (New York: Harcourt Brace Jovanovich, 1991), pp. 4–6.

7. Opinions regarding what motivates individual choices are often raised in public policy discussions. There is an often heard contention that there are no truly altruistic acts. Unselfish acts, such as volunteering to work in a soup kitchen to feed the hungry, make people feel morally correct by giving them a clear conscience. Thus actions are altruistic only at a superficial level. On closer examination, the motivation to act "altruistically" is really a motivation to achieve the self-satisfaction of thinking of oneself as being a good person.

To derive satisfaction from helping others does not make one selfish. The unselfish person does derive satisfaction from helping others, while the selfish person does not. The truly selfish person is unconcerned about the suffering of others. It is sophistry to conclude that, because an individual finds satisfaction in helping to feed the poor, she or he is selfish. If we ask *why* someone gains satisfaction from volunteering to work in a soup kitchen, the answer is that the individual cares about other people, even if they are strangers; the volunteer does not want them to go hungry, and is willing to take action to help them. If the individual were not this kind of person, he or she would receive no satisfaction in helping others; this feeling of satisfaction is a mark of unselfishness, not of selfishness. See James Rachels, *The Elements of Moral Philosophy* (New York: McGraw-Hill, 1986), pp. 56–60.

8. Rachels, *Elements of Moral Philosophy,* pp. 5–6.

9. Usually about two-thirds of those eligible to vote are registered in local elections. Thus a political entrepreneur may win an election with the support of only about 20 percent of those eligible to vote, which reduces any legitimate claim to a mandate. See Norman R. Luttbeg, "Differential Voting Turnout in the American States, 1960–82," *Social Science Quarterly* 65 (March 1984): 60–73. See also, "Elections," in U.S. Census Bureau, *Statistical Abstract 1996* (Washington, D.C.: U.S. Government Printing Office, 1996), pp. 267–292.

10. There is little disagreement with Richard Fenno's statement that candidate goals include reelection, influence within Congress, and good public policy. See Richard Fenno

Jr., *Congressmen in Committees* (Boston: Little, Brown, 1973). This is not to suggest that politicians seeking election or reelection are motivated by greed. Politicians may seek power, not as an end in itself, but as the means for implementing their visions of good public policy. But election is a prerequisite to the achievement of good policy, and therefore must be an immediate goal.

11. H. R. Haldeman, *The Haldeman Diaries: Inside the Nixon White House* (New York: G. P. Putnam's Sons, 1994), p. 221. Other presidents have also made military decisions with an awareness of potential voter reaction. President Abraham Lincoln was willing to shift troop deployments during the Civil War in a way that strengthened his chances for reelection. Troop units from states in which his reelection chances were close were either moved to the rear of battlefronts or out of the fighting altogether to reduce their casualties and the reasons that families and friends from those states would have to oppose Lincoln. Troops from states where his reelection chances were either very high or very low were moved to areas where the fighting was heaviest and the likelihood of casualties the greatest. See Gore Vidal, *Lincoln* (New York: Ballantine Books, 1984). Robert Tollison's research supports Gore Vidal's position. See Robert Tollison, *Dead Men Don't Vote* (Fairfax, Va.: Public Choice Center, George Mason University, 1989).

12. This is distinguished from a **Pareto optimum**, which is a situation in which it is impossible to make any Pareto improvement, that is, when it is impossible to make any person better off without making someone else worse off. Under unanimity rules, the individual being made worse off would veto any change.

13. Another obvious dilemma that arises with majority rule is that minorities have an incentive to break majority coalitions in order to become a part of new majority coalitions. Accordingly, in the satellite dish example, the forty-nine villagers excluded from the winning coalition might try to reform the coalition by persuading at least two members of the majority to join them in return for a side payment. Under majority rule, the search for new coalitions always continues while existing coalitions try to firm up their support.

14. The **transitivity axiom** states that if preferences are transitive, then all the alternatives can be placed in order whenever there are more than two choices. Therefore, if *a* is preferred to *b*, and *b* is preferred to *c*, then *a* is preferred to *c*. This permits ranking alternatives from the most to the least preferred.

15. Kenneth Arrow, who won a Nobel Prize in economics in 1972, produced an exceptional proof of the impossibility of formulating a democratic process for reaching a majority decision that ensures transitive and nonarbitrary group choices. See Kenneth Arrow, *Social Choice and Individual Values* (New York: John Wiley, 1951).

16. It is not clear that the net benefit to society would be greater by transferring the funds from closed bases to higher salaries and weapons systems. See Richard Halloran, "Pentagon Fights for Budget Cut (Yes)," *New York Times,* April 30, 1989, p. E5.

17. This assumes that the voters have single-peaked preferences, so that as they move away from their most preferred position in any direction, their utility of outcome consistently falls.

18. See Yoram Barzel and Eugene Silberberg, "Is the Act of Voting Rational?" *Public Choice* 16 (Fall 1973): 51–58.

19. See Arthur T. Denzau and Michael C. Munger, "Legislators and Interest Groups: How Unorganized Interests Get Represented," *American Political Science Review* 80 (March 1986): 89–106.

20. James Madison, *The Federalist* no. 10.

21. Mancur Olson, *The Rise and Decline of Nations* (New London: Yale University Press, 1982).

22. By intensifying distributional struggles and encouraging the primacy of political competition, special interest groups siphon a society's talents and energies away from the production of goods and focus them instead on winning the distributional contest. Olson claims that the postwar economic miracles in Germany and Japan were due in part to the purging of all special interest groups as a result of the war, which opened the way to rapid growth. Countries like the United States and England found their special interest groups still viable at the end of the war and experienced slower growth in the postwar era as a result.

Olson's solution would be to save democracy from its own excesses by reducing special interest groups' influence on the political process. He hopes that schools and mass media will create a widespread antipathy to special interest groups and bring about a cultural change. Perhaps society could then achieve the ideal of a state devoid of special interest politics and continually remain adaptive and innovative.

But the proposed system, lacking interest group mediation, would effectively cripple democratic institutions. Without interest groups, which are the breeding grounds for democratic opposition independent of state power, the strength of representative democracy would be weakened. Special interest groups shape social values. Group morality is defined and refined through their workings.

23. See James Buchanan, "Politics Without Romance: A Sketch of Positive Public Choice and Its Normative Implications," in Alan Hamlin and Philip Pettit, eds., *Contemporary Political Theory* (New York: Macmillan, 1991), pp. 216–228. See also William C. Mitchell, *Government As It Is* (London: Institute of Economic Affairs, 1988).

24. Ellen Coughlin, "How Rational Is Rational Choice?" *Chronicle of Higher Education,* December 7, 1994, p. A16.

25. See Brian Barry and Russell Hardin, eds., *Rational Man and Irrational Society?* (Beverly Hills: Sage, 1982).

26. Adam Smith, *An Inquiry into the Nature and Causes of the Wealth of Nations,* edited by Edwin Cannan (New York: G. P. Putman's Sons, 1877; originally published in 1776), p. 660.

27. Robert Heilbroner, "The Embarrassment of Economics," *Challenge: The Magazine of Economic Affairs,* November–December 1996.

CHAPTER 4

Ideologies and Institutional Constraints: Public Policy in the United States

Public policy in the United States must be considered in context of the peculiarities of its political institutions and its culture. If politics is the art of the possible, it is also a truism that the problems that get on the agenda and the viable policy options will be determined by the culture and institutions of the society. The framers of the Constitution fragmented power rather than concentrating it. The system of checks and balances, separation of powers, and federalism was the result of choice and the political realities of the time. By providing for a limited government and guaranteeing certain individual liberties, the framers also provided a channel through which public opinion may constrain policy.

National crises, such as the Civil War, the Great Depression, and World War II, have changed the parameters of the struggle over policy. More recently, opinion has been divided over whether the system created in 1787 can still provide for *effective* government in the twenty-first century. Many critics of the system propose schemes to streamline institutions and encourage a concentration of power. Others praise the work of the framers and the virtues of inefficient government as extolled by James Madison in *The Federalist* no. 10. This chapter examines the origins of this debate and how the conservative bias among the delegates to the Constitutional Convention was reflected in the Constitution; the role of federalism and its impact on policymaking; and U.S. political culture and public philosophy and its impact on public policy formulation. Finally, it looks at how public philosophy is related to political attitudes and peculiarly "American" values.

Ideology and Public Policy

An **ideology** refers to a structure of interrelated values, ideas, and beliefs about the nature of people and society. It includes a set of ideas about the best way to live and about the most appropriate institutional arrangements for society. As such, it invariably includes a belief that society can be improved. Ideologies include an image of the good society and the means for achieving it. Therefore, supporters of an ideology believe that if their plan is followed and the appropriate policies are adopted, the society will be improved. Ideologies thus provide a perceptual lens through which to view politics by helping to organize thoughts and evaluate policies, programs, political parties, and politicians. Ideologies are a device to simplify the complexities of political reality and therefore are never completely accurate or inaccurate descriptions of political reality.

The term *ideology* was first used during the French Revolution to describe a view of how society should be organized that was separate from religious views that were becoming increasingly controversial. Today, the term often is used to refer to the outlook of individuals with rigidly held beliefs. In fact, the mainstream of U.S. politics has never been rigidly ideological; only the far right and far left are concerned with a correct set of values and behaviors for their members. Those passionately committed to an ideology are not likely to make good policy scientists, as they often cannot dispassionately examine a problem without confusing it with their ideological goals. Ideologues find it difficult to compromise, because an ideology carries with it a commitment to try to change the society in the direction of their ideology. Policymaking becomes more difficult when issues are cast in ideological terms, because the policy problem becomes transformed into a "conservative" or "liberal" *principle* that cannot be compromised.

In the United States, more people have consistently identified themselves as conservative rather than liberal over the past twenty years.[1] People in the United States often describe themselves as liberal or conservative even while they prefer to think of themselves as pragmatic, political moderates who decide issues on their merits rather than through any ideological set of values or beliefs. Many people who call themselves liberal or conservative only accept a certain part of that ideology. Many Americans who accept the conservative view that the role of government in the economy should be reduced, want greater government involvement in the regulation of social issues, such as gays in the military. Conversely, others who view themselves as accepting a liberal position of more government intervention in the economy, feel the government should have a smaller role in the area of personal morality. Many who are conservative on social issues may be liberal on economic issues and vice versa. This is not necessarily logically inconsistent. It suggests that political ideology in the United States is rather fluid. It also suggests that an ideology is somewhat malleable to the political environment in which it exists.

A liberal or conservative orientation does not determine political postures for most people, but it is a useful means for self-identification and articulation of policy positions. The more informed people are, the more likely they are to have policy positions consistent with their ideological orientation. Since the 1980 presidential election, the Republican Party has strengthened its identification with a conservative ideology. Ideological awareness has grown in the United States in recent presidential elections, with a stronger association between ideological self-identification and voting patterns.

Most Americans, in fact, do not organize their thoughts systematically or consistently. For example, a voter may want tax cuts but would like the government to increase funding for Medicare. Many Americans view their position on one issue, such as tax cuts, in isolation from their view on another issue, such as their desire for more defense spending. Some attentive voters have difficulty finding candidates who reflect their view on a wide variety of issues, because the government is involved in an ever-wider variety of public policies.

Political entrepreneurs, including legislators, lobbyists, special interest groups, and party activists, are more likely to be ideologically committed. They often try to mobilize public opinion toward their ideology, but find that more voters may react negatively when such appeals seem too far out of the mainstream. For example, the Republican leadership turned back an attempt to make opposition to late-term abortions for party candidates a prerequisite for receiving campaign financial assistance. The "conservative" leadership learned the hard way that they drove many voters, especially women, out of their party by appearing to oppose any dissenting views. Political parties must make some accommodations with voters and ad hoc coalitions to maintain viability. This stands in stark contrast to many countries whose political parties are organized around competing political philosophies and ideologies. In those countries, political parties are more disciplined and political struggles take on the form of a protracted conflict.

Nevertheless, most voters are not at the "dead center" of a political spectrum. Rather, they have a tendency to be a "little more conservative" or a "little more liberal." Political entrepreneurs therefore try to use ideology as an organizing strategy. It is imperative to understand the main ideologies in the United States and how they influence public policy.

Today, ideological controversy is a part of the debate on the whole variety of public policy issues, from whether gay marriages should be recognized by law, to how to reduce the flow of drugs into the country, what the nation's international trade policy should be, and how to improve the educational system.

Should the government be less involved in our lives? Would it be better if people were forced to rely more on themselves and the market for their well-being? How should the government provide for economic growth and price stability? Should the government adopt a more restrictive immigration policy? How can we stop urban decay? Ideological controversy and debate are very much a part of our political process.

Two Major Ideologies

There are several different theories that try to describe how governments should behave (normative theories) or how they actually do behave (positive theories). The two major ideologies are actually theories or perspectives from which to judge government policies.

Liberalism

Liberalism is an ideology committed to a set of policies that have as their common goal greater freedom for individuals. The term "liberal" first acquired its modern political connotation from the Liberales, a Spanish party that supported a version of the French constitution of 1791 for Spain.[2] Liberal thought has two central ideas. The first is the opposition to arbitrary authority and its replacement with more democratic forms of authority. The second idea is a desire for greater overall freedom for the individual. Early liberalism emphasized freedom *from* arbitrary authority. It began with support for freedom of conscience and a demand for religious toleration.

The spirit of this rational liberalism can be traced back to John Locke and his *Two Treatises of Government* (1690). Locke's philosophical rationalism, common sense, and liberal spirit are reflected in the work, which stresses individual "natural rights," labor, property, and reason. Locke's treatises contain the basic doctrine of liberalism. Later economic liberals stressed the observation made by Locke that the first requisite for national economic growth was the protection of private property. Because unless people had a right to property, the incentive to work would dissolve and production would fall.

Adam Smith, the founder of modern economics, is often considered to be the greatest of the economic liberals. Smith published *Wealth of Nations* in 1776 in an effort to refute the mercantilists, who argued that the true wealth, or power, of nations is not determined by the amount of gold that a nation acquired, but by the amount of goods and services produced by the society. Rather than focusing on the role of the state as the mercantilists did, Smith focused on the role of the individual. Smith argued that interference with market forces by the government must lead to inefficiencies and reduced growth. The government, by directing economic resources toward one industry, must necessarily draw those resources from other areas, which are then underfunded.

There was concern that permitting everyone to follow his or her own self-interest would lead to chaos throughout society. Smith argued that the discipline of market forces would lead not to lower production resulting from the zero-sum relationships perceived by the mercantilists, but to benefits for both parties to a trade, or they would not consummate the agreement. The most efficient manufacturers will survive and the inefficient will go under. The invisible hand of market forces can regulate the market far better than the government.

Thus the idea that society should be free from government interference. Thomas Jefferson, who was a classical liberal, summed up the sentiment with his famous phrase, "That government governs best which governs least." This view was well suited to a new country that had just thrown off the shackles of arbitrary interference by King George III in political and economic decisions of the American settlers. A young vigorous nation with resources and room to expand provided an excellent foundation for an ideology of freedom from economic or political control.

Because of their experience with monarchial government, both Smith and Jefferson saw government as a threat to individual well-being. Jefferson said, "The care of human life and happiness, and not their destruction, is the first and only legitimate object of good government." Classical liberals were fearful of the heavy hand of government and sought to "free" the individual from state oppression.

Classical liberals had greater faith in the influence of markets than in the influence of governments. Both Smith and Jefferson thought that their theories would lead to an improvement in the well-being of the nation's citizens. Liberalism emphasizes a human being's reasonable nature, which leads to cooperation (such as in the social contract) and to competition in a constructive way. If society is set up correctly, we may all gain from competition. Conversely, classical liberals focused on abusive uses of power by the state. Jefferson's Declaration of Independence catalogued a list of abuses of the British government. Unlike the mercantilists, who viewed competition as zero-sum, liberals saw competition as constructive and positive-sum, that is, mutually advantageous. If two individuals meet in the market and one has brought grapes but prefers apples, and another has brought apples but prefers grapes, then both can benefit through an exchange.

The classical liberal view had a strong bias in support of the market whenever a choice was to be made between the two. Classical liberalism also became associated with a preference for democratic forms of government. Democracies were preferred because, by weakening centralized power, individual freedom was made more secure. Democratic forms of government with separation of powers and checks and balances can be more easily thwarted in any policy that requires decisive centralized decisionmaking.

The industrial revolution resulted in the rapid urbanization of Europe, rapid population growth due to better living and health standards, and the destruction of the landed aristocracy and the petty nobility, who were made irrelevant by the changes. The aristocracy was replaced by new elites comprising manufacturers, financiers, merchants, and government officials. Jeremy Bentham (1748–1832) was an observer of the changing conditions and a principal commentator on **utili-**

tarianism. Bentham joined the two threads of liberalism together by applying the concepts of utility and the marketplace to politics and the tasks of democratic government. He is well known for his observation that "nature has placed mankind under the governance of two sovereign masters, pain and pleasure" and his utility principle of the greatest good for the greatest number. However, Bentham did not identify utility with selfishness, for he says that the "first law of nature is to wish our own happiness; and the united voices of prudence and efficient benevolence add,—Seek the happiness of others,—seek your own happiness in the happiness of others."[3]

Bentham proposed that politics and law should provide a maximum of free choice and liberty for all. He believed that education, free speech, inclusive representation and an expanded suffrage, and the regular accountability of the governors to the governed—that is, politics patterned after the model of the free economy—were necessary to provide good government. His theory first combined economic liberalism with positive political action.

In the mid-1800s, more challenges were raised about this antistate view of liberalism. The goal of liberalism was individual freedom. But it was becoming increasingly clear that economic progression had brought about situations that could reduce individual freedom. For example, although political power was decentralized and pushed out of the marketplace, market power was becoming increasingly centralized. Liberals had expressed great faith in **freedom of contracts** (agreements between two consenting parties without government interference). If one party does not like the agreement, one does not sign the contract. This might not be a viable option when the bargaining power between the two parties is highly unequal. What if a powerful corporation offered a very-low-wage contract to a poor person desperate for a job to provide for his family? The contract might require a twelve-hour work day and even carry a clause in which the individual agreed never to join a union as a condition of employment. Does the person in urgent need of a job really have a choice? Corporations also claimed the right under laissez-faire to share lists of troublesome workers who might have agitated for higher wages, thus blacklisting anyone who objected to low wages. Classical liberals believed that wages would find their own natural level, even if it was at a Malthusian subsistence level.

The growth of the modern corporation and industrial technology transformed the world of Adam Smith, who had not conceived of the organizational power of large corporations. Great inequalities in the employment market made one person's economic freedom another's oppression. The market in commodities such as child labor, impure or adulterated foods, and slum housing led some to conclude that government regulation could expand freedom, especially of the poor. Some "modern liberal" political and economic writers began to suggest that in such a circumstance it was time for the government to be brought back into the marketplace to protect people from the inequities in the system. Modern liberals began to support wage and work-hour legislation, the right to unionize, and worker compensation. Other economic liberals defended the tenets of laissez-faire capitalism, transforming the means of liberalism into ends and transforming their liberalism into conservative ideology.

John Stuart Mill inherited the liberalism of Adam Smith and Thomas Jefferson as taught by his father, James Mill, a noted political economist (and friend of Bentham's). In 1848, Mill wrote his treatise *Principles of Political Economy,* which gave liberalism a new meaning. He argued that liberalism had been an important force in the destruction of arbitrary centralized power, and had provided the very foundation for democratic revolutions and reforms while invigorating individual liberty in Europe and the United States. But liberty that merely sanctioned the amassing of wealth was insufficient, according to Mill, who also wanted moral and spiritual progress. He thought that the state should take some action to correct market failures and to nudge social progress along. For example, the state should allow for individual freedom in most cases. And parents should be ordinarily free to raise their children as they see fit. However, there was a parental duty and a moral obligation for parents to educate their children. This moral obligation was to the children and also to society. This obligation of the parents to educate their children took priority over their rights to raise their children as they saw fit. The state had a right to use its coercive authority to require the education of the children. However, since some parents cannot afford the cost of educating their children, the government is obligated to provide grants to make the education of poor children possible. Mills's views on education were similar to his views on other areas of social welfare.

In his later years, Mills became increasingly willing to tolerate, or even require, government involvement in a number of social issues. The question was always when to permit government intervention, and how far the intervention should be tolerated. The Progressive period in the U.S. experience (roughly 1890–1920) signaled the willingness to use government and social institutions to improve the human condition.

John Maynard Keynes further contributed to the willingness of liberals to regulate the economy for the general welfare. His analysis showed that laissez-faire principles could lead to economic chaos and that government intervention could provide much needed order. Keynes believed that the state needed to be active to provide an improvement in society's condition (see Chapter 5 for a further explanation of his views).

Vaclav Havel, president of the Czech and Slovak republics, is often quoted as a modern liberal theoretician. He worried about the danger in placing too great a dependence on the market, which can result in tragic social consequences for the market and the individual. Moving from too powerful a state (communism) to too weak a state can risk creating a backlash that could usher in authoritarian rule. He advises moderation:

> The market economy is as natural and matter-of-fact to me as air. After all, it is a system of human activity that has been tried and found to work over centuries. . . . It is the system that best corresponds to human nature. But precisely because it is so down-to-earth, it is not, and cannot constitute, a world view, a philosophy, or an ideology. Even less does it contain the meaning of life. It seems both ridiculous and dangerous when . . . the market economy suddenly becomes a cult, a collection of dogmas, uncompromisingly defended and more important, even, than *what the economic system is intended to serve—that is, life itself.* [4]

The philosophy of John Rawls fits the modern liberal view of the proper relationship between liberty and equality. His first principle is that each person is to have an equal right to the most extensive total system of basic liberties compatible with a similar system of liberty for all. His second principle is that social and economic policies should be arranged so that they help the least advantaged at least as much as the most advantaged.

What can one conclude about liberalism today? First, modern liberalism keeps the same end of the free individual that has always guided this ideology. The means to the end have changed, but the goal of increasing human freedom remains the same. Liberalism asserts that the individual is more important than the state. But though economic man/woman is based on rational egoism, political man/woman must be concerned with the broader welfare. The state is created to serve the individual and his or her well-being. Modern liberalism does call on the power of the state, but it is in the interest of expanding freedom for all, although it may mean that some have less freedom to do as they please. The market is useful as an efficient and peaceful process to bring people together in mutually advantageous trade. However, there are some things the market does not do well. In those cases, government must step in to promote societal goals and, whenever possible, try to use market incentives to achieve them.

Conservatism

Conservatism has different aspects in the social sciences. **Temperamental conservatism** describes a cluster of attributes that most people exhibit in all societies. The major elements in the conservative temperament include habit, inertia, fear of the unexpected, the need to be accepted, and fear of being alone. These traits are often found among some of the more marginal groups in society, such as the poor, the elderly, or the ignorant.[5] A conservative temperament is given a high "value" in the gathering of knowledge and transmitting the culture from generation to generation. The maintenance of law and order would not be possible without this conservative inclination. This sentiment is also necessary for individuals to accept the division of labor and the wage structure as being better than any other system devised.

Closely related to temperamental conservatism is **situational conservatism**, which is the natural and culturally determined disposition to resist dislocating changes in the traditional pattern of living. Basically, situational conservatism is a general opposition to changes in the social, economic, political, or cultural order. The fear of change is the distinguishing characteristic of conservatism. In the political-economic arena it becomes a fear of those who would plan to change the world or to "improve" it by sacrificing the accepted societal values, institutions, and habits of living. Although the more affluent are prime candidates to be content with the established order in the society, persons at all socioeconomic levels may lament change in the status quo. For reasons that range from the instinctive to the pragmatic, many will find the security of the established order preferable to the unknown of change. The maxim "Better the devil that you know, than the one you don't" sums up this view.

Political and economic conservatism is the result of conservatives of temperament and situation being thrust into political issues. The most general meaning of the term *conservatism* refers to political conservatism (or the "right"). Political-economic conservatism refers to the attitudes that venerate the inherited patterns of morality and existing institutions, and are distrustful of the competence of popular government to provide change that will improve on the status quo. Politico-economic conservatives can be counted on to oppose liberal proposals for reform. Not surprisingly, such conservatism draws its major support from those with the greatest interest in the existing order.

Like liberalism, modern conservatism has undergone an evolution from "classical conservatism." Edmund Burke, a contemporary of Adam Smith, is the epitome of conservative thinking in the late eighteenth century. Burke agreed with Smith that a free market was the best economic system. And he was in sympathy with the American colonies and opposed sending British troops to put down the rebellion.

The liberalism of the American Revolution was a seminal event in Europe. Liberal ideas appeared to be sweeping the continent, influenced by philosophers Jean-Jacques Rousseau and Thomas Paine. The application of liberalism in America was not difficult once the British withdrew, since there was no embedded aristocracy to contend with. Democratic government fell easily into place. But in

France, a revolution based on "liberty, equality, and fraternity" met with fierce resistance from the aristocracy and the Roman Catholic Church, which received state support. The revolutionaries dealt with the intransigence with the guillotine in an effort to sweep aside all institutions.

Burke watched in horror. His *Reflections on the Revolution in France* (1790) began as a discussion of the French Revolution but expanded into an examination of the nature of reform and revolution and was to become the standard work of modern conservatism. Underlying Burke's philosophy was a deep pessimism that is visible throughout his writing. Burke realized that the French Revolution was not merely a French affair; it was a revolution in beliefs and theory. He called for a European crusade to crush this new wild, enthusiastic revolutionary spirit by force of arms. He believed that no monarchy would be safe before the tyranny of the multitude.

Burke opposed the *individualism* represented by the new philosophy. He saw society not in terms of equal individuals but of unequal groups with long-standing interests. People are not basically rational as Locke had written; they are only partly rational and are generally guided by their emotions and passions. It was to contain humanity's irrational passions that society had evolved institutions, traditions, and moral standards, such as the aristocracy, churches, and rules of morality. If these were swept aside, the result would be chaos and tyranny of the masses far worse than any injustice suffered before the revolution. Therefore these institutions were to be *conserved,* even if they were not perfect. They had evolved over hundreds of years of trial and error and people had adapted to them. Burke was not opposed to change, however; it was just that he thought change should occur gradually, allowing time for people to adapt. A state without the ability to change would not have the ability to "conserve" itself. The mission of conservatism had not been to defeat revolutions but to avert them.

Burke believed that the characteristic essence of all property, "formed out of the combined principles of its acquisition and conservation, is to be unequal."[6] The touchstone of modern conservatism is that its outlook is more pessimistic regarding the rational side of humanity's nature than is the outlook of liberalism, whether classical or modern. Conservatives emphasize the limits of rationality and the view that for most people, their intellect is subordinate to their emotions and passions. They tend to emphasize human inequality as a given and that the unequal distribution of property naturally follows from this fact.

The political and economic conservative is typically the prisoner of the pressures for change in the social process. Those proposing change keep the social process in motion, while the conservative reacts. When the pace of change is pushed by market forces through multinational corporations, computers, and automation, the conservative position illustrates that support of a social revolution can coexist with opposition to political reform.

The first principle of government for the conservatives is to protect property and maintain order. They retain the view of classical liberals that after it performs this function, government should have little regulatory authority that would impede the acquisition of property. Government should have an increased role, however, to encourage respect for tradition. For example, conservatives would like to see government take action to get prayer into schools, restrict abortion, and limit gay and lesbian rights. Modern conservatives are also traditional concerning questions of women in the military and affirmative action.

Milton Friedman, a modern conservative and Nobel Prize–winning economist, argues in favor of Adam Smith's principle of laissez-faire. President Ronald Reagan in the United States, and Margaret Thatcher in Britain, attempted to apply this aspect of classic liberalism, now frequently called **neoconservatism**. They advocated free markets at home and in international trade, and minimal state interference otherwise except in the area of national security. Reagan complained that a progressive income tax was improper and denounced policies designed to reduce inequalities as "social engineering." The top tax rate in the United States was reduced from 70 percent in 1980 to 33 percent in 1986. Critics denounced that rolling back government regulations resulted in giving away natural resources and relaxing environmental protection standards, contributing to the growing inequality in the distribution of income and wealth in the nation (see Chapter 6). For modern conservatives individual liberty is to be overwhelmingly preferred to equality. Modern conservatism continues today as a combination of the ideas of Edmund Burke and Adam Smith's idea of laissez-faire, although the problems balancing individual freedom in the market and state interests remain.

By the late nineteenth century it became apparent that the free market had several problems identified earlier by Smith. The market system produced oligopolies and monopolies, which reduced competition. Individual consumers did not benefit as Smith had hoped, when sellers could collect monopolistic rents. Inequalities in the marketplace produced great inequalities in the distribution of wealth. Left to market forces, stratified class positions were increasingly inherited. Affluent parents provided their children with the advantages that come with class: excellent educational opportunities and connections to jobs and inheritances to provide succeeding generations with appropriate privileges. At the lower end of the socioeconomic ladder, it became difficult for those at the bottom to acquire the means necessary to achieve upward mobility. Recurring sharp fluctuations in the business cycle hit the poor and working class the hardest.

As a philosophy committed to the defense of the status quo and the leadership of certain groups within the society, conservatism is an important ideology in the United States. Conservatism is thriving in the realm of ideas with a certain set of core principals. Clinton Rossiter has noted that the persistent themes of the philosophers of modern conservatism include the following:

> The existence of a universal moral order sanctioned and supported by organized religion. The obstinately imperfect nature of men, in which unreason and sinfulness lurk always behind the curtain of civilized behavior. The natural inequality of men in most qualities of mind, body, and character. The necessity of social classes and orders, and the consequent folly of attempts at leveling by force of law. The primary role of private property in the pursuit of personal liberty and defense of the social order. The uncertainty of progress and the recognition that prescription is the chief method of such progress as a society may achieve. The need for a ruling and serving aristocracy. The limited reach of human reason, and the consequent importance of traditions, institutions, symbols, rituals, and even prejudices. The fallibility and potential tyranny of majority rule, and the consequent desirability of diffusing, limiting, and balancing political power.[7]

Rossiter also notes that there is a conservative preference for liberty over equality as reflected in Burke's philosophy. Conservatism in the United States is a jumble of disparate answers to persistent questions about where to draw the line between the rights of the individual and the demands of the community. Conservatives generally support government action to protect the status quo or promote the interests of those who tend to be among the more affluent. Conservatives also are inclined to favor a decentralization of power.

Competing Perspectives of Analysis

The ideological perspectives provide an indication of how individuals holding particular views would try to work to change society. The social sciences also suggest competing theoretical viewpoints that prove useful in analyzing public policy. The pluralist and elite models, and variations on them, offer a myriad of insights into individual and collective political action and the deep-seated tensions within society. The two theories examined here adopt different units of analysis and logic of social action; they have different interpretations of data. They are often put forward as discordant approaches to analysis. However, there are so many compatible elements in both approaches that a synthesis of the two combining several aspects of each can strengthen our analytic efforts.

Pluralism

Pluralism is a theory of government that attempts to reaffirm the democratic character of U.S. society by asserting that public policy is the product of competition and negotiation between groups. It begins with the view that individuals acting in their self-interest engage in political action in an effort to obtain some benefit from the government. Individuals must compete with each other in the effort to shape policy outcomes. Pluralism, or group theory, accepts that there are shortcomings in traditional democratic theory, which emphasizes individual responsibility and control. Pluralism itself emphasizes the tendency of individuals with common interests ("factions," in James Madison's terminology) to form groups to push their demands on government. Competing groups make demands on government through political institutions. Individuals are important to the extent that they act on behalf of group interests.

The pluralist view of the world is one in which multiple centers of power compete to shape policy outcomes. Power in the United States is diffused between many groups and is fluid. The decentralized nature of politics guarantees group access to power. Competition between interest groups helps to protect individual interests by placing checks on the power groups can accumulate and preventing them from abusing the power they do achieve. Public policy at any given time results from the equilibrium achieved among the competing groups. The legislature, in this theory, acts as a referee of the group competition and records the victories of different groups in the form of statutes.[8] If the competing interest groups are roughly balanced, the policy that results roughly approximates the preferences of society in general. Overlapping group membership helps maintain the balance by preventing any single group from moving too far from societal values. Public policy tends to move in the direction of groups whose influence is growing and away from those whose influence is waning.

From the pluralist perspective, the state has no role other than to reflect and respond to the demands of participants in the political system. The government provides the representative mechanism through which groups press their demands for policy outputs. Although pluralism does not require a small state, many suggest that a minimal amount of government intervention is most compatible with the model. The government's role is primarily to be an umpire between the competing groups, interpreting and enforcing the rules agreed upon. As Milton Friedman says, "the role of the government . . . is to do something that the market cannot do for itself, namely, to determine, arbitrate, and enforce the rules of the game."[9]

Group theory does not deny that individuals by themselves have little power or influence. Individuals play only a limited role, by voting or working in interest groups. And even though the right to participate is open to everyone, active participation is heavily biased toward the most affluent members of society, who are also the better educated with higher-status occupations.[10] The poor make up a much smaller part of the activist population and their perceptions are not communicated with the clarity or urgency of the more affluent.

Neopluralists challenge the earlier pluralist idea that power is decentralized and that no single interest dominates the government.[11] Charles Lindblom holds that corporate officials in reality are a set of policymakers parallel to elected officials who act without the restraints of legislators. Elected officials are in fact very solicitous of corporate officials and their desires, because failure to accommodate them may lead to consequences, such as unemployment, that government officials are unwilling to accept. The result is that the bias within the system and the special status of business are decidedly in favor of the affluent. The neopluralists provide a bridge to the elite theory.

Elitism

Elitism is based on the straightforward empirical observation that despite the pluralist vision of diffuse and fluid power centers with open access, the reality is very different. Power is concentrated in elites drawn from business and financial centers of the society. The basic unit of analysis is not the individual or an organized interest group, but the small layer of elites who control powerful institutions, primarily financial, but also including governmental and military organizations. Elites, being rational and self-interested, use the resources to maintain order in society by managing a consensus that represents their interests—which is to say, the status quo. The elites in government try to structure the debate to quash any problem that would threaten their hold on power or that would significantly redistribute power. This model does not perceive the state as the neutral umpire of the pluralists' view.

This view accepts the idea of interest group competition that results in legislation. But the issues involved in such instances are not central to the welfare of society. The elite model holds that most election issues deal with a middle level of power. Pluralist politics, by focusing on the competition at the middle level, tends to miss the critical issues at the top, and neglects the issues at the bottom. Middle-level politics is often symbolic, while the critical issues are not open to electoral challenge but are agreed on through elite collaboration.

Every political system has inherent biases concerning who has access to it. For the United States, Founding Fathers supposedly produced a system based on the notion that "all men are created equal." But according to elite theorists, the machinery of government was not (and is not) open to all men (and certainly not to all women). There were built-in mechanisms designed to make it difficult for most groups to gain access to the government or to make changes in the way it functioned. Therefore, the idea that U.S. government reflects "the will of the people," as popularly understood, is inaccurate in the view of elite theory.

Elite theory holds that most government decisions are made by a minority elite that has enormous power. Elites derive their power from the control of key finan-

Case Study: Elites, Interests, and the Tension Between Capitalism and Democracy

A standard argument against democracy that has concerned conservatives of all stripes as well as elites is that in a true democracy there would be nothing to prevent the masses from using their democratic majority to take away the property of the relatively few haves and redistribute it to the have-nots. The concern is that the tyranny of the majority could incite unscrupulous politicians to sell out to the mob's rage for economic equality by using the tax system to confiscate the property of those who have more.

The framers of the Constitution were determined that this would not happen in the new republic. They put together a system of separation of powers, checks and balances, and federalism to safeguard individual liberty and property rights. Many of the Constitution's other key provisions, such as the indirect election of the president and senators (prior to the Seventeenth Amendment) and the appointment of judges for life, were a determined effort to limit democracy. Adam Smith had gone so far as to charge that governments were really instituted to defend the rich against the poor.

The transfer of power away from more democratic forms can also occur through bureaucratic shifts. One mechanism of government that can manage the tension between democracy and capitalism is the creation of boards that are part of the national government yet insulated from the electoral process and even largely from the control of politicians. In fact, the structure can even be justified on the notion that it should be immune from the pressures of competing self-interested pressure groups, especially since many lack the "expertise" to be involved. However, the chairman of such a board is nominated only after extensive consultation with the elite members of the particular community—for example, in the financial community, the chief executive officers of major banks.

The U.S. Federal Reserve Board (the "Fed") is the prime example of this variation on the principle of popular control over government, which reflects the fear of too much democracy and the need to protect one of the primary government functions from it. The Federal Reserve is largely insulated from democratic control. It should be noted that comparable mechanisms occur in many central banks in Europe. The Federal Reserve controls monetary policy—that is, the money supply—and through it determines some of the most important questions of the political economy. Its policies have a tremendous influence on economic growth, price stabilization, and levels of employment. Individual access to the legislature is completely lacking with regard to the Fed. It is shielded from public control in part by its own official secrecy.

The Federal Reserve was created in 1913 as an independent agency. It is integrated into the group of over 5,000 Federal Reserve member banks with national charters and twelve district banks. Major state banks are also members. The Federal Reserve banks are private, for-profit institutions. Its board of governors comprises seven members, who serve staggered fourteen-year terms as presidential appointees with the advice and consent of the Senate. The chairman of the Federal Reserve Board is appointed by the president, with Senate approval, and serves a four-year term.

cial, communications, industrial, and governmental institutions. Power flows not from the elite individuals themselves, but from the positions of authority they have in large institutions. Their power and privileged positions originate from the immense wealth of large corporations and the significance of those corporations for the overall national economy.[12]

Supporters of this view that elites and not the masses govern the United States make a strong case that it is the elites who have access to and largely determine the public policy agenda, because they have the real authority over the major institutions that shape the lives of the masses. Elite theory holds that elites govern all societies, not just the United States. Alexander Hamilton explained the existence of elites in the following way: "All communities divide themselves into the few and the many. The first are the rich and well-born, the other the masses of people. The voice of the people has been said to be the voice of God; and however generally this maxim has been quoted and believed, it is not true in fact. The people are turbulent and changing, they seldom judge or determine right."[13] The privileged aristocracy in preindustrial Europe has been generally superseded by wealthy capitalists of the present time. The common thread is that elites in every era tend to believe that what is good for them must be good for all.

Elite theory accepts upward social mobility that permits nonelites to become elites, because this openness provides stability by reducing the potential of revolution from below. Individuals who might supply the revolutionary leadership become part of the elite, and in the process assimilate the values of the ruling class they are joining. Privileged elites have a vital interest in the perpetuation of the system on which their entitlements rest. Upward social mobility means that even potential members of the elite share a consensus on the need to preserve the system by discouraging changes that would jeopardize the elites' position.[14] Competition thus occurs over a rather narrow range of issues and usually concerns means rather than ends.[15]

Consensus among U.S. elites is built around the sanctity of private property, limitations on government authority, and the economic virtues of a capitalist culture. In this view, public policy does not result from the popular will so much as it mirrors the concerns and values of the elites. Public policy changes and innovations result from shifts in elite positions. Since elites tend to be very conservative, because of their overriding interest in preserving the system, changes tend to be incremental rather than radical. Major changes take place only when the security of the basic system is jeopardized. Then elites may move swiftly to institute the reforms required to preserve the system and their privileged position within it. Elite theory does not argue that elites are unconcerned about the welfare of the masses, only that the general welfare of the masses depends on the actions of the elites. The masses rarely decide issues but accept the symbolic "democratic" institutions of voting and party membership, which gives them a means to identify with the system.[16] Thus public policy decisionmaking is limited to issues that do not imperil the elites. They organize the policy agenda so that certain kinds of decisions are eliminated from it.[17]

The theory holds that the masses are largely submissive, and indifferent to and poorly informed regarding policy issues. Elites, having more at stake and holding their positions of power, are more active and well informed. Elites generally control the communications process, which means that information generally flows from the elites to the masses. Elites will more frequently influence the masses than the masses will influence the elites.

Elites find some issues more acceptable than others, based on how the issues are perceived and presented to those with the real power. The net effect of this, according to Roger Cobb and Charles Elder, "is that new demands, particularly those of disadvantaged or deprived groups, are the least likely to receive attention on either the systemic agenda of controversy or the institutional agenda."[18] Elite theory as a tool of analysis would seem to closely conform to the conservative ideology.

Plural Elites

Both the elite and pluralist models have merit. Elite theory recognizes that the power of elites is not inherent in themselves, but flows from their positions of authority in large institutions. Different groups in society may have interests that diverge from each other as the pluralists claim. But the elite leaders of these groups, whether in politics, banking, manufacturing, insurance, construction, and so on, will typically have more in common with each other than with the organizations from which they derive their power. They may cooperate or be in conflict with other groups. Stratified interaction will take place primarily between the elite members of the organizations, who speak and negotiate on behalf of their members and are expected to keep them in line. Elites in turn must deliver at least enough to their followers to maintain their acquiescence.[19]

U.S. Government: The Decline in Confidence

Confidence in the political institutions responsible for the formulation and implementation of public policy has declined. In 1964, 78 percent of the U.S. public indicated that they could "trust the government in Washington to do what is right always or most of the time." By the mid-1990s, only about one in four Americans expressed such trust.[20] Trust in all government institutions declined, including the presidency, Congress, the judiciary, and the military. After the terrorist attacks in

2001, trust in government increased; in fact, 83 percent of Gallup Poll respondents indicated at least a fair amount of trust in the government's ability to handle international problems.[21] Many countries, including Canada, the United Kingdom, Belgium, Denmark, Italy, Japan, Spain, and Ireland, have also experienced a decline in confidence.[22] If the growing distrust was a peculiarly U.S. phenomenon, the search for the cause would be easier. However, the fact that many other countries have been similarly affected suggests a more complex problem.

The United States was born in a revolution against oppressive and arbitrary elitist monarchial power. The major issue that divided the Founding Fathers was clearly drawn between those who wanted a strong government and those who were wary lest the country exchange foreign royal oppression for local elitist oppression, and therefore believed that the less government the better, while Alexander Hamilton believed, along with many of the more affluent, that the country needed a strong central government to support fledgling commerce. The Constitution provided a decided break from European monarchies and cast government in a progressive political direction based on broad institutions and active popular participation. The compromise was a government of institutions that would sacrifice efficiency and speed of decisionmaking in favor of a more deliberative democracy to protect the liberty of a beleaguered minority. As James Madison wrote in *The Federalist* no. 10, extensive debate would be necessary before government could move. Public opinion polls are not easily translated into government policymaking.

Although confidence has declined in some institutions, like Congress, respondents typically believe their own senators and representatives deserve reelection.[23] Support has declined for medicine and schools, but people are satisfied with their own physician and local school. Majorities want the federal budget balanced but oppose cutting programs like Social Security or Medicare.[24] Some of the dissatisfaction is clearly related to how distant people feel from government. This results in a higher level of satisfaction with local government compared to the national government.

Another factor in satisfaction with government in the United States may be related to when the polls are taken. Government increased its scope of activity as a direct result of the Great Depression, World War II, and the attendant rise of the welfare state. After the government dealt successfully with such issues by taking on the responsibility of providing jobs, a minimum wage, and Social Security, confidence in government reached its zenith. Since polling began in earnest after World War II, confidence in government reached its highest in 1964, when, as mentioned above, 78 percent of the people indicated that one could "trust the government in Washington to do what is right always or most of the time."

Part of the blame for the growing cynicism can be laid at the door of the negative campaigning that constantly attacks the character and integrity of political opponents. Despite a pervasive condemnation of negative advertising in campaigns, it is used increasingly, because it has been found to be very effective in influencing perceptions regarding the political opposition. Members of Congress are often portrayed and perceived as cynical, self-promoting, and concerned primarily with their own reelections rather than with the welfare of the polity. The lower the regard in which politicians and politics are held by the public, in part as a result of negative campaign ads, the more voters respond to attack themes in those ads. However, because of a backlash against negative campaigns, candidates try to disguise their attacks as issue-related campaign advertising. The backlash against politicians produced by a politics that depicts government as the root of the problem illustrates that such methods cannot help but damage faith in and the effectiveness of political institutions. This is not to suggest that candidates should not attack their opponents' positions on such issues. Campaigns must try to simplify politics to focus voters' minds and distinguish between the various candidates' positions on such issues as health care, education, or energy and the environment. Consequently, campaigns must be loud and raucous (and expensive) to capture the attention of voters and stimulate them to vote. Low-key, low-budget decorous campaigns do not arouse people out of their lethargy to vote.

The staging of politically inspired spectacles for photo opportunities or scripted interviews, especially by the president, may get air time on the evening news, but a lack of substance is not lost on the public. Symbolic politics rather than serious policy has become the standard fare. The growing perception that money from special interest groups heavily influences political decisions has increased the gap between the politicians and the public. The numbers of those voting in presidential elections declined from 64 percent of eligible voters in 1960 to 49 percent in 1996. The staging of photo opportunities by candidates and negative campaigning reflect the increasing importance of the media in U.S. politics. Politicians have learned that the media are critical in getting elected, and in getting reelected. Endorsement by a political party is not as important as favorable press coverage of oneself and negative coverage of an opponent. The rising importance of the mass media has an almost inverse relationship to the decline in the influence of political parties. By the use of investigative reporting, politicians have become more vulnerable to critical media coverage.

Political struggles are increasingly carried on outside the electoral process, which discourages popular participation in elections. Through investigative reporting and leaks of potentially damaging information intended to negate election results, political power is splintered, denying elected officials a secure political base to effectively pursue policy initiatives. Those dissatisfied with the electoral results increasingly attempt to make public any negative information regarding elected or appointed government officials by leaks to the media. The subsequent

Case Study: Attack Politics

The break-in at the Democratic national head-quarters known as Watergate is sometimes pointed out as the first example of a steady leaking of revelations of misconduct leading to further investigations and indictment, in this case resulting in the indictment of several federal officials and ultimately forcing Richard Nixon to resign. In the Watergate example, however, there was evidence not only of a burglary, but also of the payment of large sums of money from the White House to buy the silence of those who carried out the break-in. Subsequently, the Iran-Contra affair revealed violations of the Boland Amendment, which prohibited the selling of arms to Iran. Arms from the U.S. military inventory were secretly sold to Iran and the funds that were received, rather than being returned to the Treasury, were diverted to fund the Nicaraguan contras, against the specific instructions of Congress. Several high-ranking members of the George H.W. Bush administration became subject to criminal prosecutions for their role in the affair. President Bush pardoned several administration officials before leaving office, charging that the Democrats were trying to criminalize policy differences.

Members of both political parties subsequently attacked prominent members of the opposite party in an effort to weaken their opponents. Republicans drove House Speaker Jim Wright, Democratic Whip Tony Coehlo, and Ways and Means chairman Dan Rostenkowski from office for financial misdeeds. Republican forces also scuttled the nomination of Lani Guiner as assistant attorney general for civil rights by characterizing her as a radical liberal. Those who orchestrated the attack readily acknowledged their effort and indicated that they had a score to settle with the Democrats for their opposition to the nomination of Robert Bork and Clarence Thomas to the Supreme Court.

After the Republican takeover of both houses of Congress in 1994, Republicans such as Senator Alphonse D'Amato of New York made clear their intention to embarrass President Clinton by drawn-out hearings on possible wrongdoing over investments known as Whitewater. Republicans charged that an earlier independent counsel appointed to look into Whitewater had not been aggressive enough. A new independent counsel, a well-known Republican activist, was appointed to pursue the allegations more aggressively. There was daily coverage of the investigation, which focused on charges leveled against First Lady Hillary Clinton. The official investigations were aided by unofficial legal, political, and journalistic attacks funded by Richard Mellon Scaife, heir to the Mellon banking fortune, who gave millions to conservative foundations to challenge the Clinton White House.

Republicans are not immune to charges of corruption or wrongdoing. Recently, House Majority Leader Tom DeLay was protected by his fellow Republican lawmakers. House Republicans adopted an indictment rule in 1993 that required the resignation of any House member indicted of a crime. DeLay loyalists (including House Speaker Dennis Hastert) pushed through a rule change to ensure DeLay's position, much to the consternation of House Democrats.

Despite these events, there is no reason to believe that the level of political corruption today is greater than before 1970. However, the increasing use of negative campaigning, attack politics, and damaging press leaks contributes to voter anger toward government and undermines the legitimacy and efficacy of government.

investigation often arouses hostile attitudes toward the individual or the political party targeted. Supporters become passive under the attack, lest they be viewed as favoring the alleged misconduct. Embattled supporters are strongly tempted to abandon a beleaguered politician, especially if the charges appear to be substantive. These tactics prevent an electoral winner from enjoying the fruits of their victory. The result is weakened government.

A partial explanation for the decline in confidence in government since 1964 is that its string of successes that came out of the Great Depression and World War II, particularly the commitment to maintain full employment, led to a level of confidence that was unrealistic to maintain. Confidence may decline even though performance remains the same if the government is engaged in more controversial areas of policymaking, such as the environment, health and safety, or race and gender. Even if the public generally approves of policymaking in these areas, there is likely to be a greater sense of government trespass into areas best left to private choice.

The framers of the Constitution were products of the Enlightenment, with the result that individuals were given control over such aspects of decisionmaking as religious questions. Government was to be more limited. The preamble to the Constitution superbly states the purpose and raison d'être of democratic government: to establish justice, to ensure domestic tranquillity, to provide for the common defense, to promote the general welfare, and to secure the blessings of liberty for present and future generations. This list has been used to justify government policymaking, with promotion of the general welfare having the greatest applicability.

Today, however, the U.S. government's effort to "promote the general welfare" lags behind that of many other governments in providing a basic level of education, health care, housing, or income. Clearly there is less consensus on what it means to promote the general welfare in the United States than there is in many other advanced countries.

Voters make many inconsistent demands on their political representatives. Candidates, taking the pulse of the U.S. electorate through polling, assess what will have the greatest appeal and then offer a package deal of policies to the voters in which the inconsistencies are muted. And voters are inclined to respond without scrutinizing the incompatible nature of their demands. For example, polls indicated that in the late 1990s most Americans supported increased government spending on health care, while they opposed any tax increase to pay for it; in fact, they were inclined to vote for candidates favoring tax cuts, which made it more difficult to eliminate budget deficits. In a like manner, Americans have reacted enthusiastically to the declining price of gasoline by consuming more of it, while at the same time indicating a desire for reduced dependence on oil from the Middle East. Yet they oppose any increase in taxes on gas consumption that would reduce demand for oil from the Middle East and could be used for research on alternative fuels.

The Impact of Institutions

The Founding Fathers were aware of contradictions in voter preferences that discouraged political candidates, as entrepreneurs, from considering long-range goals when seeking election. They were also concerned to protect the citizenry from the arbitrariness of dictatorial authority, with which they were all too familiar from dealings with the British monarchy. The institutional design of government put in place by the framers of the Constitution provides important pathways for policy development. Key institutions provide focal points for examining public policy in the United States. The most conspicuous feature of the U.S. political system is **institutional fragmentation** and decentralized sources of power.

A major reason for frustration in dealing effectively with society's problems is the basic design and evolution of the Constitution, which was purposely designed to make governing difficult—not to simplify political choices but to complicate them. Rather than entrusting political leaders with sufficient control, it hinders them with insufficient authority. The members of the Constitutional Convention agreed that the Continental Congress had erred in the direction of being too weak and powerless when it wrote the Articles of Confederation, which unified the executive and legislative powers; individual liberty had not been threatened, but the national government was totally dependent on the states to validate and ratify all its actions, and could not control the competitive impulses of the states that worked against the common national interest. It had also become apparent that the European powers sought to exploit the competition between states regarding overlapping claims on western territories and trade and tariff policies in order to weaken the new nation.

The failure of government under the Articles of Confederation to meet these and other challenges was the reason for the 1787 convention, held in Philadelphia. The delegates agreed on the need to develop a new form of national government that could act with more vigor and dispatch. And while there were disagreements on many features of the proposed government, there was no disagreement on the principle of **separation of powers**—the notion that the powers of government must be separated into legislative, judicial, and executive branches. They believed that this separation—"fragmentation" is probably a better description—would make a tyrannical concentration of power inconceivable. James Madison also expressed concern that a legislature could not be counted on to act for the common good when competing issues were presented.[25] Ultimately, **checks and balances** were introduced, designed to prevent any power from becoming the undisputed dominant force. Thus governmental power was divided among the three branches, and each branch was to be given authority to prevent encroachments on its power by the others. As Madison said in his famous maxim, "Ambition must be made to counter ambition."[26]

At the time of the Constitutional Convention, every state with the exception of Pennsylvania had a bicameral legislature, so the compromise, although barely adopted, was a well-known concept throughout the states. The Senate was intended to be more independent of public control than the House, so members were given longer terms. Also, senators were to be appointed by the state governments rather than elected directly by the people, in an effort to restrain too much democracy. As a compromise, to enhance its status, the House of Representatives was given exclusive power to originate revenue bills. The compromise conciliated the small states by allowing them to dominate in the Senate, and conciliated the large states by allowing them to dominate in the House.

The executive branch, which was to administer and execute the laws adopted by the legislature, was treated in a rather cursory manner, but there were fears here too. Benjamin Franklin worried that a unified executive had the potential to drift to monarchy because of a natural human tendency to prefer strong government. The Constitution says little about the powers of the presidency. Chief executives have relied on the clause that declares "the executive power shall be vested in a president" to expand their authority. The Constitution does not even define "executive power," which has allowed presidents to claim that their actions fall within the realm of inherent executive powers not precisely spelled out. The framers of the Constitution clearly designed the institutions of government to slow the policy process, through the system of checks and balances, in the belief that this would help reason to triumph over passion.

Over time, presidential power has expanded. Congress has responded to a more assertive presidency by defending and extending its own authority through more specific instructions on how public monies can be spent. Indeed, it is Congress that has created and authorized the funding of various important agencies of the government, such as the Securities and Exchange Commission, the Federal Reserve Board, the Interstate Commerce Commission, and other regulatory bodies. Presidents have consistently sought greater autonomy in dealing with these agencies. But every grant of additional authority to the president has been accompanied by protections ensuring congressional ability to shape the actions of the agency involved.

Because the Founding Fathers wrote obscurely about the nature of the federal court system, some argue that they did not want a strong judicial branch. However, the Constitution makes explicit the authority of the judicial branch to resolve disputes between state and federal laws. The federal courts' responsibility is to determine which power is exclusive to the federal government, which is exclusive to the states, and which is shared by both. The Constitution also directs the federal courts to resolve disputes between citizens of the different states. This authority grew over time because, as the U.S. national economy developed, citizens turned to the federal court system to resolve many disputes. Judicial review, or the authority to declare a law unconstitutional, is not directly mentioned in the Constitution, but it is implied. Although the court system is structured in a loose hierarchy with lower courts subject to Supreme Court decisions, it often does not work that way in reality. Differing and conflicting decisions often emerge from parallel courts. Litigants therefore "district shop" to find courts that may be more favorably disposed to their concerns. Lower courts are frequently accused of deliberately misapplying or misinterpreting higher-court rulings. And the Supreme Court hears a smaller portion of the rising tide of cases addressed at the lower levels.

The U.S. government has expanded in ways that would have astounded the Founding Fathers. However, the survival of the key features of their design—decentralization, separation of powers, checks and balances, and limited government—affirms the permanence of their effort. This fragmentation defies the effort to bring more orderly and empirical approaches to the policy process (see Figure 4.1).

Federalism and Fragmentation

One of the greatest obstacles faced by the framers of the Constitution was the knowledge that, regardless of the design of the document, they had to obtain ratification from the state legislatures for it to go into effect. Consequently, it was understood that the states would have to retain significant autonomy regardless of other governing arrangements. The difficulty, then, was to strengthen the national government so that it could carry out its will in certain necessary areas while reassuring the states that they would retain all their essential powers. The delegates crafted a system of **federalism** because that was the most they could hope the states would accept. It was recognized that under the Articles of Confederation the states had ultimate authority, leaving the national government bereft of energy for meaningful policymaking. As in other areas of constitutional debate, the Federalists were not able to agree on a precise relationship between the national and state governments.

A major concern of the delegates in Philadelphia was to design a national government with enough power to protect private property and provide economic stability.[27] Although they accepted the principle that government has a responsibility to protect everyone's rights to life, liberty, and property, it is clear that property held a preferred position. On the one hand, they wanted to place the protection of

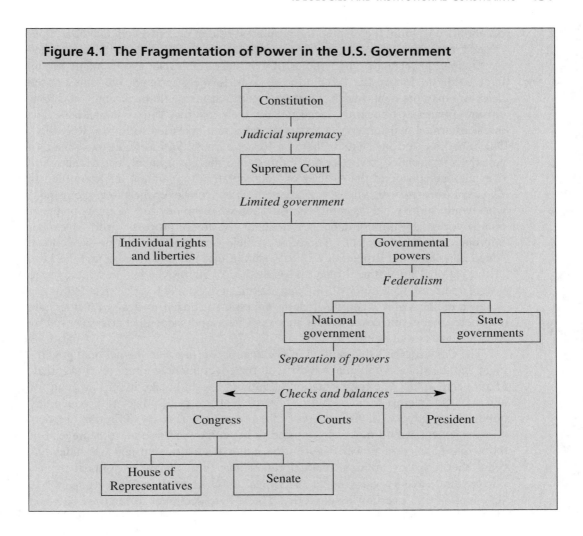

Figure 4.1 The Fragmentation of Power in the U.S. Government

property and commerce in the hands of the national government to protect them from state legislatures. But on the other hand, they wanted to ensure that the national government would not itself jeopardize commerce or private property. The delegates also specifically forbade the states to tax imports or exports, to coin money, to enter into treaties, or to impair obligations and contracts.

The Federalists were also concerned about the possibility of power being fragmented between the national government and states, since they had observed the threats to property and national unity that could occur when authority was too decentralized. While they feared the tyrannical rule of despots, they had also experienced the difficulties of a government that lacked the ability to act because it had insufficient power under the Articles of Confederation. State governments ran up huge debts to finance the Revolutionary War. In the aftermath, the states raised taxes to repay the debt, which threatened many farmers with bankruptcy and foreclosures. Farmers frequently faced jail for their inability to pay their debts. The threat of armed resistance over issues of debts and taxes led to Shays' Rebellion. The rebellion, led by Daniel Shays, a Revolutionary War veteran, on behalf of beleaguered farmers, never seriously threatened the government, but raised alarm over the inadequacy of the Articles of Confederation to maintain internal order. In *The Federalist* no. 10, Madison expressed his concern over the threat from those who would nullify debts, contracts, or taxes when he decried "a rage for paper money, for an abolition of debts, for an equal division of property, or for any other improper or wicked project." Therefore, Article 6 of the Constitution was added, which contained the **supremacy clause**, stating that the Constitution and the laws of the national government made in pursuance of its provisions are the supreme law of the land. The authority of the national government was expanded at the expense of the states when the federal government began to deal with interstate commerce, economic development and recessions, and successive crises caused by wars and military activity.

The Constitution's distribution of political power between the national government and the states would make it difficult for government at either level to threaten property rights. The fragmentation of authority would make it very difficult for any political interest to gain control of sufficient levers of power to produce any public policy adverse to the interests of the propertied class. By definition, a federal arrangement would make any unified policy very burdensome to achieve. But the actual balance of power between the national government and the states has been determined by political realities rather than through law or political theory. For the first seventy years under the Constitution, the national government was very tentative in exerting its authority. There were sectional differences between the South, which opposed effective national government, and the industrial North, which wanted greater national control of trade and tariff policies. Thus, U.S. economic development resulted in regional economies with competing and diverse interests over taxes, tariffs, and regulatory policies.

States have not retreated from the competition for power, however. Many federal policies rely on states to implement the programs. States have power through the dual banking system and many regulations imposed by states. They have become more rather than less active in passing environmental legislation, consumer protection, and occupational health and safety laws. States also often compete with each other to attract business and investment to their jurisdictions, by

Case Study: The U.S. Senate—Undemocratic and Becoming More So

The U.S. Senate is one of the least-representative legislative bodies in the Western world and is becoming more so. A basic principle of democratic representation is the equality of each person's vote. The Senate is designed to provide equal representation of states rather than the constituencies of the states. The result is that an ever-smaller minority of the electorate elects a majority of the senators. Each state is represented by two senators, yet California has sixty-six times as many people as Wyoming, and Texas has nineteen times as many people as Montana, for example.

From the eighteenth century to the present, the ratio of large- to small-state populations has grown from nineteen to one, to sixty-six to one. Today, half of the Senate can be elected by only 15 percent of the U.S. population. And the problem will get worse, because almost all of the population growth in the foreseeable future is projected to be concentrated in a few already populous states (especially California). The result is minority rule. For example:

- The Republicans controlled the Senate from 1980 to 1986. During that period, Republican senators as a group received fewer votes nationwide than did Democratic senatorial candidates. If the Senate were elected based on population, the Democratic Party would have controlled it throughout Ronald Reagan's eight years in office.
- In order to pass his 1993 budget package, President Bill Clinton had to submit to demands by senators from comparatively underpopulated states Montana, Arkansas, and Louisiana to lower the gasoline tax.

- Clinton's 1993 domestic stimulus program, which was targeted at metropolitan areas in large states like California, was killed by conservative Republican and Democratic senators from comparatively underpopulated states like Oklahoma.

The Senate was created at the Constitutional Convention to satisfy small states, like Rhode Island, that demanded equal representation. In *The Federalist* no. 22, Alexander Hamilton criticized the equal representation of the states under the Articles of Confederation as one of the worst defects of that system. Allotting representation on the basis of statehood rather than population, he wrote, "contradicts the fundamental maxim of republican government, which requires that the sense of the majority should prevail."

In the 1960s, the Supreme Court struck down malapportioned state legislatures as unconstitutional, arguing that they violated the principle of one person, one vote. In 1963 the Supreme Court rejected state arguments that they could mimic the structure of the federal legislature and have one house not based on population. The Court declared in *Gray v. Sanders* that "the conception of political equality from the Declaration of Independence to Lincoln's Gettysburg Address to the 15th, 17th, and 19th Amendments can mean only one thing—one person, one vote." Thus the Supreme Court ruled that the structural principle underlying state senates was unjust and unconstitutional.

Source: Michael Lind, "75 Stars," *Mother Jones,* January–February 1998, pp. 44–49.

offering tax exemptions, suspending regulations, and providing loan guarantees and even direct tax subsidies.

Political Parties

Political parties play a critical role in modern democratic society. In fact, mass political parties first developed in the United States with the election of 1800. Even before that, Alexander Hamilton wanted support for a national bank and tried to forge a **coalition** across the constitutionally separated branches of the executive and Congress. The checks and balances between the branches of government made competition an inherent part of the constitutional order. Hamilton's effort to join together what the Constitutional Convention had separated provided the foundation of the Federalist Party, the first political party in the United States. The political party developed into an "indispensable instrument that brought cohesion and unity, and hence effectiveness, to the government as a whole by linking the executive and legislative branches in a bond of common interest."[28] In fact, however, "What the Constitution separates our political parties do not combine. The parties are themselves composed of separated organizations sharing public authority."[29] A unified national government, in which the executive and the Congress are controlled by the same political party, has not always guaranteed cooperation, but it has given a strong impetus toward building a coalition to bridge the gap between those institutions and provide an effective vehicle for policy adoption and implementation.

The emergence of the Federalist Party brought into being a countervailing coalition of political interests. Thomas Jefferson led this coalition, composed primarily of agrarian interests, to oppose the merchant/financial interests of Hamilton and the Federalists. Jefferson was the champion of those opposed to a strong national government. They became known as the Jeffersonian-Republicans, to indicate their opposition to the Federalists led by Alexander Hamilton, who supported the monied interests who wanted a strong national government to protect them from the "excesses of democracy." The Federalists referred to Jefferson's emerging political party as the Democratic-Republicans, in an effort to link them pejoratively with the excesses of democracy. The Jeffersonians accepted the term as an indication of their faith in the ability of rational people to manage their own affairs without government intervention. They dropped the "Republican" part of the label and began calling themselves "Democrats." This is the oldest political party in the United States still in existence. The Federalists went out of existence by 1820. In the early United States, because of the extension of suffrage to a large and relatively unorganized electorate, parties became the vehicle to mobilize voters to go to the polls. But in order to mobilize the electorate to get the vote out, party elites have had to make concessions on a routine basis.

In fact, as E. E. Schattschneider notes, "Decentralization of power is by all odds the important single characteristic of the American major party; more than anything else this trait distinguishes it from all others. Indeed, once this truth is understood, nearly everything about American parties is illuminated."[30] Nonetheless, he states that "the rise of political parties is indubitably one of the principal distinguishing marks of modern government. Political parties created democracy; modern democracy is unthinkable save in terms of parties."[31]

A political party's main goal is to elect governmental office holders united under a given label. The party serves to link the elites in governmental institutions and harmonize their views to the broad outlines of a public policy agenda. Parties also serve to link individuals to government and at minimum give people the feeling that they can affect policy decisions and that they are not completely powerless. Of particular importance is the political party's effort to provide an antidote to the rational ignorance of many potential voters. Party labels evoke powerful messages about the general posture parties might take on many issues, thereby reducing the amount of specific information required of voters.

Political parties also serve as a collection place for different interest groups. Parties must represent overarching values and goals that are widely shared across the nation. By aggregating separate interest groups into one party, each group must moderate its demands to hold the coalition together to win elections. By cooperating, such groups can hope to get some of their demands met. The best-known example of providing a coalition of different interest groups that together commanded a majority was the Democratic Party coalition constructed by Franklin Roosevelt in 1932. It consisted of many groups, several of which overlapped: Catholics, Jews, organized labor, blacks, Irish, Italians, Poles, and farmers. As long as it held together, the Democratic coalition was unbeatable. It was responsible for most of the progressive legislation of the twentieth century, including labor legislation; social welfare legislation, including Social Security; and progressive economic policies. Starting about 1970, the coalition began to erode.

The Republican Party, beginning with President Ronald Reagan, formed a coalition of several economic and noneconomic conservative groups, such as the Christian Coalition, Southerners, the gun lobby, and antiabortion groups. But the Republicans have had difficulty in maintaining this coalition, because of the strong ideological fervor of some of the groups, leading them to resist compromising with other coalition members. For example, the antiabortion groups and many from the Christian Coalition want to require pledges of support and insert platform planks to provide a litmus test for candidates on the abortion issue as a requirement for receiving campaign finance assistance. The issue continues to roil through party membership.

The single-member, simple-plurality, winner-take-all electoral system of the

United States is tremendously significant for the political process. It means that the candidate with the most votes wins the election and that the winning margin is immaterial. This system encourages political parties to appeal to as broad a spectrum as possible to win a plurality of the votes. Parties with broad appeals squeeze out narrowly focused parties. Ultimately the system encourages as few parties as possible (the minimum number being two) to compete for the vital center. More recently, as noted above, conservative elites in the Republican Party have tried to mobilize public opinion in favor of a distinctly more conservative stance, instead of shifting the party to a more centrist position.

At different times in U.S. history, critical elections in response to some pronounced set of issues, such as war or economic crises, resulted in new coalitions under the banners of the two political parties. These new ruling coalitions permitted a party to pursue a coherent set of policy agendas for a period. But as the crisis faded, the coalitions tended to decay as well. While coalitions last, they may significantly influence the roles that elites play within them.

Outside the parties, interest groups mobilize to hopefully advance their interests, and at minimum to protect them. Corporations may use their resources to contribute to electoral candidates directly as well as through professional or trade associations. They may additionally be represented by professional lobbyists who represent several different corporations or businesses in general, such as the National Association of Manufacturers. Over 3,000 corporations have representatives in Washington, D.C., with over 500 professional associations and over 400 additional groups representing foreign business interests.[32] While there are approximately 100 labor organizations represented, labor has not been a credible threat to business interests in the United States.

The overrepresentation of some groups compared to others is clearly a matter of economic resources. For example, a study in the mid-1980s noted that while individuals occupying managerial and administrative positions made up only about 7 percent of the population, business associations with representatives in Washington, D.C., accounted for over 70 percent of the interest groups. Conversely, nonfarm workers made up slightly over 40 percent of the population but comprised only about 4 percent of the interest groups.[33]

The QWERTY Phenomenon

In Paul Krugman's work *Peddling Prosperity,* he points out that the layout of the keyboard on a personal computer has the same arrangement as that of an old-fashioned typewriter from the nineteenth century.[34] Why do we still have this keyboard arrangement? It is not the most efficient arrangement of keys in terms of finger movement. The QWERTY arrangement was designed for early mechanical typewriters. It was an advantage to have typists type more slowly to reduce the tendency of keys to jam. Improved designs, electric typewriters, and eventually electronic keyboards made the problem of jamming keys a thing of the past. It would make sense to shift to other keyboards with a more efficient design. But it was too late. Typists had learned on QWERTY keyboards, and manufacturers continued to make QWERTY keyboards because that is what typists knew. The QWERTY layout became "locked in" despite the advances in technology. Krugman and other economists found that stories of this phenomenon are pervasive in the economy. Many technology choices have a striking resemblance to the QWERTY tale. For example, Bill Gates and his associates developed the DOS and later the Windows software system and sold it to IBM. Since IBM was the major manufacturer of computers, all other systems had an incentive to be "IBM compatible." Although there were other operating systems with similar capabilities, the Microsoft operating system became locked in.

This led many economists to adopt a whole new way of thinking about economics. The approach led many to reject the idea that markets invariably lead the economy to a unique best solution. Rather, the outcome of market competition may depend on historical accidents. Such accidents of history force us down pathways created by earlier events. This "path dependence" limits our freedom to choose, and where we end up depends on what happened along the way. What does this have to do with public policy? Probably a great deal. The Founding Fathers designed a constitution that, despite flaws observable in perfect hindsight, is the oldest written constitution continuously in force. On the one hand, its longevity attests to the benefits and effectiveness of crafting such a document to represent the collective political will of the American people and maintain a republican form of government.

On the other hand, there is a great frustration in dealing effectively with society's problems that stems from the basic design and evolution of the Constitution. By decentralizing power and authority, the Founding Fathers designed the Constitution to make governing difficult. The result has left political leaders weak and unable to make binding decisions. Popular participation in the U.S. system is encouraged by means of picking candidates through petition drives, primary elections, and party caucuses. Since money is essential to running campaigns, and political parties cannot provide it in significant amounts, candidates must develop independent fundraising capabilities. In this system, "all politics is local" in that individuals must organize and run campaigns on local levels. This permits politicians to ignore or even oppose their party's positions on the national level.

In Europe, parliamentary democracies function much differently. The constitutional systems of Europe centralize power. In the United States, the judiciary is a powerful check on presidential and congressional actions. In Europe, courts cannot overturn acts of parliament. In Europe, candidates for office are chosen by party leaders, which makes successful candidates accountable to their parties.

At the heart of the low esteem in which the government is held in the United States is its inability to deal effectively with issues in which there is a clear national consensus. For example, public opinion polls have indicated for the past two decades that a clear preponderance of people support stricter gun control laws, but only recently has any progress been made in this area. Also, for the past decade, a significant majority of the American people have felt that the government is not sufficiently supportive of affordable housing and health care, high-quality education, and protection of the environment, although leaders of both parties solemnly profess their grave concern with these problems.

The potential veto points found in the separation of powers, checks and balances, and federalism, among aspects of the U.S. system, make it extremely difficult to respond to many felt needs of the public. Once the basic constitutional parameters are set down, the state is resistant to further change.

However, democracy is not a static political order. Rather, it is an ideal that we must constantly pursue. As Anthony Downs stated: "Democracy is a dynamic process of governance and even of living in general, not a static institutional construct. Supporters of democracy must continue to change its specific meaning and forms, without destroying its fundamental nature."[35] Democracy is something we must strive for, although, like perfection, it will never be finally achieved. A democratic society that does not constantly explore new possibilities for further democratization will tend to solidify the existing power relationships of the society. The elites will try to "freeze" the power relationships by manipulating voters through campaign contributions and opportunistic politicians.

Democratic governments vary greatly from each other because each system reflects its own unique political, social, economic, and cultural values and has evolved through its own distinct historical experience. However, despite the differences, all have been forced to address the changing interpretation of three core values central to democratic government: the right to vote and participate in a meaningful way in government, individual liberty, and equality.

We have a democratic form of government and a capitalist economic system. The evolution of a democracy joined with a capitalist political economy can develop in many different ways. A capitalist economy, like a democracy, can never stand still. It must constantly grow through processes of creative destruction, or stagnate and decay. Historically, capitalism and democracies have been thought to mutually reinforce each other, since liberal democracies have originated only within capitalist economies. The state is required to carry out the minimalist functions of enforcing contracts, maintaining civil order, protecting private property rights, and issuing and controlling money, all of which are essential for market capitalism to function well. Otherwise the state should remain aloof and neutral in the competition between individuals in their own self-interest. Market capitalism does not require a particular form of a political system to carry out these functions. Accordingly, authoritarian political systems such as those found in Singapore or Chile may also exist in a capitalist framework.

Voting and Citizen Participation

Although Thomas Jefferson, writing in the Declaration of Independence, stated that it was self-evident that "all men are created equal" and that governments derive "their just powers from the consent of the governed," the framers did not go so far as to permit all adult citizens to vote. That right was restricted to citizens who were also male property holders. In the debates at the Constitutional Convention, proposals to explicitly broaden the franchise were firmly resisted based on the notion that if the less deserving intruded their needs to the political process, it would degenerate into mob rule. If the conflict is limited to the more "gentlemanly" disagreements among the more fortunate, proper order and decorum are maintained.

The members of the political community most benefiting from this arrangement were eager to lock in these state functions as an essential requirement of "democratic government." Privileged individuals and groups attempted to defend themselves and the state from further democratization. They maintained that extending the franchise to new individuals and groups would undermine good government.[36] The rising tide of democratization with the principle of citizen participation drowned the opposition. One barrier after another was swept away before the onrushing tide: property qualifications, slavery, poll taxes, and gender restrictions. Removing legal barriers to the franchise left informal constraints in place until the last quarter of the twentieth century.

Liberty Versus Equality

The sixteenth-century Enlightenment left a legacy that held that all individuals by virtue of their membership in the human community possess natural rights, including the **right to liberty**, which refers to the individual's right to freedom from government interference with private actions. A second natural right developed by political philosophers during the Enlightenment was the individual's **right to equality**, which emphasized a disposition toward the political and social equality of all citizens. Thomas Jefferson held that liberty and equality were not incompatible rights for those pursuing egalitarian or libertarian goals.

However, it is widely held today that there is an inescapable tradeoff between these two democratic principles.[37] For example, in the United States, where liberty is achieved at the cost of significant economic inequalities, the ratio of the pay of chief executive officers to that of the lowest-paid full-time worker in their company is over 125 to 1. In Japan, a country with more egalitarian governmental policies, it is 25 to 1.

The Impact of Increased Voting Rights on the Equality Principle

The increase in voting rights has influenced the interpretation of the principle of equality. Democratic governments are agents by which private conflicts are transferred to the political arena and made into public conflicts.[38] The democratic method consists of an institutional arrangement for political decisions in which individuals are given the power to decide by winning a competitive struggle for the people's vote.[39] In this theory, the political process is an agent of socialization of disputes between special interests. When voting was limited to adult male property holders, most Americans were merely bystanders observing the debates between the elite political contenders. And political struggles between elites could ignore the disenfranchised, who were unable to affect the outcome. With each enlargement of the franchise, successive groups of bystanders were eligible to get involved in political quarrels. In fact, the bystanders had the power through their votes to determine the outcome of political disputes.

In any conflict, those who are winning would like to limit the scope of the conflict to the participants already involved, to ensure a favorable outcome. It is in the interest of those who are losing to enlarge the scope, to involve the bystanders on their behalf. In fact, the franchise was first enlarged when Thomas Jefferson, as a leader of a group of elites, found it necessary to push for an expansion in the name of a fuller liberty and equality for all. Had the Federalists been successful in maintaining a limited franchise, it is very doubtful that Jefferson would have been elected.

Since the inclusion of bystanders can change the outcome, the best time to limit the scope of the conflict is at the very beginning of the struggle, by mobilizing one's own forces to get a quick resolution before the opposition has time to mobilize new forces favoring its position. Throughout U.S. history there has been a continuing battle between the effort to privatize or limit, and the struggle to socialize or expand, the scope of political and social conflict. Many arguments are used to try to limit the scope of conflicts or even to keep the nonpropertied or poor out of the political arena altogether: the right to privacy, individual freedom, private enterprise, limited government, states' rights, and individual liberty.

As the franchise was expanded to include the poorer members of society, they gained potential political influence. Political elites were forced to compete for their votes to gain a legislative majority. To form winning coalitions, political parties had to take into consideration the interests of the less affluent and support their "general welfare." In time, a series of programs emerged, beginning with Franklin Roosevelt's New Deal, that, taken together, constitute the **welfare state**. A welfare state is a principle under which the public policy of government is to provide economic and social benefits for each citizen. The welfare state provides public assistance to those without the ability to relieve their problems of unemployment, income insecurity, inaccessible health care, physical and mental disabilities, old age, and property losses due to natural disasters.

In fact, the welfare state is a natural result of extending the franchise and democracy's equality principle. Once lower-income people also had the power to vote, they possessed at least one tool, previously an exclusive privilege of wealth, that gave them political influence to benefit themselves. The effect has been to reduce the large income inequalities that result from unregulated markets. This is accomplished primarily through a redistribution of wealth that takes place through taxes and income transfers toward lower-income individuals. The overall effect is to increase economic equality slightly.

The welfare state has not resulted so much from the pursuit of philosophical principles of social justice as it has been a natural consequence of the universal right of suffrage and the economic vagaries of market capitalism. Providing citizens with individual liberty to pursue their economic self-interest necessarily reduces economic equality. And in a capitalist political economy, economic differences breed political inequalities. Once there is economic inequality, those with more are in a stronger position to further reinforce their preferred position in relation to those who are less well off.

However, policy decisions to increase economic equality through welfare state policies must by necessity constrain certain liberties. Taxes reduce the amount of money available for consumption and transfer that authority to the government. Regulation of working conditions, health and pension programs, environmental pollution, and minimum-wage rates constrains the liberty of business owners.

Prior to giving the vote to ever-larger shares of citizens, the affluent property holders had a great deal of liberty, while the disenfranchised had very little. Laws in the eighteenth century permitted business owners to collude to hold wages down, while worker associations were outlawed. Labor laws in England prohibited a worker from moving from one parish to another to take advantage of higher wage rates.

Thus the poor, also being politically powerless, had a very qualified form of liberty. Those with money and property were not surprisingly the first to attain the ballot. The affluent have viewed with apprehension the broadening of political inclusion as weakening their power. An increase in liberty for the poor by encouraging their political participation may come at some expense of the heretofore unregulated liberties of the wealthy, even though total freedom is increased. However, the distribution of income and wealth in the United States and other countries shows that the top and bottom quintiles remain surprisingly steady in their share of economic resources. That is, the regulatory interference with individual liberties has not significantly reduced economic inequality.

There are many notions used to legitimize and encourage expanding the scope of political conflict: "whistle blowing," unions, political alliances, civil rights, equality, and justice. These tend to socialize conflict and invite outside intervention on behalf of those engaged in such struggles. A whistle blower by definition is someone who witnesses illegal or unethical behavior by superiors within an organization and therefore finds it necessary to go outside the organization for support to stop the behavior.

The Principle of Liberty

While the Constitution was a democratic document by the standards of the time, few today would maintain that a system that permitted barriers to voting based on property ownership and racial and gender considerations was a democratic system. Central to the idea of a democracy is a nation's commitment to the values of equality and tolerance. No one would concede today that any nation that permitted slavery, or did not guarantee the right to vote, was democratic. That issue was notably settled by a military conflict, because the Constitution was not able to provide a peaceful resolution of the issue. A nation approaches the democratic ideal to the extent that the people have control over the government, in what *The Federalist* no. 51 calls "a dependence on the people." The ability of the people to change the government through elections is their ultimate power. However, without an intelligent and well-informed public, this power cannot be exercised wisely. This was Jefferson's implication when he wrote: "If a nation expects to be ignorant and free, in a state of civilization, it expects what never was and never shall be."[40] Therefore the democratic ideal is more closely approached to the extent that public control is meaningful, informed, and skillfully engaged rather than symbolic or manipulated.

We would also point out that unemployment in the United States was considered primarily a personal problem (the more affluent usually judged unemployment the natural result of a debilitating character weakness, laziness, or other immorality). Under the best of circumstances it was a personal tragedy. However, since government was presumed to have no control over personal morality, it was not in either case a social problem over which it was thought to have responsibility.

The Great Depression and the election of Franklin Roosevelt did much to change those views. The response of the New Deal included public work programs to create jobs, provide unemployment insurance, and establish a bewildering variety of other government programs. As a result, unemployment came to be considered a social problem and the responsibility of the government to resolve. The Employment Act of 1946 states clearly that it is the obligation of the national government to try to create the conditions that will result in full employment. All democratic governments accept the obligation to conduct business-friendly policies to aid an expanding economy and full employment. Likewise, a government would not be considered democratic today if it did not accept responsibility for the economic well-being of its citizens.

The traditional capitalist economic system survived in the United States as a result of the alleviation of those problems that capitalism handles poorly by the intervention of the Keynesian welfare state. Capitalism cannot resolve the problems of poverty, unemployment, income insecurity, and environmental pollution. Welfare state spending increased employment during periods of economic downturns. The welfare state legitimizes the capitalist system among those at the bottom of the ladder by softening the rough edges of the system.

Conclusion

An ideology is a set of beliefs about values and the role of government. In the United States today, liberalism and conservatism dominate the dichotomy of political views and values. Other ideologies, such as communism or libertarianism, exist on the fringes and do not exert significant influence. Although most people do not identify strongly with an ideology, they do nonetheless indicate a general tendency to view politics from a slightly more liberal or more conservative perspective. Strongly held ideological convictions make it more difficult to objectively evaluate policy issues or to reach a compromise.

Classical liberals were concerned primarily with the notion that the best way to increase individual freedom was by protecting the individual *from* government. Classical conservatives were more concerned with preserving those institutions, such as the family and religion, that had grown over time and therefore had a certain legitimacy. In the liberal view, governments should contract while the private sphere should grow. By the mid-1800s it became clear that although government authority had receded in many areas, corporate influence grew to replace the vacuum left by the state. As large corporations grew, they influenced many aspects of the social and economic welfare of individuals. As a result, modern liberals began to reject laissez-faire capitalism and concluded that the government could protect and enlarge individual freedom by regulating and engaging in social welfare programs. Conservatives remained distrustful of government intervention in the economy and worried that too much would reduce the disciplines of the marketplace.

Two perspectives often utilized by policy scientists to analyze the world of public policy are the pluralist model and the elite model. The pluralist model assumes that multiple centers of power compete to influence public policy. Power in pluralist groups is wielded by those who occupy the top positions in those organizations. The second model holds that elites occupy the critical positions of power in society. They manage conflict to ensure that political debate and policy changes do not threaten their positions.

Government failure to provide a clear direction in policy formulation and implementation has caused an increase in frustration and dissatisfaction among the electorate. Politicians have exploited the lack of direction by campaigning on antigovernment platforms, which further reduces the credibility of government institutions.

U.S. public policy has been profoundly influenced by the institutions of government created by the Founding Fathers. The separation of powers, checks and balances, federalism, and limited government are a testimonial to the success of the framers' efforts to make government cumbersome and difficult to control. These barriers also contribute to the inefficiencies in policymaking that many find so frustrating. The barriers to the formulation and implementation of new policy options reflect a bias against change.

Political parties were developed to overcome the separation of powers and checks and balances put in place by the framers. The decentralized, winner-take-all pluralistic system of the United States forces political parties to fight to position themselves in the center of the spectrum.

Democracy in the U.S. political system is something that we must seek, although we never finally achieve it. The major tension in the political debate in the United States is between liberty and equality.

Questions for Discussion

1. What are the shared values of U.S. political culture?
2. Explain why many classical liberals are called conservatives today.
3. Thomas Jefferson was a classical liberal and would be considered a liberal today. Why?
4. What political institutions are most responsible for defeating coherent public policy today?
5. Why were decentralized parties a natural outgrowth of the impact of the framers' design?
6. Why is democracy something that must be forever pursued?
7. Is there a natural tension between liberty and equality? Why?

Suggested Readings

Bachrach, Peter. *The Theory of Democratic Elitism: A Critique.* Boston: Little, Brown, 1967.

Bracher, Karl Dietrich. *The Age of Ideologies: A History of Political Thought in the Twentieth Century.* New York: St. Martin's, 1984.

Cook, Karen S., and Margaret Levi, eds. *The Limits of Rationality.* Chicago: University of Chicago Press, 1990.

Dryzek, John S. *Democracy in Capitalist Times: Ideals, Limits, and Struggles.* New York: Oxford University Press, 1996.

Eisner, Marc Allan. *The State in the American Political Economy.* Englewood Cliffs, N.J.: Prentice-Hall, 1995.

Fukuyama, Francis. *The End of History and the Last Man.* New York: Free Press, 1992.

Greider, William. *Who Will Tell the People? The Betrayal of American Democracy.* New York: Simon and Schuster Touchstone, 1992.

Hamby, Alonzo. *Liberalism and Its Challengers.* 2nd ed. New York: Oxford University Press, 1992.

Hunter, James Davison. *Culture Wars: The Struggle to Define America.* New York: Basic Books, 1992.

Skidelsky, Robert. *The World After Communism: A Polemic for Our Times.* London: Macmillan, 1995.

Notes

1. See Center for Political Studies, University of Michigan, National Election Study Cumulative Data File, 1952–1992; 1994 National Election Study; and 1996 National Election Study. Those identifying as conservative or extremely conservative have averaged just over 20 percent of the population, while those identifying as liberal or extremely liberal have averaged about 18 percent.

2. David Smith, "Liberalism," in *The International Encyclopedia of the Social Sciences* (New York: Macmillan and Free Press, 1972), vol. 9, p. 276.

3. William Ebenstein and Alan O. Ebenstein, *Great Political Thinkers: Plato to the Present,* 5th ed. (Fort Worth, Tex.: Holt, Rinehart, and Winston, 1991), p. 596. The quote is from Jeremy Bentham, *Deontology, or Science of Morality* (London: Longman, 1834).

4. Vaclav Havel, "What I Believe," in Vaclav Havel, *Summer Meditations,* translated by Paul Wilson (New York: Knopf, 1992), p. 73.

5. Clinton Rossiter, "Conservatism," in *The International Encyclopedia of the Social Sciences* (New York: Macmillan and Free Press, 1972), vol. 3, p. 293.

6. Ebenstein and Ebenstein, *Great Political Thinkers,* p. 578.

7. Rossiter, "Conservatism."

8. Earl Latham, "The Group Basis of Politics," in Heinz Eulau et al., *Political Behavior* (New York: Free Press, 1956), p. 239.

9. Milton Friedman, *Capitalism and Freedom* (Chicago: University of Chicago Press, 1962), p. 27.

10. Sidney Verba and Norman H. Nie, *Participation in America: Political Democracy and Social Equality* (New York: Harper and Row, 1972), p. 336.

11. See, for example, Theodore Lowi, *The End of Liberalism* (New York: W. W.

Norton, 1972), esp. chap. 2. See also Charles E. Lindblom, *Politics and Markets* (New York: Basic Books, 1977).

12. Elite theory has been developed in many works. The classic text is C. Wright Mills, *The Power Elite* (New York: Oxford University Press, 1956). See also Michael Parenti, *Democracy for the Few*, 5th ed. (New York: St. Martin's Press, 1988); and Thomas R. Dye and Harmon Zeigler, *The Irony of Democracy*, 7th ed. (Monterey, Calif.: Brooks/Cole, 1987). Charles Lindblom, in *Politics and Markets* (New York: Basic Books, 1977), is another who argues that business has a privileged position in the U.S. political system (see esp. pp. 170–185).

13. Alexander Hamilton, *Records of the Federal Convention of 1787,* as quoted in Thomas R. Dye, *Who's Running America? The Bush Era* (Englewood Cliffs, N.J.: Prentice-Hall, 1990), p. 3. Our discussion of elite theory relies heavily on *Who's Running America?* and on Dye and Zeigler, *Irony of Democracy,* pp. 3–11.

14. Richard Hofferbert has developed a conceptual framework of policymaking that emphasizes elite influences. The policy process in his model is developed with governmental decisions being the dependent variable. The policy output is dependent on historical-geographic conditions, socioeconomic conditions, mass political behavior, governmental institutions, and most immediately, the behavior of the members of the elite itself. The model has been criticized for dealing with aggregate rather than individual choices. It also presumes that policy decisions are driven by socioeconomic conditions and mass political behavior filtered through governmental institutions and elite behavior. Other researchers, however, suggest that it is the elites who drive the policy decisions rather than merely filtering them. See Richard Hofferbert, *The Study of Public Policy* (Indianapolis: Bobbs-Merrill, 1974).

15. Dye and Zeigler, *Irony of Democracy,* p. 6.

16. Ibid., pp. 6–7.

17. Dye and Zeigler, in *Irony of Democracy,* point out that it is critical to understand what elite theory is not, as well as what it is. Elite theory does not assume that those in power are constantly at odds with the masses, or that they always achieve their goals at the expense of the public welfare. Nor does it hold that elites are involved in a conspiracy to suppress the masses. The theory does not suggest that members of the elite are always in agreement with each other, and it does not even hold that they always get their way.

18. Roger W. Cobb and Charles D. Elder, "The Politics of Agenda Building," *Journal of Politics* 33, no. 4 (November 1971): 910.

19. Robert Dahl has referred to this theory of plural elites as "polyarchy." See Robert A. Dahl, *Polyarchy: Participation and Opposition* (New Haven: Yale University Press, 1971).

20. George Gallup Jr., *The Gallup Poll: Public Opinion 1996* (Wilmington, Del.: Scholarly Resources, 1997), p. 172.

21. See http://www.gallup.com/poll/content.

22. See Elizabeth Hann Hastings and Philip K. Hastings, eds., *Index to International Public Opinion, 1987–1996,* 5 vols. (Westport, Conn.: Greenwood Press, 1997). See also Hans-Dieter Klingemann and Dieter Fuchs, eds., *Citizens and the State* (New York: Oxford University Press, 1995).

23. Gallup, *Gallup Poll.*

24. See Hastings and Hastings, *Index,* p. 124. When polled, 92 percent agreed "strongly" or "somewhat" that the federal government should guarantee a Social Security pension

to help provide for retirement. And 86 percent agreed "strongly" or "somewhat" that the federal government should provide some minimal level of health care. Another 84 percent supported nursing-home care for the elderly as well as subsidized prescription drugs.

25. In *The Federalist* no. 10, Madison stated: "No man is allowed to be a judge in his own cause because his interest would certainly bias his judgment, and, not improbably, corrupt his integrity. . . . Yet what are many of the most important acts of legislature but so many judicial determinations, not indeed concerning the rights of single persons, but concerning the rights of large bodies of citizens? And what are the different classes of legislators but advocates and parties to the causes which they determine? . . . It is in vain to say that enlightened statesmen will be able to adjust these clashing interests and render them all subservient to the public good. Enlightened statesmen will not always be at the helm."

26. James Madison, *The Federalist* no. 51.

27. The concern of the delegates to the convention about protecting private property has been well documented. See Calvin C. Jillson and Cecil L. Eubanks, "The Political Structure of Constitution Making: The Federal Convention of 1787," *American Journal of Political Science* 28, no. 3 (August 1984): 435–458. The view that the delegates' economic self-interest was the basis for private property and economic concerns was popularized by Charles Beard, *An Economic Interpretation of the Constitution* (New York: Free Press, 1913; reprinted in 1965). On economic stability, see also John P. Roche, "The Founding Fathers: A Reform Caucus in Action," *American Political Science Review* 55, no. 4 (December 1961): 799–816.

28. James L. Sundquist, "Needed: A Political Theory for the New Era of Coalition Government in the United States," *Political Science Quarterly* 103 (Winter 1988–1989): 614.

29. Richard E. Neustadt, *Presidential Power: The Politics of Leadership from FDR to Carter* (New York: John Wiley and Sons, 1980), p. 26.

30. E. E. Schattschneider, *Party Government* (New York: Holt, Rinehart, and Winston, 1942), p. 129.

31. Ibid., p. 1.

32. Marc Allan Eisner, *The State in the American Political Economy* (Englewood Cliffs, N.J.: Prentice-Hall, 1995), p. 24.

33. Robert Salisbury, "Interest Representation: The Dominance of Institutions," *American Political Science Review* 78, no. 1 (1984): 64–76.

34. This discussion of the QWERTY phenomenon is taken from Paul Krugman's discussion of this idea as it pertains to economics. We use it here because its application to politics is readily apparent. See Paul Krugman, *Peddling Prosperity: Economic Sense and Nonsense in the Age of Diminished Expectations* (New York: W. W. Norton, 1994), chap. 9.

35. Anthony Downs, "The Evolution of Democracy," *Daedalus* 116, no. 3 (1987): 146.

36. Various conservative voices have been raised in defense of the lack of participation in democratic processes by many citizens. For example, in *The Crisis of Democracy: Report of the Governability of Democracies to the Trilateral Commission* (New York: New York University Press, 1975), Michel Crozier, Samuel P. Huntington, and Joji Watanuki wrote about the need to protect government functions from too much democracy.

37. Social Darwinists such as William Graham Sumner argued explicitly that Darwinism justified the free and unregulated capitalist competition and the extreme social inequality that would result. Sumner wrote: "We cannot go outside of this alternative: liberty, inequality, survival of the fittest; not-liberty, equality, survival of the unfittest." William

Graham Sumner, "The Challenge of Facts," in Albert Galloway Keller, ed., *The Challenge of Facts and Other Essays* (New Haven: Yale University Press, 1914), p. 25.

38. See E. E. Schattschneider, *The Semi-Sovereign People* (New York: Holt, Rinehart, and Winston, 1960), for a fuller explanation of the thesis regarding the significance of the scope of the conflict for the outcome of political struggles.

39. See Joseph A. Schumpeter, *Capitalism, Socialism, and Democracy* (New York: Harper and Row, 1976), p. 269.

40. Thomas Jefferson, 1816, regarding his views on the importance of public education.

CHAPTER 5

Economic Theory as a Basis of Public Policy

Some knowledge of the nature of economic forces and economic theory is a prerequisite for thoughtful public policy analysis. It is impossible to comprehend the significance of policy choices without some understanding of the economic theory underlying market capitalism. Adam Smith's *Wealth of Nations* is based on the concept that the nation-state is a collection of people bound together in a shared responsibility for one another's mutual well-being. But the idea of a "national purpose" to promote the general welfare has come under increasing strain in recent years.

Though not every public policy of the government involves questions of resource allocation, many do. In Chapter 1 we saw that microfailures in the economy bring about situations that force government intervention to prevent free riders and to produce certain public goods. Individuals organize to distribute the costs of public goods among those people who receive the benefits. Cost sharing is necessary through government purchases to realize an ideal supply of a public good. Other failures, such as externalities, force government intervention to influence production or to determine who pays for certain goods. Members of society on occasion may decide that they are unhappy with the market determination of what, how, or for whom that society's goods are being produced. Government is also asked to intervene when real markets deviate from the ideal markets envisioned in classical economic theory.

The failures of the market provide specific justifications for government intervention through public policy. The trend of government growth and involvement in the public sector has increased dramatically in the United States since the 1930s. Until then, the government was limited primarily to the basic functions of providing for defense, administering the system of justice, and providing a postal service. Since the Great Depression, and largely because of it, the federal government has

149

become involved in a whole range of new activities, including public works, environmental regulation, education, health care, income redistribution through income-transfer programs like Social Security, and Medicare. Significant growth in government has not happened just at the federal level. State and local governments have become even more important than the federal government as sources of employment and production.

Does economic theory have anything to say about what role the government should have in policies that affect the public sector? Can economic theory suggest what effect public versus private spending will have on the economy, job creation, and social well-being? Is it supportive or negative? Can it suggest what kind of policies should be used in certain situations? This chapter will explore these questions.

Adam Smith and Classical Optimism

The year 1776 was pivotal, for the Declaration of Independence and also for the publication of Adam Smith's *Wealth of Nations*. Both were basic manifestations of the movement away from authoritarian monarchical forms of governmental control, and toward individual liberty. The American Revolution attacked not only the political control of the American colonies by England, but also the system of economic authority that made this control inevitable. The colonists—and English entrepreneurs—had already experienced what Smith argued: state domination of the economy inhibited new opportunities for increasing production and profits.

The supporters of **mercantilism**, with whom Smith took issue, advocated government regulation because they believed that the pursuit of one's own self-interest would produce chaos in society and less wealth for everyone. The mercantilists viewed competition as a zero-sum scenario in which more for one by necessity meant less for others. In 1776 Smith challenged that notion.

Adam Smith (1723–1790), a professor of moral philosophy, naturally saw economics as a branch of moral philosophy with a calling to improve the condition of humanity, especially that of the poor. Writing in the latter half of the eighteenth century, he recommended a system of natural liberty in which the individual would be free to pursue his or her own interests. By pursuing one's self-interest, each person maximizes benefits for herself or himself or for other individuals and for society as a whole.

He began by challenging the notion that economic trade was a zero-sum exchange in which, if some were better off, others must necessarily be worse off. He maintained that if Jim wants something from Kevin that Jim cannot make himself, he must produce something Kevin wants in order for them both to agree on an exchange in which both "better their condition." Both benefit because they agree to give up something that has less value to themselves personally than the products they receive. Thus the total welfare has been enhanced. Smith showed that in free competitive markets, exchange can have positive-sum results, where both parties are better off than before the exchange.

Smith, whose writing was clear and frequently amusing, stated in a famous passage: "It is not from the benevolence of the butcher, the brewer, or the baker, that we expect our dinner, but from their regard to their own interest."[1] According to his theory, self-interest and competition will eliminate two kinds of waste: unrealized trades and inefficient production. Conversely, it will encourage mutually beneficial trades and efficient production.

Smith had none of the illusions of later classical economists that associated wealth with morality. As a moral philosopher he intensely disliked and distrusted what he referred to as the "unsocial passions" of greed and self-interest exhibited by merchants who would try to enlist government to give them more power:

> To widen the market and to narrow the competition is always the interest of the dealers. . . . The proposal of Any new law or regulation of commerce which comes from this order, ought always to be listened to with great precaution, and ought never to be adopted, till after having been long and carefully examined, not only with the most scrupulous, but with the most suspicious attention. It comes from an order of men, whose interest is never exactly the same with that of the public, who have generally an interest to deceive and even to oppress the public, and who accordingly have, upon many occasions, both deceived and oppressed it.[2]

And therein lies the problem. How could a society in which merchants driven by greed and given free rein not result in great inequalities and injustice as merchants raise prices to exact the greatest profit possible? Smith noted that people of the same trade seldom are in one another's company even on social occasions, "but the conversation ends in a conspiracy against the public, or in some contrivance to raise prices."[3] He pointed out the concern of merchants only for their own self-interest: "Our merchants and master-manufacturers complain much of the bad effects of high wages in raising the price, and thereby lessening the sale of their goods both at home and abroad. They say nothing concerning the bad effects of high profits. They are silent with regard to the pernicious effects of their own gains. They complain only of those of other people."[4]

Smith said that greed and competition are the driving forces of production.[5] Further, all goods have two prices: a natural price (today referred to as a normal price) and a market price. He defined the **natural price** as the price that would have to be realized to cover the costs of production, with a small amount left over for a profit. He defined the **market price** as the price the product actually brings in the marketplace. Whenever the market price deviates from the natural price, it will be driven back in the direction of the natural price as if by an invisible hand. Every entrepreneur attempting to accumulate profits is held in check by other competitors who are also trying to attain a profit. This competition drives down the price of goods and reduces the revenue earned by each seller. In a market unrestrained by government, the competition between entrepreneurs erases excessive profits, employers are forced to compete for the best workers, workers compete for the best jobs (usually defined in terms of wages and working conditions), and consumers compete to consume products. Consequently, producers are forced to search for the lowest-cost production methods. Finally, resources are distributed to their most highly valued use, and economic efficiency prevails.

According to Smith, the owners of business tend to reinvest their profits, thereby consuming little more than the workers. The entrepreneurs inadvertently share the produce of all their improvements with the workers, though they intend only "the gratification of their own vain and insatiable desires." He continued: "[Business owners] are led by an invisible hand to make nearly the same distribution of the necessaries of life which would have been made had the earth been divided into *equal portions among all its inhabitants*."[6]

Because reality deviates from the market ideal, society experiences significant inequality and waste. Smith conceived of the idea that order, stability, and growth are intrinsic characteristics of capitalism. In the classical view, the economy is a **self-adjusting market**: it will adjust itself to any departure from its long-term growth trend. The market is self-regulating in that, if anyone's profits, prices, or wages depart from the levels set by market forces, competition will quickly force them back. Thus the market, which is the apex of economic freedom, is also an uncompromising taskmaster.[7] In a competitive economy, assumed by Smith, merchants are victims of their own greed.

Smith opposed mercantilist government intervention as a hindrance to the unfettered workings of self-interest and competition. Therefore, he has become identified with a laissez-faire economic philosophy, which is the basic philosophy of conservative-minded individuals today. His commitment to freeing individuals from the heavy hand of monarchial rule through a commitment to liberty as benefiting the general public, was a very liberal position to take in his day. Smith is a classical liberal because he tried to free the individual from the heavy hand of monarchial oppression and mercantilist policies to control the economy. This liberalism was in contrast to the mercantilism of the day, which held that government should control the economy for the interest of the state. Liberals today see the possibility in democratic governments to provide active leadership to increase freedom in the society by solving social problems and helping the needy. By that definition, Smith would be a liberal in today's political environment, because his support of laissez-faire policies was at that time not value-neutral, but designed to help those who were less well off. His sympathies were clearly on the side of consumers rather than producers when he wrote, "Consumption is the sole end and purpose of all production; and the interest of the producer ought to be attended to, only so far as it may be necessary for promoting that of the consumer."[8]

Smith did see a significant although limited role for the state. He advocated three principal uses of government: the establishment and maintenance of national defense, the administration of justice, and the maintenance of public works and other institutions that private entrepreneurs cannot undertake profitably in a market economy.

Smith's classical economic view was optimistic. According to its principles, the economy would continue to expand through growing production based on increased investment in machinery. Machinery strengthened the division of labor that was so beneficial in expanding economic output, improving the productivity of the workers. It saw the market system as an enormous power for the buildup of capital, primarily in the form of machinery and equipment, which would provide jobs and result in self-sufficiency for all. It predicted that any slowdown in the economy would be only temporary and self-correcting.

Smith was confident that the system would generate economic growth. The purpose of this growth was to improve society's welfare by extending consumption opportunities "to the lowest ranks of the people." Smith believed that free market forces would bring about an agreeable, mutually acceptable solution to the problem of individual self-interest within society as long as individuals were free to pursue their goals in a political and moral environment where everyone had equal basic rights that were acknowledged by all. This aspect of Smith's views is not usually emphasized, but in fact he was explicit in his judgment that self-interest could be destructive if it was not moderated with justice. He condemned capitalist "rapacity," and his disdain for opulence was captured in his statement that, "with the greater part of rich people, the chief enjoyment of riches consists in the parade of riches, which in their eyes is never so complete as when they appear to possess those decisive marks of opulence which nobody can possess but themselves."[9] He noted that civil "government is in reality instituted for the defense of the rich against the poor, or of those who have some property against those who have none at all,"[10] and that "all for ourselves, and nothing for other people, seems, in every age of the world, to have been the vile maxim of the masters of mankind."[11]

It should also be noted that Smith did not endorse the view that the unequal distribution of income was inherently just. He clearly indicated that coercion influences wages agreed on between capitalists and workers. Capitalists want to pay as little as possible and possess a stronger bargaining position when dealing with workers. The legal system during Smith's time also favored capitalists by permitting cooperation among manufacturers to hold wages down while prohibiting unions. Smith clearly broke with mercantilist views favoring a large working class that would be paid as little as possible to provide an incentive for hard work.

Smith also disagreed with the view that traits associated with individuals in different social classes were inherent in people's makeup, but attributed them instead to their positions in society. He held that "the very different genius which appears to distinguish men of different professions, when grown to maturity, is not upon many occasions so much the cause as the effect of the division of labor."[12] He openly sympathized with the working class over the manufacturing class and supported higher wages: "It is but equity, besides, that they who feed, cloathe and lodge the whole body of the people, should have such a share of the produce of their own labour as to be themselves tolerably well fed, cloathed and lodged."[13] In regard to raising wages of workers, he wrote: "No society can surely be flourishing and happy, of which the far greater part of the members are poor and miserable."[14] Smith argued against policies that worked against the poor. For instance, he criticized the 1662 Settlement Act, which prevented workers from moving from one parish to another to take advantage of employment opportunities.

Smith warned that the model would not work in the face of monopoly. He was particularly opposed to monopoly in all its forms and all laws that restrained competition. He charged that monopolists, "by keeping the market continually understocked, by never full supplying the effectual demand, sell their commodities much above the natural price, and raise their emoluments, whether they consist in wages or profit, greatly above their natural rate. The price of monopoly . . . is upon every occasion the highest which can be squeezed out of the buyers."[15] Smith recognized that when entrepreneurs became monopolists they were no longer the victim of market forces, but could control them to some degree, a point not lost on socialists of the nineteenth century. Smith's writings support the conclusion that he favored the workings of market forces and laissez-faire policies as preferable to government support of mercantilist policies that oppressed the poor. He left the door open for government policies to alleviate economic inequalities.

Classical Malthusian Melancholy

Despite Smith's vision of how the natural forces of a self-regulating market would lead to a constant improvement in the living conditions of the labor force, there was a nagging concern about the numbers of workers whose conditions were not improved by a market economy. The problem concerned the nature of what Smith termed **effectual demand** and its association with the distribution of income. In a nutshell, the problem is that since capitalists produce only for consumers with the money to buy, production will mirror their demand. Businesses will produce everything for those with money, and nothing for those without. It is one thing to argue that the market process is efficient. It is quite another to defend a system that produces nothing or almost nothing for the many, who after all make up the bulk of the population. The pure free market system ignored those in poverty, and indeed made it difficult for the poor to share in the benefits of an expanding market economy.

This anxiety was soon raised by the socialists, who perceived that things were not as universally rosy as Smith believed. Karl Marx was among the most famous of those to analyze the problem and offer a solution along socialist lines. But others tried to defend the market approach, with less than satisfactory results. Among these was Thomas Malthus (1766–1834), who was the first to suggest a resolution within a market economy framework. A minister by vocation, Malthus found the problem of poverty to be essentially moral in nature and therefore not susceptible to resolution by government policy. In his view, natural forces were at work and capitalists need not feel any pangs of conscience regarding wages that maintained their employees at subsistence levels.

Another economist, David Ricardo, argued there is a natural law of wages that tends toward the minimum necessary to sustain life. This occurs on the one hand because any increase in wages above subsistence results in workers procreating, and more mouths to feed means their wages in effect fall back to a subsistence level. On the other hand, if the price of food rises, workers then will force their wage rates up to pay for the necessities of their existence, thus maintaining a subsistence level. Either way, there is a natural wage rate that always tends toward the level of subsistence, which Ricardo termed the **iron law of wages**.

The conclusion for Malthus was inescapable: the population would grow until it was contained by "misery and vice." Assisting the poor would only transfer more resources to them and enable them to have more children, ultimately to the point of starvation. Providing the poor with assistance would divert wealth that should have been invested and slowed economic growth. Therefore it would be futile to look for social causes and cures for poverty. According to Malthus, if the "lower classes" do not want to be poor, all they have to do is to have fewer children. The burdens associated with poverty are a natural punishment for the failure of the lower classes to restrain their urges to procreation. Their only salvation is literally dependent on their moral reform, not government assistance. The clear implication is that the causes of poverty are not to be found in the structure of society, such as the greed combined with monopoly power that had worried Adam Smith.

A very important public policy implication of the Malthusian analysis is that no government assistance should be provided to the poor. On the contrary, a Malthusian view sees tragedies such as the miseries of poverty, famine, plague, and war as natural means of punishing and increasing the death rates of those who do not practice moral temperance. If it were not for these "natural" checks on population growth, the increasing numbers of poor would soon outstrip food production, which in turn would lead to their starvation. Malthus wrote that we should encourage the operations of nature in producing this mortality:

> And if we dread the too frequent visitation of the horrid form of famine, we should sedulously encourage the other forms of destruction, which we compel nature to use. Instead of recommending cleanliness to the poor, we should encourage contrary habits. In our towns we should make the streets narrower, crowd more people into the houses, and court the return of the plague. In the country, we should build our villages near stagnant pools, and particularly encourage settlements in all marshy and unwholesome situations. But above all, we should reprobate specific remedies for ravaging diseases; and those benevolent, but much mistaken men, who have thought they were doing a service to mankind by projecting schemes for the total extirpation of particular disorders. If by these and similar means the annual mortality were increased . . . we might probably every one of us marry at the age of puberty, and yet few be absolutely starved.[16]

Not surprisingly, Malthus recommended the abolition of the poor-laws that provided meager relief in England at the time. Thomas Carlyle, after reading Malthus's pessimistic analysis, called political economy "the dismal science." He was only partially correct, since Malthus's analysis was dismal—but only for the poor.

Malthusian analysis proved to be extraordinarily reassuring to those in search of moral justification for selfishness. It calmed their doubts and fears by asserting that the chase after wealth primarily served the interests of society. Perhaps more important, it claimed that the affluent, as well as business leaders, need not concern themselves with an undue sense of social responsibility for the conditions of the poor, since workers were the causes of their own miserable fates. By inference, the converse was also true—the affluent were morally superior to the poor. The doctrine of laissez-faire holds that the free market system has within itself the capacity to best resolve economic problems on the basis of justice and fairness for all participants. By reinforcing the commitment to a doctrine of laissez-faire, Malthus devised a superb justification for the affluent to deny any responsibility for a serious economic problem. The effects of this reassuring and convenient theory on the affluent made Malthus one of the most influential economic thinkers of his century. The fact that his theory was based on his personal pondering and was not subject to empirical verification did not cause any serious objections at the time. But subsequently it led to the scathing attack on market economics by Karl Marx.

The Haunting Specter of Karl Marx

The writings of Karl Marx (1818–1883) posed a different view of market economics than those of either Adam Smith or Thomas Malthus, and led to a radically different proposed solution for society's problems. Marx disagreed with the capitalist assumption that politics and economics could be separated. To the mercantilists, the state was a powerful force to direct the economy. To the classical liberals, the state was a threat to economic freedom. To Marx, the state was not independent of the economic structure. The real purpose of the state was to serve the interests of the wealthy owners of capital.

Marx was impressed with the ability of a capitalist economy to automatically allocate resources efficiently with no direction from the government, and to be extraordinarily efficient in producing goods and services. As Marx and his colleague Friedrich Engels commented, "The bourgeoisie, during the rule of scarce 100 years, has created more massive and more colossal productive forces than have all preceding generations together."[17] Capitalism transformed the world:

> The bourgeoisie, by the rapid improvement of all instruments of production, by the immensely facilitated means of communication, draws all nations, even the most barbarian, into civilization. . . . It compels all nations, on pain of extinction, to adopt the bourgeois mode of production; it compels them to introduce what it calls civilization into their midst, i.e., to become bourgeois themselves. In a word, it creates a world after its own image.[18]

Capitalism swept aside all former relationships and "left no other bond between man and man than naked self-interest."[19]

Marx viewed history as a continuing struggle between elites and the masses. He thought that the class struggle between capitalists and workers over profits and wages would ultimately lead to the end of capitalism. Marx, unlike Smith, saw the potential for instability and chaos in the laissez-faire market economy. His intricate analysis held that capitalists are able to increase their profits and wealth only at the expense of the workers. In his theory of **surplus value**, he argued that exploited labor generates profits, which are squeezed out through the capitalist ownership of machinery.

The significance of Marx for our purpose is that he was among the most influential thinkers to focus on the weaknesses of the market system. He emphasized the importance of the economic and social instability resulting from the tension between the opposing demands of capital and labor. In his view, the rapaciousness of business results in ever-larger business firms because small firms go under and their holdings are bought up by surviving firms. This trend toward a few large firms and the resulting concentration of wealth intensifies the struggle between labor and capital, and will eventually lead to a small group of wealthy capitalists and a mass of impoverished workers. In the end, the imbalance will be too great, resulting in the collapse of the market system. The means of production will then be centralized, that is, taken over by the government. Great inequalities and exploitation will cease.

Marxist theory has generated controversy regarding whether a pure market economy would collapse from its internal tensions. Critics of Marx point out that, despite difficulties in market economies, they have not collapsed. On the contrary, those systems that ostensibly have tried to model themselves on Marx's precepts have shown the most internal tension and in most instances have come unraveled.

Marx's contribution primarily rests on his pointing out the dynamic tensions in the market system. While market capitalism has not collapsed, it has survived in part because it has been willing to move away from a laissez-faire mode. In particular, government public policy programs have moved into many areas to ameliorate the living conditions of middle- and lower-income workers.

The Uneasy Relationship Between Politics and Economics

For more than a century following the political and economic revolution represented by the American War for Independence and Smith's writings, the state shrank as the dominant and controlling force in the economy of the United States and much of Europe. Economies grew largely with government support, but without political interference. It was widely believed that a society would prosper best when left to the free play of market forces. The basic policy principle of noninterference, or laissez-faire, logically flowed from that belief. Market forces would determine the flow of goods and capital. But economic policy, in the sense of a government's commitment to certain objectives for the economy, such as full employment, stable prices, or a satisfactory economic growth rate, did not exist. Governments were required to raise taxes to provide for national defense, administer justice, and provide for other incidental governmental functions. But there was no attempt to influence the volume of economic activity. There was no monetary policy, because the amount of currency in circulation was automatically controlled by the amount of gold or silver possessed by the government. The business cycle seemed beyond the purview of government. Unemployment rose and fell with the business cycle while government looked on from the sidelines, making no attempt to prevent and very little to alleviate its effects. The market was supposed to take care of any temporary dislocations. There was little inclination to tamper with a system that brought a growing economy and prosperity to the nation in the early twentieth century. Although progress was uneven and subject to periodic spasms, laissez-faire was validated by the upward trajectory of the U.S. economy. The idea that the economy could or should be "managed" to achieve economic growth or reduce unemployment would have seemed incomprehensible a century ago. Such perspectives on the relationship between politics and economics prevented the development of economic policy.

Despite the diminished role of government in economic matters, however, it was recognized that markets are dependent on governments for their existence. Democratic societies are based on a **social contract** in which the government is given monopoly power on the legitimate use of force in return for the state's agreement to use that power to protect people's lives and property and to enforce contracts. Smith wrote about the mutual self-interest among parties to trades in a market system. However, such a system cannot function unless there is some instrument that is entrusted to interpret and protect individual and corporate property rights. Without such a guarantor, agreed-upon trades cannot be enforced and dishonest parties can steal back the items traded, or otherwise not live up to their parts of business bargains, with impunity. This would lead to mutual distrust, a radical reduction in trade, and the collapse of the system itself. Thus the need for government as economic guarantor to establish an environment in which markets can function was recognized.

The classical view just described, identified with Adam Smith, emphasized that individuals following their own self-interest will lead to economic order, not chaos. Karl Marx, writing approximately three-quarters of a century later, saw economic trials and troubles everywhere and predicted the collapse of capitalism. John Maynard Keynes, writing still later, was also critical of the problems created by an unfettered market system, but aimed his theories not at the collapse of capitalism but its reform.

The Realist Critique of Keynes

The economist who most challenged Karl Marx's pessimistic conclusions regarding the inevitable collapse of the market system was John Maynard Keynes (1883–1946). Keynesian theory represents his effort to deal with the chaotic conditions produced by the Great Depression of the 1930s.[20] From the outset, Keynes rejected communism and agreed with Adam Smith's preference for free market alternatives.

Conservative critics of Keynes, opposing a larger role for government, charged that his views were too radical and threatened the very foundations of capitalism. Many denounced him as a socialist. Keynes, however, viewed himself as a conservative trying to defend capitalism against the growing attractions of communism. Even before the Great Depression, Keynes had observed that market capitalism had imperfections that, if corrected, would strengthen it. In a book titled *The End of Laissez-Faire,* he noted aspects of the unfettered market that lead to reduced efficiency and production and suggested how governments might exercise "directive intelligence" over the problem while leaving "private initiative unhindered":

> Contrariwise, devotees of Capitalism are often unduly conservative, and reject reforms in its technique, *which might really strengthen and preserve it,* for fear that they may prove to be first steps away from Capitalism itself. . . . For my part, I think that Capitalism, wisely managed, can probably be made more efficient for attaining economic ends than any alternative system yet in sight, but that in itself it is in many ways extremely objectionable. Our problem is to work out a social organisation which shall be efficient as possible without offending our notions of a satisfactory way of life.[21]

Keynes never faltered in his admiration of capitalism. Keynesian theory was dedicated to the preservation of the capitalist economic system and the position of those who were most favored by it. Yet his theory required some tinkering with the system by the government. The affluent were highly suspicious of any proposal that permitted government control over their interests. And they deeply resented the improved status he gave to the "working class" as an essential ingredient in the overall health of the economy. They found especially irritating his suggestion that their own privileges might actually contribute to economic instability.

The severe disturbances of the economies throughout Europe and North America shook the very foundation of those economic and political organizations. It is difficult for anyone who did not live through the Great Depression to grasp the dimensions of the catastrophe. But the statistics are staggering. It wiped out half of the value of all goods and services produced in the United States. A quarter of the labor force lost their jobs; another quarter had their jobs reduced from full to part time or had their wages reduced. Over 9 million savings accounts disappeared when banks failed, and more than 1 million mortgages were foreclosed.

The level of despair and discontent raised doubts about whether the market system could survive. Many of the more affluent who had not been seriously hurt by the depression viewed the crisis with serene detachment. They opposed the reforms proposed by Franklin Roosevelt in the New Deal as a threat to their favored status. Roosevelt's reforms were linked to many of Keynes's ideas, though more by instinct than by any philosophical commitment to Keynesian theory. The federal government entered the economic life of the nation through the New Deal to assume responsibility for the nation's economic well-being. There is a general consensus that the policies of the Roosevelt revolution not only changed the character of the national government, but also rescued the traditional capitalist economic system in the United States.

Keynes's *The General Theory of Employment, Interest, and Money,* published in 1936, was a much more complex analysis of the market economy than Adam Smith's. Undertaking a macroeconomic analysis, which Smith had not concerned himself with, led Keynes to conclude that laissez-faire was not the appropriate policy for a stagnant economy like that of the 1930s. Keynes stated his profound disagreement with the classical tradition in his one-paragraph first chapter:

> I have called this book the *General Theory of Employment, Interest, and Money,* placing the emphasis on the prefix *general.* The object of such a title is to contrast the character of my arguments and conclusions with those of the *classical* theory of the subject . . . which dominates the economic thought, both practical and theoretical, of the governing and academic classes of this generation, as it has for a hundred years past. I shall argue that the postulates of the classical theory are applicable to a special case only and not to the general case. . . . Moreover, the characteristics of the special case assumed by the classical theory happen not to be those of the economic society in which we actually live, with the result that its teaching is misleading and disastrous if we attempt to apply it to the facts of experience.[22]

The classical school of economics offered no solution to the problems facing the nation during the 1930s. But obviously, the optimistic view that the economic problems were temporary, requiring only belt-tightening and waiting for the economy to grow, was not acceptable to most of the population. Keynes asserted that classical economists

> were apparently unmoved by the lack of correspondence between the results of their theory and the facts of observation—a discrepancy which the ordinary man has not failed to observe. . . . The celebrated optimism of traditional economic theory [is] to be traced, I think, to their having neglected to take account of the drag on prosperity which can be exercised by an insufficiency of effective demand. For there would obviously be a natural tendency towards the optimum employment of resources in a Society which was functioning after the manner of the classical postulates. It may well be that *the classical theory represents the way in which we should like our Economy to behave. But to assume that it actually does so is to assume our difficulties away.*[23]

Keynes believed that the psychological and organizational conditions of the nineteenth century that permitted laissez-faire notions to work as a policy, in fact constituted a special case that was shattered by World War I. The convoluted and contrived system depended on free imports of goods and export of capital made possible by peace. It depended also on a delicate class balance between capital and labor, and a moral balance between capital and spending. In the 1920s price instability led to the unjustified enrichment of some and impoverishment of others, which cut the moral link between effort and reward. Worker acceptance of modest wages depended on the dominant business class producing job opportunities. There was also a psychological balance between saving and consumption in which saving was a great virtue. But increasingly, consumption and material outcomes constituted the measure of success—and failure. And increasingly, capitalism's driving force was a "vice" that Keynes called "love of money."[24]

It was also no longer possible to contend that people pushed into uncompensated unemployment were simply too lazy to get a job, or that they could find work if they would only lower their wage demands. Marxists of the day felt vindicated, believing that the depression was the death knell of the market system.

If Keynes was right in his analysis and prescriptions for curing the ills of capitalism, then the attraction of a planned economy as represented by communism would atrophy because people prefer to be employed and self-sufficient rather than dependent on the government for everything. His public policy solution was one in which business and government would act as partners in running the economy. The government would engage in public policies that would create a sufficient demand to maintain full employment, and profits would go to business as they had in the past. Government was the only party of this arrangement that could pull it off, however, since it alone could act in the role of a non-self-interested party. He saw government acting as a positive instrument for individual freedom by, for example, funding programs such as education that would help individuals as well as society, and for economic freedom by protecting a system whose entrepreneurs could flourish, albeit in a regulated way. Keynes maintained that economic prosperity is the only certain guarantee of a liberal political system.

Keynesian theory was a clear advancement in our understanding of market capitalism. Part of his success was also based on the fact that he addressed not only pressing problems of the moment—economic depression and unemployment—but also enduring policy concerns like growth and stability. And, like Adam Smith before him, he developed a theory that rationalized what was already being done out of necessity. Without the Great Depression, Keynes would never have written his general theory; but already by the time of its publication, Franklin Roosevelt had been elected and was implementing his New Deal, which was Keynesian in practice.

Conservative critics of Roosevelt argue that his efforts to stimulate the economy by running deficits did not get the United States out of the Great Depression. Rather, they argue that World War II ended the depression. This misses the point, however. Roosevelt's New Deal deficits were not large enough to offset the reduction in private expenditures by business, households, and state governments. It is true that it was not until World War II that the economy began to come out of the depression. But this expansion was caused by the vast increase in government purchases associated with the war that stimulated employment and aggregate demand.

This actually reinforced Keynes's theory of the role of government as employer of last resort and purchaser of goods to stimulate the economy.

Keynesian theory supplanted the classical school not only because of its more penetrating analysis, but also because the essentials of the classical school supported a basic posture of passivity regarding government public policy. Especially in crisis situations such as depressions or wars, it is not a realistic option for governments to do nothing. A major part of the legacy of Keynes is an understanding that government does bear a major responsibility for the overall performance of the economy. The questions of economic stability, employment, growth, and inflation require government leadership and cannot be left to laissez-faire inaction and faith that the system will resolve all economic problems in its own time.

Keynes's thinking was almost the opposite of Adam Smith's. Disturbances in employment, output, or prices are likely to be magnified by the invisible hand of the marketplace. A catastrophe like the Great Depression is not a rare occurrence but rather a disaster that will return if we depend on the market to self-adjust. Thus, when the economy stumbles we cannot wait for an invisible hand to provide the needed adjustments. The government must intervene to safeguard jobs and income. The total number of jobs in the economy is determined by macroeconomic variables, including levels of consumption, investment, and imports and exports. Keynes's analysis also made short work of Malthusian perspectives. The poor, he made clear, were not poor because they were less moral than the affluent; they were poor because of their position in society and impersonal economic forces.

A critical factor in determining the total number of jobs in the economy, or the "employment pie," is the relationship between employment and inflation, which constrains the number of jobs that decisionmakers can or should create. Liberal Keynesians are more concerned about high rates of unemployment than inflation. They are opposed to high interest rates, and prefer fiscal—as opposed to monetary—policy to pursue broad economic goals. Conservative Keynesians are more concerned about inflation, and therefore accept higher unemployment to reduce it, and are less willing to use fiscal policy (especially deficits) to provide full employment.

From the mid-1930s onward in the United States, a consensus emerged on government fiscal policies that accepted mild deficits. The principal goal was the achievement of **full employment**, which was loosely defined as an unemployment rate of about 4 percent. At 4 percent, existing unemployment was thought to be "frictional" or "structural" rather than "cyclical." **Frictional unemployment** refers to the temporary unemployment of new entrants to the labor force or those who leave one job while they look for a better one. **Structural unemployment** refers to unemployment due to a mismatch between the skills of the labor force and the jobs available. Frictional and structural unemployment are not considered major problems. **Cyclical unemployment**, which refers to unemployment caused by a lack of jobs in the economy due to a general economic downturn, is of serious concern.

Political leaders of both parties in the United States have long held an overwhelming presumption that in regard to election and reelection prospects, few things are more foolhardy than a tax increase or more helpful than a tax cut. The temptation to run big deficits when the economy is not in recession was reined in by Keynesian theory, which held that large deficits would result in higher inflation, requiring high interest rates to stop rising prices and bringing about a recession, which would spell disaster in elections. The perceived close connection between short-term economic trends and politics produced an arrangement that permitted deficits but kept them within a narrow range.

Keynes's analysis provided the rationale for governments to adopt public policies to keep inflation and unemployment low while encouraging economic growth. Governments would have a major macroeconomic role with their state, but there should be free trade between states. These policies were embodied in the Full Employment Act of 1946, which committed the government to an activist policy to stimulate enough growth to keep unemployment low. The 1946 legislation did not define precise goals so that policymakers would know what goals to shoot for to achieve "full employment," or acceptable levels of inflation or economic growth. The Full Employment and Balanced Growth Act of 1978 finally established an unemployment goal of 4 percent, an inflation rate of not more than 3 percent, and an economic growth rate of 4 percent.

At the core of Keynes's disagreement with the classical view was his argument that a market economy is inherently unstable. The market system could reach a position of "underemployment equilibrium" in which the economy could have a high level of unemployment and idle industrial equipment. Keynes stressed the importance of **aggregate demand** as the immediate determinant of national income, output, and employment. Demand is the sum of consumption, investment, government expenditures, and net exports. Effective demand establishes the economy's equilibrium level of actual output. A **recession** occurs when the equilibrium level of actual output is less than the level necessary to maintain full employment. The basic characteristic of a recession or depression is a decline in aggregate demand or purchasing power by consumers, business, and government. The result is an economic downturn caused by a reduction in production and the consequent increase in unemployment as employers react to reduce their costs. The significance of his theory in relation to classical theory was that it claimed there is no self-correcting property in the market system to return a stagnant economy to growth and full employment.

If his analysis was correct, the classical nostrum of tightening your belt and riding out the storm was disastrous. It meant that if demand was established at levels so low that unemployment would remain high and businesses would not be willing to undertake new investments, the situation would remain indefinitely in that depressed state, unless some variable in the economic equation was changed. According to Keynes, political management of the economy was the solution. Government spending might well be a necessary public policy to help a depressed market economy regain its vigor. According to Keynes, to the extent that there were market failures leading to insufficient demand, government should intervene through fiscal and monetary policies to promote full employment, stable prices, and economic growth. Useful government action against recessions came down to fiscal and monetary measures designed to expand consumer and investment spending. This would simultaneously improve the general social welfare by improving the position of those who are the most vulnerable in periods of economic stagnation: the unemployed.

Fiscal policy involves the use of government taxing and spending to stimulate or slow the economy, and the federal budget is the means by which fiscal policy is implemented. The government can increase or decrease aggregate demand by increasing or decreasing its share of taxing and spending. Tax cuts, especially when directed toward middle- and lower-income workers, will stimulate demand by putting more money in the hands of consumers and businesses. The increased spending results in increased employment to meet those demands. Conversely, increasing taxes, the least popular of all fiscal policies, is intended to curb spending and slow an inflationary economy.

When unemployment reaches its full-employment level (4–5 percent unemployment), we might expect universal approval. Indeed, when the jobless rate declines to full employment, the most highly paid tend to react adversely. The most well off fear inflation will be touched off when the economy presses against its production possibilities, and that it will cost more to find idle resources and bring them online. **Inflation** occurs when there is an increase in the average level of prices for goods and services (not a change in the price of any specific good or service). The conventional wisdom that says "inflation hurts us all" is simply not correct. Inflation redistributes income and wealth. Thus, while inflation will make some worse off, it must make others better off. Inflation acts like a tax in which money is redistributed from one group to another. For illustration, if the Organization of Petroleum-Exporting Countries (OPEC) doubles the price of oil, the price of a gallon of gas will go up, making the purchaser poorer, but the extra price will be transferred to OPEC countries, making others wealthier. Since inflation is an increase in average prices, not all prices rise at the same rate. Therefore, not everyone benefits or suffers equally from inflation. There are winners and losers. However, since average prices are rising, average wages must also be rising (keep in mind that a higher price to a buyer is also a higher income to a seller). To an employer, the higher cost of labor in a tight market represents a higher income to the worker selling his or her labor skills on the market. As a result, real wages on average keep up with inflation. In reality, some workers' incomes will rise faster than inflation while others may not keep up. The value of assets representing a person's wealth will also be affected by inflation. For example, in the 1990s, average prices increased by 32 percent, but the value of stocks (on average) more than doubled after adjusting for inflation, while those who invested in gold saw the value of their assets decline by over 25 percent after adjusting for inflation.

The resulting uncertainty caused by inflation can inhibit consumption and production decisions and reduce total output. **Price stability** (an inflation rate of less than 3 percent per year) is a very real concern to policymakers, whose choice of policy ultimately determines the course of the economy.

However, the determination to wring inflation out of the economy by driving up interest rates will consistently hit some groups harder than others. Lower- and middle-income workers are much more likely to become unemployed than are the more affluent members of the labor force. Stopping inflation by creating an economic slowdown does not affect everyone equally:

> Recessions are not equal opportunity disemployers. The odds of being drafted into the fight against inflation increase steadily the lower an individual's earnings and family income to begin with. The relative income losses suffered by the working heads of poor families, for example, are four to five times as great as the losses for those heading high-income families. . . . At every income level, male heads of families experience greater income losses than female heads of families, and black men suffer the most of all.[25]

The spending side of the budget is another fiscal policy tool. An increase in government spending is also an increase in aggregate demand and raises production levels. A reduction in spending reduces aggregate demand and reduces inflationary pressures. Government spending now exceeds $2 trillion a year, so changes in the federal budget can have a significant influence on aggregate demand. The spending surge to pay the costs for the war in Iraq in 2004 significantly increased aggregate demand. Combining the surge in national government expenditures with the significant tax cuts, even when directed primarily toward the affluent, significantly increased the fiscal stimulus in 2001, 2002, and 2003.

Legislation has built in what are referred to as **automatic stabilizers**, in which fiscal policy automatically responds countercyclically to certain economic events. For example, when the economy slows down and unemployment rises, tax revenues decline, while government spending for unemployment insurance benefits, food assistance, welfare, and other transfer payments rises. The budget deficit rises as a result. Tax revenues and expenditures react automatically to changing economic conditions without requiring new policy. These automatic adjustments help stabilize the economy. On the other hand, with a reduction in unemployment, tax receipts rise at the same time that expenditures for welfare decline, reducing budget deficits. Automatic stabilizers are important because they adjust immediately to a rising or falling economy and do not require any policy debate to begin working. Therefore the deficit will rise during a recession and shrink during a robust economy, even if there is no change in fiscal policy. So the same fiscal policy could result in a surplus, a balanced budget, or a deficit.

Monetary policy refers to the use of money and credit controls to shift aggregate demand in the direction needed to attain economic growth with stable prices, such as actions taken by a central bank, like the Federal Reserve (the "Fed") in the United States, to control the money supply. These actions in turn control the volume of lending and borrowing by commercial banks and ultimately by investors and consumers. In a depression, the government should increase the money supply to keep interest rates down. This policy might also be matched by reducing taxes for workers to increase demand, and increasing government spending to stimulate business investments, employment, and demand.

Some would insist that, although this is a well-established theory, it does not represent what actually happens. It may be argued that business firms borrow when they have expectations of making money and not because interest rates are low. It can be pointed out that during the recession of 2001, the Fed lowered interest rates to less than 2 percent. The housing market improved as mortgage rates declined, but business firms did not borrow to increase output without demand. The Fed may receive credit if and when there is a recovery, but as John Galbraith has written:

> The fact will remain: When times are good, higher interest rates do not slow business investment. They do not much matter; the larger prospect for profit is what counts. And in recession or depression, the controlling factor is the poor earnings prospect. At the lower interest rates, housing mortgages are refinanced; the total amount of money so released to debtors is relatively small and some may be saved. Widespread economic effect is absent or insignificant.[26]

Some policy analysts disagree over how active the Fed should be in adjusting the money supply relative to changing economic conditions. Some have argued that the Fed should be an active policymaker, while others argue for a more passive role in which the Fed would intervene to apply fixed rules regarding the money supply. It is undoubtedly true that the Fed risks making errors in applying discretionary policy. The Fed was accused of following too restrictive a monetary policy by raising interest rates excessively in late 2000, tipping the economy into a recession, which forced it to reverse its policy in 2001. A preprogrammed set of rules would also have a problem of too little flexibility and be unable to adapt to unexpected events.

From Demand-Side to Supply-Side Policies

In the early 1960s, John Kennedy became the first president to avowedly follow the Keynesian approach to shaping public policies. For nearly eight years this interventionist approach to policy was so successful in producing an uninterrupted expansion of the economy that economics was declared to be a science. The decision to extend the Nobel Prize to include an annual award in the area of economics capped this newfound prestige. But ironically, Keynesian economics was about to suffer an erosion in confidence at the moment of its greatest triumph.

Keynes's concern was with an economy, with high unemployment and low demand, that would be running well below capacity. Inflation would not be a problem with such excess capacity. But in the late 1960s inflation began to rise as unemployment declined.

The idea that unemployment could be too low to be consistent with stable inflation is of recent origin. William Phillips (1914–1976) analyzed data concerning the relationship between unemployment and inflation going back almost a century in the United Kingdom.[27] He discovered a tradeoff between unemployment and inflation, an inverse relationship that became known as the **Phillips curve**. The explanation for the relationship is implied in Keynesian theory and is intuitively obvious. Labor does respond to the market forces of supply and demand. When unemployment is high, the competition for jobs by unemployed workers allows management to fill its labor needs at relatively low wage rates. As the economy expands and unemployment declines, management must lure workers with higher wage rates. Higher wages for labor will result in higher costs of production and ultimately in higher prices. Policymakers could reduce unemployment by accepting higher inflation, or they could reduce inflation by accepting higher unemployment. Presidents of both political parties, until Ronald Reagan, chose to reduce unemployment by expansionary monetary and fiscal policies that gave people more money to spend. Increased demand meant more jobs.

Keynesian theory provides policymakers with clear options when the economy experiences a serious recession or significant inflation. There is a large area between the extremes of recession and inflation, however, such that occasionally the economy may suffer unacceptably high levels of unemployment and inflation at the same time. Dubbed **stagflation**, it became apparent that conventional policy tools might provide only a partial cure in altering the structure of supply or demand and that the economy might be forced to accept a temporary setback. Milton Friedman noted that business came to expect government policies to encourage continuous growth that would result in higher income levels. Businesses and individuals made wage, price, and consumer decisions based on the expectation of continued growth and inflation. This offset government job-creation efforts of putting more money into circulation, but it also made inflation worse. High inflation finally resulted in higher unemployment, breaking the tradeoff that existed between the two. Stagflation can also result from an external shock such as an increase in the price of oil by OPEC (as in 1979–1980 and 1999–2000), which further slows economic growth. Unemployment may also rise due to structural unemployment, such as that caused by the bursting of the dot.com bubble in 2000–2001. Policymakers were faced with an unhappy choice. To fight high unemployment, they would traditionally reduce interest rates and increase government spending. To fight inflation, they would do the opposite. In the environment of stagflation, fighting unemployment could exacerbate inflation.

By the late 1970s, a variation on classical economics began to take shape that did suggest a different way for public policy to deal with inflation and economic growth. Reagan needed an economic theory that would provide an acceptable policy doctrine as the intellectual basis for a dramatic departure from previous practice. The theory of **supply-side economics** was put forward by a loosely knit group of conservatives who claimed to have developed a solution to the problem of stagflation. Their approach reopened a debate many thought had been settled by the Great Depression when they openly proclaimed their goal to widen the gap between economic "winners" and the "losers" as an incentive to work hard, save, and invest. They placed blame for many economic problems on the policies that supported a major role for the government in the economy, rather than the preferred classical approach that favored business and suppliers over consumers and the demand side. Cynics labeled supply-side programs a return to the "trickle-down" economics of a bygone era.[28]

Supply-side proponents saw a reduction in taxes, particularly for upper-income groups, as a key ingredient to stimulate economic investments. They claimed that large reductions in marginal tax rates would stimulate enough economic growth to actually increase tax collections and balance the budget, without spending cuts. If correct, it would permit government to cut taxes and spend more at the same time—the politicians' equivalent of accomplishing the medieval alchemists' quest to turn lead into gold.

Most political economists accepted the notion that government monetary and fiscal policy must be coordinated to either reduce unemployment or reduce inflation. Supply-siders argued that monetary and fiscal policy could be split: permitting government to increase spending to stimulate job creation, while simultaneously raising interest rates to curb inflation. Despite warnings from mainstream political economists, Ronald Reagan proceeded to push supply-side policies in the

Case Study: The Appeal of Convenient Logic

The effort to understand the world through rigorous analysis is essential if we are to achieve social progress. Unfortunately, there is considerable evidence that what is passed off as objective analysis is often largely an exercise in seizing on those parts of a theory most in harmony with our financial and political self-interest. Human beings have a remarkable tendency to believe those things most in accordance with their self-interest. We resist the intrusion of reality that might suggest otherwise.

Problem-solving techniques taught in academic settings usually move from cause to effect. In real-life situations, though, when our interests are involved, we often choose the remedy that will require the least cost to us and that will require the least amount of reorganization of our other self-interested beliefs. We then reason back to a cause for which our lowest-cost remedy provides the greatest congruence. In some cases, this may require significant mental gymnastics.

By way of illustration, Adam Smith wrote hopefully that natural forces would lead to a nearly equal distribution of income between capitalists and workers in a market economy. And he heartily approved of higher wages for workers. The failure of the equalization to occur was worrisome because it raised fundamental questions about the soundness of Smith's model. Malthus's view that the poor are immoral and responsible for their own fate was a most welcome and gratifying reasoning from the effect (poverty) back to the cause (immorality) for the affluent, because it relieved them of any burden of conscience concerning subsistence wages. And it provided them with a basis for righteous indignation at any suggestion of an unwelcome obligation to transfer financial resources to the poor. Subsequently, "social Darwinism" was invoked as a self-explanatory justification through adaptation of Darwin's law of the survival of the fittest: wealth should not be passed from the wealthy (or "fit") to the poor (or "unfit"), as doing so would violate a natural law.

More recently, Keynesian analysis showed that the causes of unemployment and poverty can be found in market forces such as inadequate demand, and in economic policies that tolerate unemployment to keep a downward pressure on prices. Other studies make it clear that economic deprivation in childhood, and lack of working-adult role models, may encourage poor work habits among the young, making it impossible for them to get work. Their children in turn are without working-adult role models and it becomes difficult to untangle cause and effect.

It can no longer be claimed that poverty is caused primarily by personal immorality (or that the wealthy are more moral than the poor—recall the recent savings and loan scandals). And one might reasonably expect solutions to be proposed related to the new diagnosis of the causes of poverty—for example, economic policies that do not rely on accepting high unemployment to reduce inflation, strict enforcement of equal opportunity laws, or greater efforts to provide educational opportunities to the disadvantaged. Unfortunately, all these remedies require the affluent to incur a cost, which they find deeply disturbing. So more convenient alternatives are suggested, based on a view of causes of poverty more in keeping with solutions they wish to see implemented. Poverty is now blamed on government policy: the poor are "victims" of the well-intentioned but misguided Great Society programs aimed at

continues

Case Study   continued

helping them. This view alleges that the poor have no incentive to work because they are the beneficiaries of the welfare programs that have been lavished upon them. In other words, *the poor have too much!* So the solution to poverty, according to this view, is a reduction in public expenditures for the poor so they will be motivated to work harder.

Obviously this is a most agreeable policy proposal for the more affluent. And its logic is carried a disconcerting step further: just as the poor have too much and need to feel the misery of deprivation to spur them to work, the wealthy have not been working because they have too little. High taxes are identified as the reason for a lack of incentive for performance by the wealthy. A reduction in

taxes, especially a cut in the capital gains tax would be an excellent motivation for the wealthy. And it is claimed that this proposal favoring the affluent is motivated by compassion for the poor. It is primarily in the interest of the poor because it is alleged to create useful employment for them.

Thus, in this logic, the poor have too much to be motivated. The wealthy have too little. Therefore, benefits should be reduced for the poor and increased for the affluent.

Source: Loosely adapted from a graduation address by John Kenneth Galbraith titled "Reverse Logic" and reprinted in J. K. Galbraith, *A View from the Stands* (New York: Houghton Mifflin, 1987), pp. 34–38.

---

fond hope that he could cut taxes, increase spending, grow the economy, and reduce inflation at the same time.[29]

The supply-side tax cuts raised the national debt while an increased demand for imports expanded the trade deficit fourfold. In 1982–1983 the economy fell into the deepest recession since the Great Depression. Productivity growth actually declined in the 1980s (to less than 2 percent per year) from levels in the 1970s (3.2 percent per year). Savings and investment rates also declined significantly in the 1980s. The tax cuts contributed to unprecedented budget deficits throughout the decade. Finally, these policies contributed to the increase in inequality that occurred during the decade.

For all of these reasons, supply-side economics is no longer touted as a viable alternative to Keynesian economics. Politicians learned that supply-side policies such as major tax cuts targeting the wealthy provided tremendous political rewards despite the broader economic fiasco. Even if the theory did not hold up, many cynical neoconservative politicians saw supporting more tax cuts for the rich as a potentially forceful instrument for campaign financing.

George H.W. Bush muffled his early criticism of supply-side economics and pledged "no new taxes" in the campaign of 1988. Bush abandoned a strict reliance on supply-side arguments in favor of a call for a "kinder, gentler nation." In his inaugural address, however, he noted that "we have more will than wallet," indicating that he did not envision a larger role for government in securing that kindness and gentleness. Within two years, with deficits climbing at a dizzying pace, the economy slipping into a recession, and threats of forced spending cuts mandated by Gramm-Rudman legislation, Bush raised income tax rates on the affluent and raised the gasoline tax rate.

The state of the economy at the end of the Bush administration provided a significant boost to Bill Clinton's campaign. Unemployment was at 7.4 percent and per capita income was falling. There was a record budget deficit that year of $340 billion and a federal debt that had risen to 68.2 percent of gross domestic product (GDP). U.S. trade deficits were growing and had fluctuated between $465 billion and $109 billion during the Bush administration. Although these conditions helped Clinton win the election, he was now forced to govern under them. The size of the deficit and the national debt were the key economic problems to face Clinton. Failure to make progress on this front would crush every other policy initiative. The deficit required action because, as interest payments approached $200 billion, the government was competing with business in money markets, driving up interest rates. This made it more expensive for U.S. firms to borrow funds for capital investments to improve growth. The cost of financing the debt would also prevent the administration from pursuing any other social welfare goals requiring funding. No significant programs to improve conditions in education, health care, housing, or the environment could be initiated under such conditions. With fiscal policymakers paralyzed, the power to make economic policy would be transferred to the Federal Reserve. However, the president and the Fed serve different constituencies. The president's primary concern is with encouraging economic growth and full employment, while the Fed has very limited power in this area and is more concerned with maintaining price stability.

Clinton's campaign set two basic goals for his first term: to cut the federal budget deficit in half and to create an economic environment that would create 11 million new jobs. In his campaign for a second term Clinton could boast that the economy had created 14 million jobs, with two-thirds of those jobs paying wages above the median, and an unemployment rate that had dropped from 7.5 percent to 5.4 percent. The core inflation rate fell from 3.7 percent in 1992 to 2.7 percent in 1996.[30] And by early 1998, federal revenues as a percentage of total GDP declined to 19.9 percent. The administration's most important economic policy accomplishment was a reduction in the deficit from $290 billion in 1992 to $107 billion in 1996, a cut of 63 percent. In 1992 the U.S. general deficit (the total deficit for all levels of government) was larger in relation to GDP than were the general deficits of Japan or Germany in relation to their GDPs. By 1996 the deficit was a smaller fraction of GDP than in any other major industrialized country. It became a small surplus in fiscal year 1998 and grew each of the last three years of the Clinton administration.

In 1996 the voters rewarded Clinton by making him the first Democrat reelected to two full terms since Franklin Roosevelt. The Republican Party found it difficult to attack Clinton's economic record, so they touted the symbolic issues of the "character and integrity" of their candidate, Senator Bob Dole.

The Decline and Renewal of Keynes

Parts of Keynes's theories were inconvenient to the accepted orthodoxy of the affluent. Among other things, his analysis suggested that the poor and the unemployed are not less moral than the affluent, but rather that they too frequently fall victim to economic forces beyond their control. In fact, he insisted that insufficient demand leading to unemployment can be caused by low wages, as well as by a tendency of the affluent to save rather than to consume and invest. Such analysis legitimized policies that included increased government intervention and a progressive tax policy aimed at taking wealth from the affluent and returning it to the circular flow of the economy through, among other things, increased public expenditures that would benefit the poor. The anger of the affluent over both the analysis and the resulting policies is well known.

Despite flaws in his analysis and in his optimism about the impartiality of government, in one sense Keynes has won the debate with the classical school regarding whether or not governments should intervene in the natural processes of the market to achieve societal goals in economic and other policy matters. Several factors that cannot be ignored compel government involvement in a wide range of public policy issues and will prevent its withdrawal in the future:

1. *Democratization.* Around the world, democratic forms of government are increasingly displacing authoritarian forms. One element of democracy is greater access to government by interest groups demanding that their needs be placed on the policy agenda.

2. *Demands for economic security.* As nations have become more prosperous, demands have increased for governments to provide protection from the vagaries of market forces. Tolerance of economic disruption declined at the very time when the expansion of industrialization and modernization was increasing competition. This trend began before the Great Depression, but was legitimized by that enormous crisis. More recently, major businesses have demanded that government not let them fail, citing the potential damaging effects on the overall national economy (to say nothing of the effects on company executives). Government has been pressured to undertake measures ranging from protective legislation, to favorable tax

treatment, to business loans, to outright bailouts in the cases of Chrysler Corporation and the savings and loan industry.

It is not surprising that, if corporations can successfully plead their special right to subsidies to remain in business, ordinary citizens will plead their right for aid to alleviate the vicissitudes of poverty through assistance in unemployment compensation, health care, education, food stamps, and Aid to Families with Dependent Children, among other programs.

3. *Demands for social justice.* The demand for equal treatment before the law in the United States and throughout the world reflects the demand that gender, ethnic, racial, and religious discrimination come to an end. There is an unwillingness to endure humiliating and degrading treatment at the hands of an elite. Not infrequently, the discriminatory practices are protected by the state at the expense of victims and in favor of those not discriminated against.

4. *Urbanization.* Increased urbanization has enlarged the public sector of the economy in areas such as public health, police protection, sanitation, and education, areas that in a more rural society had been left to individuals or private groups.

5. *War.* Two world wars and a cold war in the twentieth century have resulted in a huge increase in government spending on national defense. In the absence of appropriations for a war on terror, and for foreign military operations in Afghanistan and Iraq, the U.S. military budget would have risen by 4 percent in 2003 rather than the actual increase of 11 percent. The military budget is set to continue to grow, but the rate is likely to decline over the next several years, because current levels of growth will become politically and economically unsustainable. The military budget request for fiscal year 2005 was $421 billion, which is over twenty-nine times as large as the combined spending of the seven "rogue" nations (Cuba, Iran, Iraq, Libya, North Korea, Sudan, and Syria), which spent a total of $14.4 billion. If Russia and China were added to the rogue states, the combined budget would be $116.2 billion, or 27 percent of the U.S. budget.[31] Spending at such levels will have a significant impact on the economy.

6. *Technology.* Governments have been forced to respond to problems created by new technologies that require national regulation in such areas as communications (radio, telephone, and television), aviation, legal and illicit drugs, and automobiles.

7. *Policies in other countries.* Governments in developing countries have resorted to economic planning in an effort to modernize and achieve living standards comparable with those of the Western world. Governments elsewhere engage in a variety of policies such as education to improve the quality and productivity of their labor forces. Many countries, such as Japan and Germany, have industrial policies, in which the government acts as a partner with business firms in charting

national economic development. These policies are designed to improve the economic competitiveness of the countries' firms internationally, thereby improving the national economic and social welfare. However, the U.S. government is reluctantly being pushed in this direction just to compete with these countries in international trade.

Moreover, the view popularized during the 1980s that government intervention is unneeded and that it is actually likely to be harmful, has come increasingly under question. Social problems such as homelessness, the need to improve education standards, and the need to deal with public health problems such as AIDS have contributed to this. At the same time, scandals in the banking and the securities industries have led to calls for greater government regulatory powers.

Economic Theory and Political Reality

The goal of macroeconomic theory is to explain the business cycle with all of its variables in a manner that would allow policymakers to achieve the goals of full employment, rapid economic growth, and stable prices. Yet too frequently the economy appears lackluster, or unemployment or inflation become uncomfortably high. Is economic theory inadequate? Or is it simply impossible to control all the variables that can influence the business cycle (such as oil price shocks)? In defense of theory, it must be pointed out that since World War II, economic growth has had many economic slowdowns, but they have not been as severe or as frequent as the recessions before Keynesian theory. At the same time, the U.S. economy has enjoyed longer periods of uninterrupted growth since 1945 than before. It is also clear that government intervention has reduced the severity of recessions and extended the growth periods of the business cycle. The theory has clearly helped improve the nation's economic performance.

Many economic failures are not failures of economic theory so much as they are failures caused by the real world of politicians. It is clear that Keynes, like Smith, was too optimistic in his economic views. He assumed that a better understanding of the relationship between economic variables would permit government to enter the market system to maximize social welfare. He implicitly accepted the notion that government would be neutral and benign and would intervene only to increase demand and provide employment, thus increasing output and improving income distribution. He assumed that an understanding of the shortcomings of market economics would lead to agreement about solutions. He seems not to have been aware of the degree to which governments are penetrated by self-interested groups who lobby for their own special interests rather than the general welfare of society.

Political actors may share the same goal of a growing economy, full employment, and price stability, but they often have different priorities. Politicians consider winning the next election their first priority. Therefore they will be more concerned with the need to raise money and win votes than with economic theory. Politicians are notoriously reluctant to raise taxes on potential campaign contributors. They are also reluctant, but some a little less so, to cut spending to control inflation. For example, the tradeoffs relative to a political actor's main constituents will influence whether fighting inflation or fighting unemployment will receive priority. Middle- and lower-income workers along with unions and the unemployed would urge that achieving full employment should receive the highest priority. However, more affluent communities along with bankers, and those on fixed incomes, such as retired people, will prefer that controlling inflation be given the highest priority.

Political actors also must take action without having perfect information. Economics, as a science, has been criticized because a rearview mirror is its most scientific tool. That is, economics must gather and analyze data gathered over the previous year, quarter, or month to try to determine what is happening in the economy. It is easier to say where the economy has been than where it is going. A recession is defined as two successive quarters in which the economy contracts. Because of the lag-time gathering and processing data, a recession is not confirmed until about seven to eight months into the event. Political actors are often forced to respond to problems after the fact. More effective policy occurs when politicians and economists look for signs of where the economy is headed and take action based on forecasts. Unfortunately, forecasts are based on models, all of which have their own inherent biases.

Even if political actors had almost perfect information regarding what is taking place in the economy and even where it is headed, difficulties in designing and implementing the best policy still remain. A policymaker with the best information possible may interpret information through ideological biases that will make it difficult to design the best policy. For example, a Keynesian income tax cut may be recommended to stimulate consumer spending to end a recession. A policymaker's proposal may not effectively target those most likely to place their increased income back into the economy. Or Congress may change the president's proposals in response to its own convictions and constituencies. Even if the most effective policy is formulated to resolve an economic issue, there is no guarantee it will be implemented. And even if it is implemented, by the time it moves from a plan to a selected policy, it may no longer be timely. By the time tax cut legislation is passed and implemented, the business cycle may be in the expansion phase, and a tax cut could be inflationary and would not be recommended.

The politics of economic policy may actually reward politicians for behaving irresponsibly and punish responsible economic policy. For example, tax hikes rarely win votes, and despite the fact that tax increases on the wealthiest Americans had an overall effect in reducing the deficit in 1991–1992, Democrats lost control of Congress as a direct result of that policy. On the other hand, proposing tax cuts when the economy is strong because "we can afford it," as well as when the economy is weak "to stimulate growth," has a strong appeal for voters' abiding desire for a higher after-tax income.

Advantages of Government Intervention to Correct Market Failures

Government by definition has a universal membership made up of all its citizens; it also has the power to compel obedience to its laws. Together these give it distinct advantages in attempting to correct failures in the marketplace. For example, it can avoid free rider problems in providing a public good such as highways or bridges precisely because of its universal membership. Individuals may not easily opt out of the system. It also has the power to prohibit certain activities—what we might call public "bads." For example, by law or through regulatory processes it may prevent pollution, require adequate testing of pharmaceutical drugs before they are sold, or mandate that medicine can be practiced only by particular individuals. The government also has the power to punish. It can exercise a range of punishments for violations of its laws far more severe than any that could be carried out through private arrangements.

Perhaps the government's most important advantage is that it has the power to tax. Individual insurance firms may recognize that certain behaviors increase the risks against which they provide insurance. Those firms would like to discourage smoking, for example, since it increases the incidence of health problems. Insurance companies can run ads against smoking, but the government can actively discourage the practice by raising the prices of tobacco products through taxes on them. Finally, government can improve markets having imperfect information. Business can provide information on products in ways aimed at preventing consumers from comparing differences in quality and price. The government can require that such information be provided in a standardized, easy-to-understand manner.

Conclusion

The father of modern economics, Adam Smith, tried to free the capitalist market system from the inefficiencies associated with a mercantilism in which government provided protection for and control over business. His theory promoted an economic model that claims full employment of workers and capital can be maintained without any government intervention as long as there are no monopolies or a highly unequal distribution of income does not intervene. His sympathies were decidedly on the side of the workers and against business owners. Deviations from the ideal resulting in economic slowdowns, reduced output, or unemployment will self-adjust as if an invisible hand intervenes, thus eliminating the need for government involvement. Smith's sympathies and his qualifications were largely ignored, while his views in favor of laissez-faire were accepted enthusiastically by entrepreneurs. This school concludes that government should not intervene in the economy, because any economic problem is only temporary. From this perspective, government's role should be limited as much as possible. Although there is much in Smith's analysis supportive of government intervention in the economy, today's conservatives are inclined to ignore those aspects of his writings.

Thomas Malthus focused on a problem noticed early on in market capitalism—the increasing economic disparity between the rich and the poor. His analysis led him to conclude that poverty is a moral problem: the poor lack moral restraints in reproduction. Any effort to improve their condition through government relief or higher wages will result in their producing more offspring until they fall back to subsistence levels again. This view of the iron law of wages, developed by David Ricardo, largely doomed any effort to improve the situation of workers through higher wages, government policy, or charity. The theory reinforced laissez-faire thinking and justified opposition to any policy proposal on behalf of the lower classes by the more affluent. Conversely, it can be directly linked to arguments that tax rates on the wealthy should be kept as low as possible and that it is immoral and counterproductive to take wealth from productive individuals and transfer it to those who have contributed less to the social good.

Karl Marx and his followers seized on the problems of monopoly and the inequality exacerbated by them. Marx saw threats to the continuance of the capitalist system everywhere. John Maynard Keynes's defense of capitalism against Marxism revolutionized economic theory. His analysis held that market economies are inherently unstable, and that they have no self-correcting properties. According to Keynes, government may be the only part of society capable of intervening in the economy to create the demand necessary to maintain full employment. His analysis showed the economy to be much more complex than anything suggested by the classical school. His conclusion was that there are several different areas of monetary and fiscal policy in which the government may successfully intervene. These interventions may also be geared to achieve social goals of the society other than those purely economic in nature.

It may well be that the very survival of a capitalist economy in the United States is due to the relief from some of its harshest failures (poverty, unemployment, alienation, and income insecurity) by the Keynesian welfare state. The welfare state may result less from policy choices in search of social justice than from choices to ensure the survival of a capitalist economy. Government expenditures, both national and state, now account for close to 30 percent of GDP in the United States.

The supply-side approach brought back many of the arguments of the classical school in a slightly different form. The 1980s saw a concerted effort to return to earlier policy prescriptions of reducing government involvement in social and economic issues. The policies were not successful in achieving the macroeconomic goals claimed. Although the supply-side school as an approach has receded in importance, a conservative perspective with the goal of reducing government influence and its consequent tax burden is still very much alive.

Government does have some advantages over private efforts to correct failures in the economy or to influence what, how, or to whom goods will be distributed. Changing global and domestic considerations ensure that, despite rhetoric to the contrary, big government is here to stay. The only question is whether economic theory will be acted on wisely by political decisionmakers.

Questions for Discussion

1. There is a generally held view that Adam Smith was an advocate of minimal government involvement in the economy. What evidence is there to support this view? Does this view need to be qualified? If so, how?
2. Many of Malthus's views have been discounted today, yet he was onto something when he focused on the relationship between population and a nation's economic well-being. How would you revise his theory to apply it to developing nations today?
3. Why and how did Karl Marx agree and disagree with Adam Smith?
4. How have the major tenets of the classical school been challenged by Keynesian theory?
5. In what ways has Keynesian theory been challenged or modified by subsequent writers?
6. Is there a relationship between a democracy and market capitalism? Explain why or why not.

Suggested Readings

Eisner, Marc Allan. *The State in the American Political Economy.* Englewood Cliffs, N.J.: Prentice-Hall, 1995.

Friedman, Milton. *The Optimum Quantity of Money and Other Essays.* Chicago: Aldine, 1969.

Galbraith, John Kenneth. *The Culture of Contentment.* New York: Houghton Mifflin, 1992.

Heilbroner, Robert. *The Worldly Philosophers: The Lives, Times, and Ideas of the Great Economic Thinkers.* 4th ed. New York: Simon and Schuster, 1972.

Heilbroner, Robert, and Lester Thurow. *Economics Explained.* Englewood Cliffs, N.J.: Prentice-Hall, 1998.

Keynes, John Maynard. *The General Theory of Employment, Interest, and Money.* New York: Harcourt Brace Jovanovich, 1964. Originally published in 1936.

Malthus, Thomas Robert. *An Essay on the Principle of Population.* Edited by Philip Appleman. New York: W. W. Norton, 1976.

Reich, Robert B. *The Work of Nations.* New York: Vintage Books, 1992.

Smith, Adam. *An Inquiry into the Nature and Causes of the Wealth of Nations.* Edited by Edwin Cannan. New York: G. P. Putman's Sons, 1877. Originally published in 1776. There are many more recent annotated editions available.

———. *The Theory of Moral Sentiments.* Edited by D. D. Raphael and A. L. Macfie. Oxford: Clarendon Press, 1976. Originally published in 1759.

Notes

1. Adam Smith, *An Inquiry into the Nature and Causes of the Wealth of Nations,* edited by Edwin Cannan (New York: G. P. Putnam's Sons, 1877; originally published in 1776), p. 27. Further on Smith said that there is an invisible hand that channels behavior to improve social welfare: "Every individual necessarily labours to render the annual revenue of the society as great as he can. He generally, indeed, neither intends to promote the public interest nor knows how much he is promoting it . . . he intends only his own gain and he is in this, as in many other cases, led by an invisible hand to promote an end which was no part of his intention. Nor is it always the worse for the society that it was no part of it. By pursuing his own interest he frequently promotes that of the society more effectually than when he really intends to promote it. I have never known much good done by those who affected to trade for the public good. It is an affectation, indeed, not very common among merchants, and very few words need be employed in dissuading them from it" (p. 354).

2. As quoted in Robert L. Heilbroner, *The Essential Adam Smith* (New York: W. W. Norton, 1986), p. 322.

3. Adam Smith, *The Wealth of Nations,* 6th ed. (London: Metheun, 1950), vol. 1, p. 144.

4. Ibid., p. 110.

5. Smith was against the government meddling with the market mechanism. As Robert Heilbroner has pointed out: "Smith never faced the problem . . . of whether the government is weakening or strengthening the market mechanism when it steps in with welfare legislation. . . . There was virtually no welfare legislation in Smith's day—the government was the unabashed ally of the governing classes. . . . The question of whether the working class should have a voice in the direction of economic affairs simply did not enter any respectable person's mind . . . by a strange injustice the man who warned that the grasping eighteenth-century industrialists . . . came to be regarded as their economic patron saint. Even today—in blithe disregard of his actual philosophy—Smith is generally regarded as a *conservative* economist, whereas in fact, he was more avowedly hostile to the *motives* of

businessmen than most New Deal economists." Robert Heilbroner, *The Worldly Philosophers,* 3rd rev. ed. (New York: Simon and Schuster, 1967), pp. 63–64.

6. Adam Smith, *The Theory of Moral Sentiments,* edited by D. D. Raphael and A. L. Macfie (Oxford: Clarendon Press, 1976; originally published in 1759), p. 386 (emphasis added). For excellent summaries of Smith's contribution, see Robert Heilbroner and Lester Thurow, *Economics Explained: Everything You Need to Know About How the Economy Works and Where It's Going* (New York: Simon and Schuster, 1998), pp. 26–44; Robert L. Heilbroner, *The Worldly Philosophers,* 6th ed. (New York: Simon and Schuster, 1992), pp. 42–75; Robert L. Heilbroner, *The Essential Adam Smith* (New York: W. W. Norton, 1986); and Daniel R. Fusfeld, *The Age of the Economist,* 7th ed. (New York: HarperCollins, 1994), pp. 23–36.

7. Smith's writings in *The Wealth of Nations* were at least in part an effort to refute the mercantilists' contention that the economy should be regulated by the monarchy to provide support for merchants, which would ultimately increase the nation's power. The English king was free to intervene in the most arbitrary and capricious ways as an exercise of "sovereign right." Smith wrote: "England, however, has never been blessed with a very parsimonious government, so parsimony has at no time been the characteristic virtue of its inhabitants. It is the highest impertinence and presumption, therefore, in kings and ministers, to pretend to watch over the economy of private people, and to restrain their expence, either by sumptuary laws, or by prohibiting the importation of foreign luxuries. They are themselves always, and without exception, the greatest spendthrifts in the society. Let them look well after their own expence, and they may safely trust private people with theirs. If their own extravagance does not ruin the state, that of their subjects never will." Smith, *Inquiry* (1877 ed.), pp. 227–228.

8. Heilbroner, *Essential Adam Smith,* p. 284.

9. As quoted in ibid., p. 322.

10. Smith, *Wealth of Nations* (1937 ed.), p. 674.

11. Ibid., p. 389.

12. Ibid., pp. 15–16.

13. Ibid., p. 79.

14. Ibid.

15. As quoted in Fusfeld, *Age of the Economist,* pp. 32–33.

16. Thomas Robert Malthus, *An Essay on the Principle of Population,* 6th ed., cited in E. A. Wrigley and D. Souden, eds., *The Works of Thomas Robert Malthus* (London: William Pickering, 1986), vol. 3, p. 493.

17. Robert C. Tucker, ed., *The Marx-Engels Reader,* 2nd ed. (New York: W. W. Norton, 1978), p. 477.

18. Karl Marx and Friedrich Engels, *The Communist Manifesto,* edited by Samuel Beer (New York: Appleton-Century-Crofts, 1955), p. 9.

19. Ibid., p. 12.

20. There is far more to Keynesian analysis than the few points made here. In addition to Keynes's own *General Theory of Employment, Interest, and Money* (New York: Harcourt, Brace, and World, 1936), recommended works for further reading include Dudley Dillard, *The Economics of John Maynard Keynes* (New York: Prentice-Hall, 1948); and G. C. Harcourt, ed., *Keynes and His Contemporaries* (New York: St. Martin's Press, 1985).

21. John Maynard Keynes, "The End of Laissez-Faire," in *Essays in Persuasion* (New York: W. W. Norton, 1963), p. 321 (emphasis added).

22. Keynes, *General Theory,* p. 3 (emphasis in original).

23. Ibid., pp. 33–34 (emphasis added).

24. Robert J. Skidelsky, *Maynard Keynes: The Economist as Saviour, 1920–1937* (New York: Viking Penguin, 1992), esp. chap. 7, "Keynes' Middle Way."

25. Isabel V. Sawhill and Charles F. Stone, "The Economy: The Key to Success," in Isabel V. Sawhill and John Palmer, eds., *The Reagan Record: An Assessment of America's Changing Domestic Priorities* (Cambridge, Mass.: Ballinger, 1984), p. 80. Inflation causes much more concern among the affluent. Economist Alan Blinder of Princeton University wrote: "Sometimes inflation is piously attacked as the 'cruelest tax,' meaning that it weighs most heavily on the poor. . . . On close examination, the 'cruelest tax' battle cry is seen for what it is: a subterfuge for protecting inflation's real victims, the rich. . . . [E]very bit of evidence I know of points in the same direction: inflation does no special harm to the poor. . . . The meager costs that inflation poses on the poor are dwarfed by the heavy price the poor are forced to pay whenever the nation embarks on an anti-inflation campaign." See Alan Blinder, *Hard Minds, Soft Hearts: Tough-Minded Economics for a Just Society* (Reading, Mass.: Addison-Wesley, 1987), p. 54.

26. John Kenneth Galbraith, *The Economics of Innocent Fraud* (New York: Houghton Mifflin, 2004), p. 47.

27. A. William Phillips, "The Relation Between Unemployment and the Rate of Change of Money Wage Rates in the United Kingdom, 1861–1957," *Economica* 25 (November 1958): 283–299.

28. See especially Paul Krugman, *Peddling Prosperity: Economic Sense and Nonsense in the Age of Diminished Expectations* (New York: W. W. Norton, 1994).

29. Three Nobel Prize–winning economists, James Buchanan, Milton Friedman, and George Stigler, with impeccable conservative credentials, scorned supply-side thinking. Alan Greenspan, chairman of the Federal Reserve under Presidents Clinton and Bush, also a clear conservative, is disdainful of supply-side thinking as well.

30. White House, *The Economic Report of the President, February 1997* (Washington, D.C.: U.S. Government Printing Office, 1997), p. 23.

31. See Center for Arms Control and Non-Proliferation, *World Military Spending* (Washington, D.C.: Center for Arms Control and Non-Proliferation, February 2004).

CHAPTER 6

Economic Policy: Translating Theory into Practice

As Chapter 5 indicated, prior to the 1930s most policy analysts accepted the economic theory of the time, which held that a market economy would achieve the macroeconomic goals of full employment, price stability, and productivity growth without government intervention. The Great Depression shattered such complacent beliefs. John Maynard Keynes's theories demonstrated how achieving macroeconomic goals required government intervention through monetary and fiscal policies. This was officially endorsed in the United States by the Employment Act of 1946 and reinforced by the Full Employment and Balanced Growth Act of 1978, which committed the federal government to specific policy goals for unemployment, inflation, and economic growth.

Those acts recognize the responsibility of the state for creating the economic conditions that will result in full employment and otherwise provide for the social welfare of citizens. Economic policies are the primary means by which a government provides or guarantees a range of services to protect people in circumstances such as childhood, sickness, and old age.

Promoting the General Welfare in Practice

The obligation of democratic government to "promote the general welfare" is embedded in the Constitution. As democratic revolutions spread throughout Europe after the American Revolution, they embraced this notion of government as the servant of the people in contrast to monarchial or authoritarian governments where the people were the servants of the state. The idea of the welfare state has evolved to mean different things in different countries. Most countries of the European Union and Canada use the term *welfare state* to indicate the state's responsibility for providing comprehensive and universal welfare for its citizens.

In welfare economics, welfare is thought of in terms of the utility provided by the things people choose to have. This may include social services such as health care, access to nationally guaranteed education, and even a guarantee of a minimum income. Welfare may also refer to the services designed to protect people against social problems such as crime, unemployment, learning disabilities, and social insecurity. The European Union notes that it is the obligation of the state to provide "social protection" to its citizens at the highest level possible. The European Union accepts an institutional model of welfare in which the state is to provide social protection and welfare as an individual right.

In the United States, social welfare policy is often understood to refer to "welfare provided by the state." The United States burst upon the scene in a revolution against King George III's mercantilist meddling, proclaiming the virtues of laissez-faire. Americans embraced the myth that they were the chosen people delivered from bondage and destined to be free of tyrannical government. Thomas Malthus's view of poverty as deserved punishment for moral failings was widely accepted. This perspective demanding "workfare" for recipients of welfare, and ending welfare as we have known it, was promoted by the Clinton administration.

In the United States, federalism has divided the responsibility for welfare. States are responsible for the administration of public assistance and health care programs even when most of the funding comes from the national government. When compared to other developed nations, the federal government has played a very limited role in providing social welfare policies. The national government's major foray into national social welfare was during the administration of Franklin Roosevelt in the 1930s, which provided for Social Security and most federally financed welfare programs, and the administration of Lyndon Johnson in the 1960s, which provided for Medicaid and Medicare and engaged in a wide variety of other projects at the local level such as "Operation Head Start" in the "War on Poverty." But these programs have been suspect by social and political conservatives whose goal is to dismantle the New Deal and the War on Poverty by limiting government's financial support for those programs. Social welfare systems in the United States are dependent not only on federal and state support, but also on private, religious, and corporate assistance. The resulting systems tend to be complex, inefficient, and expensive.

Several economic policy goals are generally accepted by all governments. They include full employment, price stability (low levels of inflation), and economic growth. The role of the policy analyst is to design policies that will best achieve these goals. In the United States, Congress and the president, along with a host of policy advisers, try to formulate policies to achieve the goals through the political process.

Evolution of Political-Economic Thinking

The Great Depression was the catalyst for the development and application of the Keynesian approach to economic policy. Franklin Roosevelt scrambled to turn the economy around and instinctively engaged in many policies consistent with Keynesian theory when he launched the New Deal. The New Deal signified a fundamental change in the role of government in U.S. society. For the first time, the government tried to change certain market structures to provide more socially acceptable outcomes for an economy in severe distress. The recognition that government may alter market outcomes is a significant change in political philosophy. A laissez-faire view of society no longer described the perfect model of the relationship between government and the economy. It is now widely accepted that Keynes's conclusion that, because the level of aggregate demand will not usually add up to just the right amount to achieve price stability and full employment, fiscal policy is required to achieve those goals.

The government's effort to guide the economy to maintain high levels of employment and nudge it toward growth whenever it shows signs of weakening is not a radical change to capitalism. But to business leaders and ideological conservatives, government spending is inherently wasteful. For those who believe in a social Darwinist, laissez-faire view of society, there is always a suspicion that government spending is a thinly disguised entering wedge for socialism. The debate lasted until World War II brought the unprecedented rise in expenditure, and a corresponding decline in unemployment. The federal government mobilized the nation for war, and the years of massive output led to a new attitude toward government involvement in the economy.

The new environment resulted in passage of the Employment Act of 1946, which held the government responsible for providing "maximum employment, production, and purchasing power." Most important, the law moved the debate from *whether* the government should be involved in directing the economy, to *how* to best achieve a robust economy.

The Employment Act also created the Council of Economic Advisers (CEA), to be responsible for preparing an annual economic report of the president. Although the Bureau of the Budget was completely under the control of the president, Senate confirmation of the CEA indicated that responsibility for the macroeconomic health of the nation would not be under the exclusive control of the president. The act also created the Joint Economic Committee in Congress to have legislative oversight in the area of economic affairs, which further limited the power of the president.

Differing Perspectives

Political economic policy is concerned with the interaction of political and economic forces and the way that governmental authority influences economic activity. The policy that results is the outcome of the competition between coalitions and elite demands, as constrained by institutional capacities and previous policy decisions.

Two models are generally used by officials in contemplating appropriate economic policies. The first is a variation on the classical model referred to as the neoclassical model. The classical model held that labor markets perform like other competitive markets. It assumed that there was a wage at which everyone could find employment. As the price of labor fell, demand for the cheaper labor would rise and unemployment would disappear. Ultimately it held that all unemployment was temporary or voluntary, because anyone unable to find work must be asking too high a wage. During the Great Depression the continuation of high unemployment despite falling wages was an undeniable failure of classical theory concerning labor markets finding equilibrium at full employment. The neoclassical model concedes that the state is justified in intervening only in situations of clear market failure. However, there is a presumption in favor of free market forces as being efficient and therefore legitimate.

The second model relies on the insights provided by John Maynard Keynes that, left to itself, the economy might not tend toward equilibrium at full employment. However, if policymakers were to use monetary and fiscal policies correctly, these policies could increase economic activity and reduce unemployment. According to his theory, monetary and fiscal policy could be employed throughout the business cycle to maintain low inflation and high employment. For example, the **full-employment budget**, based on calculations of what government tax revenues would be at a hypothetical state of full employment, is one fiscal policy that could be used to maintain high employment. Government expenditures would be based on the projected level of revenues at full employment. The additional spending at the level as if there were full employment would provide a measured additional demand to the economy that would stimulate job creation. Keynesian theory provided some hope that economic policy could insulate society from the wildly fluctuating business cycles of the past. More important, Keynesian theory provided an intellectual justification for active involvement by the state and social spending.

It would be difficult to overstate the importance that Keynes's economic theory had as a political doctrine. Keynesian theory provided an intellectual framework that justified state activism and social spending for policymakers. Previously, policymakers who increased spending during economic downturns were charged with being fiscally irresponsible and threatening to bankrupt the nation. Now the spending could be justified as stabilizing the economy. In fact, programs could be designed to automatically stabilize the economy by programming spending increases precisely when the economy was contracting, to limit the depth of the business cycle. When the economy begins expanding, social welfare expenditures automatically contract, reducing the potential for growth that would result in excessive inflation. This theory provided the justification for the welfare state.

Crude Policy Instruments

As noted previously, there are at least two major problems with using these fiscal and monetary instruments effectively. The first problem is that even if the goals of full employment and price stability are accepted, there is considerable debate about the best way to achieve them. Nowhere is the disagreement regarding how to achieve noncontroversial goals more apparent than in the schools of thought regarding market failure. If unregulated markets generated full employment, price stability, economic growth, and an equitable distribution of income as classical economic theory suggests, there would be no need for government intervention. However, markets do fail and governments are called on to intervene. Does government intervention accomplish its goal of economic growth and reduced unemployment and inflation? If not, government interventions also fail. In the real world, of course, nothing is perfect, so the real choice is between imperfect markets and imperfect policy interventions.

A second major problem for economic policy is that governments may be unable to achieve full employment, prevent inflation, or stimulate economic expansion, because those responsible for economic policy are either unable or unwilling to take the action required. The separation of powers fragments the responsibility for economic policy and weakens the government's ability to control the economy. While the president is by far the single most important player in economic policy, his ability to control events or policy is often overestimated. Taxing and spending is largely determined by the performance of the economy at the time the budget is introduced to Congress, and the forecast during the period of the budget. Much of the budget includes programs over which a president has little control, such as debt refinancing and various entitlement programs.

The President

The executive branch itself contains different departments at the cabinet level, such as the Departments of Commerce, Treasury, and Labor, each with different goals. In addition, the Office of Management and Budget (OMB) assists the president in preparing the budget and submitting it to Congress. The OMB tries to submit a budget that reflects the priorities of the president. But federal agencies submitting their budget requests usually believe in the value of their own programs and press for expanded funding. If the OMB reduces the budget requests of the agencies, they may appeal directly to the president or seek informal support from the Congress.

Since Article 1 of the Constitution provides that Congress alone has the power to "appropriate" money, it ensures the budgetary process will involve partisan maneuvering for political advantage. Not surprisingly, politicians often design budget projections to win support for their agendas. The most flagrant examples of predicting unrealistically low projections of inflation and optimistic projections of economic performance occurred during the first two years of the Reagan administration. Ronald Reagan began his presidency promising to eliminate the deficit, increase defense spending, cut taxes, and reduce what he perceived to be the excesses of the welfare state.[1] During a presidential election, challengers are anxious to place the blame for any economic failures on the incumbent when offering their own solutions to economic problems.

Monetary policy as a tool to control the money supply is primarily centered on the Federal Reserve banking system. By loosening or tightening the reserve requirements that banks have to maintain on their deposits, the Federal Reserve (the "Fed") is able to encourage or discourage lending money, which is the source of much economic activity. The theory also suggested that it should make more money available to the banking system to lend at low interest rates when funds were needed, and reduce the amount available when money seemed in excess supply by buying or selling bonds. The Federal Reserve did not take this action early in the Great Depression.

Presidential influence on monetary policy is based on the power to appoint individuals to the Federal Reserve's board of governors. The president's subsequent influence after appointment is largely informal, although the relationship is often much closer than press accounts would indicate. The president often works the good cop/bad cop routine with the Fed for public consumption when the latter makes a politically difficult decision. The president complains to the press that soft economic conditions are caused by a recalcitrant Fed that refuses to lower interest rates sufficiently. Or conversely, that inflation could be brought under control if the Fed would only tighten the money supply. Blame is directed toward the Fed, since its members do not run for election, while the president presents himself as a nice guy without sufficient clout to implement his more compassionate goals.

The Policymakers

Policymakers do not prefer high unemployment to full employment, inflation to price stability, or economic recessions to economic growth. But political entrepreneurs have short time horizons and may not find it in their interest to take the action required to reduce inflation, or to get a vigorous economic expansion under way. They may agree with the notion that there is no free lunch, but they are also aware that the price of lunch may be deferred. Elected officials prefer policies that provide short-term benefits before election day and bills that will not come due until after voters have cast their retrospective votes. Thus, in the U.S. political process, there is a bias in favor of policies with short-term benefits and long-term costs. This fact has profound implications for the conduct of long-term economic growth and stabilization policies as opposed to near-term policies.

In practical terms, suppose that the government increases its expenditures by borrowing rather than raising taxes. The result will be an increase in aggregate demand—the total demand for an economy's goods and services. The distributional benefits of increased output and employment will be felt almost immediately. The costs of this expansion, reflected in higher prices, will manifest themselves only months later, hopefully after an election. So from a politician's perspective, the political "goods" arrive first: an increase in employment and a rise in real gross domestic product (GDP). The political "bads" arrive later: higher debt servicing and higher inflation. Every member of the House of Representatives is never more than two years away from election and averages only one year. Every president is never more than four years from an election and averages only two years. Politicians have a very strong incentive to pursue the near-term political "goods" and put off worrying about the "bads" as long as they are in office.

To the extent that presidents do engage in economic tightening, they have a strong incentive to pursue such policies early in their terms and pursue expansionist policies as elections draw near. And to the degree that voters have short memories and limited sophistication of economic policies, they are likely to reward the political entrepreneur who engages in economic expansion just before the election.[2] Survival being a basic instinct among all politicians, these facts of political life also lead to short-term thinking.

Many recent economic problems have required the spending of more money by the government, but the string of massive federal deficits in recent years has precluded increased spending. A conspicuous solution to increased spending needs and huge deficits is large tax increases. But such increases would cause pain to taxpayers and threaten a reduction in consumer demand that could lead to greater unemployment long before a reduction in the deficit would reduce inflation or free up new government monies. In this case the political "bads" arrive rather promptly, while the "goods" would likely arrive much later and be felt only gradually. Not surprisingly, the three presidential elections in the 1980s were won by the candidate who took the hardest line against raising taxes. In 1992, presidential candidate Bill Clinton was able to neutralize the appeal of President George H.W. Bush, who had broken his pledge of "no new taxes," by indicating that he himself was a "new kind of Democrat" committed to reducing the deficit by reducing expenditures, and also to cutting taxes for middle-income taxpayers. Once in office, though, President Clinton faced pressure to initiate spending cuts but increase taxes, and to do both quickly. If the process were delayed, the fear was that it would be impossible to do either as the 1994 elections approached. Clinton barely achieved the tax increases without one Republican vote, by limiting the increases to wealthier Americans who had received steep tax decreases during the Reagan-Bush years. The political costs were enormous, however, as Republicans gained control of the House of Representatives. George W. Bush campaigned in 2000 and 2004 on the platform of cutting taxes. However, with Republicans in control of both houses of Congress and the presidency, there was considerable reluctance to directly cut expenditures also desired by other constituents.

Political entrepreneurs thus have a bias toward expansionary fiscal and monetary policies, since lower taxes and increased expenditures for special interest groups provide strong support for an incumbent's bid for reelection. Policies to reduce spending and increase taxes cause unrest among voters. Even though the optimal policy often requires long-term strategies, the political incentives for incumbents may not reflect the long-term economic interests of the nation. Political entrepreneurs find it extremely difficult to continue unpleasant policies as the exigencies of elections threaten their futures.

There is considerable irony in the fact that voters deplore the deficits and rail against the inability of governments, yet threaten to retaliate against candidates who support the painful economic measures needed to end them. The result is a built-in bias favoring lower rather than higher taxes and higher rather than lower expenditures. But cutting government spending inevitably means reducing benefits to someone who is currently receiving them. Voters who are hurt by government policies and lose benefits are thought to have long memories at election time, a notion that definitely has long-term effects on politicians' voting behavior.

Taxes as an Instrument of Policy

Through its ability to adjust taxes, especially income taxes, the government can guide the economy. The idea of monetary policy was not entirely new in the 1930s, but the idea regarding the use of taxes and national budgets as management tools of economic policy to counter economic cycles of boom and bust *was* new. Although the government borrows money to finance its operations, taxes collected from a variety of sources are the main reservoir of government expenditures.

But the question of who pays is inextricably linked to several other questions regarding tax policy. What is a fair distribution of income? What are the major issues involved in deciding who should bear the burden of taxes? What do political scientists and policy analysts take into consideration when they talk about a fair tax system? Does the U.S. tax system meet the criteria for fairness while promoting the general welfare?

Government intervention is a conscious decision not to leave the provision of certain goods or services to the marketplace. It is a determination that political, not economic, considerations will prescribe which services the government will provide. Taxes are required to finance these goods and services. Therefore, the main purpose of taxation is to move purchasing power from the private to the public sector. But in order to understand and judge these economic policies, their distributional consequences must be understood.

Antitax sentiment has always run high in the United States. Recall that the American Revolution began as a tax revolt with the dumping of tea into the Boston Harbor, because the colonists objected to the taxes levied on the tea. After the adoption of the Constitution, the government relied primarily on customs duties to fund the limited national budget. Congress enacted an income tax during the Civil War, but it expired at that war's end. In 1894 Congress passed another income tax bill. That tax was declared unconstitutional in 1895 in *Pollock v. Farmers' Loan and Trust Co.* As a result, the Sixteenth Amendment to the Constitution was passed, which was ratified in 1916 and gave Congress the power "to lay and collect taxes on incomes, from whatever source derived."

Although the personal income tax soon became the primary source of revenue for the government, the portion of income paid in taxes in the United States is still well below the percentage of income paid as taxes by workers in other countries. Figure 6.1 illustrates this fact. The data in the figure support the evidence that Americans are not overtaxed. Taxes from all levels of government are expressed as a percentage of each country's GDP, or output. This is the best measure of relative taxation, because it includes not only the tax burden, but also an indication of the ability to pay the taxes levied.

The Organization for Economic Cooperation and Development (OECD), one of the most reliable sources of data for international comparisons, found that of thirty countries examined (mostly Western, industrialized nations), only Mexico collects a smaller share of revenues as a percentage of GDP than the United States.[3] After falling in most OECD countries between 2000 and 2002, tax revenues as a percentage of GDP leveled out in 2003 and in some cases began to rise again. However, the United States experienced particularly large reductions in tax-to-GDP ratios between 2000 and 2003, from 29.9 percent to 25.4 percent.

Even though Americans are among the least-taxed people in the industrialized world, aversion to taxes runs high and politicians are usually rewarded for a vigorous and righteous defense of constituents against rapacious tax collectors. This is often accompanied by an indignant opposition to any increase in social

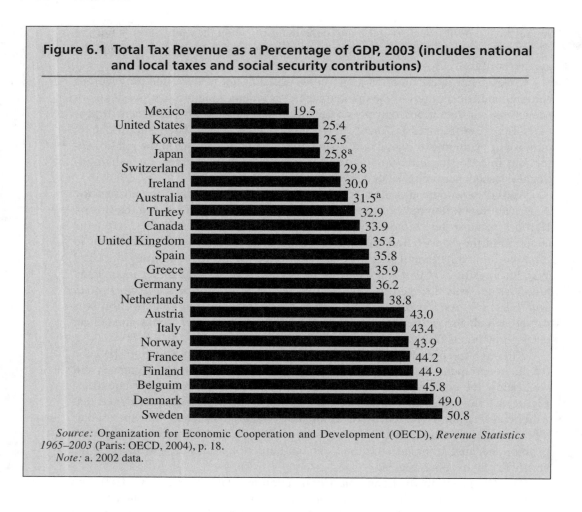

Figure 6.1 Total Tax Revenue as a Percentage of GDP, 2003 (includes national and local taxes and social security contributions)

Country	Percentage
Mexico	19.5
United States	25.4
Korea	25.5
Japan	25.8[a]
Switzerland	29.8
Ireland	30.0
Australia	31.5[a]
Turkey	32.9
Canada	33.9
United Kingdom	35.3
Spain	35.8
Greece	35.9
Germany	36.2
Netherlands	38.8
Austria	43.0
Italy	43.4
Norway	43.9
France	44.2
Finland	44.9
Belguim	45.8
Denmark	49.0
Sweden	50.8

Source: Organization for Economic Cooperation and Development (OECD), *Revenue Statistics 1965–2003* (Paris: OECD, 2004), p. 18.
Note: a. 2002 data.

welfare spending, since any increased public expenditures would entail higher taxes.

The reality is that when compared to most industrialized nations, the United States is a tax haven. Overall, government expenditures as a share of GDP remain consistently lower than in any other OECD country.

Taxation in the United States

Federal, state, and local governments obtain revenue to finance programs from taxing three basic sources: income, consumption, and wealth. The largest single source of revenue for the federal government is the **personal income tax**, followed by **social insurance tax** and **corporate income tax**. Most state governments use taxes on income and consumption. Local governments rely almost entirely on taxing property and wealth.

Taxes on income. Figure 6.2 presents a breakdown of the sources of revenue for the national government. In addition to income taxes, wages are subject to a **payroll tax**, which is levied on a company's payroll (half of which is deducted from an employee's paycheck) to finance the Social Security and Medicare programs. Payroll taxes are now the second major source of revenue.

Workers transfer part of their earnings to retired workers through mandatory payroll deductions that in 2005 amounted to 6.2 percent of wages on income up to

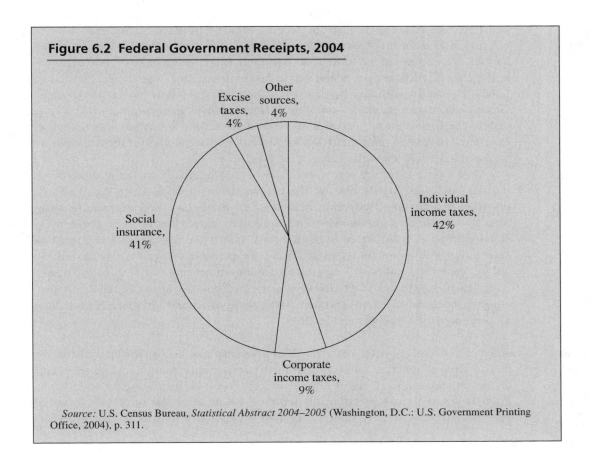

Figure 6.2 Federal Government Receipts, 2004

Excise taxes, 4%

Other sources, 4%

Individual income taxes, 42%

Social insurance, 41%

Corporate income taxes, 9%

Source: U.S. Census Bureau, *Statistical Abstract 2004–2005* (Washington, D.C.: U.S. Government Printing Office, 2004), p. 311.

$90,000. Employers contribute an equal amount. Over the past five years, payroll tax revenues have increased from 36 to 41 percent and individual income tax revenues have decreased from 44 to 42 percent, while corporate tax revenues have declined from 12 to 9 percent.

Taxes on consumption.   The most important taxes on consumption are the **sales tax** and the **excise tax**. Sales taxes are a major source of revenue for most states and many major cities. Most states raise the majority of their revenue from a combination of income taxes and sales taxes imposed on the purchase of a wide variety of goods and services (although many states exclude some essential items such as food from their sales taxes).

Excise taxes, which are taxes on specific products, are a source of revenue for state and local governments, as well as for the national government. Some items subject to federal excise taxes include gasoline, airline tickets, alcohol, cigarettes, and firearms. A tax levied on the sale of tobacco products or alcohol is often referred to as a **sin tax**, based on the idea that use of these products imposes externalities on nonusers in the form of air pollution, litter, health hazards, and increases in the cost of medical care. Some excise taxes are targeted at purchasers of certain goods who will eventually benefit when the money is spent by the government. Gasoline taxes, for example, are used to finance highway construction. An excise tax that is levied on buyers of expensive nonessential items such as yachts or expensive jewelry is referred to as a **luxury tax**, as the incomes of these people are assumed to be high enough to absorb the costs.

Most excise taxes are levied on goods with a relatively **inelastic demand**. If the demand were highly elastic, the tax would push sales down significantly, resulting in only small government revenues.[4] Politicians find that raising taxes usually costs some voter support. Therefore, they prefer that taxes be borne by as small a group as possible, or by such a large group that it is a minimal burden on each payer. Politicians find it easier to impose excise taxes than any other form of tax, because they can raise a significant amount of revenue while affecting a relatively small number of voters. Nevertheless, excise taxes have declined in importance as a source of federal revenue. Their share of federal tax revenues fell from 13 percent in 1960 to 3 percent in 2003.

Taxes on property and wealth.   The **property tax** has traditionally been the main source of revenue for state and local governments. Many local governments tax private homes, land, and business property based on its assessed market value. Some states and local governments impose taxes on the value of specific types of personal property such as cars, boats, and occasionally livestock. Property taxes account for over 75 percent of the revenue raised through taxes on wealth.[5] Other taxes imposed on wealth include inheritance, estate, and gift taxes.

Principles of Taxation: Efficiency and Fairness

Although no one likes to transfer control over part of their income to the government, most people grudgingly comply. The primary purpose of taxation is to raise revenues to carry out government policy goals, although there are other goals as well, such as discouraging the consumption of certain goods. Voluntary compliance is related to the perceived **tax efficiency** (or neutrality) and **tax fairness** of the system.

Tax efficiency. Efficiency, or neutrality, suggests that unless there is adequate justification, we should try to interfere as little as possible with the market allocation. The freest movement of goods and services maximizes economic efficiency and therefore overall economic well-being. Unfortunately, every tax invites concerted efforts to avoid it and influences economic activity and the allocation of resources, even in cases where the market process works well and needs no outside regulation. For example, the preferential treatment that allows individuals to deduct from income taxes the cost of mortgage interest and property taxes on their homes, distorts the market by increasing the demand for homeownership over rental units. Similarly, tax laws allow child care payments to be deducted from taxes owed. Such preferential treatment, referred to as a **tax expenditure** or "loophole," represents a loss in government revenue just as though the government wrote a check for the amount of the deduction.

Special interest groups that receive preferential treatment are vigorous defenders of their tax subsidies, and thus subsidies are very difficult to eliminate. This raises the issue of fairness.

Tax fairness. Political scientists, economists, and philosophers have wrestled for hundreds of years with the concept of what constitutes a just and equitable tax system. If the system is perceived as unfair, people are more likely to evade taxes, if possible, or pressure political entrepreneurs more aggressively to reduce their tax burden. There are two main principles of fairness.

Benefit principle. The **benefit principle** holds that people should pay taxes in proportion to the benefits they receive. This principle tries to make public goods similar to private goods in that payment for services is commensurate with the amount of goods or services received. If the purpose of taxes is to pay for government services, then those who gain from those services should pay. A toll bridge is justi-

Case Study: Tax Expenditures

A tax expenditure is defined as the reduction in tax revenue that results when government programs or benefits are provided through the tax system rather than reported as budgetary expenditures. The reductions are usually made by offering special tax rates, exemptions, or tax credits to programs' beneficiaries. Governments introduce tax expenditures primarily to achieve social policy objectives such as wealth transfers to lower-income families or to promote economic development and job creation.

The federal government "spends" hundreds of billions of dollars on tax expenditures each year. The largest tax expenditure—the exclusion for employer contributions for health insurance (see Table 6.1)—is also the fastest growing. The main reason the government reports tax expenditures is to improve accountability by providing a more complete picture of its spending.

Governments use the tax system to deliver programs to reduce their own administrative costs and reduce compliance costs for recipients. There are several negative aspects to tax expenditures. Their overall cost receives less public scrutiny than is the case for spending programs, because it need not be formally approved every year. The benefits of the major tax expenditures tend to go to high-income earners to an even greater degree than do entitlements. This can run counter to the objective of incorporating progressiveness into the tax system. Tax expenditures are big and automatic, and costs are often hard to control as many of the benefits tend to be more open-ended and enforcement is often more difficult than for spending programs.

fied using the benefit principle. Tolls collected are used to pay the bonds used for bridge construction and to maintain the bridge. Because those who pay the toll are the same people who use the bridge, the toll is viewed as a fair way to pay for the government service. The more they use the bridge, the more they will pay. Those who do not pay can be excluded. The major disadvantage of this principle is that it will not work for public goods from which nonpayers cannot be excluded, or where it is difficult to determine who benefits or by what amount. For example, who benefits most from law enforcement and the judicial system, the rich or the poor? Figure 6.3 indicates where the federal dollar is spent.

The benefit principle is often used to argue that the more affluent citizens should have a higher tax burden than poorer citizens, because they benefit more from public services. For example, the wealthy receive more benefit from a police force than do poor citizens because they have more wealth to protect and their losses would be much greater in the event of theft. Therefore, since police protection is more beneficial to the affluent, they should contribute more.

The welfare of the wealthy is best served by the Securities and Exchange Commission, the Federal Reserve system, national security, or by the judicial sys-

Table 6.1   Largest Tax Expenditures, 2005

Rank	Tax Expenditure	Cost to Treasury (in $ billions)
1	Exclusion for employer contributions for medical insurance	109.4
2	Exclusion of employer pension plan contribution and earnings	99.3
3	Reduced rates of tax on dividends and long-term capital gains	76.8
4	Deduction for mortgage interest on owner-occupied residences	69.9
5	Deduction of state and local government income and personal property taxes	40.9
6	Exclusion of capital gains at death	37.7
7	Tax credit for children under age seventeen	35.7
8	Earned Income Credit	35.4
9	Deduction for charitable contributions other than for education and health	28.8
10	Exclusion of Social Security benefits for retired workers	20.8
11	Exclusion of interest on life insurance savings	25.4
12	Deferral of capital gains on sales of principal residences	18.0

Source: Estimates of Federal Tax Expenditures for Fiscal Years 2004–2008, prepared for the Committee on Ways and Means by the Staff of the Joint Committee on Taxation (Washington, D.C.: U.S. Government Printing Office, 2003).

tem. If there was agreement on who benefits and by how much, then taxes could be allocated accordingly. Allocating taxes by this principle provides an incentive to insist that someone else is the main beneficiary. If these taxes could be allocated accurately, there would be no income redistribution.

Ability-to-pay principle. The **ability-to-pay principle** claims that fairness requires that taxes be allocated according to the incomes and/or wealth of taxpayers, regardless of how much or how little they benefit. According to this principle, the wealthy may benefit more than the poor from some government expenditures and less than the poor from others. But since they are better able to pay than the poor, they should pay more in taxes. This principle is justified by the argument that all citizens should make an "equal sacrifice." Fairness in this system requires both horizontal and vertical equity.

Horizontal equity means that individuals who have nearly equal incomes should have nearly equal tax burdens. This is the concept Plato had in mind when he wrote in Book One of *The Republic,* "When there is an income tax, the just man will pay more and the unjust less on the same amount of income." Horizontal equity is lacking when those with equal abilities to pay are treated differently because

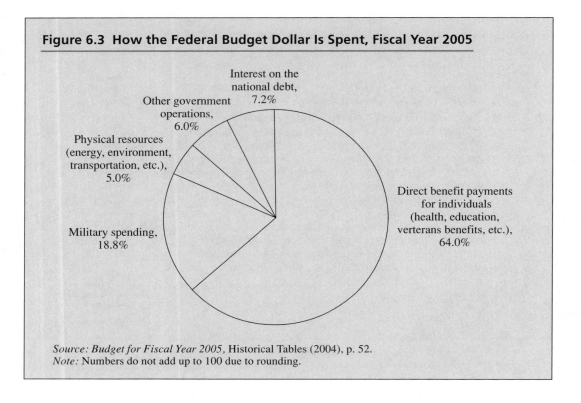

Figure 6.3 How the Federal Budget Dollar Is Spent, Fiscal Year 2005

Interest on the national debt, 7.2%

Other government operations, 6.0%

Physical resources (energy, environment, transportation, etc.), 5.0%

Military spending, 18.8%

Direct benefit payments for individuals (health, education, verterans benefits, etc.), 64.0%

Source: Budget for Fiscal Year 2005, Historical Tables (2004), p. 52.
Note: Numbers do not add up to 100 due to rounding.

of tax deductions, credits, or preferences not available to all taxpayers on equal terms.

Vertical equity means that those with higher ability to pay should pay more taxes than those with less ability to pay. There is less agreement on how much more the rich should pay. In fact, taxes are generally classified according to their incidence. **Tax incidence** is the actual distribution of the tax burden on different levels of income. Tax systems are classified as progressive, proportional (sometimes referred to as a "flat"), and regressive, as illustrated in Figure 6.4.

A **progressive tax** is one in which the tax rate rises as income rises. Wealthier taxpayers pay a larger percentage of their income in taxes than do low-income taxpayers. A progressive tax redistributes wealth from the more affluent to the less affluent. Keynesian economic theory supports a progressive income tax. Most Americans support progressive taxes on the ground that ability to pay rises more than proportionately with income.

A **proportional tax** is one in which the tax is the same through all income lev-

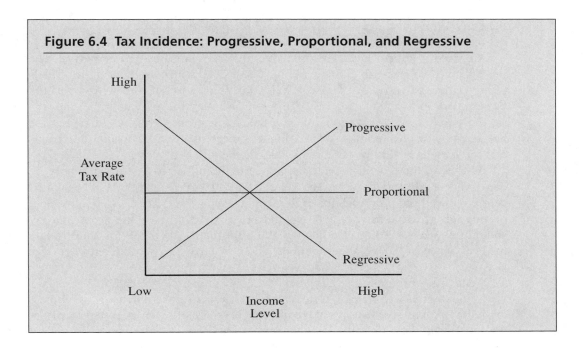

Figure 6.4 Tax Incidence: Progressive, Proportional, and Regressive

els. Ordinarily called a flat tax, a proportional tax is often praised by its supporters for its efficiency. By assessing a tax as a fixed percentage of income, a wage earner's decisions do not affect the amount of tax owed nor distort incentives. Since theoretically there are no deductions, everyone can easily compute the amount of taxes owed and there is little need to hire accountants or tax lawyers. Because the proportional tax is so efficient and imposes only a slight administrative burden on taxpayers, many argue that we should adopt it. But efficiency is only one goal of the tax system. Although some think that a system in which everyone pays the same percentage of their income is fair, others argue that is not equitable. A proportional tax is neutral in regard to income distribution.

Under a **regressive tax**, the average rate declines as income rises. It is called "regressive" because high-income taxpayers pay a smaller percentage of their income than do low-income taxpayers, even though they may still pay a higher amount in absolute dollars. A regressive tax redistributes income from the poor to the wealthy. Regressive tax systems are so manifestly unfair that few openly advocate them. A notable exception is George Gilder, a conservative writer with refreshing frankness but doubtful logic who wrote that "regressive taxes help the poor."[6] Gilder, whose work was widely and approvingly read by supply-siders of the early 1980s, also declared that "to help the poor and middle classes, one must cut the taxes on the rich."[7]

Because state and local governments often rely on sales and property taxes, these tend to be regressive. State and local sales taxes increased during the 1980s along with local property taxes. A sales tax is often confused with a flat tax because two individuals with vastly different incomes will pay the same sales tax on the purchase of ten gallons of gas. Sales and property taxes are regressive because poorer people must spend a higher percentage of their income for goods and services, as well as housing costs, than do the affluent.

In theory, the federal income tax supports the principle of vertical equity by being very mildly progressive. The tax cuts in 2001, 2002, and 2003 have significantly reduced the progressivity of the federal income tax. There is no agreement on how progressive the tax code should be, or even on how the ability to pay should be measured. For example, should adjustments be made for catastrophic medical expenses? What about families who may have several children in college at once?

Federal tax progressivity has been declining for over two decades. When taxes paid by individuals to federal, state, and local levels of government are combined, the mildly progressive features at the national level are offset by regressive taxes at the local level, resulting in a roughly proportional tax system. The trend toward inequality is attributable to the increased influence of those who argue in favor of tax neutrality (proportional tax). The avowed purpose of the tax cuts in the first term of George W. Bush was to reduce the progressive nature of the federal tax system and make it more "neutral." By primarily reducing the taxes of those in the highest brackets and cutting government funding for social welfare programs, it intended to reduce the redistributive effect of transferring wealth to the poor. Tax deductions and exemptions, often referred to as loopholes, are subtracted from personal income to determine the taxable income. All tax loopholes encourage taxpayers to engage in certain types of behavior to avoid taxes. Most loopholes primarily benefit the more affluent and therefore they erode the progressivity of the income tax. This effectively reduces the tax rate if certain conditions are met.[8]

One policy analyst, William Gale, proposes tax reform that would be revenue-neutral while broadening the tax base, reducing effective tax rates (rates paid after deductions are factored in), and simplifying the process.[9] Briefly, he contends that itemized deductions are at the heart of any serious effort at tax reform. Although they are popular and subsidize various activities thought of as "good," they create many problems. He argues that deductions largely subsidize activity that would have occurred anyway. By eroding the tax base, they require higher tax rates than would otherwise be necessary.

It may be argued that deductions under the current system are also unfair. Why should a high-income household save 38¢ on a dollar of mortgage interest while a low-income household saves 15¢? Why should homeowners with a large mortgage be able to use a tax-deductible home equity loan to buy a car, when renters with similar incomes cannot? Other deductions for state and local taxes are often justified on ability-to-pay grounds, since the taxes directly reduce household income. However, state and local taxes largely pay for services that households consume, such as schools, roads, and parks. But if taxes buy services, they should be part of the taxable income. For instance, a household that paid $30 a month for garbage collection to a private company would not expect a deduction. Why should a household that pays the same amount in local taxes for trash removal get a deduction?[10]

Many who support the neutrality of the tax system argue that efforts to redistribute wealth through tax transfers are not very effective. They maintain that a progressive income tax reduces the incentives for the more affluent to work and save. By encouraging the affluent to invest their wealth, the size of the total economic pie will be increased so that the benefits that trickle down to the poor will exceed any benefits from redistribution through tax transfers. They insist that the fact that some entrepreneurs become extraordinarily wealthy is irrelevant, because their actions have improved society.

Social Security tax (the payroll tax) is an example of a tax that is proportional in the lower ranges, but regressive for those receiving income in excess of the maximum wage for which taxes are withheld. As mentioned above, this payroll tax requires individuals and employers to pay the same rate (6.2 percent, 12.4 percent total) on wages up to $90,000 (in 2005). Above $90,000 the marginal tax rate is zero (the marginal tax rate is defined as the tax on additional income). Rather than exempting low incomes, it exempts high incomes. Once the ceiling is reached, no more payments are made for the year. Also, since only salaries are subject to the payroll tax, while income from interest is untouched, it is ultimately regressive. There is an additional Medicare payroll tax of 1.45 percent with a matching 1.45 percent paid by employers with no upper salary limit.

Broad Uses of Tax Policy

Tax policy may be used to pursue various goals simultaneously. For example, its most basic use is to achieve macroeconomic goals of expanding the economy and employment. Taxes may be used as an economic policy to provide income security, to increase investment spending, and to stimulate aggregate spending.

President John Kennedy announced his intention to provide a tax cut aimed primarily at middle- and low-income families in order to stimulate a lethargic economy. Lyndon Johnson, upon succeeding Kennedy, agreed with Kennedy's

Case Study: Lotteries as a Regressive Tax

Gambling generates enormous amounts of revenue for governments and the gaming industry. But its enchanting promises of significant benefits for the general welfare frequently do not live up to expectations.

A study by Alicia Hansen found that in 2002 the average American spent more on lotteries than on reading materials or movies. In 2003, total spending on lotteries was almost $45 billion, or $155 for every man, woman, and child in the United States. About $14 billion of that money went into state coffers.

The fact that playing the lottery is voluntary does not make the "profit" any less of a tax. It is analogous to states raising revenue from an excise tax on alcohol. The purchaser of alcohol does so voluntarily, but no one denies that it is a tax. Some then concede that it is a tax, but that a tax of choice is preferable to a tax that is paid reluctantly, and presumably the purchaser of alcohol or a lottery ticket is willing to pay the tax.

Political entrepreneurs have discovered that the average voter does not think of the lottery as a tax, which removes a major barrier to taxation. The transfer of lottery revenues to state treasuries is an implicit tax on lottery bettors. There is a consensus among researchers that state lotteries are a decidedly regressive form of taxation in that average lottery sales are highest in low-income areas and lower in areas of higher economic and educational levels.

Sponsored gambling allows many state governments to use lotteries to minimize taxes that would otherwise have to be paid by middle- and upper-income groups. The result is that states have increasingly resorted to lotteries to increase revenues as a way of sidestepping opposition to tax increases. New Hampshire started the first modern state lottery in 1964. In 2005, forty-one states and the District of Columbia sponsored lotteries.

Per capita lottery ticket sales were three times higher in inner-city Detroit than in the suburbs in 1988. Of $104 million contributed to Michigan's school aid fund by Detroit lottery ticket purchasers, inner-city schools received only $80 million. The remaining $24 million was transferred to more affluent suburban school districts. A 1988 study of the Florida lottery, which also earmarks profits from sales to go into the general education fund, found that when one includes the tax incidence (who pays) and the benefit incidence (who receives the funds), the tax was regressive for those with incomes below $40,000. The benefits of the net tax are proportionally distributed at incomes between $40,000 and $70,000 and become progressive at incomes above $70,000. Congress commissioned a National Impact Study, which found that gambling had not improved Florida's education or health services. Prior to the introduction of the state lottery, Florida allocated 60 percent of its budget for school improvement. Five years after the introduction of gambling, only 51 percent of its budget was allocated to education. The study noted that "the problem with a lottery is that lottery profits are used as a substitute for tax dollars, not as a supplement to them."

Lotteries violate the tax principles of both neutrality and equity. There is also the ethical question of exploiting human desire to extract a regressive tax on the poor.

Sources: Alicia Hansen, "Lotteries and State Fiscal Policy," Tax Foundation Background Paper no. 46 (Washington, D.C.: Tax Foundation, October 2004); Mary Borg, Paul Mason, and Stephen Shapiro, *The Economic Consequences of State Lotteries* (New York: Praeger, 1991).

logic and shifted the emphasis from expanding federal spending to boosting private consumer demand and business investment. He cut personal and corporate taxes by $11 billion, and economic activity increased exactly as the model had predicted.

Much larger tax cuts were implemented by Ronald Reagan in 1981. These cuts were directed primarily at reducing the tax burden of the affluent rather than that of middle- and lower-income workers. The top tax rate was cut from 70 to 28 percent. All told, personal taxes were cut by $250 billion over a three-year period and corporate taxes were cut by $70 billion. The deficit spending and increased consumer demand that resulted did get the economy out of its deepest recession, in 1981–1982, since the Great Depression.

President Bill Clinton won election by campaigning against policies that kept the economy lagging behind its potential, using the slogan "it's the economy, stupid." He cited the need for more fiscal stimulus during the campaign and suggested the need for middle-income tax cuts. Upon his election, however, he recognized that the economy had hit the bottom of the recession and was starting to expand. He was aware of the Keynesian multiplier at work and decided that additional stimulus might create the problem of inflation. Instead he decided to tackle the difficult and politically risky strategy of dealing with the long-term problem of the deficit and its drag on the economy. He raised taxes on the top 2 percent of income earners over the unanimous opposition of Republicans, who predicted economic catastrophe. He also cut government spending while providing tax credits for investments to stimulate economic expansion. His actions set in motion the longest uninterrupted economic expansion since World War II. (See Figure 6.5.)

President George W. Bush proposed the largest tax cuts in history. He proposed a $1.6 *trillion* cut over a ten-year period. He argued that with the government surpluses from 1998 through 2001, the nation could afford the tax cuts.[11] He argued at the same time that, because the economy was slowing down, although unemployment was hovering around 4 percent, a tax cut was needed to stimulate the economy. Finally, he argued that taxes in the United States were oppressive and people needed relief. Indeed, the 2001 tax bill was titled "The Economic Growth and Tax Relief Reconciliation Act." Congress agreed and ultimately passed a $1.35 trillion dollar tax cut over ten years. Additional tax cuts were passed in 2002 to "stimulate the economy." Tax cuts were passed again in 2003 and 2004.

The 2001–2004 tax cuts have already affected the U.S. economy in a variety of ways and will have an even larger impact in the future. The cuts have been in place long enough for analysis to provide a clearer picture of how they are affecting the economy and different income groups, and how they will influence future budgetary decisions. The Congressional Budget Office (CBO), which provides Congress with analysis of legislative action and is currently headed by a Republican, released a study that found that the Bush tax cuts will increase income inequality

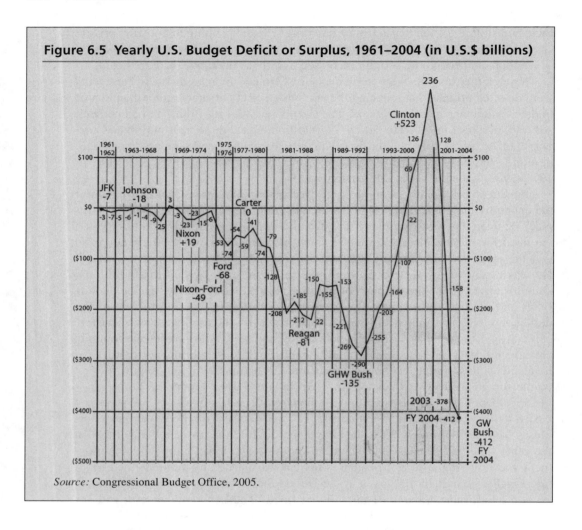

Figure 6.5 Yearly U.S. Budget Deficit or Surplus, 1961–2004 (in U.S.$ billions)

Source: Congressional Budget Office, 2005.

by raising the after-tax income of the most affluent far more than it will raise the after-tax income of middle- and low-income households.[12] Table 6.2 indicates who benefits the most from the Bush tax cuts.

Bear in mind that these calculations, based on CBO data, exclude the effects of the corporate tax cuts and the effects of the estate tax cuts. Nevertheless, those in the bottom fifth, with an average income of $16,600, received an average tax cut of $230 in 2004, while the top fifth, with an average income of $203,700, received

Table 6.2   Who Benefits from the 2001–2004 Bush Tax Cuts?

	Average Income ($)	Average Tax Cut ($)	Share of the Tax Cut (%)	Change in After-Tax Income (%)
All	80,100	1,680	100.0	2.7
Bottom quintile	16,600	230	2.8	1.5
Second quintile	38,100	720	8.3	2.2
Middle quintile	57,400	980	11.5	2.0
Fourth quintile	84,300	1,520	17.7	2.3
Top quintile	203,700	4,890	59.9	3.3
81–90 percent	116,600	2,210	13.4	2.5
91–95 percent	115,000	3,180	9.8	2.7
96–99 percent	243,100	4,830	12.0	2.8
Top 1 percent	1,171,000	40,990	24.6	5.3

Source: David Kamin and Isaac Shapiro, *Studies Shed New Light on Effects of Administration's Tax Cuts* (Washington, D.C.: Center on Budget and Policy Priorities, September 13, 2004), p. 4.
Note: Percentages may not sum to 100 due to rounding.

tax reductions averaging $4,890, and the top 1 percent, with an average income of $1,171,000, received an average tax cut of $40,990.

A more salient measurement in examining the effect of tax cuts is to assess after-tax income at different levels, since this indicates how much households have available to spend and save. This measurement also shows that the tax cuts disproportionately benefit those who are already the most affluent. According to the CBO data, the top 1 percent saw its after-tax income grow by an average of 5.3 percent, more than three and a half times the percentage increase received by the bottom quintile. Therefore, even if all households receive a tax cut, there is an increase in inequality, since after-tax income will rise by a larger percentage for more affluent than for less well-off households.

Since additional tax cuts that almost exclusively benefit affluent households, such as the elimination of the estate tax and the removal of the limitation on itemized deductions, will be phased in over the next several years, the ultimate effect will be even more unequal. Some defenders of the tax cuts have argued that everyone is a "winner" since everyone received a tax cut. However, the tax cuts have thus far been financed through growing deficits. The tax cuts must eventually be financed through either tax increases or spending cuts, because the economy cannot sustain such large and persistent deficits. In all likelihood, since the administration has ruled out raising taxes to reduce the deficit, cuts in spending will target programs that benefit middle- and lower-income households. Although advocates of the tax cuts routinely describe them as designed to be in favor of family and small business, a study by William Gale and Peter Orszag at the Brookings Institution shows, in a distributional analysis of the tax cuts, that "most families (that is, tax units with children) and most tax units with small business income will be worse off once the financing is included."[13] Since the tax cuts disproportionately benefited the wealthy, middle- and low-income households will suffer corresponding benefit losses.

The tax cuts were poorly designed to achieve their stated goal of stimulating the economy. They disproportionately benefited those with the highest incomes, the very households that were more likely to save than to spend their tax cuts. A different tax cut package that targeted middle- and low-income households would have resulted in more money flowing into the economy in the form of an increase in consumer demand, creating the stimulus sought by the administration. Lower taxes can stimulate growth by improving incentives to work, save, and invest. However, by targeting the affluent, the tax cuts created income effects that reduced the need to engage in productive economic activity. The current policy subsidizes old capital, providing windfall gains to asset holders, and undermines incentives for new activity; and by raising the budget deficit, it reduces national savings and raises interest rates. Jobs created following the tax cuts fell well below the administration's own predictions.[14] In fact, Mark Zandi, chief economist at Economy.com, points out that most Americans experienced a decline in real household incomes between 2001 and 2004. He notes that "no other President since World War II has suffered out-right job declines during their term."[15] The conclusion is inescapable that the tax cuts were poorly designed to stimulate economic growth.[16]

Data by the administration's 2004 Mid-Session Budget Review indicates that the tax cuts have played a larger role than all other legislation or policy in raising the budget deficit. That review showed that, until mid-2004, the tax cuts accounted for 57 percent of the worsening fiscal picture, more than all other policies combined.[17]

Some defenders have argued that the administration's tax cuts have actually made the tax system more progressive. They maintain that high-income taxpayers are generally paying a significantly greater percentage of federal income taxes because of the 2001–2003 tax cuts. They argue that high-income taxpayers only had a "comparable reduction" in their tax burden relative to middle-income taxpayers. This ignores taxes other than the income tax. Unlike the income tax, which is mildly progressive, other federal taxes, such as the payroll tax, are regressive, with middle- and low-income households paying a greater share of their income to these taxes than do the wealthiest taxpayers. CBO data show that 75 percent of all taxpayers pay more in payroll taxes than they do in income taxes. Analyzing tax burdens by focusing solely on the income tax and ignoring other taxes produces misleading results, as the CBO pointed out. Noting that the upper-income groups pay a higher share of taxes only tells us that the upper-income group is paying a larger share of the *much smaller amount of federal income taxes* being collected after the tax cuts. It is possible to increase the share of taxes paid by the affluent at the same time that the law makes after-tax income more unequal. Focusing on changes in the share of taxes paid misses the more meaningful after-tax income, which determines what households have at their disposal.[18]

At the beginning of the second term of George W. Bush, the effect of the changes in tax policy will be of increasing importance. By any reasonable measure, making the tax cuts permanent will be unaffordable. The tax cuts are regressive and will transfer more resources away from the poor toward the affluent. As a result, most households will be worse off. Another suggested goal of the recent tax cuts was to pave the way for a more fundamental tax reform. Many observers find that the changes may actually make reform more difficult to achieve. Some tax cut supporters justify the tax policy as an effort to reduce government spending.[19] This view claims that the cuts are justified in an effort to "starve the beast" of excessive social welfare spending. Essentially, this is an argument that reducing revenues is the best way to control spending, that the structure of the Bush tax cuts was justified by the goal of controlling spending. However, it is not clear that tax cuts are effective in cutting spending. Nor does the effort to reduce spending justify regressive tax cuts. It could be argued that since most spending cuts would be regressive (hurting the least well off the most), a tax cut aimed at reducing spending should, on fairness grounds, be progressive (that is, give greater tax cuts to households as one moves down the income ladder). Instead, the social welfare structure for those less well off is being severely curtailed. The tax cuts have not been effective in reducing spending, since spending has increased in all budget categories of defense, nondefense discretionary, and entitlement spending. Finally, even if "starving the beast" was legitimate as an original justification in 2001, when there were government surpluses, making the tax cuts permanent will create a **structural deficit** even if the economy arrives at full employment. A structural deficit occurs when government expenditures would still exceed tax revenues even if tax receipts were calculated assuming full employment.

The administration has stressed the need to make the tax cuts permanent in every budget it has presented, which will result in significantly rising costs after 2010 due to the elimination of the estate tax and the removal of the limitation on itemized deductions and the use of personal exemptions for high-income households. The baby boomers will also begin retiring at this time, putting increasing strains on health care costs. Therefore, meeting the administration's goal of cutting the deficit in half by 2009 ignores the main effect of making the cuts permanent. Since the Bush administration has ruled out any tax increase to reduce the deficit, the only remaining options are to cut spending and to grow the economy. Since the cuts are not well designed to encourage robust economic growth, spending cuts are likely to appear as the most attractive tool. The result will be that distributional issues in social welfare policies will continue to be important throughout the second term of the Bush administration.

Social Security and Reducing Poverty Among the Elderly

Until the twentieth century, few Americans could look forward to a retirement period at the end of their working lives. In 1900 the life expectancy for males was about forty-four years. Nevertheless, about two-thirds of men aged sixty-five and older were still in the labor force.[20] With insufficient savings and without a pension program, most were forced to work as long as they were physically able. By 2002, with a life expectancy of over seventy-seven years, the average age of retirement for males was just over sixty-three years.[21] Americans tend to stay in the labor force longer than the citizens of many OECD countries.[22] Advances in life expectancy and an extended retirement are clear advances in the general welfare of society. They also presents challenging public policy issues.

Since the administration of Franklin Roosevelt, the government has developed programs and, through legislation, encouraged policies to ensure that the elderly have sufficient income to provide for their needs during retirement. Social Security was initiated in 1935 to provide elderly Americans with a basic safety net. It was never intended to completely meet retirement needs. Nevertheless, this New Deal system has become the nation's main retirement program.

For most families, their primary savings for their retirement years consists of pensions and savings plans that are encouraged by tax incentives. Legislation providing tax incentives for employer-based pensions was passed in 1921. Legislation establishing Keogh accounts (1962) and individual retirement accounts (1974) expanded the eligibility for workers to participate in tax-sheltered savings plans. Nevertheless, only about half of all workers are covered by any form of a pension plan, with higher-income workers much more likely to be covered than low-income workers. The result is that for the average worker, Social Security makes up a larger part of their retirement income than private pensions, as indicated in Figure 6.6.

Currently, about 95 percent of married couples, one of whom is sixty-five or older, receive Social Security benefits. Social Security is the only form of pension income for about half of these households. Many financial planners suggest that

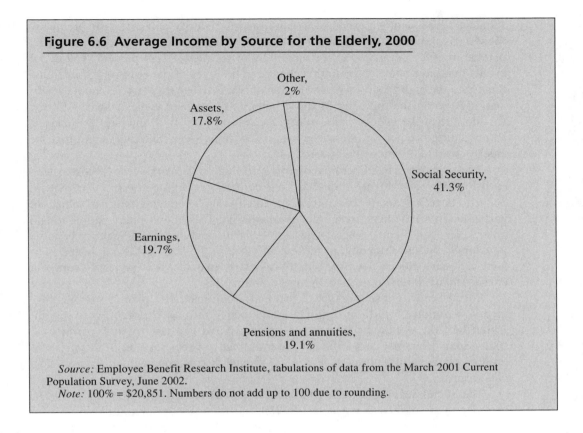

Figure 6.6 Average Income by Source for the Elderly, 2000

Other, 2%

Assets, 17.8%

Social Security, 41.3%

Earnings, 19.7%

Pensions and annuities, 19.1%

Source: Employee Benefit Research Institute, tabulations of data from the March 2001 Current Population Survey, June 2002.
Note: 100% = $20,851. Numbers do not add up to 100 due to rounding.

most families need about 70 percent of their preretirement income in order to maintain their standard of living. Currently, Social Security accounts for about 42 percent of the preretirement earnings of an average wage earner who retires at sixty-five.[23] This percentage is expected to decline, to 36 percent, until 2027, when the "normal retirement age" will reach sixty-seven. It is expected to remain at 36 percent after that.

In fact, in 2003 Social Security lifted close to 15 million above the poverty line and millions more from near-poverty. This was not always the case. In 1959 the average monthly Social Security check was $70, providing an annual income of under $1,000 per year at a time when the Census Bureau found that it would take $3,000 to provide an adequate budget for an elderly couple. In 1961 a White House conference on aging found that over half of elderly couples could not afford decent housing, proper nutrition, or adequate medical care. John Kennedy and Lyndon

Johnson subsequently pushed to expand Social Security and establish Medicare. Since 1959, poverty rates among the elderly have declined, from 35 percent to 10.2 percent in 2003, compared to the national poverty rate of 12.4 percent. The major events that have contributed to this change in the lives of the elderly in the United States are the significant increases in Social Security benefits enacted in the 1960s and 1970s, and the indexing of those benefits to average wage increases. In the first decade of the twenty-first century, the war on poverty of the elderly stands as an unqualified social welfare success story. Without Social Security, about half the elderly would fall below the poverty line.

The system has a deliberate redistributive slant to reduce poverty. Retirees who earn lower wages during their working careers get higher returns. The Social Security benefit schedule is progressive, and although some benefits are subject to partial taxation, the benefits are not means-tested. This allows many people to add other sources of income, such as pension benefits, to their Social Security benefits to achieve a level of income in retirement close to the level achieved during their working years. Social Security lifts more elderly people out of poverty—nine out of ten—than all other transfer programs combined.

Social Security also works as a national group insurance plan to provide payments to roughly 5 million disabled adults and 3 million children every month. About half the children who receive benefits have lost one or both parents. In short, Social Security is a valuable program that replaces income in the event of retirement, disability, or death, serving to reduce the income inequality across certain groups.

The Social Security system quit being a "pay as you go" program in the 1980s. In order to strengthen the system in 1983, the Reagan administration accepted a recommendation from a commission headed by Alan Greenspan to sharply raise payroll taxes to prefund Social Security's future obligations. The administration also accepted the recommendation to increase the age of full retirement to offset increased life expectancy, from sixty-five to sixty-seven, which, as mentioned above, will be fully implemented in 2027. Penalties will be correspondingly adjusted upward for early retirement at age sixty-two as well. The surplus payroll tax receipts are used to buy government bonds to be held in the Social Security trust fund. The money, and the bonds, do not belong to the government or the general public. They belong to the Social Security trust fund and to the workers whose payroll tax contributions created the Social Security surplus.[24] In essence, those who have paid Social Security payroll taxes from 1983 onward have been funding their own retirement.

The government has used the money from those bonds to fund other operations. Without the Social Security surplus, the government would have been forced to cut other programs, raise taxes, or increase the deficit. In 2019, retiree benefits will begin to exceed payroll tax receipts. At that time, Social Security tax receipts will be supplemented by redeeming some of the bonds purchased since 1983. Bonds are one of the world's safest investments. The government must pay the interest on the bonds and redeem them, because the alternative of defaulting on them would be catastrophic to its ability to sell bonds to finance its deficit.

In 2003 the Social Security Trust Fund Administration stated that the bonds would allow full funding until 2042. In the summer of 2004, using more recent data, the Congressional Budget Office projected that Social Security will be self-funding until 2052, when its bonds are to be cashed in. At that point, projected benefits would begin to exceed revenue by just 19 percent.[25] Thus "if nothing is done to the Social Security system, the average annual benefit per person would fall in the future but would remain higher in inflation-adjusted dollars than [it is] today."[26]

Bush's Proposals to Reform Social Security

President Bush has made the restructuring of Social Security the centerpiece of his second term. His Social Security Commission has put forward a plan to dramatically shrink Social Security benefits, replacing a much smaller share of preretirement wages for workers who retire in the future. While many policy analysts agree that adjustments must be made to the system, others suggest that the administration is trying to create an artificial sense of crisis that requires immediate and decisive action by the administration.[27]

Claims of a crisis in Social Security are viewed by the system's supporters as scare tactics and spin to create momentum to destroy the program in order to save it. The administration has undertaken a major public relations campaign to sell the nation on Bush's Social Security changes, because "that is where the momentum is."[28] The administration has suggested that Social Security will run out of funds in 2019, ignoring the continued worker contributions and the ability to redeem bonds. Dean Baker and Mark Weisbrot dubbed Social Security "the phony crisis" in their book by that title, wherein they maintain that Congress intends to use the money lent by buying bonds to fund the deficit and has a moral burden to redeem them, just as it does for all other bonds.[29] It would be outrageous for the government to use the money and then cut it from Social Security when it comes time to redeem the bonds. Charles Blahous, the White House's point person on Social Security, argues that that is "not much consolation to the worker of 2025 that there was an understanding in 1983 that he foot the bill."[30]

The Social Security Commission Plan

Bush has indicated that the commission's plan is a good starting point, but has not committed his administration to it at this point. This plan, which has been referred to as "privatization," would allow workers to divert up to 4 percent of the 12.4 percent payroll tax (roughly a third), up to $1,000, into a personal investment account. Proponents claim this would bring more Americans into the "ownership" society, as they would own part of their retirement. Guaranteed benefits would be cut by the amount contributed to personal accounts.

The commission's proposal would also change the benefit structure from what is referred to as "wage indexing" to "price indexing." Wages typically rise faster than prices. Over time, a household's standard of living increases, because its wages rise faster than prices. The plan's proponents frequently try to portray the change as not representing a benefit reduction but as merely curbing excessive growth in Social Security benefits.[31] The benefit formula, which would be implemented beginning in 2009, would gradually reduce benefits, which over time would be substantial. A CBO analysis found that the proposed change would save significantly more than is needed to close Social Security's long-term financing gap.[32]

Under the current formula, as mentioned above, an average wage earner who retires in 2027, when the full retirement age will be sixty-seven, will receive Social Security benefits that replace 36 percent of his or her preretirement earnings (as opposed to 42 percent for an average wage earner at age sixty-five in 2004). Under the proposal to lower replacement rates by adopting a "price indexing" rather than the current "wage indexing" formula, Social Security would only replace 27 percent of the income of the average wage earner who retires in 2042, and just 20 percent of the income of the average wage earner who retires in 2075. The result is that the standard-of-living support that Social Security would provide for retirees will decline appreciably, relative to the standard of living the worker had before retiring and relative to the standard of living the rest of society enjoys.[33]

The government would have to borrow about $2 trillion to offset the reduction in payroll taxes, in order to prevent a shortfall in payments owed to current retirees. Proponents of the plan have suggested that the $2 trillion is a necessary "bailout" of the system. However, it is the individual accounts that would create a cash flow shortfall by diverting funds away from Social Security long before benefits will be reduced. In fact, it is the private accounts that would push the Social Security trust fund into insolvency and threaten its financial condition.

Another major objection to this plan is that the stock market goes down as well as up. Obviously, as a retirement system, the stock market cannot offer the security that Social Security provides. Moreover, the less a wage earner makes, the less he or she has to invest and the smaller his or her return will be. It would be especially shortsighted to make retirement benefits more risky for those who earn low wages. In contrast, under the current system, Social Security deliberately distributes benefits to provide a slightly more generous annuity to those recipients whose incomes were low during their wage-earning years. There is also the obvious problem, especially for those less well off, of preretirement withdrawals to pay for family health or other emergencies, as well as for education. The result is that these funds would not actually provide retirement security.

The problem of achieving retirement security is compounded by the fact that the proposed shift to the stock market for Social Security corresponds to a shift in employer-provided retirement plans. In 1980, almost two out of five households (39 percent) had defined-benefit pension plans; in 2005, only about one in five (21 percent) do. Increasingly, workers in 401(k) investment plans are dependent on the vagaries of the stock market in the primary pension plan. It would make more sense to permit wage earners to add to the basic Social Security contribution with tax-deferred investment contributions, not reduce it.

The administration's view appears to be driven largely by ideology. It holds the view that private markets are more efficient. Despite the fact that over 99 percent of Social Security's current revenues go toward benefits and less than 1 percent to overhead, the administration suggests that the private sector would be more efficient. However, the CBO's own analysis shows that the administrative costs of private accounts in Social Security will incur overhead charges that would result in benefit cuts of about 20 percent.[34] And Paul Krugman has observed that the risks of privatization may make the problem worse. He notes that the government of Chile is often cited as the model for privatization; however, after more than twenty years the Chilean government must pour in additional money because it must "provide subsidies for workers failing to accumulate enough capital to provide a minimum pension."[35]

More Modest Proposals

Most scholarly opinion holds that the basic structure of Social Security is sound and does not justify a complete overhaul. If no changes are made to Social Security, it will not run out of money before 2052, allowing time to make adjustments to guarantee the program's long-term health. To put the "crisis" in perspective, a study by the Center on Budget and Policy Priorities found that the deficit in Social Security over the next seventy-five years will equal 0.4 percent of GDP, according to the CBO. By comparison, the cost over the next seventy-five years of the tax cuts enacted from 2001 to 2003 will be roughly 2 percent of GDP. If the tax cuts are made permanent, their cost will be five times larger, over the next seventy-five years, than the amount of the Social Security shortfall. Furthermore, just the cost of the tax cuts for the top 1 percent of the population, a group whose annual average income exceeds $1 million, is half again as large as the Social Security shortfall (0.4 versus 0.6 percent of GDP).[36]

Peter Orszag, a senior fellow at the Brookings Institution, and Peter Diamond, a leading scholar on Social Security at the Massachusetts Institute of Technology, propose progressive reforms. Under their plan, the payroll tax would be increased gradually from 12.4 to 13.7 percent over forty years. They propose trimming benefits by about 4 percent in 2032 and 12 percent in 2052. The increase in life expectancy has made Social Security less progressive, since those who earn higher wages tend to live longer than those who earn lower wages. To address this issue, Orszag proposes to reduce benefits to the top 15 percent of beneficiaries.[37]

Also, the proportion of earnings that go untaxed has accelerated in the past two decades, as income for the already affluent has increased rapidly while that for middle- and low-income workers has stagnated. The maximum taxable earnings base could be gradually raised about 15 percent above the current $90,000 maximum and indexed to inflation. Orszag and Diamond would also require mandatory coverage for newly hired state and local workers, which would also widen the base of workers paying into the system.

Conclusion

The theory of John Maynard Keynes provided the intellectual framework of welfare capitalism, to justify government's role in guiding the economy when it failed to live up to society's expectations. In the United States, the New Deal under Franklin Roosevelt tried to correct the weaknesses in the economy and to strengthen its workings. During the New Deal, government stepped in to manage the economy to a greater extent than had ever been done before. By the end of World War II, there was an acceptance of the idea that government had a responsibility to manage the economy to create the conditions that would provide for employment opportunities.

The experience of the war showed that economic policy could bring about high levels of employment and resulted in the Employment Act of 1946. The government is even more fully committed to these goals by the Full Employment and Balanced Growth Act of 1978, which established specific goals for unemployment (4 percent), inflation (3 percent), and economic growth (4 percent). The government has rarely attained all these goals, however. Achieving them would go a long way toward creating the conditions to promote the general welfare through various social policies. There was hope at the end of the Clinton administration that, with full employment, low inflation, and a growing economy, new programs could be undertaken to extend social welfare programs.

There are many reasons why these goals may be difficult to attain, including problems of measurement, design, and policy implementation. Perhaps even more important in the failure to achieve the economic goals that are necessary to effectively pursue social welfare policies is the increasing ideological dimension in politics. The economic theory is fairly settled, even if coordinating monetary and fiscal policies to achieve the basic goals is far from foolproof. Ideology not only provides different perspectives regarding sound social welfare policy, but it also elevates ideological commitment over pragmatic problem solving. Ideology frequently trumps practical politics. Years of conservative marketing have convinced many Americans that government programs always create inefficient, bloated bureaucracies, while private markets are always more efficient despite evidence to the contrary, as in the case of Social Security and Medicare administration. Government is seen as a "necessary evil" rather than as a "necessary good" that can improve the social welfare of the nation's citizens.

For example, the political consensus that government should take action to generally reduce great inequalities has broken down over the past several decades. The consensus of using the tools of monetary and fiscal policy to encourage a long trend of greater equalization in U.S. society receded. It is clear that the same tools can be used to increase inequality, as supply-side economics and the tax cuts from 2001 to 2003 illustrate. Considerable disagreement has arisen over what the role of government *should be* in using the power of taxation to redistribute income. And the social safety net is weakened when policies such as raising the minimum wage or expanding the Earned Income Tax Credit for the working poor are ignored.

Social Security has become the nation's greatest retirement program and is of particular importance to lower-income workers when they reach retirement. Opponents of Social Security have put forward proposals that would severely weaken its ability to provide needed support, especially for lower-income workers, who frequently are not covered by a pension. A change is of course necessary to ensure that workers reaching retirement will have sufficient assets to maintain a reasonable standard of living. Political consensus may be lacking in this crucial area of social welfare policy, as it is elsewhere in public policy. Policies proposed by the Republican majority, who currently control the White House and both houses of Congress, may unfortunately exacerbate the problems of the most needy.

Questions for Discussion

1. In what way has history provided a test for Keynes and a theory of government spending? Was it conclusive?
2. What kinds of problems do large budget deficits pose for the nation's economy? What are the different problems in the short run as opposed to the long run?

3. "Budgets are a serious problem." What additional information does a policy analyst need to make an assessment of this statement?
4. Why are investments critical in determining the level of prosperity?
5. Is a balanced-budget amendment a wise policy? Why or why not?
6. What alternative tax policies are available to the government? What are the positives and negatives associated with each?
7. What are the characteristics of a "good" tax system? Why are vertical and horizontal equity important?

Useful Websites

American Enterprise Institute, http://www.aei.org.
Center on Budget and Policy Priorities, http://www.cbpp.org.
Congressional Budget Office, http://www.cbo.gov.
Brookings Institution, http://www.brookings.edu.
Economic Policy Institute, http://www.epinet.org.
Heritage Foundation, http://www.heritage.org.
National Bureau of Economic Research, http://www.nber.org.
Office of Management and Budget, http://www.access.gpo.gov/usbudget.
Office of Tax Policy, U.S. Treasury, http://www.ustreas.gov/taxpolicy.
Organization for Economic Cooperation and Development (OECD), http://www.oecd.org.
Social Security Administration, http://www.sss.gov.

Suggested Readings

Auerbach, Alan J., and William G. Gale. "Tax Cuts and the Budget." *Tax Notes* 90 (2001).
Auerbach, Alan J., and Kevin A. Hassett. "Uncertainty and Design of Long-Run Fiscal Policy." In Alan J. Auerbach and Ronald D. Lee, eds., *Demographic Change and Fiscal Policy.* Cambridge: Cambridge University Press, 2001.
Burman, Leonard E., William G. Gale, Jeffrey Rohaly, and Benjamin H. Harris. *The Individual AMT: Problems and Potential Solutions.* Urban-Brookings Tax Policy Center Discussion Paper no. 5. Washington, D.C.: Brookings Institution, September 2002.
Congressional Budget Office. *The Budget and Economic Outlook: Fiscal Years 2003–2012.* Washington, D.C.: U.S. Government Printing Office, 2002.
Gale, William, and Peter Orszag. *The Economic Effects of Long-Term Fiscal Discipline.* Urban-Brookings Tax Policy Center Discussion Paper no. 100. Washington, D.C.: Brookings Institution, December 2002.
Kamin, David, and Isaac Shapiro. *Studies Shed New Light on Effects of Administration's Tax Cuts.* Washington, D.C.: Center on Budget and Policy Priorities, 2004.
Kogan, Richard. *How to Avoid Over-Committing the Available Surplus: Would a Tax-Cut "Trigger" Be Effective or Is There a Better Way?* Washington, D.C.: Center on Budget and Policy Priorities, 2001.
Shoven, John B. "The Impact of Major Life Expectancy Improvements on the Financing of Social Security, Medicare, and Medicaid." In Henry J. Aaron and William B. Schwartz,

eds., *Creating Methuselah: Molecular Medicine and the Problems of an Aging Society.* Washington, D.C.: Brookings Institution, 2003.

Notes

1. Reagan held that his agenda would stimulate such economic growth that enough tax revenues would be created to balance the budget by 1984. Starting with Reagan's assumption and working backward, former budget director David Stockman hastily put together a five-year plan openly referred to as the "Rosy Scenario." Stockman and his colleagues' secret calculations showed the deficit rising dramatically, but in public he insisted that his Rosy Scenario projections were valid. Later in his memoirs, Stockman stated that he "out-and-out cooked the books," inventing spurious cuts to make the deficit appear smaller. See David Stockman, *The Triumph of Politics* (New York: Harper and Row, 1986), p. 383.

2. Thomas Willett and King Banaian, "Models of the Political Process and Their Implications for Stagflation: A Public Choice Perspective," in Thomas D. Willett, ed., *Political Business Cycles: The Political Economy of Money, Inflation, and Unemployment* (Durham, N.C.: Duke University Press, 1988).

3. Organization for Economic Cooperation and Development, *Revenue Statistics 1965–2003* (OECD), p. 18.

4. The decline in sales resulting from the tax that is not offset by the tax revenue generated is referred to as a "deadweight loss," in that no one gets the money. Since a small number of voters buy cigarettes and alcohol, the price increase will not significantly affect sales. A much larger number of voters buy gas, but the political cost to an elected official of a tax on petroleum is acceptable because the deadweight losses are minimal and because the tax burden on each voter is relatively small.

5. See http://www.treas.gov/education/fact-sheets/taxes/economics.shtml, p. 3.

6. George Gilder, *Wealth and Poverty* (New York: Basic Books, 1981), p. 188.

7. Ibid.

8. An interesting tax loophole is the federal tax-exempt status of state and municipal bonds. Tax-exempt bonds are a curiosity peculiar to the United States. They are a remnant of the doctrine of state sovereignty, which originally held that the salaries of state employees must be free from federal tax. States fiercely resist any suggestion of elimination of the tax-free status because of the resulting increase in the cost of their borrowing.

9. William G. Gale, *Tax Reform Is Dead, Long Live Tax Reform,* Brookings Policy Brief no. 12 (Washington, D.C.: Brookings Institution, 2004).

10. Ibid.

11. Budget deficits declined each year of the Clinton administration and turned a surplus in 1998. In 1998 through 2001, tax revenues as a percentage of GDP were 20 percent, 20 percent, 20.9 percent, and 19.8 percent respectively. Outlays as a percentage of GDP for the same years were 19.2 percent, 18.6 percent, 18.4 percent, and 18.6 percent respectively. See *The Budget and Economic Outlook: Fiscal Years 2005–2014* (Washington, D.C.: U.S. Government Printing Office, January 26, 2004), Historic Budget Data, app. F, tab. 2.

12. Congressional Budget Office, *Effective Federal Tax Rates Under Current Law: 2001–2004* (Washington, D.C.: U.S. Government Printing Office, August 2004).

13. William G. Gale and Peter R. Orszag, "Tax Notes," in William G. Gale and Peter R. Orszag, *Bush Administration Tax Policy: Summary and Outlook* (Washington, D.C.:

Brookings Institution, November 29, 2004), p. 1280. Gale and Orszag produced eight papers analyzing and evaluating different aspects of the Bush administration's tax policy during his first term. They are an excellent resource for anyone interested in the ramifications of tax policy.

14. The Economic Policy Institute found that by September 2004, the number of jobs created after the tax cuts fell 2,668,000 short of administration predictions made in 2003. The 1.6 million jobs created constituted just 38 percent of the administration's projection. See Economic Policy Institute, "Job Watch: Tracking Jobs and Wages," http://www.jobwatch.org. Also referenced in David Kamin and Isaac Shapiro, *Studies Shed New Light on Effects of Administration's Tax Cuts* (Washington, D.C.: Center on Budget and Policy Priorities, 2004), p. 2.

15. Mark M. Zandi, "Assessing President Bush's Fiscal Policies," http://www.economy.com, July 2004. Also referenced in Kamin and Shapiro, *Studies,* p. 6.

16. Gale and Orszag, "Tax Notes," p. 1281.

17. Kamin and Shapiro, *Studies,* p. 2.

18. Ibid., p. 11.

19. Gale and Orszag, "Tax Notes," p. 1282.

20. Dan McGill, Kyle Brown, John Haley, and Sylvester Schieber, *Fundamentals of Private Pensions,* 7th ed. (Philadelphia: University of Pennsylvania Press, 1996), p. 5.

21. U.S. Census Bureau, *Statistical Abstract 2003* (Washington, D.C.: U.S. Government Printing Office, 2003), pp. 847, 857. See also *Current Population Survey for 2000.* The participation rate for women in the labor force has increased dramatically. The average age of withdrawal from the labor force for women is 63.4 years, with a life expectancy of an additional 20.4 years.

22. U.S. Census Bureau, *Statistical Abstract 2003,* p. 857.

23. *OASDI Trustees Report 2004,* tab. VI.F.

24. On this point, see Allen W. Smith, *The Looting of Social Security* (New York: Carroll and Graf, 2003).

25. Congressional Budget Office, *The Outlook for Social Security* (Washington, D.C.: U.S. Government Printing Office, June 2004).

26. Jonathan Weisman, "Revamping Social Security," *Washington Post,* January 2, 2005, p. A8.

27. Ibid.

28. Edmund L. Andrew, "Bush Puts Social Security at Top of Economic Conference," *New York Times,* December 16, 2004.

29. Dean Baker and Mark Weisbrot, *Social Security: The Phony Crisis* (Chicago: University of Chicago Press, 1999).

30. Quoted in Weisman, "Revamping Social Security," p. A8.

31. Robert Greenstein, *So-Called "Price Indexing" Proposal Would Result in Deep Reductions over Time in Social Security Benefits* (Washington, D.C.: Center on Budget and Policy Priorities, December 21, 2004), p. 2.

32. Ibid., p. 4. See also Congressional Budget Office, *Long-Term Analysis of Plan 2 of the President's Commission to Strengthen Social Security* (Washington, D.C.: U.S. Government Printing Office, July 21, 2004; updated September 30, 2004), tab. 2. Under the current formula the worker's annual earnings for each of his or her thirty-five highest-earning years are averaged and divided by twelve. The result is the worker's "average indexed monthly earnings." The individual's benefit is then determined essentially as (at full retire-

ment age): 90 percent of the worker's first $612 of average indexed monthly earnings, plus 32 percent of average monthly earnings between $623 and $3,689 (if the worker's earnings were that high), and 15 percent of any average monthly earnings covered above that. The worker's benefit level is determined at the time the worker retires. And the worker's benefit is then adjusted in each succeeding year in accordance with the annual change in the CPI (the measure of the average change in consumer prices over a period of time in a fixed market basket of goods and services).

In the proposed price-indexing method, the 90, 32, and 15 percent factors would be multiplied by the ratio of the percentage change in the CPI to the percentage change in average wages over the previous twelve months (wages usually rise faster than prices). The result is that if prices rise by 3 percent and wages rise by 4 percent in a year, the worker's standard of living rises by 1 percent. Under this formula the ratio would be 1.03 divided by 1.04, or 0.99 percent. See Greenstein, *So-Called "Price Indexing,"* p. 4.

33. Greenstein, *So-Called "Price Indexing,"* p. 4.

34. Congressional Budget Office, *Administrative Costs of Private Accounts in Social Security* (Washington, D.C.: U.S. Government Printing Office, March 2004).

35. Paul Krugman, "Buying into Failure," *New York Times,* December 17, 2004, p. A35.

36. Jason Furman, William G. Gale, and Peter R. Orszag, *Would Borrowing $2 Trillion for Individual Accounts Eliminate $10 Trillion in Social Security Liabilities?* (Washington, D.C.: Center on Budget and Policy Priorities, December 13, 2004).

37. Event Summary, *Saving Social Security: Which Way to Reform?* (Washington, D.C.: Brookings Institution, December 10, 2003).

CHAPTER 7

The Politics and Economics of Inequality

This chapter focuses on the oldest story in every society: the tension between the haves and the have-nots. As Plutarch observed early in the first millennium, "An imbalance between rich and poor is the oldest and most fatal ailment of all republics." Throughout history, elites have boldly justified their special claim to wealth, power, and privilege through the development of national myths that legitimize their position at the expense of the masses. Democracy in its most narrow formal requirement of individual freedom of expression, regular elections with full citizen participation, and a responsive government, was not possible where an aristocracy not only controlled all political power, but also had tight control over land, labor, and capital. Democracy, based on the fundamental principle of equality, sweeps aside all claims of privilege. As Supreme Court Justice Louis Brandeis said, "We can have democracy in this country or we can have great wealth concentrated in the hands of a few, but we cannot have both."[1] When great wealth is concentrated in relatively few hands that also control the institutions of governmental power, government will serve the interests of those elites first. Democratic government's stated primary purpose of serving "we the people" to "promote the general welfare" can become an illusion manipulated by the powerful to gain approval of the nonelites. Democracy is always threatened by the possible collusion between the rich to take control of government for their own benefit. When that effort succeeds, the institutions of democracy will continue to exist long after the political system has degenerated into an oligarchy.

The study of income distribution is concerned with an analysis of the way national income is divided among persons. There are several issues of normative and positive theory that crop up when examining income distribution. For economists such as Adam Smith, Thomas Malthus, David Ricardo, and Karl Marx, distribution was a central issue. At the end of the nineteenth and the beginning of the twentieth century, many policy analysts and economists were not significantly concerned with the distribution of wealth and income. The Great Depression and the theory of John Maynard Keynes renewed interest in the subject.

Major questions regarding the distribution of wealth and income include whether or not inequality is inevitable. If so, how much inequality is optimal? Is there a threshold beyond which inequality in wealth or income undermines political democracy? What kinds of public policies regarding inequalities would improve the quality of life for most citizens? Should there be a coordination of policies by democratic forms of government to reduce the variability of inequality in various nations?

The Promise of Equality in the First New Nation

Politics is often defined as the ongoing struggle over who gets what, when, and how. Throughout history much of the struggle was determined by the ability of a powerful actor, whether a warlord, a monarch, or an oligarch, to maintain his life of wealth and privilege at the expense of others. The eighteenth-century Enlightenment thinkers challenged the domination of society by a hereditary and tyrannical aristocracy. They believed that human reason was the indispensable weapon needed to battle ignorance, superstition, and tyranny and build a better world. Thinkers of the Enlightenment stressed individualism over community, and freedom replaced authority as a core value. Many Enlightenment thinkers were merchants who resented paying taxes to support a privileged aristocracy who contributed little of value to society. It was particularly galling that the aristocrats were unwilling to share power with the merchants and manufacturers who actually created the national wealth.

The intellectual leaders of the American Revolution were captivated by the Enlightenment's opposition to unchecked privilege, since they hoped to build a democracy that would require tolerance, respect for evidence, and informed public opinion. Their notion of democracy was one in which government would make decisions on behalf of the "general welfare," not for the advantage of the privileged few. The concept of equality written into the Declaration of Independence, together with the concept of "human rights," which has become an essential part of U.S. culture, has been called our "civil religion."

These notions from the Enlightenment were not seen by early Americans as naive optimism, but as the promise of the **American Dream**—the widespread belief in an open, vigorous, and progressive community committed to equal opportunities for all in which life would improve for each generation. It includes the belief that the income and wealth the economy generated would become more evenly distributed.

The leaders of the American Revolution wanted to do more than free themselves from forced obedience to a monarch; they wanted to create a government that would offer greater freedom and dignity to the average citizen. Some went so far as to propose that all free white males be allowed to vote. Other influential members of the delegation in Philadelphia in 1787 were more dubious and proposed a government administered by gentlemen of property to maintain their life of privilege at the expense of others. The constitution that resulted from all the compromises provided a system of separation of powers between the president, Congress, and the judiciary. It specifically provided for a house of representatives to represent the interests of "the people." Congress, aware of the unprecedented grant of power to the people, used the words of Roman poet Virgil in the Great Seal of the United States—"a new age now begins."[2] The principle of checks and balances resulted from the inability of the framers of the Constitution to agree on precisely how power should be distributed among the branches. Although the commitment to hold all men as being created equal and endowed by their creator with inalienable rights to life, liberty, and the pursuit of happiness was not enforced, a war on inequality began immediately to force the government to live up to the promise. Property rights for voting were abolished, but it took a civil war to free slaves, and another century passed before civil rights legislation gave substance to that freedom.

Equity and Equality

To many of the leaders of the American Revolution, democracy was looked upon as the completion of the human struggle for freedom. The framers of the Constitution were well aware of the difficulty of reconciling individuality and liberty with democratic equality. James Madison expressed his concern over the inherent conflicts a democratic society would have to address when he wrote that the "most common and durable source of factions" in society is "the various and unequal distribution of property."

Thomas Jefferson's bias in favor of equality is well known. He believed that the innate differences between men were small:[3]

> I am conscious that an equal division of property is impracticable. But the consequences of this enormous inequality producing so much misery to the bulk of mankind, legislators cannot invent too many devices for subdividing property. . . . Another means of silently lessening the inequality of property is to exempt all from taxation below a certain point, and to tax the higher portions of property in geometrical progression as they rise.[4]

He went on to say that the government should provide "that as few as possible shall be without a little portion of land" as the "small landholders are the most precious part of a state."[5]

Opponents of the trend toward equality used the vocabulary of the Enlightenment and Jeffersonian liberalism, but provided their own definitions to words like "individualism" and "progress." They even claimed support from those who were clearly concerned about the problem. For example, Charles Darwin expressed concern for the poor when he wrote, "If the misery of the poor be caused not by the laws of nature, but by our institutions, great is our sin."[6] Nevertheless, his theory of natural selection, which led to the theory of evolution, was revised by Herbert Spencer into "social Darwinism" and endorsed as a scientific finding that the destruction of the weak and the "survival of the fittest" constituted the essence of progress.

Americans have often boastfully quoted Alexis de Tocqueville's observation of "the equality of conditions" in the United States in the 1830s. U.S. culture has always emphasized equality rather than deference. Politicians, especially wealthy politicians, claim that they share the same social and cultural *values* of the average American, even if they do not share the same tax bracket. Indeed, de Tocqueville believed that the Americanization of the world in terms of the ever-increasing equality of conditions was inevitable. He realized that the creation of democratic forms of government was not the end of the struggle, but that it was a continuous process. And he believed that inevitably the rest of humanity would finally arrive at an almost complete equality of conditions. He sensed a growing "aristocracy of manufacturers" who had no sense of public responsibility and whose aim was to use the workers and then abandon them to public charity. He believed that the manufacturing aristocracy "is one of the harshest which ever existed in the world. . . . [T]he friends of democracy should keep their eyes anxiously fixed in this direction; for if ever a permanent inequality of conditions and aristocracy again penetrate into the world, it may be predicted that this is the channel by which they will enter."[7]

Writing a century later, Keynes pointed out that we could hardly expect business to act on behalf of the well-being of the workers, let alone the entire society. He noted that in democracies the government has the responsibility to protect the economic well-being of the nation. The main failure of capitalism, according to Keynes, is its "failure to provide for full employment and its arbitrary and inequitable distribution of wealth and incomes."[8] Keynes was not opposed to economic inequality. What was required, he said, was a collective management of the system that would be as efficient as possible without offending our notions of a satisfactory way of life. The problem then becomes, what is a socially optimal amount of economic inequality?

U.S. political institutions declare the equality of citizens. However, capitalism creates economic and social inequalities. The disparity between presumed equal rights and economic inequality creates tension between capitalism and the principles of democracy. Owners of capital may use money or their position of power in imperfect markets to deny others a minimum standard of living. Beginning in the Progressive era and reaching its high points during the administrations of Franklin Roosevelt and Lyndon Johnson, democratic institutions were used to keep market excesses within acceptable limits. During the 1930s, President Roosevelt inaugurated the New Deal. The Great Depression caused a national crisis that resulted in a third of the nation being ill-fed, ill-housed, and ill-clothed. The minimum wage, the eight-hour day, Social Security, trade union legislation, civil rights, women's rights, a progressive federal income tax, and civil service reform based on merit rather than a spoils system were all achieved over the vigorous opposition of business interests, which were concerned that such benefits to workers would reduce profits. The American Dream was reinforced by the notion that business prospers when workers are paid wages sufficient to allow them to buy what they produce. We prosper as "one nation, indivisible" when workers are paid wages that allowed a "middle-class" income. A broad middle class contributes to prosperity for all. Government responsibility to narrow the gap between rich and poor was largely accepted by liberals and conservatives alike after the New Deal. Others sought to preserve equality of opportunity by opposing any alliance between government and business elites. That effort, and the unsteady progress by reformers in advancing the American Dream of equality, was seriously challenged in the 1980s by a resurgence of conservatism under President Ronald Reagan. Supply-side economic thinking defended economic inequality as a source of productivity and economic growth.

The successive federal tax cuts proposed by the George W. Bush administration and enacted by Congress were for most Americans actually tax shifts that redistributed after-tax income from the bottom 99 percent to the top 1 percent, exacerbating the inequality between the rich and everybody else. The federal government has concentrated on eliminating estate taxes and reducing taxes especially for the wealthy, while ignoring social safety net policies for the poor, like raising the minimum wage, providing health care for the uninsured, or providing more funds for housing the poor.

Many of those most adversely affected by the economic changes did not respond with anger toward those primarily responsible for their economic decline. Rather than focusing their anger on the corporate and financial elite derided by Roosevelt as "economic royalists" and "malefactors of great wealth," they identified their antagonists as "liberals." Conservative strategists successfully cast the problem as "cultural" rather than "economic." These activists, with the support of conservative think tanks, pundits, lobbyists, ministers, and right-wing radio talk-show hosts, provided a smoke screen that shielded the dismantling of middle- and working-class protections while they added fuel to their anger against "liberals."

A recent study by Thomas Frank titled *What's the Matter with Kansas?* analyzes how many vulnerable Americans have been persuaded that cultural issues override economic issues, and therefore persuaded to vote against their economic and social interests.[9] Political liberals are portrayed as waging cultural warfare against a fundamentally Protestant Christian culture that is perceived as the basis of U.S. society. Conservatives argue that this is a battle to determine whether U.S. culture as we have known it can be saved. On issue after issue, they feel threatened: gay marriage, abortion rights, the Pledge of Allegiance, prayer in schools, the promiscuity portrayed in movies and television programming, to name just a few.

The economically disadvantaged segment of the U.S. population provided critical electoral support in the 2004 elections to politicians who acted against their economic interest by implementing policies that increased the gap between themselves and the affluent. Political campaigns increasingly rely on professional managers, constant polling, focus groups to test appeals to voters, and expensive television advertising. This has forced political fundraising to become increasingly dependent on large contributors. The wealthy are not surprisingly inclined to contribute money to politicians and organizations that endorse reductions in most government programs, including social welfare programs, taxes, and government regulation of business. They are very aware of the benefits of economic inequality for themselves and focus clearly on the goal of protecting their economic status when they contribute to political candidates. It is estimated that the richest 3 percent of the voting population accounts for 35 percent of all private campaign contributions during presidential elections.[10] The major corporate political action committees did not hedge their bets in the 2004 elections. They favored Republicans ten to one. Of 268 corporate political action committees that donated $1 million or more to presidential and congressional candidates from January 2003 through October 2004, 245 gave the majority of their contributions to Republicans.[11]

The nonelites are aware of the downside of economic inequality, but vote on the basis of noneconomic issues like crime, abortion, or immigration.[12] The poor are more cynical regarding government and are less likely to register and vote.[13] The federal government's response is to advance the economic interests of the wealthy and the noneconomic interests of the less affluent.

As labor organizer Oscar Ameringer observed, in such a scenario, politics becomes the art of winning votes from the poor and campaign contributions from the rich through promises "to defend each from the other."[14]

Elites' contributions give them greater political influence than less affluent voters. The process then results in economic policies that add to elites' share of total wealth and income, which is at variance with theories of democracy. The alliance between government and the rich (the U.S. equivalent of the aristocrats' relationship to King George III), so long feared by the reformers, has been realized.

Income Distribution

It has long been known that extreme inequality is a major cause of political instability in many developing countries. Even in a wealthy country like the United States, economic inequality is associated with poverty, crime, political alienation, and social unrest. Great inequality in income and wealth is a social problem and therefore an issue for the policy agenda. Whether the government should reduce the great inequality between the rich and the poor is the focus of contention. Part of the uncertainty arises from the imperfect knowledge about the relationship between inequality and economic growth. It is often held that there is a tradeoff between equality and efficiency, suggesting that policies aimed at reducing inequality reduce economic growth.

The concept of liberty and egalitarianism has been a cornerstone of U.S. social and political culture. Liberty, protected by government as the pursuit of one's own self-interest, permits each to acquire material goods according to one's circumstances and abilities. The result has been a great disparity in income and wealth that undermines equality. We hear a great deal about political equality, which typically means that individuals are equal before the law, and that regardless of ability or income, each has the right to vote. There appears to be an assumption that this narrow technical political equality is *the* significant equality in the United States, and we disregard or minimize the fact of economic inequality. Most countries of the Western world have policies designed to *reduce* the differences between rich and poor. In those countries most concede that the role of government should not be to widen the gap between rich and poor, but rather to reduce it.

How Has U.S. Income Distribution Changed?

Between 1935 and 1945 there was a clear trend toward a more equal distribution of income in the United States, primarily because of four factors. (1) The end of the Great Depression and a wartime economy provided full employment, significantly raising the wages of labor. (2) During World War II a more progressive income tax and excess-profits taxes reduced the after-tax income of the rich more than that of the poor. (3) Labor scarcity during the war reduced discrimination against minorities and increased economic opportunities for them. (4) Union membership quadrupled and increased the relative income of labor.[15]

In the decade between 1945 and 1955, the trend toward greater equality continued, but at a much slower pace as unions began meeting more resistance after the war, and as continued prosperity meant continued employment and educational opportunities for minorities. From 1955 through about 1980 the distribution of income remained relatively constant, largely because governments at all levels imposed taxes that were less progressive than in former years. Since 1980, inequality in income has increased.

Factors Contributing to Greater Economic Inequality

The gap between pay for higher- and lower-paid workers has accelerated at least since 1980, particularly among men.[16] Between 1980 and 2003, real wages fell for those at the bottom of the income distribution, while they remained rather stagnant for those close to or just above the average and rose briskly for those at the top. Women's real wages on average grew about 1 percent faster annually during the same period.

The question is, why did wage inequality expand so rapidly in the past quarter century? A variety of factors contribute to wage differentials that exist between and within the same occupation. And not surprisingly, different scholars tend to focus on different explanations. Marvin Kosters and Murray Ross emphasize supply-side factors, such as the maturing baby boom generation and the growing role of women in the labor force.[17] Others emphasize demand-side factors, such as the shift from a manufacturing to a service-oriented economy.[18]

Several policies contributed to the reversal. Since the Reagan administration, enforcement of antitrust laws has been given a very low priority. Mergers of large corporations have become a method for concentrating wealth, undertaken because of the huge payouts received by chief executive officers and senior executives when two companies merge. Historically, an increase in worker productivity resulted in a similar increase in income for the average worker. But from 1973 to 2002, median family income grew only about one-third as fast as productivity.[19] The pay gap between more highly educated workers and less educated workers has indeed increased. Those with more human capital can demand more for their more highly skilled labor, which pushes up pay levels. Highly educated (or skilled) workers are often in a more inelastic supply position, and rising demand forces up their wage rate.

Globalization is increasingly put forward as an explanation for a growing income inequality. Undoubtedly, free trade does exert a downward pressure on U.S. wages, but some scholars are skeptical that it is a major cause of rising inequality.[20] Rising inequality also results from the decline in the number of middle-class jobs and the accompanying rise in the proportion of jobs in the service sector that pay lower wages.[21]

In 1983, the first year for which comparable statistics are available, 20.1 percent of the labor force belonged to a union; by 2003 the number of private sector union members had declined to 8.2 percent of the labor force. The minimum wage of $5.15 an hour was just 34 percent of the average hourly wage in 2003, down from about 45 percent of the average wage in the mid-1970s. The decline in the minimum wage relative to the average wage is clearly a relevant factor. The coverage of workers with employer-provided pensions or health care has also declined for middle- and low-income workers over the past two decades.

Immigration policy is related to globalization. It increases the pool of labor and also exerts a greater downward pressure, particularly on middle- and low-wage workers. Many immigrants who enter the United States are attracted by the availability of jobs, even though they pay low wages by U.S. standards. But this is preferable to unemployment or even lower wages in their native countries. While they are a labor safety valve in their native countries, they clearly increase income inequality in the United States.

It is largely a matter of public choice as to how much inequality the society will permit. Growing inequality has become a politically charged topic in recent years, which raises the question, is there something public policy can or should do to reduce growing inequalities? Some conservatives have argued that significant differences in economic inequalities do not necessarily have policy implications. They argue that the wealthy are inclined to invest their money, creating jobs and contributing to faster economic growth. Conservatives accuse liberals of fomenting class warfare when they point to the growing inequality of income and wealth in society.

Others see the growing inequality as a serious threat to society's political, social, and economic well-being. They argue that income inequality causes spillover effects into the quality of life, even for those not necessarily in poverty. Wide economic disparities result in frustration, stress, and family discord, which increases the rate of crime, violence, and homicide. Robert Putnam has suggested that the breakdown of social cohesion brought about by income inequality threatens the functioning of democracy. He found that low levels of civic trust spill over into a lack of confidence in government and low voter turnout at elections.[22] There is a serious concern that too much inequality could lead to a cycle in which lack of trust and civic engagement reinforce a public policy that does not result from the collective deliberation about the public interest, but merely reflects the success of campaign strategies. In a democracy, the electorate pick their representatives. However, members of Congress increasingly choose who can vote for them through gerrymandering. In the 2004 election fewer than 3 percent of the seats were competitive.[23]

Although the current intellectual climate is less supportive of an egalitarian position than a decade or two ago, it is still true that in most Western countries, including the United States, significant majorities believe that a bias in favor of equality to reduce a large income gap accords with a democratic approach.[24]

Americans' Bias in Favor of Equality

While we may declare our sympathy for policies favoring equality, most of us would support inequality if it resulted from certain conditions:

1. *People would agree that inequality is justified if everyone has a fair (not necessarily equal) chance to get ahead.*[25] Not only would most people not object to inequality in the distribution of wealth or income if the race was run under fair conditions with no one handicapped at the start, but they would actively support it as well. However, the situation quickly becomes murky. Many people do try to compete for scarce highly paid jobs by attending college so their future incomes will be higher. Some may choose not to attend college, while others may have grown up in families who could not afford to send them to college or provide a background conducive to preparation for it. For those people, the resulting lower income is not voluntary.

What parameters make conditions fair? Of particular concern is the fairness of inheritances. What of the genetic inheritance of talent? Much of our most important human capital is carried in our genes, with the ownership of productive resources just an accident of birth. Is it fair that some individuals through their genetic endowment, a factor beyond the control of the person so equipped, have high innate intelligence, the physical ability that allows them to become professional athletes, or the physical attributes that allow them to become highly paid models, while the genetic inheritance of others determines that they will be mentally or physically limited or even both? We usually do not worry too much over this kind of inheritance, but its effects are very real.

What of the inheritance of gender? Studies make it plain that females born in the United States doing the same job as men receive approximately 70 percent of the pay received by a male. Is that fair? What about the inheritance of those who do not pick their parents wisely and grow up as an ethnic minority, in a culturally deprived family in a ghetto neighborhood, as opposed to a child born to a white privileged family who can afford the richest environment and best schools available for their children?

Then there is the income differential resulting from inherited wealth. Many of the super-rich in the United States got that way through merely inheriting large sums of money. That it should be possible to pass some wealth on from one generation to another is generally conceded, but the passing on of large fortunes virtually intact is frequently challenged. Classical conservatives tend to be most supportive of the theory of social Darwinism, which holds that society is a place of competition based on the principle of "survival of the fittest," in which those who are most fit win in the competition for material goods. Social Darwinists are opposed to the passing on of large inheritances from one generation to the next, because it nullifies the fairness of the competition. Someone who inherits a fortune may have mediocre ability, but does not have to "compete" with others and prove their ability through competition. As Barry Switzer famously said, "some people are born on third base and go through life thinking they hit a triple."[26] The wealthy who truly believe in the theory maintain their consistency by opposing the repeal of estate taxes. They are not a large group.

Any discussion of inheritances suggests the role of chance in income distribution. Chance operates not only in inheritances, but also in the wider region of income differentials. One individual hits a lottery jackpot, another finds a super-highway built adjacent to her farm, increasing its value several times, another unexpectedly finds oil on his land. On the other hand, a worker may find himself out of work for a prolonged period due to a recession beyond his control, or the victim of an expensive debilitating illness, or that a highly paid position she was trained for disappears.

2. *No one objects to inequality if it reflects individual choice.* If an individual decides to turn his back on the secular world, become a Franciscan, and take a vow of poverty, no one would object. If someone decides to take a job that offers financial incentives because of unpleasant or inconvenient working conditions, or because it is more dangerous, we will not object to her higher wages. The problem is that frequently these decisions do not result from free choices but are brought about by circumstances. A person raised in a ghetto with no opportunity to sacrifice *current* income to improve skills through education so that a *future* income will be higher, may not have the option of choosing to work in a highly paid profession.

3. *People accept inequality when it reflects merit.* Nearly everyone believes in the correctness of higher pay when we can show that it is justified by a different contribution to output.[27] Some people work longer hours than others, or work harder when on the job. This may result in income differences that are largely voluntary. Other workers acquire experience and technical skills over time that may result in their earning a higher wage. This is part of the justification for a wage differential based on seniority.

4. *People accept and even support inequality when we are persuaded that the inequality will benefit everyone.* Often the common good is thought to include an increase in the gross domestic product (GDP), since greater productivity typically means a brisk demand for labor, higher wages, and greater economic activity. Therefore, the argument is often made by some politicians and some economists that policies encouraging inequalities that benefit those with higher incomes are justified because they will lead to higher savings for the wealthy, which in turn will ultimately be translated into investments, which will create the jobs enriching the prospects of everyone else. The proposal for a lower capital gains tax is just such a suggestion. This is the **trickle-down theory**, which suggests that if the wealthy only had more money, they would be more highly motivated to invest more of it in the hope of making a profit, and these investments would then create more jobs, thus helping society in general.[28]

These four general principles describe how the unequal distribution of income and wealth *is* defended. There is no suggestion that this is the way we *should* think about inequality.

The Functional Theory of Inequality

There is a theory that maintains that inequality is functionally imperative, because no stable system can long survive without it.[29] According to the **functional theory of inequality**, society must first distribute its members into the various jobs or roles defined by the society and then motivate them to perform their tasks efficiently. Some jobs are more important than others in the sense that successful performance of them is crucial to the welfare of the whole society.[30] Additionally, some tasks require skills that are either difficult or scarce because they require special training. To ensure that the most important jobs are performed competently, every society provides a system of unequal rewards to produce incentives to channel the most competent people into the most important and difficult jobs. This ensures the greatest efficiency in the performance of these jobs.

It should be emphasized that, according to this theory, "a position does not bring power and prestige because it draws a high income. Rather it draws a high income because it is functionally important and the available personnel is for one reason or another scarce."[31] So the population comes to understand that inequality is functional. The system of unequal rewards works to the advantage of the whole system by guaranteeing that jobs essential to society's welfare are performed efficiently and competently.[32]

Milton Friedman believes that the market is the most efficient way of filling the most important positions with the most capable people. Equality of opportunity is the principle that allows the market to select the most competent individuals: "No society can be stable unless there is a basic core of value judgments that are unthinkingly accepted by the great bulk of its members. I believe that payment in accordance with product has been, and in large measure still is, one of these accepted value judgments or institutions."[33] The functional theory of inequality is intuitively appealing, but it immediately raises several problems.

Tradeoffs Between Equality, Equity, and Efficiency

Equality of income and *equity* of income are not the same. Equality deals with incomes in terms of "the same amount," while equity refers to "fairness." Equality deals with what incomes *are* and variance from a standard, while equity is the normative question of what incomes *should be*.

The main argument against an equal distribution of income is based on efficiency. An unequal distribution does provide incentives. To illustrate the point, imagine the consequences if the society decided to achieve equality by taxing away all individual income and then dividing the taxes collected equally among the entire population. Realizing that harder work would no longer lead to a higher income would eliminate an important incentive. Any incentive to forgo current consumption to purchase capital goods would also be abolished, since there would be no chance of additional income. Since all rewards for harder work, investing, entrepreneurship, and taking risks by developing capital and acquiring land would disappear, the gross domestic product would decline dramatically. This suggests that policies that increase the amount of economic equality (or reduce inequality) may reduce economic efficiency—that is, lower the incentive to produce (thus lowering the GDP).

A second argument against an equal distribution of income or wealth is based on the concept of equity. As noted earlier, people with different natural abilities and who make unequal contributions to output should not receive the same income. An equal distribution is not equitable if individual contributions are unequal. U.S. society has been based on the idea of equality of opportunity rather than equality of results.

The case in favor of an equal distribution of income must include the argument that an unequal distribution leads to unequal opportunities. Some income differences arise because of differences in wealth. Many with income-producing assets such as stocks and bonds may receive sizable incomes from them. Not only are these individuals able to acquire additional income-producing assets such as land or capital investments (i.e., more stocks and bonds), but they are also more able to invest in human capital through training and education to increase even further the amount of income they can earn in the future. A person with less wealth is, by contrast, less able to invest in other productive factors such as land and capital, or in education. Therefore, an unequal distribution tends to be perpetuated and even increased because of the unequal market power of those who already have wealth, unless the government intervenes through taxes and transfers of income.

A second argument made by those in favor of a more equal income distribution is that a highly unequal distribution that provided a great deal for the few and little or nothing for the many creates political unrest and threatens the stability of the society. When 25 percent of the population live at the subsistence level and the top 10 percent, who receive most of the income, also dominate the political and economic levers of power, the poor may be driven to rebel against the economic and political elites.

Third, it may be argued that a highly unequal distribution of income can, contrary to the conservative view, inhibit investment in capital, which is crucial to economic growth. While it is true that investment usually comes from people with higher incomes, if relatively few members of a society have most of its income, the rest of the population cannot put significant demand into the economy to stimulate growth. With a lack of investment incentives, the wealthy may opt to use their incomes for personal consumption instead.

Liberals sometimes undermine their case for more equality by denying that their proposals will have any harmful effects on incentives. Conservatives, on the other hand, undermine their case against greater equality by making greatly exaggerated claims about the loss of efficiency that would arise.

Qualifications to the Theory

The functional theory of inequality is open to some criticisms that do not demolish it, but that significantly narrow the range of inequalities that can be justified as functionally imperative:

1. *It is relatively easy to determine which skills are in scarce supply, but difficult to tell which jobs are the most important to the welfare of a particular society.* Questions of comparable worth, for example, are notoriously complex problems. After agreement is reached regarding the extremes—for example, the importance of the cardiovascular surgeon compared to the street-sweeper—it becomes very difficult to determine the relative importance of jobs more at the "center," managing a corporation versus teaching young children, for instance, or working as an accountant versus being a dentist. How does one decide?

Those supporting the functionalist approach usually shift from an assessment of the relative importance of any particular position to assessing its relative skill level and the scarcity of that skill in the society.

2. *Contrived scarcity can affect the supply of skilled personnel.* Once we shift attention from the importance of the job to the scarcity of talent, we must confront the reality that a critically located profession can control the supply of talent. Any profession tries to promote the economic interest of its members by increasing their income. Competitive conditions would attract more members, potentially developing a surplus and driving incomes down. So the profession will typically try to limit its membership through occupational licensing, creating a contrived scarcity. Many occupations require a state license. Frequently, the licensing process is very strongly influenced by the profession, whose members claim that they alone are competent to judge the criteria necessary for training and certification. Members justify their control by citing the need to exclude "quacks." But the certification, whether for architects, accountants, lawyers, or physicians, has substantial economic value. Frequently, the license is fundamentally a way to raise wages in a particular profession by limiting competition. Typically, licenses are granted by a panel of practitioners in the field, who determine how many are to be granted and to whom. The potential for conflicts of interest is apparent.[34]

Restricting competition raises the income of the rent seekers. But if those who benefit can then buy more political influence, which further increases their share of income, it undermines the democratic notion of equality of competition.

The point is that once the first criterion of the functionalists—the importance of a particular kind of job—recedes into the background, the functionalist interpretation of the second criterion—the scarcity of needed skills—becomes doubtful.

3. *Functionalists emphasize the positive side of their theory and ignore its negative aspects.* The theory does identify the value of talent and shows how rewarding various talents motivates those who possess them to work efficiently. However, it ignores the demotivating effects for those with fewer talents. Those at the higher end of the income stream can be motivated with the aspiration to bonuses, higher wages, life and health insurance benefits, promotions, and pension programs. But workers at the lower end of the income stream cannot be motivated by higher pay, for at least two main reasons. First, low income at this end of the pay scale must provide the differential to fill the higher positions with competent and conscientious workers. Second, the money needed to pay some people more must be taken from those who will be paid less. Thus, in functionalist theory, the workers on garbage trucks who are quick and efficient cannot be rewarded by higher pay or bonuses, although they may be valued employees. As these individuals get older, and slower, they must continue to work because of the need to provide for their families, even under the most adverse conditions. Consequently, low income, unemployment, and the threat of unemployment are concentrated among those jobs where the skill levels are the lowest and the supply of people having the skills is the greatest. In sum, the carrot motivating those at the upper-income levels requires the stick to motivate those at the lower levels of income. Functionalist theory rarely mentions this.

4. *For the functionalist system of inequality to operate smoothly, the society as a whole must see it as working to benefit the entire population.* Most of the population must also believe that their tasks and their income levels reflect their skills and their relative contributions to the society. The stratified system will then rest on a consensus in which even those at the lower end of the income stream understand that their low wages and the threat of unemployment are necessary motivators to keep them working. Not surprisingly, those who wholeheartedly believe in the system tend to be found at the upper end of the income stream. Those at the lower levels cannot both believe in the system *and* have a sense of self-esteem.

Trends in Income and Wealth Inequality

There is no established theory of income distribution to guide us to an optimal amount of inequality. Anyone interested in studying the social structure of the

United States must begin by examining the disparities of income and wealth. **Income** is defined as the total monetary return to a household over a set period, usually a year, from all sources of wages, rent, interest, and gifts. Income refers to the flow of dollars within a year. Labor earnings (wages) constitute an ever-larger component of total income as one moves down the income ladder. Income tends not to be as unequally distributed as wealth. **Wealth** refers to the monetary value of the assets of a household minus its liabilities (or debt), which is its net worth. Wealth includes the accumulation of unspent past income and is a source from which capital income is realized.

Income

From 2000 through 2004, average income fell for middle-income wage earners, largely due to weak demand for labor caused by the recession of 2001 and its slow recovery. At the end of 2004 the economy had not recovered all the jobs lost since the last employment peak. In addition, greater numbers of people were underemployed, that is, working at part-time jobs because full-time jobs were not available. Declines in health and pension programs eroded the income of workers, especially those in the middle- and lower-income brackets. Over the same period, executive compensation soared. From 1992 to 2003 the median chief executive officer received an 80.8 percent raise, while the median worker's average hourly wage rose 8.7 percent.[35] The unbalanced nature of the tax cuts during the George W. Bush administration has redistributed after-tax income from the bottom 99 percent to the top 1 percent.[36]

In 2003 the real median household income was $43,318, which means that half the households received more and half less. The upper income limit of the lowest 20 percent of households declined 1.9 percent between 2002 and 2003, from $18,326 to $17,984. At the other end, it took $85,941 to get into the top 20 percent in household income in 2002, which rose to $86,867 in 2003. The median earnings of men who worked full-time, year-round in 2003 was $40,668, the same as in 2002. Real earnings of women declined to $30,724 (0.6 percent) in 2003, the first decline since 1995.

Another way to look at the growth in inequality is to look at the change in real income in each quintile. The average income of households in the top quintile grew 34 percent, from $97,376 in 1980 (in 2003 dollars) to $147,078 in 2003 (see Table 7.1). During the same twenty-three-year period, the average income in the bottom quintile grew by only 6 percent, from $9,479 to $9,996. The significant gains made during the Clinton administration were only a memory and were still fading in 2004.

This unequal distribution is portrayed in Table 7.2, which reports the Gini indexes of the shares of aggregate income by each quintile. The **Gini index** pro-

Table 7.1   Mean Household Income by Quintile, 1980–2003 (constant 2003 dollars)

	Bottom Quintile	Second Quintile	Third Quintile	Fourth Quintile	Top Quintile
1980	9,479	22,876	37,652	55,439	97,376
1985	9,472	23,336	38,701	58,201	104,357
1990	9,819	24,606	40,644	61,279	118,920
1995	10,009	24,449	40,881	62,844	131,146
2000	10,849	27,090	45,113	70,130	151,969
2003	9,996	25,678	43,558	68,994	147,078

Source: Carmen DeNavas-Walt, Bernadette Proctor, and Robert J. Mills, "Income, Poverty, and Health Insurance Coverage in the United States: 2003," *Current Population Reports* (Washington, D.C.: U.S. Census Bureau, August 2004), pp. 35–36.

vides a measure of income concentration by ranking households from the lowest to the highest based on income divided into groups of equal population size (20 percent each, or quintiles). The aggregate income of each group is then divided by the overall aggregate income to determine shares. The Gini index ranges from 0, indicating a perfect equality where everyone has an equal share, to 1, indicating a perfect inequality where all the income is received by one recipient or group of recipients. The data reveal that each of the quintiles from the lowest through the fourth declined in its share of aggregate income from 1980 to 2003, with the lowest losing the most ground and each successive fifth declining by a smaller percentage. The bottom quintile saw its share of aggregate income decline by 21 percent, while the second quintile declined by 16 percent, the third by 13 percent, and the fourth by 7 percent. Only the top fifth steadily increased its share of aggregate income over this period (by 13 percent). The top 5 percent actually increased its share of aggregate income by 34 percent. Since census data do not include capital gains, the total-income figures for those at the top are actually significantly higher.

Wealth

An examination of wealth provides a more complete picture of family economic well-being than does an examination of income. The richest man in the world is Bill Gates, who in his late forties is worth an estimated $46 billion, which is equal to the combined net worth of the bottom 40 percent of U.S. households.[37] Power

Table 7.2   Share of Aggregate Income Received by Household Quintile, 1980–2003 (constant 2003 dollars)

	Bottom Quintile	Second Quintile	Third Quintile	Fourth Quintile	Top Quintile	Gini Index
1980	4.3	10.3	16.9	24.9	43.7	0.403
1985	4.0	9.7	16.3	24.6	45.3	0.419
1990	3.9	9.6	15.9	24.0	46.6	0.428
1995	3.7	9.1	15.2	23.3	48.7	0.450
2000	3.6	8.9	14.8	23.0	49.8	0.462
2003	3.4	8.7	14.8	23.4	49.8	0.464
Change, 1980–2003	−0.9	−1.6	−2.1	−1.5	+6.1	

Source: Carmen DeNavas-Walt, Bernadette Proctor, and Robert J. Mills, "Income, Poverty, and Health Insurance Coverage in the United States: 2003," *Current Population Reports* (Washington, D.C.: U.S. Census Bureau, August 2004), pp. 36–37.

also flows from wealth. Fortunes can be a source of political and social influence that goes beyond having a high income. Large holdings of wealth can also be transferred to succeeding generations, which includes the transmission of power and influence associated with it. There is a correlation, although not a strong one, between wealth and age, since older individuals typically have worked more years and have accumulated more assets. There is also a correlation between income and wealth in that those with high income generally have more wealth.[38]

Through the first three-quarters of the twentieth century, distinctions based on class became progressively less important, and opportunities for upward mobility expanded. This stopped during the 1970s, and since about 1980 both poverty and wealth have been increasing together, indicating that the distance between the rich and poor is widening.

The most recent study completed by the Federal Reserve, using data from a triennial survey of consumer finances based on data compiled from 1989 through 2001, found that wealth is highly concentrated, with the top 1 percent of the wealthiest households owning one-third (32.7 percent) of all household net worth in 2001, up from 30.3 percent in 1989 (see Table 7.3). Note that those in the bottom half saw their share of ownership of assets remain flat, while those in the top half, from the fiftieth through the ninety-fourth percentile, saw their share of ownership declined somewhat. Only the top 5 percent increased their share of the nation's assets and wealth in this period, with the largest gains going to those in the

Table 7.3 Changes in Concentration of Wealth, 1989–2001 (percentage share of total)

Item	All Families, 2001 ($ billions)	0–50% 1989	0–50% 2001	50–89% 1989	50–89% 2001	90–94% 1989	90–94% 2001	95–99% 1989	95–99% 2001	99–100% 1989	99–100% 2001
Assets	482,053	5.5	5.6	32.4	29.9	12.6	11.7	22.3	23.4	27.2	29.5
Liquid	2,380.6	6.1	6.0	32.1	32.7	13.2	13.3	21.4	21.9	27.2	26.2
Private residence	13,063.6	9.9	12.3	55.5	50.6	12.8	12.2	15.2	16.0	6.6	9.0
Other residential real estate	2,256.5	2.6	1.9	30.4	26.8	19.9	11.7	27.9	30.5	19.3	29.1
Nonresidential real estate	2,289.3	0	0.6	11.6	14.5	9.6	9.1	25.9	35.2	55.1	40.7
Stocks	4,378.9	1.3	.5	15.8	11.4	10.2	9.9	31.3	25.3	41.5	52.9
Bonds	924.1	.3	.3	7.8	4.0	11.0	8.8	29.1	22.7	51.8	64.3
Savings bonds	139.8	6.7	4.1	47.6	45.5	19.1	10.1	19.3	21.9	7.3	18.5
RetQLiquid	5,720.3	6.0	3.3	37.9	36.4	15.1	17.6	26.3	29.1	14.8	13.6
Nonmutual	2,477.8	0.9	0.9	15.3	20.5	16.2	17.9	33.6	32.6	34.1	28.1
Other managed accounts	628.8	0.4	0.3	13.3	13.0	11.4	12.1	29.4	28.3	45.5	46.2
Other financial assets	412.4	5.6	4.1	18.3	17.1	14.9	5.3	32.9	33.1	28.4	40.4
Businesses	8,148.5	0.5	0.4	8.8	9.9	10.2	6.6	27.1	24.9	53.4	58.3
Automobiles	1,656.2	25.6	27.9	48.7	48.3	9.5	9.5	10.4	9.3	5.8	9.0
Liabilities	3,429.2	25.5	5.9	49.9	47.9	9.7	.6	9.5	11.6	5.4	5.9
Private residential debt	4,370.8	21.2	3.5	57.3	51.7	9.9	.1	8.7	11.1	2.9	4.7
Installment debt	714.0	41.2	8.0	43.5	37.5	5.5	.2	6.1	5.2	3.7	3.6
Credit card debt	195.7	42.8	9.8	49.0	41.6	5.0	.2	2.8	4.9	0.3	0.5
Equity	11,348.1	1.6	1.4	20.7	21.7	11.7	14.4	29.6	29.0	36.4	33.6
Income	7,400.8	24.4	22.9	40.7	38.1	8.9	9.2	12.3	15.3	13.7	14.5
Net worth	**42,389.2**	**2.7**	**2.8**	**29.9**	**27.4**	**13.0**	**12.1**	**24.1**	**25.0**	**30.3**	**32.7**

Source: Adapted from Arthur B. Kennickell, *Rolling Tide: Changes in the Distribution of Wealth in the U.S., 1989–2001*, Working Paper no. 393 (Washington, D.C.: Board of Governors of the Federal Reserve, 2003), pp. 17, 21.

Notes: Net worth = assets – liabilities. Financial assets = liquid cash + certificates of deposit + savings bonds + bonds + stocks + non–money market mutual funds + IRAs, Keogh accounts, and other pension accounts where withdrawals or loans may be taken + cash value of life insurance + equity holdings of annuities, trusts, and managed investment accounts + value of miscellaneous nonfinancial assets (e.g., antiques, artwork, etc.). Total income = total income for the year preceding the survey year. RetQLiquid = IRAs, Keogh accounts, and other pension accounts where withdrawals or loans may be taken.

top 1 percent. As the table indicates, half the families in the country have less than 3 percent of the nation's wealth to divide between them. Those in the top 1 percent have more wealth to divide between them (32.7 percent) than does the bottom 90 percent of the people (2.8 percent + 27.4 percent). And the top 5 percent have a larger share of the wealth (57.7 percent) than 94 percent of the population combined.

The top 1 percent significantly increased their share of holdings in stocks, bonds, and business investments, including equity in commercial real estate holdings. The wealthiest 1 percent owned approximately $2.3 trillion in stocks in 2001, roughly 53 percent of all individually held shares. They also owned 64 percent of bonds and about 31 percent of all financial assets held by families (which includes cash, stocks, bonds, and other securities). For the bottom 90 percent of the households, homes (their largest investment) and automobiles were the most important assets. Mortgages were by far their major liability. Money held in checking accounts and the cash value of life insurance policies were a significant form of savings for this group. It is noteworthy that, with the significant increase in the stock market over the past several years, the share of stock and mutual funds owned by the bottom 90 percent declined between 1989 and 2001.

The effects of the Bush tax cuts are not included in Table 7.3, which includes data only through 2001. The cuts include a reduction in the top tax rate and the elimination of estate, capital gains, and dividend taxes, all of which favor the wealthy and have made money available for the stock market. While the stock market has rebounded, average real wages have continued to stagnate. Home values, which are not a major factor in the holdings of the ultra-rich, although they are the largest share of wealth for middle-income families, have surged in recent years. Interest rates could rebound with a stronger economy, sending real estate prices downward, however. President Bush's tax cut programs have especially benefited those at the top of the wealth pyramid, which will increase the gap between the affluent and the poor.

The Lorenz Curve and Income and Wealth Inequality

A **Lorenz curve** can be used to measure the degree of inequality in a given population by plotting a cumulative percentage of income against a cumulative percentage of population (see Figure 7.1). If every household had the same income and wealth, the distribution would follow the 45 degree line of complete equality. Any variance from equality will result in the graph falling below the line of equality. The shaded area shows the amount of income inequality. The larger this area, the more unequal is the distribution of income. If there were no government policies to transfer income from the rich to the poor, income inequality would be even greater.

Figure 7.1 Lorenz Curve Showing Cumulative Percentage of Income and Wealth, 1995

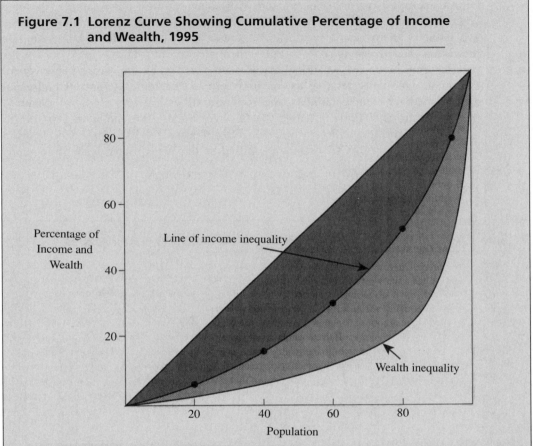

If everyone had the same income and wealth, the distribution would follow the 45 degree complete equality line. The darker shaded area shows the amount of income inequality. The lighter shaded area shows the inequality in the distribution of wealth. The larger the shaded area, the greater the inequality.

How Does the United States Compare with Other OECD Countries?

The United States consistently ranks as one of the most unequal countries when compared to other developed countries. However, since each country develops unique policy approaches for underwriting various social welfare programs, cross-country comparisons must be treated with some caution. For example, in some countries, like the United States, the poor may receive monetary benefits for housing, while in another country subsidized housing may be provided. Many countries provide a mix of goods (e.g., health care for everyone), largely paid for by tax receipts. Any given cross-national comparison based on income alone may over- or understate inequality relative to consumption. In developing countries and especially for lower-income families, income inequalities are very close to consumption inequalities.[39] Table 7.4 uses the Gini coefficient, the standard statistic, to measure income inequality in nineteen Organization for Economic Cooperation and Development (OECD) nations identified by the World Bank as "high-income" nations.

Table 7.4   Gini Index Comparison of High-Income OECD Nations, 2003

	Average Annual Real Growth (% of GDP), 1990–2003	Gini Index	Percentage Share of Income or Consumption	
			Lowest 20%	Highest 20%
Denmark	2.0	24.7	8.3	35.8
Japan	−0.5	24.9	10.6	35.7
Sweden	1.8	25.0	9.1	36.6
Belgium	1.8	25.0	8.3	37.3
Finland	2.0	26.9	9.6	40.2
Germany	1.6	28.3	8.5	36.9
Austria	1.7	30.0	8.1	38.5
Korea, Rep.	4.8	31.6	7.9	37.5
Spain	3.8	32.5	7.5	40.3
Netherlands	2.4	32.6	7.3	40.1
France	1.5	32.9	7.2	40.2
Canada	1.5	33.1	7.0	40.4
Switzerland	1.1	33.1	6.9	40.3
Australia	1.9	35.2	5.9	41.3
Greece	7.5	35.4	7.1	43.6
Italy	3.4	36.0	6.5	42.0
United Kingdom	2.8	36.0	6.1	44.0
New Zealand	1.6	36.2	6.4	43.8
United States	2.0	40.8	5.4	45.8

Source: World Bank, *World Development Report 2005* (New York: Oxford University Press, 2004), pp. 258–261.

The data indicate that someone in the top quintile in Denmark received an income 4.3 times that of someone in the bottom quintile. The average gap between the highest and lowest OECD quintiles is 4.8 to 1.0. By comparison, in the United States the same income ratio was 8.4 to 1.0, or 40 percent greater. The proportional distance between the bottom and top quintiles is about twice as large in the United States as in Denmark, Japan, Sweden, Belgium, and Finland. The household income ratio of the ninetieth percentile to the tenth percentile was 11.22 to 1.0.[40] In the United States, income inequality is much greater than in most OECD nations, and is more unequally distributed than in any other high-income OECD nation. The greater inequality cannot be said to have stimulated faster economic growth of GDP in the United States, which averaged 2 percent after inflation while the average growth rate of OECD countries was 2.4 percent.

The variation in the Gini index in each country is illustrative of the fact that the distribution of income is fundamentally the outcome of the political and economic choices made by decisionmakers. There has been a pattern of an increase in inequality throughout the OECD nations. However, the increase has been greatest in those nations that emphasize a laissez-faire approach to capitalism, such as the United States and the United Kingdom.

Those OECD countries that have more corporatist institutions, such as Belgium, Sweden, and Denmark, together with a greater tendency to intervene with social welfare programs, have experienced much smaller increases in inequality. The resurgence of income inequality in U.S. society is abrupt enough to be called the "great U-turn" by Bennett Harrison and Barry Bluestone, who place the beginning of the increased inequality in the early 1970s.[41]

The most comprehensive analysis of income inequality has been developed by the Luxembourg Income Study project, which uses census survey data from OECD nations and finds that the most corporatist countries have a less unequal distribution of income. The study confirms that inequality generally declined throughout all the OECD countries until about 1974, after which inequality began to rise. Since that time "the living standards of the least well-off families tended to decline as overall inequality rose."[42] The study also finds evidence that the income shares of the middle classes have declined.

Child poverty is a particular concern of all governments, because children are not responsible for their life situation. It is also generally accepted that deprivation may limit cognitive and social development of children, limiting their life chances. As might be expected from the tables above, the highest child poverty rates are found in the United States, Turkey, Italy, and the United Kingdom, and the lowest are found in the Nordic countries and Belgium (see Table 7.5).

Children living in the richest U.S. households are by a large margin the most affluent of any industrialized country. Those children living in poor U.S. house-

Table 7.5 Variation in OECD Child Poverty Rates

	Child Poverty Rate	Single Parent, Working	Two Parents, One Worker	Two Parents, Both Working	Employment Rate (%)
Finland	2.1	3.0	3.5	1.5	67.7
Sweden	2.7	3.8	6.0	0.8	75.3
Denmark	3.4	10.0	3.6	0.4	75.9
Belgium	4.1	11.4	2.8	0.6	59.7
Norway	4.4	4.6	3.9	0.1	77.5
France	7.1	13.3	7.3	2.1	62.0
Netherlands	9.1	17.0	4.7	1.2	72.1
Germany	10.6	32.5	5.6	1.3	65.9
Australia	10.9	9.3	8.9	5.0	68.9
Greece	12.3	16.3	15.1	5.0	55.6
Canada	14.2	26.5	18.1	3.7	70.9
United Kingdom	18.6	26.3	19.3	3.3	71.3
Italy	18.8	24.9	21.2	6.1	54.9
Turkey	19.7	16.3	17.8	14.4	45.1
United States	23.2	38.6	30.5	7.3	73.1
OECD (15)	10.7	16.9	11.2	3.5	66.3

Source: Society at a Glance: OECD Social Indicators (Paris: OECD, 2003), pp. 53, 31.
Note: Poverty is defined as the share of children living in households earning less than 50 percent of the median income.

Case Study: Global Inequalities

Not only are the gaps between rich and poor in the United States wider than in the past, but similar pressures that increase inequality are being felt worldwide as well. United Nations (UN) surveys have concluded that the wealthiest and the poorest people—both within and among countries—are living in increasingly separate worlds. The UN's *Human Development Report 2002* found that incomes are distributed more unequally across the world population (with a Gini coefficient of 0.66) than in countries with the highest inequality (e.g., Brazil has a Gini coefficient of 0.61). The world population's richest 5 percent receive 114 times the income of the poorest 5 percent. The world's richest 1 percent receive as much as the poorest 57 percent. The wealthiest 25 million Americans have as much income as almost 2 billion of the world's poorest combined.

continues

Case Study   continued

The UN's *Human Development Report 1996* found that many of the most equitable societies are in Asia, where economic growth has been the fastest and division of national wealth has been the most equitable. Several economies in Asia, including Japan, Indonesia, Hong Kong, Malaysia, the Republic of Korea, and Singapore, have maintained rapid economic growth together with relatively low inequality. The report found that during the past three decades, "every country that was able to combine and sustain rapid growth did so by investing first in schools, skills and health while keeping the income gap from growing too wide."

A central theme of the UN's 2002 report is that, contrary to the conventional wisdom, income and wealth inequality are harmful to economic growth. "The new insight is that an equitable distribution of public and private resources can enhance the prospects for further growth."

The 2002 report also found that:

- The net worth of the world's richest 358 billionaires is equal to the combined annual incomes of the poorest 45 percent of the world's population (2.3 billion people).
- Eighty-nine countries are worse off economically than they were a decade ago. Seventy developing countries have lower incomes than they did twenty-five years ago. In nineteen countries, per capita income is below the 1960 level.

Branko Milanovic analyzed data on a global scale using household surveys and concluded that an important increase in inequality, from 1988 to 1993, was caused by slower growth of rural incomes in populous Asian countries compared to OECD countries, as well as by rising urban-rural income differences in China and by falling incomes in transition countries. Xavier Sala-i-Martin produced a study based on aggregate income and estimates of within-country distributions of income between rich and poor, suggesting that income inequality was actually falling in the 1980s and 1990s.

Amartya Sen, a Nobel Prize–winning economist, replied to the debate regarding whether inequality is increasing or decreasing by noting:

> Even if the poor were to get just a little richer, this would not necessarily imply that the poor were getting a fair share of the potentially vast benefits of global economic interrelations. It is not adequate to ask whether international inequality is getting marginally larger or smaller. In the contemporary world—or to protest against the unfair sharing of benefits of global cooperation—it is not necessary to show that the massive inequality or distributional unfairness is also getting marginally larger. This is a separate issue altogether.

Sources: United Nations Development Programme, *Human Development Report 1996* (New York: Oxford University Press, 1996); United Nations Development Programme, *Human Development Report 2002* (New York: Oxford University Press, 2002), pp. 10, 19, 34; Branko Milanovic "True World Income Distribution, 1988 and 1993: First Calculation Based on Household Surveys Alone" (New York: World Bank, 1999); Xavier Salai-i-Martin "The World Distribution of Income" (estimated from individual country distributions) (New York: Columbia University Press, 2002); Amartya Sen, "How to Judge Globalism," *American Prospect,* January 2002.

holds are poorer than the children of any other country except Mexico. The gap is greater in the United States largely because U.S. taxes and transfer programs are less generous than in other OECD countries. In the United States, taxes and transfers reduce the Gini coefficient by 23 percent (from 0.48 to 0.37).[43] If the United States redistributed as much income as do the other OECD countries, the dispersion of disposable incomes would be close to the middle range of the countries represented.

Through the beginning of the twenty-first century, actual market incomes in the United States were very comparable to those in France or Germany. The reason for this anomaly is that although senior U.S. business executives receive much higher compensation than their counterparts elsewhere, other countries provide many more benefits for those who are unemployed. As a result of low government transfers to the unemployed in the United States, unemployment has more serious consequences than in most European nations. Since job loss is more disastrous in the United States, labor is more inclined to accept wage cuts than in Europe, where more generous public social expenditures make the prospect of losing a job altogether less severe. The compensation for employment for many Americans who work for low wages is not very large. Nonetheless, when the relatively high number of individuals with zero earnings are included in OECD national averages, the Gini coefficient for the United States is not too dissimilar from coefficients for other high-income countries. Since 1980, inequality has increased somewhat in all OECD countries. About half the countries have taken steps to prevent a significant increase in inequality. Actions taken in the United States and the United Kingdom have, as a whole, actually reduced the equalizing effects of taxes and transfers.[44]

What Is the Relationship Between Inequality and Economic Growth?

Simon Kuznets received the Nobel Prize in 1971 for research on economic growth and income distribution. He found that economic growth in poor countries increased the income gap between rich and poor people. However, once a threshold level of maturity was crossed in its transition from a rural to an industrial and urbanized society, economic growth would reduce income disparity. Thus Kuznets argued that income distribution follows a U-curve in which economic expansion makes poor people relatively poorer during the initial stage of a country's development. The concentration of workers in urban areas encourages both union and political organizations to press for worker rights, the regulation of business, progressive taxes, and public social expenditures, all of which reduce inequality. Kuznets presented historical data to show, for example, that income inequality in the United States peaked in the 1890s, and did not begin to decline until after World War I.[45] Later research by Robert Lampman on the distribution of wealth, as opposed to income, found a similar pattern of increasing inequality of wealth, with a decline in the gap occurring between the late 1920s and continuing through the next several decades.[46]

However, the United States is something of an anomaly since it is the richest OECD country and has the most inequality. But as Gary Burtless and Christopher Jencks point out, "If we eliminate the United States and look at the sixteen remaining big OECD countries, the richer ones have *less* inequality than the poorer ones, as the Kuznets model predicts."[47] Nevertheless, a model that would predict lower inequality in the United States, which is at variance with the facts, is inadequate.

Some investigators have found evidence of a cycle in which wealthy power elites wage a counteroffensive to reestablish their dominant control.[48] Noted economist John Galbraith suggests that there is struggle in which the elites, in defense of their social and economic advantage, must now persuade the majority of voters in a democracy that government must accommodate the needs of the haves.[49] The late Arthur Okun focused on ways in which economic inequality can affect growth. He noted that political institutions proclaim the equality of individuals and distribute rights and privileges universally.[50] Economic institutions inevitably create inequalities in material welfare. The political principles of democracy and the economic principles of capitalism create tensions. Whenever the market denies a worker a minimum standard of living or when the wealthy use their power and privilege to obtain more of the rights that are supposedly equally distributed, then "dollars transgress on rights," in Okun's expression.

Efforts to solve the problem involve a tradeoff in which greater equality has been achieved only at heavy costs in efficiency, while in other cases greater efficiency has been achieved only by severely restraining civil liberties. In Okun's view the U.S. system of mixed capitalism is a workable compromise in which the market has its place as long as democratic institutions are able to keep it within acceptable boundaries. He felt that the democratic concern for human dignity could be directed at reducing economic deprivation in the United States through progressive taxes and transfer payments, and removing certain barriers to capital.

Although there are many theories on the relationship between inequality and growth, the evidence regarding whether or not inequality reduces growth is inconclusive. There is some evidence that inequality can reduce growth by preventing the poor from providing an adequate health diet for their children, thereby limiting their potential. Many will have insufficient capital to invest in education or to launch a small business. If returns to these investments would have been high, their lack of availability will limit growth. Or the unequal economic status may breed strong social tensions that discourage productive capital investments.

How Does Economic Inequality Threaten Democratic Equality?

Aaron Bernstein wrote an article summarizing research indicating that social mobility has declined in recent decades.[51] Corporate strategies to control labor costs, such as hiring temporary employees, fighting unions, dismantling internal career ladders, reducing benefits, and outsourcing, are successful in restraining consumer prices. Unfortunately, these tactics trap about 34 million workers, over a quarter of the labor force, in low-wage and usually dead-end jobs. Many middle-income employees face fewer opportunities as work is shifted to temporary agencies and outsourced jobs overseas. The result, according to Bernstein, has been an erosion of one of the most cherished values in the United States: the ability to move up the economic ladder over one's lifetime.

The myth of income mobility has always exceeded the reality. But it is true that there has been considerable intergenerational mobility. One study cited by Bernstein shows, for example, that 23 percent of men from families in the bottom 25 percent of the economic ladder make it into the top 25 percent by the end of their working careers. Bernstein cites a new survey that finds that this number has dropped to only 10 percent. Fewer children of lower-class families are making it to even moderate affluence.

A study by the Federal Reserve Bank of Boston analyzed families' incomes over three decades and found that the number of people who stayed in the same income bracket—whether the bottom or the top—jumped to 53 percent in the 1990s, up from 36 percent in the 1970s. The income bracket persisted even after accounting for the major growth of two-earner families. For mobility to increase in relative terms, someone has to move down the pecking order to make room for another to move up. The new reality has a greater impact on those at the bottom, who tend to stay poor because of the creation of millions of jobs that pay rates at around the poverty-line wage of $8.70 an hour. A college degree remains out of reach for most students from low-income families. The number of poor students who get a degree—about 5 percent—has been stable for almost thirty years.

Business strategy is putting a lid on the intergenerational progress that has been a part of the American Dream, but public policy also plays a role. Paul Krugman speculates about what policies someone who controlled government and wanted to entrench the advantages of the haves over the have-nots might engage in.[52] One policy initiative would definitely be to get rid of the estate tax, to allow fortunes to be passed on to the next generation untouched. Other policies would include a reduction in tax rates on corporate profits and on unearned income such as dividends and capital gains. Tax rates would be reduced on people with high incomes, shifting the burden to the payroll tax and other revenue sources that bear most heavily on people with lower incomes. On the spending side, he suggests that one should cut back on health care for the poor and on federal aid for higher education, which would result in rising tuitions and make it more difficult for people with low incomes to acquire the education essential to upward mobility.

Current policies of closing off routes to upward mobility lead Thomas Piketty and Emmanuel Saez to conclude that current policies will eventually create "a class of rentiers in the U.S., whereby a small group of wealthy but untalented children controls vast segments of the U.S. economy and penniless, talented children simply can't compete."[53]

Economic Inequality and Life Expectancy

The United States is the wealthiest major country in the world in terms of per capita GDP (and second only to Luxembourg overall). Since longevity is associated with income, we might hypothesize that Americans would have a longer life expectancy than those living in other large industrialized and relatively wealthy OECD states. However, we find that life expectancy in the United States, at age sixty-five for both males and females, is just about in the middle of the thirty OECD countries. Throughout the twentieth century until about 1980, the United States was the leader in increases in life expectancy due to improvements in public health and medicine. Since then, life expectancy has increased more rapidly for citizens of all other industrial nations.

A higher GDP per capita would suggest that the United States has more resources that it can dedicate to education, medical care, and other services associated with longevity. However, while the average GDP per capita is high, those in the top quintiles receive a much larger share compared to other OECD nations. At the lower levels of the income distribution, U.S. incomes now fall in the middle of the OECD countries. Median family income growth has slowed dramatically since 1980, at the very time inequality in the distribution of income began to surge in the United States.

Richard Wilkinson's original research, focused on the relationship between overall levels of inequality (rather than individual income levels) and mortality across OECD countries, has inspired much of the subsequent research on the subject.[54] In a series of papers, Wilkinson found negative associations between inequality and mortality that persisted even after he controlled for cross-country differences in median income.[55] Several scholars have focused on the United States and have documented similar findings between mortality rates and inequality across states and metropolitan areas within the United States after controlling for income level.[56] Metropolitan areas with low per capita incomes and low levels of income inequality have lower mortality rates than metropolitan areas with high median incomes and high levels of income inequality. Although many studies now show that inequality and health are linked in OECD countries, the reasons for the association are still debated in the United States, the United Kingdom, and Brazil.

Wilkinson and his colleagues suggest several reasons for the association. They suggest that the larger the income gap between the rich and the poor, the more reluctant the affluent are to pay taxes for public services they will likely never use or for which their payment in taxes will significantly exceed the benefit they expect to receive. A reduction in public expenditures on public health, hospitals, schools, or other basic services will be negligible on the life expectancies of the wealthy, but it will significantly impact poor people's life expectancies. Second, an income gap is inversely related to social cohesion (i.e., the larger the income inequality, the lower the social cohesion in society). Greater socioeconomic equality is associated with higher levels of social involvement. Social isolation, which increases with inequality, is a documented health risk factor.[57]

Various researchers have challenged Wilkinson's conclusions and insist that it is not clear that inequality is due to the rich getting richer rather than the poor getting poorer. They maintain that while it is demonstrable that the rich are getting richer, the poor, it is alleged, are not getting poorer in absolute terms, but only in "relative" terms. They concede that in theory the rich may be less inclined to support taxes for items that will not benefit themselves, or that the poor will find their concerns being crowded out by the demands of the affluent. But benefits may also result from positive externalities created by the wealthy, who may demand the development of more advanced medical technology or crime prevention.

Michael Marmot has written extensively on the study of social inequality and health and finds that diseases that are commonly thought of as diseases of affluence—like heart disease, associated with high-calorie and high-fat diets and lack of physical activity—are actually most prevalent among the least-affluent people in rich societies.[58] He claims that social inequality frequently shadows the more immediate cause of death, whether it is listed as heart disease, diabetes, accidental injury, or homicide. The lower one is in the socioeconomic hierarchy, the worse one's health and the shorter one's life is likely to be. Most of the top causes of death are not "equal opportunity killers." They tend to strike poor people at an earlier age than they do rich people, the less educated more than they do the highly educated, people of color more than they do white people—generally, those people lower rather than higher on the income ladder. A poor person with a health problem is about half as likely to see a physician as a high-income individual. Adults living in low-income areas are more than twice as likely to be hospitalized for a health problem that could have been treated with timely outpatient care, compared to adults living in high-income areas.[59]

Marmot's best-known research is a study of health among British civil servants. Since civil servants share similar office work environments and job security, he expected to find only very minor health differences among them. However, he found an unexpected significant increase in mortality with each step down the job hierarchy—including from the highest to the second highest grade. Over a decade, employees in the lowest grade were three times as likely to die as those in the highest grade. Those in the lower grades had a higher incidence of risk factors such as smoking, unhealthy diet, and lack of exercise. But even after controlling for these "lifestyle" risk factors, over half the mortality gap remained. Those at lower levels were less likely to express satisfaction with their work situation and were more likely to indicate they felt they had less "control over their working lives," while those at a higher level were likely to complain of working at a fast pace. Marmot concluded that psychosocial factors—the psychological costs of being lower in the hierarchy—played a significant role in the mortality gap.[60]

Research has definitely found a relation between economic inequality and life expectancy. Cross-country research clearly suggests that economic inequality may reduce life expectancy for lower-income workers. The reduction in life expectancy is difficult to calculate and projections are very tentative. Burtless and Jencks estimate that inequality reduces life expectancy for low-income individuals by about five months.[61] In this debate, poverty and inequality are closely related. Whether public policy focuses primarily on the elimination of poverty or on reduction of income inequality, neither goal is likely to be achieved without the other.

Economic Inequality and Justice

When Thomas Jefferson wrote that it was self-evident and that all men are created equal and are endowed by their creator with certain inalienable rights, and that government's purpose was to promote the "general" welfare, he was expressing principles of justice that are the essence of U.S. democracy. Politics would be the method by which average citizens would work out common problems through the instrument of government, whose function would be to promote the safety and happiness of the people. The American Revolution ushered in a democracy that gave hope to the exploited and downtrodden as the enemy of unchecked privilege.

This was not an empty idea, and Americans have made great strides toward equality in several areas. For example, Americans embrace the notions of equality before the law; one person, one vote; and equality of opportunity. As the income gap has increased, however, awareness that economic inequalities may undermine all the various forms of equality has increased.

The political system of democracy has a bias in favor of equality. The principle of individual freedom finds its expression for many in capitalism, which leads to vast economic inequalities and threatens to bring about an aristocracy of wealth. Power flows from wealth. And those who control vast amounts of money may translate their economic power to political power to increase their dominance.

As the functional theory of inequality suggests, inequality can perform a positive function in society by motivating individuals to produce more under the hope of financial reward. On the other hand, the functional theory must be qualified, since it assumes perfect market conditions and does not take into account the differences in inheritances, power, or economic rent seeking that occur in imperfect markets. That is, much of the inequality is not based on merit in that many members of society have no control over the conditions of the competition. Nor is it clear that the rewards for "winning" and the penalties for "losing" are fair. The conclusion is that we do not want perfect equality, or a society that is so equal as to be unjust. We are left to search for an optimal amount of inequality.

Many who argue in favor of a progressive income tax, an inheritance tax, or social welfare programs seldom emphasize Keynesian arguments based on economic theory.[62] They usually support increasing taxes on capital gains or other sources of income, because they believe the current level of income and wealth inequality is unfair. Although sound economic principles may be called on to support a national health insurance program, a higher minimum wage, or more college tuition assistance for low-income families, usually moral arguments are stressed. People should not be denied medical care or the ability to go to college because their parents cannot afford it. Such moral arguments are often supplemented by practical arguments that point out that investments in college subsidies for low-income individuals will allow them to become more productive and pay more in taxes. Raising the minimum wage helps keep families together and reduces welfare dependency. But these arguments often appear to be secondary. Egalitarians would probably favor national health care and a higher minimum wage even if it had no effect on longevity or did not reduce welfare dependency.

Those opposed to the proposals for less inequality do not defend large disparities in income as positive. Their economic arguments tend to be limited to concerns, expressed by Arthur Okun, that the transfer of resources from one group to another has inherent inefficiencies that exact a tradeoff between equity and efficiency. Their main contention tends to be that the market is fairer at distributing income than is the government. Empirical evidence that redistribution has fewer costs than they assumed is rarely persuasive. Like their egalitarian rivals, they argue from a moral perspective that emphasizes their belief that government interference unfairly punishes those who have been more successful in competing for money while it rewards dependent behavior.

Philosophers have debated the issue of justice and the distribution of income throughout history. John Rawls's answer to the problem of determining a fair distribution of goods states the egalitarian position well. He contends that the fairest distribution of goods is one that individuals would freely choose, or agree to, if they had no knowledge of their own ultimate position in society.[63] If individuals were behind a "veil of ignorance" and did not know their race, sex, social class, innate talents, and psychological propensities, they would only agree to those inequalities that benefited everyone, but especially the least advantaged. Such inequalities would be those required to call forth sufficient talent and effort in the production of social goods that would improve the lot of the least advantaged as much as the most advantaged. Rawls's attention to the least advantaged originates from a desire to protect against the worst outcome that we can imagine for our-selves. Since it is possible that we could find ourselves at the bottom of society, we would want to ensure that it is not a terrible place to be. His assumption is that most are risk-adverse and would want to avoid a very bad outcome even if that meant doing with less should we be fortunate to end up near the top.

Robert Nozick makes the opposite case, pointing out that most people may not be as risk-adverse as Rawls assumes.[64] Also, the process of redistributing income from the more to the less advantaged requires interfering with the basic liberties of those who happen to begin (whether for reasons of history, individual effort, or inheritance) with certain advantages. As long as the *process* is fair, everyone should be permitted to keep whatever they have.

John Kennedy lamented the practical problem for public policy when he said, "If a free society cannot help the many who are poor, it cannot save the few who are rich."[65] Distributive justice is basically an ethical problem. The National Conference of Catholic Bishops issued a statement that noted, "The moral measure of any economy is not simply the information shared, the wealth created, the trade encouraged, but how the lives and dignity of the poor and vulnerable, the hungry and destitute are protected and promoted."[66]

Policies to Reduce Poverty and Inequality

The fact that an economy is efficient says nothing about the distribution of income. Competitive markets may give rise to a very unequal distribution, which may leave some individuals with insufficient resources on which to live. One of the more important activities of democratic government is to reduce poverty and redistribute income. This is the express purpose of policies such as the Earned Income Tax Credit, Medicaid, and Social Security.

Conclusion

The American Revolution ushered in a new age of democracy. The democratic ideal, based on the fundamental principle of equality, sweeps aside all claims of special power and privilege. Democracy as a form of government is an ideal to be pursued rather than a goal fully achieved merely through recognition of the rights to free speech or the right to vote. The framers of the Constitution dedicated themselves to the proposition that all men are created equal, even though some were slaves and others without property were denied the right to vote. The United States became more democratic when it abolished ownership of property as a requirement to be a voting member of society. U.S. democracy advanced further when the Civil War abolished slavery, and when civil rights legislation a century later gave substance to the ideal of political equality.

Democracy, as the Constitution attests, is based on compromise between society's elites and nonelites. The elites, not surprisingly, resist with every means at their disposal any movement toward greater equality that challenges their interests. Control over the political institutions is always central to the struggle, since the elites can use the political institutions to influence the perceptions, values, and political preferences of the nonelites by their dominant position as opinion-makers in mass communication. Through money and organization, the elites more than make up for their small numbers, while the poor, lacking both resources and organization, are not as powerful a political group as their numbers might suggest.

In a capitalist society, power flows from money. The financially powerful naturally seek ways to leverage their wealth and status into political power. Through the late nineteenth and early twentieth century, theories of laissez-faire capitalism were put forward as justification for preventing the federal government from "interfering" in the economy, despite the fact that monopolistic and oligopolistic market power was clearly being used to increase the political power of those who ran the giant corporations. Government should not interfere in business, corporate leaders said, because government was not competent, and the interference was undemocratic in that it limited the freedoms of those who were creating the nation's wealth. The gap in income and wealth distribution grew in the 1920s.

The Great Depression encouraged a rethinking of economic theory. Keynesian theory showed that excessive economic inequality could not only hinder economic growth and stability, but also threaten the very survival of democratic systems. because the overwhelming majority of Americans also depend on employment for their economic security, Franklin Roosevelt embarked on a series of policies, such as adoption of a minimum wage, pro–labor union legislation, unemployment compensation, and Social Security, that worked to reduce economic inequality. Since about 1980, inequality in both income and wealth distribution has increased markedly. The increase, which has been greater in the United States than in other OECD countries, is due to a variety of factors, including globalization, oligopolistic power, and changes in tax and social welfare legislation designed to redistribute income toward those already at the top.

The functional theory of inequality holds that economic inequality has a beneficial effect in a capitalist society. The theory has several drawbacks, however, that justify government involvement to redress the power imbalance of dominant economic groups. Economic theory makes no claim that capitalism distributes income and wealth in a just fashion.

To the extent that the political apparatus becomes dependent on a financial elite, democracy is undermined. In the extreme case, the old hereditary aristocracy is merely traded for a financial aristocracy. An economic elite with inordinate political power moves the democratic ideal of meaningful political equality further from our grasp.

Let us be clear that some inequality is not only inevitable but also even necessary. However, a healthier democracy would result from less inequality than now exists. Policies that would reduce inequality would include raising the minimum wage, strengthening antipoverty programs such as the Earned Income Tax Credit, strengthening the social safety net to include health care, and increasing rather than decreasing progressiveness in the tax code. Some of these policies will be addressed more fully in the next chapter.

Questions for Discussion

1. Democracy is based on the principle of equality, while capitalism as an economic system inevitably leads to inequality. Are the two systems incompatible and destined to produce frustration or even cynicism? Will either capitalism or democracy dominate?
2. What are the strengths and weaknesses of the functional theory of inequality? Do the qualifications destroy the value of the theory? Why or why not?
3. Can you explain what public policy decisions were made throughout Europe and the OECD countries that have resulted in greater equality than is present in the United States?
4. If you were to recommend public policies to reduce inequality in the United States, what would you recommend? What are the negative consequences of your proposals?
5. Is there such a thing as an optimal amount of inequality? What criteria would you use to determine it?
6. Why is inequality increasing in the United States?

Useful Websites

Bureau of Labor Statistics, Consumer Expenditure Survey, http://stats.bls.gov/cex/home.htm.
Census Bureau, http://www.census.gov/population/socdemo.

U.S. Office of Management and Budget, http://www.whitehouse.gove/omb/budget.
World Trade Organization (WTO), http://www.wto.org.

Suggested Readings

Arjons, Maxime Ladaique, and Mark Pearson. *Growth, Inequality, and Social Protection.* Labor Market and Social Policy Occasional Paper no. 51. Paris: Organization for Economic Cooperation and Development, 2001.

Burtless, Gary. "Effects of Growing Wage Disparities and Changing Family Composition on the U.S. Income Distribution." *European Economic Review* 43 (May 1999).

Burtless, Gary, and Timothy Smeeding. "The Level, Trend, and Composition of Poverty." In Sheldon Danziger and Robert Haveman, eds., *Understanding Poverty: Progress and Problems.* Cambridge: Harvard University Press, 2001.

Danziger, Sheldon, and Jane Waldfogel, eds. *Securing the Future: Investing in Children from Birth to College.* New York: Russell Sage, 2000.

Forster, Michael, and Michele Pellizzari. *Trends and Driving Factors in Income Distribution and Poverty in the OECD Area.* Occasional Paper no. 42. Paris: Organization for Economic Cooperation and Development, 2000.

Gerreira, Francisco H.G. *Inequality and Economic Performance: A Brief Overview to Theories of Growth and Distribution.* Washington, D.C.: World Bank, 1999.

Kawachi, Ichiro, and Bruce P. Kennedy. *The Health of Nations: Why Inequality Is Harmful to Your Health.* New York: New Press, 2002.

Notes

1. *Labor Journal,* October 17, 1941, p. 18.

2. See Page Smith, *A New Age Now Begins* (New York: McGraw-Hill, 1976), for a detailed discussion of the importance of this idea.

3. Garry Wills develops the thesis that the idea of all men being created equal was more than just rhetoric. See Garry Wills, *Inventing America: Jefferson's Declaration of Independence* (New York: Doubleday, 1978).

4. Thomas Jefferson, *The Papers of Thomas Jefferson,* vol. 8, edited by Julian P. Boyd (Princeton: Princeton University Press, 1953), p. 682.

5. Ibid.

6. See http://www.quotegarden.com/poverty.html.

7. Alexis de Tocqueville, *Democracy in America,* cited in William Ebenstein and Alan Ebenstein, *Great Political Thinkers* (New York: Harcourt Brace, 1991), p. 641.

8. John Maynard Keynes, *The General Theory of Employment, Interest, and Money* (London: Macmillan, 1936), p. 372.

9. Thomas Frank, *What's the Matter with Kansas? How Conservatives Won the Heart of America* (New York: Metropolitan Books, 2004).

10. Robert Putnam, "The Strange Disappearance of Civic America," *American Prospect,* Winter 1996, pp. 34–48. See also Sidney Verba, Kay Schlozman, and Henry Brady, *Voice and Equality: Participation in American Politics* (Cambridge: Harvard University Press, 1996).

11. Associated Press, "Corporate PAC's Backed Republicans 10 to 1," *New York Times,* November 26, 2004.

12. Gary Burtless and Christopher Jencks, "American Inequality and Its Consequences," in Henry J. Aaron, James M. Lindsay, and Pietro S. Nivola, eds., *Agenda for the Nation* (Washington, D.C.: Brookings Institution, 2003), p. 62.

13. The Pew Research Center for the People and the Press reports that 84 percent of those making $75,000 or more are registered to vote, compared to just 66 percent of those earning $20,000–$29,000, and only 60 percent of those earning less than $20,000. See Pew Research Center for the People and the Press, *Evenly Divided and Increasingly Polarized: 2004 Political Landscape* (Washington, D.C.: Pew Research Center for the People and the Press, November 5, 2003), pt. 6, "Cynicism, Trust, and Participation," p. 5.

14. See http://www.quotegarden.com/politics.html.

15. See James Willis, Martin Primack, and Richard Baltz, *Explorations in Economics*, 3rd ed. (Redding, Calif.: CAT, 1990), p. 43.

16. Martin Dooley and Peter Gottschalk, "Earnings Inequality Among Males in the United States: Trends and the Effects of Labor Force Growth," *Journal of Political Economy* 92, no. 1 (1984): 59–89. For women the annual increase in wages was about 1 percent faster than for men. The gap between high- and low-wage females is increasing as well, just not as rapidly as for men.

17. Marvin Kosters and Murray Ross, "The Influence of Employment Shifts and New Job Opportunities on the Growth and Distribution of Real Wages," in Phillip Cagan and Eduardo Somensatto, eds., *Deficits, Taxes, and Economic Adjustments* (Washington, D.C.: American Enterprise Institute, 1987).

18. See Barry Bluestone and Bennett Harrison, *The Great American Job Machine: The Proliferation of Low Wage Employment in the U.S. Economy,* Report to the Joint Economic Committee of the U.S. Congress, December 1986.

19. Jared Bernstein, "Facts and Figures: Income," in Jared Bernstein, *The State of Working America 2004/2005* (Washington, D.C.: Economic Policy Institute, 2005), http://www.epinet.org, p. 2.

20. See Gary Burtless, "International Trade and the Rise in Earnings Inequality," *Journal of Economic Literature* 33 (June 1995): 800–816.

21. For a time, there was debate among scholars over whether wage inequality was increasing, and whether real wages had declined in absolute terms. The trends and data are now clear, and there is general agreement that both trends are occurring. See especially Bennett Harrison, Barry Bluestone, and Chris Tilly, "Wage Inequality Takes a Great U-Turn," *Challenge* 29 (March–April 1986): 26–32. See also Bennett Harrison and Barry Bluestone, *The Great U-Turn: Corporate Restructuring and the Polarizing of America* (New York: Basic Books, 1988).

22. Robert Putnam, "Bowling Alone: America's Declining Social Capital," *Journal of Democracy* (January 1995): 34–35.

23. See http://www.cookpolitical.com/races/report_pdfs/2004_house_competitive_oct8.pdf.

24. See, for example, Pew Research Center for the People and the Press, *Evenly Divided.* See also http://www.trinity.edu/mkearl/equalize3.jpg; *U.S. News and World Report,* August 7, 1989, p. 29; and more recently, Marc Suhrcke, *Preferences for Inequality: East vs. West,* Working Paper no. 89 (Florence: Unesco Innocenti Center, October 2001).

25. See especially Robert Heilbroner and Lester Thurow, *Economics Explained,* rev. ed. (Englewood Cliffs, N.J.: Prentice-Hall, 1994), pp. 216–218. Our discussion on the bias in favor of equality relies heavily on this source.

26. See http://www.quotegarden.com/humility.html.

27. Economic discrimination occurs when duplicate factors of production receive different payments for equivalent contributions to output. This definition is difficult to test because of the difficulty of measuring all the relevant market characteristics. For example, the average female earns less than the average male. Women are less likely to have majored in a technical subject than are men. It might not be discrimination if a woman with a high school diploma receives a lower salary than a man with a college degree (although discrimination might help in explaining their educational achievements). It is too simplistic to try to measure discrimination by merely comparing the typical incomes of different groups. The question is not, "Do women earn less than men?" but rather, "Do women earn less than men *with like market characteristics* (work experience, age, education, etc.)?"

28. We could achieve the same goal without yielding to inequality by financing the investment through taxation and government purchases (public investment) rather than through private investment through savings.

29. The functional theory of inequality is a variation on the **marginal productivity theory** (MPT) of distribution, which holds that the income of any factor will be determined by the contribution that each factor makes to the revenue of the endeavor. Its income will be higher or lower depending on the ability and willingness of the suppliers of land, labor, and capital to enter the market at different prices. But at each price, factors will earn amounts equal to the marginal revenue they produce. The result, in theory, is that there cannot be exploitation of any factor in a perfect market.

The functional theory challenges the assumption of the MPT that a perfect market exists. If it does not, then the earnings of each factor may not reflect their contribution to output. The MPT cannot explain the variation of incomes due to nonmarket factors such as discrimination, imperfect markets, and other factors.

30. Kingsley Davis and Wilbert Moore, *Some Principles of Stratification,* Reprint Series in Social Science (New York: Columbia University Press, 1993).

31. Ibid, p. 37.

32. James Madison, in *The Federalist* no. 10, clearly states that it is a primary function of governments to protect individual freedom, which will lead to inequalities in income based on differing abilities and interests. He notes that this is the basis for factions, which he laments. The most common and enduring source of factions is the unequal distribution of property. This poses a major dilemma for governmental administration.

33. Milton Friedman, *Capitalism and Freedom* (Chicago: University of Chicago Press, 1962), p. 167.

34. See Doug Bandow, "Doctors Operate to Cut Out Competition," *Business and Society Review,* no. 58 (Summer 1986): 4–10. Bandow illustrates that entry into the medical profession is essentially controlled through the use of licensing arrangements, which increase health care costs and decrease the options available to patients.

35. Bernstein, "Facts and Figures: Income."

36. Jared Bernstein, "Facts and Figures: Inequality," in Bernstein, *State of Working America 2004/2005.*

37. Mary H. Cooper, "Income Inequality," *CQ Researcher,* April 17, 1998, p. 341. See also *Forbes,* 2004 list of world's richest people, http://www.forbes.com/lists/results.jhtml.

38. Edward N. Wolff, *Top Heavy: A Study of the Increasing Inequality of Wealth in America* (New York: Twentieth Century Fund, 1995), p. 6.

39. Timothy Smeeding, *Globalization, Inequality, and the Rich Countries of the G-20: Evidence from the Luxembourg Income Study* (Syracuse, N.Y.: Maxwell School of Citizenship and Public Affairs, July 2002), p. 7.

40. Carmen DeNavas-Walt, Bernadette D. Proctor, and Robert J. Mills, "Income, Poverty, and Health Insurance Coverage in the United States: 2003," in U.S. Census Bureau, *Current Population Reports* (Washington, D.C.: U.S. Government Printing Office, August 2004), p. 36.

41. Harrison and Bluestone, *Great U-Turn.*

42. Francis Green, Andrew Henley, and Euclid Tsakalotos, *Income Inequality in Corporatist and Liberal Economies: A Comparison of Trends Within OECD Countries,* Studies in Economics (Canterbury, UK: University of Kent, November 1992), p. 13.

43. Burtless and Jencks, "American Inequality," p. 77.

44. Ibid., p. 80.

45. Simon Kuznets, "Economic Growth and Income Inequality," *American Economic Review* 45, no. 1 (March 1955): 1–28.

46. Robert J. Lampman, *The Share of Top Wealth-Holders in National Wealth, 1922–1956* (Princeton: Princeton University Press, 1962). Other research confirmed the Kuznets-Lampman research in various countries. See Peter Lindert and Jeffrey Williamson, *Explorations in Economic History* 22 (1985): 341–377.

47. Burtless, "International Trade," pp. 80–81 (emphasis in original).

48. Kevin Phillips, *Arrogant Capital: Washington, Wall Street, and the Frustration of American Politics* (Boston: Little, Brown, 1994). Phillips continues the theme in *American Dynasty: Aristocracy, Fortune, and the Politics of Deceit in the House of Bush* (New York: Viking, 2004). William E. Simon's *A Time for Truth* (New York: Reader's Digest Press, 1978) is sometimes cited as a call to arms for U.S. business to recover the privileges it lost after 1929.

49. See John Kenneth Galbraith, *The Culture of Contentment* (New York: Houghton Mifflin, 1992).

50. Arthur M. Okun, *Equality and Efficiency: The Big Tradeoff* (Washington, D.C.: Brookings Institution, 1975).

51. Aaron Bernstein, "Waking Up from the American Dream," *Business Week,* December 1, 2003.

52. Paul Krugman, "The Death of Horatio Alger," *The Nation,* January 5, 2004, p. 16.

53. As quoted in ibid.

54. See especially Richard G. Wilkinson, *Unhealthy Societies: The Afflictions of Inequality* (London: Routledge, 1996). See also B. Kennedy, I. Kawachi, and D. Prothrow-Stith, "Income Distribution and Mortality: Cross Sectional Ecological Study of the Robin Hood Index in the United States," *British Medical Journal* 312 (1996): 1004–1007.

55. See Ichiro Kawachi, Bruce Kennedy, and Richard Wilkinson, eds., *The Society and Population Healthreader,* vol. 1, *Income Inequality and Health* (New York: New Press, 1999).

56. George Kaplan, E. Pamuk, J. W. Lynch, R. D. Cohen, and J. L. Balfour, "Inequality in Income and Mortality in the United States: Analysis of Mortality and Potential Pathways," *British Medical Journal* 312 (1996): 999–1003. See also John Lynch, George Davey Smith, George Kaplan, and James House, "Income Inequality and Mortality: Importance to Health of Individual Income, Psychosocial Environment, or Material Conditions" *British Medical Journal* 320 (2000): 1200–1204.

57. See Thad Williamson, "Social Movements Are Good for Your Health," *Dollars and Sense,* May 2001, p. 7. See also Robert Putnam, *Bowling Alone: The Collapse and Revival of American Community* (New York: Simon and Schuster, 2000). Putnam analyzes

the decline of social ties in the United States. He argues that social ties and strong communities are important to human well-being, particularly in the area of health.

58. Michael Marmot, "The Social Pattern of Health and Disease," in David Blane, Eric Brunner, and Richard Wilkinson, eds., *Health and Social Organization: Towards a Health Policy for the Twenty-First Century* (New York: Routledge, 1996).

59. Alejandro Reuss, "Cause of Death: Inequality—Mortality Statics Analysis, United States—Statistical Data Included," *Dollars and Sense,* May 2001.

60. Marmot, "Social Pattern."

61. Burtless and Jencks, "American Inequality," p. 95.

62. See ibid., pp. 98–102, for an excellent discussion of these issues.

63. John Rawls, *A Theory of Justice* (Cambridge: Harvard University Press, 1971).

64. Robert Nozick, *Anarchy, State, and Utopia* (New York: Basic Books, 1974).

65. Inaugural address, January 21, 1961.

66. U.S. Conference of Catholic Bishops, "Labor Day Statement" (Washington, D.C.: Office of Domestic Social Development, September 3).

CHAPTER 8

Crime: Different Issues, New Concerns

Public opinion polls in the mid-1990s showed crime overtaking the economy as the biggest perceived problem facing the nation. U.S. citizens read daily newspaper accounts of car thefts, muggings, child abuse, robberies, murders, drug sales, and vandalism. This, along with sensational stories of bombings and shooting sprees, made Americans clamor for public policies to thwart the "crime wave." In the wake of September 11, 2001, however, much has changed; new problems and new fears have emerged. Ironically, while everyone agrees that crime remains a serious problem, few have a clear perspective on it. Most public reaction to crime reflects anecdotal experience springing from fear, not reasoned thinking. In this chapter we explore the crime problem by asking how much crime is out there, what its causes are, and how policies can be created that prevent crime, punish criminals, and protect the innocent from becoming victims.

New Fears: Changing Attitudes

Former president Bill Clinton recounted that during his first presidential primary campaign in 1992, he met a Greek waiter working in New York City whose remarks made a lasting impression on him. The man lamented how "in Greece, we were poor but we were free. Here, my boy can't play in the park across the street alone or walk down the street to school by himself because it is too dangerous. He's not free."[1] While campaigning for the presidency, Clinton responded to this fear by describing himself as tough on crime. According to scholar Alfred Blumstein, "toughness seems to be the panacea that has the most political appeal."[2] Clinton realized this message with passage of the 1994 Violent Crime and Law Enforcement Act. The omnibus crime bill channeled $30 billion into various federal programs, the most prominent of which were the Brady Bill, a ban on assault weapons, and the Department of Justice's COPS program, designed to improve relations between law enforcement and communities and committed to putting thousands of local police officers on a street beat. A decade later, U.S. attitudes about crime have changed. That earlier, often unrealistic fear of crime has given way to a different type of fear. Who could have predicted to that Greek waiter appealing to President Clinton that by 2002 many Americans would be living in fear for a very different type of security?

In the mid-1960s, U.S. concern for "law and order" propelled President Lyndon Johnson to initiate federal legislation to combat crime. Public Law 89-197, the Law Enforcement and Assistance Act, was passed in 1965, setting up a special office within the Department of Justice to fund local projects experimenting with new methods of crime control and law enforcement. In 1968 the federal government's role in local jurisdiction grew again with the passing of Public Law 90-351, the Omnibus Crime Control and Safe Streets Act. This act lived up to its name by granting funds to state and local jurisdictions for recruitment and training of law enforcement personnel and crime prevention education. Eventually the grants were phased out, though they left Americans with an expectation for a larger federal role in local crime control and prevention. No longer were Americans satisfied with the Federal Bureau of Investigation's (FBI's) "Ten Most Wanted" list as a way to combat crime and build public awareness, though it is interesting to note that today's "most wanted" list includes Osama bin Laden and offers a reward of up to $25 million for information leading to his apprehension.

Federal activity renewed in the 1980s. Over the next ten years Congress passed three comprehensive crime bills dealing with different aspects of what Americans then perceived as a terrible crime problem. In 1984, Public Law 98-473, the Comprehensive Crime Control Bill, overhauled federal sentencing procedures and created a new grant administrative agency, the Office of Justice Programs. In 1990, Congress passed Public Law 101-647, the Crime Control Act, which authorized $900 million for local law enforcement assistance and included a "victim's bill of rights." Four years later, President Clinton added his solutions to the crime problem with passage of the omnibus bill described earlier. From then until September 11, 2001, Americans thought about and fought crime locally and asked the federal government to help pay the bill.

The attack on the World Trade Center in 2001 altered perceptions about the federal government's role in combating a different violent crime, terrorism. It also invigorated the Department of Justice, whose authority and direction were expanded and refocused. Gallup polls now show that Americans no longer cite violent crime as a top government priority. In February 2003, just 2 percent of respondents to a national Gallup poll cited violent crime as an important problem facing the country, compared to 37 percent in January 1993. More Americans now fear war, nuclear war, and international tensions (35 percent).

The new U.S. perspective on violent crime may in fact be more accurate. Since 1929 the FBI has published an annual report on crime titled the *Uniform Crime Report (UCR)*. This statistical summary, compiled from data supplied by state and local agencies, presents a detailed breakdown of criminal activity in the United States. For years, the most commonly cited *UCR* statistic was the **crime index,** a highly aggregated measure of the volume and rate of reported crime, but in June 2004 the FBI decided to stop publishing the crime index because it was inaccurate. Instead the agency broke the crime statistics into two measures, total violent crime and total property crime. The FBI yearly snapshots reveal that violent crime and property crime actually have declined in the United States.

How Much Crime?

The 2003 *UCR* (see http://www.fbi.gov) and a preliminary 2004 report proudly announce that the level of U.S. crime is down overall, particularly violent crime. Though over 1.3 million violent crimes occurred in 2003, the *UCR* finds that violent crime is down 3 percent from 1999 and 24 percent from 1994.[3] Most violent crime, which includes murder, forcible rape, robbery, and aggravated assault, occurs during the heat of July and August. Aggravated assault is the most common category (62 percent of violent crime); murder is the violent crime least often committed (12 percent of violent crime). In 2003, 44 percent of those arrested for violent crimes were under twenty-five years of age; most were men (82 percent), and by race, more were white (60.5 percent) than black (37 percent). Firearms were used in 27 percent of violent crimes reported, which is relatively constant with earlier data. Knives were used in 15 percent of cases. According to the *UCR,* crime is highest in the metropolitan areas, highest in the southern United States, and lowest in rural counties.

Murder nationwide reached a high in 1991, with 24,703 incidents reported.[4] By 2003 the number of criminal homicides was down to 16,503. Most murder victims, like offenders, were male (77 percent) adults (90 percent). Altogether, the murder rate for U.S. cities was 7.1 per 100,000 residents; the murder rate increased for larger cities (over 250,000 residents) by nearly double (13.2 percent).[5] Seven out of ten murders involved the use of firearms. Most murder victims knew or were related to their assailants; most were family affairs. Nearly one-third of the murders resulted from arguments. Juvenile gangs, brawls involving alcohol or drugs, and sniper activity counted for about 20 percent of homicides.[6]

Nearly one-third (30 percent) of violent crimes were robberies, with most occurring during the December holidays. The 2003 *UCR* found that over $500 million was lost to robberies, and the average monetary value of property taken was about $1,200. According to *UCR* data, all types of robberies declined 25 percent from 1994, except for a modest increase in residential robbery.[7] Research by David T. Lykken reports that those at highest risk of violent crime are the young, between fifteen and twenty-four years old. The young are ten to fifteen times more likely than those over age sixty-five to be assaulted, robbed, or murdered.[8]

Loss from nonviolent, property crime, which includes larceny theft, burglary, and motor vehicle theft, equaled $17 million in 2003, a decline of 14 percent since 1994.[9] Over $8 billion was estimated to have been lost to motor vehicle theft; the FBI estimates 60 motor vehicle thefts per 100,000 people.[10] Table 8.1 displays a regional breakdown of U.S. crime categories.

As part of these *UCR* summary statistics, the FBI also reports **clearance rates**. These are offenses cleared by arrest or "other exceptional means."[11] The 2003 clearance rate for violent crimes was not quite half (47 percent), including 62 percent of murders. Typically, property crime has a lower clearance rate, 16 percent in 2003. In 1994 the FBI began collecting hate crime statistics. Hate crimes are not distinct crimes but are motivated by prejudice based on race, religion, ethnicity, sexual orientation, or disabilities both mental and physical, and are committed against persons, property, and society. The *UCR* reported in 2003 that racial bias represented the largest proportion of hate-motivated offenses. Most hate crimes take the form of intimidation against persons and vandalism against property.

While the overall *UCR* data present an encouraging summary of crime in the United States, the puzzle for analysts is finding the reason for the decline. International comparisons offer some clarification and perspective. Cross-national comparisons of crime rates indicate that "lethally violent crime is much higher in the United States than in other nations . . . in contrast, the United States has lower rates of serious property crime than other similar nations."[12]

Though tempting to conclude that the drop in overall crime statistics indicates progress in the "war on crime," data alone fail to give the full picture. Much data underreport the extent of particular crimes. For example, the *UCR* reports that rape has dropped to its lowest level since 1989. Yet two studies conducted in the 1990s found a significantly higher incidence of rape victimization than *UCR* data reflect.[13] Looking at existing data, criminologist Elliott Currie comments, "While guarded optimism may be in order, complacency is not. And there is no guarantee that the respite that we are now enjoying will last."[14]

Table 8.1 Index of U.S. Crime, Regional Offense, and Population Distribution, 2003 (percentages)

Region	Population	Violent Crime[a]	Property Crime[b]	Murder/ Nonnegligent Crime[c]	Rape	Robbery	Aggravated Assault	Burglary	Larceny Theft	Motor Vehicle Theft
NE	19	16	13	14	13	20	14	11	13	13
MW	19	19	21	20	25	19	18	20	22	19
S	36	41	41	44	38	39	43	45	41	35
W	23	24	25	23	24	23	24	24	24	34

Source: Federal Bureau of Investigation, *Uniform Crime Report 2003* (Washington, D.C.: U.S. Government Printing Office, 2004).

Notes: a. Violent crimes are offenses of murder, forcible rape, robbery, and aggravated assault.

b. Property crimes are offenses of burglary, larceny theft, and motor vehicle theft. Data are not included for the property crime of arson.

c. Nonnegligent crimes are offenses such as nonnegligent manslaughter, which is the willful killing of another human being.

NE = Connecticut, Maine, Massachusetts, New Hampshire, New Jersey, New York, Pennsylvania, Rhode Island, Vermont.

MW = Illinois, Indiana, Iowa, Kansas, Michigan, Minnesota, Missouri, Nebraska, North Dakota, Ohio, South Dakota, Wisconsin.

S = Alabama, Arkansas, Delaware, District of Columbia, Florida, Georgia, Kentucky, Louisiana, Maryland, North Carolina, Oklahoma. South Carolina, Tennessee, Texas, Virginia, West Virginia.

W = Arizona, Alaska, California, Colorado, Hawaii, Idaho, Montana, New Mexico, Oregon, Utah, Washington, Wyoming.

Because of rounding, column percentages may not sum to 100.

Case Study: How Accurate Are the Numbers?

Conventional wisdom says that no data are better than bad data. How accurate are crime statistics? The most commonly reported numbers are those collected by the FBI in its *Uniform Crime Report (UCR)* and the Census Bureau in its *National Crime Victimization Survey (NCV)*. Both data collections are compiled annually. Both report on similar crimes, though the *NCV* surveys do not include arson and homicide. Both collections also suffer from errors of measurement and bias, and both underreport crime.

The *UCR* data are based on police reports. Underreporting is largely due to unwillingness on the part of citizens to call the police. Not surprisingly, much petty theft (like someone stealing your wallet) goes unreported. Most people wager the police cannot do much about the loss, so why bother? A second source of inaccuracy comes from the reporting methods used. Some police departments do a better job reporting crime than others. Perhaps their collection techniques are better. Sometimes it is in a department's best interest to report crime; it reflects a job well done. It might even help the department's budget allocation. On the other hand, sometimes a police department would rather not report as much crime. It raises questions about the competence of the police force. If the FBI discovers intentional underreporting, it refuses to publish the statistics of the offending agency until the discrepancies are corrected. Further, when the *UCR* data are collected the police report all crimes committed in a given locality. Consequently, big cities, like New York, which experience lots of commuters and visitors, report high crime rates. Police reports also emphasize certain types of crimes and not others. Selling drugs, for example, is not included. And if several crimes are committed by a criminal at once, only the most serious is counted.

Victimization studies are equally flawed. The Bureau of the Census randomly selects households for inclusion in the study and it too underreports crime, but for different reasons. *NCV* studies only count personal and household crimes, not crimes against business. Consequently, the studies are not as sensitive to crime rates overall, nor are the rates they report as volatile as *UCR* statistics. On the other hand, *NCV* studies report up to three times the number of crime victims that police reports do. It makes sense that if five people are robbed at gunpoint, the victim study presents a different tally than the police report.

Other factors also skew the data collected in each report. Victims are likely to report some kinds of crime to the police, and others, like rape, to interviewers. Women are more likely to report to interviewers that they have been robbed than that they have been assaulted (possibly by a relative). Over time, people also forget or grow confused about when a crime occurred, so human error tends to creep into *NCV* data, since these studies collect information longer after a crime than do most police reports. Further, *NCV* interviews include data from the previous year. All this makes data from the two sources difficult to compare. Moreover, any comparisons should keep in mind that *UCR* data report perpetrators while *NCV* data report victims.

So, are no data better than bad data? It depends. Certainly if crime statistics are used for political convenience, the public is not well served. But if policymakers use the data with an awareness of their inaccuracies and a sense of appropriateness to the crime issue, then they serve a valuable purpose. The data from year to year probably do not indicate

continues

Case Study   continued

much. Large differences probably do indicate something. These widely cited studies give researchers some sense of the amount of crime occurring throughout the country. As noted by James Wilson, they do not specify the prevalence of crime or the incidence of crime. In other words, they do not indicate what proportion of a given population consists of criminals or the number of crimes committed per year by the average criminal,

indicators that would give a more valid measure of crime in the United States. Wilson warns that the best statements about crime are those supported by as many different measures as possible.

Sources: James Q. Wilson, ed., *Crime and Public Policy* (San Francisco: ICS Press, 1983); U.S. Department of Justice, *Criminal Victimization in the United States 1992* (Rockville, Md.: Bureau of Justice Statistics, March 1994), p. 9.

Crime: A Definition

In their book *Crime and Human Nature,* Harvard University scholars James Wilson and Richard Herrnstein explore the meaning of **crime**.[15] Wilson and Herrnstein tell us that crime is not easily measured, categorized, or defined. For example, categories of crime, like property crime, crime against persons, white collar crime, victimless crime, or public corruption, fall short because they are not mutually exclusive. Crimes have different social costs. Most people fear property loss from street crime, yet the financial loss from white collar crime is far greater. Obviously, some crimes are more abhorrent and more destructive to the social fabric than others. Wilson and Herrnstein use a legalistic definition of crime: "any act committed in violation of the law that prohibits it and authorizes punishment for its commission."[16] A serious crime is aggressive, violent behavior categorized as murder, rape, assault, and theft. The legalistic definition of crime is the least ambiguous, though not all scholars are happy with it. Critics complain that criminal law reflects the values of society's most powerful. What is a crime and who is criminal can vary over time and differ between societies. Clive Coleman and Clive Norris illustrate this point by recounting the U.S. experience with Prohibition during the 1920s, noting that it "represented a political victory for the moral code of one segment of American society at the expense of another." They emphasize that "the more complex society [is], the more likely that norms [will] come into conflict."[17] When reviewing lists of acts that have been defined as crimes over history, it seems evident that criminal law and crime are social constructions and very problematic.

One way to gain an understanding about crime is to look at the **causes of criminal behavior**. This approach focuses attention on the criminal and his or her relationship with the rest of society. A second approach explores the processes and characteristics of the **criminal justice system**, established to deal with crime. Here one asks how effectively the system protects the innocent and punishes offenders. This perspective concentrates largely on the legal system. When looking at the criminal justice system, one also asks how well it operates in reducing the level of crime.

Causes of Crime: What Do We Know?

Judging from the amount of crime reported, many observers feel very little is known about causes of criminal behavior. Wilson and Herrnstein argue overall that "crime is as broad a category as disease, and perhaps as useless. To explain why one person has ever committed a crime and another has not may be as pointless as explaining why one person has ever gotten sick and another has not."[18] But in fact, scholars who study the determinants of criminal behavior know quite a bit about its etiology or origin. This scholarly endeavor forms the field of **criminology**. Social scientists have learned more about why some people commit crimes than they have about the overall crime rate.

Criminologists have proposed many scientific, empirically testable theories of criminal behavior, often based on multidisciplinary research. Recently, research has drawn on fields like economics and biology. The field has a long history. Since the eighteenth-century Enlightenment period, scholars have focused attention to the nature of crime, criminal behavior, and the criminal justice system. As recounted by Coleman and Norris, early researchers "opposed the unpredictable, discriminatory, inhumane and ineffective criminal justice systems that were to be found in their day, systems that often left much to the discretion of judges (including the frequent use of 'mercy' and 'pardons'), employing barbaric, cruel methods of punishment (and torture for extracting confessions) and seemed to any intelligent observer to be very ineffective in preventing crime."[19] Facilitated by publication of national crime statistics, first in France in the early 1900s, moral statisticians looked for patterns in criminal behavior and attempted to design models comparing their work to that of the natural sciences. Later in the nineteenth century, Italian Cesare Lombroso claimed to have discovered actual physical differences in the anatomical makeup of criminals. Though thoroughly discredited, Lombroso's work helped to further establish the academic and scientific nature of criminology.[20]

George Vold and Thomas Bernard, in their book *Theoretical Criminology,* assign criminologists as social scientists to one of three essentially different ways of thinking about crime: "Two frames of reference focus on the behavior of criminals. The first argues that behavior is freely chosen, while the second argues that it is caused by forces beyond the control of the individual. The third frame of reference views crime primarily as a function of the way criminal law is written and enforced."[21]

Given these different points of departure, it is no wonder there is a great deal of scholarly disagreement among criminologists over the causes of crime. Those who see a **criminal behavior as freely chosen** describe people as rational. A criminal act is considered like any other act—as a rational purposeful choice whose aim is to promote one's best self-interest, much as a choice is described by public choice theory. This "classical," deterrence view is highly legalistic and emphasizes ways society can maximize the cost and minimize the benefits of criminal behavior. More recent analysis of crime by economists like Gary Becker has integrated key economic concepts into research on criminal behavior. Economic ideas like **expected utility** represent an offender's expected reward compared to the likelihood of punishment.[22]

The second perspective, **criminal behavior as caused**, is deterministic. In other words, it proposes that people behave as they have been determined to behave biologically. This perspective dominated the early field of criminology. Contemporary positivists argue that social scientists will never be able to say what causes a person to commit a crime, but research can determine what factors predispose or increase the risk of a life of crime. These theories explore the relationship between socioeconomic settings and emotional, psychological, and physical factors. Some of the criminologists holding this view even question the efficacy of punishment in dealing with criminal behavior and emphasize the value of psychological therapy and counseling. The last perspective, the **behavior of criminal law**, emerged in the 1960s, when, as Vold and Bernard explain, "some criminologists [began] to address a very different question: why some individuals and behaviors are officially defined as criminal and others not."[23] These scholars ask why, given a place and time, certain people and behaviors are defined as criminal. Those who focus on crime as an opportunity emphasize crime incidents rather than offenders, along with victims' lifestyles, which might expose them to offenders.

Thus the field of criminology offers compelling theoretical arguments and divergent explanations. Some criminologists argue that crime relates to intelligence, hyperactivity, or chromosomal characteristics. Others assert that poverty and economic inequality lead people to criminal behavior. A traditional view, associated with sociologist Emile Durkheim (1858–1917), argued that in the process of social change and modernization, societies became highly differentiated. A consequence of differentiation was **anomie**, or a breakdown in social norms and rules. Crime is one normal consequence of anomic society. It is a price society pays for progress. Many criminologists and sociologists in the tradition of Durkheim look to society as a whole to explain criminal behavior.

More recent explanations, like **strain theory**, offer the intuitive appeal of a causal relationship between social inequality, lack of economic opportunity, and crime.[24] Some see crime as learned behavior. Others offer a Marxist or feminist interpretation. All theories of criminal behavior have been extensively criticized. They are afflicted with a large number of theoretical and empirical problems, and many offer limited guidance to the policymaking community.

In the introductory chapter to their book on crime, Wilson and Herrnstein summarize the facts we do know:

> Predatory street crimes are most commonly committed by young males. Violent crimes are more common in big cities than in small ones. High rates of criminality tend to run in families. The persons who frequently commit the most serious crimes typically begin their criminal careers at a quite young age. Persons who turn out to be criminals usually do not do very well in school. Young men who drive recklessly and have many accidents tend to be similar to those who commit crimes. Programs designed to rehabilitate high rate offenders have not been shown to have much success, and those programs that do manage to reduce criminality among certain kinds of offenders often increase it among others.[25]

For the policymaker, individual indicators of crime like age, gender, personality, or intelligence do not translate easily into practical policy. Even policies emphasizing the deterrence of **criminogenic factors** like drugs, alcohol, and guns are hotly debated (see later sections of this chapter).[26] As a result, policy attention shifts to an area more easily identified and controlled, the criminal justice system. Here, consideration is given to the relative costs of legal protection and punishment and the efficient delivery of criminal justice services.

Characteristics of the Criminal Justice System

There is no single criminal justice system. What exists is a jumble of legal avenues that, when mapped out, look more like a very poorly designed interstate road system than a carefully constructed legal structure. The U.S. criminal justice system is **decentralized**. It consists of local, state, and federal jurisdictions. Again, this reflects the U.S. historical experience; when drafting the Constitution, the Founding Fathers left most criminal law to the states. They wanted criminal law to reflect community standards and enforcement to be localized. The consequence is variability in laws and consequences throughout the fifty U.S. states, resulting in challenges to equity and justice.

The Courts

Generally, state and local criminal jurisdictions follow similar organizational patterns, although they often use different names to describe similar functions. The design and size of jurisdictions vary. To fully explain all the systems of each jurisdiction would require a separate look. Nevertheless, they all share basic similarities

Case Study: Youth Gangs

Two weeks before the Christmas holiday in 2004, residents of Charles County, Maryland, woke to a $10 million fire burning homes in a new subdivision, named Hunters Brooke. The fire destroyed ten large houses and damaged sixteen others. Police investigators quickly seized on arson as the motive and found their culprits, members of a local youth gang named the Unseen Cavaliers. Members of the gang held grudges against the builder and, during meetings in the parking lot of a fast food restaurant, purportedly planned to set the blaze.[27]

Youth gangs are on the rise in the United States according to the National Youth Gang Center. Law enforcement agencies report over 20,000 youth gangs nationwide. Different from the "teddy boys and the mods" of the 1960s, with their curious combination of pop culture and high art, youth gangs today bear a stronger resemblance to gangs in the 1920s. Historically, gangs originated in the United States after the Revolutionary War. By the 1920s, they consisted mainly of Irish, Jewish, and Italian groups. From the 1960s to 1990s, the demographics changed, with African American and Hispanic gangs gaining prominence. Gangs today are more dangerous because of access to lethal weapons. The old tactics of hit-and-run have given way to frightening "drive-by shootings." Gang members today are both older and younger (average age of seventeen years), more likely to have prison records, and more likely to use drugs and alcohol. Significantly, a rise in female gangs has accompanied the trend in

gang activity, with many female gang members acting as auxiliaries to male gangs.

Categorizing gangs troubles sociologists, who represent them by their degree of organization, from the loosely formed teenage groups "hanging out" in shopping malls, to street gangs, to semistructured criminal organizations that often feed into organized crime groups. Gangs are not isolated to the inner city, though Los Angeles's Hispanic gangs and Chicago's African American gangs record the highest memberships. Recent data indicate that gang formation has cascaded to the suburbs and rural areas, where members participate frequently in property crime often marked by gang graffiti. The most established megagangs and specialty gangs deal drugs and fight over their geographic control of territory.

While African Americans, Hispanics, and Asians disproportionately join gangs, studies show that they are not predisposed to rebellious or illegal activity. Rather, groups like Chicago's Black Gangster Disciples Nation are often carriers of community traditions and offer their members an identity they frequently crave. Studies point to the roots of gang formation in low neighborhood integration, faulty parental supervision, lack of stable work opportunity, poverty, and for many, the excitement and prestige of gang membership. Contemporary sociologists point to gangs as symptomatic of problems in the wider social context. The U.S. Department of Justice funds its National Youth Gang Center to demonstrate its commitment to a communitywide approach to gang prevention and suppression.

in organization and process. Generally, at the bottom of each state system are courts of **limited jurisdiction** (or "special" jurisdiction). They hear civil cases and criminal misdemeanors.[28] The next level of courts has **general jurisdiction**. Here the state prosecutes individuals accused of serious crimes—felonies and certain types of important civil cases. The **appeals courts** review and rule on the legality of decisions made by the lower courts. State **supreme courts** are the top appellate courts within this judicial system.

Organizationally, the federal court system is divided into ninety-seven district courts and ten courts of appeal. Again, cases originate in federal district court and move upward in the appeals process to the U.S. Supreme Court. The Supreme Court hears only those cases with far-reaching policy implications.

Many people take part in the administration of justice. Key participants include police officers, prosecutors, public defenders, judges, wardens, psychiatrists, and parole officers. Often, they have competing goals. Some seek to protect citizens' rights under the law; others see that punishment is effectively carried out. Ultimately, there is a struggle between speed and due process of law, between protection and punishment.

Our criminal justice system seeks to investigate and arrest, prosecute, determine guilt or innocence, and punish and/or rehabilitate. The process from arrest to sentencing has changed little from colonial times. A crime is investigated and an arrest is made by the police. The prosecutor seeks an indictment and an arraignment follows. A trial consists of the admission of evidence and questioning of witnesses until a verdict is reached. If guilt is determined, a judge or jury establishes the appropriate sentencing. From there, the penal system takes over.

Understand too that most criminal cases never follow this process; rather a **plea bargain** is forged. Here a defendant pleads guilty to a certain charge in exchange for the court dropping more serious charges or in exchange for the promise of a lighter sentence. In the United States, if a defendant pleads guilty, there is no trial. By reducing court loads and avoiding long and costly trials, plea bargaining expedites the judicial process. Critics argue that the plea bargain works against those who insist on the constitutional right to trial by jury. But trials too can work against defendants. As noted by one author, "If defendants exercise this right, they risk a harsher sentence."[29]

The Role of the Police

Because the police are the most visible part of the criminal justice system, much attention focuses on their effectiveness. One author writes that the police represent "that 'thin blue line' between order and anarchy."[30] The United States has no national police force, and state and local police agencies operate autonomously. Local autonomy has its roots in historical opposition to any type of standing army in the United States. Today the FBI catalogs 13,032 police agencies, or 2.3 law enforcement officers per 1,000 inhabitants.[31]

The chief function of the police is keeping the peace, not enforcing the law.

Police officers share a subculture not unlike the military subculture. Police departments are organized to follow a chain of command, and regulations and discipline govern police behavior. As peacekeepers, the police use patrolling techniques to protect public safety and enforce the law.

Many argue that the police have been restricted in their ability to exercise their **investigative and arrest powers**. These powers, to stop, question, detain, use force, and search, have been constrained by Supreme Court decisions. Much public policy debate about the criminal justice system centers on legal decisions critics claim have tied the hands of law enforcement agencies.

During the tenure of Supreme Court Justice Earl Warren (1953–1969), a revolution in **procedural rights** occurred. Because the rights of the accused are the same as the rights of the innocent, constitutional protections against unjustified searches, admission of hearsay as evidence, and inadequate legal defense apply. Since the 1960s the rights of the accused have been expanded. This expansion may have been stopped by the appointment of more conservative justices to the Supreme Court during the Reagan-Bush years.

The exclusionary rule. Once such expansion involved the **exclusionary rule**, which prohibits illegally obtained evidence from being introduced in a court of law. Despite the arguments by critics that the rule protects only the guilty, the Supreme Court fully extended the principle to the state justice systems in *Mapp v. Ohio* (1961).[32] *Mapp* produced immediate reactions from enraged police departments throughout the country, which felt it seriously diminished their legal investigative powers. Conservatives feared that criminals would now be able to walk away due to mere legal technicalities.

The exclusionary rule was eventually set back by the **good faith exception**, enunciated in *U.S. v. Leon* (1984). Here the Supreme Court ruled that, even if a search was determined to have been technically illegal, if the police acted in good faith, the evidence obtained could be introduced in court.

Custodial interrogation. The Supreme Court extended the right to counsel at state expense to all felony cases with *Gideon v. Wainwright* (1963). Shortly afterward the Court moved even further to protect defendants by addressing police conduct during arrest and interrogation in *Escobedo v. Illinois* (1964), when it decided suspects have the right to counsel back to the point of arrest. And two years later, in *Miranda v. Arizona* (1966), it required police to inform every suspect of their constitutional rights upon arrest. These cases and others represented the belief that convictions often resulted from confessions obtained through inappropriate interrogations by the police—in other words, from defendants who were unaware of their constitutional rights in regard to criminal matters. Since most convictions result from confessions, once again bitter reactions followed. New York City's police commissioner argued that "if suspects are told of their rights they will not confess."[33]

Many argue that the *Miranda* decision has reduced the effectiveness of confessions as a crime-fighting tool and symbolizes an obsessive concern for the rights of the accused. However, the original strength of the *Miranda* rule has been diluted through decisions reached in cases beginning with the 1970 Burger Court.[34] Chief Justice Warren Burger, a Nixon appointee, espoused a "law and order" position. More recently, concern with custodial rights has centered on the use of plea bargaining, as discussed earlier. Today the number of defendants deciding to "cop a plea" far exceeds those opting for jury trials. Some critics maintain that the practice subverts justice by violating constitutional protection against self-incrimination and the guarantee of a fair jury trial. But its widespread use also lessens pressure on the criminal justice system.

Often manipulated, blamed, or even hated, police departments are caught in the crossfire of criminal justice policy debates. The police find it difficult to balance the demands for more aggressive anticrime measures, which require more expenditures and greater intrusiveness on people's lives, with demands that they adhere to constitutional protections that ensure proper investigative and arrest procedures. Increasingly the police are forced to use discretion, or **selective enforcement of the law**, in doing their job.

Police Theory

In September 1994, President Clinton signed a $30 million crime bill into law. Critics of the law denounced its lack of coherence and proposed benefits, while its proponents argued that the law represented a fundamental change in the role the federal government played in fighting crime. The centerpiece of the law was the **Community-Oriented Policing Services** (COPS) program, which proposed hiring 100,000 new police officers. Community-oriented policing represents a change in police strategy. The first large, organized police force was set up in London in 1830; New York and other large cities followed.[35] Before that, policing was a voluntary, citizen-based effort. To these early police departments, a policy of high visibility and low response time was very effective. According to criminologist Lawrence Sherman, "There is substantial evidence that serious violent crime and public disorder declined in response to the 'invention' of visible police patrol."[36]

Over the past twenty-five years, research has shown that police visibility really does not matter anymore. An influential experiment was done by the Kansas City, Missouri, police department that compared crime rates in three groups of patrol beats. One group was given two to three times as much coverage as the others, another group no coverage, and a third group normal police coverage. Results showed no difference in crime across the groups.[37] Researchers speculate that changes in population density resulting from the growth of suburbs in the 1950s and 1960s have reduced the effectiveness and practicality of police visibility and quick response time. As Carl Klockers explains, "it makes about as much sense to have police patrol routinely in cars to fight crime as it does to have firemen patrol routinely in fire trucks to fight fire."[38]

Yet police visibility does make a difference if it is concentrated and directed at "hot spots"—areas and times of high crime. For example, police crackdowns—sudden and massive increases in police presence or enforcement activity—are very effective, especially if they are short in duration and unpredictable.[39]

Today the police are adopting strategies that emphasize "security guard" and "public health" activity. Community-based policing treats a neighborhood the same way a security guard treats a client's property, by looking for risk factors for crime. Security guards, however, protect private property, while the police protect public space. The police cannot use trespassing laws to protect public space. They rely on programs that address risk factors, like traffic stops to control handguns, repeat offender programs to track parolees, and curfews and truancy regulations to monitor juveniles. Using public health strategies, police departments consider long-term trends and "situational factors" that contribute to crime. They use this analysis, for example, to make recommendations to communities for siting automatic teller machines or determining business closing hours. Both of these approaches represent a new philosophy of policing, one that emphasizes prevention, problem solving, and peacekeeping alongside traditional law enforcement. Gradually, police strategy is moving toward a balance between the taxpayer demand for "fair share" approaches to policing, and focused, risk-reduction strategies.

Prisons: Perspectives on Punishment and Correction

By the 1960s not only had the orientation of the courts changed, but so had public attitudes toward crime. The decade was in many ways a turning point in criminal justice policy. Citizens had come to fear crime as never before, in part due to increasing street crime, drug use, and civil rights protests. Consequently, President Lyndon Johnson declared a "war on crime" and established a presidential commission to study the psychology and sociology of crime in the United States, and appropriate policy responses to it. Commission recommendations led to passage of the Omnibus Crime Control and Safe Streets Act in 1968. This act was viewed by some as a way to offset criticism that the country had gone soft on crime.

The emphasis on law and order continued through the 1970s. President

Richard Nixon supported increased funding to local governments via the Law Enforcement Assistance Administration for researching and conducting programs directed at crime abatement.[40] By the 1980s, both President Ronald Reagan and President George H.W. Bush fought hard for strict law enforcement policies along with protection for victim rights and stricter drug laws. And the emphasis has not been just at the federal level. A recent study reports: "Criminal justice is the fastest growing area of state and local spending, expenditures grew 232% between 1970 and 1990. In comparison, public expenditures on hospitals and health care increased 71%; public welfare, 79%; and education, 32%."[41] In 1984, Congress created the U.S. Sentencing Commission (USSC) to launch federal sentencing guidelines. The USSC's purpose was to make sentences more uniform by providing judges a "grid with the offense for which the defendant has been convicted on one axis and the offender's history and other details on the other. The grid gives the judges a range of possible sentences and the system instructs them [judges] to go above that range if they make certain factual findings."[42]

In January 2005 the U.S. Supreme Court decided that federal sentencing guidelines were unconstitutional because they violated a defendant's Sixth Amendment right to trial by jury. Essentially, sentencing guidelines empowered judges to increase sentences beyond those set by a jury. The Supreme Court justices opposing the decision argued that Congress's original intent when passing the Sentencing Reform Act in 1984 was to ensure that similar sentences were given to those committing similar crimes. Now, they argued, allowing juries to set the sentences shifted "too much power to prosecutors."[43] Ironically, many judges, too, have complained about the USSC guidelines, particularly when they want to show more leniency. As a result of the Supreme Court decision, the USSC will continue to exist, but its guidelines will be advisory. Members of Congress reacted by promising to respond with hearings as they continue to compete with the judiciary for control over the criminal punishment process.

In 1994, President Clinton launched passage of a crime bill that represented a shift in philosophy for the Clinton administration. Frustrating his Republican counterparts, Clinton took up the crime issue and campaigned on it as a central pillar of his presidency. Among the "new Clinton" proposals were a "one strike, you're out" rule for violent criminals and drug offenders living in public housing, proposals for school uniforms and curfews, statements inveighing against the entertainment industry's showcasing of drugs and violence, and allocation of nearly $8.7 billion spread over six years to help states build more prisons.[44] Policies like "one strike, you're out" have had costly consequences. As illustrated in Table 8.2, incarceration rates in the United States are many times higher than those in other, comparably industrialized countries. According to data collected from the International Centre

Table 8.2   International Comparison of Prison Populations, 2003

	Prisons per 100,000 Population
United States	714
Russia	548
South Africa	402
Israel	209
Mexico	169
England and Wales	141
China	119
Canada	116
Australia	114
Germany	96
France	95
Sweden	75
Japan	58
India	29

Source: The Sentencing Project, December 2004, www.sentencingproject.org.

for Prison Studies (www.prisonstudies.org), U.S. incarceration rates are comparable to those of countries like Cuba, Belarus, and Belize.

According to Marc Mauer, assistant director of "The Sentencing Project," criminal justice policies in the United States continue to become more punitive.[45] The higher incarceration rate can be tied directly to the shift to mandatory and determinate sentencing. Crowded prisons, housing in excess of 2 million inmates in 2002, have placed a tremendous financial burden on the states and the federal government. Fully two-thirds of those in prison are ethnic and racial minorities. Most of those newly incarcerated are there for nonviolent, drug-related charges, often associated with crack cocaine. The federal prison system has grown to the third largest in the United States, after the state systems of Texas and California. To offset the expense of the massive federalization of crime, a shift to private prisons has been considered. Claiming more efficiency and cost savings, proponents maintain that the private market should take on the prison problem. Philosophically, though, a private prison system can lead to serious conflicts of interest. Any private claim to incarceration would have a vested interest in sentencing policies that encourage longer sentences and a large prison population. The cost of public oversight of private prisons would likely offset any savings.

Despite recent trends, no explicit philosophy serves as an underlying rationale for U.S. criminal justice policy. Traditionally, such policy has been based on one of four competing philosophical attitudes about punishment—retribution, incapacitation, rehabilitation, and deterrence. Emphasis on which particular attitude reigns at any given time depends on shifting national values and growing or waning fears about crime.

Retribution is the age-old philosophy of "an eye for an eye." Now often referred to as a policy of "just deserts," it emphasizes punitive sanctions: criminals must pay their debts to society through punishment that "fits" the crime. Somewhat related is the philosophy of **incapacitation**, which postulates that, through restraint or incapacitation, criminals are removed from society so that they can no longer endanger others. Incapacitation emphasizes citizen protection and crime prevention.

Rehabilitation seeks to reintegrate criminals into society through corrections programs and services. More humanitarian in its outlook, this philosophy looks to social causes to explain crime. As noted earlier, rehabilitation dominated most twentieth-century thinking and policymaking about crime.

In recent years **deterrence** philosophy has come to the fore. Here, some argue that the effective use of sentencing will function as an example to deter would-be offenders (general deterrence) or to convince criminals not to commit another crime (specific deterrence).

Often the appeal of a particular philosophy is tied to our assumptions about human nature. In an effort to sort through competing policy approaches, David Gordon has laid out the logical flow of conventional criminal justice policy.[46] He notes that liberal and conservative philosophies about crime correspond to liberal and conservative positions on other social issues. Both liberals and conservatives share the assumption that criminal behavior is irrational. To a conservative, the problem and the solution are for the most part straightforward. Social order, as reflected in the law, is rational. Because criminal behavior is irrational, it must be met with a response that protects public safety. Policies to combat crime must emphasize forces that deter crime. This translates into more police, more equipment, and more prisons.

On the other hand, liberals, although they agree that criminal behavior is irrational, also see imperfections in the social order. And because the system is imperfect, they note, some people are more likely to be driven toward a life of crime. As Gordon states, "Criminality should be regarded as irrationality, but we should nonetheless avoid blaming criminals for irrational acts."[47] Liberals postulate relationships between poverty and racism and crime. Consequently, their answer to crime is found in more research, more technology, and more professional help for criminals. Liberals argue that societies will never rid themselves of crime until the root causes are discovered and eliminated.

The conservative emphasis on law and order and protection leads to policies promoting incapacitation and deterrence. The liberal emphasis on justice and equality has a stronger connection to rehabilitative techniques.

Sometimes laws contradict ideological integrity. For example, all but three states—Kentucky, Nebraska, and New Mexico—have enacted a version of **Megan's Law**, which requires convicted sex offenders to register with their local police after their release from prison and allows officials to publicize names of some offenders. Despite a string of court challenges that argued that the registration represented an additional punishment, appeals courts have determined that the law is an administrative action and not a criminal penalty. Some, including members of the various state civil liberties unions, oppose the registration, arguing that the decision about how to characterize an offender (one of three groups ranging from low to high risk; all information on high-risk offenders, including name, address, physical description, and detailed criminal history, is published) can lead to prejudice and mistakes. Liberals and conservatives alike are torn between offender and victim rights.

More recent economic analysis of crime began to question traditional liberal and conservative assumptions in another way.[48] These scholars challenge the assumption that criminal behavior is irrational. Building on nineteenth-century utilitarian thinking, they argue that criminal behavior is a rational choice, as follows: "A person commits an offense if the expected utility to him exceeds the utility he could not get by using his time and other resources at other activities. Some persons become 'criminals,' therefore, not because their basic motivation differs from that of other persons, but because their benefits and costs differ."[49]

The rational choice model of crime claims that criminals rationally calculate the cost/benefit ratio of an act. In doing this, they consider the likelihood of being caught, the probability of punishment, and the length and nature of their possible punishment. Solutions to crime from this perspective can be found in an analysis of why criminals make the choice they do and in the development of cost- or punishment-optimizing policies to deter people from making that choice. Public policy should thus aim at raising the cost of crime disproportionately to its potential benefits.

Still, notions of deterrence pervade current policy for combating crime as evidenced by the continued enthusiasm for definite and determinate sentencing policies. A **definite sentence** sets a fixed period of confinement that allows no reduction by parole, while a **determinate sentence** is a fixed confinement, set by the legislature, with parole eligibility. The more customary **indeterminate sentence** offers more court discretion and is based on a correctional (not deterrent) model of punishment. Recent **truth-in-sentencing** rules mandate that a prisoner must serve at least 85 percent of his or her sentence. As noted above, all of these practices have led to large-scale crowding and considerable expense.

The Implications of Punishment and Reform

Many find fault with the increased emphasis on deterrence and especially question the assumption of criminal rationality. They argue that even if individuals know that the risk of being caught for committing a crime is low, most people would not commit a crime, particularly a violent crime. Further, critics point out that the assumption that criminals understand and weigh the possible costs and punishments for their criminal acts lacks empirical support. Many analysts argue that it takes more than the threat of punishment to keep people in line.[50] Those who defend deterrence argue that, while **particular deterrence**, or the effect of deterrence on criminals, may be hard to prove, it is likely to have a great effect of **general deterrence**. They claim that the average citizen is less likely to commit a criminal act because of the "demonstration effect" of punishment.

Some assert a relationship between the **certainty and severity of punishment** and crime levels.[51] They claim that criminal behavior is deterred if the punishment is swift, certain, and severe. This proposition helped build arguments against the more traditional rehabilitative policies. Research has found that traditional rehabilitation has achieved only limited success. Alfred Blumstein explains that by the mid-1970s, studies showed that rehabilitation programs had a "null effect."[52] In other words, corrections programs broke even on reducing **recidivism**.[53] Recidivism seems more closely associated with personal characteristics of the criminal and the outside environment to which the prisoner returns upon release. As Robert Blecker explained, this is what led policymakers to pass laws like the Sentencing Reform Act of 1984, in which Congress rejected rehabilitation as an outmoded philosophy.[54]

But tougher sentencing has not had the desired deterrent effect either. Data since 1975 show that longer sentences have not reduced the level of crime. As noted in a National Research Council study: "if tripling the average length of incarceration per crime had a strong deterrent effect, then violent crime rates should have declined in the absence of other relevant changes. While rates declined during the early 1980s, they generally rose after 1985, suggesting that changes in other factors . . . may have been causing an increase in potential [violent] crimes."[55]

Some even argue that longer sentences may have aggravated the crime problem. A number of experts fear that jail houses and prisons have become "schools for crime." Blumstein points out how some critics argue that "prison is harmful because it socializes prisoners, especially younger ones, into a hardened criminal culture."[56] Table 8.3 describes the current prison population.[57]

How society finds a suitable mix of retribution, incapacitation, rehabilitation, and deterrence to fight crime is a practical issue, but it also has important moral dimensions. Blecker makes the following trenchant critique: "What actually happens to prisoners—their daily pain and suffering inside prison—is the only true measure of whether the traditional concepts have meaning, the traditional goals are fulfilled, the traditional definitions apply."[58] Equally important are the ethical questions associated with incarceration rates that disproportionately represent ethnic and minority populations. For example, as a result of highly publicized crack cocaine use in the 1980s, two federal laws were passed that have resulted in more serious consequences for crack users than for users of regular powder cocaine. Crack is cheaper and sold in the streets, and thus is more likely to involve inner city residents. It is no coincidence that the increased incarceration of nonviolent drug offenders, especially for crack use, involves low-income minorities.

Ingredients of Violence: Drugs, Guns, and Poverty

Crime abatement has been linked with policies aimed at low levels of drug and gun use, along with policies designed to lift people out of poverty. The relationship between these factors and crime is controversial. Politicians often proclaim such policies because they appeal to voters. But prudent analysis shows that the connection between drugs, guns, poverty, and crime is not obviously direct or causal.

Table 8.3   Who Is in Prison?

	Prisoners per 100,000 Population (2001)
Whites	235
Blacks	1,815
Latinos	609
Asians	99
Native Americans	709

Source: *The Prison Index: Taking the Pulse of the Crime Control Industry*, www.prisonpolicy.org.

The War on Drugs

The shattering effects of drug dependency lead citizens to endorse just about any program directed at eliminating illegal drug use. Public drug policies are based on medical, commercial, and moral concerns, and increasingly they are connected with crime policy. Most Americans support the "war on drugs" and believe that any efforts to decriminalize drug use are morally bankrupt. But the links between drugs and crime are unclear, and the empirical evidence demonstrating their relationship is weak.

Supply and demand considerations govern current drug policies. Reducing drug supplies through interdiction and the punishment of drug traffickers, and reducing demand through the education, incarceration, and rehabilitation of drug users, form the basis of the government's antidrug strategy. This strategy relies heavily on the criminal justice system, particularly the Department of Justice's Drug Enforcement Agency, for its effective implementation. Most Americans buy into the argument that drugs and crime are closely related. Consequently, they support employing the resources of the criminal justice system to fight the war on drugs. But is doing so justified?

Illegal drugs today include a wide range of psychoactive products such as opiates, cocaine (and its derivative crack), amphetamines, PCP, and hallucinogens. Medical research reveals that the behavioral response to these various drugs differs significantly from one person to the next and from one drug to another. But setting up good scientific research on drug use and behavior is difficult. Reactions to drugs are highly individualistic and depend on factors like how much and how often a drug is taken.

Scientists do know that different drugs elicit different reactions.[59] For example, heroine and opiates tend to inhibit behavior, though it is not at all clear what happens during periods of withdrawal. The chronic use of these drugs may affect the central nervous system and lead to aberrant social behavior. Drugs like cocaine, LSD and PCP, and amphetamines produce effects not unlike alcohol. In small doses, individuals tend to act out in a disruptive fashion, while higher doses lead to more disorganized, clumsy behavior that may have an inhibiting effect on social interaction. Crack cocaine may lead to a psychotic state, though no direct relationship has been established. Essentially, the analysis of individual drug use and crime levels shows no consistent relationship. As explained by researcher James Inciardi, "New York, with the highest cocaine prevalence of the five cities [Detroit, Los Angeles, New York, Miami, Washington, D.C.], and Los Angeles, with the second lowest, have the lowest homicide rates. The New York, Miami and D.C. data resemble, if anything, an inverse relationship between homicide rates and arrestees' cocaine use."[60]

While the physiological connection between drugs and crime is not verifiable,

Case Study: Capital Punishment—The Enduring Debate

In October 1993 the state of Maryland began preparing for its first criminal execution in more than twenty-five years. Despite the legal and moral debate that has threatened the use of **capital punishment**, most Americans still support it. But the death penalty raises a number of problems, including proportionality of punishment, consistency of state statutes, and the vagaries of sentencing.

When the Bill of Rights was added to the Constitution, few intended the Eighth Amendment's "cruel and unusual punishment" to preclude capital punishment. The concern was to ensure that punishment be proportional to the offense. Flagrant acts of punishment, like burning at the stake, were outlawed. The use of capital punishment continued historically. It peaked in the 1930s and began to decline precipitously in the 1960s. Critics denounced the variability in state statutes and pointed out that the poor, blacks, and underrepresented groups were more likely to be executed. By the 1960s, the National Association for the Advancement of Colored People and the American Civil Liberties Union had mounted a campaign against the use of capital punishment, making the issue one of public policy debate.

Beyond the question of arbitrary use, others raised the larger question of "evolving standards of decency." They argued that, though our colonial ancestors found no moral distaste in imposing the death penalty, perhaps contemporary standards of decency had changed. These two concerns, combined with growing worry that juries lacked sufficient directions in imposing the death penalty, led to a virtual moratorium on its use by the late 1960s.

Perhaps inevitably the question came before the Supreme Court. The first challenge to the death penalty addressed questions like the legality of "death-qualified juries," that is, jurists selected for their willingness to impose the death penalty. The Court ruled such juries unconstitutional. The Court also invalidated the death penalty as mandated under the Federal Kidnapping Act.

The major challenge to the death penalty occurred in the 1972 case *Furman v. Georgia.* The Supreme Court temporarily struck down the death penalty because of the "arbitrary, capricious, and racist manner" in which it had been applied. Essentially the Court reacted to how the death penalty had been used, not to the death penalty per se. Though the decision was complex, it did leave two legal avenues open to the states. They could pass laws that established a bifurcated procedure for the death penalty. Here defendants would face a trial to establish culpability. If found guilty, then a second proceeding would follow to establish grounds for the death penalty. The other legal avenue available to states was to make the death penalty mandatory for certain crimes.

The Supreme Court ruled on the legality of the two-step procedure in *Gregg v. Georgia* (1976). In this case, the Court ruled that the death penalty for murder did not necessarily constitute cruel and unusual punishment. Further, it declared the bifurcated system constitutional. However, the Court ruled in *Woodson v. North Carolina* (1976) that the death penalty may not be made mandatory.

Despite the fact that the *Gregg* case upheld the constitutionality of the death penalty, a series of rulings has eroded the jury discretion in applying the statutory guidelines. In addition to these fundamental legal questions, other objections have been voiced regarding the cost and effectiveness of the

continues

Case Study   continued

death penalty. While some are persuaded that it is a cost-effective form of punishment, others point out that, given the need to guarantee procedural safeguards, its costs are much higher than are those of other forms of punishment. In other words, the studies show that the deterrent effect of the death penalty is far from proven. Comparisons show few differences in crime rates for those states with the death penalty and those without it. And in states with the death penalty, comparisons of the crime rate before and after an execution show no differences. Many conclude that the death penalty is popularly supported by Americans and politically useful. Some elected officials, however—among them the former governor of New York, Mario Cuomo—

have argued forcefully for life in prison without parole as a preferable sentence. As noted by Cuomo in a *New York Times* editorial, "That alternative is just as permanent, at least as great a deterrent and—for those who are so inclined—far less expensive than the exhaustive legal appeals required in capital cases."

Sources: Mario M. Cuomo, "New York State Shouldn't Kill People," *New York Times,* June 17, 1989, p. 23; Donald D. Hook and Lothar Kahn, *Death in the Balance: The Debate over Capital Punishment* (Lexington, Mass.: D. C. Heath, 1989); Bonnie Szumski, Lynn Hall, and Susan Bursell, eds., *The Death Penalty: Opposing Viewpoints* (St. Paul, Minn.: Greenhaven Press, 1986).

---

economic arguments are persuasive. Do drug addicts steal or kill to feed a drug habit? Again, good data to confirm this proposition are hard to come by. One study found the empirical support for economic violence to be very inconclusive. But the report's first author, P. J. Goldstein, further concluded from a study done on the New York City Police Department that drug-related violence can be categorized as **systemic violence** rather than just **economic violence**.[61] That is, it can be understood as the result of factors concerned with the overall drug "marketplace," in line with the following analysis: Current public policy aims at minimizing the supply of drugs. An artificial drug scarcity results, which drives up the price of drugs. Dealers capture these excess profits, and drug users are forced to find ways to pay the contrived high prices. Among the reactions to this systemic condition is violence resulting from territorial disputes, gang warfare, battles with police and informers, the creation of black markets, and the lure of corruption. Prostitution increases, and drug dealers enter the school yards. A logical extension of this argument is the **iron law of prohibition**. If all drugs are prohibited, dealers have a greater incentive to traffic in the more profitable and more dangerous drugs. In other words, if the punishment for dealing marijuana is the same as that for dealing cocaine, then logically it is preferable to deal cocaine, which is more profitable.[62] Analysts point to the rising use of expensive "designer drugs" as an indication of this trend.

One public policy direction consistent with this reasoning is **decriminalization** of drugs. Not surprisingly, some elected officials have concluded that, given the costs of combating drug use, decriminalizing them makes the most sense. Proponents of this position argue that studies fail to confirm that drug use causes crime, and that maybe coincidentally criminals just use drugs. In addition, some worry that effective drug programs will infringe on civil liberties.

Decriminalization has only a small following. Most Americans simply will not accept the risk. It is estimated that as many as 6 million people already use drugs, and that legalizing them could lead to even greater numbers. Yet the costs of treating drug use as a crime are also great. Prison overcrowding, caseload pressure, and ballooning police and military budgets raise practical questions about the policy. Some argue that de-emphasizing the crime connection and re-emphasizing the public health aspects of drug use is a more viable and appropriate course.[63] This approach would target education and rehabilitation rather than interdiction and prosecution as its main goals. The growing use of anabolic steroids, particularly among professional athletes, is an interesting example of a public health problem that has become a crime problem. These performance-enhancing drugs can promote uncontrolled bursts of violence known as "roid rage," thus daring new responses from the war on drugs.

Gun Control

Like drugs, guns represent something tangible that policymakers can control in the fight against crime. Policymakers point to the experience of other countries, like England, which have tough gun control policies and far lower crime rates. But the relationship between guns and crime is very complex. While analysts concede that tough gun laws could mitigate crime, they argue that those laws would not work unless all states agreed to the same standards.

Gun control policies affecting the availability, use, distribution, and deadliness of guns are already in place in the United States. Legislation dating to the 1930s regulated the use of machine guns and required gun sellers to be licensed. In 1968, Congress passed the Federal Gun Control Act in reaction to public outcries over the assassinations of Senator Robert Kennedy and Reverend Martin Luther King. The act emphasized restrictions on the availability and distribution of guns. It banned mail order sales of guns and outlawed sales to convicted felons, fugitives, and individuals with certain mental illnesses. It restricted private ownership of automatic and military weapons. The law required that gun dealers be licensed by the Bureau of Alcohol, Tobacco, and Firearms (ATF) and that the serial numbers on all guns sold by licensed dealers be recorded. Finally, it required that individuals buying guns from licensed dealers must show proof of identification and residency and certify their eligibility to own guns. In 1986, Congress set mandatory penalties for those convicted of using guns in a federal crime and prohibited the use of bullets that could penetrate bulletproof clothing: "cop-killer" bullets. The import and manufacture of semiautomatic assault weapons was banned in 1990.

Despite this effort to control the distribution and availability of guns, gun ownership today is widespread. The ATF estimates that 150 to 200 million firearms are privately owned, mostly used for hunting, sport, or self-protection. Twenty-four percent of privately owned guns are easily concealed handguns, which are used disproportionately in homicides. Estimates provided by the FBI indicate that in 1989 about 60 percent of all homicides resulted from gun attacks and that the cost of gun injuries was about $14 billion.[64] These frightening statistics led to a ground swell of support for more effective gun control. Many states tightened their gun ordinances by insisting on waiting periods before purchase, licensing of purchasers, and laws against carrying concealed weapons. But these stricter requirements were often undercut by the less demanding regulations of neighboring states. Such frustration mounted that Congress finally passed the popular **Brady Bill**. The bill, named after presidential press secretary James Brady, who was seriously wounded in the 1981 assassination attempt on President Ronald Reagan, required a background check and a five-day "cooling off" period prior to purchasing a gun.

Despite widespread popular support, particularly among law enforcement, the Brady Bill has met with ongoing congressional opposition. Its original passage came only after a threatened filibuster attempt by Senate members and an aggressive advertising campaign mounted by the National Rife Association (NRA). Both failed to sway public sentiment. In an emotional ceremony, President Clinton signed the Brady Bill shortly after Thanksgiving 1993. Despite this, the Brady Bill initiatives have been rolled back. The five-day waiting period and required background checks were found unconstitutional, as the Supreme Court argued in *Printz v. United States* (1997) that they infringed on states' rights. A national computer system now provides background checks, so the need for a waiting period no longer exists. The ban on assault weapons expired in 2004 despite considerable political pressure to extend its duration.

Gun enthusiasts complain that legislation like the Brady Bill misses the point. Their common refrain, "Guns don't kill people, people kill people," reflects their belief that gun control will not solve the crime problem. Further, they argue that gun control violates individual rights. Supported by the aggressive lobbying of the NRA, gun control opponents challenge any attempt to curtail their right to own and use weapons. They base their opposition on the right to bear arms as protected by the Constitution's Second Amendment and on what they perceive as a common-sense judgment that ownership of guns is uncontrollable. They find efforts to control certain types of guns—for example, the ban on imported assault rifles imposed by President George W. Bush—to be illogical, particularly when no such ban was placed on similar domestic-made weapons. Opponents also point to studies that show no difference in crime patterns between jurisdictions with strict gun laws and those without.[65]

Despite this opposition, U.S. public opinion still insists that policymakers do something to counteract gun availability.[66] Recent horrifying school violence—such as two boys aged eleven and thirteen killing four schoolmates and a teacher and injuring ten others in Jonesboro, Arkansas, in 1998—has led to renewed demand for gun control.[67] Children with access to firepower, perhaps spurred by the indiscriminate violence absorbed from television, movies, and video games, alarm even die-hard opponents of gun control. Scholars point out that gun use tends to be an instrumental act much more than an intentional act. They point to the fact that firearms are rarely used by serial killers. Tragically, gun availability has changed victimization patterns. Empirical evidence supports the conclusion that, while guns do not increase the overall levels of crime, they seem to increase the seriousness of criminal attacks.[68] One study concludes:

> Where guns are available, commercial targets are robbed more than individual citizens, and young men more frequently than elderly women. Similarly, in domestic assaults husbands are more frequently the victims. Thus the most important effects of guns on crime are that they increase the seriousness of criminal attacks and affect the distribution of victimization; they do not seem to markedly increase the overall levels of criminal attack.[69]

Poverty and Crime

Does poverty cause crime? The connection between these two societal illnesses is far from simple. Yet many propose that the antidote to crime is the elimination of poverty. Unfortunately, what research tells us about the relationship between poverty and crime is inconclusive and sometimes misleading.

Much of the research about crime and poverty takes as its starting point assumptions about criminal behavior. In this model, individuals choose crime over employment when crime seems a more expedient course of action. They do this particularly if the risk of being caught is low and the utility (money) to be gained is high. It follows, then, that the appropriate reaction to this rational choice is to increase the deterrent (punishment) for prospective criminals. A further implication is that poor people are more likely to make this rational calculus than are members of other segments of society. They have less to lose than those who have sufficient income sources.

Empirical research advanced to confirm this rationale is common but methodologically weak. Many studies use unemployment statistics to measure poverty, but these have proven to be very unrefined measures, neither reliable nor valid. Time-series studies comparing crime rates and unemployment statistics fail to explain mounting crime rates, nor do they show that unemployment causes crime. Cross-sectional studies comparing crime rates and unemployment trends across different geographic areas are even more difficult to interpret. States and cities differ widely in the nature and extent of the crimes committed within their jurisdictions. Fluctuations in differing labor markets make unemployment figures difficult to compare. Nonetheless, the intuitive sense that if individuals have jobs they are less likely to commit crimes has resulted in politicians promoting job programs as an antidote to crime. The consequences of these policies have been unclear, leading some to wonder if the causes of unemployment and crime are the same, if some people simply cannot succeed economically no matter what help they receive, or if the problem is simply that criminals choose a life of crime (a return to rational choice notions). Analysts continue to struggle with these questions. Though unable to explain how crime factors relate, researchers continue to point to correlations between delinquency, homicides, and the socioeconomic characteristics of communities.

Indicators like population density of households, residential mobility, family disruption, the presence of gangs, gun density, and drug distribution typically characterize low-income communities. All correlate with high crime rates. Studies point out that population density of households, residential mobility, and disrupted family structures, in particular, are significant indicators of crime.[70] They are typical of communities with high numbers of teenagers and single-parent households.

Research concludes that poverty today goes hand in hand with significant social disorganization. In his study *The Truly Disadvantaged: The Inner City, the Underclass, and Public Policy,* William Julius Wilson writes of the social isolation of the inner city.[71] Beyond the extreme racial segregation of inner cities in relation to other parts of the social fabric, there is a further breakdown within these communities themselves. People live side by side but do not know one another. Great mistrust exists among neighbors. In these communities, unlike poor communities of the past, parenting becomes highly individualistic. Everyone is a stranger. Intergenerational relationships fall apart. There are no positive identifications with a neighborhood, no explicit community norms, and no sanctions against delinquent behavior. A street culture develops with its own set of norms and symbols. Embedded in this culture is a deep distrust for established institutions such as the police, schools, and businesses. Furthermore, given the current ongoing structural economic change toward service production and away from traditional industrial production, little opportunity exists in these communities to find good jobs and move out of the inner city culture. Crime is convenient, pervasive, and attractive.

The crisis for policymakers is where and how to break into this cycle. In the

1970s, theories proposing the concept of "defensible space" took hold.[72] Here the objective was to create a more livable and more easily protected environment. City planners took hold of these ideas and experimented with better architectural design, improved lighting, and more green space. Thirty years later, these experiments have met with mixed success. While still aware of the need to make communities more hospitable, studies now recommend the use of more informal social controls. Community watch programs, beat police patrols, and exact-change requirements for public transportation are all examples of the changing emphasis. Increasingly, policymakers have come to consider crime and poverty as social illnesses that need not just deterrence, but also improvements in areas such as public health. The complex relationship between crime and poverty defies any simple solution. Better studies, improved social and anticrime programs, and better economic opportunities may help shed light on the issue.

White Collar Crime

White collar crime is defined as illegal activity conducted in the course of one's occupation. It differs from **organized crime**, which is economic gain through illegal business practices like gambling, loan sharking, prostitution, and narcotics. Organized crime *is* one's occupation; white collar crime is perhaps more insidious. The activities of white collar criminals cut across business and politics, the professions and labor organizations. The scope of white collar crime is broad, including financial, environmental, safety, and consumer affairs misconduct.

In 1939, U.S. criminologist Edwin Sutherland studied these crimes not "ordinarily included within the scope of criminology" and defined white collar crimes as those "committed by a person of respectability and high social status in the course of his occupation."[73] Sutherland's definition and research were controversial at the time, but are less so today. The financial corruption and scandal associated with the economic boom of the 1990s affected many unsuspecting Americans. They found themselves caught up in the misdeeds of corporate white collar executives who exploited their privileged positions at the expense of many.

Too often white collar offenders hide behind corporate or professional sanctuaries, leading to claims that white collar criminals experience more lenient penalties. Critics say that white collar crime is just a "better racket." Unfortunately, the criminal justice system reacts differently to white collar crime than to street crime. Some criminologists theorize that judges and criminal justice personnel are often reluctant to view white collar crime as seriously because they identify with the socioeconomic standing of these offenders. To illustrate this, consider the savings and loan (S&L) crisis of the 1980s. After the Reagan administration deregulated the S&L industry, some S&L owners and executives violated laws and regulations by engaging in fraudulent, unsafe business practices that resulted in billions of dollars of losses.[74] Table 8.4 compares prison sentences for S&L offenders with those of selected federal offenders. The authors of this study concluded that the latter offenders often received longer sentences, "despite the fact that these crimes almost never approached $500,000, the average S&L offense."[75] White collar offenders typically have the resources to mount a good defense and, as argued by Richard Posner, because the "social stigma" associated with white collar crime is so great and the civil law procedure so costly, white collar criminals are best punished by "monetary penalties—by fines . . . rather than by imprisonment or other 'afflictive' punishments (save as they may be necessary to coerce payment of the monetary penalty)."[76]

In part, the legal system's historical reaction to white collar crime reflects the difficulty in conceptualizing and measuring it. These crimes do not fit easily into wider definitions of crime. On the sidelines of criminology, they are often complex and easily concealed, and present measurement problems. Responsibility for these crimes is easily diffused and sadly, victims are often unaware of what actually has happened to them. A recent *New York Times* article by journalist Floyd Norris

---

Table 8.4   Prison Sentences for Savings and Loan Offenders and Selected Federal Offenders

	Mean Prison Sentence (months)
Savings and Loan offenders	36.4
All federal offenders, convicted of:	
Burglary	55.6
Larceny	27.5
Motor vehicle theft	38.0
Counterfeiting	29.1
Federal offenders, with no prior convictions, convicted of:	
Property offenses (nonfraudulent)	25.5
Public order offenses (regulatory)	32.3
Drug offenses	64.9

Sources: Federal Criminal Case Processing, 1980–90 (Washington, D.C.: U.S. Department of Justice, Bureau of Justice Statistics, 1992), p. 17; *Compendium of Federal Justice Statistics, 1988* (Washington, D.C.: U.S. Department of Justice, Bureau of Justice Statistics, 1991), p. 43.

derides the chief executive officer (CEO) of a large international corporation who claimed he "didn't know" about the company's wildly inflated revenues and hidden expenses. The executive's defense: "He worked on the strategy vision part, talking to key clients, being on the outside of the company." As Norris concludes about bosses walking away while their subordinates go to jail, "It's good to be the king."[77]

Classifications of white collar crime include financial manipulations known as "theft after trust," fraud (including tax fraud), corruption such as acceptance of bribes, and "restraint of trade" such as phony limited partnerships and pyramid schemes. Embezzlement is crime by an individual in a subordinate position against a strong corporation. Corporate crime includes price fixing and "collective embezzlement," or crime *by* a corporation *against* a corporation. Some occupations are more easily susceptible to crime, especially those in frequent contact with money or those that require specialized, technical information. Some industries, like the automobile or pharmaceutical industries, are more vulnerable. The car dealer wants to sell that used car for as much as possible; the pharmaceutical company can so easily falsify a result.

In their study of the savings and loan crisis of the 1980s, *Big Money Crime,* researchers Kitty Calavita, Henry Pontell, and Robert Tillman explain that, "'collective embezzlers' were not lone, lower-level employees," but thrift owners and managers, acting within networks of co-conspirators inside and outside the institution. Indeed, this embezzlement was company policy."[78]

Corporate crime is distinctive because its primary objective is to advance corporate interests, and thus Calavita and colleagues find many similar characteristics between corporate and organized crime. Both are premeditated, organized, continuous, and develop connections to public officials to avoid prosecution. These types of crimes reflect the dark side of the business subculture of competition and profit maximization. Crimes like false advertising, misuse of campaign funds, and occupational and environmental violations are further examples of betrayals of the public trust by business and political leaders. Ironically, most citizens worry little about or are unaware of the effects of this activity. In fact, the systematic, empirical study of white collar crime did not take hold until recently.[79] Yet while the average bank heist nets a robber $10,000, the average computer crime has reached a figure of $430,000.[80] Another study reports that "about 30 percent of business failures were the result of employee dishonesty . . . about 15 percent of the price paid for goods and services goes to cover the costs of dishonesty."[81]

Of similar interest are recent theories about white collar crime. Some economists apply rational choice theory to the white collar criminal, claiming that self-interest in the absence of control best explains why it occurs. Others disagree, arguing that the wider social context must be explored. Financial performance, the search for profitability, the values of individualism, and the pursuit of wealth—all features of U.S. capitalism—give rise to white collar crime, a notion first identified by sociologist C. Wright Mills in his work *The Power Elite* in the 1950s.[82] Author D. Quinn Mills argued that psychological traits like obsession with power lead to large-scale misuse and abuse are evident in recent white collar crimes.[83]

The general lack of documentation and prosecutorial activity regarding white collar crime is not surprising. Its nearly invisible and very diffuse nature complicates investigation. One investigator complained that it was like "doing someone else's checkbook."[84] Paper trails are papered over, increasingly with the help of computers and other sophisticated forms of technology. Nevertheless, the FBI has established a special branch of forensic accountants and lawyers to investigate and prosecute white collar criminals. In 1987, Congress enacted the Computer Fraud and Abuse Act, which has been supplemented by various state laws to counteract computer fraud and abuse. Computer specialists are now routine members of law enforcement agency staffs. This, combined with new tougher sentencing guidelines, means the criminal justice system is starting to focus on these illegal operations.

Nothing prepared the U.S. public for the white collar crime spree of the 1990s. An array of prominent corporations confronted charges of large-scale financial abuse, stock price manipulation, and theft. Beginning with the inflated sales and profits of Sunbeam Corporation's CEO Alfred J. Dunlap, and continuing to ENRON's notorious creative accounting schemes, the result has been millions of dollars lost to small investors. ENRON began as a gas pipeline company and grew into an Internet company involved in energy trading. Company officials, with the help of the Arthur Anderson company's accounting wizardry, concealed losses from investors and made a fortune by running off balance-sheet partnerships. Anderson, which ceased to exist after the ENRON fiasco, pioneered an accounting procedure named the "integrated audit." Essentially, the practice allowed Anderson accountants to work a company's books both on the inside and on the outside. In the absence of auditor independence, the accounting industry was compromised so seriously that Congress passed legislation to regulate the profession. Historically, the industry had relied on peer review, but as of 2002, with the creation of the "Public Company Accounting Oversight Board," established under the Sarbanes-Oxley Act, auditing guidelines and professional discipline will be imposed on the accounting profession. Corporations including WorldCom, TYCO, Adelphia, and Imclone (which ensnared Martha Stewart) have been charged with egregious white collar crimes—egregious in the sense that the leaders of these large corporations stood to profit whether stockholders prospered or not. In a summary study conducted for the American Bar Association, John Cassidy states, "From the beginning of 1999 to the end of 2001, senior executives and directors of these doomed companies walked away with some $3.3 billion in salary, bonuses, and the proceeds from sales of stock and stock options."[85]

CEO compensation skyrocketed by the end of the twentieth century. Peter Drucker once suggested that the ratio of CEO to average employee compensation should be no higher than twenty times. As Drucker argues, when the salary gap goes beyond this amount, it makes a mockery of the contribution of the ordinary employee.[86] Today's chief executive and chief financial officers prosper by way of stock options, which they can exercise to vastly increase their salaries. Historically, CEO salaries were tied to the size of a company, but in the late 1970s this switched to stock profitability. Based on models developed by two University of Chicago graduates, Michael Jensen and William Meckling, the use of the stock option was promoted as a way to better tie the CEO incentive structure to the company's profitability. Whereas in the past the CEO worried about employees and customers, this concern was refocused to shareholder value. A **stock option** is a legal contract that grants the owner the right to buy stock in the future at a certain price. These largely unregulated stock options marked the course for corporate irregularity, as they led to creative accounting that overvalued corporate stock.

The betrayal by corporate leaders of many trusting employees and investors has alerted the policymaking community to the need for different regulatory devices in the areas of finance and securities. Regrettably, the role of lawyers and accountants is too easily compromised when part of their job is determining just how much a company can get away with.

With the white collar crime price tag estimated at approximately $200 billion per year, society can no longer afford to allow professional and business standards alone to regulate the workplace.[87] In the aftermath of the savings and loan crisis, which cost U.S. taxpayers about $180 billion, the heavy artillery of criminal law is increasingly being used.[88] Many Americans have yet to learn that there is a much greater property loss associated with white collar criminal activities than with street crime. Paradoxically, crime prevention funds are allocated in just the opposite way.

Conclusion

While Americans are united, often passionately, over the need to fight crime, no public policy problem is more elusive. Science offers advances in medical treatment and environmental protection, but tells us little about how to keep peace in our streets.

How much crime is there? Newspaper accounts give the impression that crime-free, safe neighborhoods no longer exist. The days of unlocked cars and houses are of another era. Systematic studies of crime like FBI and police reports,

Case Study: Napster Mania—New Spin on an Old Crime?

In the late 1990s, middle-aged Americans shook their heads in confusion over the entertainment industry's outcry about a computer "invention" named Napster. The brainchild of young computer whiz Sean Fanning, Napster was allegedly costing the recording industry millions of dollars in losses. Worried parents cautioned their college-aged children not to do whatever Napster purportedly did, so that they would not be caught in a sting operation and land in jail for copyright infringement. The clamor has quieted for now. A federal court order shut down Napster, but many wonder for how long and, more importantly, what caused all of the controversy. To understand this "new age" crime, a short lesson in intellectual property rights policy is important.

Copyrights and patents protect creative, including intellectual, property. Unlike other things that an individual owns, intellectual or creative properties, in theory, become public goods unless they are protected. Without protection, there is nothing to stop an individual from seizing an idea, a song, or even a better way of doing something, using it for profit, and escaping any associated "fixed costs"—financial investments made in creating a property. Recall that classical liberal philosopher John Locke reasoned that property had meaning when an individual mixed his or her labor with it. He used the analogy of the apple orchard and argued that after being picked from a tree, apples became the property of the gatherer. Unfortunately, intellectual property is not easily guarded. It cannot be placed in a basket and then baked in a pie for sale in the market. Intellectual property takes on a life of its own, out in the airwaves, on the stage, or in the case of Napster, on the computer.

To counteract this dilemma, U.S. law extends a limited monopoly on creative and intellectual property. Despite their historical dislike of monopoly power, early policymakers realized that without protection, little financial incentive existed to create and invent.[89] Why not just copy? Discussion of copyright and patents quickly enters the realm of the technical and legal, though the fundamental arguments are quite understandable. Copyright protection allows copyright holders to maintain their ownership long enough to recover their fixed cost. Many argue though that the terms of protection are too long—for example, in the music industry a ninety-five-year copyright is issued for "work made for hire." A composer is given seventy-five years of protection for intellectual property after his or her death. Technically, any time a band wants to sing a song, or a high school or church group wants to perform a play, some royalty must be paid to the owners of the copyrighted material. For any copyrighted material used in this very book, whether a cartoon or a direct quotation, permission must be obtained, credit must be attributed, and in the case of the cartoon, royalty must be paid.

Some property is not easily protected. For example, most classical ballet (with the exception of the work of George Ballanchine) is not protected, and on a more mundane level, neither are recipes or clothing. (On the other hand, the Ralph Lauren Polo logo is protected. It is the brand name that garners the profit.) The invention of radio and later cable television set up new challenges for copyright law, all of which have been met with different and specific protections.

This is the fundamental problem. Copyright protection tends to be very specific and ad hoc. When the need arises, demand for new protection begins. Powerful interest groups, like the Record Industry Association of America (RIAA) and the Motion Picture Association of America (MPAA), mount powerful offenses to protect the value of their

continues

property. Without much legal finessing, the ubiquitous VCR would never have survived the television and movie industries' assault on its ability to record TV programs and movies.[90] Manufacturers of VCRs convinced the courts that their primary function was "time shifting," that is, recording for later viewing. The fact that the machines are used for more than this was not as compelling.

Essentially, technology continues to throw up new challenges for prevailing interests to protect. Such was the case for Napster, which turned out to be not as successful in mounting its defense as were the makers of the household VCR. Maybe if more middle-aged adults understood the issue, the outcome would have been different. Napster allowed a "peer to peer" (p2p) transfer of music files. File sharing of this sort had been around for some time, primarily among users of chat rooms. One protocol in particular, Internet relay chat (IRC), was used prior to Napster and is still used today. A protocol is basically a set of guidelines that establish the rules of communication between two computers. Sean Fanning (whose chat nickname was "Napster") used IRC to transfer files before founding his company.

Computers today use the file format MP3, a sophisticated computer algorithm that permits more dense storage than in the past with little quality lost. In the recent past, music files took up a lot of computer storage. In computer parlance, they were "hogs." Music files also took a long time to transfer, but with the creation of MP3s, files took up less space and transferred in about five to ten minutes. The stage was set. People, mostly teens and the college aged, recognized the potential immediately and began to "rip" tracks from CDs (in other words, convert the music on CDs into MP3 format) and send them to one another through the IRC and file transfer protocol (FTP) servers. Industrious Sean Fanning set up Napster to streamline

what was already happening. He established a central computer server complete with search terms. People signed on to Napster, searched for the music they wanted, then made contact with another "peer" to transfer the music. Napster facilitated but did not distribute the music.

Napster exploded. Servers, especially at colleges, slowed to a crawl as students clogged bandwidth with downloaded files. The music industry cried foul. It threatened to sue colleges, arguing that as Internet service providers (ISPs), they enabled the activity. Some schools complied by penalizing students and even shutting down servers. The RIAA went after individuals and made headlines by prosecuting college-aged students, whom they considered excessive users of Napster.[91] Ironically, many in the music industry embraced the Napster concept. They argued that this was the way of the future and that it actually helped increase sales. Other groups, like the heavy metal band Metallica, fought alongside the RIAA and eventually met Napster in a federal court in California. In the end, Napster was shut down and sold. Now, if people want MP3s, they pay a fee to download their favorite song. The clamor has quieted, but not without raising important questions about the nature of copyright and the inexorable march of technology. Supporters of Napster railed against the music industry, complaining that overpriced CDs encouraged the proliferation of MP3s. Further, they claimed that copying music files was hardly a crime. Stealing a song was not like stealing a car; after all, the owner still had the song. The Napster case is a precursor of what lies ahead as technology enhances the ability to copy, store, communicate, spy on, and imitate owners of property. These cases are changing the face of copyright law and creating greater challenges to ownership than ever.

along with academic studies, confirm this impression and tell us that violent crime in particular has reached record levels. The associated physical, emotional, and financial costs have forced policymakers at all levels to put crime at the top of their agendas.

What are the causes of crime? Efforts to answer this question have so far offered minimal direction to policymakers. Diverse theories point to a range of possible origins, but none explain conclusively why some individuals commit criminal acts and others do not. More is known about specific conditions associated with crime, like the use of drugs, the availability of guns, and poverty. Unfortunately, policy recommendations based on this knowledge are controversial and too often aimed at achieving political aims rather than true solutions.

How can the U.S. criminal justice system create effective policies to control crime, punish offenders, and protect the innocent? The criminal justice system is the crossroads for testing our resolve to protect the rights of the victims and of the accused before conviction, yet to punish offenders. Often bogged down by its own size and complexity, the system is characterized by the right to legal appeals, pervasive plea bargaining, and complex sentencing requirements. The police, the front line in fighting crime, typically suffer "whiplash" from the need to observe procedural safeguards, protect victims, and respond to society's demand that they catch the criminals.

Consequently, crime abatement creates a policy quagmire. There is no consensus and there are no viable remedies. A rough starting point is the healthy uneasiness about current crime control practices voiced by individuals like Attorney General Janet Reno. Reno calls for redirection in fighting crime to emphasize prevention and the welfare of children, rather than tougher punishment. Despite this, President Clinton's $30.2 billion crime bill passed after an aggressive partisan battle over what some representatives saw as "social pork." The resulting crime bill, the biggest in history, suggested few links between public health and education. It called for $13.4 billion in grants to localities to hire more police, $9.9 billion to build more prisons, and just $5.5 billion for crime prevention programs—the pork. The bill also banned nineteen more types of assault weapons, increased to sixty the number of federal crimes punishable by death, and introduced the so-called three strikes penalty for repeat offenders. It appears that the future portends stronger gun control laws, more prisons, new antidrug campaigns, and increased police visibility as the plan of action.

This chapter's discussion calls for a warning: finding the answer to crime has proven as intractable as eradicating any of humanity's most deadly diseases. Like disease, crime rots the social system. Analysts know that until the true root causes of this social illness are determined, money spent and prisons built will only treat the symptoms.

Questions for Discussion

1. Is there a relationship between public expenditure and crime abatement?
2. How accurate are crime statistics? Why is crime underreported?
3. Compare and contrast leading theories of criminal behavior. What policy guidance have they offered?
4. Describe the competing philosophies of criminal justice. How does deterrence differ from other philosophies?
5. Discuss contemporary police theory. What policies reflect these new approaches?
6. What are the implications of a decentralized criminal justice system?
7. Is the "war on drugs" winnable? What is the theory underlying decriminalization?
8. Do "guns kill people" or do "people kill people"? Discuss.
9. Why are Americans less concerned about white collar crime? How important is the "fear factor" in our criminal justice policy?

Suggested Readings

Andreano, Ralph, and John J. Siegfried, eds. *The Economics of Crime.* New York: John Wiley and Sons, 1980.

Bedau, Hugh Adam. *The Death Penalty in America.* 3rd ed. New York: Oxford University Press, 1982.

Cole, David. *No Equal Justice.* New York: New Press, 1999.

Coleman, Clive, and Clive Norris. *Introducing Criminology.* Portland: Willan, 2000.

Croall, Hazel. *Understanding White Collar Crime.* Philadelphia: Open University Press, 2001.

Currie, Elliott. *Crime and Punishment in America.* New York: Henry Holt, 1998.

Inciardi, James A. *Criminal Justice.* 3rd ed. New York: Harcourt Brace Jovanovich, 1990.

Jacoby, Joseph E., ed. *Classics of Criminology.* Prospect Heights, Ill.: Waveland Press, 1988.

LeVert, Marianne. *Crime in America.* New York: Facts on File, 1991.

Mills, D. Quinn. *Wheel, Deal, and Steal.* New York: Prentice-Hall, 2003.

Poveda, Tony G. *Rethinking White-Collar Crime.* Westport, Conn.: Praeger, 1994.

Reiman, Jeffrey. *. . . And the Poor Get Prison.* Needham, Mass.: Allyn and Bacon, 1996.

Reiss, Albert J., Jr., and Jeffrey A. Roth, eds. *Understanding and Preventing Violence.* Washington, D.C.: National Academy Press, 1993.

Tyler, Tom R. *Why People Obey the Law.* New Haven: Yale University Press, 1990.

Vold, George B., and Thomas J. Bernard. *Theoretical Criminology.* 3rd ed. New York: Oxford University Press, 1986.

Wilson, James Q., ed. *Crime and Public Policy.* San Francisco: ICS Press, 1983.

Wilson, James Q., and Richard J. Herrnstein. *Crime and Human Nature.* New York: Simon and Schuster, 1985.

Wilson, James Q., and Joan Petersilia, eds. *Crime.* San Francisco: ICS Press, 1995.

Notes

1. Bill Clinton, *My Life* (New York: Alfred A. Knopf, 2004), p. 390.
2. Alfred Blumstein, "Criminal Justice Policy," in Jodi Lane and Joan Petersilia, eds., *Criminal Justice Policy* (Northhampton, Mass.: Edward Elgar, 1998).
3. Federal Bureau of Investigation (FBI), *Uniform Crime Report 2003* (Washington, D.C.: U.S. Government Printing Office, 2004), p. 11.
4. Ibid.
5. Ibid., p. 16.
6. Ibid., p. 23.
7. Ibid., p. 27.
8. David T. Lykken, "The Causes and Costs of Crime and a Controversial Cure," *Journal of Personality* 68, no. 3 (June 2000): 565.
9. FBI, *Uniform Crime Report 2003*, p. 42
10. Ibid., p. 49.
11. Examples of "exceptional means" include death of the offender or denial of extradition.
12. James Lynch, "Crime in International Perspective," in James Q. Wilson and Joan Petersilia, eds., *Crime: Public Policies for Crime Control* (Oakland, Calif.: ICS Press, 2002), p. 17.
13. A 1992 study titled *Rape in America,* conducted by the National Crime Victim Center and the Crime Victims Research and Treatment Center at the Medical University of South Carolina, found that every year in the United States, 683,000 women are forcibly raped. Partly in response to this finding, the Bureau of Justice Statistics completed a redesign of its National Crime Victimization Survey and documented in *Violence Against Women: Estimates from the Redesigned Survey* (August 1995; NCJ-154348) that women report about 500,000 rapes and sexual assaults to interviewers every year.
14. Elliott Currie, *Crime and Punishment in America* (New York: Henry Holt, 1998), p. 4.
15. James Q. Wilson and Richard J. Herrnstein, *Crime and Human Nature* (New York: Simon and Schuster, 1986).
16. Ibid., p. 22.
17. Clive Coleman and Clive Norris, *Introducing Criminology* (Portland: Willan, 2000), p. 7.
18. Wilson and Herrnstein, *Crime and Human Nature,* p. 21.
19. Coleman and Norris, *Introducing Criminology,* pp. 18–19.
20. Cesare Lombroso, *L'Uomo Delinquente* (Milan: Hoepli, 1876).
21. George B. Vold and Thomas J. Bernard, *Theoretical Criminology* (New York: Oxford University Press, 1986), p. 9.
22. Gary Becker, "Crime and Punishment: An Economic Approach," *Journal of Political Economy* 76, no. 2 (March–April 1968): 169–217.
23. Vold and Bernard, *Theoretical Criminology,* p. 13.
24. For an excellent discussion of strain theories, see ibid., pp. 185–204.
25. Wilson and Herrnstein, *Crime and Human Nature,* p. 19.
26. Mark H. Moore, "Controlling Criminogenic Commodities: Drugs, Guns, and Alcohol," in James Q. Wilson, ed., *Crime and Public Policy* (San Francisco: Institute for Contemporary Problems, 1983), pp. 125–143.

27 Rick Lyman and Gary Gately, "Behind the Maryland Fires: A County in Transition," *New York Times,* January 7, 2005, p. A11.

28. In a civil case, individuals bring action against one another in the hopes of recovering financial damages. A misdemeanor is a crime that is less serious than a felony and punishable by less than a year in jail.

29. Marianne LeVert, *Crime in America* (New York: Facts on File, 1991), p. 116.

30. James A. Inciardi, *Criminal Justice,* 3rd ed. (New York: Harcourt Brace Jovanovich, 1990), p. 168.

31. FBI, *Uniform Crime Report 1992,* p. 289.

32. In 1957, Cleveland police officers sought entrance to the home of Dollree Mapp, in search of a man suspected of an earlier bombing and of possessing gambling paraphernalia. The police forced their way into Mapp's home, forcibly arrested her, and conducted what was later established to be an illegal search. The Supreme Court ruled that evidence seized from Mapp's home was illegally obtained and therefore not admissible in any courtroom in the country.

33. Robert F. Cushman, *Cases in Constitutional Law* (Englewood Cliffs, N.J.: Prentice-Hall, 1979), p. 400.

34. For example, in 1975 the Supreme Court ruled that, even if a suspect asserts the right to remain silent during interrogation, the police can commence questioning him or her about another crime (*Michigan v. Mosley*). Beginning in the 1980s, a series of cases were heard that dealt with issues of public safety. In *Berkemer v. McCarthy* (1984) the Court held that roadside questioning of suspected drunken drivers does not require *Miranda* warnings.

35. Lawrence Sherman, "The Police," in James Q. Wilson and Joan Petersilia, eds., *Crime* (San Francisco: ICS Press, 1995), p. 330.

36. Ibid.

37. George L. Kelling, Tony Pate, Duane Dieckman, and Charles Brown, *The Kansas City Preventive Patrol Experiment* (Washington, D.C.: Police Foundation, 1974).

38. Carl Klockers, ed., *Thinking About Police* (New York: McGraw-Hill, 1983).

39. Sherman, "Police," p. 332

40. The Law Enforcement Assistance Administration (LEAA), now defunct, grew out of the earlier Office of Law Enforcement Assistance, set up within the Department of Justice. The LEAA was set up to financially assist local governments in fighting crime.

41. U.S. Advisory Commission on Intergovernmental Relations, *Guide to the Criminal Justice System for General Government Elected Officials* (Washington, D.C.: U.S. Government Printing Office, 1993), p. 11.

42. Linda Greenhouse, "Supreme Court Changes Use of Sentence Guides," *New York Times,* January 13, 2005, p. A27.

43. Ibid.

44. David Johnston with Steven Holmes, "Experts Doubt Effectiveness of Crime Bill," *New York Times,* September 14, 1994, p. 16.

45. Marc Mauer, "Thinking About Prison and Its Impact in the Twenty-First Century," fifteenth annual Walter C. Reckless Memorial Lecture, Ohio State University, April 14, 2004.

46. David M. Gordon, "Capitalism, Class, and Crime in America," in Ralph Andreano and John J. Siegfried, eds., *The Economics of Crime* (New York: John Wiley and Sons, 1980).

47. Ibid., p. 98.

48. See, in particular, Gary S. Becker, "Crime and Punishment: An Economic Approach," *Journal of Political Economy* 76, no. 2 (April 1968): 169–217; and Gordon Tullock, "An Economic Approach to Crime," in Andreano and Siegfried, *Economics of Crime.*

49. Quoted from Gordon, "Capitalism," in Andreano and Siegfried, *Economics of Crime,* p. 100.

50. See James Q. Wilson, *The Moral Sense* (New York: Free Press, 1993), which argues that to combat crime, societies need to nurture more private virtue.

51. See studies noted in Albert J. Reiss Jr. and Jeffrey A. Roth, eds. (of the National Research Council), *Understanding and Preventing Violence* (Washington D.C.: National Academy Press, 1993), pp. 291–294.

52. Alfred Blumstein, "Prisons: Populations, Capacity, and Alternatives," in James Q. Wilson, ed., *Crime and Public Policy* (San Francisco: ICS Press, 1983), p. 232.

53. Recidivism refers to recurring criminal behavior.

54. Robert Blecker, "Haven or Hell? Inside Lorlon Central Prison: Experiences of Prison Justified," *Stanford Law Review* (1990): 1149–1249.

55. Reiss and Roth, *Understanding and Preventing Violence,* p. 292.

56. Blumstein, "Prisons," p. 232.

57. See U.S. Advisory Commission on Intergovernmental Relations, *Guide to the Criminal Justice System,* p. 30.

58. Blecker, "Haven or Hell?" p. 1152.

59. For a detailed summary of the leading scientific research on drugs and their effects, see Reiss and Roth, *Understanding and Preventing Violence.*

60. Quoted in ibid., p. 188.

61. P. J. Goldstein et al. (of the National Institute on Drug Abuse), *Drug Related Involvement in Violent Episodes: Final Report* (New York: Narcotic and Drug Research, 1987). See also P. J. Goldstein, "Drugs and Violent Crime," in N. A. Weiner and M. E. Wolfgangs, eds., *Pathways to Violent Crime* (Newbury Park, Calif.: Sage, 1989).

62. This argument is presented in David Boaz, "The Case of Legalizing Drugs," in Herbert Levine, ed., *Point Counter Point Readings in American Government,* 4th ed. (New York: St. Martin's Press, 1992).

63. In October 1993, Attorney General Janet Reno agreed to a new approach to fighting the war on drugs. Drug offenders arrested in Washington, D.C., would come before a "drug court" rather than the D.C. Superior Court. The drug court would supervise intensive treatment for nonviolent drug offenders. The goal, as expressed by Reno, was to deal with the underlying problems of drugs rather than adjudicate for criminal charges. Other drug court experiments have been set up in Florida's Dade and Broward counties.

64. Dorothy P. Rice et al., *Cost of Injury in the United States: A Report to Congress 1989* (San Francisco and Baltimore: Institute for Health and Aging, University of California, and Injury Prevention Center, Johns Hopkins University, 1989).

65. The National Research Council reports estimates showing that only one out of six firearms used in crimes is legally obtained. Charles F. Wellford, John V. Pepper, and Carol V. Petrie, eds., *Firearms and Violence* (Washington, D.C.: National Research Council, 2004).

66. A study of children's hospitals reported in the *Washington Post* (November 26, 1993) estimated the average cost of treating a child for a gunshot wound at more than

$14,000. One study reports that gunshot wounds are the fifth leading cause of death for children under fourteen.

67. On March 24, 1998, in Jonesboro, these two boys opened fire on classmates. In April 1998, a fourteen-year-old boy killed a teacher and wounded two students and another teacher when he opened fire at an eighth-grade graduation dance in Edinboro, Pennsylvania. And on May 22, 1998, a fifteen-year-old Springfield, Oregon, high school student killed three of his classmates in the school cafeteria and wounded twenty-six.

68. Mark H. Moore, "Controlling Criminogenic Commodities: Drugs, Guns, and Alcohol," in Wilson, *Crime and Public Policy,* p. 130.

69. As noted in ibid., p. 130.

70. Reiss and Roth, *Understanding and Preventing Violence,* p. 133.

71. William Julius Wilson, *The Truly Disadvantaged: The Inner City, the Underclass, and Public Policy* (Chicago: University of Chicago Press, 1987).

72. Oscar Newman, *Defensible Space: Crime Prevention Through Urban Design* (New York: Macmillan, 1973).

73. Edwin H. Sutherland, *White Collar Crime* (New York: Holt, Reinhart, and Winston, 1949), p. 9.

74. Charles Keating, Don Dixon, and Erwin Hansen were the three best known of the thrift defendants.

75. Kitty Calavita, Henry N. Pontell, and Robert H. Tillman, *Big Money Crime* (Berkeley: University of California Press, 1997), p. 164.

76. Richard Posner, "Optimal Sentences for White Collar Criminals," *American Criminal Law Review* 17 (Winter 1980): 410.

77. Floyd Norris, "Chief Executive Was Paid Millions, and He Never Noticed the Fraud," *New York Times,* January 7, 2005, p. C1.

78. Calavita, Pontell, and Tillman, *Big Money Crime,* p. 63.

79. "White collar crime" as a term was first used by Edward Sutherland in an address to the American Sociological Society in 1939.

80. Paul W. Keve, *Crime Control and Justice in America* (Chicago: American Library Association, 1995), p. 33.

81. Charles R. Wagner, *The CPA and Computer Fraud* (Lexington, Mass.: Lexington Books, 1979).

82. C. Wright Mills, *The Power Elite* (New York: Oxford University Press, 1956).

83. D. Quinn Mills, *Wheel, Deal, and Steal: Deceptive Accounting, Deceitful CEOs, and Ineffective Reforms* (New York: Prentice-Hall, 2003).

84. Comment quoted by reporter for "Sheriff's Investigation Follows More Paper Trails," *St. Petersburg Times,* August 30, 1993, p. 1.

85. John Cassidy, "The Greed Cycle: How the Financial System Encouraged Corporations to Go Crazy," *New Yorker,* September 23, 2002, p. 64.

86. As cited in Peter Schwartz, "The Relentless Contrarian," *Wired Magazine,* August 1996.

87. See Chantico Publication Company, *Combating Computer Crime: Prevention, Detection, Investigation* (New York: McGraw-Hill, 1992). See also Francis T. Cullen, William J. Maakestad, and Gray Cavender, "The Ford Pinto Case and Beyond: Assessing Blame," in Michael Braswell et al., *Justice, Crime, and Ethics* (Cincinnati: Anderson, 1991).

88. See Congressional Budget Office, *Resolving the Thrift Crisis* (Washington, D.C.:

U.S. Government Printing Office, April 1993). See also F. Stevens Redburn, "The Deeper Structure of the Savings and Loan Crisis," *PS: Political Science and Politics* 24, no. 3 (September 1991): 436.

89. James Boyle, "The Second Enclosure Movement and the Construction of the Public Domain," http://www.law.duke.edu/pd/papers.html.

90. The case in point is *Sony Corp v. Universal City.* See www.eff.org/legal/cases/sony_v_universal_decision_html.

91. All of the *RIAA v. Napster*–related cases are available online at http://www.eff.org/ip/p2p/napster. The briefs include information about the record industry's alleged losses due to Napster.

CHAPTER 9

Education Policy: Low Grades for National Effort

Surveys on policy issues consistently show that education ranks among the top concerns. Those without children in the school system are just as likely as parents to cite education as their primary concern. Generally, parents think their children's schools are better than other schools in their community and that public schools nationally have even more serious problems. There is broad agreement that the education system should be improved, that academic standards should be enforced, that teachers should be paid more, and that run-down buildings should be fixed up. The major problems in public education nationally include concern over disruptive students in the classroom and violence, along with overcrowded classrooms and lack of parental involvement. There is strong public support for educational reforms in these areas even if it requires higher taxes. Proposals to reform public school funding by providing equity in financing, using vouchers, or instituting charter schools are much more controversial. Apathy and complacency among the public have been replaced with increasing interest as education has become a policy issue of national importance. Alarm over policy issues in education often has many different and contradictory sides. Many believe that investing more in education would solve the unemployment problem in the United States and help it regain its competitive edge in international trade.

Public opinion is less concerned about colleges and universities. Many U.S. institutions of higher learning are regarded as the best in the world. There is increasing concern about the rising cost of higher education, and whether lower-income Americans lack the financial resources to pursue a postsecondary degree, thus contributing to the unequal distribution of income and wealth.

Education is a distinct departure from other services provided by the government. Unlike social welfare or health care, which are concerned with the maintenance of human capital, education seeks to *develop* it. Americans agree that providing a quality education is one of the most important items on the public policy agenda. Policies that remove obstacles to achieving a quality education, such as reducing school violence or discouraging disruptive behavior, receive widespread support. Beyond these areas of obvious agreement, the unity quickly dissolves when more fundamental questions are raised. Education policy provokes debate because no policy issue is more important to the nation's future. For example, what should be the purpose of the educational endeavor? Is it primarily to help individuals succeed to their full potential? Or is its main ideal to contribute to the public good by creating a more skilled labor force? Or perhaps it is some combination of both propositions. These two separate ideas are the basis for conflicting educational goals and policies. The first view suggests that parents have a right to give their children the best education possible, one that will give them access to the most important jobs available (or allow them to pass on their privileged position in society to their children by giving them education advantages). The second proposition leads to the view that education should promote the public good, which is best achieved by a dedication to educational equality. Many hold both views simultaneously. The result is widespread dissatisfaction with the U.S. educational system. Unfortunately, little consensus exists about *what* should be done to resolve the problems and *who* has the primary responsibility for taking corrective action.

Education: A Quasi–Public Good

In Chapter 1 we pointed out that competitive markets are very efficient mechanisms for meeting consumer demand. Why, then, should government be involved in providing education when a competitive market is such an efficient mechanism? After all, education has some elements of a private market; for example, education brings private rewards to individuals through higher income, more satisfying work, and more pleasant working conditions.

Public support of education has long been touted because of its positive impact on society. **Functionalism** holds the view that society can exist in harmony because its institutions spring from a shared culture. Consequently, the family, the educational system, and the economy, among other institutions, perform specific "functions" necessary for the survival of society. The function of education is to (1) transfer societal values, (2) produce a more informed citizenry, (3) produce workers with more productive skills, and (4) provide for "equal opportunity" by providing everyone, regardless of circumstance, with basic education skills. School serves as a halfway house to assist a child's passage between the familiar world of the family and the impersonal world of adult careers and community life.[1] The belief that formal education correlates with good citizenship has assimilated into U.S. culture.

Functionalism supports the notion in that all members of society should have an equal chance for educational and economic success. This meritocratic ideal strongly supports equality of *opportunity,* but not equality of *outcomes.* Supporters of the theory contend that a public education system fosters greater equality because it provides the knowledge and skills necessary to perform those jobs that society rewards highly. Thus, wealthier members of society are not able to monopolize access to highly paid jobs. By broadening the equality of opportunity, education encourages social mobility. We will return to the critics of this view after discussing the implications of human capital theory.

Education also has characteristics of a **quasi–public good** in that important positive externalities result from an educated society. A more highly educated and skilled work force is more productive and produces more wealth than a poorly educated one. Individuals demand education based on their expectations of personal benefit without regard to the larger benefits to society. The result is that private decisions about how much education to buy will not lead to a socially optimal level of output. The external benefits justify that government provide education for everyone through subsidies.

Human Capital Theory

To most people the notion of **capital** means a factory, shares of stock, or a bank account. They are forms of capital in that they are assets that provide income in the future, as opposed to **consumption**, which provides immediate benefits but does not increase one's ability to earn future income. **Human capital theory** contends that expenditures on education, medical care, and training make individuals inherently more productive and therefore more highly valued workers. Adam Smith and John Stuart Mill realized that there must inevitably be a link between education and economic growth. Smith pointed out that education was an investment that would improve the future productive capacity of workers, and their future earnings, just as an investment in machinery or a factory will generate future income. He said that the capital stock of a nation includes the

> useful abilities of all the inhabitants or members of the society. The acquisition of such talents, by the maintenance of the acquirer during his education, study, or apprentice-ship, always costing a real expense, which is a capital fixed and realized, as it were, in his person. Those talents, as they make a part of his fortune, so do they likewise of that of the society to which he belongs. The improved dexterity of a workman may be considered in the same light as a machine or instrument of trade which facilitates and abridges labour, and which, though it costs a certain expense, repays that expense with a profit.[2]

During preindustrial periods the value of individuals to society was measured primarily in physical productivity rather than mental ability. The size of a nation's population was a strong indicator of its power. With the advent of the industrial and commercial revolutions, it became apparent that a nation's power was less dependent on physical labor and more dependent on skills. A country with the largest population was not necessarily the most productive or powerful. The ability of colonial England and France to control far more populous territories illustrated this.[3]

Education can be thought of as human capital because individuals cannot be separated from their knowledge or skills the same way they can be separated from material assets. Just as a corporation commits some of its profits to buying new equipment to generate more profits at a later date, the individual may reduce current income (and consumption) by investing in education in the hope of increasing future income. By obtaining a college degree, you anticipate that you will acquire useful knowledge and skills that will improve your employment opportunities and lifetime earnings, resulting in a more pleasant job than a high school friend who did not continue his or her education would have.

The Rate of Return to Human Capital

The theory holds that those with more human capital should be more productive than those with less. The productivity and quality of labor will be largely determined by the education and skill of the work force. The educational process replicates many of the skills the job market rewards generously in the form of wages. Most efforts to measure the rate of return to investment in education concentrate on direct monetary benefits and ignore the spillover benefits that accrue to society because of the difficulty in measuring them. The fact that private rates of return to educational investment are higher and more easily measured than the social rates of return, especially for higher education, has been used to justify adding tuition fees and student loans at the university level.

There is a positive relationship between education and lifetime earnings. High school graduates ordinarily have higher lifetime earnings than those without a high school degree, and college graduates will earn more during their lifetime than high school graduates (see Table 9.1). This leads to the conclusion that one is better off with more rather than less education. That more education *correlates* with higher lifetime earnings does not prove that higher education *causes* the higher earnings.

Further, estimates of educational benefits may be too low because of the difficulty of distinguishing between consumption and investment benefits.[4] Education is not only an investment, but also a consumption good in that many enjoy learning during the process.

Table 9.1   Average Income by Highest Degree Earned, 2002

	Not a High School Graduate	High School Graduate Only	Associate's Degree	Bachelor's Degree	Master's Degree	Professional Degree	Doctorate
All	18,826	27,280	34,177	51,194	60,445	112,845	89,734
25–34 years	19,235	26,278	30,662	42,623	48,598	75,247	62,190
35–44 years	22,324	30,259	37,440	58,267	63,758	123,811	88,818
45–54 years	21,231	31,251	39,167	60,680	67,096	126,230	112,538
55–64 years	24,761	30,893	34,848	55,057	62,640	132,372	81,166
65 and over	18,949	27,519	34,331	51,612	61,151	114,981	91,771

Source: U.S. Census Bureau, *Statistical Abstract 2004–2005* (Washington, D.C.: U.S. Government Printing Office, 2004), p. 142.

Costs and Benefits of Human Capital Investment

Who pays for the costs of education? In regard to the public school system, government at the federal, state, and local levels underwrites the costs of education through tax **subsidies**, especially at the elementary and high school levels, where compulsory attendance is required at least through age sixteen. Individuals during the years of their elementary and high school education forgo minimal income, since the law precludes significant employment below the age of sixteen. All taxpayers, including parents and those without children in the affected age groups, absorb the cost of the educational subsidy.

A college education is far more expensive, since the government does not fully subsidize its costs. The student, or his or her impoverished parents, must pay directly for room, board, tuition, books, and other assorted fees. In addition, the individual receiving the education can forgo significant income during the typical four- to five-year period it increasingly takes to complete a college degree. And after the college education is completed, it may take time before college graduates surpass high school graduates in income levels, since the latter have already acquired four years of seniority and experience on the job. The variation in income as related to gender and education, indicated in Table 9.2, is striking.

Human capital theory maintains that education provides skills and technologies, such as reading, writing, mathematical calculation, and problem solving, that are directly related to the production process. Education therefore raises productivity and the earning capacity of the individual worker. This is called the **marginal**

Table 9.2   Average Income by Highest Degree Earned and Factors of Gender and Racial/Ethnic Background, 2002

	High School Graduate Only	Associate's Degree	Bachelor's Degree	Master's Degree	Professional Degree	Doctorate
All						
Male	32,673	42,392	63,503	73,629	138,827	99,607
Female	21,141	27,341	37,909	47,368	61,583	66,426
White	28,145	34,876	52,479	60,787	115,523	92,125
Male	33,920	43,494	65,439	74,426	140,965	103,787
Female	21,388	27,480	37,903	47,209	60,944	64,106
Black	22,823	30,391	42,285	51,974	96,368	69,780
Male	25,582	36,028	47,018	60,647	(B)	(B)
Female	20,209	26,940	38,741	47,765	(B)	(B)
Hispanic[a]	24,163	31,710	40,949	58,814	81,186	(B)
Male	27,992	37,365	46,115	59,901	90,767	(B)
Female	18,810	25,888	35,357	57,447	(B)	(B)

Source: U.S. Census Bureau, *Statistical Abstract 2004–2005* (Washington, D.C.: U.S. Government Printing Office, 2004), p. 142.

Notes: a. Persons of Hispanic origin may be of any race.

(B) = base figure too small to meet statistical standards for reliability of a derived figure.

productivity theory, which states that an employer will be willing to pay a worker only for what he or she adds to the firm's utility.

Higher educational attainment provides the individual not only with higher income, but also with greater job security. One way to measure job security is to compare unemployment rates and educational attainment, as in Table 9.3.

As less developed countries have dramatically increased their own supply of college graduates, businesses have found that many highly skilled jobs can be sent overseas. For example, India is now producing over four times as many engineers annually as is the United States. Many jobs that rely on highly skilled and educated Americans can now be contracted out at far lower costs. The result is that higher education is less able to provide the safeguard against economic shocks that it once did. As pressure to cut costs rises, U.S. businesses are replacing high-quality,

Table 9.3 Unemployment Rates by Educational Attainment, 1992–2003

	Total	Not a High School Graduate	High School Graduate Only	Less Than a Bachelor's Degree	College Graduate
1992	6.1	11.5	6.8	5.6	3.2
1995	4.3	9.0	4.8	4.0	2.4
2000	3.0	6.3	3.4	2.7	1.7
2003	4.8	8.8	5.5	4.8	3.1

Source: U.S. Census Bureau, *Statistical Abstract 2004–2005* (Washington, D.C.: U.S. Government Printing Office, 2004), p. 396.

high-wage workers in the United States with high-quality, low-wage workers abroad.

Objections to Human Capital Theories

Early theories of human capital that claimed precise relationships between education and economic growth, both at the individual level and at the national level, have been forced to acknowledge that supportive empirical evidence is weak.

One social science theory that broadly supports the human capital theory maintains that education functions to distribute workers into the jobs for which they are best suited based on their educational skills. Critics of functionalism accuse it of disregarding the social class divisions in society perpetuated by the educational system. They charge that students are separated into vocational, general education, and college prep programs along the general class lines of their families. One researcher suggested a similar sorting mechanism takes place in the way curriculums are presented in different communities.[5] Many hoped that as education became more available and equally distributed, children from disadvantaged families would get as much education as those from advantaged families. That has not happened. Therefore, the critics claim, while education can provide social mobility, it tends to "transmit inequality from one generation to another."[6] One study shows that high school graduates who are in the top quarter in socioeconomic status are almost twice as likely to go on to college as those in the bottom quarter.[7] The gaps in educational achievement are a major factor in the transmission of inequality. Another study, by Christopher Jencks and his colleagues, found that about 40 percent of the association between male childhood family background and adult occupational status was due to students' educational attainments, after controlling for the effects of IQ test scores. In other words, upper-class graduates receive higher-status jobs than do working-class graduates, because the former receive more education and not because of greater innate ability.[8]

Pierre Bourdieu, a French sociologist and leading critic of higher education, has focused on the glaring inequalities in the distribution of wealth and status that persist despite the expansion of educational opportunities for everyone.[9] He is concerned with how inequalities of position endure over generations. Bourdieu argues that individuals use education to maintain their positions of privilege. The educational system has displaced the family, church, and workplace as determinant variables for the transmission of **social stratification**. Since democratic societies originated in a rebellion against privilege and therefore affirm a belief in the essential equality of individuals, privileged groups cannot openly claim a right to dominating positions. Modern democracies rely on indirect and symbolic forms of power rather than physical coercion to maintain authority. Dominant groups have found that higher education can transmit social inequalities by converting them into academic hierarchies.[10] Several points are stressed in Bourdieu's research. His investigation supports other findings that academic performance of students is highly correlated with parents' cultural background. This further relates to degree of success in the labor market, which hinges on both the *amount* of education received and the academic *prestige* of the institution attended. Ultimately, educational institutions frequently develop their own academic interests and agendas. These may differ significantly from those proclaimed by the existing social order.

Class Conflict Model

Another explanation for the expansion of education in the United States argues that education grows to meet the rising technical skill requirements of jobs. Given this premise, the **class conflict model** claims that employers use education to *screen* workers, although no demonstrable connection exists in most cases between education and job performance. According to this model, formal education developed to meet the growing problems created by industrialization and urbanization in the United States. Rather than meeting objectives like supplying workers with more complex technical skills or reducing social inequality, public education has provided social control by instilling behavior attributes like obedience, discipline, and respect for and compliance with authority.[11] Thus, employers are willing to give a preference to more educated workers in hiring and salary because those workers are more willing to accept traditional corporate values.[12] Thus, education serves to legitimize inequalities rooted in the economic structure of society.

Research by Gregory Squires concluded that the upgrading of the educational requirements related to work cannot be explained in terms of the increasing technical skill requirements of jobs.[13] He points out that the Census Bureau reports that the increasing educational achievements of workers show that educational accomplishments have risen faster than technical skill requirements. He states that there is a misconception that a change from farm laborer to assembly line worker or from blue collar worker to white collar worker necessarily represents an increase in skill requirements. Although an assembly line worker may use more sophisticated machinery than the farmer, the assembly line worker is not necessarily a more highly skilled worker.[14] Employers frequently raise the educational specifications of jobs in reaction to an increase in the supply of better-educated workers. And better-educated workers receive the preferred positions within the job structure. With the expansion of schooling, both employers and occupational groups increasingly require formal education as an entry requirement.[15] One result is that individuals have responded by acquiring higher levels of educational achievement to improve their competitive position within the job market, thereby continuing the ever-higher spiral of educational credentials and requirements.

As the gap between the supply and the demand for college graduates continues to increase, competition between them extends further down in the labor market, leaving those with less education with even fewer job opportunities. Thus the wage gap between those with high school degrees and those with college degrees increases, while both groups experience underemployment. More highly educated workers receive higher pay, but it is based on the amount of education rather than the content of learning or the skills required for the job.

Human Capital Theory and Its Limits

Since supporters of human capital theory believe that there is a linear relationship between formal education and economic growth at the individual (micro) level and national (macro) level, education emerges as a major policy field. In the context of economic policy, higher unemployment, declining international competitiveness, and a generally weaker economy, education (or lack of it) is identified as the cause of the problem. It also suggests a solution—more education—to resolving U.S. economic problems. Education is viewed as a form of economic and not social policy. In fact, the need for education to level the playing field in improving the life chances of those born into poverty, or to strengthen the social fabric of society or provide for a more informed democratic citizenry, increasingly tends to be ignored. Supporters of human capital theory justify an emphasis on education policy to produce the economic drive needed to reverse the declining fortunes of the national economy.

Alan Greenspan, Chairman of the Federal Reserve, provided the standard

Case Study: Education as Market Signaling

Human capital theory suggests that college graduates should receive an increased income that at least compensates them for their extra investment in education. It assumes that students acquire skills as they successfully complete high school, and gain even more skills improving their productivity as they invest in a college education.

Other social scientists challenge this view of how education raises income. One view claims that the educational process teaches students little in the way of relevant knowledge or skills for subsequent job performance. Rather, the educational system *sorts* people according to ability. Supporters of this view claim that competencies like perseverance, intelligence, and self-discipline are needed to succeed in college and also correlate with success in the labor force. A college degree indicates to employers that the individual is a high-quality worker who can be trained easily, thus lowering productivity costs. Employers are therefore willing to pay a differential to more highly educated workers because they will be more productive on average.

Academic credentials thus provide a mechanism by which better-educated workers may separate themselves from those with less education. Suppose the labor force is divided equally between low- and high-skilled workers: a low-skilled worker has a **marginal revenue product** (MRP) (the additional revenue when the firm uses an additional unit of input) of $300 per week, and a high-skilled worker has an MRP of $500 per week.

If an employer cannot be sure whether a new worker has the qualities of a high- or low-quality worker when first hired, the wage will be based on the *anticipated* MRP. Thus the firm will calculate that a new hire has a 50 percent chance of being a high-quality worker and a 50 percent chance of being a low-quality worker, and pay a wage based on the expected MRP of $400 ($[0.50 \times \$300] + [0.50 \times \$500] = \$400$).

Since firms pay the average MRP, low-quality workers are better off, since they receive $400 rather than $300, while high-quality workers are worse off, since they receive $400 rather than $500. High-quality workers would like to signal to the firm that they possess the characteristics associated with high productivity in the labor force. The educational system provides the means for them to signal the firm in a way that low-quality workers would be unable to do. Employers are aware of the correlation and screen workers based on their education. Although education by itself does not increase a worker's productivity, it signals to the employer the probable possession of other qualities that improve productivity. Signaling does not change the *average* wage, only its distribution. It has a positive effect on the income of the more highly educated workers, and a negative effect on the incomes of those less educated.

A more radical view holds that the wealthy are able to buy the best education regardless of ability. Education thus sorts people according to social class, not ability. In this way, education is a device by which the privileged members of society are able to pass on their favored position to their already privileged successors while providing the appearance of legitimacy for higher wages. In this model, education does not enhance ability, but does cultivate noncognitive traits like discipline, respect, obedience, and acceptance that are valued in the business culture.

Source: A. Michael Spence, "Market Signaling: Informational Transfer in Hiring and Related Screening Processes," in *Harvard Economic Studies*, vol. 143 (Cambridge: Harvard University Press, 1974).

human capital theory in testimony before the House Committee on Education and the Work Force when he said that the U.S. economy is best served through competition in the global economy. Therefore, to ensure that as many Americans as possible have the opportunity to receive the benefits that flow from this engagement, one critical element is the "provision of rigorous education and ongoing training to all members of our society." He went on to say that, unfortunately, the United States has "a shortage of highly skilled workers and a surplus of lesser-skilled workers."[16] At the same time, Greenspan rejected the notion that the quality of the education system is directly linked to how much government spends, and warned against "overcommitting" to certain levels of expenditure. "Putting money in is not necessarily an accurate measure of the output. However, he said, "we have to increase the skills every year or we will fall behind."[17]

Jared Bernstein of the Economic Policy Institute agrees that highly educated workers are far more likely to be employed and to be well compensated than those with less education. However, there is little evidence of a shortage of highly skilled U.S. workers; the problem is a lack of jobs. Highly skilled jobs are moving overseas, including jobs for computer software engineers, architects, radiologists, and financial analysts. Such workers are among the most highly educated in our country. Many less-developed countries have been producing many more skilled workers, which results in the exportation of jobs and an erosion of our comparative advantage. This increased supply of skilled workers abroad brings a downward pressure on the earnings of skilled workers at home, who have a significant wage advantage over workers with similar skills abroad. Human capital investment theory assumes that by further educating our most skilled workers, we will justify once again the wage differential in our favor in the global labor market with even more workers with even higher skills than were previously available.[18] But since these workers are already among the most skilled workers in the country, they would require education beyond anything now contemplated. Bernstein concludes that although the educational system has problems, the "problems do not stem from a national lack of quality, but rather from inequities in the distribution of that quality."[19]

Current Policy Goals

In the United States the goal is to reposition the nation and its economy around the free market forces of free competition, deregulation, and private enterprise as opposed to social welfare approaches. Supporters claim that education reforms in the 1970s and 1980s lost their rigor as a result of education policies being taken over by teachers, parents, and students who were allowed too much control. The need for schools to provide a skilled work force as justified in human capital theory is now central to U.S. education policy. The National Commission on

Excellence in Education produced a document titled *A Nation at Risk,* which criticized the "educational reform" that had occurred in the educational system. It claimed that "if an unfriendly foreign power had attempted to impose on America the mediocre educational performance that exists today, we might well have viewed it as an act of war."[20]

The report found that society and its educational institutions had lost sight of the basic purposes of education and the disciplined effort needed to achieve them. This state of affairs resulted from schools, teachers, and parents having gained too much authority, the result being that policymakers had to regain control to secure U.S. economic interests. Since the commission's report, educational policy has been closely tied to economic policy concerns for U.S. global competitiveness. The commission proposed restructuring education through a series of reforms to focus on the "basics," and measuring learning and progress toward certain goals through standardized testing. If progress was not swift enough, schools, teachers, and students could be quickly identified and appropriate remedies applied.

Implementing education policy in the United States is particularly cumbersome. There is an increasing effort at the national and state levels to determine policy, set educational targets and direction, evaluate outcomes, and provide teacher appraisals on the basis of achieving the measurable goals. Simultaneously, there is an effort to shift responsibility for achieving policy goals to the local level, as funds appropriated to the schools are tied to the achievement of, for example, attrition rates, standards, and competencies as measured by distant policymakers.

The Structure of U.S. Public Education: An Overview

The success of U.S. education in the nineteenth century, especially when compared to European nations, reflects the nation's revolutionary origins. The Founding Fathers rejected the idea of a hereditary aristocracy and emphasized the equality of all citizens. Around the time of the American Revolution, much of education was the responsibility of the family. This **informal education** took place primarily in the home, with relatives and friends serving as teachers. Learning in this context took place largely through the socialization process and through imitating the behavior of elders. This was because in an economy based on tradition, production techniques changed at a glacial pace, and the needed knowledge and skills would be passed from one generation to the next through apprenticeships and work experience.

In more advanced market economies, however, production techniques change more rapidly, requiring greater adaptability to the new skills needed by workers. Productivity growth is fostered by workers with more education who can more easily adapt to new work requirements than can workers with less education. Modern societies have developed **formal education** systems in which professional teachers guide the learning process. The state has become largely responsible for transmitting culture, literacy, and technical knowledge.

Most modern societies spell out the right to education in their constitutions. However, education is not mentioned in the U.S. Constitution, which was drafted in 1787, when formal education was a rarity and not perceived as critical to society or its citizens. Thomas Jefferson believed that democratic government required an educated citizenry. He wrote that "if a nation expects to be ignorant and free, in a state of civilization, it expects what never was and never will be."[21] Jefferson thought education was essential to maintaining a free government. As such, the primary purpose of education was to enlighten the citizenry so that they could assume the responsibilities of democratic citizenship. Jeffersonian scholar Saul Padover maintained that ensuring political liberty was a major goal of Jefferson's plan, which was based on the principles that (1) democracy cannot long exist without enlightened citizens, (2) democracy cannot function without wise and honest officials, (3) talent and virtue, critical to a free society, should be educated regardless of accidents of birth and wealth, (4) and the children of the poor must be educated at common expense.[22]

Jefferson was so concerned about the political necessity of an educated electorate that in his State of the Union address in 1806 he submitted an amendment to the Constitution to provide federal support.[23] Jefferson's proposed amendment was never seriously considered, so after leaving the presidency he developed an extensive education plan for Virginia covering elementary, secondary, and university levels. At a time when most education was informal, Jefferson believed that the elementary school plan was the most important, because it was "safer to have the whole people respectfully enlightened than a few in a high state of science and many in ignorance as in Europe."[24]

In the early years of the nation, education was the responsibility of the ministry of the various congregations. As a result, elementary and secondary education, funded by tuition payments from parents, was not begun within states until the early 1800s. Alexis de Tocqueville, in the early nineteenth century, noted that equality was the dominant value in U.S. society, along with a culture of individualism that supported personal freedom to pursue interests without hindrance by the government. In this view, social conditions should enable individuals, whatever their pedigrees, to compete for positions on the basis of merit (though in the nineteenth century gender and race were sufficient grounds for exclusion from all higher-level positions).

Most businesspeople of the early nineteenth century opposed efforts to require compulsory school attendance, as well as taxation to support public education. The struggle to create publicly funded school systems in the various states was taken up as a crusade by educational reformers in the 1830s. Paradoxically, the drive to provide public schools, financed by property taxes, was given a boost by immigration. Successive waves of immigration generated the fear that unless the new arrivals were "anglicized," the "American character" would be destroyed. The arrival of Catholics and Jews in increasing numbers caused growing concern among the established elites. In fact, the "Know-Nothing" party of the 1840s developed from fear of a Catholic takeover. Catholic and other religiously affiliated schools were founded not only to reinforce religious values, but also to escape societal religious discrimination.

Providing schools where foreigners learned U.S. customs, morals, and language meant the system had to be tuition-free for all newly arrived poor immigrants as well as for second- and third-generation Americans. A public school system reflecting U.S. nativism was designed to anglicize recent arrivals. Public education was justified as a public good that reduced distinctions between people and created a unified citizenry.

There is still uneasiness in the United States regarding parochial schools. Critics see these institutions as maintaining religious and cultural identities different from mass culture. Still, the United States has the largest number of religious and private elementary and secondary schools, and universities, in the world. Private and parochial schools enroll 14 percent of all elementary school children, 11 percent of all secondary school students, and 33 percent of all college students.[25] Many are hardly distinguishable from public schools. Others are known as elite academic institutions. Many elite prep schools, which began with a religious purpose, have dropped any formal religious affiliation. These boarding schools (such as Phillips Exeter, Groton, and Choate) provide the children of families of established wealth and distinction with advantaged access to the most prestigious universities, and from there, with access to corporate and political leadership.

One goal of the U.S. educational system, which can be traced back to Jefferson, is to equalize differences in wealth and circumstances so that individuals can progress according to their abilities. Unfortunately, according to critics, the results of U.S. public education in the past reflected differences in the wealth of students' parents, and often do so today:

> For despite the promise of American education, it was organized in such a way that it acted as an overwhelmingly powerful mechanism for preserving and promoting racial and social class segregation. Today its effects are so pervasive that probably no other public policies or government actions are as important in preserving inequality from one generation to the next.[26]

The method of financing public education has contributed to the inequality of the system. As recently as 1920, over 80 percent of public education revenue still came from local government. State assistance was generally limited to a flat grant per pupil. The Progressive movement of the early twentieth century, with its concern over unequal educational opportunities between school districts, proposed various plans for states to finance public schools. Between 1920 and 1980, most state governments developed some form of assistance to local school districts. The state government share of the education budget has grown to an average of 49.7 percent of all public school funds spent within states. Traditionally, once having developed education systems funded by tax revenues, states have jealously defended their authority and control over public education.

The long tradition in the United States of local control includes not only what is taught but also how schools are funded. Since school districts are typically funded by local property taxes that are matched on a per pupil basis by the state, the school district's spending is highly correlated to the wealth of the community. Not surprisingly, there are many states where pupils in the most affluent districts receive more than double the funding that students in poorer districts receive. The public educational system historically provided one school per community for children from all social levels (segregation by race was a glaring anomaly). Limitations in transportation kept residents, their workplace, and schools in close proximity. Since World War II, the automobile has fostered the separation of workplace from residence, and the development of large, socially homogeneous school districts. This coincided with the erosion of the egalitarian principle that underlay the notion of public education. It also led to the erosion of traditional local control of education.

Local property taxes within the districts, which often are identical with local political boundaries, typically provide less than half of school finances. But dependence on local property taxes resulted in highly unequal funding available per student between property-rich and property-poor districts. Lawsuits challenging the fairness of relying on local property taxes for funding have resulted in states steadily increasing their contribution to local school districts.[27] Today and overall, states provide more funding than do local districts. In 2001–2002, states contributed 49.7 percent of the money needed for public elementary and secondary education, as noted earlier, while local districts contributed 42.9 percent. The federal government contributed 7.5 percent.[28] States generally establish standards for education within their boundaries, while local control is exercised within the constraints permitted by state governments.

The U.S. method of financing public schools primarily through property taxes perpetuates inequality. School district boundaries reflect societal divisions between affluent and poor, and between white and nonwhite students. Central city school systems tend to receive fewer funds and have disproportionate numbers of poor and minority students. Children attending these schools typically exhibit poorer academic performance than students attending suburban schools. "White flight" to suburban school districts, the result in part of efforts to escape mandated desegregation of inner city schools, has introduced a racial and ethnic factor into these educational problems. Concern over the strong association between family background and success in scholastic performance has led to much research and a number of theories.

Despite the promise of the Supreme Court in the landmark case *Brown v. Board of Education* (1954), the condition of public education in the United States still tends to be separate and unequal. And despite the virtual elimination of de jure segregation, most minority children today still attend de facto racially segregated schools. Public schools, for all their virtues, have not been very helpful to those children who need it most. The same educational system that once was seen as a poor child's ticket out of the slums is seen by many as part of the system that today traps the poor in the slums.

Several California school districts sued the state over unequal funding of school districts. In *Serrano v. Priest* (1971), the California Supreme Court found the inequities in the school funding system, based on property taxes, to be so egregious as to violate the state constitution's equal protection clause. The court said that the funding scheme invidiously discriminated against the poor because it made the quality of the child's education a function of the wealth of his or her parents and neighbors. The court ruled that property tax rates and per pupil expenditures should be equalized and the difference in base revenue limits should be less than $100 by 1980.[29] In 1979, California adopted Proposition 13, which shifted control of the property tax from school districts to the state. This effectively transformed school funding from a local system to one in which the state has control over the bulk of school revenues. The result has been a decline in average spending per pupil, and has not equalized quality across districts.

Many hoped that the *Serrano* decision would provide the foundation for a successful challenge of many state finance systems before federal courts. However, the U.S. Supreme Court dashed those hopes with its decision in *Rodriguez v. San Antonio School District* (1973), in which it held that an unequal school financing plan in Texas was not a federal issue. In the *Rodriguez* case the Supreme Court rejected the idea that education is even a federal responsibility, since education is not a fundamental right guaranteed by the Constitution. This decision made clear that such matters are in the jurisdiction of state courts.

The effect of *Rodriguez* was that equity lawsuits were brought before over forty additional state courts; in nineteen of these cases, the school funding system was found to violate the state constitution. The courts in many cases followed along the lines of *Serrano* and required school districts to spend within a certain range per pupil. The courts have tried to provide a range of equity based on a principle of reasonable variation. Policymakers in various states have been required to spend a lot of time trying to define "relative equity" and devising plans regarding how to achieve it.[30] Since the 1990s the equity issue has been overshadowed by concern over "finance adequacy." The concern here is to define what minimal level of funding is needed in order for every school to effectively teach.

The Federal Government's Role

President Lyndon Johnson enacted the Elementary and Secondary Education Act (ESEA) as a component of the war on poverty. It was the first program to provide significant federal funds targeted toward the educationally disadvantaged children from kindergarten through grade twelve because of social and economic conditions. The act created a range of educational programs for economically and culturally disadvantaged children. The act was originally authorized through 1970, but it has been reauthorized every five years since then and has undergone various name changes with different presidents. The basic purpose of the law remains.[31] The programs that have been funded by the act include Head Start, Native American Education, Bilingual Education, Class Size Reduction, Education Technology, and Title I (the latter of which assists the disadvantaged in meeting high standards).

President George W. Bush reauthorized the ESEA, now renamed "No Child Left Behind" (NCLB), which was signed into law in January 2002. The NCLB law strengthens Title I accountability by requiring states to put accountability systems in place to cover all public schools and students. These systems basically require states to administer standardized tests in reading and mathematics for all students in grades three through eight. These test results and state progress objectives must be categorized by poverty, ethnicity and race, and limited English proficiency and other disabilities, to make sure that no group is in fact left behind. Schools that fail to make adequate annual progress toward statewide proficiency goals will be subject to corrective action and restructuring.

The centerpiece of the NCLB law is that it gives children who are attending failing schools the opportunity to attend public schools, within the local area, that have attained acceptable standards, which may include charter schools. The district must provide transportation to and from the new school.

Charter schools are self-governing public schools frequently run by corporations operating outside the authority of local school boards. Most operate in urban areas in poor neighborhoods. These schools were originally hailed by conservatives as a way to force public schools into competition with the institutions based on the private school model. The NCLB law was expected to stimulate an exponential growth rate in charter schools.

However, the 2003 National Assessment of Educational Progress, usually referred to as the "nation's report card," provided data to the American Federation of Teachers revealing that charter schools are failing to provide the remedy to poor schools that the administration clearly hoped for. Data reported in the *New York Times* shows that fourth-graders attending charter schools are performing about half a year behind students in other public schools in both reading and math.[32] This means that 25 percent of the fourth-graders attending charter schools were proficient in reading and math, against 30 percent who were proficient in reading and 32 percent in math at traditional public schools. This report is the first national comparison of children attending both types of schools.

Charter schools were once hailed by conservatives as a kind of free market solution offering parents an escape from failing public schools. Yet around the country over eighty charter schools were forced to close because of financial problems and poor performance. And in California, the state's largest charter school operator announced the closing of sixty campuses, stranding 10,000 children just weeks before the start of the fall 2004 school year.[33]

The original ESEA program was designed to offset the inequality of per pupil spending within states. But there is in fact a greater inequality in the per pupil expenditures between rich and poor states. There is little likelihood that the federal government will push to target increased funding to alleviate this problem, since it has not requested sufficient funds to fully implement the NCLB law, its own flagship policy proposal in education. Resistance can also be expected from states reluctant to surrender control over their major public policy. However, it is the financial inequity in per pupil spending between states that is perhaps more serious than intrastate inequalities. An argument for a greater funding role for the federal government comes from an analysis of interstate inequalities of school financing, which has risen sharply since 1982.[34] The complexity of the problem of equalizing per pupil spending between states would have to take into account a number of factors. For example, the purchasing power of money varies between states. High-spending states are typically states where the purchasing power of a dollar in education buys less than in many lower-spending states. Also, any national plan would have to adjust funding on the basis that it costs more to educate disadvantaged and high-risk students than advantaged children. To encourage states to use federal aid as a supplement and not a replacement, any plan would have to determine taxing ability versus taxing effort (this distinguishes the taxes levied consistent with one's ability to pay versus low tax rates levied in a state with incomes comparable to states with higher tax rates). A precise computation of such differences is impossible, but estimates of cost of living and other indicators suggest that the real spending gap between most high- and low-spending states is less than the raw numbers would indicate, but the gap is still significant. Most Organization for Economic Cooperation and Development countries have constitutions that were drafted since

World War II. These constitutions refer to education as being the national government's responsibility. As a result, they do not face the great disparity in per pupil funding between geographical divisions that is found in the United States.

Table 9.4 suggests the difficulty of comparing the state effort in education with its ability to tax and with the decision of how much of its budget to put into education. The second column (spending per pupil) indicates the state average without taking into account the intrastate inequalities. Even if all intrastate spending were equalized at the "average," high-poverty districts in rich states would spend much more than low-poverty districts in poor states.[35] Currently, per pupil spending on education in the lowest-spending states is roughly half the expenditures in the highest-spending states.

Assessing Factors in Learning

How can we evaluate the quality of education offered by a school system? How can parents be confident that their son or daughter will receive a quality education from a particular school? How can a local school board, legislator, or governor be confident that they can evaluate the effectiveness of the education offered within a school, the educational district, or the state? The most difficult provision of the NCLB law is the requirement to assess student progress in order to hold schools accountable. States are required to set goals for learning and to present a plan to measure success in reaching those goals.

States have been slow to set out their goals on yearly progress and accountability. They are concerned that, if areas for improvement are identified in many schools and in many areas, they could compound the problem by trying to aid so many schools and spreading their resources so thin that they would be unable to provide extra resources and help to the schools and students most in need. States are also concerned that if they set higher goals than do other states, they may unintentionally penalize themselves, because their schools will have a more difficult time achieving complete efficiency, while states that put forward lower goals might have an incentive to keep them low.

Improving qualifications of teachers and paraprofessionals.

The NCLB law requires teachers of core academic subjects to be highly qualified as defined by the law. Whether raising these qualifications will improve the educational process is unclear. Presumably, if state certification requirements are more rigorous, it will contribute to better teaching.

Although the NCLB law mandates that schools employ "highly qualified" teachers, and although new studies reaffirm the importance of quality teaching, new research also shows that pay for teachers from kindergarten to grade twelve is

Table 9.4 Spending per Pupil as a Percentage of State General Spending and Personal Income

	Educational Spending per Pupil ($ 2002–2003)	Rank	Educational Spending as Percentage of General State Budget ($ FY 2000)	Rank	Educational Spending as Percentage of Personal Income ($ FY 2000)	Rank
Alabama	5,418	47	35.2	27	7.7	36
Alaska	9,569	8	23.2	50	9.9	1
Arizona	5,197	48	33.8	34	6.5	46
Arkansas	5,789	46	38.0	11	7.4	45
California	7,244	29	32.5	40	6.4	22
Colorado	7,428	25	35.1	29	6.2	24
Connecticut	11,378	2	31.4	44	5.2	12
Delaware	10,270	5	36.6	19	7.4	5
Florida	6,411	40	30.3	46	5.4	50
Georgia	8,238	17	38.8	7	6.9	29
Hawaii	7,455	24	25.4	49	5.7	47
Idaho	6,378	41	36.6	18	7.5	41
Illinois	9,376	9	35.3	26	6.0	25
Indiana	8,307	16	39.8	4	7.4	20
Iowa	6,974	33	38.3	10	8.1	10
Kansas	7,620	21	37.9	12	6.9	27
Kentucky	7,274	28	33.5	36	6.9	44
Louisiana	6,698	38	32.3	41	7.2	43
Maine	9,289	10	32.0	42	7.2	35
Maryland	8,124	20	36.6	16	6.0	16
Massachusetts	10,691	4	30.3	47	5.2	30
Michigan	8,166	18	41.4	2	8.1	3
Minnesota	8,628	14	33.0	39	7.0	9
Mississippi	5,822	45	34.6	31	8.4	37
Missouri	6,819	37	37.2	14	6.4	40
Montana	7,368	27	36.3	22	8.4	26
Nebraska	7,203	31	38.9	6	7.2	15
Nevada	6,128	43	31.0	45	5.4	48
New Hampshire	8,151	19	36.4	21	5.5	39
New Jersey	11,103	3	39.8	5	6.5	4
New Mexico	6,857	35	36.6	17	9.7	11

continues

Table 9.4   continued

	Educational Spending per Pupil ($ 2002–2003)	Rank	Educational Spending as Percentage of General State Budget ($ FY 2000)	Rank	Educational Spending as Percentage of Personal Income ($ FY 2000)	Rank
New York	11,515	1	29.0	48	6.6	7
North Carolina	6,547	39	35.0	30	7.1	33
North Dakota	4,773	50	34.2	33	8.5	14
Ohio	7,518	22	35.8	23	6.7	28
Oklahoma	6,829	36	42.4	1	7.6	38
Oregon	7,242	30	32.0	43	7.2	19
Pennsylvania	8,331	15	35.3	25	6.8	18
Rhode Island	9,889	7	33.4	37	6.4	32
South Carolina	7,403	26	35.2	28	7.8	31
South Dakota	6,924	34	35.4	24	6.6	42
Tennessee	6,048	44	33.1	38	6.0	49
Texas	7,152	32	41.0	3	7.3	21
Utah	4,907	49	38.4	9	8.5	17
Vermont	9,942	6	38.6	8	8.7	6
Virginia	6,316	42	37.8	13	6.4	23
Washington	7,516	23	34.5	32	6.6	13
West Virginia	8,722	13	36.4	20	8.4	34
Wisconsin	9,019	12	37.1	15	8.0	8
Wyoming	9,232	11	33.8	35	8.9	2
All fifty states	7,415		34.8		6.7	
District of Columbia	13,355		18.8		4.7	
United States	7,829		34.7		6.7	

Source: Kendra A. Hovey and Harold A. Hovey, *CQ's State Fact Finder 2004* (Washington, D.C.: Congressional Quarterly Press, 2004), pp. 216, 217, 218.

significantly lower than for other workers, and that the wage gap is growing.[36] Research has found a pay gap between teachers and workers with similar education and skills, with no improvement in benefits that offset the growing wage disadvantage. The erosion of teachers' pay will make improving their quality more difficult; it cannot be done on the cheap.

Most efforts to assess quality in education from kindergarten through college try to evaluate the effect of the educational experience on the individual's education. Assessment of the value added by an educational institution is difficult, because education has many different dimensions. Different primary and secondary educational institutions may have different educational missions. Public schools may vary in their vocational, technical, or arts focus. When private and parochial schools are added into the comparison, the missions become even more varied and complex. Although money is not the solution to every educational problem, most aspirations to improve the value added do have tangible costs associated with them.

Assessing outcomes.   One strategy for assessing quality is to measure the outcome of education as students move from one grade to another and as they graduate. For example, the Scholastic Assessment Test (SAT) is often cited by institutions as a good way to measure the educational attainment of their high school graduates.

Less that half of all high school graduates take the SAT and a slightly higher number take the American College Test (ACT). SAT scores began to decline in the late 1960s and reached a low point in the early 1990s. Average math scores dropped from 516 in 1967 to a low of 492 in 1980, but bounced back to 506 in 1995 (see Table 9.5). Average verbal scores fell from 543 in 1967 to 500 in 1990, and have only begun a modest rebound since. In 1994 the College Board recentered SAT scores at 500, based on the levels established in 1990. By accepting the new standard, critics point out that it validates the mediocre performance of 1990.

Why SAT scores have declined is a matter of debate. Some dismiss the decline as a shift in the pool of students taking the SAT. They contend that a smaller and more elite percentage of high school students were college bound in the 1960s. As college admission has opened up to a larger percentage of high school graduates, a

---

Table 9.5   Average Scholastic Assessment Test (SAT) Scores, 1967–2004

	1967	1970	1975	1980	1985	1990	1995	2000	2004
Verbal	543	537	512	502	509	500	504	505	508
Math	516	512	498	492	500	501	506	514	518

Source: U.S. Census Bureau, *Statistical Abstract 2004–2005* (Washington, D.C.: U.S. Government Printing Office, 2004), p. 162.
Note: Scores for 1995 and prior years have been recentered by the College Entrance Examination Board.

growing number of less well prepared students have been included in the pool. But declines also occurred at the top end of the distribution. For example, in 1972, 116,585 students (11.4 percent of those taking the SAT) scored above 600 on the verbal test. By 1983 only 66,292 (6.9 percent of the total) scored above 600. Since that time, the proportion scoring above 600 has languished at around 7 percent.[37]

There is no relationship between the diversity of test takers and the decline in test scores. In 1980, math scores reached their lowest level, when less than 20 percent of those taking the test were from minority backgrounds. In the late 1990s almost a third of the test takers were from minority backgrounds, yet math scores had increased significantly. One reason for the improvement in the math scores may be attributed to the "New Basics" math requirements. Because of these requirements, in the past fifteen years the number of high school graduates who have taken geometry increased from 45 to 70 percent. However, they have also resulted in students taking a wider variety of courses in "language arts" rather than courses that emphasize grammar, syntax, and spelling.

One study suggests that the drop in SAT scores may explain the decline in the productivity rate in the labor force over the past two decades.[38] To the extent that test scores do measure intellectual achievement, even imperfectly, the decline results in a slowed growth of U.S. productivity. There is a cost to the nation, in forgone productivity and earnings, that can be associated with the low academic achievement of the average person who joins the work force after high school.[39]

International Comparisons

U.S. students have often been criticized for lagging behind their contemporaries in other countries overall and among the most advanced students. The most recent and largest international comparison of student achievement ever administered is the Trends in International Math and Science Study (TIMSS), conducted in 1995, 1999, and 2003. In 1995, U.S. eighth-graders scored well below the international average in mathematics and only slightly above the mean in science. In 1999, U.S. eighth-graders rose to nineteenth out of thirty-eight countries in mathematics and eighteenth in science. In 2003, Singapore, Hong Kong, Taipei, and the Republic of Korea led in science and math test scores, but U.S. students made progress against forty-eight other countries. U.S. eighth-graders closed the gap in science, ranking ninth among all nations while trailing Singapore by fifty-one points. The international average for eighth-grade science was 474, and the United States scored 527. The international average for eighth-grade math was 467, and the United States scored 504. U.S. fourth-graders were twelfth in math and sixth in science. The international math average was 495, and the United States scored 518. The international average for fourth-graders in science was 489, and the United States scored

536.[40] Despite the 2003 improvements, these are disappointing scores when one considers that the United States spends more money per capita on education than any other country except Finland. Only in the United States, however, are a majority of those who work in education not teachers.[41] A survey in 1991 by the Organization for Economic Cooperation and Development found, for example, that in Australia, Belgium, Japan, and France, teachers made up 80 percent of all education workers.[42]

Student- Versus School-Centered Approaches

Researchers have developed two general approaches for analyzing educational achievement: student-centered and school-centered.

Student-Centered Analysis

Education at the individual level is inherently a student-oriented system. The **heritability thesis** suggests that there is a natural inheritance of genes that, according to Arthur Jensen, determines about 80 percent of one's IQ. Thus, according to this view, there is little point in intervening to try to reduce this difference.[43] A slightly different thesis was put forward by Richard Herrnstein and Charles Murray, who contend that genes for IQ are becoming correlated with class. Their view may be summarized as follows: if differences in ability are inherited, and if acquisition of wealth and prestige requires high abilities, then social inequalities will be based on inherited inequalities.[44] In the United States the ideal of equality can be reached when each individual can go as far as their talent and hard work can take them, without the worst forms of social inequality barring the way and the abolition of privilege. The result would be a class stratification system.

Critics point out that Herrnstein and Murray failed to mention the many more comprehensive studies that give a much lower estimate of heritability. Nor do they mention studies that show the extreme sensitivity of estimates of heritability to the inclusion of factors such as cultural transmission. Heritability does not provide us with any information regarding the effectiveness of any social policy on a trait. Nor does the view suggest how we may structure the learning experience for different individuals so that each can maximize their potential. The **bell curve thesis** revives the essentially racist propositions of an earlier period that would provide us once again with the convenient logic to release us from any obligation to devise policies to improve the lives of every citizen.[45]

Cultural deprivation theory counters the heritability thesis by focusing on the environment. It examines the relationship between a child's experience and cognitive development and holds that lower-income or "working-class" culture is different from "middle-class" culture. These elitist interpretations emphasize the qualities of the student, as brought into a learning environment.

Basically, many of these arguments suggest that a **cultural deficit** works to provide poor and working-class students with behavior patterns and attitudes different from those of the white middle- or upper-class culture reflected in the public educational curricula.[46] The theory holds that working-class and nonwhite students perform poorly because they are raised in a culture that fails to develop the skills that encourage school success. Conversely, middle-class culture does prepare children adequately for educational success. For example, Melvin Kohn discovered class differences in culture in the 1950s, when he found middle-class parents more likely to encourage independence of mind for their children, and working-class parents more likely to value obedience.[47] In the late 1950s, Oscar Lewis introduced the idea of a **culture of poverty**, in which poor people develop lower-class cultural values to enable them to survive poverty, and so children in poverty are "deprived" of preparation for the demands of academic success and achievement.[48] Individuals in this subculture grow to feel helpless and powerless to change their circumstances. By the age of six or seven, the cultural resources of lower-class children are insufficient to ensure educational success, while the cultural resources of middle- and upper-class children go a long way toward ensuring their relative success. The effectiveness of the elementary and secondary educational systems depends on the quality of the home environment, which becomes increasingly important in secondary school. This view is in theoretical conformity with the notion of a **cycle of poverty**, and is supportive of C. Wright Mills's concept of **elite self-recruitment**.[49] The members of the elite class protect their interests and those of their children by sending them to the best schools, where they acquire the social skills to rise to the most powerful positions in society.

The cultural deprivation theory suggests that there is something in the cultural background of lower-class children, irrespective of gender, race, or ethnic background, that needs changing. If something in the lower-class culture holds children back, then we need to identify the characteristics that create failure and modify them. If schools cannot be significantly changed, we must change those aspects of the deprived culture of lower-class families.

Student-centered analysis has been attacked for letting schools escape criticism by focusing blame on the deprived children. In the 1960s, people were surprised to learn that almost 50 percent of men reporting for military service from a background of poverty were educationally or physically unfit. President Johnson declared a war on poverty based on the view that poverty could be cured through education in the correct attitudes needed for success. The policy was based on the notion that the poorest people are not only culturally deprived, but also trapped in a cycle of poverty. It was hoped that compensatory education could offer poor children some of the educational advantages of the more affluent children and change their attitudes and values. Head Start combined health care, social services, and education. Even though there was some disappointment in that Head Start did not live up to some of its exaggerated expectations, it is generally viewed as an unqualified success in improving the well-being of many poor children.

Cultural difference theory rejects cultural deprivation theory. It claims that the lack of educationally important skills is not due to any inadequacy in working-class or minority households, but results from children being raised in oppressed subcultures. It sees the low educational aspirations and achievements of working-class and minority students' achievement reflected in the inequalities inherent in the class structure.[50] Those who have little education are also likely to have little income, forcing them to live in communities where their children attend inferior schools.[51] Rapidly rising college tuitions and federal financial-aid policies tilt toward the more affluent, making it very difficult for low-income students, even if well prepared, to pursue a college degree. Studies that control for academic achievement find that the "dumbest rich kids have as much chance of going to college as the smartest poor kids."[52]

Some critics of student-centered analysis see school failure as a long-term effect of elitist and meritocratic school procedures that lead to different educational conditions for the advantaged and the disadvantaged. This view accounts for low student achievement by attributing it to individual inadequacies, rather than to schools that do not serve their students well. Whatever their weaknesses, student-centered interpretations do delineate the differences between the skills and characteristics that students bring to school and those that lead to success in classroom settings.

School-Centered Analysis

School-centered analysis shifts the focus to the educational process. Until the mid-1960s, this approach started from the premise that a major reason disadvantaged students receive less education is because they go to inferior schools, while in contrast, middle- and upper-income students attend schools having substantially more resources and more experienced teachers. This explanation has an appealing inherent logic.

Researchers began to investigate schools commonly considered effective and compared them, where possible, with schools commonly regarded as ineffective. This approach provided insight into the critical performance factors within the larger population of schools. By the late 1970s and early 1980s, a number of studies reached the inescapable conclusion that school organization does have an important impact on learning.

Case Study: Justice and Educational Equality

John Rawls and Robert Nozick offer two conflicting philosophical approaches for considering the problem of inequality in education. Rawls holds that only those inequalities that are to the benefit of the least advantaged are justified—that is, inequalities of position or resources that result in greater productivity and thereby provide greater benefits to all. Rawls would attempt to delete the "accidents of birth" wherever possible, thus creating a full equalization of opportunity for each child. By moving toward equality, individual liberty is lost to the central authority that imposes that equality.

Robert Nozick's position is based on the entitlement of the individual to whatever property he or she has legitimately acquired. Accordingly, for him the imposition of equality in benefits signifies a loss of rights for the affluent as well as the poor. The extreme position of Nozick would suggest no public education. Public education is by definition redistributive. But according to Nozick, in regard to education each child is entitled to the untaxed benefits of his or her family's resources to the extent that the family chooses to apply those resources to the child's education. This would make all education private and paid for by each family according to its ability and desires. By moving in the direction of individual liberty, equality is lost to the variations in market power enjoyed by different individuals.

Because of the issue of school financing, parental choice of schools based on residence conflicts with the attempts by states and federal agencies to reduce inequality. This problem arose because schools were no longer primarily financed from independent towns and cities. The schools reflected the social diversity within their communities, so the poor and affluent had access to the same program of studies, which encouraged Rawlsian equality. But each school district was thought to be entitled to its own resources even if there was inequality between districts, which accorded with Nozick's position. The decision to levy taxes for public schools resulted in the surrender of control over resources to government authority.

With the shift in recent decades of the responsibility for financing public education away from local government to the state and federal levels, the issue of liberty versus equality has become more prominent. But now it involves the liberty of the local school district (not the individual) to freely allocate its own resources, versus equity among school districts (not individuals), restricting district liberty. The basic conflict is between those who appeal for financing by the state based on principles of equity, versus those who protest that resources should not be redistributed to other districts. For this issue there are policy alternatives that tend toward the positions of Rawls or Nozick, and a third that is somewhat of a compromise. The first, in tune with Rawls's views, would emphasize equality by providing full funding by the states. This extreme position precludes the liberty of individual districts to spend more on education by taxing themselves more heavily, insisting on complete equality of funding for all children. The second option, more closely in tune with Nozick's views, would maintain local funding and local decisions regarding the level of expenditure. State and national funds would supplement local financing but without regard to the level of the local tax burden for education.

The third alternative would encourage some aspects of both Rawls's and Nozick's

continues

Case Study   continued

principles. Rather than taking away rights from those who feel entitled by their economic power to opt for the school of their choice through residence, those rights might be expanded to include others who do not have this choice. Permitting choice would increase equality rather than inequality by allowing individuals otherwise effectively excluded by economics from the residential area of the school to choose a school other than that of closest residence. By exercising this right, inequality is reduced. Full equality is not realized, however; the liberty of the affluent to maintain socially homogeneous schools is restricted. Importantly, however, a new liberty (option) is provided for the less privileged, who previously were without it.

Source: James Coleman, "Rawls, Nozick, and Educational Equality," *Public Interest* 43 (Spring 1976): 121–128.

Interestingly, one of the major arguments in favor of the significance of school organization on the learning process came from the late James Coleman. In a study whose results were published in 1982, Coleman and his colleagues at the University of Chicago used the *High School and Beyond* data set to conduct a comparative study of public, parochial, and private schools.[53] They concluded that parochial school students generally received the highest scores on achievement tests, followed by private school students and then public school students. This finding remained constant even when background characteristics of students, such as family income or parental education, were controlled. The study also found that parochial schools, primarily those serving inner city racial minorities, were more integrated than public schools.[54] Parochial and private schools on average did a better job of educating the typical student than public schools. The superior performance seems clearest in inner city settings, where lower-income students have fewer options. Coleman recognized the difficulty of separating the performance of these schools from the selection decision. That is, because attending public school is an option, but because parents of some students invest additional resources for a private or parochial school, students who attend the latter schools are different from public school students with otherwise identical characteristics. When the selection issue is taken into account, various studies conclude that there is still an advantage from attending parochial schools but not for attending elite private schools.[55] Caroline Hoxby provided evidence that public schools react to outside competition by performing better in areas with concentrations of Catholic schools than in areas without outside alternatives.[56] The more affluent can seek higher-quality schools by selecting their residential location in terms of school quality.

Coleman's findings generated considerable debate. Many in the public educational community rejected the study out of hand. But Coleman and his colleagues established an important theoretical point that schools matter. "Effective schools research," as studies of school organization came to be called, suggest that it should be possible to identify how structural features of schools can condition teacher behavior and expectations and influence student success. Using this approach, schools whose students perform much better than typical for comparable students elsewhere are identified. Researchers then try to isolate those factors that differentiate such atypically effective schools. Comparing "effective schools" with those commonly regarded as "ineffective" also provides insight into the general elements of effectiveness within the educational system.

No single factor makes a school exceptional. Effective schools, these studies have concluded, are characterized by several ingredients that conventional wisdom has all along suggested to be important:[57]

- *Clear school goals.* Effective schools have clear goals and a strong principal or school-based leadership. In other words, schools should have a mission rather than operate from force of habit.
- *School autonomy.* Effective schools are free from extensive outside bureaucratic controls.
- *High expectations.* Effective schools have high expectations for student performance, from teachers as well as principals.
- *Vigorous leadership and involvement.* In effective schools, the principal plays a leading role in the instructional program.
- *Rigorous academic standards.* Effective schools employ teachers with high expectations for students—that they graduate from high school, go to college, become good readers, and become good citizens.
- *Professionalism among the teachers.* In effective schools, teachers spend their time actually teaching and monitoring their students, and providing feedback to them. Teachers rely on tests they have developed in judging student achievement.
- *Experimentation and adaptation.* In effective schools, principals and teachers are able to experiment and adapt techniques and procedures in response to the circumstances encountered.

The research on effective schools came at a time when dissatisfaction with the educational system reached a critical level. It is consistent with the views of those who suggest a "back-to-basics" approach that accentuates order and discipline, emphasizing basic skills, more testing to measure progress, and higher educational standards. Coleman and others found in their research that Catholic parochial schools tend to be more effective and provide a significantly better education than public schools, due to their focus on just such aspects of education.[58] This research has been challenged, along with its policy implications, by several researchers.[59]

In the private education sector the formal right to control a school is vested with a church, a corporation, or a nonprofit agency that has the legal right to make all the educational decisions. In the public education sector, different interests struggle over educational decisions. Ironically, though, a basic market or "choice" principle gives parents and students a more influential role in private sector schools than in the public educational system. Those who run private or parochial schools have a strong motivation to please their clientele, because they know that if people do not like the educational services they receive, they can switch. This is invariably a strong possibility, since the low-cost public school system is always an alternative. Moreover, private sector schools that cannot attract a clientele of sufficient size must be able to pass along the higher per pupil charges to the families of the students they are able to attract or to their sponsoring organizations. Otherwise they will go out of business.[60] This is a strong financial motivator to be responsive to parents and provide a good education.

Coleman's conclusions have been supported and reinforced by the more recent research findings of Anthony Bryk and his colleagues, as reported in their work *Catholic Schools for the Common Good*.[61] Their most significant finding is that Catholic schools have been particularly effective in educating inner city minority students with profiles very similar to those associated with failing public schools. These parochial schools are typically more racially integrated and operate at a per capita cost of between 50 and 60 percent of public schools. Most would agree that racial equality can be achieved only by eliminating the differences in the average academic performance of blacks and whites. However, half of all African Americans, but only 20 percent of whites, in public school attend inner city schools. In the largest U.S. cities, the racial differences between inner city and suburban schools are even greater. In Chicago, Dallas, Detroit, Houston, Los Angeles, and Washington, D.C., over 85 percent of public school students are minorities.[62] In fact, today's private school students are more integrated than those attending public school. According to 1992 Department of Education data, 37 percent of private school students are in classrooms whose share of minority students is close to the national average, compared to only 18 percent of public school students.[63]

Other researchers, such as Richard Rothstein, maintain that holding schools accountable can only be a part of the solution. Rothstein's concern is that effective schools research entirely neglects the earlier concern regarding cultural differences.[64] It is simplistic to think that even the most effective schools could overcome the black-white or the rich-poor achievement gap. His research emphasizes how different child-rearing practices, ways of communicating, and disciplining methods will influence children's performance in school. Poor families have occupational, economic, psychological, health, and personality traits that predict lower achievement in academic and other settings for children compared to families from more affluent levels of society. Therefore. school reform must be assisted by a comprehensive compensatory program along with after-school, summer, and prekindergarten programs.

School Choice and Vouchers

In 1990, John Chubb and Terry Moe published *Politics, Markets, and America's Schools,* which is now a classic in U.S. education.[65] Their work was controversial, as its findings helped initiate a national movement in support of **vouchers**. Their research findings suggest that factors are at work in the public educational system that directly conflict with several of the indicators that make for effective schools. The voucher issue remains the most controversial topic in U.S. education today. For example, Chubb and Moe concluded that a public educational system with low or declining quality may not keep parents from moving into a school district, and it is even less likely to cause existing residents to leave. Rather, it might prod them to consider a private school. If they choose that option, it reduces the number of disgruntled parents in the public school system and reduces the average dissatisfaction of those left in the public sector.[66] The major disincentive to leaving is that public education has a very low out-of-pocket cost. Therefore, private or parochial schools must be far superior to public schools to attract students. Or stated differently, the low cost of public schools permits them to attract students without being particularly good at teaching them.

Once parents make a choice in favor of a public school despite their apprehensions, they may try to correct perceived problems in methods or performance through the democratic process. The political struggle for control over the public schools involves parents, student advocacy groups, teachers, teacher unions, administrators, business groups, local school boards, state governments, and the federal government. Victory comes in the form of tenuous compromises regarding goals that could vanish with a shift in political power. Thus schools will be directed to "pursue academic excellence, but without making courses too difficult; they will be directed to teach history, but without making any value judgments; they will be directed to teach sex education, but without taking a stand on contraception or abortion. They must make everyone happy by being all things to all people— just as politicians try to do."[67] The winning coalition inevitably sets up a bureaucratic arrangement to force compliance upon the losers and to ensure against the risks of future defeat by opponents who would like to impose their own rules. Bureaucratic control means that teacher behavior will be regulated in minute detail and through enforcement procedures set up by the winners that permit verification of teacher compliance with rules and standards.

Thus the tendency to blame the public education bureaucracy for educational problems is to misunderstand the nature of the problem. It is true that bureaucrats are rewarded for devising rules and regulations and setting standards based on policies and programs defined in the past. But the bureaucrats are put in place by the victors of the political struggle to enforce compliance with their vision of what education should be. Not to put bureaucrats in place would result in an uncertain political victory and an inability by the victors to enforce their terms.

Nor are teachers necessarily to blame for problems in public education. Good teaching consists of skilled operations that are extremely difficult to measure in formal bureaucratic assessments. Educational output results from the interaction between a teacher and a student. This is the primary relationship in education. Professionalism requires that teachers have the freedom to exercise their judgment in applying their knowledge and teaching skills to the specific students and circumstances they encounter. When the system is bureaucratized, the most important relationship for the teacher is with the supervisor, not the student. Increasing bureaucratic regulations and reporting standards guarantee that teacher discretion will be reduced and initiative stifled.[68]

The Debate over Market-Oriented Reforms

The obvious implication of the "effective schools" type of research is that policy alternatives need to be implemented that will move the educational system in the direction of decentralized educational "markets." Public schools would be forced to compete with other private and parochial schools. Advocates argue that this would give parents more choice in selecting schools for their children and force schools to compete for the financial support that would come through parental choice. As a necessary component of choice, proponents point out, schools must be given greater autonomy in deciding their academic programs, principal, and staff, and how to compete for students. Thus they would resemble private and parochial schools more closely. The projected benefits would be a public education guided more by markets and less by politics, and therefore it would be less prone to the debilitating effects of excessive bureaucratic controls. By subjecting schools to fewer bureaucratic requirements, but to more competition, the market mechanism would reward clear goals and efficiency. Finally, proponents argue, the choice exercised by the consumers of education, parents and students, should foster more positive and cooperative affiliations between parents, students, and the school.[69]

The firestorm of controversy generated by these studies demonstrates that education is not an issue that neatly divides liberals and conservatives. Much of the subsequent literature is subordinate to ideological considerations and has not been particularly scientific.[70]

Chubb and Moe's research led them to conclude that Americans like public schools. They are also reasonably satisfied that their local school system is performing well. Most Americans also support a public school ideology, meaning that they have a set of values that lead them to think that having good public education is worthwhile. However, many Americans, especially supporters of vouchers, also think that private and parochial schools are better than public schools in terms of relative performance. Further, they think that the education system tends to be inequitable and that parents do not have enough influence. They also believe that many schools are too big and that generally they do poorly in teaching moral values. They also think that competition would be a healthy thing for schools.[71]

Many critics of vouchers are fearful that they would have the greatest appeal to the affluent and that, if adopted, there would be an exodus of advantaged students from the public system, which would exacerbate the existing social biases of the schools. There is a legitimate fear that "elitists" want to separate themselves from lower classes. Moe's research found evidence that parents think primarily about finding a good school for their children, and not about race or elitism. In fact, choice has the greatest appeal to parents who are low-income and minority (especially black and Hispanic), and who reside in disadvantaged school districts.

Supporters argue that vouchers would be a better system, especially for poor children most in need of choice. As they see it, this would give the disadvantaged more of the choices that the affluent already have. With affluence comes the ability to buy homes in the preferred public school district or to opt for private school alternatives. The affluent have also been able to press for the best principals, teachers, and facilities. It is only equitable to provide an open enrollment plan (market oriented) to give the disadvantaged families the same market power to choose that the affluent have always had. Currently, the poor have little choice. The idea of giving the poor the same options as those exercised by the more affluent members of society appears inherently democratic.

One concern frequently expressed is that conservatives are attempting to use the research findings and recommendations for "choice" to rig the system against the poor and divert more resources to the affluent. The contention is that the No Child Left Behind bill applies *testing* not only to students but also to schools. Schools can "fail" just as students can. Failing schools are overwhelmingly in poor districts with the attendant funding and student problems. Failing schools would be "punished" by cuts to their funding, which would make it more difficult for them to improve, and many would face elimination. The failing public schools would be replaced by a voucher system that would be insufficient to provide payment to good private schools. The voucher would be a "transfer slip" for a poor student to another poor school. The wealthy could convert their tax payment for public schools to a voucher to be used as partial payment in a private school, reducing the cost of the private school by the monetary value of the voucher.

It would contravene the policy goal of leveling the playing field between rich and poor if vouchers were to permit affluent parents to select the private school of their choice and give it their share of what had been their tax payment for public schools. The objection basically concerns why the taxpayer should have to subsidize the parents who want to use their taxes to pay a significant portion of the high tuition that elite schools charge. Low-income families would not be able to pay the difference between the value of their voucher and the tuition costs of elite academies. Legislators in Wisconsin provided one solution to the problem by limiting eligibility for state vouchers to families whose income did not exceed 175 percent of the federal poverty level. Means-testing the program does eliminate a concern over the wealthy taking advantage of the system to subsidize their leaving the public educational system. Another proposal to thwart the affluent using the voucher as a tax deduction would be to require the receiving school to accept the voucher as "payment in full," which would eliminate affluent private schools while still permitting some parochial schools to take part.

Strict separationists argue that school choice or voucher programs that would include parochial schools would have the "primary effect" of advancing religion and would therefore be unconstitutional. The Supreme Court has continued a prohibition against direct public assistance to religious institutions, but in recent years has provided standards that would permit parents to receive aid to send their children to religious schools. Three basic requirements for aid to be permissible are, first, that the assistance must be provided to the parent or child rather than to a religious institution; second, that any benefit that accumulates to a religious institution must result from a parental decision; and third, that funds must be appropriated on a neutral basis regarding religion and made available to everyone regardless of whether they attend a public, private, or parochial school.[72] The Rehnquist Court has stressed that parents who wish to have their children attend sectarian schools are entitled to the same rights and privileges as those who desire a public education for their children. The Supreme Court held that a Minnesota tax deduction for educational purposes, whether for secular or parochial schools, did not "establish a religion." Nor did state-provided scholarships "establish a religion" as long as they could be used at any school, whether Catholic, Protestant, Jewish, Muslim, or secular.[73] Supporters argue that if religious schools accept vouchers, they should be required to admit students of any religion.

In the United States, the Democratic Party, which has long felt that education is its issue, finds itself torn between its desire to defend the educational establishment and its desire to support its working-class members who want choice.

Republicans have eroded the Democrats' advantages by appealing to traditional Democratic Party constituents, especially ethnic minorities and Catholics, and by supporting choice.

Leaving Children Behind: The Dropout Crisis

Policy concern over high school dropouts stems primarily from the importance of having an educated work force. Technological advances have increased the demand for skilled labor to the point that a high school education is increasingly a minimum requirement to enter the work force. Students who drop out of school before completing their high school education exact a high cost on themselves and U.S. society. On average, dropouts have higher rates of unemployment and earn lower wages than those who graduate. The average annual income of dropouts is approximately 69 percent of the income of high school graduates ($18,826 versus $27,280 in 2002).[74] Women who drop out of high school are more likely to become pregnant at an early age, and are more likely to become single parents.[75] They are also more likely to receive public assistance. Half of all families on welfare are headed by high school dropouts.[76] The stress and frustration associated with dropping out mean an increased risk of turning to crime for financial support; dropouts account for about half the prison population and over half of death row inmates.[77]

There is no doubt that completing high school is an important highlight in an individual's academic career, as well as an indicator of social and economic advancement. For all these reasons, graduation rates are an important indicator of the performance of the school system. The passage of the NCLB law in January 2002 focused attention on calculating a high school's "on-time graduation rate" rather than the "dropout" rate, which can be subject to various state definitions. The law for the first time requires that school systems be held accountable not only for academic assessments, but for graduation rates as well.

The Urban Institute compiled and analyzed data from the U.S. Department of Education's "Common Core of Data" to compute graduation rates for the high school class of 2001 in nearly every public school district in the nation.[78] Its findings are discouraging. Nationally, only 68 percent of ninth-grade students graduated in four years. Graduation was defined as on-time with a regular diploma. When results are separated out by race and ethnicity, 77 percent of white and Asian students graduated on-time compared to only 50 percent of black students, 51 percent of American Indian students, and 53 percent of Hispanic students. Male students complete high school at a rate about 8 percentage points below that of females. Therefore, minority on-time graduation rates for males were less than 50 percent. In school districts that are predominantly minority, highly segregated, and socioeconomically disadvantaged, the graduation rates were 15 to 17 percent lower than rates in more affluent school districts. For example, New York City had a 38 percent completion rate, Houston and Atlanta had a 40 percent rate, while Oakland and Cleveland had a 30 percent completion rate.

Congress recognized the seriousness of the dropout problem by including accountability provisions for graduation rates in the NCLB law. In a contentious decision, Roderick Paige, secretary of the Department of Education, reduced the effectiveness of the provisions by issuing regulations that permit states to "bundle" dropout rates for accountability reporting, which conceals the alarming data regarding socioeconomic and minority status. The Department of Education also approved state plans that set a "soft" adequate yearly progress (AYP) goal, which allows states to avoid sanctions by providing evidence of the slightest improvement from one year to the next. As a result, California set a goal of 100 percent on-time graduation, but reports AYP for "any improvement"—even one-tenth of a percentage point. If California were to disaggregate its graduation data and require progress by all major racial groups, it could take the state over 500 years to reach its goal. In contrast, the Department of Education enforces a more rigid test score accountability in determining AYP. This creates an incentive for administrators to improve their school's test profile by "pushing out" low-performing students rather than providing resources to keep them in school. Low-income and minority students are most vulnerable to these practices.[79]

Growing up in poverty does not determine school failure. But when the difficulties of deprivation are not alleviated by the dedication of substantial resources and the commitment of concerned adults, it is extremely difficult to succeed. There is little help in many poor rural communities and inner city schools. As Theodore Sizer, a former dean of the Harvard School of Education, wrote:

> The hard fact is that if you are the child of low-income parents the chances are good that you will receive limited and often careless attention from adults in your high school. Most of this is realism that many Americans prefer to keep under the rug, of course; it is no easy task for the poor in America to break out . . . of their economic condition. But a change of status that is a matter of moderately poor odds becomes impossible when there is little encouragement to try.[80]

Higher standards usually do not come with funding for remedial programs. Increasing the number of required courses and upgrading course content may result in teachers adding units to a course but allowing less time to aid students who are falling behind. There are many programs with substantial funding to promote "excellence" in education, but few that take "equity" into account, which may be essential in helping potential dropouts to remain in school.

Students drop out of school for reasons that are largely unchanged over several decades. In the *High School and Beyond* study, researchers found that the most often cited reason for leaving school is poor academic performance. High-risk students frequently find school to be a hostile environment where they are confirmed as failures daily. School agendas prize uniformity, harmony, regulation, and intellectual competition. These behaviors are often especially difficult for high-risk students. Their rebellion against those behaviors leads to truancy, suspension, or other forms of misconduct within school. They are more likely to report that they are not popular with their classmates, are less likely to take part in extracurricular activities, and feel estranged from school life. Males who are older than average for their grade (who tend to have repeated a grade at least once) and racial and ethnic minorities (other than Asian Americans) are more likely to experience "disciplinary" problems and become dropouts. Dropouts by and large are capable of doing the academic work, however, though they are inclined to be underachievers, as indicated in the *High School and Beyond* survey, which found that their tested achievement levels were seven to twelve percentiles higher than their grades.

A variety of programs have been developed to increase pupil retention. First, programs should address those school practices that discourage high-risk students and substitute practices and arrangements that encourage them to remain in school until graduation. Recommendations of several studies include the following.

1. *Higher requirements should be accompanied with support for low-achieving students.* Higher standards without additional assistance for those with lower aptitudes and achievement will reinforce their sense of failure and negative views of school.

2. *Promotion policies.* The dropout rate among students who have repeated a grade is more than double that of those who have not been held back. This connection begins as early as the first grade. Research shows that holding a child back a grade in elementary school is less cost effective than providing the special services the student needs to perform at the grade level. Several states are instituting standardized tests to determine competence for promotion and graduation. If such programs are implemented without remedial programs, they may simply divide "winners" and "losers" without identifying where help is needed. Retaining a student without remedial help is a form of punishment.

3. *School and class size.* The larger the school and classes, the more problems reported by both teachers and students with the quality of teaching. Teacher workloads are increased with overcrowded classrooms, making it difficult to provide individual attention or remedial help with learning difficulties. Students experiencing problems in overcrowded classrooms find teachers less accessible, increasing their feelings of frustration and alienation. The greatest overcrowding occurs in poorer school districts, where there is insufficient funding to provide extra classroom space or hire the additional teachers needed.

4. *Lack of support for minorities.* Many ethnic minority students, primarily Hispanic, suffer from attending schools that do not provide sufficient bilingual education. Few Hispanic children with limited English proficiency, even in areas where they make up the majority of the class, are placed in a bilingual program.

5. *Work-study programs.* Schools should develop programs to provide relevant work experiences for students who are faced with the necessity of helping to provide a family income.

Evaluation of Current Federal Education Policy

The "No Child Left Behind" law is an extension of Lyndon Johnson's Elementary and Secondary Education Act of 1965, which was intended to provide aid to low-income children, though it tended to become general federal aid to education. Reform measures undertaken by Bill Clinton required more focus on aid going to poor children. The NCLB law goes further in making schools accountable for the achievement of poor children. In reality, the NCLB law is a sweeping nationalization of school policy. The law took its name from Marian Wright Edelman's Children's Defense Fund slogan "Leave No Child Behind." Its stated goal was to require schools to close the huge achievement gaps in U.S. education between poor and minority children and those attending primarily suburban affluent and mostly white schools. It was to do this by creating an accountability system of tests, on-time graduation rates, and other indicators that would force schools to make significant progress by raising overall test scores as well as every major subgroup of students (low-income, African American, Hispanic, special education students, and those learning English) to a state-defined level of competence. School districts were to issue annual report cards on the system, and each school was to provide information on the quality of its education. Schools were to ensure the presence of "highly qualified" teachers in every classroom by 2005–2006. "Failing schools" were to face sanctions until their performance once again satisfied their annual goals. Children in "failing schools" were to be allowed to transfer to better public schools (including charter schools if available). For its part, the federal government was to provide the necessary resources to fund the reforms required to implement the policy.

The law has several problems. The major complaint is that although the administration can argue that funding for education is up, appropriations fall seriously short of what Congress has authorized and what states claim are necessary to achieve the goals. Many educators see the law as essentially an unfunded federal mandate. States have been spending more money even while their tax receipts have fallen, and the federal government is not providing the funding it promised. Several state legislatures have considered withdrawing from the NCLB program even though they would lose whatever federal money is available under the law. A wave of lawsuits have been filed by parents and school districts demanding that states provide the resources necessary to achieve the standards that they have imposed.

The law is also criticized for failing to live up to its own provisions. Many students of "failing schools" have found there is nowhere to transfer to, because other schools are already overcrowded. Other school districts have complained that schools with large numbers of English learners are in a no-win situation. If foreign students (primarily Spanish-speaking) become proficient on English tests, they are redesignated as being proficient in English and are no longer counted in the "English learner" group. But new students enter who are not proficient, so it is difficult to show statistical improvement. In fact, in areas with rapidly growing Latino populations, it may appear that schools are regressing. The law mandates putting "highly qualified" teachers in every classroom, but has not been able to get many school districts to even report on teacher qualifications.

Some cynics have suggested that the NCLB accountability system was adopted as a conservative ploy to show the school system's failures and open the door for vouchers. Former governor Howard Dean says the purpose of NCLB "is to make the public schools so awful, and starve them of money, just as he's [Bush's] starving all the other social programs, so that people give up on the public schools."[81] Most observers, while critical of underfunding the program, approve of a process that puts more pressure on schools to be more accountable to the achievement of poor children.

Conclusion

There is widespread evidence that the quality of elementary and secondary education in the United States is lagging behind that of many other countries. The United States is atypical in that education is primarily a state and local policy issue. Constitutionally, states are responsible for educational systems. The federal government's ability to influence policy is primarily through the carrot of financial assistance. The result is that education policy has never been a major aspect of national policy. It is frequently a matter of symbolic politics. As recently as 1980, Ronald Reagan campaigned on the platform of abolishing the Department of Education, since education was not a question for national policy.

There are several theories regarding the benefits of education. Functionalism stresses that education prepares individuals for various positions in the job market. Other theories contend that education should promote equality, but that the system in fact reinforces social stratification. Human capital theory is one of the major justifications for government intervention and for treating education as a quasi–public good.

Recent studies to improve the quality of education have focused on the factors that affect learning. Student-centered and school-centered factors are both involved in the learning process. School-centered approaches are the primary interest of "effective schools" research, which suggests that decentralized systems that encourage market competition are strongly correlated with effectiveness in educational achievement.

Because evolution of the educational system in the United States occurred long after the drafting of the Constitution, education has been primarily a state and local responsibility. This is decidedly unlike the systems in many other countries, where education is a function of national governments based on more recently drafted constitutions. Countries noted for educational excellence, such as Japan, have strongly centralized education ministries that set national standards. Germany and Britain are exceptions. Germany vests its Lander (states) with educational authority in a manner similar to the arrangement in the United States, while Britain gives its Local Educational Authorities considerable autonomy. A strongly centralized system will not work in the United States, since states and local governments are jealous of their authority over education.

There are almost 16,000 school districts in the United States, none of which uniformly turns out students that outperform their foreign counterparts. The system of school choice might introduce an element of market competition among U.S. schools that would make them more effective.

High school dropout rates are reflective of serious social stratification problems in society and a need for remedial assistance to encourage greater equality of educational opportunity.

Questions for Discussion

1. Has the "No Child Left Behind" law lived up to expectations regarding the measurement of student learning and holding schools accountable? What are the major criticisms of the law?
2. Does the economy grow because of its investment in human resources, or does it invest in education because it is growing and can afford it?
3. Acquiring high levels of education was assumed to guarantee job security. What evidence is there that this may no longer be as valid as in the past? Does that mean that investment in education is no longer as valuable as in previous years?
4. What is the concept of "human capital investment"? In what ways can edu-

cation and training be considered investment? In what ways can they be considered consumption?

5. Should parents be able to apply school vouchers to public schools only, or should they be able to use them for private or parochial schools as well? What are the arguments for and against their use in public schools, let alone private or parochial schools?

6. How could we provide for equality in public education? Is there a realistic chance of resolving the issue?

Useful Websites

American Association for Higher Education, http://www.aahe.org.

American Federation of Teachers, http://www.aft.org.

Center for Education Reform, http://www.edreform.com.

Children's Defense Fund, http://www.childrensdefense.org.

Democratic Committee on Education and the Workforce, http://edworkforce.house.gov/democrats.

Education Policy Analysis Archives, http://epaa.asu.edu.

Educational Resources Information Center, http://www.ericsp.org.

Educause, http://www.educause.edu.

House Committee on Education and the Workforce, http://edworkforce.house.gov.

National Center for Public Policy and Higher Education, http://www.highereducation.org.

National Center for Education Statistics, http://www.nces.ed.gov.

National Education Association, http://www.nea.org.

U.S. Department of Education, http://www.ed.gov.

Suggested Readings

Applebee, Arthur N., Judith A. Langer, and Ina V. Mullis. *Crossroads in American Education: A Summary of Findings.* Princeton: Educational Testing Service, 1989.

Arrow, Kenneth, Samuel Bowles, and Steven Durlauf, eds. *Meritocracy and Economic Inequality.* Princeton: Princeton University Press, 2000.

Chubb, John E., and Terry M. Moe. *Politics, Markets, and America's Schools.* Washington, D.C.: Brookings Institution, 1990.

Cohen, David K., and Eleanor Farrar. "Power to the Parents? The Story of Education Vouchers." In Nathan Glazer, ed., *The Public Interest on Education.* Cambridge, Mass.: Abt Association, 1984.

Coleman, James S., Thomas Hoffer, and Sally Kilgore. *High School Achievement: Public, Catholic, and Private Schools Compared.* New York: Basic Books. 1982.

———. *Public and Private Schools.* Washington, D.C.: National Center for Education Statistics, 1981.

Finn, Chester E., Jr., Bruno V. Manno, and Gregg Vanourek. *Charter Schools in Action: Renewing Public Education.* Washington, D.C.: Brookings Institution, 2002.

Heckman, James J., and Alan B. Krueger. *Inequality in America: What Role for Human Capital Policies?* Cambridge: MIT Press, 2003.

Hill, Paul T., and Robin J. Lake. *Charter Schools and Accountability in Public Education.* Washington, D.C.: Brookings Institution, 2002.

Kasen, Stephanie, Patricia Cohen, and Judith S. Brook. "Adolescent School Experiences and Dropout, Adolescent Pregnancy, and Young Adult Deviant Behavior." *Journal of Adolescent Research* 13, no. 1 (January 1998).

Moe, Terry M. *Schools, Vouchers, and the American Public.* Washington, D.C.: Brookings Institution, 2001.

Odden, Allan, and Lawrence Picus. *School Finance: A Policy Perspective.* 2nd ed. New York: McGraw-Hill, 2000.

Peterson, Paul E., and Bryan C. Hassel, eds. *Learning from School Choice.* Washington, D.C.: Brookings Institution, 1999.

U.S. Department of Education, National Center for Education Statistics. *Dropout Rates in the United States.* NCES 97-473, by Marilyn McMillen, project officer. Washington, D.C.: U.S. Government Printing Office, 1997.

Viteritti, Joseph P. *Choosing Equality: School Choice, the Constitution, and Civil Society.* Washington, D.C.: Brookings Institution, 1999.

Witte, John F. *The Market Approach to Education: An Analysis of America's First Voucher Program.* Princeton: Princeton University Press, 2000.

Notes

1. Kevin J. Dougherty and Floyd M. Hammack, *Education and Society* (New York: Harcourt Brace Jovanovich, 1990), pp. 13–14.

2. Adam Smith, *The Wealth of Nations,* edited by Edwin Cannon (New York: G. P. Putnam's Sons, 1877), bk. 2, chap. 1, p. 377. Smith did not develop this idea beyond the statement quoted. Theodore Schultz and Gary Becker are usually given credit for developing human capital theory. See Theodore W. Schultz, "Investment in Human Capital," *American Economic Review* 51 (March 1961): 1–17; and Gary Becker, *Human Capital* (New York: National Bureau of Economic Research, 1964).

3. Roe J. Johns, Edgar L. Morphet, and Kern Alexander, "Human Capital and the Economic Benefits of Education," in Dougherty and Hammack, *Education and Society,* pp. 534–535.

4. Many look upon their school days, especially their college years, as the most rewarding years of their lives. Therefore, if half the cost of education is assigned to consumption, then the benefits derived, compared to investment, would be doubled. The share assigned to consumption and investment might vary with the focus of the education. Vocational training, on-the-job apprenticeships, work-study and other programs, and training designed for a particular job may have less consumption and more investment aspects. On the other hand, the study of art, drama, music, and the humanities may have a higher consumption portion than the study of some of the sciences. In any case, the difficulty of assigning portions of educational cost to consumption and investment has resulted in most studies attributing all cost to investment, thus underestimating the rate of return to education.

5. For example, one study of three communities—an affluent community with politically active adults, a lower-middle-class community with reduced levels of involvement, and a working-class neighborhood with primarily apolitical adults—concluded that the students in each community were being taught to play "different" political roles. Only in the

affluent community were students taught the subtleties and nuances of decisionmaking and given the expectation that they should be a part of the process. The lower-middle-class neighborhood covered mechanics and procedures without stressing the utility of participation. See Edgar Litt, "Civic Education, Community Norms, and Political Indoctrination," in Richard Flacks, ed., *Conformity, Resistance, and Self-Determination* (Boston: Little, Brown, 1973), pp. 136–141.

6. Dougherty and Hammack, *Education and Society,* p. 248.

7. Ibid.

8. Christopher S. Jencks et al., *Who Gets Ahead?* (New York: Basic Books, 1979), pp. 224–227. See also more recent confirming research: Sanders Korenman and Christopher Winship, "A Reanalysis of the Bell Curve: Intelligence, Family Background, and Schooling," in Kenneth Arrow, Samuel Bowles, and Steven Durlauf, eds., *Meritocracy and Economic Inequality* (Princeton: Princeton University Press, 2000), pp. 136–178. See also Samuel Bowles and Herbert Gintis, "Does Schooling Raise Earnings by Making People Smarter?" in Arrow, Bowles, and Durlauf, *Meritocracy,* pp. 118–136.

9. See Pierre Bourdieu, "The School as a Conservative Force: Scholastic and Cultural Inequalities," in John Eggleston, ed., *Contemporary Research in the Sociology of Education* (London: Methuen, 1974), pp. 32–46.

10. Pierre Bourdieu and Jean-Claude Passeron, *The Inheritors: French Students and Their Relation to Culture* (Chicago: University of Chicago Press, 1979), p. 153.

11. Gregory Squires, "Education, Jobs, and Inequality: Functional and Conflict Models of Social Stratification in the United States," *Social Problems* 24, no. 4 (April 1977): 436–450.

12. Ibid.

13. Ibid., p. 445.

14. Ibid., p. 551.

15. Floyd M. Hammack, "The Changing Relationship Between Education and Occupation: The Case of Nursing," in Dougherty and Hammack, *Education and Society,* pp. 561–573. Hammack points out that requiring greater educational achievement and "credentials" increases the prestige of a profession while encouraging higher pay and control over access to the profession.

16. Alan Greenspan, testimony before the House Committee on Education and the Workforce, U.S. House of Representatives, March 11, 2004.

17. Ibid.

18. Jared Bernstein and Amy Chasanov, *Viewpoints* (Washington, D.C.: Economic Policy Institute, April 2, 2004).

19. Jared Bernstein, "School's Out," *American Prospect Online,* March 18, 2004, http://www.prospect.org.

20. National Commission on Excellence in Education, *A Nation at Risk: The Imperative for Educational Reform* (Washington, D.C.: U.S. Government Printing Office, April 1983).

21. Quoted in Saul K. Padover, *Thomas Jefferson on Democracy* (New York: Appleton-Century, 1939), p. 89.

22. Saul K. Padover, *Jefferson: A Great American's Life and Ideas* (New York: Harcourt, Brace, and World, 1952), p. 43.

23. Padover, *Thomas Jefferson,* p. 87.

24. Merrell D. Peterson, *The Jefferson Image in the American Mind* (New York:

Oxford University Press, 1960), p. 241. Jefferson felt so strongly that only an enlightened citizenry could preserve freedom that he was willing to require a literacy test for the franchise. Note that Jefferson, who opposed any restriction on personal liberty, was proposing just such a restraint by tying the right to vote to the literacy provided by the state in the form of a free public education. The Virginia Assembly ignored Jefferson's egalitarian proposal to educate the masses and provided funding for the more elite University of Virginia instead.

25. Figures for 2005 projected from U.S. Census Bureau, *Statistical Abstract 2003* (Washington, D.C.: U.S. Government Printing Office, 2003), p. 147.

26. David B. Robertson and Dennis R. Judd, *The Development of American Public Policy: The Structure of Policy Restraint* (Boston: Scott Foresman, 1989), p. 246.

27. See John Augenblick, "The Current Status of School Financing Reform," in Van Mueller and Mary McKeown, eds., *The Fiscal, Legal, and Political Aspects of State Reform of Elementary and Secondary Education* (Cambridge, Mass.: Ballinger, 1986).

28. Kendra Hovey and Harold Hovey, *CQ's State Fact Finder 2004* (Washington, D.C.: Congressional Quarterly Press, 2004), p. 220.

29. *Serrano v. Priest* (1971).

30. The definition of educational equity generally includes a collection of various concepts. Obviously, equity principles use students as the target group and equalize either per pupil expenditures, the tax base, or the expenditure needs of a district. Expenditure needs can vary between school districts depending on differences in cost-of-living and the relative number of special needs students within a district, that is, students with limited English proficiency, or the number of students in poverty. Equity standards will also depend on whether the goal is to have school districts equalize resources or achieve certain results.

31. In 1965, Johnson provided $1 billion in funding, which grew rapidly in succeeding years. Although some participants start out far behind the national achievement averages and never catch up, students typically gain a year in reading and math achievement for each year of participation in elementary grades and thus do not fall further behind their more advantaged peers.

32. Diana Jean Schemo, "Nation's Charter Schools Lagging Behind, U.S. Test Scores Reveal," *New York Times,* August 17, 2004.

33. Ibid.

34. Helen F. Ladd and Janet S. Hansen, eds., *Making Money Matter: Financing America's Schools* (Washington, D.C.: National Academy Press, 1999), esp. chap. 3.

35. Richard Rothstein, "Closing the Gap: How the Federal Government Can Equalize School Spending Between the States" (online anthology from *American School Board Journal*), http://www.asbj.com/school.

36. Sylvia Allegretto, Sean Corcoran, and Lawrence Mishel, *Teacher Pay Lags Behind* (Washington, D.C.: Economic Policy Institute, 2004).

37. Diane Ravitch, *Student Performance Today,* Brookings Policy Brief no. 23 (Washington, D.C.: Brookings Institution, 1997).

38. John Bishop, "Is the Test Score Decline Responsible for the Productivity Growth Decline?" *American Economic Review* 79 (March 1989): 178–197.

39. Charles Schultze, *Education: A Memo to the President* (Washington, D.C.: Brookings Institution, 1992).

40. The top finishers in mathematics that scored significantly higher than the United States were Singapore, the Republic of Korea, China (Taipei), Hong Kong, Japan, Belgium-

Flemish, the Netherlands, the Slovak Republic, Hungary, Canada, Slovenia, the Russian Federation, Australia, and Finland. Those that scored significantly higher than the United States in science included China (Taipei), Singapore, Hungary Japan, the Republic of Korea, the Netherlands, Australia, the Czech Republic, England, Finland, the Slovak Republic, Belgium-Flemish, Slovenia, and Canada. See National Center for Education Statistics, *Trends in International Mathematics and Science Study* (Washington, D.C.: U.S. Government Printing Office, 2004); and Emily Berg, "American Students Struggle to Catch Up," http://www.vvdailypress.com/2004/110312137877322.html.

41. U.S. Census Bureau, *Statistical Abstract 2003*, p. 167.

42. Ravitch, *Student Performance Today.*

43. Arthur R. Jensen, "How Much Can We Boost IQ and Scholastic Achievement?" *Harvard Educational Review* 39, no. 1 (1969): 1–123.

44. Richard J. Herrnstein and Charles Murray, *The Bell Curve: Intelligence and Class Structure in American Life* (New York: Free Press, 1994).

45. See especially James R. Flynn, "IQ Trends over Time: Intelligence, Race, and Meritocracy," in Arrow, Bowles, and Durlauf, *Meritocracy,* pp. 35–60. See also Marcus Feldman, Sarah P. Otto, and Freddy Christiansen, "Genes, Culture, and Inequality," in Arrow, Bowles, and Durlauf, *Meritocracy,* pp. 61–85.

46. Dougherty and Hammack, *Education and Society,* p. 340. The geneticist argument has been thoroughly dismantled primarily on the basis of cultural biases of tests and social factors including family upbringing and schooling.

47. Melvin Kohn, *Class and Conformity: A Study in Values* (Homewood, Ill.: Dorsey Press, 1969).

48. Oscar Lewis, *La Vida: A Puerto Rican Family in the Culture of Poverty—San Juan and New York.* (New York: Random House, 1966).

49. C. Wright Mills, *The Power Elite* (New York: Oxford University Press, 1956).

50. Dougherty and Hammack, *Education and Society,* p. 342.

51. Richard D. Kahlenberg, "Schools of Hard Knocks," *American Prospect Online,* May 4, 2004, http://www.prospect.org.

52. Ibid.

53. James S. Coleman, Thomas Hoffer, and Sally Kilgore, *High School and Beyond* (Pittsburgh: National Center for Education Statistics, November 1981). This was a longitudinal study of U.S. high school seniors' and sophomores' academic preparation in different settings.

54. A Rand Corporation study in 1990 concluded that parochial schools had particular success with disadvantaged and minority students. Although minority students score lower than their white classmates in Catholic and public schools, the gap decreases significantly by the eleventh grade. However, in Catholic schools, children in single-parent homes drop out only at the same rate as those in two-parent homes.

Although the educational level of parents of parochial school students exceeds that of parents of public school students, Catholic schools' achievement advantage over public schools is the greatest for children whose parents have the least education. Reported in Tim Baker, "Successful Schools Are Right Under Our Noses," *Baltimore Sun,* June 3, 1991.

55. J. T. Grogger and D. Neal, "Further Evidence on the Effects of Catholic Secondary Schooling," in W. G. Gale and Pack J. Rothenberg, eds., *Brookings-Wharton Papers on Urban Affairs* (Washington, D.C.: Brookings Institution, 2000), pp. 151–193.

56. Caroline Minter Hoxby, *Do Private Schools Provide Competition for Public Schools?* (Cambridge, Mass.: National Bureau of Economic Research, 1994), p. 53.

57. For a good review of the characteristics of effective schools research, see Stewart C. Purkey and Marshall S. Smith, "Effective Schools: A Review," *Elementary School Journal* 83 (March 1983): 427–452.

58. See, for example, James S. Coleman, "Families and Schools," *Educational Researcher* 16 (August–September 1987): 32–38. For research comparing public and private schools, see Coleman, Hoffer, and Kilgore, *High School and Beyond;* and James Coleman and Thomas Hoffer, *Public and Private High Schools* (New York: Basic Books, 1987).

59. *Sociology of Education* 55 (April–July 1982) and *Harvard Educational Review* 51 (November 1981): 481–545, were devoted to a critique of Coleman, Hoffer, and Kilgore, *High School Achievement.*

60. John E. Chubb and Terry M. Moe, *Politics, Markets, and America's Schools* (Washington, D.C.: Brookings Institution, 1990), pp. 32–33.

61. Anthony Bryk, Valerie Lee, and Peter Holland, *Catholic Schools for the Common Good* (Cambridge: Harvard University Press, 1993).

62. Paul E. Peterson and Jay Greene, "Race Relations and Central City Schools: It's Time for an Experiment with Vouchers," *Brookings Review,* March 22, 1998.

63. Ibid., p. 36.

64. Richard Rothstein, *Class and Schools: Using Social, Economic, and Educational Reform to Close the Black-White Achievement Gap* (Washington, D.C.: Economic Policy Institute, 2004).

65. Chubb and Moe, *Politics.*

66. Ibid., p. 33. Chubb and Moe provide an excellent analysis of the problems of public education and alternative approaches to resolving them.

67. Ibid., p. 54.

68. The problem of increased bureaucratic control has increased as responsibility for funding has moved from localities to the states and with the growth of federal regulation with such initiatives as NCLB. Court decisions on funding equity and racial integration have also contributed to the trend. Increased regulation contributes to instruction taking a smaller portion of educational expenditures.

69. See John E. Chubb and Eric A. Hanushek, "Reforming Educational Reform," in Henry J. Aaron, ed., *Setting National Priorities: Policy for the Nineties* (Washington, D.C.: Brookings Institution, 1990), pp. 223–224.

70. See "Schools, Vouchers, and the American Public," a discussion by Terry Moe at the Brookings Brown Center on Education Policy, http://www.brookings.edu/comm/transcripts/2001.

71. Ibid.

72. Joseph Viteritti, "Stacking the Deck for the Poor: The New Politics of School Choice," *Brookings Review* 14, no. 3 (Summer 1996).

73. *Mueller v. Allen* (1983).

74. U.S. Census Bureau, *Statistical Abstract 2003,* p. 457.

75. Marilyn McMillen, *Dropout Rates in the United States, 1995,* NCES 97-473 (Washington, D.C.: U.S. Department of Education, National Center for Education Statistics, 1995).

76. Karl L. Alexander, Doris R. Entwisle, and Carrie S. Horsey, "From First Grade

Forward: Early Foundations of High School Dropouts," *Sociology of Education* 70, no. 2 (1998): 87.

77. U.S. Census Bureau, *Statistical Abstract 2003,* p. 220.

78. Christopher B. Swanson, *Who Graduates? Who Doesn't? A Statistical Portrait of Public High School Graduation, Class of 2001* (Washington, D.C.: Urban Institute, Education Policy Center, 2003), p. v.

79. See ibid. and Christopher Edley Jr. and Johanna Wald, *The Hidden Dropout Crisis* (Washington, D.C.: Center for American Progress, February 27, 2004), http://www.americanprogress.org.

80. Theodore B. Sizer, *Horace's Compromise: The Dilemma of the American High School* (Boston: Houghton Mifflin, 1984), pp. 36–37.

81. As quoted in Peter Schrag, "Bush's Education Fraud," *American Prospect* 15, no. 2 (February 2004). See also Robert Kuttner, "Stranglehold: The Right-Wing Push for a One-Party State," *American Prospect* 15, no. 2 (February 2004).

CHAPTER 10

Health Care: Diagnosing a Chronic Problem

Health care issues consistently surface as one of the most important policy concerns facing the United States today. Americans spend more money on health care than does any other nation in the world. Yet health care seems to be a topic of constant controversy. Who gets health care and how much they receive is an ethical and a practical problem in society. We do not want to get ill but want proper treatment when we need it. Why is it that, despite spending huge sums of money, we never seem to have the health care we want? It is so costly that almost 45 million Americans are without health insurance and do not have access to high-quality care. Whatever the amount we spend on health care, how can we spend it efficiently so that we get the most effective health care for a given commitment of resources? Efforts to control rising costs are held in check by new treatment technologies, which drive up the cost. Various business and lobby groups prefer the status quo over changes that might limit their influence. Political power is divided among the executive, various congressional committees, states, and political parties. Finally, there is an ideological conflict between those who see health care as just another "market" good and those who think government should guarantee health care as a right based on need.

The Rising Cost of Health Care

The cost of health care is the single most important concern of most Americans when they think of health care problems. After housing and transportation, health care spending and food claim the largest share of average household spending. American health is a study in contrasts. A baby girl born to an affluent family can expect to live for about eighty-two years, but a girl born to a poor family without health insurance will have a much shorter life expectancy. The affluent child can expect to receive adequate nutrition and attention to health needs, and be given every educational opportunity. If she becomes a mother, she and her child will benefit from high-quality maternity and prenatal care. As she grows older, she may fall victim to chronic diseases, but insurance and personal resources will ensure that she receives the best treatment and rehabilitation services available. Almost no medical treatment recommended by her physician will be turned down.

Meanwhile, the poorer girl born to a poor mother without prenatal care will more likely be an underweight child throughout childhood. Living in poverty will increase the likelihood that the child will develop asthma or other diseases that may be a chronic condition largely left untreated. She will probably have poorer dietary habits and a lower level of education. She will more likely marry at an earlier age and will have a greater likelihood of having inadequate insurance and thus continuing the pattern of inadequate maternity and prenatal care and counseling. If she develops chronic diseases later in life, she is much less likely to have access to adequate treatment. Her chronic health problems will lead to a shorter life span, on average, than that of the affluent child.

The contrasting scenarios are at the crux of what good medicine can achieve and the unmet needs of those without access to good health care. A goal of health care in the United States today is to close the gap between the health care inequalities.

Spending on health and health care has risen dramatically in the United States and most other Organization for Economic Cooperation and Development (OECD) countries in the first several years of the twenty-first century. Slower economic growth along with increased health spending drove the share of health expenditure as a percentage of gross domestic product (GDP) from 13 percent in 1997 to almost 14.9 percent by 2002 in the United States.[1] Health spending increased 2.3 times faster than GDP during that period. Meanwhile, the OECD average increase in health expenditures increased from 7.8 percent in 1997 to 9.3 percent in 2002. Health expenditures exceeded average annual OECD rates by 1.7 percent. In 1997 the average American spent $3,939 on health care. By 2002, health care spending in the United States reached $5,440 per capita, over twice the OECD average of $2,144.[2] Health care is valued highly in the United States, as demonstrated by the nation's sizable investment in it. The nation provides health insurance in the form of Medicare for those over sixty-five and offers tax subsidies to support health insurance for workers, which taken together benefit about 85 percent of the population.

Why has the demand for health care grown so much? Obviously the desire of people to remain healthy has led to a continuous growth in the demand for health care. But there are more specific reasons for the continued increase in demand for health care. There has been a shift from a focus on infectious diseases to more costly chronic diseases.[3] With the development of vaccines and antibiotics, the incidence of infectious diseases decreased and concern shifted to chronic ailments, such as heart disease, diabetes, and cancer, for which cures are not available. People with chronic diseases often undergo treatment for the rest of their lives, which is more costly.

Improvements in medical technologies is a second factor that has driven up the cost of health care. New and more expensive drugs permit the treatment of a number of conditions, such as asthma, that previously were essentially untreatable. Technology that permits heart bypass surgery, kidney dialysis, and chemotherapy and radiation for cancer may not cure or even arrest chronic diseases, but may permit a much longer and higher quality of life. Other expensive technologies are used with increasing frequency, such as magnetic resonance imaging (MRI) for diagnostic purposes.

A third major factor contributing to cost escalation is the changing age structure. Countries like the United States have an aging population, which increases the demand for health care. The elderly (defined as those sixty-five and older), who require more health care than younger age groups, now constitute over 12 percent of the population and are the fastest-growing age group. As baby boomers begin to reach retirement age within the next few years, this segment will expand significantly.

Rising real incomes have resulted in many people deciding that they no longer have to endure the pain, discomfort, or lack of mobility associated with conditions like osteoarthritis of various joints. People now demand a hip or knee replacement operation rather than accept the reduced mobility that used to be associated with those conditions.

Finally, traditional health insurance systems have contributed to the increase in demand for health care (and therefore its costs). Employer-based health insurance grew rapidly in the decade after World War II and provided a ready supply of cash to finance technical developments in medical care.

Nevertheless, now over 15 percent of the U.S. population has no health insurance, about one in six people, while virtually 100 percent of citizens in all other OECD countries are covered by their respective national health care systems. As mentioned above, Americans spend more on health care, both per capita and overall, than do citizens in any other country in the world, and that spending continues to grow faster than GDP. The proportion of GDP spent on health care may rise to 18 percent by 2013.[4] This is unsustainable. Any increase in health care spending must be accompanied by offsetting reductions in other sectors of the economy such as housing and education.

The Problem: Access to Health Care and the Uninsured

Despite the large sums of money spent as a nation on health care, a growing number of Americans lack access to health care because they cannot afford basic health insurance. The U.S. Census Bureau concluded that the share of the population without health insurance rose from 41.2 million in 2001 to 45 million in 2003, or 15.6 percent of the population.[5] How large is 45 million? It is more than all African Americans (about 37 million), all Hispanic and Latino Americans (about 40 million), or all Americans age sixty-five and older (about 36 million). The uninsured population is about the same size as the number of Americans living in California, Washington, and Oregon combined. The percentage of people covered by employment-based health insurance dropped from 62.6 percent to 60.4 percent between 2001 and 2003, in what has become a clear trend.

There is a general stereotype that the uninsured are unemployed and on welfare. The truth is somewhat more complicated. Considering the eighteen- to sixty-four-year-old population, workers are somewhat more likely to have health insurance than are nonworkers. But over 74 percent of nonworkers have insurance.[6] Among employed workers, the proportion who have employment-based policies in their own name has been declining, to 55 percent in 2002. There are several key demographic factors related to health insurance coverage. Age is a significant indicator. Young adults (ages nineteen to twenty-four) compose a larger share of the uninsured than do workers (21 percent versus 10 percent).[7] Since almost everyone over sixty-five is covered by Medicare insurance, over 99 percent of the elderly have health coverage. For other age groups, employment-based insurance coverage increases with age. The likelihood of having health insurance also increases as educational levels rise. The same is true with income. While 20 percent of all workers have low family incomes (defined as an income less than double the federal poverty level [FPL]), over half of uninsured workers have low incomes. Almost half of poor workers (an income equal to the FPL) and a third of near-poor workers (an income equal or greater to, but less than double, the FPL) have no health insurance.[8]

In 2002 there were 143 million workers aged eighteen through sixty-four, of which 55 percent had employment-based health insurance. The proportion of workers with insurance increased with the size of the company. Only 31 percent of the workers in firms employing twenty-five or fewer people had employment-based insurance, compared to 65 percent of those employed by firms with one hundred workers or more. Not surprisingly, the uninsured are also more likely to be minority, either black (20 percent) or especially Hispanic (32 percent). The uninsured also vary significantly by state. Texas has one of the nation's lowest rates of employer-sponsored coverage and the highest rate of uninsured (24 percent) in the country. In 2002, over 1.4 million children were uninsured in Texas. In contrast, just 8 percent of Minnesota's population was uninsured. The uninsured tend to be young workers in low-skill jobs working for small companies that often do not offer health insurance to their employees.

Those without insurance lack *access* to quality health care. Without insurance, the out-of-pocket expenses put all but the most routine health care out of reach. Not surprisingly, the uninsured get significantly less care than do insured people. The Institute of Medicine estimates that 18,000 people between the ages of twenty-five and sixty-four die prematurely each year because they are uninsured.[9] The institute also found that the amount the uninsured pay for services out of pocket, along with worker compensation, charity, and insurance payments for partial coverage is over $100 billion per year. When they do receive services, the uninsured are often charged a higher price and pay more of the total cost themselves than do people with health insurance. The lack of health insurance is costly to society. Uninsured children lose the opportunity for normal development and educational achievement when preventable health conditions are left untreated.[10] Families lose peace of mind because of the uncertainty of the medical and financial consequences of an illness or injury. The economic vitality of the country is diminished by productivity lost as a result of poorer health, disability, or premature death of uninsured workers. This is bothersome for both ethical and medical reasons. As David Cutler has written, "In a country as rich as ours, it is difficult to accept that not everyone has health insurance. Other countries insure everyone, and at lower cost. Why can't the United States do the same?"[11]

Quality of Health Care in the United States

Is the quality of health care in the United States what we would expect from an investment of 15 percent of GDP? It is not unusual to hear the boast that health care in the United States is the best in the world. But critics make the claim that it is scandalously inferior to what the average citizen in other developed democracies has come to expect. Unfortunately, both claims may be simultaneously valid. In the Dickensian sense it is "the best of times, and the worst of times." For the affluent and the well insured, access to health care of the highest quality is readily available, while for the poor and uninsured, access is limited and the quality of health care they receive is decidedly inferior.

According to the U.S. government, health care spending rose to $1.6 trillion in 2002, a growth rate of 9.3 percent, or 5.7 percentage points faster than the overall economy.[12] Governments must rely on tax revenue to fund health care programs. When tax rates remain constant, tax revenue will generally increase at the same rate as GDP. However, health care costs continue to accelerate at a faster rate than GDP, which must result in a rising portion of GDP going to health care. One policy dilemma is that taxes must be raised to pay for increased health costs or government deficits will rise. However, recent government policy leans heavily in the direction of reducing taxes, which makes it increasingly difficult to pay for rising health care costs. Another possibility is that the government might seek ways to have the private sector pick up an increasing portion of the expense. Another obvious policy dilemma is that more resources put into health care means that there are fewer resources for other sectors of the economy. Private industry is opposed to absorbing more health care costs because it already feels itself at a competitive disadvantage with foreign competitors.

Figure 10.1 indicates that private sources funded over half the national health expenditures in 2003, with private health insurance contributing 36 percent of the total ($550 billion). Out-of-pocket payments contributed $212 billion, or 14 percent of all expenditures. The public sector accounted for 45 percent of all health payments, with Medicare providing 17 percent, at $267 billion and Medicaid 16 percent, at $249 billion, of total spending, and other public spending equaling 12 percent. Figure 10.1 also indicates where the money was spent.

Since we pay more for health care than any other country both per capita and as a percentage of GDP, one might expect that our society would lead the world in indices of what constitutes health. We are also the *only* developed democratic capitalist state that leaves most of health care up to market forces and the *only* country without national health insurance. The fact that Americans spend 14.9 percent of GDP on health care while other developed countries spend approximately 8 percent would suggest that, by paying so much more, we would have more services available than do other countries. Unfortunately, the United States lags behind most countries in several leading health indicators. Table 10.1 illustrates the problem.

Despite paying so much more than other OECD countries for health care, the United States ranks below most of those countries in key areas. For example, the United States had 2.4 doctors per 1,000 people, compared with a median of 3.1 in other OECD countries. Even more striking is the fact that the United States lags behind every other OECD nation in infant mortality rates, with 6.9 deaths per 1,000 live births versus an OECD average of 4.4. Or consider life expectancy at birth for the U.S. population compared to that for other developed countries, as indicated in Table 10.2.

Female life expectancy in the United States is the lowest of the fifteen nations listed in Table 10.2, while males in the United States rank fourteenth, just ahead of Portugal. OECD projections also indicate that the United States will rank fourteenth on the overall life expectancy indicator in 2010. OECD data also suggests other anomalies. For instance, the United States has only 2.9 hospital beds per 1,000 people, while the OECD average is 3.9.[13] An American is also likely to

**Figure 10.1 U.S. Health Care Spending: Where It Came From and
Where It Went, 2003**

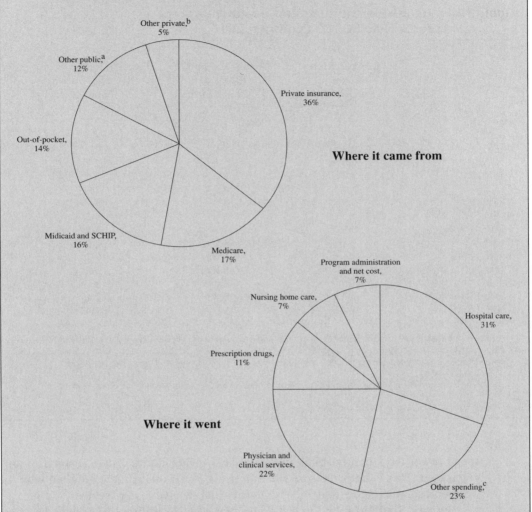

Other private,b
5%

Other public,a
12%

Private insurance,
36%

Out-of-pocket,
14%

Where it came from

Midicaid and SCHIP,
16%

Medicare,
17%

Program administration
and net cost,
7%

Nursing home care,
7%

Hospital care,
31%

Prescription drugs,
11%

Where it went

Physician and
clinical services,
22%

Other spending,c
23%

Source: Centers for Medicare and Medicaid Services, Office of the Actuary, National Health Statistics Group, 2003.

Notes: a. "Other public" includes programs such as worker compensation, public health activity, Department of Defense, Department of Veterans Affairs, Indian Health Service, state and local hospital subsidies, and school health.

b. "Other private" includes industrial in-plant, privately funded construction, and nonpatient revenues, including philanthropy.

c. "Other spending" includes dental services, other professional services, home health care, durable medical products, over-the-counter medicines and sundries, public health activities, research, and construction.

Table 10.1 Health Expenditures and Health Indicators for Selected OECD Countries, 2002

	Total Expenditures on Health (% of GDP)	Infant Mortality (deaths per 1,000 live births)	Practicing Physicians (Density per 1,000 population)
Australia	9.1[a]	5.0	2.5
Austria	7.7	4.1	3.3
Belgium	9.1	4.9	3.9
Canada	9.6	5.0	2.1
Finland	7.3	3.0	3.1
France	9.7	4.2	3.3
Germany	10.9	4.3	3.3
Greece	9.5	5.9	4.5
Italy	8.5	4.7	4.4
Japan	7.8[a]	3.0	2.0
Netherlands	9.1	5.0	3.1
Portugal	9.3	5.0	3.2
Spain	7.6	3.4	2.9
United Kingdom	7.7	5.3	2.1
United States	14.9[b]	6.9	2.4

Sources: Organization for Economic Cooperation and Development (OECD), *OECD Health Data 2004: A Comparative Analysis of 30 Countries* (Paris: OECD, 2004); Center for Medicare and Medicaid Services; U.S. Census Bureau, *Statistical Abstract 2003* (Washington, D.C.: U.S. Government Printing Office, 2003).
Notes: a. 2001data.
b. Revised upward from 14.6 as originally reported by the Center for Medicare and Medicaid Services.

---

spend fewer days in a hospital and less likely to be admitted to a hospital in any given year. This is not necessarily bad in itself, but if this is the case, then why do we spend so much more than other countries and receive fewer services?

Barbara Starfield found that the fact that over 44 million Americans have no health insurance is well known, but seems to be tolerated under the assumption that better health results from more expensive care. Her research concluded that, in fact, Americans do not have anywhere near the best health in the world.[14] Of thirteen countries in her study, the United States ranks twelfth on sixteen available health indicators, lagging behind Japan, Sweden, Canada, France, Australia, Spain, Finland, the Netherlands, the United Kingdom, Denmark, and Belgium.[15] Evidence

Table 10.2   Life Expectancy at Birth, 2002

	Females at Birth (years)	Males at Birth (years)	Male and Female Projected to 2010 (years)
Australia	82.6	77.4	81.0
Austria	81.7	75.8	(NA)
Belgium	81.1	75.1	79.4
Canada	82.2	77.1	80.7
Finland	81.5	74.9	(NA)
France	82.9	75.6	80.3
Germany[a]	81.3	75.6	79.4
Greece	80.7	75.4	79.8
Italy	82.9	76.8	80.3
Japan	85.2	78.3	81.6
Netherlands	80.7	76.0	79.6
Portugal	80.5	73.8	77.4
Spain	83.1	75.7	80.2
United Kingdom[a]	80.4	75.7	79.2
United States[a]	79.8	74.4	78.4

Source: Organization for Economic Cooperation and Development (OECD), *OECD Health Data 2004: A Comparative Analysis of 30 Countries* (Paris: OECD, 2004); U.S. Census Bureau, *Statistical Abstract 2003* (Washington, D.C.: U.S. Government Printing Office, 2003).

Notes: a. 2001 data.

(NA) indicates data not available.

of the deficiency of U.S. medical care has been reinforced by the World Health Organization (WHO), which ranked the United States fifteenth out of twenty-five industrialized countries.[16] The WHO created a single measure of the overall quality of national health systems by integrating measures of child survival and life expectancy with differences across social groups in experiences with health care systems and the level of public financing (versus out-of-pocket expenditures for health care). The evidence from international comparisons, according to Starfield, is "incontrovertible," and the U.S. position is declining not improving. Research suggesting the relatively poor position of the United States, when compared to other developed, democratic, capitalistic nations, is not dependent on the particular measurements used. Thus the data in Table 10.1 suggest that about 4 percent of GDP (about $600 billion a year), the amount we spend beyond what other countries spend, is essentially wasted.

What Is the Relationship
Between Money and the Health of Society?

The criticism of health care in the United States cannot be that we spend too little. Rather, it is that we get too little for what we spend. The evidence is conclusive that the United States spends more of its GDP than does any other advanced democratic, capitalist nation. The most recent data available from the World Health Organization confirm this point (see Table 10.3).

Research also shows that Americans receive on average fewer health care resources than the average person in an OECD country. Yet the state of health of Americans ranks well below the average for OECD countries. What can account for this result?

One view is that there is a dynamic tension between the competing needs of cost, quality, and access. Any attempt to address one of these fundamental problems, adversely affects the other two.[17] Donald Barr points out that if the policy choice is to control the *cost* of care, we must inevitably either reduce the *quality* by cutting the services available, or reduce *access* by providing coverage to fewer people. Conversely, if the policy decision is to improve access by providing coverage for the uninsured, we must increase the overall cost of care. If we try to improve access while trying to hold down cost, quality must suffer. Finally, if we try to improve the quality of health care by introducing new technologies, treatments, or medications, we will increase the cost, which many think is already excessive, by depriving more people of access, a result of their being driven into the ranks of the uninsured.[18] Thus a proposal to deal with one problem (i.e., cost, access, or quality) will face defenders of the status quo from the other two, which has prevented serious reform.

Evolution of Health Care in the United States

That health care is a scarce economic good is attested to by the fact that 45 million Americans are uninsured. In a free market, health care would be allocated according to consumers' demand (i.e., their ability and willingness to pay). By contrast, a command model would allocate health care according to a predefined basis such as "need." What has ultimately developed in the United States is a model that leans heavily toward the free market with only a trace of a command model to include the poor, the elderly, and the military. Medical care in the United States is treated as a private consumer good distributed primarily according to one's ability to pay, while the poor might be guaranteed a minimal package of care.[19] The United States is alone among democratic capitalist nations in approaching health care as primarily a market commodity.

Policy analysts would suggest two criteria to judge the performance of the dis-

Table 10.3 Measured Levels of Expenditures on Health, 2001

	Total Expenditures as % of GDP	Government Expenditures as % of Total Health Expenditures	Private Expenditures as % of Total Health Expenditures	Government Expenditures as % of Total Government Expenditures	Out-of-Pocket Expenditures as % of Private Expenditures	Private Insurance as % of Private Health Expenditures
Australia	9.2	67.9	32.1	16.8	59.6	24.2
Austria	8.0	69.3	30.7	10.7	61.3	23.3
Belgium	8.9	71.7	28.3	13.0	58.8	6.8
Canada	9.5	70.8	29.2	16.2	52.3	39.3
Finland	7.0	75.6	24.4	10.7	82.7	8.3
France	9.6	76.0	24.0	13.7	42.6	53.1
Germany	10.8	74.9	25.1	16.6	42.4	33.5
Greece	9.4	56.0	44.0	11.2	73.9	4.4
Italy	8.4	75.3	24.7	13.0	82.1	3.6
Japan	8.0	77.9	22.1	16.4	74.9	1.4
Netherlands	8.9	63.3	36.7	12.2	24.1	42.4
Portugal	9.2	69.0	31.0	13.7	58.5	4.3
Spain	7.5	71.4	28.6	13.6	82.8	14.1
United Kingdom	7.6	82.2	17.8	15.4	55.3	17.2
United States	13.9	44.4	55.6	17.6	26.5	64.1

Source: World Health Organization (WHO). *World Health Report 2004: Statistical Annex*, tab. 5, pp. 136-141, http://www.who.int/whr/2004/annex/topic/en/annex_5_en.pdf.

tribution system. The first criterion is efficiency: Does the system allocate resources in a manner that meets the Pareto efficiency criterion (i.e., an allocation that makes one person better off must not make someone else worse off)? The allocation is efficient if the tradeoffs lie on the production possibilities frontier (see Chapter 1). The second criterion is normative in that it depends completely on people's values. Does the system meet society's view of justice? Although this criterion is more subjective, it has been determinative in other industrialized nations, where notions of the prerequisites to create a just and humane society have resulted in adoption of a policy of health care as a basic right for all citizens.

The concept of fairness here is analogous to our discussion of horizontal and vertical equity in tax policy (see Chapter 6). Horizontal equity in health care would provide equal treatment for those in equal need. Horizontal equity would require that two individuals with the same medical condition receive the same treatment. Treatment would not differ according to financial circumstances, for example. Vertical equity holds that people in unequal circumstances should not be treated equally. Accordingly, in health care we would expect unequal treatment for unequal circumstances. A severely injured victim of an accident should be given more treatment than a walk-in patient with a minor complaint. And as in taxation, it might include the government financing health care based on ability to pay, such as through a progressive tax.

The determination of what kind of health care to provide, how to finance it, as well as how and to whom to deliver it, is deeply influenced by the unique culture and peculiar political system of the nation concerned. Especially in the United States, health policy is very broad and encompasses much more than just the federal government and bureaucracies like the Center for Medicare and Medicaid Services. States also play a major role, especially in financing care for those in poverty and in licensing medical practitioners. Insurance companies, which are private businesses, provide health insurance to other corporations. Thus corporations in the United States are key players in determining the way health care is financed and delivered. They are also deeply involved in pressuring government at all levels to accept a market-based approach. Private professional organizations such as the American Medical Association (AMA) have been a major force behind the creation of the private-practice **fee-for-service** model for health care delivery providers. Private businesses that attempt to compete with physicians to hold down prices as an alternative to traditional prepaid private insurance, known as **health maintenance organizations** (HMOs), have also become very influential. Accordingly, the United States is unique in treating medical care as a market commodity to be bought and sold in the marketplace rather than as a social good that should be made available to all on the basis of need.

The first policy decision to profoundly affect the way health care evolved in the United States was the result of a commission report that attempted to restructure and standardize medical education. In the early 1900s there were few standards regarding medical education in the United States. The **Flexner Report** of 1910, titled *Medical Education in the United States and Canada,* was very critical of the quality of medical education at the time and encouraged strict standards of education as a requirement to become a certified practitioner of medicine. The report promoted the AMA as the primary authority over medical practice, and so government at all levels began to rely on the AMA for advice regarding policy matters. The AMA effectively closed down inferior medical schools while improving the economic status of physicians by limiting the number produced. The sovereignty of the U.S. medical profession was not seriously challenged at the time, because health care was a relatively minor concern in most people's lives. Insurance companies and corporations were not yet players in the health care arena. In the early part of the twentieth century, physicians were seen as professionals who provided care to everyone without regard to ability to pay. Hospitals were often run by religious or charitable organizations and charged fees to those who could pay, but provided care to everyone despite financial ability. It was this view that led state and local governments to defer authority to the medical profession over how medicine was practiced. Physicians were able to demand the autonomy of a fee-for-service system because of their specialized knowledge and the fact that there were no other major players in the field. A critical view contends that the medical profession began using its power to limit the size and number of medical schools and thereby limit entry into the profession. The AMA was able to restrict the supply of physicians by placing limits on medical schools and on the number of physicians trained, and ultimately on the supply of doctors in active practice.[20] As Table 10.1 illustrates, the United States ranks near the bottom in number of physicians available to the population. The AMA also prevented doctors from advertising, which prevented consumers from gaining the information needed to make a rational choice in a free market.[21]

The fee-for-service system defended the right of physicians as entrepreneurs to charge patients a separate fee of whatever the market would bear. In providing health care, physicians presumably had the desire to make decisions that would be in the interest of the patient as well as in their own financial interest. The higher the quality of medical care for the patient would also improve the personal income of the physician.

The AMA accepted the original prepaid indemnity plans as not conflicting with the fee-for-service notion. An **indemnity plan** allows the enrollee to use any licensed doctor and provides the same coverage no matter which physician or hospital the enrollee uses. It reimburses for covered medical services, as long as the expenses are reasonable and customary. A physician's willingness to supply these services and then bill the insurance company leads to the problem shown in Figure 10.2's simple supply/demand curve.

The fee-for-service system also provided a powerful incentive to develop new surgeries or devices to improve health. Research funds flow from such organizations as the National Institutes of Health, hospitals, pharmaceutical firms, and insurance companies. The expected return for successful research is obviously high. Insurance companies as a major source of such funds found themselves facing increasing costs to generate benefits and to pay for their use once established. It is not easy to convince employers to pass the cost on to workers in the form of higher premiums (which ultimately result in lower wages).

The economic success the medical profession enjoyed after establishing control over the organization of medical care and gaining acceptance of the fee-for-service system ultimately brought about its own countervailing power. According to Gerard Anderson and colleagues, the reason for the high level of spending is that Americans with access to health care pay much more for prescription drugs, while hospitals, doctors, and administrative expenses are higher than in most industrialized countries.[22] This puts an upward pressure on insurance costs. Employers increasingly resist higher costs for health insurance to prevent further erosion of their competitiveness with foreign corporations that do not face similar health care

Figure 10.2 Implications of User and Third-Party Payer Health Care

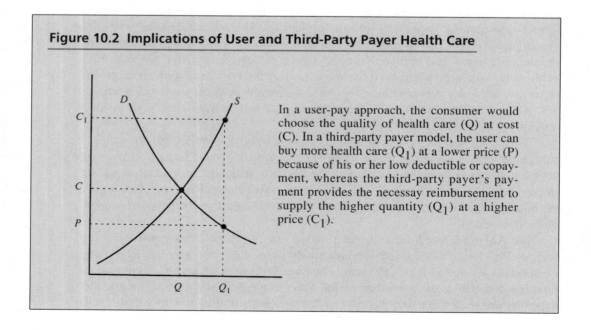

In a user-pay approach, the consumer would choose the quality of health care (Q) at cost (C). In a third-party payer model, the user can buy more health care (Q_1) at a lower price (P) because of his or her low deductible or copayment, whereas the third-party payer's payment provides the necessay reimbursement to supply the higher quantity (Q_1) at a higher price (C_1).

costs because of national health insurance. Governments also find that Medicare and Medicaid costs rise faster than tax revenues, even when the economy is growing. A slow growth economy, or even a contracting one, results in deficits, and tax cuts further exacerbate the problem.

The Growing Consensus on the Need for Change

The growing public awareness that health care costs have climbed so high that more and more Americans can no longer afford basic health insurance has forced health care onto the policy agenda. A survey by the Henry J. Kaiser Family Foundation in 2004 found that 73 percent of survey respondents said health care would be "very important" or "one of the most important issues."[23] There is also increased concern that the government could do more to ensure both improved access to and quality of health care for all Americans.[24]

Theodore Roosevelt proposed a publicly financed universal health care system in the United States when he ran for president in the Bull Moose Party in 1912, but it garnered little support. Although private health insurance was introduced in the early part of the twentieth century, it was not until 1929, when Blue Cross offered hospital insurance, followed a few years later by Blue Shield's offering of prepaid physician care, that health insurance began to grow. Before then, very few Americans had prepaid health insurance that covered hospital or doctor bills. In the 1930s and 1940s, labor unions, strengthened by New Deal legislation, pressed for higher wages *and* fringe benefits. President Franklin Roosevelt considered adding medical care to the Social Security legislation in 1935, because so many poor and unemployed during the Great Depression had no secure access to health care. Blue Cross developed a vigorous campaign to persuade the middle class that the availability of private insurance made national health insurance unnecessary and even illegitimate in that private, not public, programs were the American way. Roosevelt decided that adding health care to legislation already deemed radical by opponents would destroy the chance for passage of Social Security by Congress.

The situation changed rapidly during World War II, when unemployment virtually disappeared. Companies were not allowed to raid rival corporations' workers by offering higher pay, because strict wage controls to fight inflation were in effect. However, the tax code, after energetic lobbying efforts by a growing insurance industry and labor unions, allowed employers to claim the cost of health insurance as a tax-deductible business expense. Insurance premiums were not counted as wages, or taxable income, to workers. This policy continued after the war.

The employee actually pays for the health insurance fringe benefit, since it is part of overall compensation. If he or she did not receive it as insurance coverage, it would be paid in higher wages. But an employee would rather receive $100 as an untaxed health care benefit than $100 in wages, which would be subject to federal, state, and payroll taxes (Social Security and Medicare). As a result, almost every major company provided health benefits to its employees as a standard fringe benefit by the end of the 1950s. Since employees receive a subsidized (i.e., untaxed) benefit, they have an incentive to buy more insurance coverage than if they had to pay the premium out-of-pocket as well as a tax on the income.

After World War II, the recipient of health care services usually had to pay only a minor deductible or copayment, and the insurance company became the major payer for care itself. Under this **third-party-payer** system, both consumers and physicians had little incentive to consider costs when seeking or providing medical care. And the more medical services the physician performed, even questionable procedures, the more his or her total personal income increased.

Employment-sponsored, prepaid private health insurance became the standard, so that shortly after the war, lack of medical insurance coverage was seen as a problem primarily of the poor and the elderly. In 1945 and again in 1948, President Harry Truman proposed national health insurance to cover those without employment-related insurance. His program was defeated, largely because the AMA launched a well-financed and harsh attack to defeat Truman and his congressional sponsors of "socialized medicine." The AMA continued its assault on Truman and his congressional supporters even after the Democrats regained control of the House and Senate in 1949.[25]

A discussion of health care brings up the obvious differences in the ability of individuals to pay for health care. The affluent are more able to buy health insurance and to pay for more esoteric medical treatment than are those in poverty. Fifty years ago, most physicians would provide medical services for the uninsured by a process known as **cost shifting**, in which physicians would absorb some of the cost of seeing indigent patients, and offset some of the cost by a somewhat higher fee billed to insurance companies or more affluent patients. The rising costs of medical care resulted in insurance companies tightening their oversight on billing while raising their rates. The health needs of the uninsured quickly exceeded the ability of physicians to supply them. Since many medical advances have been assisted by health insurance, it has become increasingly expensive. And because most affordable insurance for families with modest incomes is through their employment, one's employment is often a deciding factor regarding health insurance coverage.

Health Care and Market Failure

In theory, markets respond to impersonal forces of supply and demand and produce the services that we want at the lowest (i.e., most efficient) cost. Sometimes, however, market imperfections may result in what policy analysts call market failure.

For example, most health care decisions are made by the physician (the supplier) on behalf of the patient (the consumer). Once the patient selects the physician, the physician determines most of the patient's health expenditures by prescribing medications, ordering tests, and if deemed necessary, admitting the patient to a hospital, as well as charging for their own services.

A model of perfect competition requires that buyers have perfect information and that sellers produce the good or service at the lowest possible price and earn only normal profits. Here the sellers have the power to influence both the price and the total amount of health care consumed. Physicians and other suppliers of health care usually have significantly more power than does the consumer.

Most of us think in terms of what sort of health care we would want for ourselves *if we needed it*. We tend to value treatment for potential health care needs. Our concern is often for health care that we may someday need. We typically do not know if or when we will need it, only that some people may and it could be us. How would we pay for care if we were in an automobile accident, suffered a stroke, or found out that we, or a member of our family, had cancer? Since we cannot know all of our future health care needs, we try to prepare for such eventualities by purchasing insurance and paying the premiums whether we need health care or not. We only know that not buying health insurance is risky. Consumers purchase insurance to remove risk and uncertainty. A free market in health care will also require an efficient health care insurance market. Unfortunately, moral hazards and adverse selection may cause a market failure here as well.

The need for medical resources is potentially unlimited, but the supply of those resources is not. In a market-driven system there are not enough providers or money to give care to everyone. Initially, those with adequate insurance received whatever care they needed and were not significantly affected by rising costs. To keep costs low, insurance companies made it expensive and difficult for those most needy of health care services to get insurance. The health needs of the uninsured promptly exceeded the ability of humanitarian caregivers to supply them. And rising health care costs meant that almost any health care was prohibitively expensive for the uninsured. Some in the health care industry were still committed to the notion of providing health care to all who needed it, despite their ability to pay. The system tried to meet the need by spreading out the cost of caring for the poor and uninsured, through increasing the charges to those with insurance. This drove up health care costs for providers, employers, and insurance companies, and created a larger division between the haves and the have-nots in health care coverage.

Recent Steps Toward Cost Control
The health care system in the United States really consists of separate markets. The system has responded to the haves, whose well-funded insurance plans encourage

Case Study: Health Care and Moral Hazards

A **moral hazard** refers to the reduced incentive of policyholders to protect themselves from what they are insured against. The point is that once we have purchased health insurance, we may change our behavior in ways that will drive up insurance costs. As already noted, consumers who are insured have incentives to seek more care than they would if they were paying the entire cost out-of-pocket.

Part of what is claimed to be a moral hazard is a subjective judgment, however. A jogger, with insurance, who falls and twists an ankle while running may have x-rays taken to determine if there is a fracture. Without insurance, the person may hope it is just a sprain that will heal in a few days by giving the ankle rest. Whether seeking medical attention in such a situation is excessive or not is unclear. It is also unlikely that possessing health insurance would increase one's incentive to take risks that might lead to cancer.

As well, the concern with the insured consumer as the focal point of a moral hazard may be misplaced. The major choice made by the patient noted above is typically that of choosing a physician. After that choice, the physician is also affected by moral hazard when he or she acts as the patient's agent and decides what diagnostic tests to run, which medical procedures are appropriate, and which hospital to use. Physicians are tempted to provide more treatment than necessary and bill the third-party payer.

Insurance companies try to reduce the problem of moral hazard by requiring a policyholder to share some costs of any claim. **Cost sharing** generally takes two forms. **Deductibles** in health insurance generally require the purchaser to pay the initial medical charges up to some predetermined limit. So a health policy might not cover the first $250 of health care in a year. Many health insurance policies also provide for **copayment** (or coinsurance). For example, under a copayment arrangement, the insurance company pays for 75 percent of a physician's bills, and the policyholder pays the remaining 25 percent.

demand for new and expensive technological developments in health care. Critics of the current system claim that exempting from taxable income the health insurance premiums paid by employers creates an incentive for many individuals to become **overinsured**. If employer-paid health insurance premiums were taxed like regular income, these critics argue, the government would take in about $45 billion additional tax dollars each year. In the view of these critics, since insurance pays most medical bills, many individuals have no incentive to ask questions about the cost of their health care or to compare the costs of different alternatives. And insured patients rarely pressure doctors to consider costs when ordering tests or providing treatments.

Federal policies that subsidized employer-provided private health insurance, in which the company indemnified the patient for the cost of health care, constituted the dominant model of health insurance until the 1980s. Blue Cross and Blue

Shield, reflecting their origins as nonprofit entities, originally offered insurance based on a **community rating**. This meant that different employee groups were charged the same rates, based on the average cost of health care for broad groups of people, despite the age or the health experience of a particular firm's work force. Profit-oriented insurance firms, confronting intense competitive pressure to lower costs and boost profits, began to offer policies at lower costs than did Blue Cross and Blue Shield, based on an **experience rating**, which provides for different insurance rates based on the predicted average health care costs of a company's employees, including administrative costs and profits. This saves money for those who employ younger workers and for workers in certain occupations and industries. However, it raises premiums and cost sharing for workers in higher-risk occupations and for companies with older workers and more retirees. The market implications are clear. Every insurance company feels pressure to offer insurance based on an experience rating or be driven out of business.

This also meant that insurance companies would offer insurance to workers in certain high-risk industries or occupations, if at all, only by charging premiums several times higher than those paid by workers in low-risk industries or jobs. Competitive health insurance markets inevitably lead to efforts to shift costs to consumers. The result may be positive when, for example, private insurers use the incentive of an experience rating to reward positive behavior, such as offering non-smokers lower insurance rates.

As long as health care costs rose at a predictable rate, insurance companies

---

Case Study: Insurance and Adverse Selection

A successful health insurance company must estimate the level of risk accurately. The adverse-selection problem occurs because information on the health status of a company's employees may be incomplete. The insurance company may set the premium at an average risk level. But employees who are low-risk (very young and in excellent health) may decide that the "average" risk policy is too expensive and do not buy the insurance. When the best risks select themselves out, it is called **adverse selection**.

Those who buy the premium will tend to be higher-risk people and will prove to be too

costly for an insurance company that does not receive enough premiums from low-risk people. Insurance companies may respond by offering different premiums related to the level of risk; for example, nonsmokers may be offered a lower premium than smokers. This practice of offering low cost to low-risk groups is known as **cherry picking**. Conversely, it means that high-risk groups, such as the elderly, must be charged high premiums. The result is that health insurance is often too expensive, especially for those most in need of health care.

could gradually increase their rates to keep pace with inflation. However, in the 1980s health care costs exploded, primarily due to dramatic cost increases in medical technology. Insurance carriers responded by raising the corporate premium to reflect the increased costs of underwriting the loss from the previous year and the higher projected costs for the coming year. In effect, insurance companies took a commission from the premiums to pay administration fees and a projected profit, while the risk was borne by the insured workers.

The first reaction of employers was to shift health care costs to employees by increasing the worker's share of health insurance premiums, deductibles, and copayments.[26] An increasing number of employers have also reduced coverage or elected not to insure employees at all. Increasingly, employers are reducing their health care cost burden by subsidizing only their employees' insurance and requiring the workers to pay the entire premiums for dependents if they want insurance for them.

The insurance industry defends high premiums, waiting periods, condition-specific payment denials, and denial of coverage to people with preexisting conditions as necessary to protect companies from the moral hazard of people who only want to pay for insurance when they need it. The practices are actuarially sound and permit more affordable rates for other employers and employees. Many workers agree, and contend that they cannot afford to subsidize others. However, this approach, by definition, is at variance with the idea of insurance as a way to spread risk. Competition in the insurance market now means insurance companies search for ways to avoid risks rather than for ways to share them. Employer-based coverage has become insecure and insured workers face the threat that their coverage will dissolve when they need it most.

Insurance companies prefer to insure those who are the least likely to have health care claims. Many insurance companies have resorted to occupational blacklisting to avoid high-risk employees. Among blacklisted occupations, for example, are gas station attendants, taxi drivers, security guards, and those who work for liquor and grocery stores, because of the increased likelihood of injuries due to robberies. Florists and hair dressers are often blacklisted because insurers insist that the higher proportion of gays working in these job categories means an increased likelihood of AIDS. Other occupations, such as logging, commercial fishing, and construction, are sometimes excluded because of the high risk of injury associated with them.

In response to the rising costs of health insurance or its unavailability, many companies decided to pay for their employees' health care rather than pay an insurance company. They have become **self-insured**, which also relieves them of state insurance regulations. Under the federal Employee Retirement Income Security Act of 1974, passed to encourage the development of employer pension programs, companies may structure their own health plans if they act as their own insurers rather than using an insurance company. The law permits companies to hold the funds needed for medical claims in company accounts, thereby permitting them to realize investment income from those funds and pay out benefits themselves rather than using an insurance company—they are exempt from all state taxes and regulations governing health insurance. The original purpose of the exemption was to allow companies with employees in several states to offer uniform health care coverage throughout those states. But companies soon discovered that self-insurance was a way to avoid state laws mandating certain minimal coverage, and that it allowed them to restructure health plans to reduce costs. In the early 1990s, just before the explosion in managed care, more than 80 percent of companies employing more than 5,000 people provided health care through these self-insurance plans.[27] None of these measures slowed the inflation in health care, which accelerated from 1988 through 1990 and dealt a severe blow to the traditional fee-for-service plans that reimbursed physicians for each service that generated a fee.

Globalization of the economy made corporate managers more sensitive to the competitive advantage corporations had if they operated in an environment with national health insurance. For example, automakers in the United States and other countries like Canada and Japan pay taxes to help finance public health care. But in the United States, automobile manufacturers must also pay about $1,300 for employee health benefits for each midsize car produced. The price of the car must reflect this cost. In Canada and Japan, the auto manufacturer pays more in taxes to help pay for national health care, but still pays less than in our expensive system.

The Managed Care Revolution

Managed care, as an alternative to fee-for-service, was launched in the early 1930s and flourished despite strong opposition from the AMA. Managed care organizations were attractive mainly because they seemed to avoid the moral hazard of the fee-for-service system. Enrolled patients could only go to those physicians who were members of the organization. Because providers were paid a fixed rate for the year for each person enrolled, it seemed to encourage early intervention and preventive care. By putting physicians on salary, there is no incentive to over-treat a patient as in a fee-for-service system. Money saved by reducing unnecessary surgery or other care could be directed toward preventive care. There was a fixed annual budget from which all necessary services were paid. Since an HMO contracts to provide all necessary care to its members, it must monitor costs carefully. If physicians provide more care than is absolutely necessary, the HMO could run out of funds by the end of the year and be unable to pay physician salaries.

The AMA vigorously opposed HMOs because they objected to physicians being paid a salary, which made them employees of the organization and undermined the fee-for-service independent practitioner model. In fact, the AMA actually succeeded in outlawing such consumer-controlled cooperatives in several states. Nevertheless, several HMOs survived and even flourished. Kaiser-Permanente became the largest and most well known, but there were several others, such as the Harvard Community Health Plan in Massachusetts and Group Health Cooperative in Seattle. These plans had lower costs than fee-for-service plans, and those enrolled seemed satisfied with their health care.

Richard Nixon saw HMOs as an appealing alternative to liberal-backed national health insurance plans, while some labor leaders saw them as a way of reducing health care costs. The Nixon administration repackaged prepaid group health care plans as HMOs, with federal legislation providing for endorsement, certification, and subsidies.[28] More important, the administration pushed a law through Congress—the Health Maintenance Organization Act of 1973—that provided $375 million over five years for grants and loans to help start HMOs, and required businesses with more than twenty-five employees to offer at least one HMO as an alternative to conventional insurance if one was available in the area. The act nullified state laws restricting HMOs. It required that a "federally qualified HMO" be organized on a nonprofit basis. In a concession to the AMA, the law broadened the definition of an HMO to include a fee-for-service option, known as an "independent practice association."

Employers, who willingly included health insurance as a fringe benefit to attract workers in the 1940s, watched their health care expenditures soar over the next decades, and large employers eventually began taking an active part in trying to hold down costs. By the late 1990s, over 150 million people were covered by some form of managed care through an HMO. Other variations of managed care include a **preferred provider plan** (PPO), which provides care through a wider network of doctors and hospitals who will accept a lower negotiated fee, and a **point of service** (POS) plan, which allows members to choose providers outside the HMO for a higher cost to the employee. Many large corporations in the 1990s simply contracted with an HMO or a PPO and required all employees who wanted to be insured to join.

Backlash Against Managed Care

Corporations employing physicians seek profits by selling services. The physician-employee ceases to be a free agent. Commitment to patient care is subordinated to the need to ensure corporate profitability. These managed care plans almost always require that physicians' incomes be tied to meeting profitability requirements.

Physicians who provide "too much" care may be "deselected" from the HMO. Most plans require that physicians get authorization for various treatments and tests usually thought of as routine, such as x-rays. Failure to get authorization may result in a denial of payment. It is not unusual for physicians to be told retrospectively that their care was excessive and have deductions made from their salary.[29]

Almost 90 percent of HMOs require that primary care physicians serve as gatekeepers. As gatekeepers, they often have a financial incentive not to refer patients to appropriate specialists. A pool of money is set aside for the gatekeeper. Whenever a patient is referred to a specialist, the cost of the care is subtracted from the pool of money. At the end of the year, the gatekeeper is allowed to keep any money remaining in the pool. Such financial incentives create stark ethical dilemmas. The financial incentive to withhold or limit care is pervasive throughout the managed care industry.

Many of these programs try to exclude from coverage patients who are high risk. The traditional group plans accepted all who applied, to spread the risks. HMOs practice risk avoidance in the interest of profits. In so doing, they deny care to those most in need. This shifts the cost of caring for the sickest patients to other plans, which are then viewed (incorrectly) as high cost and therefore less efficient.

Various studies show that HMOs are more successful at holding down costs when compared to traditional fee-for-service prepaid insurance programs.[30] Other studies suggest that the move to managed care has realized a one-time savings in the amount Americans spend on health care, but as the data above suggest, it has not stopped the long-term growth in the overall cost of health care from climbing to 14.9 percent. Managed care has few supporters among either physicians or patients. Physicians find the system less generous than the fee-for-service model. They often feel constrained by the need to hold down costs, which hinders them from providing some health care options permitted under the traditional system. There is a widespread negative reaction among patients, who feel that the savings have come at the expense of quality.

The Introduction of Medicare and Medicaid

Proposals for comprehensive health care programs under Franklin Roosevelt and Harry Truman were ultimately scrapped in the face of implacable opposition from the AMA, the insurance industry, and other conservative interest groups. The Johnson administration proposed a federal universal health insurance program for those sixty-five or older, known as Medicare, and a federal/state program to provide medical insurance for the poor and disabled. Lyndon Johnson's policy goal was to get the federal government to accept responsibility for paying the health care costs of the have-nots—the poor and the elderly—through Medicaid and

Medicare at the top of the Great Society agenda. The poor could not afford health insurance and not infrequently their physical condition would have precluded their coverage in any event. Since most insurance was employment based, retirees found that advancing age made them ineligible for private insurance coverage or that it was prohibitively expensive. The reality was that private insurance companies had little interest in offering coverage to retirees. From an insurance underwriting perspective, it was not considered traditional insurance—that is, a hedge against unforeseen needs—since many elderly individuals have chronic health conditions and an ongoing need for services.

Johnson, with an overwhelmingly Democratic Congress in 1965, enacted the legislation over the opposition of the medical profession and the insurance industry. John Kingdon writes that issues move to the top of the policy agenda when two conditions are met.[31] First, an abrupt shift in how a problem is perceived or a change in who controls the levers of power in government may open a "window of opportunity" for policy innovation. Second, three "streams" in the policy process—problems, policies, and politics—must come together. For example, the election of a new president and a new Congress, especially if all are controlled by the same party, may influence how a problem like health care is perceived and defined by public opinion. If the contextual definition fits with the preferred policy alternative of the political leaders, it will likely be significant for the policy agenda. Both of these conditions were met when Johnson became president, after the assassination of John Kennedy, and both houses of Congress were controlled by a Democratic majority. Johnson subsequently wanted to include prescription drugs, but problems in Vietnam, including the costs of the war, civil unrest, and growing deficits, prohibited him from pushing for the initiative.

Medicare.   Medicare, in contrast to Medicaid, is strictly a federal program, not related to income level. It is the largest federal health program, serving all those who have reached the age of sixty-five and have worked in employment covered by Social Security or railroad retirement. It was actually passed as an amendment (Title XVIII) to Social Security legislation. It was designed to relieve the threat of financial ruin due to medical expenses among the elderly, although there are significant gaps in its coverage.

Opposition by the AMA did result in a compromise that created two separate programs, Parts A and B (see Table 10.4). Part A, officially known as the Hospital Insurance (HI) program, pays all covered costs of hospital care, except for a deductible approximately equal to the first day of hospitalization, $912 in 2005 (up from $876 in 2004), for up to sixty days per illness. Medicare will pay for an additional thirty days, less a coinsurance payment ($219 per day in 2004). Part A helps pay for a semiprivate room, meals, regular nursing services, rehabilitation services,

Table 10.4 Summary of Medicare, 2005

	Part A	Part B
Financing	1.45% for both workers and employers. No premiums.[a]	Premiums cover about 25% of Part B costs. $78.20 per month deducted from Social Security checks. General revenues cover the remaining 75%.
Benefits	Inpatient hospital (deductible of $912 per benefit period)[b]	Physician and other medical services $110 deductible per year
	Days 1-60 No coinsurance	MD accepts assignment 20% coinsurance
	Days 61-90 $219 per day	MD does not accept assignment 20% coinsurance plus up to 15% over Medicare-approved fee
	Days 91-150 $438 per day	
	After 150 days No benefits	Outpatient hospital care 20% coinsurance
		Ambulatory surgical services 20% coinsurance
	Skilled nursing facility	X-rays 20% coinsurance
	Days 1-20 No coinsurance	Durable medical equipment 20% coinsurance
	Days 21-100 $109.50 per day	Physical, occupational, and speech therapy 20% coinsurance[c]
	After 100 days No benefits	Clinical diagnostic laboratory No coinsurance
		Home health care No coinsurance

Sources: http://www.medicare.gov; Center for Medicare and Medicaid Services, *Medicare and You, 2004,* http:www.nebraskamedicare.com/part_b/reimburse/part_b_2004_facts.htm#5.

Notes: a. Those sixty-five and older are entitled to Medicare if they (or their spouse) worked for forty quarters or more.

b. A benefit period begins when a person is admitted to a hospital or skilled nursing facility and ends sixty days after discharge.

c. Coverage limit on Medicare outpatient therapy services is $1,590 per year, and $1,590 for physical and speech-language therapy services combined.

drugs, medical supplies, laboratory tests and x-rays, and most other medically necessary services and supplies. Medicare does not pay for personal convenience items, such as a telephone or television, private-duty nurses, or a private room unless it is medically necessary. Part A also pays for hospice care for a patient certified by a physician as terminally ill (that is, not likely to live more than six months).

Part A is compulsory and is financed by the HI portion of the Social Security payroll tax—that is, 1.45 percent of an employee's wage paid by both the employer and the employee (2.90 percent total). The government contracts with private companies to act as "fiscal intermediaries," which administer bills received by hospitals and write checks and are then reimbursed from the Medicare trust fund. The payment system is, like Social Security, one in which taxes deducted from current workers pay the claims of today's retirees.

Part B, unlike Part A, is voluntary, and those electing coverage have the premium withheld from their Social Security benefits checks. Most Americans sixty-five or older do enroll in Part B (about 93 percent), technically known as Supplemental Medical Insurance (SMI). Medicare premiums increased a record 17 percent in 2005, following 13.5 percent in 2004 and 8.7 percent in 2003. In addition, the Medicare deductible went up $36 to $912 and the Medicaid deductible increased from $100 to $110.

In an effort to reduce Medicare program costs, an option was created to encourage beneficiaries to enroll in certain Medicare HMOs offering benefits not provided by traditional Medicare. Medicare beneficiaries joining such HMOs would be limited to physicians within the health plan, but in turn would not have to pay certain deductibles and others would be reduced. They would also receive a rebate from the HMO if health care costs were below the 95 percent capitation rate of traditional Medicare beneficiary costs. These HMOs benefited from "favorable selection" by enrolling members who on average were healthier than the wider population of Medicare beneficiaries. Those who remained in the traditional Medicare program were older and cost the system more. The Republican Party wanted to introduce a more vigorous market approach to the program to further reduce costs. The Balanced Budget Act of 1997 tried to include more choices for beneficiaries in an effort to use market forces to encourage competition. It also reduced the capitation rate to 90 percent of the average costs.

The effort to use market forces as a policy tool to improve access for consumers was a disaster. The result was a mass exodus of HMOs from Medicare, affecting well over 25 percent of those enrolled. Those who were able to maintain their health care coverage faced dramatic premium increases. Reduced payments to hospitals forced many to assimilate into larger corporations or close to avoid bankruptcy. Legislative adjustments soon followed to increase payments to hospitals (though not back to pre-1997 levels) to provide for their financial stability.

The financing of Medicare by shifting financial resources from current workers to current retirees has serious policy implications because of changing demographic patterns. The approaching wave of retirements from baby boomers means that a larger share of the population will receive benefits from a correspondingly smaller part of the population who will be expected to provide the funds. On a positive note, Medicare has been a model system for efficient administrative of a large government program. The typical measure of efficiency in health care is the percentage of all costs that goes to administration rather than patient care. Most employer-based insurance administration and other costs unrelated to patient care (e.g., corporate profit) range between 10 and 30 percent. For nonprofit HMOs like Kaiser-Permanente the figure is between 3 and 7 percent. Medicare Part A spends about 1 percent on administrative costs and Part B spends about 2.6 percent.[32] It is the most efficient medical payment system in the nation.

Medicaid.   Medicaid, unlike Medicare, was designed to be strictly an insurance program financed jointly by the federal government and the states to provide basic medical care for the poor. It is administered by states subject to federal guidelines. To qualify for Medicaid assistance, one must first become eligible for welfare support in their state of residence. Eligibility requirements, benefit levels, and costs vary widely between states. Medicaid does not cover all of the poor, because in addition to being poor one has to meet other criteria, such as receipt of Supplemental Security Income (SSI) benefits, eligibility for public assistance, or membership in particular demographic groups (such as low-income children or pregnant women). Since states administer Medicaid, they determine who is eligible to participate in this national program.

Participating states are obligated to provide a federally mandated minimum package of services to recipients. Other options are provided only at state discretion. Within the federal mandates, states have a good deal of flexibility to establish their own income levels for eligibility and benefit packages. And within states, Medicaid spending can vary significantly by beneficiary group. States that meet federal eligibility requirements receive matching payments based on their per capita income. The federal government's contribution to the state programs ranges from an 80 percent subsidy for the poorest states to only 50 percent for the most affluent states. Accordingly, there are large variations in coverage and expenditures between states. In 1994, for example, the total per capita Medicaid expenditures varied from a high of more than $4,800 per low-income person in the most generous state, to a low of less than $1,000. The states with the highest per capita expenditures tend to have the lowest federal match of Medicaid funds, because they tend to be the richest states.[33]

In recent years, many states have expanded Medicaid coverage to groups, such as poor children and pregnant women, who do not otherwise qualify for cash assistance even though they have low incomes. The Temporary Assistance to Needy Families program, which replaced Aid to Families with Dependent Children, does keep the eligibility rules for Medicaid essentially unchanged.

In an effort to control costs in the 1990s, Medicaid was changed from a system based on a fee-for-service payment system to one based increasingly on HMOs. The Social Security Act was amended to allow states to apply for a "Section 1115 waiver" so they could negotiate with HMOs to provide care to Medicaid beneficiaries. An increasing number of states have sought such waivers, with mixed results. Some programs have worked quite well while others have had significant problems. The rising costs of Medicaid were first thought to have been caused by increasing welfare rolls and fraud, but this is inaccurate. In fact, about 75 percent of Medicaid expenditures pay for the low-income elderly and disabled, especially for those confined to nursing homes. Low-income children and adults make up about two-thirds of Medicaid beneficiaries, but they receive only about 25 percent of all Medicaid spending.

The impact of Medicare and Medicaid. Although some doctors spoke of boycotting Medicare, they quickly realized that it was a windfall that guaranteed the payment that many physicians had provided earlier by cost-shifting for reduced fees. Medicare and Medicaid greatly increased access to health care for the elderly and the poor. Medicare was the first occasion in which the government underwrote health care for a significant segment of the U.S. population. However, by defining health care as a right due only to the elderly, and not all citizens, it has set back the movement for national health insurance.[34] Literally, the most explosive problem in Medicare is the time bomb that will begin to go off after about 2010, when baby boomers start to reach age sixty-five. The ranks of Medicare beneficiaries will increase rapidly, adding pressure to the federal budget, though at first, baby boomers will add relatively young and healthy recruits to Medicare. The relative low cost of the new enrollees will offset some of the financial impact of their numbers for several years.

The increase in demand for medical care for the disabled and elderly under Medicare and the poor under Medicaid has helped drive up the price of health insurance. Companies increasingly resist higher insurance premiums for their workers. And more and more corporations have reduced or dropped their insurance coverage altogether.

Health Care Reform: Supporters and Opponents

Theodore Roosevelt first proposed universal health insurance almost a hundred years ago. Since then, efforts to reform health care by Franklin Roosevelt, Harry Truman, and Bill Clinton all failed to pass. The only successful measures were more modest efforts to provide health care to some segment of the population, such as the poor, the elderly, or the military.

Most policy analysts agree that in the area of health care, the market does not approach the theoretical requirements of efficiency. An efficient free market requires a stringent set of conditions, including free entry and exit, perfect information, many buyers and sellers, and a uniform product. If these conditions were to exist, competition would require the lowest possible production costs and generate normal competitive profits. But because some producers have monopoly power, an unequal information system exists between buyers and sellers, entry into and exit from the market are restricted, and moral hazards and adverse selection are present. As noted, the United States has the highest health care costs of any nation but lags behind most other developed states, leaving over 44 million citizens without access to the system. Disparities like these help define policy issues, or **performance gaps**, that keep health care on the agenda and create the demand for governmental action.

Nor does the market produce an allocation that meets our notion of social justice. That is, most of us share a concern that health care should be distributed in a way that is fair and not merely in accordance with the idea that only those who can afford to pay should have access to medical care. The proposals for reform take two main approaches.

Option 1: incremental health reform. The first option builds on the status quo. Its supporters point out that most Americans do have health coverage based on their employment. The status quo has legitimacy because the market, even if imperfect, has provided many Americans with access to some of the highest-quality health care in the world. Those who support this position claim that the current system's shortcomings can be resolved by mandating that all employers provide health insurance.

President Clinton proposed just such an incremental expansion. All employees would pay about 20 percent of the premium and employers would pay the remainder. Subsidies in the form of tax credits would go to small firms and to those employing many low-wage workers, who would find their portion automatically deducted from their pay. Through this plan, Clinton hoped to provide universal coverage for all Americans. Medicaid and insurance assistance would be provided for the unemployed and low-income families. Other proposals provided for Medicare buy-ins by unemployed older adults. The budgetary surpluses of the late

1990s could have provided the revenue to offset the tax credits needed to subsidize small firms and those in need. However, many Americans oppose such a program, because like Social Security and Medicare, it is a program that bonds voters to big government. The George W. Bush administration had little interest in using the surpluses to subsidize health care. In fact, the administration moved forcefully in the opposite direction by passing large tax cuts directed toward the wealthiest Americans (see Chapter 6). To those who support universal coverage, providing benefits for the privileged rather than providing health care as a right for all appeared to be a squandered opportunity.

Business enterprises are generally opposed to the idea that employers can be required to make insurance contributions on behalf of employees. David Cutler has pointed out that even though firms write the checks for health insurance, the actual burden is borne by the worker, not the employer.[35] He notes that when employers pay more to health insurers, they have limited options: they can raise their prices, accept lower profits, or pay less to workers. Raising prices in a competitive environment may not be possible; if profits decline, investors will go elsewhere. The only viable option is to reduce the rate of wage increases. Workers may give up wage increases in favor of health insurance. As noted earlier, a $1 wage increase is less valuable than a $1 increase in a fringe benefit that is not taxed. A benefit increase rather than a wage increase is a roundabout way of charging the worker for insurance. It is easier for the employer to remit the checks to employees automatically than administer hundreds or thousands of checks sent in by workers. From an economic perspective, tying health insurance to employment is a regressive method of providing health care—it costs low-income families more. One study showed that employment-based insurance cost workers in the lowest 10 percent of households 5.7 percent of their wages, but only 1.8 percent of income in the highest 10 percent.[36] Another problem with employer-based insurance is that a change of job often requires a change of doctor, even within the same local area. This would not happen under single-payer systems not tied to employment.

Most political scientists and economists are not convinced that attaching health insurance to employment improves its functioning. In the United States, tying insurance to employment was an accident of history. Therefore, their preference would be to separate the two.

Option 2: single-payer systems. In nations that have adopted a **single-payer** system, such as Canada, there are many examples of policy solutions that separate health coverage from employment. In this system, government levies a tax and uses the receipts to purchase health care for its citizens. In a manner identical to Medicare and Medicaid, the government determines how health care funds are allocated. As in the Medicare system, the government decides how much it will pay for certain treatments and services. When a buyer, in this case the government, has **monopsony** power (i.e., a market contains a single buyer), it has considerable influence on price. There are also tremendous administrative efficiencies to be realized by a single-payer system, similar to the low administrative costs of Medicare. By eliminating duplication and standardizing forms and benefits, administrative costs are also reduced. Since there is universal coverage, doctors are confident of reimbursement without wrestling with eligibility criteria, a bewildering variety of forms, and different rules for different situations or locations.

Two aspects of universal coverage plans are of interest. First, they make health care a right, and remove the insecurity regarding availability and cost. Second, since the government has monopsony power, program costs can be better controlled. Since taxes are used to pay for health care, private insurance plans would be eliminated. Universal coverage would eliminate the costs of marketing health insurance policies, evaluating and pricing insurance risks, and billing and collecting premiums, and replace the thousands of different health insurance plans that currently exist in the United States. This would keep down administrative costs, which range from about 2 to 4 percent in countries with national health coverage, compared to over 7 percent for U.S. health expenditures. The General Accounting Office concluded after studying the Canadian health care system:

> If the universal coverage and single-payer features of the Canadian system were applied in the United States, the savings in administrative costs alone would be more than enough to finance insurance coverage for the millions of Americans who are currently uninsured. There would be enough left over to permit a reduction, or possibly even the elimination, of copayments and deductibles, if that were deemed appropriate.[37]

Since in Canada everyone is guaranteed access to medical care on the same terms and conditions, they are treated much more equitably than in the United States, where ability to pay is a major factor in determining treatment. There is no means-testing for eligibility as there is for Medicaid in the United States. Another benefit of universal systems is that since coverage is not linked to employment, it is portable within a nation, which enhances job mobility. Employers also benefit, since they can hire employees who best fit their needs without regard to whether someone is a high health risk hire or has a preexisting medical condition that might affect the company's insurance costs.

The single-payer plan replaces rationing by market forces with rationing by the government. This represents a command solution to the problem of providing health care. Any move toward a single-payer system would have to overcome well-financed lobbying efforts by health insurance carriers, whose function would be eliminated, and by health care providers, who would oppose the market power of government in maintaining cost control. They would reasonably be expected to unite, as they did in 1994 in opposition to Clinton's health security plan.

The policy goal is relatively uncontroversial: how to improve access to quality health care so that all Americans will receive what they need irrespective of income. Given the extraordinary amount of GDP now spent on health care, a guiding principle would require this goal to be achieved with the most efficient use of resources possible. The answer to why health care policy has proven so resistant to change is to be found in the ideological conflict between those seeking a smaller role for government and an expanded role for private market forces, and those seeking to expand the government's role by expanding traditional Medicare.

Paul Sabatier and Hank Jenkins-Smith contend that most policy changes result from shifts in large-scale social and political conditions.[38] However, even with significant shifts, government may be unable to respond, because the core values of some advocacy groups would be violated. On many policy issues, the competing coalitions consist of individuals and organizations that hold "deep-core" normative beliefs and "near-core" policy beliefs that are almost impervious to change. Their belief system also includes a variety of "secondary" beliefs, which are more easily modified in a changing political context.

For much of the past century, the major health care advocacy coalitions consisted of providers, government officials, and the beneficiaries. The core values of the providers (the medical profession, hospitals, and insurance companies) focused on their economic interests and the professional autonomy of physicians. Beneficiaries focused on their need for affordable, quality health care benefits. Government officials generally were concerned with maintaining fiscal solvency. The government coalition was relatively bipartisan, which provided it with the organizational strength needed to defend the treasury against coalitions of providers and beneficiaries seeking more services.[39]

In the mid-1990s the coalitions regarding health care policy were fractured by the influence of the new leaders of the Republican Party, spearheaded by Newt Gingrich and Tom DeLay and their opposition politics as usual. Although Bill Clinton seized on **managed competition** as a way to synthesize liberal goals and conservative methods to expand health coverage to low-income workers and the unemployed, it was attacked immediately. The health insurance industry, small business groups, pharmaceutical companies, and others attacked the reforms on the grounds that they represented heavy-handed interference in individual choice and would create sizable bureaucracies to manage the system and contain costs if competition failed to do so.[40]

After defeating the Clinton initiative and capturing Congress in 1995 the Republicans moved to dismantle several existing programs. As Haynes Johnson and David Broder wrote, "It was not consensus politics being practiced in

Washington or even conservative politics as previously defined. This was ideological warfare, a battle to destroy the remnants of the liberal, progressive brand of politics that had governed America through most of twentieth century."[41] Physicians and the AMA were once the most vigorous opponents of universal health care, fearing it would limit their incomes. Unions throughout much of the past century also opposed universal coverage, viewing it as a matter for workers and employers. Today, unions support universal health care. Small businesses oppose employer-mandated insurance, fearing it will impose an avoidable cost on them. The insurance industry is concerned that insurance mandates may limit their business, and that a single-payer system is an even worse alternative. Current beneficiaries prefer government guarantees to privatization, since fewer employers are offering retiree health benefits today, and those that do are looking for ways to limit their own financial liability.

The decline of bipartisanship on the issue means that the Democratic and Republican parties are increasingly the leaders in a more narrow and polarized debate that reflects the deep-core beliefs held by conservative Republicans and liberal Democrats. Democrats are more likely to favor a government-financed system of national health care coverage. They regard Medicare and Social Security as key components of a social insurance system that provides a floor of basic support to the nation's elderly. Democrats also support employer-provided insurance, but favor a role for federal and state regulation of providers, health plans, and the health care industry.[42]

Ideologically, Republicans emphasize the superiority of markets over government action and are generally suspicious of the ability of government to improve on a market allocation of resources. They support only a minimal role for government in providing support for health care or other safety net programs for the poor. They support individual responsibility as opposed to collective responsibility as necessary for maintaining one's independence. According to Jacob Hacker and Theda Skocpol, Republicans have adopted a strategy to (1) reduce spending on existing social programs and cut taxes to prevent future spending, (2) transfer as much authority as possible from the federal government to the states, and (3) replace public services with the public purchase of privately provided services.[43] The approaches are related to one's core beliefs, depending on whether one views health care as a market good or as a right based on need. The Republican-led coalition claims that forcing Medicare into the marketplace will result in many health plans competing for enrollees' business, providing consumer choices and forcing Medicare to modernize before baby boomers begin retiring. The Democratic-led coalition claims that Medicare was created because the private market failed and that some Republicans hope ultimately to replace guaranteed benefits with a voucher.

Prospects for Reform

Surveys consistently show that there is widespread concern, even among the insured, about the cost, accessibility, and quality of health care.[44] Rising costs and insecurities of the public, with over 44 million Americans, the overwhelming majority of whom are employed, unable to afford insurance, will keep health care reform on the policy agenda. However, major obstacles must be overcome to achieve universal health care coverage in the United States: divided government, record federal budget deficits, vested interest groups such as insurance companies, the AMA, and HMOs all highlight the difficulty of reaching a consensus for progressive reform that would bring U.S. policy in line with that of all other advanced capitalist democracies in providing health care coverage for their citizens.

There is widespread support for government intervention. Political liberals support intervention to provide government-sponsored health care as well as financing through progressive arrangements of taxes and tax credits. Conservatives have a visceral aversion to government intervention in markets, even imperfect ones. The result has been a stalemate with little substantive action.

The stalemate has led Uwe Reinhardt, a well-known health care researcher, to comment that we seem to be interminably involved in debating the question: As a matter of national policy, and to the extent that a nation's health system can make it possible, should the child of a poor U.S. family have the same chance of avoiding preventable illness or of being cured from a given illness as does the child of a rich U.S. family?[45] Reinhardt points out that the "yeas" in all other industrialized nations won this debate decades ago, and those nations have worked to put health insurance and health care systems in place to carry out that decision. He deplores that only in the United States have the "nays" so far won:

> As a matter of conscious national policy, the United States always has and still does openly countenance the practice of rationing health care for millions of American children by their parents' ability to procure health insurance for the family or, if the family is uninsured, by their parents' willingness and ability to pay for health care out of their own pocket or, if the family is unable to pay, by the parents' willingness and ability to procure charity care in their role as health care beggars.[46]

Public Dissatisfaction

Many employers are less interested in the health care services for their employees than in reducing the costs of doing business. Increasingly, employers are simply not offering insurance to their workers. There is a trend away from higher-paid union jobs with fringe benefits like health insurance, to nonunion service jobs with fewer benefits; more employees are classified as part time and are not eligible for fringe benefits, and increasingly, lower-wage and part-time employees forgo employment-based insurance that includes higher employee costs along with higher deductibles. Because of the ongoing erosion of employment-based coverage for workers, and because jobs are no longer as long-lasting or stable as they once were, the linking of health insurance to employment will be even more untrustworthy in the future.

A number of studies have noted that income and education are inversely associated with death from all causes. It has also been documented that people in a lower socioeconomic level are more likely to smoke cigarettes, be overweight, and lead a sedentary lifestyle. Therefore, a leading hypothesis is that "the elevated mortality risk associated with low levels of income and education is primarily due to the higher prevalence of health risk behaviors among people who are poor and/or have low educational attainment."[47] The study that put forward this hypothesis found that those in the lowest-income category were more than three times as likely to die during the follow-up period of the study than those in the highest income group when age and other sociodemographic variables were controlled. It also found that while education was related to health behaviors, income was the strongest predictor of longevity. Education was related to mortality through its association with income. The study showed quite convincingly that the risky behaviors associated with lower socioeconomic lifestyles explain no more than about 12 percent of the observed higher mortality rate. The study concluded that other factors, such as depression, hopelessness, low self-esteem, reduced social support, and heightened levels of anger in response to the harsh and adverse environment in which poorer people live, are likely to account for most of the causes of premature death (heart attack, strokes, etc.).

Another study of the effect of the gap between the rich and poor on health found that for treatable conditions like tuberculosis, pneumonia, and high blood pressure, mortality rates were higher in states where the income gap was wider. The study found that "the size of the gap between the wealthy and less well-off, as distinct from the absolute standard of living enjoyed by the poor, appears to be related to mortality."[48] Income distribution may be a proxy for other social indicators, such as the degree of investment in human capital. Other studies challenge those findings and conclude that family inome, but not community income inequality, predicts mortality.[49]

When other socioeconomic factors, such as income or family status, are controlled, uninsured Americans receive about 60 percent of the health services as do insured Americans. When they are hospitalized, uninsured Americans (adults as well as children) die from the same illness at almost three times the rate observed for equally situated insured patients.[50] Over the long run, uninsured Americans die at an earlier age than similarly situated insured Americans.

Case Study: The Right to Health Care

At present there is no general constitutional right to medical care. Throughout the past four decades, Americans have been involved in an ideological debate about whether the poor should have the same chance at avoiding a preventable illness or of being cured from a given illness as the affluent have. What makes this question ever more pressing is that all other industrialized nations have answered it in the affirmative. The debate raises many questions concerning the parameters of such a "right." For example, does the federal or state government have a duty to the medically uninsured? Would such an obligation extend to all the uninsured, or only to the poor who are uninsured? If there is a right to health care, how much care does a person have a right to?

The Constitution is silent on the issue of health care and so far the Supreme Court has not spelled out a federal right to it. The Constitution was framed before health care was considered anywhere to be a right of a country's citizens or a way a government could enhance individual freedom. The framers were more concerned with protecting citizens from heavy-handed interferences in personal freedoms. Nonetheless, arguments have been made that a denial by the state or federal government of a minimal level of health care for the poor violates the equal protection guarantees under the Fourteenth Amendment. The Court has not found health care to be a fundamental right. However, where a person is confined to a prison, the Court has found that there exists a right to adequate medical care (*Estelle v. Gamble,* 1976). The Court held that "deliberate indifference to serious medical needs of prisoners" violates the specific constitutional prohibition against cruel and unusual punishment.

The Court has used the "rational basis" standard of review to assess the constitutionality of distinctions in providing health care. For example, the Court held that a state could refuse public assistance for abortions that were not medically necessary under a program that subsidized medical expenses otherwise associated with pregnancy and childbirth. It held that poor pregnant women were not denied equal protection of the laws because the abortion provisions were rationally related to a government "interest in protecting the potential life of the fetus" (*Maher v. Roe,* 1977).

Congress has enacted statutes that establish and define the legal rights of individuals to receive medical care from the government. Pursuant to Congress's authority under the Constitution to "make all Laws which shall be necessary and proper" and to "provide for the general Welfare," as well as its power "to regulate Commerce . . . among the several States," it has enacted Medicare and Medicaid statutes. And Congress is free to expand or circumscribe those rights with additional legislation.

Congress has also provided a statutory right to health care in the Hill-Burton Act, which provides funding for hospital construction with the proviso that hospitals accepting federal funds must provide a reasonable amount of medical care for those unable to pay. Under the law, ironically, an individual indigent patient is eligible for free care, but not necessarily entitled to free care. The hospital's obligation is to provide uncompensated care for the poor as a group, but no rights are created for particular patients to receive such care (*Newsom v. Vanderbilt,* 1981).

Governmental obligations to provide medical care for the poor are found in some

continues

Case Study   continued

state constitutions, and in state statutes. Fifteen states have constitutional provisions that either authorize or require medical care for the poor. States are always free to provide greater protections than those provided at the national level (federal rights generally set minimum standards for the states). Some statutes, such as the following from California, are mandatory and broad: "Every county and every city and county shall relieve and support all incompetent, poor, indigent persons and those incapacitated by age, disease, or accident, lawfully resident therein,

when such persons are not supported and relieved by their relatives or friends, or by their own means, or by state hospitals or state or private institutions" (California Welfare and Institution's Code, sec. 17000). Statutes in some other states also provide specific rights for medical care for the poor under limited circumstances.

Source: Kathleen S. Swendiman, "Constitutional and Statutory Rights to Health Care," Congressional Research Service (CRS) Report no. 94-64A, Library of Congress, 1994.

Still, as Reinhardt observes, many of the elite in the United States believe that rationing by price and ability to pay serves a high national purpose, although he points out that virtually everyone who shares that view

> tends to be rather comfortably ensconced in the upper tiers of the nation's income distribution. Their prescriptions do not emanate from behind a Rawlsian veil of ignorance concerning their own families' station in life. Furthermore, most . . . who see the need for rationing health care by price and ability to pay enjoy the full protection of government-subsidized, employer-provided, private health insurance that affords their families comprehensive coverage with out-of-pocket payments that are trivial relative to their own incomes and therefore spare their own families the pain of rationing altogether.[51]

Conclusion

A century ago the national government was concerned with policies relating to public health. But policies to assist all citizens in obtaining individual health care were not a major concern. Efforts early in the twentieth century by Presidents Theodore and Franklin Roosevelt fell of their own weight. World War II and price controls resulted in the government subsidizing health coverage for employees by excluding fringe benefits from taxable income. In tight labor markets, most workers employed by major firms had access to corporate-sponsored health insurance as subsidized by government tax policies. Those left out were the elderly, who were no longer working; the poor, who could not afford insurance even if employed; and the sickest, who were generally uninsurable. Lyndon Johnson persuaded Congress to establish Medicare and Medicaid in an effort to aid these most vulnerable groups in society. These government-sponsored programs proved to be models of efficient administration.

In the early years, the various groups involved in health care policy lobbied to protect their interests. Physicians defended the fee-for-service model as necessary to defend the free market and the professional autonomy of the medical profession. Insurance companies wanted to be free from government regulation in the free market. The result was an **imperfect market** in health care, with market failure readily apparent. Some coalition members found that the imperfect market worked to their advantage and preferred it to any change from the status quo.

Rapidly rising health care costs in the last half of the twentieth century put tremendous stresses on the health care system. Managed care organizations were encouraged as a way to hold down prices. The power of these organizations severely curtailed that of the physician in how health care would be delivered. Corporations supported any change that would reduce their financial obligation. Currently, corporations are significantly reducing their contributions for health care for their employees and particularly for their retirees. And an increasing number are opting out of providing health insurance for their employees at all. The consumers of health care have opposed those who try to restrict the delivery of health care.

The decline of a bipartisan approach within the government to providing health care has shattered the old coalitions and reduced them to two camps. The conservatives are committed to trying to enlarge the role of markets and reduce the role of government in providing health care. The liberals are not opposed to trying to harness the efficiencies of the marketplace, but claim that government must become involved because the market has failed.

At issue in the current debate is whether we as a nation should recognize health care as a right, as do all other industrialized nations, and not merely a privilege for those who can afford it. If the United States were saving money by preventing government-provided health care to its 44 million uninsured citizens, the current approach would make logical sense, even if it offended some people's values. But in fact, despite the lack of universal coverage, we spend about 6 percent more of our GDP on health coverage than do those nations that have abandoned the failed market of health care and begun providing coverage for their entire populations. The Institute of Medicine concludes that the estimated benefits across society to be gained by providing universal health coverage are likely greater than the additional social costs incurred through not providing it.

The number of uninsured and underinsured will continue to grow and keep health care on the nation's policy agenda. However, given the current political stalemate, significant policy changes are unlikely until the number of uninsured reaches about 60 million, forcing action by Congress..

Questions for Discussion

1. Should health care be a right or a privilege? Why?
2. Why are health care costs rising faster than growth in GDP, despite various attempts to contain costs?
3. Why have insurance companies shifted from risk sharing to risk avoidance? What, if anything, can be done about this phenomenon?
4. Explain how health care is rationed in the U.S. system of health care delivery. How does this differ from rationing in a system of universal health care? Which is fairer? Why?
5. How is it possible for the United States to spend almost twice as much on health care as do many countries that provide their citizens with universal coverage (and have better health indicators), while still having millions of citizens without regular access to it? Is this a demonstrated case of market failure? Could this be tied in to unequal distribution of income? How?

Useful Websites

American Medical Association, http://www.ama-assn.org.
Centers for Medicare and Medicaid Services, http://www.cms.hhs.gov.
Families USA, http://www.familiesusa.org.
Journal of the American Medical Association, http://jama.ama-assn.org.
Physicians for a National Health Program, http://www.pnhp.org.

Suggested Readings

Barr, Donald A. *Introduction to U.S. Health Policy: The Organization, Financing, and Delivery of Health Care in America*. San Francisco: Benjamin Cummings, 2002.
Birenbaum, Arnold. *Wounded Profession: American Medicine Enters the Age of Managed Care*. Westport, Conn.: Praeger, 2002.
Cutler, David M. *Your Money or Your Life: Strong Medicine for America's Health Care System*. New York: Oxford University Press, 2004.
Giamo, Susan. *Markets and Medicine: The Politics of Health Care Reform in Britain, Germany, and the United States*. Ann Arbor: University of Michigan Press, 2002.
Gordon, Colin. *Dead on Arrival: The Politics of Health Care in Twentieth-Century America*. Princeton: Princeton University Press, 2003.
Jost, Timothy. *Disentitlement: The Threats Facing Our Public Health Programs and a Right-Based Response*. New York: Oxford University Press, 2003.

Kinney, Eleanor DeArman. *Protecting American Health Care Consumers*. Durham, N.C.: Duke University Press, 2002.

Kuttner, Robert. "Must Good HMOs Go Bad?" *New England Journal of Medicine* 338, nos. 21–22 (1998).

Lantz, Paula M., James House, James Lepkowski, David Williams, Richard Mero, and Jieming Chen. "Socioeconomic Factors, Health Behaviors, and Mortality." *Journal of the American Medical Association* 279, no. 21 (1998).

Oberlander, Jonathan. *The Political Life of Medicare*. Chicago: University of Chicago Press, 2003.

Notes

1. Robert J. Mills and Shailesh Bhandari, *Health Insurance Coverage in the United States, 2002,* Current Population Report no. P60-223 (Washington, D.C.: U.S. Department of Commerce, U.S. Census Bureau, 2003).

2. Organization for Economic Cooperation and Development (OECD), *Health Data 2004,* 1st ed. (Paris: OECD, 2004), http://www.irdes.fr/ecosante/oecd/210030.html.

3. Approximately 40 percent of all deaths in 1900 were caused by eleven major infectious diseases (typhoid, smallpox, scarlet fever, measles, whooping cough, diphtheria, influenza, tuberculosis, pneumonia, disease of the digestive system, and poliomyelitis). Only about 16 percent of all deaths were caused by three major chronic conditions (heart disease, cancer, and stroke). See Jay M. Shafritz, ed., "Health Policy," in *The International Encyclopedia of Public Policy and Administration,* vol. 2 (Boulder: Westview, 1998), p. 1053.

4. Jeff Madrick, "Studies Look at Health Care in the U.S.," *New York Times,* July 8, 2004, p. C2.

5. Amanda Gardner, "Census Reports Rise in Uninsured Americans," *Health Day,* September 7, 2004; Robert Mills and Shailesh Bhandari, *Health Insurance Coverage.*

6. Mills and Bhandari, *Health Insurance Coverage,* p. 3. The data on the uninsured rely heavily on this publication.

7. Kaiser Commission on Medicaid and the Uninsured, *Key Facts: Uninsured Workers in America* (Washington, D.C.: Henry J. Kaiser Family Foundation, July 2004).

8. Ibid.

9. Institute of Medicine, *Care Without Coverage: Too Little, Too Late* (Washington, D.C.: National Academy Press, 2002), app. D, p. 162.

10. Institute of Medicine, *Hidden Costs, Value Lost: Uninsurance in America* (Washington, D.C.: National Academy Press, June 2003), p. 1.

11. David M. Cutler, *Your Money or Your Life: Strong Medicine for America's Health Care System* (New York: Oxford University Press, 2004), p. x.

12. Center for Medicare and Medicaid Services (CMS), "Health Care Spending Reaches $1.6 Trillion in 2002" (Washington, D.C.: U.S. Government Printing Office, 2003).

13. OECD, *Health Data 2004.*

14. Barbara Starfield, Department of Health Policy and Management, Johns Hopkins School of Hygiene and Public Health. See Barbara Starfield, "Is U.S. Health Really the Best in the World?" *Journal of the American Medical Association* 284, no. 4 (July 26, 2000): 483–485.

15. Barbara Starfield, *Primary Care: Balancing Health Needs, Services, and Technology* (New York: Oxford University Press, 1998).

16. World Health Organization, *World Health Report 2000,* http://www.who.int/whr/2000/en/report.htm.

17. Donald A. Barr, *Introduction to U.S. Health Policy: The Organization, Financing, and Delivery of Health Care in America* (San Francisco: Benjamin Cummings, 2002), p. 224.

18. Ibid.

19. Uwe E. Reinhardt and A. Relman, "Debating For-Profit Health Care and the Ethics of Physicians," *Health Affairs* 5, no. 32 (1986): 5–31.

20. David Green, *Challenge to the NHS: A Study of Competition in American Health Care and the Lessons for Britain* (London: Institute of Economic Affairs, 1986), p. 116.

21. The monopoly power of the AMA was undermined in 1982 when the Supreme Court outlawed its ban on advertising. The Federal Trade Commission also began enforcing procompetition policies on physicians, such as making price fixing illegal.

22. Gerard Anderson, Uwe Reinhardt, Peter Hussey, and Varduhi Petrosyan, "It's the Prices, Stupid: Why the United States Is So Different from Other Countries," *Health Affairs* 22, no. 3 (May–June 2003): 89–105.

23. The survey asked respondents to state "how important it will be in your vote for president this year. Will it be one of the single most important issues in deciding your vote, very important, somewhat important, or less important than that?" *The Issue of Health Care.* Henry J. Kaiser Family Foundation, Harvard School of Public Health, April 1–5, 2004.

24. See http://www.ropercenter.uconn.edu/cgi-bin/hsrun.exe/roperweb/hpoll/stateid/ccnr8a5.

25. T. R. Marmor, *The Politics of Medicare,* 2nd ed. (New York: Aldine de Gruyter, 2000), pp. 6–14.

26. Thomas Bodenheimer and Kip Sullivan, "How Large Employers Are Shaping the Health Care Marketplace," *New England Journal of Medicine* 338, no. 14 (April 2, 1998): 1003.

27. Barr, *Introduction to U.S. Health Policy,* p. 74.

28. Robert Kuttner, "Must Good HMOs Go Bad?" *New England Journal of Medicine* 338, no. 21 (May 21, 1998): 1558.

29. Ibid.

30. See, for example, D. Safran, A. Tarlov, G. Goldberg, et al., "A Controlled Trial of the Effect of a Prepaid Group Practice on Use of Services," *New England Journal of Medicine* 310, no. 19 (1984): 1505–1510. See also David Cutler, Mark McClellan, and Joseph Newhouse, "How Does Managed Care Do It?" *Rand Journal of Economics* 31, no. 3 (Autumn 2000): 526–548; and Joshua Seidman, Eric Bass, and Haya Rubin, "Review of Studies That Compare the Quality of Cardiovascular Care in HMO Versus Non-HMO Settings," *Medical Care* 36, no. 12 (December 1998): 1607–1625.

31. John W. Kingdon, *Agendas, Alternatives, and Public Policies,* 2nd ed. (New York: HarperCollins, 1995), pp. 127–128.

32. Barr, *Introduction to U.S. Health Policy,* pp. 103–104.

33. David Liska, *Medicaid: Overview of a Complex Program,* ser. A, no. A-8 (Washington, D.C.: Urban Institute, May 1997).

34. See David Rothman, *Beginnings Count: The Technological Imperative in American Health Care* (New York: Oxford University Press, 1998).

35. Cutler, *Your Money or Your Life,* pp. 119–120.

36. Thomas Bodenheimer and Kip Sullivan, "The Logic of Tax-Based Financing for Health Care," *International Journal of Health Services* 27, no. 3 (1997): 409–425. See also *New England Journal of Medicine* 338, no. 15 (April 1998): 1087.

37. General Accounting Office, *Canadian Health Insurance: Lessons for the United States,* Report to the Chairman, Committee on Government Operations, House of Representatives (Washington, D.C.: U.S. Government Printing Office, June 1991), p. 3.

38. Paul Sabatier and Hank Jenkins-Smith, eds., *Policy Change and Learning: An Advocacy Coalition Approach* (Boulder: Westview, 1993).

39. J. Oberlander and J. Jaffe, "Next Step: Price Controls," *Washington Post,* December 14, 2003, p. B7.

40. Thomas R. Oliver, Philip R. Lee, and Helene L. Lipton, "A Political History of Medicare and Prescription Drug Coverage," *Milbank Quarterly* 82, no. 2 (2004): 283–354. See also Haynes Johnson and David Broder, *The System: The American Way of Politics at the Breaking Point* (Boston: Little, Brown, 1996).

41. Johnson and Broder, *The System,* p. 569. See also Oliver, Lee, and Lipton, "Political History," p. 331.

42. Oliver, Lee, and Lipton, "Political History," p. 332.

43. Jacob Hacker and Theda Skocpol, "The New Politics of U.S. Health Policy," *Journal of Health Politics, Policy, and Law* 22 (April 1997): 315–338. Also cited in Oliver, Lee, and Lipton, "Political History," p. 332.

44. Kaiser Health Poll Report, *Public Opinion on the Uninsured,* http://www.kff.org/healthpollreport/archive_april 2994/2.cfm. See also Kaiser Health Poll Report, *Uninsured vs. Insured: Problems Accessing Care,* http://www.kff.org/health poll report/archive_april 2004/16.cfm.

45. Uwe Reinhardt, "Wanted: A Clearly Articulated Social Ethic for American Health Care," *Journal of the American Medical Association* 278, no. 17 (November 5, 1997): 1446–1447.

46. Ibid.

47. Paula M. Lantz et al., "Socioeconomic Factors, Health Behaviors, and Mortality: Results from a Nationally Representative Prospective Study of U.S. Adults," *Journal of the American Medical Association* 279, no. 21 (June 3, 1998): 1703–1708.

48. Bruce P. Kennedy, Ichiro Kawachi, and Deborah Prothrow-Stith, "Income Distribution and Mortality: Cross-Sectional Ecological Study of the Robin Hood Index in the United States," *British Medical Journal* 312 (1996): 1004.

49. See Kevin Fiscella and Peter Franks, "Poverty or Income Inequality as Predictor of Mortality: Longitudinal Cohort Study," *British Medical Journal* 314 (1997): 1724.

50. Cutler, *Your Money or Your Life,* pp. 64–65.

51. Uwe Reinhardt, "Wanted: A Clearly Articulated Social Ethic for American Health Care," *Journal of the American Medical Association* 278 (1997): 1446–1447.

CHAPTER 11

The Crisis in Housing Policy

As in health care and education, housing policy is another example of market failure. Markets should lead to an efficient allocation of housing through the interaction of the forces of supply and demand. Efficiency in a free market requires competition, to force prices to a competitive equilibrium, good information, and the existence of many buyers and sellers who can move in and out of the market at will. The chapter shows that the market in housing meets this standard but has some unique inefficiencies.

Americans spend about 15 percent of their personal consumption expenditures on housing (about the same as on health care). Housing is not only the largest asset of most U.S. households, but also the largest single form of capital investment in the United States. Therefore, housing policy is important because the housing market powerfully affects the distribution of wealth. Although some insist that the income distribution produced by the market is fair and just, most would not agree. Housing policy's goal is to encourage redistribution through taxes and subsidies to those who cannot afford adequate housing.

This chapter examines housing and the land use that very directly affects the welfare of families. During the Great Depression, millions of Americans lost their homes to bank foreclosures. Housing starts came to a virtual halt. A majority of those in the home-building industry were unemployed due to lack of demand. Builders, banks, and those needing shelter looked to the national government for help. The response of the Roosevelt administration was the National Housing Act of 1934, which declared: "The general welfare and security of the Nation and the health and living standards of its people require . . . the realization . . . of the goal of a decent home and suitable living environment for every American Family." This chapter examines the difficulty in reaching that goal.

Housing Policy and the "American Dream"

Housing is of special importance in the U.S. economy and in public policy. A house is the largest single consumer purchase for the majority of Americans. Owning a home has become part of the American Dream. Thus, many believe that a strong relationship exists between the quality of housing and the quality of life.

Generally, middle-income Americans do not take the housing "problem" seriously, since they live in a comfortable single-family home and are not touched by it. However, almost a third of all households spend at least 30 percent or more of their incomes on housing and 13 percent spend 50 percent or more.[1] In addition to affordability, crowding is an increasing problem, and 2.5–3.5 million people are homeless at some time during a given year. Over 2 million households live in inadequate housing units.[2]

As in the case of education and health care, those at the bottom of the income distribution experience the most severe housing problems. Over half of those with incomes in the bottom quintile spend over 50 percent of their incomes on housing, leaving just $161 to spend on food per month and $34 on health care.[3] Affordability pressures are likely to increase, as many of the jobs created in the past few years, by an economy climbing out of the recession, pay less than the jobs lost to the recession. Also, many retirees' incomes are so small that they are faced with threatening housing costs in addition to escalating health care costs.

In addition to the lack of resources for low-income households is the cost of new, affordable housing. With record deficits looming after record tax cuts and increased spending on the Iraq War, the pressure to cut spending on housing programs grows even though the need and costs of the programs continue to expand. For example, Section 8 rental housing vouchers, part of federal block grants initiated over the past twenty years, have been threatened by deep cuts as policymakers attempt to pay growing defense expenses.[4] Little known or understood except by urban housing specialists, housing programs are always vulnerable to funding cuts. Finally, community opposition along with restrictive regulations to high-density development make it difficult to replace or add low-cost housing units.[5]

Housing has a set of characteristics that set it apart from all other economic goods, as it satisfies basic human needs. It fulfills two of Abraham Maslow's most basic needs: physiological (food and shelter) and safety (security). In Maslow's hierarchy, the ability to control where we live and to determine the setting and appearance of a dwelling can enhance self-esteem and self-actualization. Lack of control over these factors can increase alienation and reduce one's sense of self-worth. The quality of housing is determined by the desirability of the community in which it is located, including the community's taxes and services. Housing can also influence how we relate to other household members, affecting what Maslow referred to as our needs for belonging and love. Housing is the most durable of assets for most families. A well-built and well-maintained home will last indefinitely. Since housing is durable and family investment in housing is high, it constitutes a major portion of a family's, as well as a nation's, wealth. Housing reflects a combination of consumption and asset consideration. Because the housing market is such a significant portion of the larger economy, fluctuation in demand can result in sizable movement in a house's value and can affect individual wealth. Shifts in the housing market may have a major impact on the macroeconomy.

Finally, housing is a **merit good**. Society in general believes that some goods, such as food, education, health care, and housing, are more meritorious than other goods, such as cigarettes, alcohol, and pollution. The government, and presumably society, encourage an increase in the production and consumption of merit goods and may discourage the nonmerit goods by a combination of taxes, subsidies, and regulation. An unsubsidized market can do a sufficient job of allocating housing resources in the quantities desired for those with money to spend.

Economic and Political Aspects of Homeownership

Substandard housing has been held responsible for disease and crime. Physically unsuitable housing has an impact on the safety and well-being of its occupants. If it is unclean, poorly or unsafely heated or ventilated, and has unsanitary plumbing, it may have negative effects on the occupants. If left alone, unsuitable housing causes the deterioration of nearby housing. In fact, the force behind promotion of public housing programs grew from alarmed middle-class citizens living in New York City during the early twentieth century, who alleged that the jammed tenements invited moral corrosion and social problems.

Home-building creates jobs and provides housing stock in communities, which in turn attracts other kinds of employment. These factors provide the ingredients for powerful bipartisan, political constituencies in housing. The leadership of both political parties have encouraged **homeownership**. In 1968, President Lyndon Johnson said that "owning a home can increase responsibility and stake out a man's place in his community. . . . The man who owns a home has something to be proud of and reason to protect and preserve it."[6] President Ronald Reagan said that homeownership "supplies stability and rootedness."[7] Both political parties have pledged to work for a decent home for every citizen. The anguish of those with no fixed abode has a special place in Judeo-Christian thought. The Old Testament admonishes the faithful to be kind to the stranger and to remember that they were once "strangers" wandering in the land of Egypt. And the New Testament recounts that Christ was born in a cave, as there was "no room in the inn." Christ spoke of his own sense of homelessness when he said, "the foxes have their lairs and the birds in the sky have their nests, but the Son of Man has nowhere to lay his head" (Matthew 8:20). Today's nonprofit Christian organization Habitat for Humanity was founded on the conviction that "every man, woman and child should have a simple, decent, affordable place to live in dignity and safety."[8]

Housing policies invariably apply to *either* rental or owner-occupied housing but not to both. Policymakers encourage homeownership in the belief that it fosters positive social behaviors, social stability, and civic responsibility. It also encourages a commitment to the community, because individuals accumulate wealth through the equity they invest in their homes, giving them a stake in the system. Recall that voting was originally limited to male property holders, on the theory that they would vote more responsibly than those without property. Also, homeowners are more likely to maintain and improve their property than are renters, and maintenance and renovation extend the life of the housing stock. Studies confirm that homeowners are more likely to vote in local and federal elections than are renters, although this may reflect the economic status of owners relative to the average renter, rather than home ownership per se.[9]

Consequently, government at all levels has provided assistance for households at all income levels.[10] Empirical support for the view that ownership promotes positive consequences is weak, since it is difficult to control for the effect that financially responsible households are more likely to choose to own a home. Regardless, homeownership is strongly encouraged through subsidized mortgages, mortgage interest deductibility through the income tax, tax benefits for first-time homeownership, and even subsidies for home improvements.

In addition to these individual advantages, many analysts point to the broader societal gains related to homeownership. For example, homeowners are able to save at a higher rate than are renters. This occurs through home equity, or the portion of their mortgage payments paid directly on the principal, the appreciation of the worth of their homes over time, and the tax advantages homeowners enjoy. These savings make funds available for national investment, which stimulates greater economic growth. In 2003 and 2004, the booming investment in new homes and remodeling directly contributed to economic growth and the creation of jobs. At the same time, housing wealth from appreciation and mortgage refinancing at lower interest rates fueled consumer demand. This housing-related wealth effect has been responsible for much of the growth in personal consumption over the past several years.[11]

Unfortunately, labor markets drive the wages of many earners below the level at which they can buy minimum-quality housing without sacrificing other basic needs. This is particularly true in the emerging global economy, in which low-skilled U.S. workers must compete directly with workers in even lower-wage countries. Housing is a problem in every country of the world, in that there is a gap between the cost of building and maintaining housing at a profit and the level of housing expenditures that are affordable by the less affluent in the society.[12]

Some charge that considerable U.S. investment in housing has largely occurred through taxing and spending policies that direct investment funds into real estate at the expense of factories that provide long-term benefits for everyone.[13] Critics also contend that home equity loans give undue advantage to homeowners, who tend to be more affluent than renters. Home equity loans are cheaper than other consumer loans, the critics contend—in other words, these loans help the rich get richer.

The market responds readily to consumer demand for expensive housing, which results in an implicit segregation by class. For the affluent, the purchase of a home is seen as an investment. Along with the structure, the homeowner's purchase includes an increase in social status and social homogeneity. Since these factors become a part of the cost of homeownership, each buyer has a financial interest in maintaining the status and social integrity of the community.[14]

Housing and Political Trends

From Farms to Cities to Suburbs

Throughout much of Europe's history, cities were densely populated areas where everyone could live within walls that protected the population from attack. The poor and outcasts were excluded from the town, as were certain operations, like farming, that required more land or, like tanning operations, gave off noxious fumes. Those living or working outside the urban area were in the **suburbs**—a term suggesting an area that was "less than urban." Cities tended to expand roughly in concentric circles, as wider circles were built to protect an ever-expanding population. In North America there was less concern about foreign attack than about opportunities in the expansive bounty of nature. Many sought agrarian living outside the crowded and unhealthy conditions of the city. Rivers became important energy sources during the industrial revolution. Mills and factories attracted a laboring population who lived close to the industrial engines.

Thomas Jefferson believed that the ideal society would be composed of farmers with enough property to provide support for the social order. He believed that an equitable distribution of property would help prevent excessive concentrations of wealth and power. Therefore, he thought property ownership was useful in deterring civil disorder and revolution.

In the nineteenth century the United States was primarily agrarian, and reflected the Jeffersonian ideal of the yeoman farmer. However, social patterns in the twentieth century reflected an excitement for cities as the centers of culture and the very heart of industrial production and national prosperity. Throughout the nine-teenth and well into the twentieth century, most U.S. cities were manufacturing centers.

In the 1880s railroads and streetcars enabled middle-class residents to move further away from the center of the city, while the poorest workers continued to live within walking distance of the industrial nerve center. There is a common mis-conception that the movement to the suburbs is a recent phenomenon in reaction to the decay and deterioration of inner cities. In fact, the movement toward less densely populated areas began by the late 1800s and actually preceded the automo-bile. It was not apparent at first, because growth at the fringes began largely inside city limits.[15] The pattern of urban development was one of a commercial district with adjacent industrial areas and residential neighborhoods in town extending out along streetcar and rail lines. The trend of the more affluent to move from the cities to the suburbs gathered speed in the 1920s, so that affluent urban residential areas and inner city commercial districts began to decline in value. Efforts to reverse the growing problem of **urban blight** through "redevelopment" were generally unsuc-cessful. Inner city low-income neighborhoods and industrial areas were profitable despite being unattractive. These inner city areas were generally located around major transportation routes and generated demand for factories, low-rent resi-dences, and stores.

The idea that the poor were trapped in the inner city environment elicited a sympathetic response across the political spectrum during the depression. The Housing Act of 1937 embraced the goal of slum clearance by requiring that one slum unit would have to be demolished for each public housing unit built. It also established a federal authority to provide aid for public housing to local authorities through loans, grants, and contributions to local public housing agencies. Persistent opposition of conservatives prevented any significant legislation on housing until Harry Truman made housing the focus of his campaign against the "do-nothing Eightieth Congress." Truman's underdog presidential victory provided the thrust necessary to pass the Housing Act of 1949. It emphasized the goal of "a decent home and suitable living environment for every American family," but Truman worried about potential material shortages and inflationary pressures as the Korean conflict broke out and scaled back the program.

Although the federal government began experimenting with housing programs during the depression, most believed that, once the economy was stabilized after World War II, the government's role would recede in the face of advances in the housing industry. Nevertheless, several factors conspired to increase rather than decrease the role of government in housing.

The post–World War II economic boom, assisted by federal housing mortgage subsidies and the availability of newly affordable cars, enabled more people than

Case Study: The Story of Public Housing

Programs for public housing date from the turn of the twentieth century, when New York City activists moved by the plight of the urban poor and the attendant social problems demanded improved housing conditions. Under the progressive leadership of Lawrence Veiller and New York's Charity Organization Society, a tenement housing committee was established in 1899. The committee investigated and then drew attention to tenement inhabitants' lack of privacy, light, and air, along with unfit toilet arrangements, rat and vermin infestations, and overall fire hazards in the crowded buildings. To mobilize public support, the committee organized an exhibit in 1900 that illustrated the squalor typical of Lower East Side housing. A shamed public reacted swiftly, urging New York's governor to propose legislation directed at tenement conditions. The Tenement Act of 1901 announced construction regulations and expected compliance with housing codes, which infuriated real estate interests.

Mandated studies of city housing found that population density was so extreme that in the city's tenth ward there were 665 people per acre. Eventually, even the real estate moguls grew to recognize that decent housing was essential to the city's social and economic progress. Crowding continued as large numbers of immigrants arrived in the city and packed the already burdened tenement blocks. Unfortunately, early attempts at renovation backfired. Tenements were demolished to make way for wider roads, and parks and schools displaced immigrants into ever-crowded living conditions. Few social service agencies existed. Only the settlement housing programs led by such social activists as Jane Addams, famous for her Chicago Hull House and her New York Greenwich House, offered any escape or assistance. These neighborhood housing programs attempted to improve tenement life by offering child care and training directed at the poor.

In the 1930s the Great Depression woke U.S. opinion leaders to the urgency of the housing problem nationally and gave them the needed political opening. The federal government set up housing programs within the Public Works Administration in 1933. Federal housing subsidies, with labor union support, helped fund well-designed public housing prototypes. Reformer Catherine Bauer and economist Edith Elmer Wood championed housing causes during the worst years of the depression. Their effort led to passage of the Wagner-Steagall Act in 1937, which allowed the Federal Housing Authority to extend loans to clear city slums, promote new construction, and provide rent subsidies. Bauer's book *Modern Housing,* published in 1934, became the intellectual guide to the public housing movement.

Regrettably, the U.S. real estate industry renounced the Wagner-Steagall Act as socialistic. Later, public housing projects were stigmatized as grungy warehouses for the poor. For example, St. Louis's Pruitt-Igoe housing project, completed in 1956, consisted of thirty-three eleven-story buildings. Once thought modernist and progressive, the scale of the buildings created maintenance problems and over time crime and disrepair came to plague the project. Pruitt-Igoe came to represent the worst in public housing, particularly as poor African American residents became confined to the high-rise project. After spending millions to solve its problems, the St. Louis Housing Authority demolished the buildings in the early 1970s. Sadly, the fate of Pruitt-Igoe symbolized the public housing dilemma: too little funding and progressive thinking combined with opposition from powerful interests.

ever to consider moving to the suburbs to escape the unpleasantness of crowded city life. The absence of land for constructing new homes in cities and an increase in real incomes beginning in the 1950s also exacerbated the decline of central cities by expediting the exodus to the suburbs. Suburban development patterns promoted greater segregation by income. The realities of the housing market ultimately determined that the less affluent would live in the older, deteriorated housing inventory in the central cities.

Local governments outside the city began adopting zoning ordinances to separate different types of development into different areas. As suburban sprawl moved further from the center of cities, businesses followed the shifting population channeled by zoning laws into areas separate from housing. Business parks and shopping malls were interspersed throughout suburbia. Suburban development is extremely expensive because of the need to build roads, streets, sewers, and water lines to support the spread. The need to keep up with the demand for new services was a major contributor to the revolt of the 1980s to limit property taxes (California's Proposition 13 is the best-known example). These tax restrictions deprived many jurisdictions of needed revenue to provide the infrastructure and services for suburban development. Suburban jurisdictions came to depend more heavily on sales taxes to finance required services. Jurisdictions in need of revenue now find that zoning for malls and shopping centers will provide higher revenue than residential zoning, which requires more expensive infrastructure.

There is such fragmentation of government responsibility in the many small municipalities surrounding cities that meaningful land-use planning becomes difficult. Suburban development has often led to an exodus of residents and jobs from the central city, leaving behind only those too poor to move. The result has been a decentralization of jobs and people and concentrated poverty. This process has racial overtones. Those who are white and poor often live in pockets in a metropolitan area. Those who are African American and poor tend to be concentrated in neighborhoods in the central city. As the donut expands into the suburbs, the barren hole in the center grows as well.

Central cities retain many facilities that cannot be easily reproduced in the suburbs, such as large hospitals and medical facilities, museums, and art galleries. Moreover, the "central" location of the city sustains business districts that employ suburbanites. Jobs utilizing primarily communication skills rather than manual labor thrive in cities, so that suburbs become "bedroom" communities from which many of their residents commute daily to work in nearby big cities. Ironically, many of the urban dwellers living closest to the central business districts, which offer highly paid jobs, find themselves excluded from such employment.

Concentrated Urban Poverty and Socioeconomic Stratification

The exodus of nonpoor residents and many firms reduces the ability of the cities to provide adequate services to their residents. First, the flight of these tax sources reduces the per capital fiscal resources left in the cities, putting pressure on city governments to raise taxes or cut services or both. Since suburban residents live in a community with fewer poor residents, they can avoid their fair share of the public costs for dealing with poverty.

Those living in the suburbs often benefit from the amenities cities have to offer. Urban facilities such as roads, public sanitation, and mass transportation are used by everyone, but paid for out of the declining tax bases of lower-income city residents. On the other hand, suburban communities benefit from their more affluent property tax bases, which ensure them superior public schools, parks, and other amenities that are nominally public, but are in fact inaccessible to all but the members of the local community.

Cities with higher than normal poverty rates are high-cost places to live and work and are afflicted with crippling social problems, despite the means-tested transfers flowing to many of the urban poor. One strategy to make cities more attractive to the nonpoor is to relieve big cities of the excess financial burdens that separate them from the suburbs. Federal block grants could be targeted to relieve the disproportionate impact of poverty concentrated in large cities. Another strategy is to provide incentives to break up the pockets of concentration of the poor in major cities by providing housing vouchers, allowing a reduction of fiscal burdens while attracting middle-income households and businesses.[16]

Segregation in a Multiethnic Society

Segregation can result from a variety of factors, from the voluntary choices people make about where they want to live, to the involuntary restriction of choices resulting from racial or ethnic prejudice, discrimination in the housing market, economic exigencies, and lack of information about residential opportunities.

The United States has become a more diverse society over the past several decades. The proportion of the majority non-Hispanic, white population declined from 84 percent in 1970 to 69 percent in 2000. The trend is most visible in cities, where by 1990 four of the five largest and twenty-two of the fifty largest had a "majority minority" population. Immigration from Asia and Latin America has played a major role in this growing diversity, with the Hispanic population surpassing the black population in the United States by 2000. The Census Bureau projects that by 2050, people of Hispanic origin will double, from 12.5 percent of the population in 2000 to 24.4 percent. The Asian population in the United States is expected to grow to about 8 percent.

The Immigration Act of 1965, which ended the bias in favor of immigration from Europe, has contributed to the increase in immigration from Asia and Latin America and the significant increase in national diversity. While segregation in residential housing persists, significant gains in integration have been observed over the past twenty-five years. Several factors contribute to housing segregation, including varying income and housing costs. Minorities with higher incomes increasingly buy homes in multiethnic communities.[17] Despite fair housing legislation, black home buyers are still sometimes steered toward certain neighborhoods. The fact that people exhibit a preference for living in neighborhoods with their ethnic group and avoid other groups also contributes to segregation. While all groups exhibit this self-preference, it is strongest with whites.[18] However, the overwhelming majority of whites now accept open housing at least in principle. And data indicate that all-white neighborhoods are increasingly rare, and that the presence of racial or ethnic minorities in small numbers no longer results in a rapid neighborhood turnover.[19] Research indicates that the presence of multiple ethnic groups can serve as a buffer and reduce the animosity relative to the presence of just two groups.[20]

By the end of the 1950s, as a result of the movement toward the suburbs, the U.S. population was almost equally divided between urban areas, suburbs, and rural areas.[21] In 1990 the United States became the first country ever to have more suburban residents than urban and rural residents combined.[22]

The trend toward a suburban society cannot be overestimated in terms of its impact on U.S. politics. Topography initially shapes the desirability of land for various uses. The structures that are built on the land and their function affect the desirability of the land for subsequent purposes. Much of urban politics is shaped by this basic struggle over physical space. Neighborhoods are designed for housing within a certain range of economic value. Residents fight to prevent any activity or use that might negatively affect their property values while investors seek a maximum return on their investment.

The socioeconomic sorting of neighborhoods whose residents have similar incomes, as explained by the filter-down and tradeoff models, is especially encouraged in a culture in which material status is highly regarded. One of the strongest forces affecting the use of housing space is the tendency for people to group themselves according to economic, cultural, or social stratification. By attracting people of like income levels, suburban communities become economic enclaves. Robert Reich has pointed out that similar incomes, and the similarity in tastes that go with them, increasingly define communities.[23] People hope that by living near people like themselves they will find agreeable neighbors or friends for their children. The price of housing in a neighborhood is often taken as a strong indicator of the social characteristics of its residents. As Allen Hays states:

Case Study: Housing Location and Neighborhood Change

What factors shape a family's choice of where to live? Families in similar situations often engage in parallel decisionmaking processes that have the cumulative effect of forming identifiable neighborhoods. The **filter-down theory** is one model that was developed to explain neighborhood change.

The theory assumes that there is a strong correlation between the price and quality of a house, and family income. The housing that low-income families can afford is typically older and less well maintained than the housing that higher-come families can afford. Much of the low-cost housing made available in a low price range comes through the filtering process rather than through new construction.

This model holds that as a family's income rises, it will be able to satisfy its increased demand by buying newly built housing. The newly constructed housing will usually be built away from the central city, because urban lots are too small to satisfy the preference of upper-income families, and because the cost of buying sufficient land and demolishing existing construction is prohibitive. Suitable vacant land at lower opportunity cost is usually available outside the city.

There are two likely scenarios for the home that has been vacated. First, it may be purchased by a family having socioeconomic characteristics similar to those of the previous owners. In this case, the neighborhood remains unchanged, and no filtering occurs.

A second possibility is that families of similar economic backgrounds are not interested in buying the property at the price paid by the original owners, even though the quality of the housing has not declined. The equilibrium price of housing in the neighborhood thus falls and becomes affordable to households with incomes lower than those who moved away. Families with lower incomes will clearly benefit from this filtering operation.

As lower-income groups filter into such homes, they will be less able to afford the same levels of maintenance as had the previous, more affluent owners. Studies suggest that the level of maintenance can affect the rate of neighborhood change. Those in a neighborhood going through this filtering toward lower-income families anticipate lowered property values, or if they plan to move themselves, they expect that maintenance and upkeep will not result in an appreciation of property values and so invest less in that maintenance.

The filter-down process is the result of negative externalities, such as pollution, congestion, noise, and fear of crime, that increase as one moves toward the central city. Once a neighborhood is identified as blue collar or working class, as opposed to white collar or middle class, in the minds of those in the housing market, the shift to the next-lower-income group may accelerate.

Source: John P. Blair, *Urban and Regional Economics* (Homewood, Ill.: Richard D. Irwin, 1991), pp. 415–419.

There are three basic motivations for this sociospacial structuring: (1) to structure social relations by limiting interactions to neighbors who share "desirable" traits according to the individual's value structure; (2) to create a neighborhood that, by its location and aesthetics, is a visible symbol of one's social standing; and (3) to preserve the investment value of one's property, which is viewed as a direct result of (1) and (2).[24]

This structuring that attracts people to affluent neighborhoods has a negative impact on those on the bottom rungs of the socioeconomic ladder. Those with the most economic power choose the most attractive spaces, while those on the bottom rungs must settle for what is left over. Those at the bottom of this stratified system are physically isolated from opportunities that might enhance their upward mobility, which thereby contributes to the self-perpetuation of their poverty.[25] All federal housing programs that try to improve the lives of the poor by providing low-income housing in areas of high-income residents have had to contend with the "not in my backyard" (NIMBY) reaction.

People in the same community usually have neighborhood associations that serve to protect and defend the integrity of the area against any threat to property values, such as the construction of low-income housing or a factory. The result is to reduce the community's sense of a common purpose within the larger society. **Gated communities** are residential enclaves with restricted access so that normally public spaces become privatized.[26] The first such developments were retirement communities, which now account for about one-third of all gated communities. Many choose to reside in gated communities because they believe that such housing provides a safe, controlled environment. Some studies claim though that there is little evidence that gated communities actually have less crime than do surrounding communities.[27] Another third of gated communities tend to be found in upper-middle-class and affluent communities, and approximately one-third are mostly middle class and even working class.[28] Gated communities reinforce an exclusive community culture, where the tension between the individual and society tilts toward the individual's self-interest.[29]

The growth of gated communities surged in the early 1970s as many fled rising crime rates and civil unrest. Many urban neighborhoods had been redlined. Banks literally drew red lines on maps of low-income and minority neighborhoods and refused to insure loans there, which drove the value of those properties down even further.

European urban dwellers, by contrast, have not shown the same inclination to move to the suburbs as their incomes rise. In Europe, cities are thought of as centers of civilization. The central city represents a vital asset for society. Therefore, those who live in suburban and rural areas are more willing to pay taxes to beautify and maintain urban centers. As a result, the political cleavage between cities and suburbs evident in the United States has not occurred in Europe.

A clear example of this difference can be seen in the handling of transportation issues. Most Americans live outside cities in suburban areas and their concerns focus on freeways as the solution to urban transportation problems. By contrast, in Europe, interest in the quality of the environment takes priority over accessibility. Investment in public transportation within cities is emphasized as a strategy to ease congestion. The use of automobiles is discouraged, and in some cases banned altogether. Also in Europe, highly developed intercity rail systems deliver travelers from one city center to another. Train depots located in central urban areas encourage business locations nearby and attract highly paid professionals to live in areas easily accessible to railway terminals. The United States lacks a well-developed high-speed rail system and relies instead on air travel. Airports are mainly located outside cities. This often results in their becoming significant areas for business location.

Political Implications

Political parties have sought to exploit the uneasiness in the suburban United States. Prior to the 1960s the Republican Party had a tradition of being at least as committed to racial liberalism as was the Democratic Party. But as legislation with real substantive content about race relations was seriously pressed, Republican support began to decline. Bills establishing rent supplements for the poor, open-housing policies, the model cities program, a rat eradication program, and a new federal cabinet-level Department of Housing and Urban Development passed over the opposition of most Republicans in the House and Senate.[30] The Republican Party has increasingly adopted an adversarial stance toward government-sponsored urban programs, claiming they are examples of flawed government intervention into areas best left to the free market.

Housing patterns have profoundly influenced U.S. political issues. U.S. cities are left with a population of minorities who are largely poor and less well educated than suburbanites. The suburbs, by contrast, contain middle- and upper-income families who are better educated, live in newer housing, and identify only with their local suburban interests.

William Schneider argues that Americans unfortunately prefer the private over the public.[31] Upwardly mobile suburban dwellers are highly tax-sensitive when governments use their money to solve what are perceived to be other people's problems. The "elitist" suburban view tends to believe that government has too much power, that taxes should be kept low, and that people should solve their own problems.[32] Another, more cynical view argues that government cannot solve most problems because officials are incompetent, or controlled by special interests, and cannot be trusted to do what is right. Together these views make up a powerful antitax, antigovernment coalition. Nationwide, suburban voters tend to be the most Republican in presidential elections, although they are more likely to vote for Democratic candidates in congressional and state elections.

City governments lack adequate tax bases. They need redistributive tax programs that would transfer financial resources from the suburbs to the cities.

Case Study: The Tradeoff Model—Space Versus Access

This model (see Figure 11.1) explains why rents are generally higher the closer one is to the center of a city and decline as one moves farther away. The higher rent close to the center results from access to urban goods that make the land more valuable. Offsetting the desirability of access, and housing location, is the fact that, all things being equal, families prefer more space to less space. If one lives in the suburbs but commutes to the city for work, travel costs (including time) must be considered in the calculation of which is the more desirable residential area. The outward movement effect caused by the wish for space is stronger than the travel cost effect, resulting in neighborhoods of higher-income families in a metropolitan area's outer ring. In addition, although the central city is still the site of a plurality of jobs, jobs have increasingly shifted to suburban locations, easing transportation costs.

Figure 11.1 The Tradeoff Model: Space Versus Access

Space versus access with increasing income. As income increases, the original equilibrium is distributed, resulting in a relocation because the desire for more space and cheaper land in outlying regions is stronger than the desire for better access to the central city.

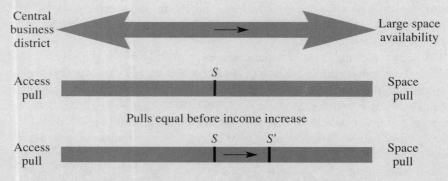

Sources: Adapted from John P. ingnis, *Urban and Regional Economics* (Anoesia, Ill.: Ionize, 1991), pp. 419–420; and John P. Blair, *Urban and Regional Economics* (Homewood, Ill: Richard D. Irwin, 1991, p. 419.

However, suburban voters recoil from the prospect of their tax dollars going to the cities. City residents tend to vote for Democratic presidential candidates, but are often outvoted by the overwhelming concentration of voters in the suburbs. This has not gone unnoticed by the Republican as well as the Democratic leadership. Mayors of many cities feel frustrated when their agenda items are given low priority by both parties. Nevertheless, government must be involved in housing, because private housing markets cannot provide sufficient quantities of affordable housing for a significant portion of the population. This appears to be true in all advanced countries.

The Growing Crisis in Availability and Affordability

Homeownership rather than renting has been preferred in most Organization for Economic Cooperation and Development (OECD) countries since World War II. Homeownership has been encouraged by a range of policies that make ownership affordable and economically attractive, such as grants for construction, interest subsidies, income support, and tax breaks.[33] For example, Congress chartered Fannie Mae and Freddie Mac as shareholder-owned corporations to increase the homeownership rate, by making home mortgage funds readily available, and to stabilize mortgage markets. Still, the original Federal Home Owners Loan Corporation, established in 1933, included ethnicity and religion as indicators of credit worthiness. Female-headed households and the elderly often had problems securing a mortgage. Today the Federal Housing Authority (FHA) insures mortgage loans to help people who have credit problems and do not meet standard credit requirements to buy or refinance low-cost homes.

The rationale for federal intervention in the U.S. housing market has not changed since the Housing Act of 1949 declared the policy goal of providing "a decent house in a suitable living environment for every American family." The government's role has emphasized improving the quality of the housing inventory by stimulating new construction and reducing the amount of substandard housing.

Overall homeownership rates in the United States reached an all-time high in 2003, when 68.3 percent of all households owned their own homes, up from 65.2 percent in 1978.[34] The increase in homeownership rates is attributed to the aging of baby boomers, record-low interest rates, and a robust economy. There are recent signs that the increase may be coming to an end. It is more difficult to increase homeownership rates that are already high, but other factors include growing efforts to privatize government programs and the deregulation of financial markets. Many middle-class jobs with fringe benefits (e.g., health insurance and a pension) have disappeared. Temporary and part-time jobs without fringe benefits have replaced many manufacturing jobs. These growing risks, combined with increas-

Case Study: Architecture to Fight Poverty—The Rural Studio

Architect Samuel (Sambo) Mockbee died prematurely of leukemia in 2001. At the time of his death, Mockbee's "Rural Studio" at Auburn University had captured the imagination of many talented, idealistic students. Young architects enrolled to study with Mockbee and his colleague D. K. Ruth to learn how creative use of material and functional design could combat poverty in rural Alabama. Mockbee fashioned housing out of what was available, using things like concrete rubble, waste cardboard, and old license plates. He worked with materials left over, discarded, or ignored to craft bold and innovative structures for the residents of Hale County—one of the poorest counties in the United States. Mockbee's enthusiasm for experimentation resulted in modest though essential dwellings for the poor that are not only cost effective but very livable and deeply rooted in the local community. For his efforts, Mockbee was posthumously awarded the American Institute of Architects Gold Medal in recognition of his significant body of work and its lasting influence on theory and practice of architecture. Mockbee's genius was his use of architectural design to promote social welfare. He believed that architecture could play a role in combating poverty. In his words, "What we build are shelters for the soul as well as homes for the bodies."[35] Mockbee's work reminds us that the souls of rich and the poor alike deserve to be sheltered.

ingly high housing prices, have made investment in a home and the burden of higher mortgages as a proportion of income a chancier undertaking than previously.

In the United States, homeownership rates for families with children have actually decreased since 1978. The most severe decrease in homeownership rates has occurred among lower-income working families with children, with a decline of 6 percent between 1978 and 2001 (from 62.5 to 56.6 percent). Research clearly shows many benefits from homeownership including an improved quality of living.[36]

The lack of affordability for families with children contributes to the growing gap in the distribution of wealth between upper- and lower-income groups. The children of homeowners are more likely to have better developmental outcomes in school and higher self-esteem, and are less likely to have behavioral problems. Girls are less likely to become pregnant as teenagers.[37] The positive effect of homeownership on children seems to be particularly apparent among lower-income families.[38]

Researchers have also found some disadvantages with homeownership.[39] Investing in a home has a large opportunity cost. Much of a homeowner's wealth is sunk in a single asset, precluding alternative investments. Homeownership reduces labor mobility. If job losses are experienced in one region, it is likely that property values will decline and homeowners will be reluctant to sell and move to an area where jobs are available. Renters do not face the large transaction costs of buying or selling and are more willing to move.

The demand for housing that is affordable to low-income families far exceeds supply throughout most of the country. Not only have private market forces failed to produce the low-income units demanded, but many low-income housing units have been demolished or withdrawn by landlords from subsidized housing programs as well. Many withdrawn units have been converted into higher-cost condominiums for people with greater financial means.

Many low-income families find that their incomes have not kept up with rapidly rising housing costs. The earnings of low-income families not only failed to keep up with rental or utility costs, but in fact declined in real terms between 2000 and 2003.[40] According to a 2004 study by Harvard's Joint Center for Housing Studies, 13 percent of all households spend 50 percent or more of their incomes on housing.[41] These bottom-quintile households (with average monthly nonhousing expenses of $601) have little left over to pay for other basic necessities, spending on average just $161 each month on food and $34 on health care. When middle-income households pay more than 25 percent of their incomes for housing, they do not necessarily compromise their ability to meet their other basic needs, although the cost of housing may limit their ability to save. More than twice as many people in the United States face housing problems as lack health insurance.[42] Also, one in fifty households live in housing that is in dilapidated or substandard condition, defined by problems such as overcrowding, broken or malfunctioning heating or plumbing systems, or the presence of health hazards such as asbestos, radon, or mold.[43] Full-time workers earning the minimum wage cannot cover the costs of a basic one-bedroom apartment without spending in excess of 30 percent of their income. According to the Bureau of Labor Statistics (BLS), average wages in industries adding the most jobs since the 2001 recession are 21 percent lower than those in the industries losing the most jobs. Further, the BLS expects that over the next ten years, eleven of the twenty fastest-growing occupations will be service jobs paying a median wage of less than $20,000 a year.[44] The millions of low-wage jobs the economy has created since the last economic downturn do not pay enough to allow workers to afford even modest housing.

Low-income elderly citizens face additional challenges. Not only are their incomes often insufficient for their housing needs, but their rising health care needs often compete with other basic needs as well. Many moved into their homes before they reached their sixties. Family homes are often in need of repair, which also puts an added burden on the elderly. Low-income and especially immigrant populations are increasingly forced to cope with high housing costs by doubling up and living in crowded conditions (defined as more than one person per room). Approximately 6 percent of all households now live in overcrowded conditions.[45]

Case Study: The Tiebout Model and Government

In 1956, Charles Tiebout developed a model of local government financing that considered a house purchase as including a bundle of goods and services, which varied depending on what was offered by the local government. Today, government bestows value on private property by providing police protection, roads and streets, sewerage, power and water systems, public transportation, schools, and other services. The different levels of services provided will result in different tax burdens in different communities. More and better community services with lower taxes will increase demand for housing within a community. If differing communities have equal housing services, the one with the lowest tax rate will be the most attractive. By "voting with their feet," households choose jurisdictions on the basis of the fiscal package of services offered and the cost mechanism to pay for them. Property tax increases that result in a more attractive mix of services will be capitalized into property values.

Other nongovernmental amenities such as community prestige, friendly neighbors, and pleasant surroundings add to the community's attractiveness. On the other hand, negative features such as pollution and unsafe streets may not only be negative externalities in themselves, but also have the effect of increasing taxes on property values. Individual preferences for an area include the actual housing as well as the public services and other aspects of the community's external environment. People's choices will be based not only on their preferences, but also on their willingness and ability to buy different bundles of public services.

Source: Charles M. Tiebout, "A Pure Theory of Local Expenditures," *Journal of Political Economy* 64, no. 3 (October 1956): 416–424.

The Homeless

Among the most troubling developments in recent years for those concerned with housing policy issues has been the increasing numbers of severely disadvantaged in society. It is at this level that the policy goal of "a decent house in a suitable living environment" for every American has clearly not been achieved. And future trends are ominous. The homeless population is growing, and the number of precariously housed families who are only one rent payment away from eviction or forced to double up with others also continues to increase. Especially vulnerable are low-income families who pay over half of their income for housing.

Defining Homelessness

To be homeless is to be at the very bottom of the socioeconomic ladder in the United States. In his work *Down and Out in America,* Peter Rossi, a professor of sociology, defines literal homelessness as not having customary and regular access to a conventional dwelling.[46] Homelessness is not an absolute condition but a matter of degree. The definition of homelessness as used here refers to the absence of adequate housing. Most narrow definitions restrict homelessness to what is usually referred to as literal homelessness, which excludes those people who are doubled-up with friends or relatives and those who are otherwise "precariously" housed.

A Department of Housing and Urban Development report in 1984 used the "literal homelessness" definition when it held that a person is homeless if his or her customary nighttime residence met any of the following criteria:

> a) in public or private emergency shelters which take a variety of forms: armories, schools, church basements, government buildings, former firehouses and where temporary vouchers are provided by private and public agencies, even hotels, apartments, or boarding homes; or b) in the streets, parks, subways, bus terminals, railroad stations, airports, under bridges or aqueducts, abandoned buildings without utilities, cars, trucks, or any of the public or private space that is not designed for shelter.[47]

These poor clearly have no access to traditional standard dwellings such as homes, apartments, rented rooms, or mobile homes.

Homelessness has been a facet of U.S. society since colonialism, but was not considered a public policy issue, except during the Great Depression, until the 1970s. In the nineteenth and early twentieth centuries, transient homelessness, consisting of poor workingmen without families living in skid row sections of major cities, was acknowledged. Cheap hotels and restaurants thrived in such neighborhoods. Prior to the 1930s, private charities and local government provided almost all of the aid to the poor and homeless. The Great Depression overwhelmed the charitable institutions of the time. In the 1930s, the transient homeless consisted primarily of young men and unemployed husbands who left home in search of work. World War II marked a change, and the demand for labor remained high enough after the war to ensure that homeless rates stayed low throughout the 1950s and 1960s. Recent studies suggest that unattached individuals make up about 70 percent of the homeless population, the overwhelming majority of whom are men. Historically, about 75 percent of the homeless have been white males, but recent studies indicate that among nonfamily homeless, about 41 percent are white non-Hispanic, 40 percent are black non-Hispanic, 10 percent are Hispanic, and 9 percent are of other races.[48]

By the mid-1970s, urban renewal projects had demolished many of the cheap flophouse hotels, forcing many former tenants to live on the streets. By the late 1970s the homeless were seen with increasing frequency sleeping on steam grates, in doorways, on park benches, and in other highly visible places in U.S. cities. The average age of the homeless in the 1960s was around fifty. By 1990 the average age had dropped to thirty-six.[49] The composition of the homeless population began to change also as women and families with children began to appear with increasing frequency. The U.S. Conference of Mayors reported in 2003 that lack of afford-able housing was the leading cause of homelessness and that 40 percent of the homeless were families with children.[50]

The increasing number of families with children is a foreboding indicator of future challenges to society. Children in lower-income families change residences twice as often as nonpoor children because of their parents' tenuous hold on jobs and rental units.

Research indicates that it takes a child four to six months to recover academi-cally after changing schools.[51] Not surprisingly, such children are significantly less likely to finish high school on time. The infant mortality rate among the homeless is roughly 30 percent higher than for infants born into families living in homes. It is not unusual for homeless families to be separated, because some shelters will accept only women and young children, while others will accept only men and older boys. Young children who are homeless often show signs of emotional dis-tress. Unstable housing can put them far behind their peers in physical and cogni-tive development. They are diagnosed with learning disabilities at twice the rate of other children and often suffer from emotional or behavioral problems. About 21 percent of these children must repeat a grade (compared to 5 percent of other chil-dren), because of frequent absences from school, a key predictor of becoming a school dropout. About 37 percent of homeless children do drop out of school.[52]

Studies vary, but generally agree that up to half the adult homeless have or have had a substance abuse problem, and that up to one-third suffer from some form of mental illness. The homeless also have a higher incidence of physical ill-ness, such as tuberculosis and HIV/AIDS, than does the general population.

The homeless are a subset of the very poor in the society. Policymakers need a reasonable estimate of the extent of the problem of homelessness in order to effec-tively deal with it. Unfortunately, methodological problems make it difficult to count people who lack a fixed address. A person may be on the street one night, in a shelter the next, and in a voucher motel after that. Many of the "hidden" homeless, who avoid shelters and are often missed in homeless counts, are those who stay in vehicles, boxcars, boxes, or tents. The best approximation on the homeless popula-tion comes from the Urban Institute, which states that about 1 percent of the U.S. population—3.5 million people, 1.35 million of them children—are likely to experi-ence homelessness in any given year.[53] Recent studies suggest that there has been a significant increase in homelessness over the past two decades. And the market sys-tem is producing homelessness at a higher rate than previously considered.

Major Factors Contributing to Homelessness

Various explanations have been advanced to explain the surge in homelessness in the past two decades. One explanation holds that rising homelessness has been caused by the falling incomes of low-skilled workers. The economy has replaced many higher-paid manufacturing jobs with low-paying service sector jobs. As a result, the economy has benefited those workers situated securely in the upper-income ranges, while those with lower skills have not benefited. A related explanation refers to the reduction in social welfare benefits, such as unemployment and housing assistance. Moreover, states have reacted to federal cutbacks by reducing their funding for welfare programs. States reacted to the recession of 2001–2002 by even further reducing their commitment to social welfare spending. These cutbacks erased the only margin of protection that had kept some from becoming homeless. Many of the mentally ill were deinstitutionalized without providing adequate care to permit them to function in a noninstitutionalized setting. Certainly the reduction in availability of housing for low-income families is also a significant factor. Those at the bottom of the wage scale have been forced to compete more aggressively for a reduced number of low-cost units. The result for many is homelessness. For those who manage to avoid homelessness, the result is higher-cost housing and an increased risk of homelessness. Finally, there are the individual pathologies of alcohol and drug use. Each of these explanations also applies, although perhaps not as critically, to those who are precariously housed and to those who are low-income renters and homeowners.[54]

Homelessness cannot be explained away by charges like individual laziness, lack of skills, alcohol abuse, or deinstitutionalization of the mentally ill. Clearly, structural factors like a changing economy and policy decisions are as much a part of the explanation as are the individual characteristics of the homeless person.

Policy Response for the Homeless

Prior to the 1930s, homelessness tended to be viewed by most policymakers as a personal pathology and a problem for local organizations. But by the late 1970s the homeless were seen as a serious policy issue. The initial response by religious organizations, charitable groups, and some local governments was to join together in a "coalition for the homeless," and to focus on immediate relief through soup kitchens and homeless shelters.

The term *homeless* suggests that the policy issue would be solved if those without a fixed abode could be provided affordable housing. But for many others the issue involves personal responsibility and accountability. As Christopher Jencks wrote:

> If no one drank, took drugs, lost touch with reality or had trouble holding a job, homelessness would be rare. But if America had a system of social welfare comparable to that of Sweden or Germany, homelessness would also be rare. In those countries job training is far better, unskilled jobs pay better, benefits for the unem-

ployed are almost universally available and the mental health system does much more to provide housing for the mentally ill. It is the combination of widespread individual vulnerability and collective indifference that leaves so many Americans in the streets.[55]

The Housing Voucher Program

The **housing voucher** program, usually referred to as "Section 8," after the section of the U.S. Housing Act that authorized it, was created in the 1970s and has become the largest federal housing assistance program. The federal funds are distributed to low-income families with children, the elderly, and the disabled by 2,600 state, regional, and local housing agencies known collectively as public housing agencies (PHAs). Federal rules ensure that vouchers are targeted at the families who need them most. PHAs are required to ensure that 75 percent of the households admitted to the program have incomes at or below 30 percent of the area median. Approximately 61 percent of voucher recipients are families with children. Nationally, 30 percent of the median income is $18,850 for a family of four, which is roughly the poverty level.[56] When a family receives a voucher, it has sixty days to find housing in the private market. After a family identifies a unit, the PHA inspects the unit to ensure that it meets the program's housing quality standards and to certify that the rent is consistent with rents for comparable units in the local area. A family with a voucher is required to contribute 30 percent of its income for rent and utilities. The program has grown with the population over the past two decades, such that there are currently over 2 million housing vouchers. Nevertheless, vouchers are not an entitlement and limited funding means that only about 25 percent of households eligible for vouchers receive any form of housing assistance. By 2003, with the average wait for a voucher in many areas over thirty months, many housing agencies stopped accepting new applications. Landlords are under no obligation to rent to families with vouchers and only about two-thirds of all voucher holders are successful in finding acceptable units. Vouchers can also be used to help families buy homes.

Vouchers are a highly effective form of housing assistance. Research finds that voucher holders in low-income neighborhoods are more likely to succeed in the workplace and nearly twice as likely to leave welfare as those without housing assistance.[57] Studies also show that using vouchers to move from high- to low-poverty neighborhoods improves educational outcomes for children. Children in these families are also less likely to become involved in violent crime as either perpetrator or victim.[58]

Unfortunately, the George W. Bush administration has proposed shifting responsibility for the housing voucher program away from the federal government and to state and local authorities. The administration has also proposed cutting the program by 30 percent by 2009, which would reduce the number of families currently served and push others into vulnerable living situations or homelessness. The problem is made even worse by the housing boom and local zoning laws that cap development in many high-income areas, forcing builders to put expensive housing elsewhere. This pushes the working poor farther from centers of employment and transportation, and pushes the poorest out of housing and into overcrowded shelters.

The Stewart B. McKinney Homeless Assistance Act of 1987 designated the Department of Housing and Urban Development (HUD) to be the lead federal agency in providing grants to states and localities to increase subsidies for housing and shelter support in an effort to alleviate some of the problems for the homeless. President Bill Clinton issued a plan to reduce the homeless population by one-third by spending $2.15 billion in 1995. His plan recommended a "continuum of care" that combined shelter, education, substance-abuse counseling, job training, and medical treatment.[59] Many of the homeless are workers with little education and few working skills. Job-training programs that develop interpersonal skills and job responsibility attitudes would offer significant hope for reducing homelessness. A liberalization of welfare benefits, which have not kept pace with inflation, and a relaxation of eligibility rules for those benefits, would make housing more affordable for many. There is some evidence that U.S. sympathy for the homeless is receding. Recent surveys by the National Law Center on Homelessness and Poverty found that many cities have enacted or enforced restrictions on occupying public spaces, or otherwise selectively enforced laws rarely applied to the non-homeless. The center conceded that some concerns about the use of public space are legitimate in that city residents do not want people living or begging in the streets.

The homeless are merely the most visible portion of the population experiencing housing deficiencies. Many of the homeless eventually do obtain housing, either on their own or when taken in by friends or relatives for varying lengths of time. A much larger portion of the poor population do not move into the streets but double up with relatives or friends. Such displaced people have to be considered in the overall determination of housing needs.

Housing Markets for the Middle- and Upper-Income United States

Overall, exceptionally strong income and job growth characterized the last half of the 1990s, up to the 2001 recession, for those in the middle- and especially for those in the upper-income groups. Despite the cyclical slowdown, 1.3 million new households have been formed each year since the turn of the twenty-first century. Home sales, single-family housing starts, homeownership rates, and refinances

have reached new peaks. Economic expansion over the past decade has given support to rising house prices. Low-interest rates have also allowed middle- and
upper-income families to hold down mortgage payments of more expensive homes,
and have encouraged rising home prices. High demand has contributed to a rapid
increase in housing values, which in turn has generated wealth effects through
home price appreciation. As interest rates declined during the economic slowdown,
families were able to refinance and even borrow on home equity, which helped sustain consumer demand. This strong demand resulted in house prices in the more
affluent market rising faster than household incomes. Builders eagerly responded
to the increased demand by building more profitable, larger homes with more
amenities and, of course, higher price tags. Table 11.1 indicates how homes have
changed over the past three decades.

The trends indicate increases in square footage, the number of bathrooms, the
percentage of new units with central air conditioning, and the number of units having parking facilities. Every category of amenity has grown. It is noteworthy that
the size and price of homes are increasing at a time when households are getting
smaller. The number of single-person households increased from 18 to 28 percent
between 1980 and 2002, while the number of two-person households increased
from 25 to 36 percent.[60] The trend toward smaller households will continue with
the coming surge in retirement by the baby boomers.

There is a widespread misconception that housing subsidies are aimed primarily at the poor and the homeless, when in fact the middle and upper classes have
been the primary target population of the most generous government assistance.
Most government policies encourage a higher level of ownership than the market
would produce.

The major subsidy for owner-occupied housing comes in the form of tax concessions. The goal of various administrations to balance the budget while reducing
marginal tax rates has not seriously threatened housing tax concessions. The major
concessions include:

1. Allowance of mortgage interest deduction on owner-occupied homes.
2. Deductibility of local property taxes from federal tax returns on owner-
   occupied homes.
3. Nontaxation of the first $250,000 ($500,000 for a married couple) of capital
   gains realized on the sale of an owner-occupied home.
4. Nontaxation of net imputed income from owner-occupied homes.[61]

These concessions are a significant fiscal burden on the federal budget. The mortgage interest deduction (MID) is a common tax feature in OECD countries, with
about half allowing it. The real estate tax deduction and MID were historical acci-

**Table 11.1 Characteristics of New Privately Owned
Single-Family Houses Completed 1970–2003**

	Percentage of Units		
	1970	1980	2003
Floor area (square feet)			
Under 1,200	36	21	5
1,200–1,599	28	29	17
1,600–1,999	16	22	21
2,000–2,399	21	13	19
2,400+		15	38
Bedrooms			
2 or fewer	13	17	12
3	63	63	51
4 or more	24	20	37
Bathrooms			
1 or fewer	20	10	5
2	32	48	38
3 or more	16	25	56
Central air conditioning	34	63	88
Fireplaces, 1 or more	35	56	58
Parking facilities			
Garage	58	69	88
Carport	17	7	1
Median square feet	1,385	1,595	2,137

Sources: U.S. Census Bureau, *Statistical Abstracts 1993, 1997, 2004–2005* (Washington, D.C.: U.S. Government Printing Office, 1993, 1997, 2004).

dents. They were embedded in the first Internal Revenue Code, in 1913, with little attention to their effect on homeownership, because the tax rates were very low and the proportion of households that paid no income tax at all was very high. During World War II, with rising incomes and rising tax rates, their impact on home purchases became significant, after which they were defended as sacrosanct because they had always been there. Taxation of capital gains on home sales did not become an issue until after the war.[62]

Easily the largest housing subsidy is the ability of homeowners to take a deduction on mortgage interest and local property taxes from their federal income taxes. A tax deduction is an amount of money that may be subtracted from income before a taxpayer computes his or her taxable income. The ability to avoid paying taxes on income spent on mortgage interest and property taxes may substantially reduce taxes and gives homeowners preferential treatment when compared to renters. Since homeowners are, on average, more affluent than renters, this special treatment reduces the progressivity of the income tax. The tax deduction often more than compensates for the real interest paid on mortgages.[63] Therefore, upper-income households have a particularly strong incentive to buy homes. For them, a home is viewed "primarily as an investment rather than as necessary shelter."[64] The combination of tax deductions and inflation can result in a distortion of the housing market in which builders provide too many large houses to produce tax shelters for the affluent, and too few low-priced houses for the poor.

Tax deductions on the interest paid on home mortgages are available to all who can afford to buy a home. The recipients do not have to compete for the benefit as if there were limited funds available. And the amount of the subsidy is related to the amount of interest paid. Those who can afford to carry larger mortgages or pay higher local property taxes receive larger subsidies.

Housing subsidies in the form of tax deductions that reduce the cost of owning a house for middle- and upper-income families amounted to $112.8 billion in 2002. In fact, the mortgage interest deduction alone was almost three times the size of the entire budget for the Department of Housing and Urban Development in that year. This tax expenditure would be more acceptable if most of the money went to help a majority of the people. But it does not. There are virtually no tax benefits to home-ownership for median-priced homes in dozens of mid-American cities, where the median home is priced below $170,000, because tax deductions from ownership will not exceed the standard deduction already allowed. For example, a family that buys a $140,000 house with about a 20 percent down payment receives no tax benefits. As the price of the home rises, tax benefits escalate. Those with the highest incomes and the most expensive houses get the largest tax breaks.

Since the income tax laws do not require homeowners to report imputed income, it would be consistent to not permit homeowners to take deductions from unreported income. Owner-occupied housing is an income advantage in that rent does not have to be paid. Central to this issue is whether owner-occupied housing is mostly a durable consumption good (such as a car) or mostly an investment (such as shares of stocks). A pure investment good only provides a monetary return; durable consumption goods also provide nonmonetary values. Yet despite all the critical analysis recommending the elimination of the mortgage interest deduction, Congress ignores the proposal.

Defenders of MID argue that it helps many people become homeowners by making housing more affordable, and that it increases the number of housing units built by the home-building industry without resorting to direct subsidies.

Defenders also argue that eliminating the MID would depress housing values, resulting in unfair losses for those whose purchase of a house was based partly on the availability of the deduction. Opponents point out that the primary purpose of the MID is to increase the homeownership rate. But two other nations have a similar homeownership rate without such favorable tax treatment, Australia, at 69.8 percent in 1996, and Canada, at 64.0 percent, compared to 65.4 percent in the United States in that year. Kenneth Rosen concluded that without the MID, the homeownership rate in the United States would have been 62 percent.[65] What is clear is the fact that low-income families benefit least from the deduction. Critics often challenge each of these points, and insist that the MID provides unfair benefits to high-income households at the expense of low-income households and renters.[66] Finally, they contend that it increases housing expenditures among the more affluent households that do not need a subsidy to acquire adequate housing. The higher the incomes of homeowners, the larger the mortgages they are likely to have, since they can deduct their mortgage interest and local property tax against the federal taxes they owe on their incomes.

Figure 11.2 shows distribution of housing subsidies by income quintile. The bottom quintile receives about $25 billion in outlays from government spending on public housing, vouchers, and other spending programs, and receives 17.8 percent of the subsidies. The next quintile only receives 2.7 percent, as their income is in many cases too high to qualify for subsidies but insufficient to receive tax deductions from home purchases. Those in the third quintile receive about 3.1 percent of all subsidies. At this income level, many who are able to buy a modest home find that taking the standard deduction is more advantageous than itemizing expenses, so they do not receive a significant MID from a home purchase. The fourth quintile receives 13.8 percent of all MIDs. But it is those in the top quintile who receive the most generous subsidy. This income group finds it advantageous to itemize, and as a result they receive 62.5 percent of all mortgage interest deductions. Although the home mortgage deduction is usually defended politically as a major tax break for the middle class, the statistics clearly indicate that it mainly benefits upper-income homeowners.

Over the past several years, the Congressional Budget Office (CBO) has recommended options to reduce the federal deficit. One recommendation it has consistently made is to eliminate the mortgage deduction entirely for second homes. The CBO contends it is unfair to provide tax breaks for vacation and investment homes when many cannot afford a modest home for basic shelter. It would save the government over $400 million annually. However, this proposal would run into determined opposition from the vacation industry in many states, and in particular such states as Maine, Florida, Colorado, and Arizona. No proposal to limit MID has been put forward in Congress since 1996.

Figure 11.2 Estimated Distribution of Housing Subsidies by Income Quintile, 2002 (constant 2002 U.S.$ in billions)

Quintile	Tax Expenditures	Housing Outlays	Total	Percent	Quintile Income Limit	Quintile Average Income
Bottom	0.1	25.4	25.5	17.8	16,532	9,461
Second	0.7	3.2	3.9	2.7	31,192	24,188
Thrid	3.9	0.6	4.5	3.1	49,584	40,472
Fourth	19.6	0.1	19.8	13.8	76,935	62,594
Top	89.3	0.0	89.3	62.5	n/a	132,455
Total	113.7	29.2	142.9	100.0	n/a	53,858

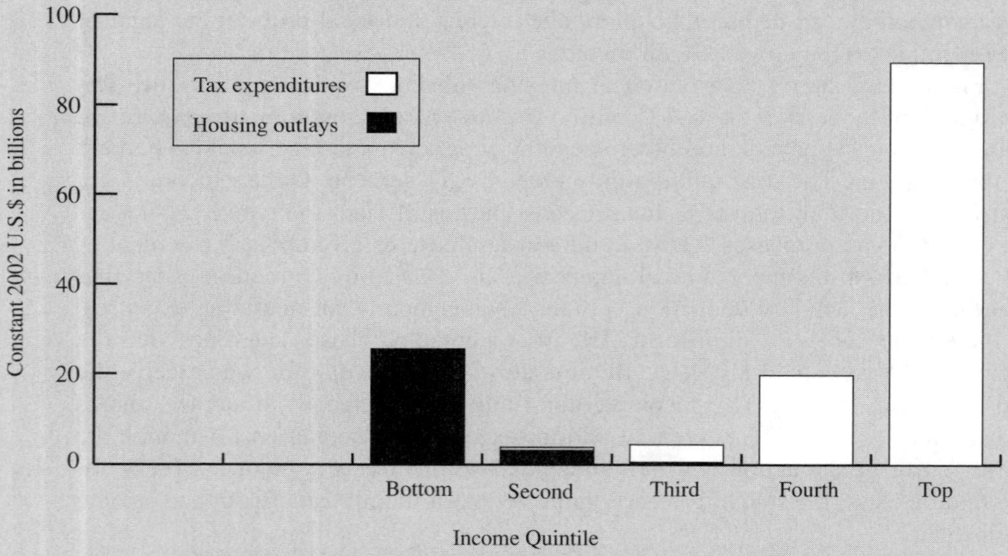

Source: Cushing N. Dolbeare and Sheila Crowley, "Changing Priorities: The Federal Budget and Housing Assistance, 1976–2007," National Low-Income Housing Coalition, August 2002, p. 4.

Also, since over 65 percent of households own their own home, homeowners form a very powerful interest group. Many nonowners also aspire to homeownership. These groups successfully argue the convenient logic that Congress should continue to encourage homeownership as a support for responsible citizenship.

Case Study: Home Mortgage Tax Deductions and Horizontal Equity

Mortgage and property tax deductions by homeowners are tax expenditures from the perspective of the government. A tax expenditure, or "loophole," is a provision of the tax code that reduces an individual's tax bill, and hence reduces revenue collections by the government.

The tax deductions associated with homeownership are also held to violate a tax principle that those who are equals in all pertinent tax respects should be treated equally. For example, suppose than Jim and Katherine are neighbors, each earning $50,000 per year. The only difference is that Jim owns his home while Katherine is renting her house. Since they have equal incomes, most observers would say that they should pay the same income tax. Because of the favorable tax treatment of homeowners, however, they

probably will not. Suppose Jim pays $3,000 in property taxes and has a $100,000 mortgage at 10 percent interest, which costs him about $10,000 a year in interest costs. Since the property taxes and mortgage interest are tax-deductible, he is able to deduct $13,000 per year in housing costs. Katherine pays $13,000 per year in rent, which is not tax-deductible. Her tax burden is significantly higher than Jim's.

The inequity could be remedied in several ways. One would be to allow renters to deduct their rent from their income tax. Or the mortgage and property tax deductions could be disallowed. A third alternative would be to require the homeowner to add the value of housing (or imputed rent), which is calculated by adding mortgage and property tax payments to income.

They also argue that tax deductions raise home values higher than would be the case without the deductions, and that repealing them would reduce those values and thus ultimately the demand for homeownership. The tax advantages of homeowners remain untouchable to politicians. However, reductions in the marginal tax rates have resulted in reductions in the size of this type of tax expenditure.

Conclusion

In this chapter we have reviewed the origins and evolution of U.S. housing policy since the early twentieth century. Homeownership has been looked upon as a goal of most citizens throughout the nation's history. Government has supported homeownership since the early 1900s. That support became more direct during the Great Depression. After World War II, the Housing Act of 1949 reflected the renewed goal during the Truman administration that the United States could raise living standards and provide for urban renewal in cities that had been neglected since the 1930s. The act concentrated on building more housing units but did not address the social and economic problems of an increasingly stratified society. By the late 1950s, policymakers began to back away from urban renewal projects that threat-

Case Study: Housing—How Much Can Households Afford?

One method of determining how much a family can afford for housing is based on percentage of income. This is the most widely used standard for housing affordability. The standard rule of affordability rose from 20 percent in the 1950s, to 25 percent in the 1960s, and to 30 percent in the 1970s. Since 1981, families receiving government subsidies have been required to contribute 30 percent of their income toward their housing costs.

The major criticism of this approach is that fixed percentages are arbitrary; the maximum affordable percentage will actually vary with income and household size and type. Since housing costs constitute a fixed basic claim on a household's disposable income, subsequent expenditures must adjust to what is left after housing expenses have been met. On a sliding scale, some low-income households might be able to afford less than 30 percent of their income for housing. At upper-income levels, over 50 percent of net income could be spent on housing, and the remainder would more than adequately cover other expenses.

A second method approaches the problem in reverse and determines the market costs of basic necessities such as food, clothing, and health care first. These are viewed as making a fixed claim on the disposable income of a household, with the remainder being taken as what the household can "afford" for housing. This is usually considerably less than 30 percent. However, most of the poor do not receive housing subsidies and must pay more than 30 percent of their income for housing. Renters usually have higher cost burdens than owners.

Sources: James Poterba, *Housing Price Dynamics: The Role of Tax Policy and Demography,* Brookings Paper on Economic Activity (Washington, D.C.: Brookings Institution, 1991), vol. 2, no. 2, pp. 184–203.

ened not only middle- but also low-income urban dwellers. As government retreated in its commitment to rebuild inner cities, Section 8 became the focal point of low-income housing policy. Funds for vouchers became the main policy for low-income individuals seeking to purchase or rent housing. Proposals by the current administration to reduce funds for vouchers threaten the program's viability. Congress examines every detail of the budget for government outlays to support low-income families and is under increasing pressure to reduce funding in its effort to balance the budget. More Americans are spending an ever-increasing percentage of their incomes on housing, leaving them with insufficient means to purchase other necessities such as food, clothing, and health care.

Data indicate that about half of working poor families with children who receive no housing subsidy pay at least half their income for rent. High housing costs leave many low-income families trying to move into the work force with insufficient money for the increased costs that often accompany employment, such as additional clothing and food, child care, and transportation. Reducing low-income workers' housing cost burden can provide some families with the stability they need to get and retain a job. Homeownership has a positive impact especially for low-income families with children.

For more affluent homebuyers, tax concessions that were included in the Internal Revenue Code in 1913, with no thought to the value of the expenditure and with both inflation and tax increases during World War II, are accepted as being sacrosanct. Congress does not appropriate any funds for these tax expenditures. The revenue losses attributable to the tax laws that allow a special exemption, exclusion, credit, or deduction are determined primarily by a more affluent taxpayer's calculation regarding how expensive a home is within his or her means. These tax expenditures impoverish the treasury as much as a direct outlay by the government. The result is that, since there is a nontaxation of imputed rent from a mortgage, a mortgage insurance deductibility, a real estate tax deductibility, and an exemption of most capital gains, the top 20 percent of income earners receive over three-fifths of all housing subsidies. Minimally, a cap on the deductibility of mortgages over a limit like $100,000 and a denial of mortgage deductibility altogether for second homes would seem fair. Calculations indicate that exemptions do not result in a significant increase in homeownership. This is in direct contradiction of the goals of housing policy. There are excellent reasons why reductions in some of these tax concessions could be used to redirect policies toward lower-income families.

The outcome of the housing market in the United States leaves much of the public dissatisfied. The policy outcomes tend to be a series of narrow interventions by the government designed to deal with individual aspects of the problem. Therefore, the greatest challenge for policy analysts is to develop an analytical framework to indicate which alternatives best address specific issues and to evaluate those policies implemented.

Policies may be classified according to the critical choices implicit in their purpose. As already indicated, one classification is the population targeted. We often think of housing assistance as aimed primarily at the poor, because housing projects are more visible, while in fact those in the middle class and the affluent are the beneficiaries of the most generous programs encouraging homeownership.

The exponential growth of suburban and ex-urban areas has major implications for housing and urban development concerns. Today, the suburbs are the major job generators in the new economy, being responsible for over 85 percent of the jobs in the lower-paying and lower-skilled service and retail trade sectors. Not surprisingly, unemployment rates in central cities are frequently one-third to one-half higher than in the surrounding suburbs. Also, cities today continue to lose middle-class families, which destabilizes neighborhoods and increases the concentration of the poor in urban ghettos. This is perhaps the most disturbing housing trend in the United States, and is largely ignored in the welfare and housing debate.

Questions for Discussion

1. Why are so many people homeless in the United States compared to most European nations?
2. What evidence is there that federal tax laws provide far more generous subsidies to the affluent homebuyer than to those in the bottom 40 percent of the U.S. population? What policies would you suggest to redistribute the subsidies more equitably?
3. Is housing in the United States becoming less racially segregated? Is it becoming more segregated by income? Explain how this works.
4. What is the significance of the growth in gated communities at different levels of income?
5. How does the fragmentation of power between federal, state, and local authorities complicate housing policy?

Useful Websites

American Bar Association Commission on Homelessness and Poverty, http://www.abanet.org.

Beyond Shelter, http://www.beyondshelter.org.

National Association of Housing and Redevelopment Officials, http://www.nahro.org.

National Coalition for the Homeless, http://www.nationalhomeless.org.

National Low-Income Housing Coalition, http://www.nlihc.org.

Urban Institute, http://www.urban.org.

U.S. Department of Housing and Urban Development, http://www.hud.gov/homeless/index.cfm.

Suggested Readings

Bauer, Catherine. *Modern Housing*. New York: Houghton Mifflin, 1934.

Blair, John P. *Urban and Regional Economics*. Homewood, Ill.: Richard D. Irwin, 1991.

Burt, Martha R., and Barbara E. Cohen. *America's Homeless: Numbers, Characteristics, and Programs That Serve Them*. Washington, D.C.: Urban Institute Press, 1989.

Ehrenreich, Barrbara. *Nickel and Dimed: On (Not) Getting By in America*. New York: Metropolitan Books, 2001.

Green, Richard K., and Stephen Malpezzi. *A Primer on U.S. Housing Markets and Housing Policy*. Washington, D.C.: Urban Institute Press, 2003.

Hopper, Kim. *Reckoning with Homelessness*. Ithaca: Cornell University Press, 2003.

Jones, Jacqueline. *The Dispossessed: America's Underclasses from the Civil War to the Present*. New York: Basic Books, 1992.

Kozol, Jonathan. *Rachel and Her Children: Homeless Families in America*. New York: Crown, 1988.

Miller, Henrey. *On the Fringe: The Dispossessed in America*. New York: Lexington Books, 1991.

Momeni, Jamshid A., ed. *Homelessness in the United States*. Vols. 1–2. New York: Greenwood Press, 1989.

National Law Center on Homelessness and Poverty. *Homelessness in the United States and the Human Right to Housing*. Washington, D.C.: U.S. Government Printing Office, January 14, 2004.

Rossi, Peter. *Down and Out in America: The Origins of Homelessness*. Chicago: University of Chicago Press, 1989.

Struyk, Raymond J., Margery A. Turner, and Makiko Ueno. *Future U.S. Housing Policy: Meeting the Demographic Challenge*. Report no. 88-2. Washington, D.C.: Urban Institute Press, 1988.

Tucker, William. *The Excluded Americans*. Washington, D.C.: Regnery Press, 1990.

Vogel, Ronald K. *Handbook of Research on Urban Politics and Policy in the United States*. Westport, Conn.: Greenwood Press, 1997.

Williams, Mary E. *Poverty and the Homeless*. St. Paul, Minn.: Greenhaven Press, 2004.

Notes

1. Joint Center for Housing Studies, *The State of the Nation's Housing, 2004* (Cambridge: John F. Kennedy School of Government, Harvard University, 2004), p. 4, http://www.jchs.harvard.edu..

2. Ibid.

3. Ibid.

4. Jonathan Fanton, "Signs of Hope for America's Cities," *Washington Post,* November 4, 2004.

5. Ibid.

6. Lyndon B. Johnson, "The Crisis of the Cities," President's Message to Congress on Urban Problems, February 12, 1968.

7. Ann Mariano, "Action Urged to Keep Public Housing Units Available to Poor," *Washington Post,* July 13, 1985.

8. See http://www.habitat.org/how/christian.html.

9. See Raymond J. Struyk, *Should Government Encourage Home Ownership?* (Washington, D.C.: Urban Institute, 1977).

10. The government has supported homeownership beginning with the Homestead Act in 1860, extending through the federal income tax in 1913, up to tax policies currently in effect. However, it is debatable that homeowners are more responsible than renters in all respects: there is some evidence that free rider behavior leaving neighborhood improvements to others extends across both groups.

11. Joint Center for Housing Studies, *State of the Nation's Housing,* p. 7.

12. Allen R. Hays, "Housing," in Ronald K. Vogel, ed., *Handbook of Research on Urban Politics and Policy in the United States* (Westport, Conn.: Greenwood Press, 1997), p. 294.

13. Alfred L. Malabre, *Beyond Our Means* (New York: Vintage Books, 1987), pp. 42–43. Malabre contends that housing policy has encouraged excessive indebtedness and overspending, as more and more Americans have been going into deeper debt by borrowing against equity in their homes (p. 44).

14. Hays, "Housing," p. 294.

15. See William G. Grisby and Thomas Corl, "Declining Neighborhoods: Problem or

Opportunity," *Annals of the American Academy of Political and Social Science* 465 (January 1983): 90.

16. Joseph Gyourko and Anita A. Summers, *A New Strategy for Helping Cities Pay for the Poor,* Brookings Policy Brief no. 18 (Washington, D.C.: Brookings Institution, 1998).

17. John R. Logan, Richard D. Alba, Tom McNulty, and Brian Fisher, "Making a Place in the Metropolis: Locational Attainment in Cities and Suburbs," *Demography* 33, no. 4 (1996): 443–453.

18. William A. Clark, "Residential Preferences and Residential Choices in a Multiethnic Context," *Demography* 29, no. 3 (1992): 451–466.

19. Nancy Denton and Douglas Massey, "Patterns of Neighborhood Transition in a Multi-Ethnic World: U.S. Metropolitan Areas, 1970–1980," *Demography* 28, no. 1 (February 1991): 41–63.

20. John Iceland, "Beyond Black and White: Metropolitan Residential Segregation in Multi-Ethnic America," Housing and Household Economic Statistics Division, U.S. Census Bureau, paper presented at the American Sociological Association meetings, Chicago, August 16–19, 2002, p. 6.

21. The definition of what constitutes a city, or what is a rural area, is complicated by the growth of suburban areas (neither rural or urban). In 1910 the Census Bureau defined any incorporated town with 2,500 residents as urban. By 1980 the definition shifted so that an area had to have a minimum population of 50,000 and have "built-up" characteristics to be classified as urban.

The U.S. Census Bureau and the American Housing Survey now use what are termed metropolitan statistical areas (MSAs) in an effort to create more useful boundaries for urban areas. MSAs typically include cities and nearby suburban areas. However, they are rather imprecise and also present research problems. For example, some MSAs include entire counties that have close economic relationships with central urban areas. In the western United States, some counties are so large that an MSA may extend, for example, from coastal Seattle to the Cascade Mountains, fifty miles inland.

22. Kenneth Jackson, "America's Rush to Suburbia," *New York Times,* June 9, 1996.

23. Robert B. Reich, *The Work of Nations* (New York: Vintage Books, 1992), p. 278.

24. Hays, "Housing," p. 293.

25. Ann C. Case and Lawrence Katz, *The Company You Keep: The Effects of Family and Neighborhood on Disadvantaged Youths* (Cambridge, Mass.: National Bureau of Economic Research, 1991).

26. E. J. Blakely and M. G. Snyder, "Divided We Fall: Gated Communities in the United States," in N. Ellin, ed., *Architecture of Fear* (New York: Princeton Architectural Press, 1997), p. 85.

27. S. M. Low, "The Edge and the Center: Gated Communities and the Discourse of Urban Fear," *American Anthropologist* 103, no. 1 (March 2001): 45–58.

28. E. J. Blakely and M. G. Snyder, *Fortress America. Gated Communities in the United States* (Washington, D.C.: Brookings Institution, 1997).

29. Robert E. Lang and Karen A. Danielsen, "Gated Communities in America: Walling Out the World?" *Housing Policy Debate* 8, no. 4 (1997), http://www.fanniemaefoundation. org/housingresearch/abstracts/hpdebate.

30. Thomas Byrne Edsall and Mary D. Edsall, *Chain Reaction: The Impact of Race, Rights, and Taxes on American Politics* (New York: W. W. Norton, 1991), p. 62.

31. William Schneider, "The Dawn of the Suburban Era in American Politics," *The Atlantic* 270, no. 1 (July 1992): 37.

32. Ibid.

33. J. Yates and C. Whitehead, "Introduction to the Focus Issue," *Housing Studies* 16, no. 2 (2001): 141–146.

34. Center for Housing Policy, *Working Families with Children: A Closer Look at Homeownership Trends* (Washington, D.C.: Center Pieces, May 2004).

35. Andrea Oppenheimer Dean, "The Hero of Hale County: Sam Mockbee," *Architectural Record Digital,* February 2001.

36. W. Rohe, S. van Zandt, and G. McCarthy, "Home Ownership and Access to Opportunity," *Housing Studies* 17, no. 1 (2002): 51–61.

37. Richard Green and Michelle White, "Measuring the Benefits of Homeowning: Effects on Children," *Journal of Urban Economics* 41, no. 3 (1997): 441–461; Donald R. Haurin, Toby Parcel, and R. Jean Haurin, *Impact of Homeownership on Child Outcomes* (Cambridge: Joint Center for Housing Studies, Harvard University, 2001); Nicolas Pauyl Retsinas and Eric S. Belsky, eds., *Low-Income Homeownership: Examining the Unexamined Goal* (Washington, D.C.: Brookings Institution, 2002).

38. Center for Housing Policy, *Working Families with Children,* p. 1.

39. E. Glaeser and J. Shapiro, *The Benefits of the Home Mortgage Interest Deduction,* Discussion Paper no. 1979 (Cambridge: Harvard University, 2002).

40. Joint Center for Housing Studies, *State of the Nation's Housing.*

41. Ibid.

42. Ibid.

43. Children's Defense Fund, *The Bush Administration: Set to Exacerbate Growing Housing Crisis for Families with Children* (Washington, D.C.: U.S. Government Printing Office, January 2005), p. 3.

44. Joint Center for Housing Studies, *State of the Nation's Housing.*

45. Ibid., p. 28.

46. Peter Rossi, *Down and Out in America: The Origins of Homelessness* (Chicago: University of Chicago Press, 1989), p. 11.

47. U.S. Department of Housing and Urban Development, *A Report to the Secretary on the Homeless and Emergency Shelters* (Washington, D.C.: Office of Policy Development and Research, 1984). "Literal homelessness" is also the definition used in the Stewart B. McKinney Act, which is the principal legislation regarding homelessness.

48. Ralph S. Hambrick and Debra J. Rog, "Homelessness: United States," in Neil J. Smelser and Paul B. Baltes, eds., *International Encyclopedia of the Social and Behavioral Sciences* (New York: Elsevier, 2001).

49. Rossi, *Down and Out.* This is still one of the best discussions of the characteristics of the homeless.

50. U.S. Conference of Mayors, *Sodexho Hunger and Homelessness Survey 2003,* http://www.usmayors.org. Also cited in Children's Defense Fund, *Bush Administration,* p. 3.

51. Children's Defense Fund, *Bush Administration,* p. 4.

52. Hambrick and Rog, "Homelessness: United States."

53. Urban Institute, *A New Look at Homelessness in America* (Washington, D.C.: Urban Institute, 2000), http://www.urban.org.

54. See William Tucker, *The Excluded Americans: Homelessness and Housing Policies* (Washington, D.C.: Regnery Gateway, 1990), pp. 4–10.

55. Christopher Jencks, "The Homeless," *New York Review of Books,* April 21, 1994, p. 22.

56. *Federal Register* 69, no. 30 (February 13, 2004): 7336–7338.

57. Center on Budget and Policy Priorities, "Introduction to the Housing Voucher Program," Washington, D.C., May 15, 2003, p. 7.

58. Ibid.

59. Richard L. Worsnop, "Helping the Homeless," *CQ Researcher* 6, no. 4 (January 1996): 73–96.

60. U.S. Census Bureau, *Statistical Abstract 2003* (Washington, D.C.: U.S. Government Printing Office, 2003), p. 61.

61. **Imputed income** is the single largest tax concession for owner-occupied housing. If a family invests $25,000 in a government bond, they will be taxed on the interest earned. But an individual who invests $25,000 in a home is not taxed, even though the home yields a return. A homeowner receives a return in shelter services. For example, if an owner buys a house for cash (and almost 40 percent of all houses are owned free of mortgage debt), the owner would have no mortgage payment and would receive what is referred to as "imputed" income—the noncash income in shelter benefits. That could be calculated by estimating how much the house would rent for and subtracting cash expenses such as taxes and insurance. The remainder would be the imputed shelter income, which is not taxed. Not taxing imputed rent may be criticized on the grounds of simple fairness and that it results in a misallocation of resources. Nontaxation reduces the cost of investing in owner-occupied housing below the cost of investing in other forms of capital, resulting in too much investment in housing and not enough in other productive sectors like capital plants and equipment. As William Vickrey, a Nobel Prize winner in economics, said in his presidential address to the American Economic Association in arguing for the inclusion in taxable income of the rental value of owner-occupied homes: "This would not only improve the equity and progressivity of the income tax but also go a substantial way toward making more units available for rental and, to a modest extent, promoting the construction of additional affordable rental housing and abating the problem of homelessness." Quoted in Steven C. Bourassa and William G. Grigsby, "Income Tax Concessions for Owner-Occupied Housing," *Housing Policy Debate* 11, no. 3 (2000): 527–528.

62. Ibid., p. 522.

63. The **real rate of interest** is defined as the nominal rate of interest minus the rate of inflation. The **nominal rate of interest** is defined as the interest rate actually paid in current prices.

64. Anthony Downs, *Rental Housing in the 1980s* (Washington, D.C.: Brookings Institution, 1983), p. 33.

65. Kenneth Rosen, *The Mortgage Interest Tax Deduction and Homeownership,* Working Paper no. 89-159 (San Francisco: University of California, Center for Real Estate and Urban Economics, 1989).

66. Bourassa and Grigsby, "Income Tax Concessions," pp. 529–530. See also William C. Baer, "On the Making of Perfect and Beautiful Social Programs," *Public Interest* 39 (Spring 1975): 80–98; and Peter Dreier, "The New Politics of Housing: How to Rebuild the Constituency for a Progressive Federal Housing Policy," *Journal of the American Planning Association* 63, no. 1 (1997): 5–27.

CHAPTER 12

Environmental Policy: Domestic and International Issues

Environmentalism is a relatively new social movement that challenges institutionalized politics. The purpose of environmental policy as a field of study is to inform policy choices regarding the relationship between human society and the environment. The more specific purpose of environmental policy is to protect the natural environment from overexploitation and degradation. It recognizes that Earth's resources are finite and that excessive exploitation through overpopulation, pollution, or resource extraction imposes costs on society and should be recognized as an inefficiency. The environment has been altered by industrial waste, reckless use of technology, and government indifference. Until recently, many environmentalists had directed their efforts to persuading the public that there was in fact an environmental crisis. The public awakening to environmental issues has fostered an urgency in certain quarters to the need for environmental policies. Measurable degradation of air and water quality, oil and sewage spills, and contaminated beaches and drinking water have served to dramatically focus attention on the environment. Public opinion polls now regularly reveal that overwhelming majorities of Americans place a high priority on environmental policies. Environmental policies are not designed to preserve the environment in its unaltered state as much as they are designed to protect the environment while promoting the social and economic welfare of the nation's inhabitants.

Environmental policy is distinctive because of the scientific nature of the fundamental questions raised. Environmental issues are complicated and multifaceted, and environmental choices are often intertwined with consequences for energy policy. Moreover, the technical nature of scientific debates may discourage some from trying to inform themselves on the issues. Nevertheless, energy and environmental issues have a very real impact on the average person's daily life. Those who support major initiatives typically want ensured energy resources at reasonable prices with acceptable environmental consequences. This is very difficult to accomplish in fact.

Despite increased awareness and growing efforts to protect the environment, disruptions have surfaced with increasing frequency. Environmental issues have emerged in different forms, including projected scarcities of energy resources, damage from releasing harmful substances and pollution into the environment, deforestation and soil erosion, water shortages, depletion of the ozone layer, the greenhouse effect, and global warming.

Evolving Environmental Themes

Most approaches to environmental problems can be categorized as protection or regulation. The first is based on the notion that there are finite limits to Earth's resources. This approach springs from **conservationist** and **preservationist** beliefs. The conservationist stance began in the early to middle 1800s, when various writers such as Thomas Malthus and Henry David Thoreau viewed Earth's resources as existing for the benefit of mankind but also recognized the limits to natural resources and believed in an ethical obligation to use them wisely and efficiently rather than squandering them.

In contrast, preservationists, as the name indicates, want to preserve rather than conserve the natural environment. Concerned about the well-being of all nature, both living and nonliving, they view the world as containing many species, not just humans, that have an equal right to live on the planet. Saving various species, whether whales or the great apes, as well as protecting them from hunting, is supportive of this view. For this reason, preservationists support biodiversity among plants as well as animals. The natural environment in its pristine state, encompassing such features as mountain ranges, rivers, and wetlands, has a value that is not reducible to the people or the wildlife that live within its confines. John Muir, the founder of the Sierra Club in 1892 is often looked upon as the founder of the preservationist movement.

The Sierra Club and the Audubon Society were organized to call attention to the environmental destruction caused by unrestricted and destructive exploitation of the nation's resources. The preservationist movement had an interest in protecting natural areas from the encroachment of industrialization. Few political elites got involved, nor did most Americans seem to take seriously the damage that unregulated growth and development were inflicting on the environment.

President Theodore Roosevelt, a leader of the conservationist movement, prevailed over the preservationists of the time. Roosevelt and a few politicians and scientists were largely motivated by a concern for resource conservation and management. The movement was driven by a fear of resource exhaustion and a need to manage natural resources before they were destroyed. This approach tried to make rational choices based on utilitarian principles of the greatest good for the greatest number, from an economic perspective. Such mid-twentieth-century projects of the Roosevelt administration as the Tennessee Valley Authority and the Civilian Conservation Corps reflect this desire to use nature for society's benefit.

Although the conservationist movement emphasized the efficient consumption of resources while the preservationists emphasized the long-term protection of animal and plant life, they shared a goal of protecting and managing the environment to achieve maximum **sustainable development**. The essential idea of sustainable development, while difficult to define precisely, emphasizes the need for policymakers to include a consideration of environmental, social, and economic factors in policy decisions. Policymakers will further take into account the interest of current and future generations and attempt to provide intergenerational equity. Policies should give a preference to strategies that provide the maximum sustainable yield of benefits. An application of this principle is the setting of maximum levels for fish catches. While no one owns the ocean and the fish and other animals that live within it, everyone has an incentive to exploit these resources but no incentive to manage or conserve them. The problem of the "commons" may be dealt with by setting up regulations and incentives to encourage the management of the common stock in question to its maximum sustainable yield. This principle is consistent with the goal of protecting those most vulnerable to the spillover effects of policy choices as well. Since later generations are vulnerable to present-day choices, setting maximum sustainable yields guarantees that succeeding generations are provided with benefits roughly equal to those enjoyed today. This principle also encourages renewable energy sources such as solar, wind, and wave over the use of scarce nonrenewable forms of energy.

The concept of sustainable development has been included in several environmental treaties and is now viewed as an essential principle of international environmental and development policy. However, both industrialized and developing states are not in complete agreement on the obligations the concept imposes.

Environmental policy is also concerned about **environmental justice**. Lower-income groups are much more likely to face the hazards associated with pollution than are more affluent groups. Poor communities far more often have a chemical plant, incinerator, sewage treatment plant, landfill, or other polluting or unhealthy industry located nearby than do affluent communities. Many environmentalists believe that the unequal distribution of financial resources is a crucial cause of environmental degradation. Society must first alleviate the vastly unequal distribution of wealth in order to provide a more equitable distribution of polluting industries. The environmental justice movement includes the notion that all communities are entitled to equal protection and enforcement of laws that affect the environmental quality of life. Environmental justice means that policies should give special consideration to those most vulnerable to the consequences of policy choices. Too often, the poor may find themselves at the mercy of decisions made by the more economically powerful members of society. But no socioeconomic or racial group should bear a disproportionate share of environmental degradation resulting from industrial or municipal operations or decisions. Protesters, particularly minorities, rail against what they claim is "environmental racism," and organize "not in my backyard" (NIMBY) demonstrations against the placing of environmentally polluting factories or other waste sites in their neighborhoods and against locally unwanted land uses (LULUs) that could locate environmentally noxious waste sites in their communities.

Many environmental problems extend beyond national boundaries and require international responses. International problems of environmental degradation frequently mirror domestic problems writ large. This is especially the case concerning the unequal distribution of wealth. Many if not most threats to the global environment can be traced to the wealthy nations' demand for goods, while much of the actual pollution occurs in poorer countries attempting to supply the goods demanded. Activists in many developing nations organize to protect their natural resource base of forests, minerals, and rivers, as well as their culture, from the pressures of globalization. These movements parallel the movement for environmental justice in the United States. These groups often see themselves at odds with their political elites, who are perceived as being in the pockets of multinational corporations. These environmental groups oppose globalization and hold that environmental justice goes beyond the calculation of the marketplace.

Market Failure and the Environment

Government has a function of providing the legal framework within which economic activity takes place. Public policy scholars often debate the extent to which governments need to intervene in the market. Those who prefer free market solutions contend that government intervention should be kept to a minimum, while more centrist scholars believe that there are many examples of a need for intervention.

Until recently, this debate relied heavily on Garrett Hardin's notion of the tragedy of the commons (see Chapter 3), which illustrates the conflict between individual and communal interests. Hardin's parable suggests that communal ownership of resources (rather than private ownership) will lead to depletion. Each individual will treat communal property as free goods and maximize their advantage by using as much of a resource as possible. Individual self-interest will lead to behavior to maximize private gain and prove suboptimal for the community in the long run. Therefore, if communal property were turned over to private owners with property rights over the resource, they would have an intrinsic interest to preserve the resource over a longer period of time. Over a century ago, large landowners made the argument for their taking control of the commons that remained, for a modest fee, to bring order to an unregulated and chaotic situation. In the current environmental debate the pollution of air and water, global warming, and the exhaustion of ocean fisheries seem to reinforce the notion that private property rights rather than community ownership will guarantee efficient management of resources. Ironically, people may worry about the need to save the whales that are not privately owned, but because cattle and chickens are privately owned, no one worries that they will become extinct.

The tragedy of the commons is an example of market failure, which can occur for several reasons. First, the environment may be thought of as a public good. Communal property where there are no established property rights, such as the oceans beyond national jurisdiction, provides little incentive to manage the resources of the sea. Or farmers who cut down trees to gain more arable land in Brazil may not incur a business cost, though the new farmland can no longer be used for preserving wildlife.

Second, the production and consumption of goods may involve external costs or negative externalities that affect people other than those producing or consuming the good. One of government's primary policy roles is to provide remedies for the inefficiencies resulting from externalities. We noted earlier that externalities exist when a producer or a consumer does not bear the full cost (negative externality) or receive the full benefit (positive externality) of economic activity. Since externalities do not pass through the market system, the market cannot allocate them. The fact that externalities, whether positive or negative, do not pass through the market system, results in some of our most intractable problems.

Pollution is the classic example of an externality problem. Pollution is the production of wastes that we do not want, such as industrial wastes, smoke, congestion, or noise. These externalities exist for various reasons. The first is technical: we do not know how to produce some goods without creating waste products. Second, even if we do know how to produce goods without creating waste, their production or consumption may be very expensive without those externalities. For example, an automobile manufacturer may find it cheaper to drain industrial waste into a nearby river than to ship it to a waste dump. Neither the factory owners nor the customers pay for this use of the river. The river is a scarce resource, however, and degrading it does not take into account the rights of those downstream to fish or swim in it, or enjoy it for other forms of recreation or natural beauty. Consequently, the cost of the pollution is borne by the public at large. If these external costs could be taken into account and charged to the producer or consumer, it would result in a higher price and a necessarily lower output equal to the socially efficient level of output. This is an external cost—a cost not reflected in market prices. That cost, moreover, is imposed on the public without its consent. In the example of the automobile, since the cost of such pollution is not reflected in the price of the car, the factory will tend to produce more cars (and pollution) than is socially desirable.

Third, as in the case of health care, markets fail when lack of information results in decisions that do not meet the criteria of rationality. For example, scientists conducting the first nuclear tests were unaware of the devastating effects that radiation had on human health. If they had been, different decisions might have been made.

And finally, self-interest, a major principle of the free market, fails to take into account the future interests of the community. There should be a preference for policies that are not irreversible. A fisherman catching an endangered species may not worry about the impact of the extinction of the species on future generations. Many individual choices will make it very difficult to go back and choose an alternative that was rejected. But policy choices should not be of the sort that irrevocably close out other options. For example, many conservationists feel that policies aimed at preserving endangered species from extinction should rank above those aimed at maintaining jobs, since new jobs can be created but once a species is extinct its loss is irreversible.

Thus there arise demands for the government to intervene and change the market outcome through laws and regulations. Those who argue against government intervention to control externalities emphasize that business is, or can be, socialized to be responsible through voluntarism. But there are many instances where feelings of social responsibility and voluntarism are not sufficient. In the early 1960s, despite mounting public pressure to reduce auto pollution, car manufacturers lobbied against legislation to mandate pollution control devices. The auto makers in a public relations campaign gave assurances that they were conducting research, but solving the problem was extremely difficult. In 1963, California passed a law requiring pollution control devices on all new cars sold within one year after a state board had certified that at least two systems were available at reasonable cost. California certified four devices, made by independent parts manufacturers, and mandated their requirement on 1966-model cars. Although automobile manufacturers had insisted that they would not be able to produce such devices before 1967 at the earliest, they announced that they would be able to install emission control devices on their 1996-model cars.[1]

We have already seen how positive externalities, such as those resulting from education, will tend to be undersupplied in the market. In such cases, government may respond to raise output to a socially optimal level by subsidizing their cost through student loans or research programs. Likewise, government must oversee solutions to negative environmental externalities. As Figure 12.1 suggests, economic efficiency requires greater expenditures on environmental protection than would occur in a free market. The equilibrium price (E) does not include the positive benefits received by others. If a firm installs pollution control equipment in its smokestacks, it will have a social marginal benefit higher (E') than its private marginal benefit. A firm that takes only its private interests into account will operate at point E, and not voluntarily install equipment to provide a situation where margin-

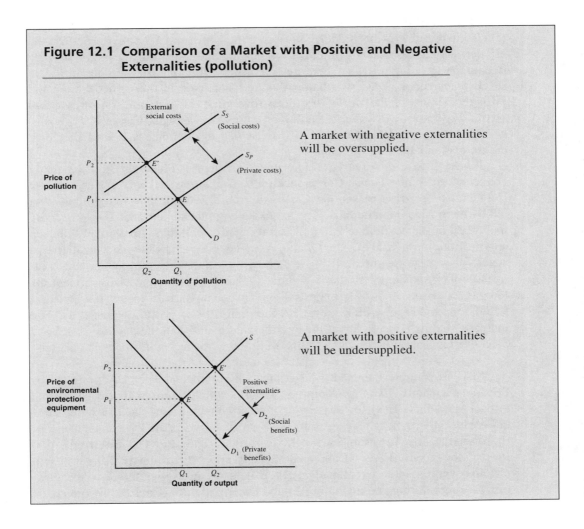

Figure 12.1 Comparison of a Market with Positive and Negative Externalities (pollution)

A market with negative externalities will be oversupplied.

A market with positive externalities will be undersupplied.

al social benefits equal the marginal costs for society, at point E'. A major public policy role for the government, then, is to correct for market inefficiencies that result from externalities.

Environmental Politics in the United States

Growing affluence after World War II resulted in ever-increasing numbers of people spending leisure time traveling, hiking, and camping outdoors, which increased their commitment to preserving wildlife and areas of natural beauty. Scholars also began documenting scientific evidence of environmental degradation. The publication of Rachel Carson's book *Silent Spring* in 1962 was an important contribution to the modern environmental movement. She warned of the effects of toxins as they move up the food chain, and argued that a fragile balance in nature was being upset by the excessive use of DDT on bird reproduction. As a result of her book, DDT was banned as an insecticide in the United States and throughout most of the world. The disastrous effect of pesticides on birds was a warning of the risk of chemical pollution to humans as well. Carson's work suggested the interconnectedness of all life, which has become a central theme of environmentalists.

Reacting to the increased environmental concern, President John Kennedy convened the White House Conference on Conservation in 1962. Kennedy and a Democratic Congress passed the Clean Air Act of 1963 despite fierce opposition led by the business community. The act had a complicated enforcement procedure that relied on state action to initiate lawsuits against polluters. In 1965 the Johnson administration passed the Water Quality Act. Federal grants were made available to states for sewage treatment plants to improve water quality. But again, conservatives wrote provisions into the law allowing states to formulate plans to meet the federal standards. In 1969 a major oil spill in Santa Barbara received significant television coverage, which increased the visibility of pollution disasters. The increased public concern about the environment resulted in the passage of several pieces of legislation in the early 1970s. Both Republicans and Democrats vied with each other to prove themselves as the real champions of the environment.

In 1969, Congress passed the National Environmental Policy Act (signed by President Richard Nixon on January 1, 1970), which requires an environmental impact statement (EIS) for any major federal construction. The EIS must show either that government projects will not significantly impair the environment or that satisfactory steps can be taken to mitigate damage. The Environmental Protection Agency (EPA) was created in 1970; prior to that, many different agencies in several federal departments, such as Interior and Agriculture, had responsibility for monitoring and regulating air and water pollution. The EPA was given the responsibility to enforce environmental laws regulating toxic waste, air and water pollutants, as well as solid waste and pesticides.

In 1970, Congress renewed the Clean Air Act and set national standards for ambient air quality. Congress also set a timetable for the reduction of auto hydrocarbon, carbon monoxide, and nitrogen oxide emissions. The 1970 act was intended "to protect and enhance the quality of the Nation's air resources so as to promote the public health and welfare."[2] The EPA was directed to promulgate the National Ambient Air Quality Standards (NAAQS) in an effort to limit the amount of certain pollutants in the atmosphere that adversely affect public health—sulfur oxides, particulates, carbon monoxide, hydrocarbons, nitrous oxides, and photochemical oxidants. The act required states to adopt plans to meet NAAQS requirements. After approval by the EPA, each state was required to enforce its plan. The EPA was given the authority to prepare and enforce a state plan if it did not meet federal requirements. The EPA was also to set exhaust emission standards for the auto industry and require the use of catalytic converters and the use of fuels with reduced lead.

The Water Pollution Control Act amendments of 1972, passed over President Nixon's veto, attempted to limit the discharge of pollutants into navigable waters by 1985. It provided $25 billion in grants for local governments to build waste treatment plants and to install the best-available technologies by 1983. The Clean Water Act of 1977 allowed for more flexibility in meeting compliance deadlines and effluent limitation requirements.

Industrial expansion after World War II resulted in the disposal of enormous amounts of solid and hazardous wastes into the atmosphere, into the water, and onto the land. The potentially dangerous impact on the atmosphere and groundwater of hazardous waste dumping was apparent. Since the states controlled waste disposal, some industries were encouraged to shop for states with the weakest regulatory controls. Congress finally responded with the Resource Conservation and Recovery Act of 1976, which required that hazardous waste storage and disposal be regulated so as to minimize the threat to public health and the environment. The EPA was authorized to establish standards for the disposal of hazardous waste.

A serious weakness in several pieces of environmental legislation in the 1970s was that the EPA had to negotiate with states and local governments to obtain compliance. The agency simply did not have the personnel or the budget to force compliance in an efficient manner.

Nonetheless, many states began to complain that they were overburdened by these environmental laws. By the late 1970s, critics began complaining that environmental legislation was causing inflation and slowing down economic growth. Business and conservation groups began mounting a counterattack against environmentalists. They ultimately argued that, while the excesses of the past could not continue, "reasonable" future controls would allow the environment to purify itself. They pointed out how a certain amount of pollution is inevitable in a growing economy. Therefore, they claimed, the benefits of any environmental regulation must be balanced against the economic costs to business. There was general acceptance of the view that little additional legislation to protect the environment was necessary. Ronald Reagan wove these views into his campaign for president in 1980; he was not opposed to "reasonable" environmentalism, he said, but the government had gone too far.

Reagan interpreted his victory as clear support for a reversal of the federal government's role in environmental protection. His administration moved immediately to repeal several regulations approved by the Carter administration. He appointed individuals who were openly hostile to the federal government's role in environmental policy, such as Ann Gorsuch Burford to head the EPA and James Watt as secretary of interior.[3] Several thousand EPA employees were fired, including many attorneys experienced in environmental law. The entire staff of the President's Council on Environmental Quality, whose views were unapologetically environmentalist, was fired.

The Reagan administration required that any new EPA regulation clear a cost-benefit analysis hurdle, one with a built-in bias against regulation. The administration claimed that it was using cost-benefit analysis as a neutral tool to make sure that the dollar benefits of any proposed regulation exceeded the dollar costs. The problem was that no uncontested dollar value could be assigned to the value of a human life, let alone to the value of an endangered species like the spotted owl or the beauty of a natural setting, while the costs incurred by industry were more precisely quantifiable. As a result, most new regulations were predestined to fail the test of cost-benefit analysis. The Reagan administration was less interested in protecting the environment than in encouraging industrial growth through reduced regulation. Reagan's antagonism toward environmental policy galvanized renewed support for environmental organizations and policy.

In 1988, George H.W. Bush campaigned for vigorous action to improve the environment. He indicated that he wanted to be known as "the environmental president." Indeed, one of his more famous charges against his opponent, Michael Dukakis, was that he had not cleaned up the pollution of Boston Harbor. During the first two years of his term, President Bush supported amendments to the Clean Air Act, put areas of the U.S. coastline off-limits for oil exploration, approved an increase in the EPA budget, and was generally supportive of other environmental issues. In 1990, Congress approved Clean Air Act amendments that provided far stricter regulations than those Bush had proposed. Bush reluctantly signed the amendments but indicated his reluctance to enforce them.

Environmentalists became disenchanted during the last two years of Bush's term. They charged that his administration had undermined the most dynamic provisions of the Clean Air Act by waiving rules that would have restricted pollutants from automobile, chemical, and pharmaceutical industries. Bush also refused to support an environmental treaty at the 1992 Earth Summit, held in Rio de Janeiro, until its provisions designed to slow global warming were watered down. As well, he refused to sign a second treaty at the same summit designed to protect endangered species. In the 1992 presidential campaign, Bush dismissed his Democratic opponents, Bill Clinton and Al Gore, as dangerous "environmental crazies." Clinton campaigned on a pledge to take an activistist stance on the environment and reverse his Republican predecessors' weak record.

The new administration did install forceful administrators committed to environmentalism, such as Secretary of Interior Bruce Babbitt, in critical agencies. But for most of Clinton's two terms he was confronted with an aggressive congressional majority controlled by Republicans intent on frustrating most of the president's policy initiatives. Clinton was forced to back down and was defeated by Congress in several of his environmental efforts. For example, administration proposals to elevate the EPA administrator to the cabinet, to overhaul the Clean Water Act of 1972, and to strengthen the "superfund" effort to clean up hazardous waste sites were all defeated by Congress. After the Republican takeover of both houses in 1994, the Republican majority set out to implement its "Contract with America," proposing legislation to reduce the federal government's ability to enact regulations. President Clinton was thrown on the defensive and took a policy stance designed to neutralize the Republican momentum of environmental deregulation. Clinton took up international environmental policymaking negotiations, the most notable being a commitment to the Kyoto Protocol to control global warming. However, the Senate refused to give its consent to the treaty, thereby preventing its ratification.

The environmental movement was united in opposition to the election of George W. Bush and his vice presidential candidate, Dick Cheney, who had a record, as a congressman and as the chief executive officer of Halliburton, of opposition to government regulation. The new president insisted he was a moderate on environmental issues and would support reasonable reforms. However, the worst fears of many environmentalists seemed to be validated from the beginning of Bush's presidency, when the administration filled critical policymaking jobs in the EPA and the Departments of Energy, Justice, Interior, and Agriculture with individuals from the very industries they were to regulate. By the end of Bush's first term in 2004, the environmental community was unanimous in its criticism of the administration's environmental record.

Antienvironmental Politics

In 2002, the Natural Resources Defense Council (NRDC), an environmentalist organization, began publishing an annual report documenting the antienvironmental actions of the Bush-Cheney administration.[4] The report is a devastating indictment of troubling policy decisions.

Failure to enforce.   Criminal penalties against polluting industries dropped during the first two years of the administration by more than one-third (to $62 million), while new referrals dropped by over 40 percent and civil penalties dropped by almost half (to $55 million).[5] Bush's budget requests to Congress have called for cuts in hundreds of enforcement personnel positions. The EPA administrator meanwhile lauded the agency's "smart enforcement approach," which emphasizes voluntary compliance rather than punishing corporations for violating pollution laws.[6] One example that received wide publicity was the EPA's lack of enforcement of the Safe Drinking Water Act, including inspections and administrative penalties, against the District of Columbia's Water and Sewer Authority (WASA), which declined significantly after President Bush took office. In 2003, studies found significant levels of lead in the water in about two-thirds of the homes tested. The EPA chose not to levy fines against D.C.'s city government and declined to force WASA to take action. The EPA opted to give D.C. officials almost fifteen years to replace the lead pipes causing the problem. Nor did the EPA require WASA to inform residents about the health hazard posed by the city's lead problem. The *Washington Post* published a series of articles indicating that the EPA and the city knew about the dangerous level of lead in the water for over two years and did nothing. Local health officials, responding to pressure from the newspaper articles, not the EPA, recommended that pregnant women and children under the age of six should not drink unfiltered tap water and should have their blood tested for lead.[7]

Sewage in waterways and drinking water.   During the Clinton administration, the EPA proposed to address the problem of the contamination of beaches and rivers by bacteria, fecal matter, and other wastes from sewage releases through new Clean Water Act rule-making. A consensus agreement was reached after exhaustive hearings and negotiations that included environmentalists and federal, state, and local authorities. The Bush administration, upon taking office in January 2001, shelved the proposal for three years of "internal review." The administration ultimately proposed to legalize the release of inadequately treated sewage into waterways, as long as it was diluted with treated sewage, a process the EPA delicately labeled "blending."

The state of Florida is injecting treated sewage into deep wells despite concerns that contaminants such as cryptosporidium and giardia, bacteria that cause illness in humans, could migrate up into the drinking water supply. Studies have in fact found that this is precisely what is happening. Although the Safe Drinking Water Act rules require waste injection to be stopped in such situations, the EPA has proposed a special exemption for Florida to allow the injection of treated sewage to continue.[8]

Mercury pollution. Power plants and other industries discharge over 150 tons of mercury into the air each year. Because methylmercury accumulates in the blood, it is particularly dangerous for pregnant women, as it disrupts the brain development of fetuses, causing attention disorders, learning disabilities, and mental retardation. Fetuses and children are especially at risk to mercury because of their developing nervous systems. This hazardous air pollutant is deposited in lakes and streams and enters the food chain through a buildup in fish. In 2003, forty-four states issued warnings for eating mercury-tainted fish, a 63 percent increase from a decade earlier, when twenty-seven states issued such warnings. Utility officials often claimed they were unaware they were in violation of the EPA's interpretation of the law until the agency began filing high-profile enforcement lawsuits in 1999. Internal electric utility documents made public in 2004 disclosed that the industry knew for more than a decade that enormous increases in mercury pollution violated the Clean Air Act.

The Bush administration refused to regulate mercury through the same standards applied to other hazardous air pollutants under the Clean Air Act. The administration proposed weaker regulations for mercury emissions, essentially pardoning an industry that withheld potentially harmful information from the public. Substantial parts of the administration's mercury proposals were taken verbatim from recommendations from the lobbyists representing the electric utility industry.[9]

Wilderness preservation program. The federal policy at the heart of the wilderness preservation program protects public lands while federal land managers assessed them for possible inclusion as officially designated wilderness areas. In 2003 the EPA settled a suit with the state of Utah in which the administration "renounced the government's authority to conduct wilderness inventories on public lands or to protect more areas for their wilderness values."[10] The settlement was made without public comment or input. This reversal of federal policy jeopardizes millions of acres of public lands and allows industry to apply for drilling, mining, road-building, and other development rights.

Lobbyists, scientists, and administration policy choices. Environmentalists were particularly exasperated that the Bush administration made a public pretense of support for environmentally friendly policies, while secretly allowing major polluters to help draft policy. For example, an analysis of the administration's plan to regulate mercury emissions from coal-fired power plants revealed that at least a dozen paragraphs were lifted from law firm memos that represented the utility industry.[11] Federal judges have a long history of deference to the EPA's technical expertise in these scientifically complex issues and have refrained from overturning agency decisions on the environment. However, federal judges have halted EPA actions in several cases that were found to be blatantly inconsistent with existing environmental laws.[12]

In an unprecedented event in 2004, over 4,000 scientists, including 48 Nobel Prize winners and 127 members of the National Academy of Sciences, accused the Bush administration of suppressing, distorting, or manipulating scientific fact and misleading the public to suit its own partisan political objectives.[13] Among other examples, the administration's bending of science to policy includes:

- Ordering substantial changes to a section on global warming in the EPA's 2003 environment report. The entire section was subsequently deleted.
- Replacing a Centers for Disease Control and Prevention fact sheet on proper condom use with a warning emphasizing condom failure rates.
- Ignoring advice from Department of Energy nuclear materials experts who warned that aluminum tubes imported by Iraq were not suitable for use in making nuclear weapons.
- Suppressing a Department of Agriculture microbiologist's finding that potentially harmful drug-resistant bacteria float in the air in the area of large hog farms.
- Excluding from regulatory advisory panels scientists who receive federal grants, while permitting the appointment of scientists from regulated industries.[14]

The administration rejected these criticisms as misleading and politically motivated. Political reaction to the administration's antienvironmental policies revealed the weakness of the environmental lobby.

Protest Politics
A well-known environmental slogan is "Think globally, act locally." And in fact, many of the successes of the environmentalist movement have been at the local or national rather than the international level, although international efforts have been

growing. The inability to prevent the Bush administration from reversing many environmental initiatives with impunity reflects the tendency of much environmental action to occur in the form of protest politics, whose main action often takes the form of street marches and demonstrations. But protest politics are often associated with human rights movements, such as those for feminist, gay, and lesbian rights, that often pursue their goals outside the ordinary channels of political parties and legislative assemblies. This may reduce their political influence.

Policy Debates on Environmental Issues

As with other public policy issues examined in this book, there is spirited debate regarding what role, if any, the government should play in environmental policy. Most people admit to being concerned about environmental degradation at some level. But individual views differ markedly about the perceived level of threat to the environment from different sources (such as global warming, ozone depletion, or deforestation). Experts often differ regarding the nature of the threats as well as the most effective responses to them. Frequently, there is sufficient scientific uncertainty to allow people to reach different conclusions based on the same evidence.

Global Warming: Clear Facts and Hazy Conclusions

Over a century ago, Swedish chemist Svante Arrhenius theorized that all the carbon dioxide and other gases being released from burning vast amounts of coal were trapping solar heat in Earth's atmosphere, similar to the way the glass roof and walls of a greenhouse trap solar energy. He predicted that **global warming** would occur: industrialization would release more gases into the atmosphere, trapping increasing amounts of solar heat and causing global temperatures to rise several degrees. Only in recent years, however, has scientific study proven that Earth is getting warmer due to the environmental effects of **greenhouse gas** (GHG) concentrations. Greenhouse gases are atmospheric gases that are almost transparent to incoming solar energy, but trap infrared energy reflected from Earth's surface. There are about twenty such gases, but scientists primarily focus on carbon dioxide (CO_2), the predominant greenhouse gas, which occurs naturally, as do other GHGs such as methane, nitrous oxide, and water vapor. Each greenhouse gas differs in its ability to absorb heat in the atmosphere. For instance, methane traps over 21 times more heat per molecule than does carbon dioxide, and nitrous oxide absorbs 270 times more heat per molecule than does carbon dioxide.[15] The primary greenhouse gases are considered **stock pollutants**, which means that they have a long lifetime in the atmosphere and therefore can build up over time. Carbon dioxide, for example, has an atmospheric lifetime of between 100 and 200 years.[16] Given the long lifetime of GHGs, they tend to be well mixed in the atmosphere, independent of where they were emitted. This suggests that problems associated with GHGs must ultimately be addressed on an international scale.

As solar radiation, or heat from the sun, approaches Earth, about 30 percent is absorbed by the atmosphere and by Earth's surface; the rest is reflected back into space. GHGs permit solar radiation to pass relatively freely to Earth's surface, but then trap significant amounts in the atmosphere that would otherwise be reflected back into space. Without the **greenhouse effect** to prevent some radiation from escaping, life on Earth would be impossible. The GHGs produce the greenhouse effect, without which Earth's temperature would be about sixty degrees Fahrenheit colder. At the other extreme, a runaway greenhouse effect, extremely unlikely, could change long-term weather patterns and make Earth unbearably hot.

In 1995 the United Nations Intergovernmental Panel on Climate Change, a worldwide network of 2,500 leading scientists, announced that the evidence of global warming was "undeniable." Nor is there any doubt that the buildup of GHGs is largely the result of human activities. According to the EPA, the United States emits more greenhouse gases per person (approximately 6.6 tons, or about one-fifth of all global GHGs) than does any other country.[17] About 82 percent of the emissions result from burning fossil fuels to generate electricity and to fuel our cars. The remaining emissions are from methane from landfill waste, livestock, natural gas pipelines, coal, and other industrial chemicals and sources.

According to the National Academy of Sciences, average global temperatures have risen about one degree Fahrenheit in the past century. Accelerated warming has occurred during the past two decades and there has been an unexplained jump in carbon dioxide levels since 2002.[18] The ten warmest years of the twentieth century all occurred after 1985, with 1998 being the warmest year since records have been maintained. Global warming is greatest in the polar regions, where average temperatures are rising more than twice as fast as they are elsewhere. Snow cover, glaciers, and ice in the polar regions have retreated, which accelerates global warming. Melting glaciers contribute to rising sea levels and threaten low-lying areas with erosion and coastal flooding. Over the past century the sea level has risen about six inches. Scientists project as much as a three-foot sea-level rise by 2100. That increase would flood over 22,400 square miles of land along the Atlantic and Gulf coasts in the United States alone. For example, a three-foot rise would extensively flood New York City, Houston, Charleston, South Florida, and many coastal towns along the East Coast. Many other countries, such as the Netherlands, Egypt, Bangladesh, and China, would face even more extreme problems.

There are strong possibilities that a warmer world would lead to more frequent and intense storms, such as hurricanes. There is some evidence that once hurricanes are formed, they will be stronger if the oceans are warmer. Projections also suggest that the temperature in some areas will rise between three and ten degrees Fahrenheit. An increase of that magnitude could cause severe problems and disruptions for human society.

Now that global warming has moved from an abstract threat to an urgent reality, the policy debate concerns what to do about it. We do not know precisely how much and how fast global warming will occur. Nor is it clear what the beneficial and adverse effects will be. We do not know if we can determine the cost of reducing GHGs, or if the computer-generated models of global warming are accurate.

Most political leaders around the world have been reluctant to act on the early warnings, for fear that reducing emissions of carbon dioxide would require actions that would undercut economic growth. International pressure to take action has begun to build, however. For example, deforestation in Brazil increases the amount of carbon dioxide in the atmosphere by destroying the trees necessary to absorb it. When the trees are burned, even more carbon dioxide is added to the atmosphere.

Since most GHGs come from power plants and vehicles, the most effective way to reduce heat-trapping gases in the atmosphere is to burn fewer fossil fuels. The technology already exists to make cars that run cleaner and get better gas mileage. Power plants can be modernized to reduce pollution. Buildings and appliances like refrigerators and air conditioners can be designed to use less power. Senators John McCain and Joe Lieberman proposed legislation to reduce global warming by requiring a reduction in carbon dioxide emission to 2000 levels by the year 2010. The bill proposed capping overall GHG emissions from electricity generation, and would allow utility, transportation, and industrial firms to trade pollution credits based on the successful acid rain trading program of the 1990 Clean Air Act. Although the Bush administration opposed any action on global warming, the bill was defeated by a relatively narrow margin of forty-three to fifty-five, which many took as a sign of growing support for action.

Greenhouse Gases and the Climate Treaty

In the summer of 1992, the Conference on Environment and Development, better known as the Earth Summit, was held in Rio de Janeiro. It focused attention on the environmental concerns of developing countries. The Rio Declaration on the Environment and Development set forth twenty-eight guiding principles to reinforce global environmental authority. The George H.W. Bush administration was severely criticized for its refusal to support the declaration and the work of other industrial nations to produce timetables and goals for the reduction of the greenhouse gas emissions that cause global warming. The Clinton administration proved to be much more positive in its support for environmental regulations, and in par-

Case Study: Acid Rain

Acid rain is any precipitation, whether rain, snow, sleet, hail, or fog, that is acidic. Acidic water has a pH lower than the 5.6 average of rainwater. The term **pH** refers to the free hydrogen ions (electrically charged atoms) in water and is measured on a scale from 0 to 14. On this scale, 7 is considered neutral; measurements below 7 indicate acidity, and those above indicate alkalinity. Each point on the scale represents a tenfold increase over the previous number. For example, a pH of 3 is ten times more acidic than a pH of 4, and a pH of 9 is ten times more alkaline than a pH of 8.

Actually, rain is naturally acidic, because carbon dioxide, which is found normally in Earth's atmosphere, combines with water to form carbonic acid. "Pure" rainwater's acidity is about 5.7, but actual pH readings vary depending primarily on the sulfur dioxide (SO_2) and nitrogen oxides (NO_x) present in the air. Rainfall with a pH below 5.6 is considered acidic. Some acid rain falling in the eastern U.S. has been in the range of pH 3.5. Sulfur dioxide and nitrogen oxides are pumped into the atmosphere by coal-fired electric utilities, smelter smokestacks, and motor vehicle exhausts. About half of the acidity in the atmosphere falls back to Earth's surface as dry deposition of acidic particles and gases. These dry deposits can be washed from trees and other surfaces by rainstorms. When this happens, the runoff water adds to the acid in the rain. When these pollutants combine with water vapor, they form either sulfuric or nitric acid and then return to Earth's surface as acid rain. In the United States, electric utilities are responsible for over two-thirds of all sulfur oxides, and motor vehicles are responsible for over 40 percent of all nitrogen oxides. Sulfur dioxide

is about twice as acidic as nitrogen oxides. Predictably, NO_x emissions are more evenly dispersed around the nation than sulfur oxides, which are concentrated in the Ohio Valley. However, high smokestacks, electric utilities, and industries in the valley have reduced local sulfur dioxide concentrations. Typically, these oxides are then carried by the prevailing winds for hundreds of miles in a northeasterly direction before returning to Earth's surface as precipitation.

Acid rain contributes to the deterioration of metal and stone in buildings and statues. It has also been linked to health problems like asthma, emphysema, and chronic bronchitis. The New England states and Canada have linked the acidity of rivers and lakes, and the resultant destruction of aquatic life and forest, to emissions originating in the Ohio Valley. Aquatic plants grow best in water that has a pH of 7 to 9. But as acidity increases, aquatic plants begin to die, depriving waterfowl of their food source. At a pH of about 5.5, the bottom-dwelling bacteria that decompose leaf and organic debris begin to die. As undecomposed organic leaf-litter increases, toxic metals such as aluminum and mercury accumulate, harming people who drink the water or eat its tainted fish. Most frogs, insects, and fish die when the water reaches a pH of 4.5.

The amendments to the Clean Air Act of 1990 did establish goals and deadlines for a two-phase reduction in sulfur and nitrous dioxide emissions, and caps on future sulfur dioxide emissions; they also created a system of marketable "allowances" for allocating reductions from different emissions sources. Since 1995, electrical utilities must obtain a permit for each ton of sulfur dioxide they emit. These permits are distributed in limited supply to utilities each year by the govern-

continues

Case Study   continued

ment, and can be resold among the utilities. They roughly reflect the per ton costs of pollution control. It was expected in the early 1990s, when the permits were being designed, that the per ton cost would be about $1,100. By 1997 they were selling for around $100. Compliance costs have been less expensive than either industry or the EPA had predicted. George W. Bush alarmed environmentalists when he proposed the construction of 1,800 new electric power plants while relaxing regulatory controls on new fossil fuel–burning electric utilities.

Sources: Adapted from Sharon M. Friedman and Kenneth A. Friedman, *Reporting on the Environment: A Handbook for Journalists* (Bangkok: Asian Forum of Environmental Journalists, 1988); and Thomas H. Moore, *Acid Rain: New Approach to Old Problem,* Editorial Research Report no. 9 (Washington, D.C.: Congressional Quarterly Press, March 9, 1991).

---

ticular for the timetable and emission targets to reduce greenhouse gas emissions in the 1997 Kyoto Protocol. On Earth Day in 1993, President Clinton announced his Climate Change Action Plan, which included a series of voluntary programs to persuade companies to cooperate with federal agencies to improve energy efficiency and reduce GHGs. The goal was to have the United States meet is goal of reducing its carbon emissions to 1990 levels by the year 2000 through voluntary actions rather than mandatory regulations. In 1996 the United States announced that it had abandoned its call for voluntary steps to reduce GHG emissions and would press instead for legally binding targets and timetables in the treaty negotiations in Kyoto, Japan, where negotiators would try to produce a treaty on climate change.

The United Nations Framework Convention on Climate Change was adopted in Kyoto in 1997. It was to enter into force only after at least fifty-five parties to the convention, the sum of whose CO_2 emissions accounted for at least 55 percent of the world total, had ratified it. Many industries in the United States were adamantly opposed to bound targets and timetables, and aggressively sought help in Congress to defeat any agreement that would require mandatory cuts in GHG emissions. Although Clinton had signed the protocol, George W. Bush, shortly after his inauguration in January 2001, announced that his administration had no interest in implementing it. The announcement infuriated U.S. environmentalists and European nations. The Bush administration, forced to respond to both domestic and international environmental opposition, defended its actions by pointing out that restrictions in the United States would be greater than in developing countries. Many complained that the U.S. refusal would slow the ratification process, which it did. The United States emits more CO_2 than any other country, with 22 percent of global CO_2 emissions (almost all from fossil fuel combustion). In the fall of

2004, the convention finally came into effect when Russia ratified it, bringing the number of signatories to over 100 and the sum of their CO_2 emissions to over 55 percent of the world total. Commitment was popular in Western Europe, which had become frustrated with a series of foreign policy decisions by the Bush administration that reflected disinterest for that part of the world.

Environmental policy is often caught between the competing concepts of sovereignty over domestic resources (e.g., domestic business and financial sectors that want to lower the cost of production by reducing environmental controls), and the international legal obligation not to damage the environment of other states. Many environmental problems, such as acid rain, are transboundary; for example, a downstream nation may bear the major brunt of the pollution produced by an upstream nation. International environmental diplomacy is just beginning to emerge as a force to mitigate the force of unbridled sovereignty and encourage the development of a global environmental consciousness. There is growing pressure to consider environmental issues within international diplomacy, rather than after issues of national security and economics have been resolved. Environmentally concerned states and organizations have forced the Bush administration to reluctantly acknowledge the significance of international environmental concerns.

Ozone Depletion

Stratospheric ozone depletion is undoubtedly the best example of the international community accepting the scientific characterization of an environmental problem and successfully mobilizing a global response.

Ozone (O_3), a molecule that comprises three oxygen atoms, is the most frequent chemical implicated in depletion of the stratosphere. Ninety percent of all atmospheric ozone is found in the stratosphere, which ranges from approximately twelve to thirty-five miles above Earth's surface. Most of the upper-level ozone is concentrated about fifteen miles above Earth's surface in what is known as the "ozone layer." Ozone occupies only a small fraction of Earth's atmosphere, but its existence is extremely important to all forms of life, since it is the only gas that absorbs most lethal ultraviolet-B (UV-B) radiation from the sun and reduces it to reasonably safe levels. Depletion of the ozone shield allows more UV-B to reach Earth's surface, producing increased rates of skin cancer, eye cataracts, and weakened immune systems in humans. It also damages ecosystems, resulting in decreased photosynthesis in plants and reduces crop and fish yields. While ultraviolet radiation is necessary to synthesize vitamin D, it also damages DNA, which is the protein code necessary for cell reproduction. Animal and plant life on Earth has adapted to "natural" levels of UV-B. Without such UV protection, most life forms experience cell damage. Without the ozone layer, much higher levels of UV-B would reach Earth's surface, wiping out most life on the planet.

Chlorofluorocarbons (CFCs), first created in 1928, are a family of nonreactive, nontoxic, and nonflamable gases and liquids. Their properties soon made them valuable for use as refrigerants, in urethane and polyurethane foam for insulation, and in fast food wrappings, aerosol sprays, and other convenience items. Because CFCs are nonreactive, unlike ozone, they have expected lifetimes of twenty-five to thirty years per molecule and may drift in the environment for years until they reach the stratosphere. They are insoluble and therefore unaffected by rainfall. Scientists estimate that it takes six to ten years for the average CFC molecule to reach the stratosphere through convection and diffusion. Once there, UV radiation decomposes the CFCs, producing chlorine, which acts as a catalyst—a compound that can be used repeatedly in a reaction without being consumed—in breaking down ozone. Consequently, the resulting chlorine atom is not used up in the process. One chlorine atom can break down well over 100,000 molecules of ozone before it becomes part of a less reactive compound and is precipitated out of the stratosphere in water. The level of chlorine in the atmosphere is estimated to be about six times higher now than it was at the turn of the century. Other CFCs, like halons, which are primarily used in fire extinguishers, have far more ozone-depleting capabilities than does chlorine.

Ozone, an unstable atom, is primarily produced over the tropics, where solar radiation is strongest, and then diffused through air circulation toward the polar regions. Therefore, ozone tends to be spread thinner at the poles. Although we often refer to an "ozone layer," what actually exists is a diffusion of O_3 throughout the upper reaches of the stratosphere, not a "layer" of pure ozone. If the ozone in the stratosphere were compressed to surface pressures, the layer would be less than two inches thick.

By the mid-1970s, laboratory studies demonstrated the ability of CFCs to break down ozone in the presence of UV light, and projected that CFCs would deplete the ozone layer by about 7 percent within sixty years. In 1985 a team of British and U.S. scientists confirmed the existence of a "hole" in the ozone layer, covering an area greater than the United States, that lasted for several weeks of the Antarctic spring. Subsequent discoveries of ozone depletion over other areas. especially over the Arctic, led to considerable research to determine the specific forces behind ozone destruction. Studies by the National Aeronautics and Space Administration found by 1988 that the ozone layer around the entire globe was decreasing by 8 percent, a rate much faster than had been previously suspected. In 2000 the area of the ozone hole reached a record 18 million square miles. While no hole has appeared elsewhere, the ozone layer over the North Pole has thinned by up to 30 percent, while the depletion over Europe and other high latitudes varies from 5 to 30 percent.[19]

In 1985 the Vienna Convention for the Protection of the Ozone Layer encouraged international cooperation on research, systematic observation of the ozone layer, and monitoring of CFC production. A stronger agreement, to limit CFCs, could not be reached, because some members of the United Nations wanted a phaseout of CFCs while others wanted production caps. In 1987 a compromise was reached and the Montreal Protocol, signed by 184 countries, placed quantitative limits on the production and consumption of CFCs and halons. The protocol was designed so that the phase-out schedules could be revised on the basis of periodic scientific assessments. Funds were also provided to pay the incremental costs incurred by developing countries in phasing out their production of ozone-depleting substances. The protocol was amended on five different occasions to introduce new control measures and to add new controlled substances to the list; ninety-six chemicals are now controlled for. Governments are not legally bound until they ratify the protocol as well as each successive amendment.

The results of the protocol have been most gratifying. Without it, ozone depletion by 2050 had been projected to double the amount of UV-B radiation reaching Earth's surface in the northern middle latitudes, and to quadruple the amount of radiation in the southern latitudes. Without the protocol, the ozone-depleting chemicals in the atmosphere would be five times greater by 2050, resulting in a staggering 19 million more cases of nonmelanoma cancer, 1.5 million more cases of melanoma cancer, and 130 million more cases of eye cataracts.[20] Instead, the total consumption of CFCs worldwide dropped from about 1.1 million tons in 1987 to about 110,000 tons in 2001.

The Montreal Protocol has been hailed as an extraordinary success. Scientists now predict that ozone depletion will reach its worst point during the next few years and then decline until the ozone layer returns to normal around 2050. The success of the international community's intervention was possible because science and industry were able to develop alternatives to ozone-depleting chemicals, allowing countries to end the use of CFCs more quickly and with less cost than originally anticipated. However, there is no room for complacency, since some countries have not yet ratified various amendments, and the global economic slowdown has made it difficult for others to comply. At the same time, illegal trade in CFCs has increased. Although all new CFCs are banned in developed countries, millions of CFC-dependent refrigerators and other equipment are still in service. Although there are alternatives to this equipment, they are often more expensive. Also, many chlorofluorocarbon-based refrigerators are being exported to the developing world by countries that have phased out the use of CFCs.

As well, CFCs are being replaced by hydrofluorocarbons (HFCs), such as ammonia and hydrocarbons, which have no ozone-depleting properties. However, HFCs have a high global-warming potential and are included in a basket of six greenhouse gases that are to be reduced by the industrialized states.

There are several lessons to be learned from the Montreal Protocol that can be applied to other environmental issues. First, a precautionary principle was applied. It was agreed that, to avoid potentially irreversible damage, the world had to take immediate action despite lacking complete scientific proof. Second, the negotiators sent consistent signals by adopting legally binding phase-out schedules so that industry had an incentive to develop efficient alternative technologies. The negotiators also took pains to ensure that improved scientific understanding could be easily incorporated in the treaty provisions. The negotiators encouraged broad participation by recognizing that while all had a common interest in the protocol, developed countries had a responsibility to provide the financial and technological support to developing countries to ease their cost of phasing out CFCs.

Hazardous Wastes

Most toxic and hazardous wastes are the direct result of the chemical revolution during and after World War II. Today, literally a ton of hazardous waste is produced for every person in the United States per year. Although most chemical wastes are harmless to humans and the ecosystem, many chemicals have not been thoroughly tested to determine their toxicity. However, cancer is probably the most widely dreaded impact of toxic wastes, and over 300 chemicals have been shown to be carcinogenic. Hundreds of other chemicals have been linked to other debilitating and even fatal diseases. Widely used pesticides have been identified as highly toxic, with many types having ingredients containing carcinogens.

Awareness of the dangers from toxic waste dumps was symbolized by public reaction to the discovery that a subdivision of Niagara Falls, New York, known as Love Canal had been built directly over a 20,000-ton highly toxic chemical waste dump. Many of the residents of Love Canal suffered a wide range of serious illnesses, from birth defects to cancers, as a result of the toxic contamination of the area. Their struggle motivated Congress to pass a law to clean up hazardous waste in 1980 known as the "superfund" legislation, which provided $1.6 billion to clean up the worst of the abandoned and hazardous waste sites. The legislation also provided a superfund corporate tax. The legislation required the EPA to prioritize a list of the nation's most dangerous hazardous waste sites, and begin cleaning up sites based on their ranking. By 1995, the year the superfund corporate tax expired, polluters were paying 85 percent of cleanup costs. In 2004, 79 percent of the superfund cleanup costs were paid by U.S. taxpayers while corporate polluters picked up the remainder.[21] By 2004 nearly 900 sites had been cleaned and removed from the list. Unfortunately, new sites are added as others are removed.

Because of the high costs involved, the debate over who should pay has been contentious from the start. Many in industry claim that since all Americans have profited from cheaper consumer goods that resulted from the improper disposal, taxpayers should pay for the cleanup. Environmentalists argue that since polluters have most directly profited from imposing negative externalities on the general public, they should be liable for the cleanup. The Comprehensive Environmental Response, Compensation, and Liability Act of 1980, however, is based on the "polluter pays" principle by holding anyone who produces or handles hazardous wastes strictly, jointly, and severally liable for cleanup and damages caused. When the federal regulations were enacted, however, no one understood the tremendous expense that would be involved in hazardous waste cleanup. Industry critics claim that many regulations impose unacceptable costs for the strict control of substances based on fragmentary evidence of risk. In their view, Congress and the EPA are overly risk-averse, preferring to err in the direction of stringent control and accepting the most pessimistic projection based on tenuous scientific evidence. Indeed, critics in both Bush administrations argued that costs and benefits should be given more weight in determining whether a substance should be regulated.

In the 1990s the scientific community began focusing on a long list of human-made synthetic chemicals known as endocrine disruptors, which can interfere with the endocrine system with catastrophic consequences. The endocrine system is composed of glands that secrete hormones that, together with the nervous system, integrate many different processes that allow the human body to function. Endocrine disruptors, if they are present in the right concentrations, can adversely effect hormone balance. According to the EPA's working definition, endocrine disruptors "interfere with the synthesis, secretion, transport, binding, action, or elimination of natural hormones in the body that are responsible for the maintenance of homeostasis (normal cell metabolism), reproduction, development, and/or behavior."[22] Many of the disruptors appear to accumulate in human tissue over long periods of time. The various health problems may include cancer of the reproductive system, reduced sperm counts in males, abnormalities of fetal development leading to learning and behavioral disorders, and other pathologies associated with hormonal malfunctions.[23] The chemical industry argues that risk aversion too often results in a regulatory intolerance for minimal health risks and excessive regulatory costs. The political chemistry, environmentalists claim, is one in which negatively inclined administrations combined with industry have slowed progress on the regulation of toxic and hazardous wastes beyond any justification.

Population

The sheer numbers concerning the world's population growth raise the specter of a collision between the expanding needs of human beings and the limits on human ability to increase production. Understanding the relationship between population, pollution, and poverty is necessary before one can consider policies to deal with these issues.

Throughout most of human history, the population has grown very slowly, with the net death rate nearly equal to the net birth rate, both of which have been high. The crude birth rate minus the crude death rate equals the increase in population for a given year. Mortality started to decline just as life expectancy started to increase, beginning in the late seventeenth century in Europe. Improving infant survival rates lead to potentially much larger populations to produce the next generation of children.

The world's population reached 1 billion around 1830. By 1900, Earth had a population of about 1.6 billion people. The global population quadrupled between 1900 and 2000. The population increase between 1990 and 2000 was equal to all those who lived in the seventeenth century. Significantly, 80 percent of the growth had taken place in the world's developing nations. It took several million years of human history to reach the first billion, about 130 years to reach the second, and today a new billion is added in less than about ten years. World population now stands at 6.5 billion, and is growing by about three people every second, or more than a quarter of a million people every day. As an illustration, the world is adding a city the size of New York every month. Between 90 and 100 million people— roughly equivalent to the population of Mexico—will be added each year of this decade. A billion people, almost the population of China, will be added over the decade. About 97 percent of the world's population growth now takes place in poorer and developing countries. In some countries, the rate of increase is over 3 percent per year, which means the population will double within twenty years. The result is that social dislocations caused by population growth are more severe in the poorer countries, which also tend to have the fewest natural resources. Several million will migrate to more industrialized countries, but most will remain in the country of their birth, taxing natural resources and adding to the burden of the local society.

Global Projections

The recent population growth has resulted not from increased birth rates but from worldwide decreases in the death rate. In the preceding millennia, plagues, famines, and epidemics kept normal death rates high and population growth rates very low. Although all living beings eventually die, it is mortality at an early age that keeps population growth rates low. With the decline of famines and epidemics and improvements in hygiene, death rates were significantly reduced in the industrialized states by the beginning of the twentieth century.

Throughout most of history, a large and growing population was invariably regarded as a sign of a robust and prospering society, while a small or declining population indicated decay. In the colonial eras of the eighteenth and nineteenth centuries, many believed that population size and national power were closely related. Even in the twentieth century, Nazi Germany initiated a pronatalist policy urging German women to produce more children. At the same time, Germany invaded neighboring states to appropriate additional living space for its growing population. To be sure, skeptics began pointing out that in the modern world, economic and technological superiority contributed more to national power than did population. It was on that basis that a small country like Great Britain could dominate the much larger populations of India and the Middle East. Since World War II, improved water and sewage treatment and the availability of antibiotics removed the major checks to population expansion, resulting in unprecedented growth.

Poor countries have traditionally sustained high levels of population growth to support agricultural production. But the modernization of agricultural production in those countries has displaced labor-intensive sharecropping systems in favor of mechanized farms using seasonal wage labor. As a result, urban areas have grown rapidly as unemployed farm workers search for jobs in cities. Continued population growth in many poorer countries has led to overcultivation and the destruction of rainforests in a search for new arable land. Desperately poor people are often driven to further ravage the environment in their struggle to survive. In many cases, the consequence is an actual decline in per capita agricultural production and a further increase in poverty. The gap between rich and poor widens. Hence, all too often, agricultural development has not only failed to eliminate poverty but also increased it, with unfortunate consequences for population growth and the environment.

Almost one-third of the world's 6.5 billion people are age fourteen or younger. Population growth will continue because of the momentum of large numbers of young people just reaching their reproductive years. An international environmental disaster characterized by starvation, unemployment, poverty, and civil unrest is not idle speculation. The basic concern regarding population growth has been put forward by the U.S. National Academy of Sciences and the UK Royal Society: "If current predictions of population growth prove accurate and patterns of human activity on the planet remain unchanged, science and technology may not be able to prevent either irreversible degradation of the environment or continued poverty for much of the world."[24] Because population growth rates are not evenly distributed around the world, there will be significantly altered population densities. For example, Europe and North America made up about 22 percent of the world population in 1950, but by 2025 they will make up less than 9 percent. By contrast, Africa, which made up 9 percent of the world's population in 1950, will make up approximately 20 percent in 2025. Over 90 percent of the global population growth over the next thirty-five years will occur in the developing countries of Africa, Asia, and Latin America. The sheer numbers indicate that there will be an increasing impact on the environment.

Migration from one country to another is also at an all-time high. In the mid-1990s about 125 million people, mostly in developing countries, lived outside the country in which they were born. At the same time, there is a systematic shift from rural to urban living. Problems arise when cities grow so rapidly that governments cannot provide the necessary public services, such as adequate housing and sanitation, and when the job market is unable to absorb all those who move to the cities.

There was a fear that continued population growth would lead to mass starvation, internal conflict, and perpetual poverty. In the late 1960s, fear of impending famine and environmental degradation encouraged the development of the first population policies. The idea that the state would provide family planning services to reduce the rate of population growth was a novel idea. Prior to this time, most contraceptives were awkward or illegal. The contraceptive pill in 1960 resulted in a revolution in sexual behavior and the idea of family planning in the United States.

In 1973, in *Roe v. Wade,* the Supreme Court struck down the laws outlawing abortion as a violation of the right to privacy inferred from the Fourth, Fifth, and Ninth Amendments to the Constitution and applied to the states through the due process clause of the Fourteenth Amendment. The Court held that states had no "compelling interest" to ban abortions during the first trimester, when abortions performed by qualified medical personnel are safer for the mother than is childbirth. During the second trimester, states may regulate abortions, as they become more dangerous as pregnancy progresses. During the third trimester, a fetus may survive outside the womb and therefore becomes a new "compelling interest" for the state.

By the 1990s the revival of the religious right challenged both the Court decision and the abortion providers. The Republican Party backed away from most family planning programs. The leaders of the Republican Party began to appeal explicitly to religious fundamentalists and to conservative Catholics on an antiabortion agenda that opposes all forms of family planning. The Democratic Party has consistently supported family planning and the right of women to make choices in this area.

International Population and Environmental Policies

There are two views of the ability of developing countries to adjust to changes in the environment and population growth to avoid economic decline. One is the **Cornucopian** position of Julian Simon, who opposes all attempts to restrain population growth. He believes that people are the highest resource, so it is unbeliev-

---

Case Study: U.S. Population Trends

The United States is the most populous of the developed countries and also has one of the highest population growth rates of the industrialized nations: about 1 percent annually. The Census Bureau reported that the U.S. population grew by 32.7 million people between 1990 and 2000, the largest single-decade population increase in the nation's history. In fact, between 1980 and 2000, population growth in the United States equaled the entire population of France (55 million people). This adds 2.75 million people to the population each year. The annual growth is equal to a city about the size of Chicago. The United States is almost the only advanced industrialized state with such a high rate of population increase.

There is a new birth in the United States about every seven seconds, a death about every thirteen seconds, and one net migrant gain every twenty-four seconds, which produces a net gain of one person every ten seconds.

The United States is undergoing a significant change in its geographic distribution.

The stream of immigrants into the country is highly directed toward six states—California, New York, Texas, Florida, New Jersey, and Illinois. And within these states the flow is primarily to a few metropolitan areas. The population within the United States is also shifting to the south and the west.

The nation is also undergoing significant changes in ethnic composition. Forty percent of the present population of the United States now comprises African American, Asian, and Hispanic minorities. Hispanics are now the largest minority, at 13.7 percent of the population, or 39.9 million (not counting 3.9 million in Puerto Rico). The Hispanic population is projected by the Census Bureau to rise from 13.7 percent of the population in 2004 to 24 percent by 2050 due to a combination of immigration and higher fertility.

Sources: U.S. Census Bureau, Public Information Office, http://www.census.gov/press-release; Carl Haub, "Global and U.S. National Population Trends," *Consequences* 1, no. 2 (Summer 1995).

---

able that a society can have too many people. According to Simon, people will use their creativity to develop technologies to provide for ever-growing population. Cornucopians historically have been right in that technological progress has allowed most Western economies to avoid the dire warnings of Malthus, because output has grown faster than population. Food production has increased faster than expected because of technological improvements, and populations have grown more slowly than anticipated. Higher standards of living and improved health care have increased life expectancy and reduced infant mortality. These factors have contributed to population growth. They have been offset, however, by the fact that children become an economic liability in developed societies. This has encouraged family planning and has contributed to the stabilization of populations in developed countries. Developed countries have also benefited from improved health care. There are fewer incentives for family planning in developing societies, where children are an economic asset as a source of labor. In countries without pension programs or social security, children may also be a source of support for parents in their old age. Unfortunately, many less developed agrarian countries have not been able to avoid Malthusian predictions because of diminishing marginal productivity. As more people live on a fixed amount of land, the output per worker declines. Even though the economies are growing, per capita growth is negligible or even declining.

The other view is known as **neo-Malthusian**, and as its name implies, its proponents believe that in the long run population will exceed the means of subsistence. Populations will increase to the limit that natural resources can support.

Paul Ehrlich is a leading exponent of the neo-Malthusian view. He developed an "impact equation" to explain the relationship between human beings and their environment: $I = P \times F(P)$, in which I is the total impact, P is the population, and F is a function that measures the per capita impact.[25] The larger the population, the greater the impact on the environment. A world population of less than 1 billion people in the 1600s had less of an environmental impact than did a population of 6 billion people at the end of the twentieth century. A larger population puts more stress on clean water and air than does a smaller population.

In addition to the size of the population, lifestyles have an impact on the environment. The lifestyle of an individual in an affluent country like the United States creates more of an environmental burden than the lifestyle of the typical Ethiopian. Americans make up about 6 percent of the world's population but are responsible for producing over two-thirds of the world's atmospheric carbon monoxide and almost one-half of its nitrogen oxide emissions.

Many charge that there are ethical implications for such affluence. They argue that if Americans ate less meat, more land could be used to raise grain to feed hungry people abroad. Currently, about one-quarter of world cropland, and 38 percent of grain production, are devoted to feeding livestock. In the United States this amounts to about 135 million tons of grain annually out of a total production of 312 million tons, sufficient to feed a population of 400 million people on a vegetarian diet.[26] A move away from diets high in animal protein toward a diet higher in vegetable protein would result in more grain being available for populations in poorer countries.

"Overpopulation" provided a rationale for advanced as well as developing nations to explain poverty's hold on much of the third world. It was easier to ascribe the lack of development to excessive population than to confront economic inequality, female subjugation, or other social, religious, or governmental factors that contribute to poverty and underdevelopment. When population issues did come to the fore, population control caught the attention of many Western nations, since it required few changes in the international social and economic structure. Many elites in developing countries also embraced overpopulation as an explanation for their societies' underdevelopment, and population control as the solution, since it provided them with a justification for their elite status and relieved them of responsibility for society's failures.

During the 1970s the United States encouraged developing countries to voluntarily limit population growth before it began to seriously erode living standards. In 1974 the United Nations held an intergovernmental conference on population. The United States lent its strong endorsement to the program and actively encouraged nations to adopt education programs for family planning; it was a major donor to the United Nations Population Fund, the International Planned Parenthood Federation, and other family planning programs in developing countries. At the conference, many developing countries criticized the U.S. position, arguing that poorer countries needed more economic assistance, not contraceptives. At a similar conference a decade later in Mexico City, the positions were reversed. Most developing countries were now in favor of family planning programs and actively sought assistance for that purpose. However, in the 1980s, Ronald Reagan and George H.W. Bush stopped all financial assistance for family planning and refused to cooperate with multilateral efforts to reduce population growth. Some nations that were usually closely allied with the United States, such as Canada, the United Kingdom, Japan, and Germany, increased their donations to the United Nations Population Fund to try to fill the void.

There are several reasons why the threat of population growth fails to attract our attention as a critical problem. The world's population grows by over 250,000 people a day, every day. What networks report as news usually involves climactic occurrence rather than daily happenings. Nevertheless, many of the consequences of overpopulation, such as deforestation, malnutrition and starvation, and toxic waste, do make the news on a daily basis.

Another reason overpopulation does not seem a serious threat is that Thomas Malthus's dire warnings of economic collapse resulting from growing populations have so far failed to materialize. While many aspects of the Malthusian analysis have proven wrong, Malthus did focus on at least two important points: that growing populations could be a problem, and that there is a relationship between population size and poverty. A growing population within a nation means that the national economy must grow by at least the same rate just to maintain the same standard of living. A country with a population growth rate of 2.7 percent a year must maintain economic growth of 2.7 percent just to maintain the status quo. Continual economic growth rates above that level are very difficult to maintain. It is rather like running up a down-moving escalator. Since much of the population growth rate is occurring in underdeveloped countries, it means that their industrial revolutions can be undone by a Malthusian revolution. Another factor that militates against the perception that population growth is a problem is that many individuals and businesses benefit from population increases. Landlords, banks, manufacturers, and merchants all stand to benefit by providing a growing population with goods and services.[27]

Population Policy Choices

Population, poverty, and pollution are related in complicated ways. World population has grown beyond an optimal level of "carrying capacity" at the present stage of technological development. At least 1.8 billion people today, over one in five, live in absolute poverty.

People do create wealth and earn incomes, and without people there would be neither. But the more people there are, the greater the impact on the environment. And larger populations often reduce the income per person and the output of economic goods produced per worker. A country can reduce poverty by increasing income while holding its population constant, or by holding income steady while decreasing its population.

Reduction of poverty is seen by many policymakers as a moral obligation. It is also necessary for the preservation of the environment and the health of the world economy. A healthy environment can more easily support the present or growing population than can a devastated one, so policies to protect the environment are necessary to reduce poverty. Because pollution and poverty are twin problems, economic development programs to reduce poverty must take into account the necessity of environmental protection. But it is not easy to work toward the seemingly antithetical goals of reducing pollution while promoting economic development. Poorer countries have few incentives to limit greenhouse gases. They do have an incentive to transfer the added costs of pollution to the global environment as an externality, giving themselves a cost advantage in the process.

Although threats to the environment are global and thus require international cooperation, political power often lies with the wealthier members of society, who have much at stake in accommodating the current economic interests of business leaders. Political leaders in most countries tend to remain fixated on narrow aspects of sovereignty and feel they are accountable solely to their domestic constituents. Moreover, nations differ in their contributions to environmental degradation. The wealthier nations of the North make a greater per capita contribution to environmental degradation by emissions of GHGs through the burning of fossil fuels. In poorer countries, overpopulation contributes to environmentally unsound deforestation. The destruction of watersheds by bringing less arable land under cultivation threatens many ecologically fragile areas, along with the economic viability of the countries in question.

To reduce world poverty, per capita income in poor countries must be raised. However, there is no realistic way poor countries can achieve the economic development needed for them to significantly raise their standards of living unless their population growth rates are decreased. Population control is an important first step in reducing poverty levels, but other steps are needed also. One possibility would be to encourage technology transfers of low-population, energy-efficient production procedures to poorer countries. In addition, subsidizing the investment costs of installing the equipment needed to implement those procedures would be beneficial.

Environmental Policy Responses

Politics is said to be the art of the possible. The task of the political scientist engaged in policy analysis, then, is to devise solutions derived from principles that different interests share. Policy responses that result in non-zero-sum solutions are generally to be preferred. For example, many businesses view environmentalists' concerns with alarm, fearing that any regulatory measures will drive costs up to intolerable levels. Business leaders tend to dismiss negative externalities as inevitable byproducts of market forces. Environmentalists, for their part, tend to view businesses as callous for pursuing profits without sufficiently considering the needs of the environment. The ideal solution would accommodate the needs of both sides, not sacrifice one set of needs to the other.

Command and Control

Diametrically opposed views such as those just described lead to bitter struggles and political polarization. Simply put, government finds itself pressured to outlaw a negative externality, even though many oppose any regulation. Thus the government may adopt direct regulation in which it determines permissible levels of pollution, and may fine or shut down firms that exceed them while allowing pollution by other firms that remains within the defined limit.

This regulatory technique is usually referred to as the **command and control** approach, because it requires such heavy government involvement. It requires the government to determine the maximum safe level of emissions and then set uniform standards for every smokestack or waste pipe. Policy analysts are uncomfortable with it because the standards promulgated are usually "all or nothing" in nature and do not necessarily reach their stated goals as efficiently or as fairly as possible. The standards require every company to meet the same target regardless of differing costs. This is inefficient because some businesses may have to use more expensive technologies to control pollution than others. Perhaps more important, businesses have no incentives to reduce pollution below the standards set by the government. They have no incentives to develop or utilize technologies to exceed the regulated targets. Money that might be used to develop technologies to further reduce pollution is often diverted to fighting the standards or getting an exemption based on the threat of eliminating jobs if the standard is imposed.

Market Incentive Programs

Huge budget deficits, anemic economic growth, and sharp foreign competition have inspired searches for policies that reduce bureaucratic intrusion into business decisions. At the same time, policymakers wish to be sensitive to the need for cost-effective solutions to get a high rate of return for the regulatory effort.

Political scientists recognize that pollution externalities represent a failure of the market in which the production of a good exceeds the optimal level. Business and consumers tacitly agree to pass some costs on to the public. Since firms can pass the costs of pollution on to society, they have little incentive to consider them in business decisions. To the contrary, any firm that unilaterally tried to reduce external costs would be less competitive in the market. However, rather than rejecting market mechanisms as a source of help in favor of direct regulation, or forsaking pollution control by returning to laissez-faire economic policies, policy analysts recognize that **market incentives**—trying to make the market price of a good include the cost of any negative externality—might suggest creative solutions. There are several ways to ensure that environmental costs are included in choices made by firms and individuals.

Tax incentives. A **tax incentive** uses taxes to provide incentives for individuals to pattern their behavior in a way that achieves the desired goals. This tactic charges a fee (tax) on the amount of good consumed that generates pollution, or imposes effluent charges. The threat of taxes is a stick to encourage the desired behavior to protect the environment.

For example, suppose that 100 gallons of gasoline are consumed each month in a society consisting of just three people. And suppose they mutually agree that total gas consumption should be reduced by 15 percent. Let us assume Mrs. A uses 50 gallons per month, Mr. B uses 35 gallons, and Ms. C uses 15. Direct regulation would require that each decrease their consumption by an equal percentage (15 percent each) to achieve the reduction. The difficulty with this approach is that it does not reward anyone for saving more than he or she is required to save. It may be that Mrs. A could easily reduce her consumption by 10 gallons with little inconvenience, and Mr. B can easily reduce his by 15 gallons, while Ms. C has always been frugal and would find it difficult to reduce her consumption by more than 1.5 gallons (10 percent) per month.

On the other hand, if they agree to levy a tax of 25¢ per gallon on the gasoline they consume, each will have an incentive to reduce consumption. Mrs. A will likely reduce her consumption by 10 gallons (20 percent) and pay $10 in taxes, Mr. B will reduce his consumption by 15 gallons (42 percent) and pay $5 in taxes, while Ms. C will reduce her consumption by 1.5 gallons (10 percent) and pay $3.38 in taxes each month.

In this illustration, the tax achieves the goal more efficiently than does direct regulation. Since the incentive to conserve is included in the price, each person has to choose how much to reduce their consumption. Each is influenced by the marginal utility of consuming an additional gallon. Those who consume less, pay less in taxes. The tax gives individuals an incentive to reduce their consumption as much as possible, and to find new ways of reducing consumption. For example, they may buy more fuel-efficient cars, use carpools, consider public transportation alternatives, or consider walking short distances instead of driving.

A variation on this market-based incentive is to provide a subsidy (a carrot rather than a stick). For example, a business could receive a tax credit for installing pollution abatement equipment, such as a scrubber, in a smokestack. Society is still better off, with less pollution, since the gap between the market price and the social costs is reduced. Businesses almost invariably prefer subsidies to taxes. Policy analysts typically prefer tax incentives, because they encourage companies to seek greater efficiency in reducing consumption or reducing pollution rather than just achieving a defined standard.

Marketable permits.   Through a **marketable permit**, the government establishes an upper limit of allowable pollution and allows businesses to emit some fraction of that total. If companies reduce their pollution (or consumption) below the level allocated to them, they receive a permit, which they can then sell to another firm that has chosen not to reduce its emissions to less than its allowable amount. For example, a utilities firm may want to expand production, but under an emissions cap may be unable to do so unless it can purchase permits to increase its emission of pollutants.

This method is aimed at encouraging firms to significantly reduce their pollution in order to generate marketable permits for other firms that, for one reason or another, do not find such a reduction worthwhile. The 1990 Clean Air Act explicitly used this market incentive to deal with pollution. The act provided for a 10-million-ton reduction in sulfur dioxide emissions from the 1980 level by the year 2000. Nitrogen oxide emissions were to be reduced by 2 million tons in that time frame. The law also provided a cap that limited emissions to about 50 percent of 1990 levels by 2000. To meet these goals by the year 2000, the EPA issued permits designed to reduce the amount of pollution allowed each year. Utilities were forced to take a number of actions to reduce the levels of emissions: install scrubbers, switch to low-sulfur coal, implement conservation measures, close down obsolete plants, use renewable energy sources such as hydroelectric power where feasible, and build new, more efficient utilities and transfer the emission allowances to the new plant. The act also contained a system of pollution allowances that encouraged utilities to exceed their required reduction of pollutants and recover their costs by selling their marketable certificates to other companies.

Assessing Policy Approaches

Market incentive policies like taxes, subsidies, and marketable permits are attractive to policy analysts for many reasons. They reduce the market inefficiency of pollution by discouraging undesirable activities that produce externalities. Charges levied for pollution require that businesses share the cost burden of externalities, and therefore include consideration of externalities in their daily business decisions. Firms for which pollution reduction is cheapest will reduce pollution more, while those for which reduction is expensive will reduce it less. Such policies also make the price that consumers pay for an externality more closely reflect its cost.

Since pollution cannot be reduced to zero, many see market-based incentives as a pragmatic approach to achieve the optimal level of pollution. The optimal level of anything produced from a purely economic perspective is the point at which its price reflects the marginal costs of its production. The difficulty is in accurately determining the marginal social cost of pollution and setting the incentives appropriately. If properly set, firms will pursue pollution abatement to the point that its marginal cost equals its marginal benefit to society. If the tax is too low, firms will commit to insufficient environmental protection, while if it is too high, production of the good will be excessively cut back.

Market approaches to controlling pollution are rapidly gaining acceptance among many policymakers. For example, many states have instituted market-based incentives known as "bottle-bills": a deposit must be made on the purchase of beverages in aluminum or plastic bottles, which is refunded when empty containers are returned. The effect has been to reduce litter and promote recycling.

Nevertheless, there is still significant skepticism regarding market-based incentives, for several reasons. Many environmentalists oppose them because it seems that selling permits to pollute legitimizes pollution. Many business firms oppose market approaches because they involve taxes, which are associated negatively with government interference. Also, businesses and their lobbyists often prefer direct-market regulation, because they have become very effective at countering this approach. For example, they can appeal for a delay in the implementation of regulatory rules by citing economic hardship and the possibility of layoffs due to increased costs, and they often get what they want.

Ethics and Environmentalism

The appeal of market approaches to encourage environmentally sound policies is their efficiency. The market provides a framework in which trade takes place based on the choices of individuals between a given supply and demand for goods. Through cost-benefit analysis the government can try to set policy while relying on the efficiency of the market even as decisions aimed at protecting the environment are incorporated into the market process. This is built on the assumption that the policy goals embody an ethical consensus that can be promoted better by market mechanisms than by any other means.

There are problems with this utilitarian approach. Cost-benefit analyses are carried out by individuals, and individual preferences may provide a weak foundation for policymaking. Individual preferences are the result of personal experiences, which are necessarily limited and based on incomplete information. Even if we were willing to accept individual preferences, we may have a problem in translating the aggregate conflicting preferences into a single policy decision. Another major objection to this form of utilitarianism is that it may result in decisions that are an affront to our sense of justice. Cost-benefit analysis would permit the loss of income of thirty families at $30,000 per year each, rather than the loss of one person's income at $1 million. That is, cost-benefit analysis does not require (or preclude) us from taxing distribution. Cost-benefit analysis, then, cannot be the sole guide to decisionmaking on environmental matters.

Policies should also give special consideration to those most vulnerable to their consequences. For example, the poor may find themselves at the mercy of decisions made by the more economically powerful members of society. Dolphins, whales, or spotted owls are affected by human choices. And later generations will have to live with results of decisions made today regarding the use of fossil fuels versus nuclear energy.

The poor have always suffered more than the affluent because of the deleterious effects of inferior living conditions, and industrialization has only added to their burden. We have noted how housing policy generally stratifies society, with the poor living in deteriorating urban areas close to factories and pollution, while the wealthy move to the suburbs. Discrimination against minorities can compound the problem, making the poor even more likely to live in areas where hazardous waste and other toxins make for unhealthy living conditions. Poor nonwhite Americans are disproportionately impacted by environmental degradation.

When the environmental movement began in the 1970s, it largely reflected the views of some of the more prosperous upper-income people in the United States. However, since the mid-1980s, minorities and the poor have increasingly assumed a leadership role.[28] President Clinton assumed office in 1993 promising to restore the role of the government in environmental protection. The following year he issued Executive Order 12898, requiring all federal agencies to include the achievement of "environmental justice" as part of their mission.

Conclusion

Environmental issues have taken center stage in public policy debates only in the past three or four decades. Almost every environmental issue is related to the impact of humanity on the environment. Nature everywhere tends to be treated as a mine or a dump. As we make more and more demands on the environment, we use up natural resources, destroy habitats for wildlife, increase biological extinction, and increase environmental pollution. Earth's natural systems, such as climate and temperature, the ozone layer, and water supply, have all been affected by human demands that outrun its capacity.

Although many other countries initially lagged behind the United States in environmental regulation, many have now overtaken us. "Green parties" have emerged in Europe to push standards beyond those of the United States.

It is increasingly recognized that global environmental degradation requires global solutions. Meaningful actions are difficult to achieve, however, when populations resist any increase in cost as a threat to material affluence. Markets do not provide an efficient outcome when negative externalities exist, because business firms have a market incentive not to take the marginal social costs into account in their business decisions. To do so would put them at a competitive disadvantage.

Business interests usually react negatively to any government regulation that they fear will drive up prices. Politically, the Republican Party has emerged as the standard bearer of those who would dismantle the environmental regulation that is in place as damaging to U.S. competitiveness.

The world faces tradeoffs regarding the environment. Eliminating all pollution would be impossible. However, the planet does appear to be nearing a real environmental crisis. When private people cannot solve externalities such as pollution, the government has a responsibility to step in. The problem is that special interest groups resist any regulation that would limit their negative externalities. The crucial problem in devising market-based programs is to determine the level of incentives needed to achieve the optimal policy outcome, which is where the marginal cost of the program equals its marginal benefit.

Questions for Discussion

1. Distinguish between environmental protection and environmental regulation. How are these practices informed by moral principles, particularly utilitarian principles?
2. What is meant by sustainable development and what environmental problems threaten this goal?
3. Compare the concept of a public good with the NIMBY attitude. What incentives can government offer to protect public goods and avoid NIMBY?
4. When and why did environmentalism become part of the political agenda? Did any specific events help to "politicize" the environment?
5. Discuss the plight of public interest groups devoted to the environment. What sources of funding do they have and how do they compete with private sector interests?
6. Much criticism is leveled about the "greenhouse" effect. What criteria do scientists rely on to evaluate scientific findings regarding the environment? Is science always objective?

Useful Websites

Audubon Society, http://www.audubon.org.
Clean Air Task Force, http://www.catf.us.
Environmental Integrity Project, http://www.environmentalintegrity.org.
Institute for European Environmental Policy, http://www.ieep.org.uk.
U.S. Department of Energy, http://www.energy.gov.
U.S. Department of the Interior, http://www.doi.gov.
U.S. Energy Information Administration, http://www.eia.doe.gov.
U.S. Environmental Protection Agency (EPA), http://www.epa.gov.
U.S. Environmental Protection Agency, Global Warming site, http://www.epa.gov/globalwarming.

Suggested Readings

Anselmo, Joseph C. "Energy Overhaul: Not Much Difference After a Decade." *Congressional Quarterly Weekly,* November 8, 2003.

Bohringer, Christoph, Michael Finus, and Carsten Vogt, eds. *Controlling Global Warming: Perspectives from Economics, Game Theory, and Public Choice.* Northampton, Mass.: Edward Elgar, 2002.

Brainard, Jeffrey. "How Sound Is Bush's 'Sound Science'?" *Chronicle of Higher Education,* March 5, 2004.

Carson, Rachel. *Silent Spring.* Boston: Houghton Mifflin, 1962.

Environmental Protection Agency. *Draft Report on the Environment 2003.* Washington, D.C.: U.S. Government Printing Office, June 23, 2003.

Green, Kenneth P. *Global Warming: Understanding the Debate.* Vancouver: Enslow, 2002.

Harrison, Neil E., and Gary C. Bryner. *Science and Politics in the International Environment.* Lanham, Md.: Rowman and Littlefield, 2004.

Kolbert, Elizabeth. "Clouding the Air." *New Yorker,* September 29, 2003.

Layzer, Judith A. *The Environmental Case: Translating Values into Policy.* Washington, D.C.: Congressional Quarterly Press, 2002.

Lomborg, Bjorn. *The Skeptical Environmentalist: Measuring the Real State of the World.* New York: Cambridge University Press, 2001.

Rosenbaum, Walter A. *Environmental Politics and Policy.* 5th ed. Washington, D.C.: Congressional Quarterly Press, 2002.

Simon, Julian. *The Ultimate Resource 2.* Princeton: Princeton University Press, 1996.

Vig, Norman J., and Michael E. Kraft. *Environmental Policy: New Directions for the 21st Century.* Washington, D.C.: Congressional Quarterly Press, 2002.

Weart, Spencer. *The Discovery of Global Warming.* Cambridge: Harvard University Press, 2003.

Notes

1. Lawrence White, *The Regulation of Air Pollutant Emissions from Motor Vehicles* (Washington, D.C.: American Enterprise Institute, 1982), p. 14.

2. Public Law 91-604, 84 Stat. 1713 (1970).

3. Ann Burford had been a vocal critic of all environmental regulation from Colorado before going to the EPA. She was forced to resign in 1983 after evidence was made public that strongly suggested secret collusion between the EPA and the industry it was to regulate. For example, amendments to the Clean Air Act of 1977 were based on public health concerns. Agency records showed that there were thirty high-level meetings between officials of the EPA and the oil industry before leaded gasoline standards were set, but that no meetings were held with public health officials about leaded gasoline standards.

James Watt was a leader of the "Sagebrush Rebellion," which was an effort by businesspeople, lobbyists, and state officials to persuade the federal government to ease its regulation and thereby the costs of public land used by cattle, mining, and real estate interests. As secretary of interior, Watt antagonized environmentalists when he sold and leased federal lands to mining and timber interests at a fraction of their commercial market value.

4. Robert Perks, *Rewriting the Rules: The Bush Administration's Assault on the Environment,* 3rd annual ed. (Washington, D.C.: Natural Resources Defense Council, April 2004), p. 101.

5. Ibid., p. 1.

6. Ibid.

7. Ibid. D.C. officials agreed to distribute free water filters to 10,000 of over 23,000 homes fed by lead lines and to accelerate the replacement of the lead pipes. See also David Nakamura, "EPA Failed to Hold D.C. Accountable, Some Say," *Washington Post,* February 23, 2004.

8. Perks, *Rewriting the Rules,* p. iv.

9. Ibid., p. 7. See also Eric Pianin, "Proposed Mercury Rules Bear Industry Mark," *Washington Post,* January 31, 2004. The EPA's plan would require a 30 percent reduction in mercury emissions over the next fifteen years, rather than enforcing previous proposals that would have required a 90 percent reduction over three years. The EPA's proposals involve a cap-and-trade program that would allow "dirty" utilities to purchase credits from "clean" utilities, in order to reach an overall target for the electric utility industry. This would allow mercury hotspots in areas where credits had been purchased.

10. Perks, *Rewriting the Rules,* p. iv.

11. Ibid., p. v.

12. For example, courts overturned the Department of Energy's attempt to relax energy efficiency standards for new air conditioners; they overturned Department of Interior rules allowing broad snowmobile access to Yellowstone National Park; and they stopped the EPA's efforts to relax the Clean Air Act's requirement for power plants and factories to install modern pollution controls when they upgrade equipment. See Perks, *Rewriting the Rules,* p. vi.

13. Elizabeth Shogren, "Researchers Accuse Bush of Manipulating Science," *Los Angeles Times,* July 9, 2004.

14. Seth Borenstein, "Bush Administration Accused of Suppressing, Distorting Science," *Knight-Ridder,* February 19, 2004.

15. U.S. Environmental Protection Agency, *Global Warming: Emissions,* http://yosemite.epa.gov/oar/globalwarming.nsf/content/emissions.html.

16. Ross Gelbspan, "A Global Warning," *American Prospect,* March–April 1997, p. 37.

17. U.S. Environmental Protection Agency, *Global Warming.*

18. Alister Doyle, "Greenhouse Gas Jump Spurs Global Warming Fears," Reuters, October 11, 2004.

19. United Nations Environment Programme (UNEP), "Basic Facts and Data on the Science and Politics of Ozone Protection," August 2003, p. 1. See also http://www.unep.org/ozone.

20. UNEP, "Basic Facts," p. 4.

21. Perks, *Rewriting the Rules,* p. 45.

22. "Questions About Endocrine Disruptors," http://extoxnet.orst.edu/faqs/pesticide/endocrine.htm.

23. Walter A. Rosenbaum, *Environmental Politics and Policy* (Washington, D.C.: Congressional Quarterly Press, 2005), p. 228.

24. U.S. National Academy of Sciences and Royal Society of London, "Population Growth, Resource Consumption, and a Sustainable World," joint statement, February 27, 1992.

25. Paul R. Ehrlich and John Holden, "Impact of Population Growth," *Science* 171 (March 26, 1971): 1212–1217.

26. Henry W. Kindall and David Pimentel, "Constraints on the Expansion of the

Global Food Supply," *Ambio* (Royal Swedish Academy of Sciences) 23, no. 3 (May 1994): 198–205.

27. Garrett Hardin, "Population Policy," *E: The Environment Magazine* 1, no. 6 (November–December 1990): 5.

28. Mary H. Cooper, "Environmental Justice," *CQ Researcher* 8, no. 23 (June 1998): 537.

CHAPTER 13

U.S. Foreign Policy

For those who conduct foreign policy, the beginning of the twenty-first century is the best of times and the worst of times. At the end of World War II, the consolidation of Soviet power in Eastern Europe, with its clear challenge to the West, prevented President Harry Truman from withdrawing all U.S. troops from Europe. The ideological conflict between communism and capitalism and the logic of the bipolar model defined the relations between the Soviet Union and the United States until the unexpected dissolution of the Soviet bloc in the late 1980s. U.S. political leaders accommodated themselves to a military policy of **mutual assured destruction** and a foreign policy of **containment**, which conveniently constrained the policy options of many regional powers. Political leaders, regardless of political identification, accepted the general rubrics of containment policy and became comfortable with predictable policies toward world communism. The geopolitical concern of providing for European security against the threat of a Soviet invasion and for containment, which had dominated foreign policy thinking since the 1940s, quickly evaporated with the implosion of the Soviet Union. U.S. goals of advancing democracy and market economies over communism and planned economies had been accomplished, and even China's economic system submitted to market forces. Suddenly the United States was unchallenged as the world's dominant military and economic power.

At the turn of the twenty-first century the United States was in its longest period of economic expansion in history. The stock markets reached record highs while unemployment and inflation fell to negligible levels. There was a brief period of optimism that democracy was now dominant in the world and conversely that nondemocratic regimes were in retreat. Many believed that fatal flaws had become evident in nondemocratic governments, while the flaws in democracies, and especially U.S. democracy, resulted primarily from the incomplete implementation of freedom and equality. Francis Fukuyama wrote that the world was entering a new age,[1] and that "what we may be witnessing is not just the end of the cold war, or the passing of a particular period of history, but the end of history as such, that is, the end point of mankind's ideological evolution and the universalization of Western liberal democracy as the final form of government."[2] U.S. prestige was at its zenith as many foreign governments tried to model its democratic reforms. U.S. culture, from capitalism to music and language, was admired and copied throughout the world. The sheer predominance of the United States was without historical precedent.

Ominously, there were areas of regional conflicts and internal power struggles, suppressed by the Cold War, that flared up with the withering away of the Soviet Union. A civil war erupted in Somalia. U.S. military intervention to provide relief, along with efforts by the United Nations (UN), resulted in U.S. casualties and prompted withdrawal. The end of the Cold War also resulted in a revival of ethnic and religious intolerance in the imploding state of Yugoslavia. Bill Clinton, despite considerable opposition in Congress, intervened to stop the "ethnic cleansing." The United States ended the bloodshed in Bosnia-Herzegovina and Kosovo while limiting exposure of U.S. troops to enemy fire. Once military operations ended, Clinton turned over the rebuilding efforts to multilateral institutions.

The shift away from engagement and toward unilateralism gained momentum when the Republican Party won control of both houses of Congress for the first time since the Eisenhower administration. In 1998 a Republican-led Congress defied President Clinton and refused to appropriate funds to pay a backlog of U.S. dues owed to the UN in excess of $1 billion. At the same time, reductions in U.S. foreign aid programs left the United States, the world's largest economy, with the lowest aid contributions as a percentage of gross domestic product (GDP).

President Clinton, whose primary interest was domestic policy, nevertheless embraced the notion that a new world order populated by national democracies would be more peaceful and cooperative and less prone to war. Economic cooperation and globalization were also encouraged through the elimination of trade barriers and support of free trade. Clinton believed that free market principles would be facilitated by the institutions of multilateral economic cooperation, such as the World Bank and the International Monetary Fund (IMF). He supported the creation of the World Trade Organization (WTO) in 1995 to enforce free trade reforms negotiated in the last decades of the century. Clinton believed the nation would be more secure and prosperous in "a more tightly knit world whose nations shared common values, interests, and political institutions."[3] Clinton's national security policy of **engagement and enlargement** was designed to forge closer relations between countries, particularly on economic matters, in the hope that by providing collective benefits it would discourage smaller countries from challenging the primacy of the United States.

Presidents of both political parties sought to achieve foreign policy goals through diplomacy, to encourage democratic institutions and increase their economic and military power. The primary approach was to offer economic and military aid, and negotiate a reduction in trade barriers with the ultimate goal of free trade. Since U.S. power would on occasion lead to inevitable resentment, it was understood that the nation should try to be "nonoffensive" in foreign policy. The United States should try to curb military spending through arms control and encourage increasing reliance on collective peacekeeping and peaceful means of conflict resolution. The strategy emphasized the attempt to engage states in the progressive building of a world community through the development of international organizations like the United Nations and the strengthening of principles of international law.

In 1999 a Republican-led Senate denied President Clinton's request for consent to ratify the Comprehensive Nuclear Test Ban Treaty. Although Clinton pledged that the United States would maintain its policy of not conducting nuclear tests, the Senate's unwillingness was clearly out of step with the more than 150 nations that supported the treaty.

The election of George W. Bush in 2000 spelled the end of engagement and enlargement and advanced **unilateralism**. The new president surprised most observers by aggressively rejecting U.S. policy goals, pursued since World War II, of encouraging the progressive development of an interdependent world community. Bush came into office with the intention of pulling back from what he and many Republican politicians regarded as excessive engagement and **nation building**. He made clear that he would pursue a narrower view of the "national interest" and be more selective in overseas involvement.

The new president ultimately adopted the views of a neoconservative group who advocated a more "muscular" foreign policy. They believed that a competitive posture based on a strong military and a foreign policy that "boldly and purposefully promotes American principles abroad," under national leadership that accepted the "global responsibilities" of the United States, would effectively achieve the nation's goals.[4] President Bush turned his back on several international agreements that had been negotiated over several years and made clear his belief that a unilateral approach would best advance U.S. interests. The willingness to be abrasive in pursuit of perceived U.S. interests became a defining characteristic of the administration.

The attacks of September 11, 2001, and the resulting war on terrorism led the president and his advisers back to global involvement. The administration also came to believe that the war against Islamic terrorism required democratic reform and even nation building in the Middle East. The desire to promote democracy grew out of the conviction that U.S. security interests are aided by democratic forms of government. The administration's goal of supporting democracies for their own sake represents a return to the universalist principles that have usually shaped U.S. foreign policy.[5]

The United States in the Twenty-First Century

The United States is the world's greatest military power. However, because the United States is also the world's largest economic power, defense spending today is actually a smaller share of GDP than it was during the Cold War. The military budget request for fiscal year 2005 was $420.7 billion, about 19 percent of the federal budget, but only about 4 percent of GDP.[6] Traditional military threats to the United States are rather remote, as most former enemies and allies do not pose a danger. The most likely form of threat to the United States today is through terrorism, rather than conventional warfare, although most military spending is still directed toward conventional confrontations. Nevertheless, U.S. military spending is more than the combined spending of the next twenty-three ranked nations and roughly twenty-nine times the combined spending of the seven "rogue" states (Cuba, Iran, Iraq, Libya, North Korea, Sudan, and Syria), which collectively spent 14.4 billion.[7] To achieve such a dominant military position while spending less than during the Cold War is remarkable.

The size of the U.S. economy is the single most important factor in the country's influence throughout the world. The United States produces almost one-third of the world's total output. U.S. economic output in 2004 was $10.2 trillion, equivalent to that of the next five ranked national economies combined (Japan, Germany, the United Kingdom, France, and China), at $10.3 trillion.[8] The nation exports more than any other nation, about $1 trillion in 2004 (about 15 percent of total world exports). It also imported over $1.5 trillion in 2004 (about 20 percent of the world's imports). And although foreign direct investment (FDI) in the U.S. economy has slowed in recent years, more money flows into U.S. investments than into the investments of all other countries.

The military and economic primacy of the United States is unlikely to be jeopardized over the next two or three decades. Militarily, it is unlikely that any group of nations will spend enough money to compete with the United States over the next twenty-five years. The Soviet Union once defined itself in terms of its military and economic rivalry with the United States. Now a smaller Russia tries to emulate Western Europe and the United States. China's economic transformation toward a market economy and away from aspirations of becoming a military superpower is equally positive. With Russia and China and other countries increasingly interconnected with ties that are for the most part irreversible, there are many hopeful signs for the future. Other major nations have no incentive to try to match the United States militarily, and most countries lack the resources. It is this reality that makes terrorism the weapon of choice for poor and excluded nations or groups.

Economically, the United States is unlikely to lose its preeminent position. The U.S. economy has shown itself to be extremely resilient and flexible in adapting to a changing economic environment. And there are indications that Europe and Japan will face greater challenges in dealing with aging populations than does the United States. However, it is also unlikely that the United States will maintain its share of global output indefinitely, since modernizing nations experience more rapid average growth rates than do mature economies.

Power in the Age of Globalization

Most people are familiar with the two most obvious forms of national power, military and economic. Niccolo Machiavelli famously advised monarchs that it was more important to be feared than to be loved. Writing at a time in history when there were no democracies, and princes were engaged in a fratricidal struggle to gain and then to keep power, that was excellent advice. But today much of the advanced world consists of democracies with major economic assets. It is now important to be loved as well as feared. The "hard" military power of the United States was invaluable in providing security in the long struggle in the Cold War. But it is of limited value when the nation cannot achieve economic goals without the cooperation of the European Union, Japan, China, or even the World Trade Organization. The hard power of military power is not a significant threat in such negotiations.

Joseph Nye has coined the term **soft power** to indicate the ability to get others to want the same outcomes that you want through cooperation rather than coercion.[9] It is difficult to run complex organizations by simply issuing commands. It is essential to get others to accept the values of the organization. Nye points out that soft power is the staple of daily democratic politics. The ability to achieve goals tends to be associated with the acceptance of a culture, political values and institutions, and policies that are perceived as legitimate or having moral authority.[10] Soft power is more than influence, which may rest on the **hard power** of military threats. In behavioral terms soft power is "attractive power." Hard and soft power are related because they are aspects of the ability to achieve a goal by affecting the behavior of others.

The soft power of a country flows from three main sources: the attractiveness of its culture, its political values (when it lives up to them at home and abroad), and its foreign policies to the extent that they are perceived as legitimate and having moral authority.[11] A culture that includes universal values and government policies that promote principles that others share conforms to the interests and desires of other peoples and attracts their support. Conversely, policies that are not in harmony with widely held values may undermine a nation's soft power. For example, weak gun control laws and government acceptance of capital punishment reduce U.S. soft power.

The social changes that have occurred inside advanced democracies have also raised the costs of using hard military power. Postindustrial democracies tend to be more focused on social welfare than on military glory. In most advanced democracies, the use of force now requires an elaborate moral justification to attract popular support. War is still an option, but it is less acceptable now than it was even fifty years ago.[12] Soft power is crucial in the calculation of terrorism. Terrorists are dependent on their ability to convince the bystanders to a conflict that they should join in on the side of the underdogs who support the right values, as much as they rely on an ability to destroy their enemy's will to fight.

After September 11, 2001, the neoconservatives believed that U.S. military power could be used to export democracy to Iraq and would result in a transformation of the entire Middle East. The war would become legitimate by the democratic changes that would result. As Republican strategists William Kristol and Lawrence Kaplan write, "What is wrong with dominance in the service of sound principles and high ideals?"[13]

Although the outcome of the military effort to topple Saddam Hussein was never in doubt, other states tried to stop the United States by denying President George W. Bush the legitimacy of a UN Security Council resolution authorizing the action. When the United States acted outside the UN Charter, world opinion shifted to concern about its unbridled use of power and away from any threat posed by Hussein. Some neoconservatives thought that a properly working UN would offer the United States official sanction for the "preemptive" U.S. use of force in Iraq.[14] Since it did not, they hoped that a quick victory would remove Saddam and show the UN to be a failure, leading to its replacement by the United States in an alliance with England and Russia.

Other states, unable to prevent the hard power invasion of Iraq by the United States, countered by denying the legitimacy of a Security Council resolution authorizing the action. Lacking the soft power of legitimacy by the UN has made action by the Bush administration much more difficult and costly. Turkey and Saudi Arabia refused to allow the United States to use their territory to stage operations against Iraq. By ignoring the UN, the United States has had to spend over $300 billion on the Iraq War, the equivalent of assessing each household an additional $3,000 tax by the fall of 2005. In most military operations, including the

Clinton interventions under UN auspices and the 1991 Gulf War, the United States has been responsible for 15 and 20 percent of the military costs respectively.[15] Without UN authorization, most countries refused to participate in the U.S.-led war against Iraq. For those countries that did agree to participate—such as Poland, Ukraine, Nicaragua, El Salvador, and Honduras—it was estimated that the United States would have to spend $250 million to win their support and underwrite their commitment.[16]

Joseph Nye makes a powerful case that the neoconservatives who advised President Bush focused too heavily on using U.S. hard power to force other nations to do the country's will. They failed to appreciate the importance of soft power in dissuading moderates from joining terrorist organizations, and in encouraging other states and international organizations to confront critical global issues through multilateral cooperation rather than unilateral approaches.

Harbingers of Domestic and International Stress

Many U.S. foreign and domestic policies, some beginning before the George W. Bush administration, have been overwhelmingly disapproved by the world community as well as large segments of the U.S. population. The following is only a partial list:

• On taking office in 2001, President Bush criticized his predecessor's multilateral approach. To emphasize the point, Bush announced the withdrawal of the United States from the Anti-Ballistic Missile (ABM) Treaty in August 2001, insisting that the United States must maintain an unrestricted ability to defend itself from nuclear attacks by rogue nations and terrorists. At the same time, Bush announced plans to move forward with a controversial national missile defense system in direct violation of ABM Treaty.

• President Bush rejected the Kyoto Protocol, which was signed but not ratified during the Clinton administration. Bush claimed that it was harmful to U.S. business and the overall economy, because it exempted 80 percent of the world, especially China and India. It commited the principal countries responsible for climate change to reduce their emissions of greenhouse gases by 5 percent a year until reaching 1990 emission levels. The treaty has been ratified by 128 nations, including nations in the European Union and Russia, and went into effect in early 2005.

• President Bush increased tariffs on imports of foreign steel in violation of the World Trade Organization agreements. The European Union appealed to the WTO, which found against the United States. The administration was forced to repeal the steel tariffs to avoid retaliation by the European Union.

• In 2002 the Bush administration announced that it did not consider itself bound by President Clinton's signature on the treaty to create the International Criminal Court (ICC). The administration raised concerns that U.S. service members could be brought before the court in politically motivated cases. Ninety-four countries ratified the treaty by summer 2004, however, and the ICC came into force despite U.S. opposition.

• Prisoners in the custody of U.S. occupation forces were abused in Afghanistan, Iraq, and Cuba. News that a White House adviser had prepared memos about the abusive treatment indicated that it stemmed from more than a few misguided guards.

• The Bush administration advocated "preemptive" war in violation of the UN Charter's provisions on the use of military force. The administration bypassed the United Nations when it could not muster the Security Council votes needed for authorization, and under threat of veto from France and Russia.

• The Bush administration asserted in March 2003 that preemptive war was justified because Iraq possessed weapons of mass destruction (WMD), as well as chemical and biological weapons, and was reconstituting its nuclear weapons program. In January 2005 the Iraq Survey Group submitted a report contradicting nearly every prewar assertion that the Bush administration made about Iraq's possession of weapons.

These and other controversial decisions—the result of what Pope John Paul II called an "arrogance of power"—have damaged U.S. ties to European allies and tarnished the image of the United States throughout the world.[17]

International Law and the UN Charter

The decision to invade Iraq severely strained relations between the United States and most of its closest allies, and also damaged U.S. relations with the United Nations. U.S. approval ratings dropped precipitously in Europe and the Middle East following the invasion.

The United States has a long history, going back to its founding, of supporting the progressive development of international law. The framers of the Constitution explicitly recognized the binding nature of the **law of nations**. As the United States grew into a world power, it insisted, although with some lapses, that conflicts had to be settled by peaceful means. In launching World War II, the German and Japanese governments acted with contempt for treaties they had signed that renounced war as an instrument of policy. The treaties also committed the signatory states never to seek the settlement of disputes except through peaceful means. The treaties merely made explicit what the customary international law already required—a prohibition against launching a war of aggression. The chief U.S. prosecutor at Nuremberg, Supreme Court Justice Robert Jackson, emphasized that the defendants were on trial not because they lost the war, but because "they started it."

In its resort to force against Iraq, the Bush administration has been widely criticized for abandoning the previously championed principles of international law. This is a major departure from past administration policies. The United States had a major role in the creation of the United Nations and its basic Charter (which is a treaty now binding 191 nations as of 2005). Having just experienced the horrors of World War II, peace was the paramount concern of the framers of the Charter. It obligates UN members to "refrain in their international relations from the threat or use of force" against any state. Article 51 provides the one unequivocal exception: "Nothing in the present Charter shall impair the inherent right of individual or collective self-defense if an armed attack occurs."[18] The United States has encouraged the progressive development of international law through treaties and international organizations including the United Nations. Persuading the world community to abide by international law advanced the interests of the United States as well. It outlawed the aggressive use of force and encouraged an interdependent world community.

Much of the world has been persuaded of the value of international law, which contributed to the soft power of the United States as the primary supporter of the values of a more global perspective. Thus President Bush provoked widespread criticism for a speech at the U.S. Military Academy when he indicated that the United States would "impose preemptive, unilateral, military force when and where it chooses."[19] These recent justifications of preemptive war are in conflict with the UN Charter's provisions on the use of force. Only the Security Council may authorize the use of force to deal with any threat or breach of the peace. This is the reason why the Security Council refused to authorize the use of force against Iraq, despite significant pressure by the United States for an authorizing resolution.

The law of the Charter is very close to domestic law on issues regarding the use of force. There is a monopoly on the legitimate use of force that resides in the community. No one may use violence against another person without breaking the law. Conversely, although a person may use force for self-defense, there is no legal right to attack another person in anticipation that they may use violence. One may go to the legal authorities to prevent an attack.

Critics of the restrictions of Article 51 insist that it may not be realistic, especially when dealing with terrorist threats, as opposed to a Cold War scenario that provided the lead time necessary to get the UN involved. However, since the search for Iraq's alleged weapons of mass destruction has shown that the United States was not genuinely threatened, this argument is weakened.

The United States claimed to be threatened by Iraq and Saddam Hussein, who was alleged to be amassing an array of weapons of mass destruction, including chemical and biological weapons. The Security Council voted unanimously to require Hussein to permit inspections to determine if the allegations of WMD were true, but refused the Bush administration's request for an authorization to use force. The administration claimed that there was no time to wait for the evidence of a smoking gun, which might come in the form of a mushroom cloud from an Iraqi nuclear weapon. The Secretary-General of the United Nations, Kofi Annan, has stated clearly that the U.S.-led war in Iraq and the Bush doctrine of the right to use preemptive, unilateral military force are illegal.[20]

President Bush also claimed the right to try foreigners charged with terrorism. He signed an order authorizing detainees to be held by the military in Guantanamo Bay, Cuba, without the right to any legal review by any U.S. or international court. Protection under the Geneva Conventions was not to be extended to the detainess, who could be held without trial for the duration of the "war on terror." The U.S. secretary of state, Colin Powell, responding to diplomatic pressure and criticism from major allies such as Britain and Australia on behalf of citizens of theirs who were being detained, advised the administration to release or transfer those detainees whose offenses were uncertain or minor.[21] The administration's claim that it had the exclusive right to determine the legal status of the detainees was later rejected by the Supreme Court in a six-to-three ruling that federal courts do have jurisdiction to hear prisoners' legal challenges.[22]

The administration vehemently denied allegations of torture at Guantanamo and insisted that the cases of prisoner abuse that surfaced at Abu Ghraib in Iraq were the result of actions by individual personnel, not of U.S. policy. The nomination of Alberto Gonzales to replace John Ashcroft as U.S. attorney general emphasized what many saw as a lack of sensitivity to the toll that the "war on terror" had taken on the image of the United States both at home and abroad, because Gonzales had endorsed the view that the president was not bound by treaty obligations in war and had authored position papers indicating that measures against prisoners would not constitute torture.

U.S. Foreign Policy Making

Who has responsibility for the conduct of foreign policy? And how is foreign policy made in the United States? This chapter can only briefly consider the primary policymakers and some of the more important instruments they use to implement their policies.

The President and Congress

The Founding Fathers were concerned about the accumulation of too much power in any one branch of government. They were especially careful to circumscribe the powers given to the president, to ensure against the acquisition of dictatorial powers. Article 2 of the Constitution gives the president the right, with the advice and consent of the Senate, to make treaties and to appoint ambassadors. The Founding Fathers also designated the president as the commander in chief of the military and indicated that the executive could receive foreign ambassadors. These powers do not justify the conclusion that those at the Constitutional Convention thought the president should dominate in making foreign policy. In fact, foreign policy was viewed as a minor matter by the framers. The new nation was thousands of miles from the European cauldron. George Washington's well-known farewell warning to avoid entangling alliances is indicative of the framers' attitudes.

Although the president was designated commander in chief of the military, only Congress was allowed to declare war. The drafters of the Constitution specifically gave Congress the responsibility to "provide for the common defense." They further gave Congress a role to play in the confirmation of all high-level diplomatic and military officials. Finally, they gave Congress the authority "to make all Laws which shall be necessary and proper for carrying into Execution the foregoing Powers, and all other Powers vested by this Constitution in the Government of the United States."

The Constitution's grant of authority to the president had potential for expansive interpretation by chief executives as opportunities presented themselves. Historically, presidential power in foreign policy has expanded during wars. Presidents have also found that being perceived as "defending" the United States can reap great rewards in terms of prestige at home to pursue other domestic policies. Many were convinced that quarrels between the president and Congress would provide openings for U.S. adversaries. Therefore, Congress and other groups had an obligation to unite behind the president, as politics should "stop at the water's edge" and critics should remain silent. Since dissenters run the risk of being perceived as unpatriotic and aiding the enemy, the president typically has a freer hand to conduct foreign as well as domestic policy. There is a clear causal connection between the tremendous growth of presidential power and the fact that the United States has been at war almost continuously during the past century, having fought two world wars and a cold war, and engaged in intermittent hot conflicts, like Korea and Vietnam and now Iraq.

The deference accorded to a president who appears to be defending the nation's security can become critical in political campaigns. President George W. Bush appeared eager in 2004 to portray himself as a "war president" and stressed the need for a president to take strong unilateral action when necessary. Democratic Party candidate John Kerry urged the pursuit of diplomatic rather than military solutions to conflicts, and a return to collective security instead of unilateral action.[23] This position was ridiculed by Bush, who implied that Kerry would require UN approval to defend U.S. security, while he himself would "never seek a permission slip to defend the security of our country."[24]

Prior to the terrorist attacks of September 11, 2001, political and nongovernmental foes openly challenged Bush's shift toward a unilateral foreign policy. After the attacks, critics in Bush's own party as well as the Democratic Party muted their misgivings regarding his approach and gave him full support in responding to the attack. Congress provided the requested appropriations to provide relief to the victims of terrorism, expand government authority to oppose terrorism domestically, expand the government's power to arrest and detain suspects, and strengthen the military. Congress also supported using force to overthrow the Taliban, which had allowed Al-Qaida terrorists to train in Afghanistan. Subsequently, Bush claimed that he did not require congressional approval to overthrow Saddam Hussein. However, in an effort to acquire as much legitimacy as possible, especially in light of foreign opposition, he did request support. Congress responded with a resolution authorizing the president to use military forces "as he determines to be necessary and appropriate in order to defend the national security of the United States against the continuing threat posed by Iraq."[25] This deference to presidential authority bears a striking resemblance to the Gulf of Tonkin Resolution, by which Congress gave President Lyndon Johnson unlimited authority to expand military operations in Vietnam.

Congress's surrender to the president of its foreign policy authority in response to the threat or use of force has resulted in what historian Arthur M. Schlesinger argued is an "imperial presidency" within the United States, in which presidents conduct foreign policy by fiat.[26] A foreign policy problem that involves the use of force, is by definition a crisis. It may provide a president an opportunity to appear to be rising above politics in "defending national security" while conveniently enhancing approval ratings. That such actions by the president can so strongly support the interests of the executive branch, given the ritual view of political life that only a strong leader can save the nation from peril, is a temptation for resolute action. To presidents, this may represent the natural, even righteous view of what best serves the larger national interest. The spillover rewards to presidential authority in other policy areas are but secondary to the rewards of self-benefiting action. Presidents are especially alert to situations that might permit a short, inexpensive, and victorious use of force to strengthen their hand in domestic affairs. Some scholars have suggested that presidents may actually seek conflicts to boost their public approval ratings.[27] Republicans accused President Bill Clinton of using this tactic by intervening in Kosovo to divert attention away from the Monica Lewinsky scandal.[28]

The terrorist attacks of September 11, 2001, resulted in a significant boost in George W. Bush's approval ratings, which averaged 53 percent prior to the attacks. After the attacks, his approval soared to over 90 percent,[29] which was higher than Franklin Roosevelt's after the Japanese attack on Pearl Harbor.[30] Support for Bush was exaggerated by the public's misunderstanding of certain facts regarding Saddam Hussein and Iraq. Polls found that most Americans believed that Saddam Hussein was linked to Al-Qaida and the attacks of September 11, that Iraq possessed weapons of mass destruction, and that world public opinion favored military action against Iraq. Various administration officials, including Vice President Dick Cheney and Secretary of Defense Donald Rumsfeld, made a number of public comments that lent support to those misunderstandings. Those misperceptions were also related to the source of news the public was attentive to.[31] Bush's public approval drifted downward, but spiked to about 70 with the invasion of Iraq, then drifted down again to about 50 percent as the war has dragged on and he began his second term.[32]

The fact that news travels around the globe instantaneously heightens the awareness of individuals outside the United States of the country's foreign policy, and world public opinion judges the appropriateness of that policy. Significantly, mistrust of the United States, and particularly of President Bush, has grown in Western Europe. In a 2004 survey, most foreign respondents said that Washington, D.C., acts on its own without taking into account the interests of other nations.[33] World opinion regarding the trustworthiness of the United States as a leader declined sharply after the invasion of Iraq.

Unfortunately, foreign policy problems have a disconcerting unpredictability regarding their outcome. For example, as the war in Vietnam dragged on and casualties mounted, many Americans became disillusioned. They did not think the war was unwinnable so much as they thought it was not winnable at a price they were willing to bear. The long-term effect on President Lyndon Johnson's presidency was devastating.

The similarity of the Iraq War to the Vietnam experience is significant. What was promised to be a short war drags on, with an ongoing loss of U.S. lives and no victory in sight. U.S. soldiers have suffered more casualties after the declaration of "mission accomplished" by President Bush than before the declaration of victory.

The foreign policy process often involves only a small elite group who provide input based on their supposed expertise. This is in contrast to the formulation of most domestic policy issues, where the emphasis is on a broad democratic participation in the process. Most problems involving crisis management issues require the formation of quick responses and are dealt with by experts at the top of the executive branch's foreign policy bureaucracy. Presumably they formulate the best strategy to deal with each problem.

When a policy question involves a combination of international and domestic concerns (often referred to as **intermestic** issues), it is more likely to resemble domestic policy formulation. That is, it involves a wide spectrum of interest groups claiming a right to be heard. For example, the involvement of interest groups in the congressional debate over the North American Free Trade Agreement greatly expanded the scope of the debate and encouraged negotiations and compromises.

The president has policy institutions to advise him on foreign and military issues. The Department of State is the oldest of all the cabinet departments, which makes the secretary of state (Thomas Jefferson being the first) the ranking cabinet member. Its primary objective is to carry out foreign policy to promote the long-range security goals of the country. U.S. ambassadors, along with over 8,000 foreign service officers who work for the State Department, represent the United States at foreign embassies and international organizations around the world.

The secretary of state is the president's primary foreign policy adviser. Secretaries of state have only as much policymaking authority as the president chooses to delegate. Presidents like Dwight Eisenhower and Ronald Reagan gave their secretaries of state broad discretion to make foreign policy decisions. Others, like John Kennedy and Jimmy Carter, took a more active role in foreign policy decisionmaking.

Those who favor a more robust U.S. foreign policy complain that the State Department is excessively timid in promoting U.S. interests because of its determination to maintain friendly relations with foreign governments. Former secretary of state James Baker claims that this desire to maintain good relations can result in some foreign service officers losing sight of the national interest.[34]

Colin Powell's prestige uniquely qualified him to rejuvenate morale at the State Department when he became secretary of state in the first George W. Bush administration. However, regarding the preemptive attack on Iraq, Powell urged the administration to return to the UN Security Council to get its endorsement to use force against Saddam Hussein, as it had before launching an attack against Afghanistan. It was clear that it would be more difficult to convince other nations of the legitimacy of preeemptive war. But President Bush challenged the UN to authorize force against Iraq or risk becoming "irrelevant." The Security Council refused to draft an authorizing resolution and instead called for a new round of UN inspections for weapons of mass destruction in Iraq. Bush, armed with a congressional resolution endorsing his authority to use military force, became impatient with the failure of UN weapons inspectors to find WMD. Powell was left to make the case that there was clear evidence that Hussein possessed stockpiles of WMD, including chemical and biological weapons, and was working toward achieving nuclear weapons capability. Rejecting the UN's request for more time for its inspectors, President Bush launched an attack in March 2003.

Bush was clearly more attuned to foreign policy advice from the neoconservatives, including Vice President Dick Cheney, Deputy Secretary of Defense Paul Wolfowitz, adviser Richard Perle, and Secretary of Defense Donald Rumsfeld. Not only was Colin Powell marginalized as the odd man out in giving foreign policy advice to the president, but the State Department clearly lost its role as the president's primary foreign policy adviser as well.

Despite intensive searches by the U.S. government throughout Iraq, no banned weapons were found after the fall of Hussein's government. A special group sent to search for prohibited weapons concluded that Iraq's WMD program was destroyed in 1991 and that Hussein ended the country's nuclear program after the Gulf War. This confirmed the UN weapons inspection team's findings prior to the launching of the war. Nevertheless, Bush maintained the correctness of his actions despite the findings, saying, "He was a threat we had to confront, and America and the world are safer for our actions."[35]

National Security Organizations

National Security Council (NSC). The NSC was created in 1947 to help presidents integrate the domestic, foreign, and military policies that affect national security. The NSC's statutory membership includes the president, vice president, secretary of state, and secretary of defense. The director of the Central Intelligence Agency (CIA) and the chairman of the Joint Chiefs of Staff (JCS) serve as advisory members. The president's assistant for national security affairs serves as the day-to-day director of the NSC. Technically, the agency does not make decisions, since that is the responsibility of the president, but it does offer policy guidance and advice. Its statutory designation indicates that it has advisory authority only. It does not have any operational authority. The NSC system is flexible and responds to the form that each president finds most useful.

Under President Bush, National Security Adviser Condoleezza Rice tended to remain in the background until thrust into the spotlight to defend Bush's foreign policy decisions. White House officials and Rice resisted testifying before the 9/11 Commission regarding her conversations with the president prior to the attack. They claimed that testimony concerning failure to warn the public about the terrorist threat prior to September 11, 2001, and other matters would violate the separation of powers and was beyond Congress's authority and that a national security adviser's conversations are privileged, as such an adviser would not give candid advice if knowing it could become public. Rice's loyalty to the president led to her appointment as secretary of state, replacing Colin Powell, at the start of the second Bush term.

Department of Defense (DOD). The secretary of defense officially presides over the Department of Defense and is the president's main military adviser. The DOD comprises all the military services and is responsible for about 70 percent of the government's equipment purchases. The commanding officers of each of the services, together with a chairman, comprise the Joint Chiefs of Staff, who advise the secretary of defense as well as the president. Friction frequently develops between the members of the JCS as they try to strengthen the roles of their respective services in military planning.

The Department of Defense is easily the largest and most expensive organization in the federal government. Direct defense spending in the United States will exceed $450 billion dollars in 2005. In addition to 2.3 million military personnel and almost 750,000 civilian employees, the defense industry employs millions of other contractors and workers to provide various goods and services to the military.

The constitutional design of civilian control over the military is often a source of tension. Each military service is overseen by a civilian secretary, and the Department of Defense is overseen by a civilian, the secretary of defense, who answers directly to the president. In 1986 the Defense Reorganization Act (generally known as the Goldwater-Nichols Act) strengthened the power of the chairman of the JCS, who became the primary military adviser to the secretary of defense and the president. Tensions can still become very public when there is a disagreement on policy matters between uniformed military leaders and civilian leaders.

For example, before September 11, 2001, the secretary of defense, Donald Rumsfeld, wanted to exploit changes in technology to take advantage of satellite-guided munitions, unmanned surveillance drones, rapid deployment of troops, and concentrated firepower. Rumsfeld felt vindicated with the success of these techniques in Operation Enduring Freedom in Afghanistan in 2001. However, when General Eric Shinseki, the U.S. Army chief of staff, testified before Congress that "several hundred thousand troops" would be needed to provide security and stabilization after the initial combat phase was over in Iraq, he was publicly criticized by the civilian leadership. Military leaders also thought Rumsfeld unnecessarily antagonized North Atlantic Treaty Organization allies who opposed the Iraq War, derisively referring to them as "Old Europe," and increased their disinclination to assist the United States later when the administration realized that their help was sorely needed. Finally, the military believed that Rumsfeld set in motion the systems and procedures that led to the prisoner abuses in Afghanistan, Abu Ghraib, and Guantanamo. The *Army Times* published an editorial harshly condemning both

Rumsfeld and JCS chairman General Richard Myers, who was selected to replace Shinseki because of the latter's disconcerting outspokenness in his misgivings about the Iraq venture. The editorial stated: "On the battlefield, Myers' and Rumsfeld's errors would be called a lack of situational awareness—a failure that amounts to professional negligence. . . . This was not just a failure of leadership at the local command level. This was a failure that ran straight to the top. Accountability here is essential even if that means relieving top leaders from duty in a time of war."[36] Rumsfeld's views appeared to be consistent with the commander in chief's, however, as Bush had refused to increase the size of military forces operating in Iraq. To have required Rumsfeld's resignation would have implied mistakes in the planning and execution of the war, which President Bush was loath to acknowledge. Rumsfeld was one of only a few cabinet members asked to stay on into the second term.

The Intelligence Community

"Intelligence" refers to the process of collecting, analyzing, protecting, and using information to further national interests. The origins of U.S. intelligence policy can be traced to its skillful exploitation by George Washington, which was largely responsible for the improbable success of his colonial army against the vastly superior forces arrayed against him. Secret intelligence agencies are something of an anomaly in a democratic society, which is based on openness and transparency. The requirements of national security provide a justification for a carefully regulated intelligence capability.

Prior to the surprise attack on Pearl Harbor, the United States had no centralized agency for intelligence gathering. During World War II, President Franklin Roosevelt created the Office of Strategic Services (OSS) to analyze intelligence to aid in military planning. After World War II, the OSS was disbanded and the small Central Intelligence Group provided information to the government. The Central Intelligence Agency was created by the National Security Act of 1947 to advise and make recommendations to the departments of government about issues and situations related to national security. **National intelligence** is the term for intelligence that is of value to more than one department or agency and provides the basis for national security policymaking.[37] The CIA was supposed to centralize intelligence gathering and analysis in a way that had not been done prior to the attack on Pearl Harbor. It was to direct, collect, and analyze intelligence about foreign countries and disseminate it to those in the government who needed the information for their decisionmaking. The intelligence community makes use of classified sources of information, but most information is collected from open sources such as news stories, public documents, and diplomatic reporting. Intelligence is distinguished, however, by its sources and methods, which are not openly available. Some intelligence agencies, particularly those housed in the Department of Defense, make use of highly technical collection efforts with a view to providing analytical and technical support to consumers outside the DOD as well as senior defense officials, to the Joint Chiefs of Staff, to combat commanders, and to joint task forces worldwide. Included in this category would be the National Reconnaissance Office (NRO), established in 1960. The NRO is staffed by DOD and CIA personnel to design, build, and operate the reconnaissance satellites that collect intelligence information and images of Earth's surface.[38] The National Security Agency, created in 1952, collects, processes, and analyzes foreign intelligence in order to support national policymakers and operational forces. The National Geospatial-Intelligence Agency, established in 1996, provides topographic data and imagery intelligence to DOD users and other officials responsible for national security.

The basic tension between the goal of centralized authority under a director of central intelligence (DCI), who is also the director of the Central Intelligence Agency, and decentralized intelligence gathering has been particularly troubling. During the Cold War, the goal was to aggressively pursue U.S. covert action and counterintelligence capabilities against communism. Army general James Doolittle argued that setting aside the U.S. ideal of "fair play" was justified in the struggle to prevent Soviet world domination.[39] The intelligence community was widely criticized for a succession of failures and for violating its legal authority. The missteps included the role of intelligence during the Bay of Pigs and in Vietnam (during the Bay of Pigs, U.S. intelligence underestimated the popular support for Fidel Castro, and during Vietnam, army intelligence underestimated the size of the Vietcong forces, rejecting the CIA's larger troop estimates), as well as the attempted assassination of foreign leaders and the surveillance of U.S. citizens. Congressional investigations into the activities of the intelligence community did result in a rededication to the need for congressional oversight and involvement. Increased congressional oversight has for the most part been resisted by presidents, who tend to think of intelligence as a function of the executive branch and perceive Congress as "meddling."

Nevertheless, the general trend has been toward more thorough oversight by congressional committees as well as by the executive branch. The DCI is the primary spokesman for the intelligence community to the president and the National Security Council. However, the DCI does not have "line" authority over any intelligence agency other than the CIA. Since the DOD has many more intelligence agencies, its influence is all-inclusive.

The failure of the intelligence community to warn the public about the terrorist threat prior to the attacks of September 11, 2001, and the lack of accurate intelligence information regarding alleged WMD in Iraq, brought new demands for reorganization of the intelligence community. Congress amended the National Security Act to establish a director of national intelligence (DNI), separate from the DCI, to be appointed by the president with the advice and consent of the Senate. The legislation, signed in December 2004, makes the DNI responsible for determining the annual budgets for all national intelligence agencies and to direct how those funds are spent. Otherwise, the new law will preserve the existing chain of command. The DNI does have greater authority over intelligence agencies in the DOD than did the DCI; however, there will be a continued requirement for close coordination between the DNI and the DOD.

Politicized Intelligence

The purpose of intelligence policy is to provide decisionmakers with the most accurate and up-to-date information available. But decisionmakers are responsible for creating and making policy decisions, and are free to make decisions that run counter to the analysis provided. Decisionmakers are often tempted to leak intelligence analysis that is supportive of their own policy agenda, to undermine political opposition, but are quick to cry foul if the political opposition leaks information that undermines their own goals.

The issue of politicization often arises from concerns that intelligence officers may slant their intelligence, which is supposed to be unbiased, to support the outcome preferred by decisionmakers. In this case the analyst produces intelligence different from what their objective analysis would support. Analysts may have several motives for slanting their intelligence to coincide with the decisionmaker's known preferences, such as avoiding the displeasure of having their analysis rejected and enhancing their career chances. As well, lack of professional distance from the decisionmaker and loss of objectivity may result in bias. DCI George Tenet was strongly criticized for having indicated to President Bush that the likelihood of Saddam Hussein possessing nuclear weapons was a "slam dunk." His support was widely quoted by the administration as a justification for the use of aggressive military force against Iraq. In fact, most analysts were very doubtful that Iraq had WMD. Subsequent congressional testimony by Richard Clarke and others revealed many CIA failures to properly vet intelligence information both prior to and after September 11, 2001. Although Tenet resigned from the CIA under pressure from critics who blamed him for providing President Bush with inaccurate statements about Iraq in his 2004 State of the Union address, he was subsequently awarded the Presidential Medal of Freedom, the highest civilian governmental award. The choice of Porter Goss to replace Tenet as director of central intelligence was criticized because of Goss's reputation for aggressive political partisanship. Several high-level resignations at the CIA in the weeks after Goss was confirmed heightened concern over the CIA's ability to provide good intelligence.

From the perspective of intelligence policy, objectivity is a core goal. Having altered and politicized intelligence may be worse than not having intelligence at all, because it provides fabrications, distortions, and propaganda rather than the "truth."

The most controversial aspect of intelligence often concerns **covert action**, which involves secret operations designed to influence events in other countries while the sponsoring government's involvement is concealed. Covert action may include propaganda and political, economic, and paramilitary operations. Many scholars argue that covert action is not intelligence per se. However, it is a function that most governments assign to their intelligence branches, because their ability to collect clandestine information makes them well suited for many forms of covert action.

The U.S. Self-Image: Myth and Reality

The founding of the United States was rather unique in that the country was the first "new nation" drawing its population from various parts of the world. Its government was established on political principles rather than any ethnic identity. The United States has traditionally perceived itself as the world's first modern democracy to espouse the principles of egalitarianism. European concepts of nobility and heredity had no place in the new nation. Americans believed that individual freedom and social justice would lead immigrants to improve their stations in life. The lack of hereditary status or rank placed an individual's responsibility for their station in life squarely upon their shoulders. Status and prestige would be measured by merit rather than an inherited social position. In the Old World, status, money, and prestige were the consequence of one's inherited position, not of intelligence or merit. Thomas Paine pointed out in *Common Sense* that the natural result of such a system was that ignorance and stupidity prevailed in affairs of state in Europe.

Americans have a collective self-concept that embraces what Richard Hughes refers to as the "myths America lives by."[40] These myths are the ways that Americans learn to view the world. A myth is not a story that is patently untrue; rather it is a story that speaks of purposes and meaning. **National myths** are the means by which citizens affirm the meaning of their country. Hopefully, U.S. national myths provide us with the ideals we try to uphold as a nation. Caution warns us not to naively confuse the ideal of the myth with the reality actually achieved by the nation.

The first myth is the **myth of the chosen people**, the notion that God chose the American people for a special role in world history, which arose in the notion of being "chosen" for the good of one's fellow man. From the earliest days of the Republic, Americans have believed that they have a special destiny to become a beacon of hope to the rest of the world. A system based on freedom, opportunity, social justice, and faith in the goodness and rationality of all human beings was thought to be obviously morally superior to European concepts based on hierarchy, exploitation, and war. John Quincy Adams depicted it most vividly: "Wherever the standard of freedom and independence has been on shall be unfurled, there will be America's heart, her benedictions and her prayers. But she goes not abroad in search of monsters to destroy. She is the well-wisher to the freedom and independence of all. She is the champion and vindicator only of her own."[41]

Americans have believed it their obligation to encourage the spread of freedom and social justice throughout the world. In theory, as John Quincy Adams suggests, this propagation of freedom and justice was to come through modeling behavior for others to emulate. The United States was never to impose its democracy on others. More recently, the neoconservative "idealism" in the Bush administration holds that the United States should be forceful in establishing democracy in the Middle East. And President Bush has called on the Middle East to join "the global democratic revolution" and has vowed to build a democracy in Iraq.[42]

A closely related myth is the **myth of the millennial national**, which also emerged early on in U.S. history. Struck with the wonders of freedom, many believed that the United States would usher in freedom for all the peoples of the earth. An additional consequence of being a new nation with an emphasis on individualism was that there was not a set pattern or traditional way of doing things. Americans quickly established a penchant for inventiveness and creativeness in solving problems. This utilitarian approach led to the conclusion that whatever works is good. Americans were admired for their "Yankee ingenuity" and their ability to get things done, not for "Yankee wisdom." Individual freedom is closely related to political freedom. That is, individuals and nations should be free to choose what works best for them without outside interference.

A third myth prevalent throughout U.S. history is the **myth of the Christian nation**. At its best it encourages Americans to embrace policies in keeping with the teachings of Jesus. In particular it suggests a dedication to the issues of social justice, to helping the poor and the less fortunate both at home and abroad.

Richard Hughes notes that these myths may result in an unwarranted sense of moral superiority. In the extreme, the ideal of the myth may be confused with a reality that does not actually exist. In believing that the nation has achieved its ideals and is therefore superior to the reality one sees beyond U.S. shores, there is a temptation to support those goals abroad, even by coercion.

For example, the myth of the chosen people can be distorted to suggest not that Americans should benefit their fellow man, but that Americans have been chosen for special privileges and blessings in the world. The perversion of the myth may be seized upon, not to extend compassion to the poor, but as a badge of cultural superiority.[43] This notion was ultimately fused with the myth of the Christian nation and evolved into a belief that God had chosen the United States for special privilege precisely because it was thought to be a Christian nation. And the emphasis on individual freedom and pragmatism can become an emphasis on conformity. There is an expectation that other nations would want to adopt our system if they were free to do so. This myth has also been twisted into a willingness to *force* others to be free. Hughes notes that capitalism in the United States was a doctrine grounded in the absolute forms of these earlier national myths. Capitalism can promote hard work and individual effort and holds the potential for good, but its excesses can nurture greed and exploitation of the economically deprived. This was certainly the case in the late nineteenth century, when self-interest and greed were promoted as being inherently Christian and as another attribute of the United States as the chosen nation. The distorted forms of these myths actually work to undermine the promise of the United States.[44]

A case in point is the conflicting views regarding aid to poor nations. Americans are frequently surprised at what they feel is unjustified criticism of U.S. policy by foreign nationals. The UN's 2003 summit on global poverty in Mexico produced the "Monterrey Consensus," which urged rich nations to contribute 0.7 percent of their national income to development aid for poor nations. That would amount to a little over 70¢ a day per American. President Bush endorsed the Monterrey Consensus, noting that "opportunity is a fundamental right to human dignity" and that providing hope to the poor aids the struggle against terrorism.[45] However, the United States is currently providing the smallest amount of development aid from the world's twenty-two wealthiest nations. By contrast, many other wealthy nations give a far greater share. The United States provides about 15¢ a day per person, while Norway, the most generous nation, gives about 92¢ a day per person (see Table 13.1).

President Bush has indicated that the recipients of aid should be "accountable" for the money they receive. To be eligible for U.S. aid, the recipient country should establish a democratic government with a market economy, while government intervention in the economy should be minimized and barriers to free trade should be removed. As a result of the need to rebuild Iraq after the U.S. military intervention, that country became the major aid recipient since 2003. Although the administration increased foreign aid spending in 2004 to $21 billion, the share of U.S. economic output devoted to foreign aid was still the lowest of all industrialized countries.[46] While the United States was the world's biggest spender in absolute

Table 13.1   Development Assistance, 2004

	Governmental Assistance in ¢ per $100 of National Income	Total Governmental Assistance in Millions of U.S.$	Nongovernmental Assistance in ¢ per $100 of National Income
Norway	92	2,042	11
Denmark	84	1,748	(NA)
Luxembourg	81	194	2
Netherlands	80	3,981	6
Sweden	79	2,400	1
Belgium	60	1,853	4
France	41	7,253	(NA)
Ireland	39	504	16
Switzerland	39	1,299	8
Finland	35	558	1
United Kingdom	34	6,282	2
Germany	28	6,784	4
Australia	25	1,219	7
Canada	24	2,031	5
New Zealand	23	165	3
Spain	23	1,961	(NA)
Portugal	22	320	< 1
Greece	21	362	< 1
Austria	20	505	3
Japan	20	8,880	1
Italy	17	2,433	< 1
United States	15	16,254	6

Source: Washington Post, January 15, 2005, p. A18.
Note: (NA) indicates data not available.

terms, it was also the most miserly when the degree of national sacrifice was taken into account. The government defends itself by noting that the United States spends more than any other country in absolute terms and that the United States helps other economies by being the world's largest importer of goods and services.

International Trade

International trade has become a significant part of the U.S. economy only in the past fifty years. Sales of domestically produced goods and services abroad, or

exports, now amount to 10 percent of what the U.S. economy produces. Purchases of goods and services produced abroad, or **imports**, have increased dramatically in the past twenty years. Imports have exceeded exports consistently since 1975.

Whenever nations engage in international trade, there are potential problems. International trade differs from domestic trade in that a foreign entrepreneur's right to sell in another country's domestic market can be limited by **tariffs**, or taxes, on imports. Tariffs result in higher prices for consumers. Other regulatory restrictions on imports, called **nontariff barriers** (NTBs), such as requirements that a percentage of the products must be assembled within the host states, imposed quotas, and environmental or food and drug restrictions, also limit trade. Governments impose NTBs because they are frequently more responsive to business interests, or to the interests of organized labor, than to consumer interests.

One reason policymakers today must be concerned with international trade issues is because of the current U.S. trade balance, the gap between the value of exports and imports. When the value of exports exceeds the value of imports, a country runs a **trade surplus**. Conversely, when the value of imports exceeds that of exports, a country runs a **trade deficit**. From the end of World War II until the early 1980s, the United States consistently exported more than it imported. Then in the early 1980s, persistent and massive trade deficits emerged. The United States ran a record trade deficit of over $600 billion in 2004.[47]

Why Worry About Trade Deficits?

Running a trade deficit has similarities to running a budget deficit. It allows a nation to consume (import) more than it produces (exports) by spending past savings, or by borrowing. When the United States runs a trade deficit, it must make up the difference by selling assets like real estate, stocks, bonds, and even whole corporations. From World War I until the 1980s, the United States was the major creditor nation. It ran large trade surpluses with other countries, lending large sums abroad and acquiring large amounts of foreign assets in the process. Net U.S. foreign investment reached a peak of $141 billion at the end of 1981. Then in just four years, the total accumulated investments of over sixty years were undone. By the end of 1985, foreign assets in the United States exceeded U.S.-held assets by $112 billion.[48] Since then, the United States has become the world's biggest debtor nation, and instead of receiving interest income, it must pay out interest every year while getting nothing in return.

An important factor in determining whether a country runs a trade deficit or surplus is its ability to produce goods more cheaply than can other countries. Through the 1950s and 1960s, U.S. workers were highly competitive even though their wages were higher than those of their foreign counterparts. U.S. productivity was great and U.S. goods were of higher quality and lower price and thus were more desirable than foreign goods. That began to change in the late 1970s as Japan and the developing countries invested heavily in their industrial bases. With so much at stake, foreign governments were not about to allow natural market forces to determine outcomes. Governments intervened to subsidize much of the research and development necessary for business growth and manufacturing. In the process, they proved that governmental intervention can strengthen national markets. Foreign manufacturers with new and modern industrial facilities and lower wages—in the steel industry, for example—began with increasing frequency to compete effectively with U.S. manufacturers.

Other trade pressures magnify a trade deficit. When a trade deficit occurs, imports rise and exports fall. A fall in exports means that domestic production falls, which means that domestic workers have less income; consequently, demand for goods falls and unemployment rises. Higher unemployment means that workers spend less and incomes fall even further. Conversely, in a nation that exports more than it imports, like Japan, as production rises citizens have more income to spend on consumer goods or investments, resulting in high employment levels so that ultimately the country's incomes rise even further. The effect of exports on income creates export-led economic growth. That is, a trade surplus stimulates higher incomes.

Protectionism

Free trade has its critics, who argue that trade restrictions would directly reduce the deficit. They claim that free trade is unfair because of the resultant low foreign wages and government subsidies. However, if U.S. producers benefited from tariffs, consumers would lose. Consumer prices would rise with tariffs, while the quality of domestic products would fall, reducing the standard of living. Trade restrictions also invite retaliation. If one country erects trade barriers, other countries respond with restrictions of their own.

The economic arguments in favor of free trade are forceful, but are challenged by those who argue that it may be in the public interest to restrict or suspend free trade. There are several arguments advanced in favor of trade restrictions.[49] First is the argument for national defense, which contends that it would be foolhardy to rely on imports for items necessary to the nation's security. Combat ships and aircraft, along with munitions, are critical to national defense. It would be too risky to leave weapon production to commercial trading partners. Although the argument undoubtedly may have some legitimacy, it is often misapplied. The national defense argument has been stretched to include agriculture, fishing, and other tangentially related industries.

Second is the argument against dumping, in which "dumping" is defined as the sale of goods abroad at a price lower than their sale in the domestic market, or below their average cost, and which claims that dumping is an unfair trade practice because it is done to drive out domestic producers and then raise prices. However, this is a questionable market strategy, because once dumpers have driven out the competition and raised their prices, the domestic competition will return. Meanwhile, the dumping nations would have only a string of losses to show for their effort of selling below cost to drive out competition. During this period, domestic consumers would be the beneficiaries, due to their ability to buy products at very low prices.

Third is the argument for infant industry, which is probably the most blatant appeal for special interest protection. The argument is that new industries may need protection until they have grown and become competitive with more mature foreign competitors. Critics point out that an infant industry grown to maturity is more powerful and even more insistent that benefits not be taken away.

Fourth is the argument for saving domestic jobs, which masquerades in different guises. One form of the argument is that domestic producers cannot compete with foreign producers because of the higher wages received by U.S. workers relative to those paid by foreign producers. Without protection, domestic producers will be forced to shut down and domestic jobs will be lost. However, the argument ignores the point that the higher productivity of domestic workers is why the U.S. worker earns more compared to the low wage of a less productive worker. If a U.S. capital goods worker earns $25 per hour with benefits and produces 100 widgets per hour, the labor costs per unit will be lower than that for a foreign worker who receives $3 per hour but produces only 4 widgets per hour with minimal assistance from machinery. That is, a high-wage disadvantage may be offset by a productivity advantage. Conversely, a country's advantage of low wages can be negated by its low-productivity disadvantage. Another variation on the argument for saving domestic jobs is that foreign governments subsidize foreign exports. When government subsidies lower the costs to foreign producers, the result is that domestic producers cannot compete, leading to failure and the loss of domestic jobs.

Conclusion

U.S. foreign policy has generally consisted of a blending of idealism and realism. The idealist aspect of foreign policy emphasizes the aspirations of the United States as the first new nation advancing individual human and political freedoms at home and abroad. The realist strain tends to emphasize and justify the advancement of U.S. interests while subordinating the concerns of the world community to that goal.

Foreign policies of different administrations, such as Woodrow Wilson's or John Kennedy's, have been noted for the prominence given to the idealist goals of encouraging democratic principles around the world and strengthening the development of international law and human rights. At other times, such as during the Cold War, idealist goals have tended to be overshadowed by concerns over military competition. Even during that period, the Untied States tried to give careful consideration to the interests and perspectives of other nations to encourage their support in a bipolar struggle, as well as from a belief that democratic procedures are to be preferred to nondemocratic ones.

After World War II the United States appeared to be genuinely reluctant to shoulder the burden of defender of the peace for the Western world. The United States shouldered the burden in the name of its own ideals, as enshrined in the UN Charter. Some did express their concern that the connection was so close that the United States used the United Nations as an instrument of its foreign policy. Many principles in the Charter embodied U.S. ideals that all members subscribed to upon admission into the body. Many newly emerging states looked to the United Nations and the United States for support and security in their struggle for independence, democratization, and development. Various documents, on topics ranging from universal human rights to arms control, were adopted under the auspices of the UN and supported by the United States during this period. During the Vietnam era there was a loss of some legitimacy for the United States because of the gap between its ideals and its use of military force over the opposition of much of the international community. However, there remained a consensus during the Cold War that U.S. power was necessary to preserve the peace and protect the developing community of states. U.S. power was accepted as necessary and legitimate.

The dramatic loss of presumed legitimacy for U.S. power and foreign policy initiatives under President George W. Bush must be understood in this context. Upon assuming office, the new president indicated that he intended a sharp break with the Clinton administration's policy of engagement and enlargement and nation building. The administration embraced the philosophy of the neoconservatives.

Without an opposing superpower, international law was seen as having limited utility. John Bolton, the undersecretary of state for arms control and international security, noted a few years earlier that "it is a big mistake for us to grant any validity to international law even when it may seem in our short-term interest to do so because, over the long term, the goal of those who think that international law really means anything are those who want to constrict the United States."[50] This reflected a rejection of the principles that had previously provided the basis for the legitimacy of U.S. soft power.

After September 11, 2001, the Bush administration drew a line in the sand, declaring to the world that "you're either with us, or you're with the terrorists" and heaping scorn on those unwilling to use force as part of "old Europe." The administration made clear its intention to use force against Iraq even if the UN Security Council opposed it, warned that the UN would become irrelevant if it did not accede to the U.S. demand to authorize force, and proclaimed a doctrine of preventive war to replace the policy of containment and deterrence that had discouraged the use of force since 1945.

The principles that had been the mainstay for U.S. policy after World War II—support for the progressive development of international law, multilateral democratic decisionmaking processes, and opposition to the use of force outside of the UN framework—were swept away. Without another superpower to rein it in, the United States suddenly appeared much more threatening to much of the world. Much of the criticism has centered on the neoconservatives, still held in high esteem in some circles. The neoconservatives in turn defend themselves by pointing to precedents in earlier administrations where arbitrary or illegal conduct occurred. However, earlier lapses in U.S. policy were treated as just that—lapses—or as unique situations, and were not trumpeted as fundamental changes in policy.

Questions for Discussion

1. How does the neoconservative foreign policy of the current administration blend realism and idealism?
2. What particular features of terrorism threaten conventional policy strategies?
3. What role does international law play in the twenty-first century?
4. What are the implications of U.S. and European soft power?
5. Why have intelligence failures occurred?
6. What can be done to reduce U.S. dependence on imports?

Useful Websites

Center for the Study of Islam and Democracy, http://www.islam-democracy.org.
Center for Foreign Policy Studies, http://www.dal.ca/~centre.
Foreign Policy Research Institute, http://www.fpri.org.
Institute for Foreign Policy Analysis, http://www.ifpa.org.
International Studies Association, http://www.isanet.org.
National Center for Policy Analysis, http://www.ncpa.org.

Suggested Readings

Hook, Steven W. *U.S. Foreign Policy: The Paradox of World Power.* Washington, D.C.: Congressional Quarterly Press, 2005.

Nye, Joseph S., Jr. *Soft Power: The Means to Success in World Politics.* New York: PublicAffairs, 2004.

Notes

1. See Francis Fukuyama, *The End of History and the Last Man* (New York: Penguin, 1992).

2. Francis Fukuyama, "The End of History?" *National Interest* 16 (Summer 1989): 3–18.

3. Steven W. Hook, *U.S. Foreign Policy: The Paradox of World Power* (Washington, D.C.: Congressional Quarterly Press, 2005), p. 51.

4. Thomas Donnelly, "Rebuilding America's Defenses: Strategy, Forces, and Resources for a New Century" (Washington, D.C.: Project for the New American Century, September 2000), p. 2.

5. Robert Kagan, "A Higher Realism," *Washington Post,* January 23, 2005.

6. Office of Management and Budget, *Budget of the United States Government, 2005* (Washington, D.C.: U.S. Governmet Printing Office, 2005), Historical Tables 2004, p. 52.

7. See http://www.globalissues.org/geopolitics/armstrade/spending.asp.

8. World Bank, *World Development Indicators 2004* (Washington, D.C.: International Bank for Reconstruction and Development, 2004).

9. Joseph S. Nye Jr., *Soft Power: The Means to Success in World Politics* (New York: PublicAffairs, 2004).

10. Ibid., p. 6.

11. Ibid., p. 11.

12. Nye does not suggest that military force is not important in international politics today, especially in those areas not constrained by democratic institutions. Ibid., chap. 1.

13. William Kristol and Lawrence Kaplan, *The War over Iraq: Saddam's Tyranny and America's Mission* (San Francisco: Encounter Books, 2003), p. 112.

14. David Gelernter, "Replacing the United Nations: Make Way for the Big Three," *Weekly Standard,* March 17, 2003.

15. Lael Brainard and Michael O'Hanlon, "The Heavy Price of America's Going It Alone," *Financial Times,* August 6, 2003. Also cited in Nye, *Soft Power,* p. 27.

16. Nye, *Soft Power,* p. 27.

17. Daniel Williams, "Pope Urges Dialogue to Counter 'Arrogance of Power,'" *Washington Post,* January 11, 2005.

18. See also Article 2, para. 4, of the UN Charter.

19. President George W. Bush, address to U.S. Military Academy graduates, May 2000.

20. Patrick E. Tyler and Felicity Barringer, "Annan Says U.S. Will Violate Charter If It Acts Without Approval," *New York Times,* March 11, 2003, p. A8.

21. Tim Golden, "Administration Officials Split over Military Tribunals," *New York Times,* October 25, 2004, p. A1.

22. *Rasul v. Bush* (2004).

23. John F. Kerry, "Making America Secure Again: Setting the Right Course for Foreign Policy," speech before the Council on Foreign Relations, New York, December 3, 2003.

24. George W. Bush, State of the Union address, White House, January 20, 2004.

25. "Joint Resolution Authorizing the Use of United States Armed Forces Against Iraq," http://www.whitehouse.gov/news/releases/2002.

26. Arthur M. Schlesinger Jr., *The Imperial Presidency* (Boston: Houghton Mifflin, 1973).

27. Jack Levy, "The Diversionary Theory of War: A Critique," in Manus Midlarsky, ed., *Handbook of War Studies* (London: Unwin Hyman, 1989), pp. 259–288.

28. Hook, *U.S. Foreign Policy,* p. 202.

29. See http://www.pollingreport.com/bushjob.htm.

30. This unique spike in Bush approval ratings was in part due to his low standing in the polls prior to September 11, 2001. Roosevelt, in contrast, was very popular prior to December 7, 1941, but his pre–December 7 approval rating of 72 percent did not allow as significant a bounce in the polls. See Matthew A. Baum, "The Constituent Foundations of the Rally-Round-the-Flag Phenomenon," *International Studies Quarterly* 46 (June 2002): 263–298.

31. Steven Kull, Clay Ramsay, and Evan Lewis, "Misperceptions, the Media, and the Iraq War," *Political Science Quarterly* 118 (Winter 2003–2004): 569–598. See also *Outfoxed Fox,* video, directed by Robert Greenwald (Disinformation Company, 2004).

32. Peter Wallsten, "Bush Approval Rating at Historic Low: Unpopular Iraq War Dampens Effect of Reelection Win," *San Francisco Chronicle,* December 29, 2004.

33. See http://www.globalissues.org/geopolitics/waronterror/opiniongap.asp.

34. James A. Baker III and Thomas M. DeFrank, *The Politics of Diplomacy: Revolution, War, and Peace, 1989–1992* (New York: Putnam, 1995), p. 29.

35. Barbara Starr and Elise Labott, "Official: U.S. Calls off Search for Iraqi WMDs," January 12, 2005, http://www.cnn.com/2005/us/01/12/wmd.

36. Editorial, "A Failure of Leadership at the Highest Levels," *Army Times,* May 17, 2004.

37. Richard A. Best Jr., "Intelligence Community Reorganization: Potential Effects on DOD Intelligence Agencies," Congressional Research Service, December 21, 2004, p. 3.

38. Ibid., p. 2.

39. Richard A. Best Jr., "Proposals for Intelligence Reorganization, 1949–2004," Congressional Research Service, September 24, 2004.

40. Richard T. Hughes, *Myths America Lives By* (Chicago: University of Illinois Press, 2003).

41. John Quincy Adams as quoted by George Kennan, testimony before the Senate Foreign Relations Committee, February 10, 1966, in *Supplemental Foreign Assistance Fiscal Year 1966—Vietnam: Hearings Before the Senate Foreign Relations Committee,* 89th Congress, 2nd session (Washington, D.C.: U.S. Government Printing Office, 1966), p. 336.

42. Kenneth Josat and Benton Ives-Halperin, "Democracy in the Arab World," *CQ Researcher,* January 30, 2004.

43. Ibid., p. 6.

44. Ibid., p. 7.

45. Robin Wright, "Aid to Poorest Nations Trails Global Goal," *Washington Post,* January 15, 2005, p. A18.

46. Hook, *U.S. Foreign Policy,* p. 350.

47. See http://www.bea.doc.gov/bea/newsrel/tradnewsrelease.htm.

48. Paul Krugman, *The Age of Diminished Expectations* (Cambridge: MIT Press, 1992), p. 40.

49. Arguments are adapted from Roger A. Arnold, *Economics,* 3rd ed. (St. Paul, Minn.: West, 1996), pp. 752–758.

50. As cited in Robert W. Tucker and David C. Hendrickson, "The Sources of American Legitimacy," *Foreign Affairs,* November–December 2004.

Index

About the Book

This accessible yet challenging introduction to public policy navigates the concepts and methods of the policymaking process, as well as the values influencing policy choices.

The authors first cover the basics: How do issues reach the policy agenda? How are policies crafted and implemented? Who pays and who benefits? How is the effectiveness of a policy determined? They then apply this foundation to a range of contemporary policy areas: the economy, welfare, education, crime, health care, housing, the environment, foreign policy, domestic security, and more. Throughout, they emphasize the essential relationship between individual self-interest and national well-being. Notably, the text:

- Explains complicated ideas clearly—but without oversimplifying.
- Uses "everyday" examples to illustrate challenging concepts.
- Stresses the importance of values in economic cost-benefit analyses.
- Considers liberal and conservative positions in a balanced way.
- Compares U.S. approaches with those of other countries.
- Challenges students to rethink their assumptions about "the public good."

Engaging with controversial issues that bring the subject alive, this up-to-date new edition of *Public Policy* provides the ideal tour of the field—offering the perfect combination of theory and application.

Charles L. Cochran is professor of political science and past chairperson of the department at the U.S. Naval Academy. He is also an adjunct faculty member of The Johns Hopkins University graduate school. His main fields of teaching include public policy, political economy, and macroeconomics. He has authored numerous articles, contributed several chapters to books, and edited and coauthored a book on civil-military relations. He has served as a consultant to the Departments of Energy, Commerce, and Transportation, and has worked at the Defense Intelligence Agency. **Eloise F. Malone** is professor of political science at the U.S. Naval Academy. She previously worked at the U.S. Department of State where she analyzed public opinion. Her primary fields of teaching and research include political philosophy, quantitative methods and policy analysis, and the use of computer applications in political science. She is author or coauthor of numerous articles ranging from public opinion analysis to ethics, and psychological preferences.